# Leslie Marmon Silko

---

*A Literary Companion*

---

Mary Ellen Snodgrass

McFarland Literary Companions, 10

McFarland & Company, Inc., Publishers
*Jefferson, North Carolina, and London*

LIBRARY OF CONGRESS CATALOGUING-IN-PUBLICATION DATA

Snodgrass, Mary Ellen.
Leslie Marmon Silko : a literary companion / Mary Ellen Snodgrass.
p.   cm. — (McFarland literary companions ; 10)
Includes bibliographical references and index.

ISBN 978-0-7864-4853-1
(softcover : 50# alkaline paper) ∞

1. Silko, Leslie, 1948– — Criticism and interpretation.
I. Title.
PS3569.I44Z95   2011      813'.54 — dc22        2010051899

British Library cataloguing data are available

On the cover: Leslie Mamon Silko (photograph © Nancy Crampton);
background © 2011 Shutterstock

Manufactured in the United States of America

*McFarland & Company, Inc., Publishers
Box 611, Jefferson, North Carolina 28640
www.mcfarlandpub.com*

For Lotsee Patterson

# Acknowledgments

I would like to acknowledge the advice and assistance of the following:

Paulita Aguilar, reference,
University of New Mexico Library,
Albuquerque, New Mexico

Esther Antonio, Laguna Council,
Laguna, New Mexico

Meghan Fallon, publicity,
Viking/Penguin,
New York, New York

Janice Kowemy, director,
Laguna Public Library,
Laguna, New Mexico

Nyal Niemuth, engineer,
Arizona Department of Mines and
Mineral Resources,
Tucson, Arizona

Lotsee Patterson, archivist,
University of Oklahoma,
Norman, Oklahoma

James Rosenzweig, reference,
University of Washington,
Seattle, Washington

Jeff Savage, reference,
Great Falls Public Library,
Great Falls, Montana

Graham Sherriff, reference,
Beinecke Library, Yale University
New Haven, Connecticut

Joel D. Valdez, reference,
Pima County Library,
Tucson, Arizona

I owe special thanks to reference librarians Mark Schumacher of the University of North Carolina at Greensboro Library, Burl McCuiston of the Lenoir Rhyne University Library, Martin Otts and Mary Sizemore of the Patrick Beaver Library, and Wanda Rozzelle of the Catawba County Library. My work gets a collegial boost from the advice of webmaster Patty Johnson and of my press agent and fellow writer Joan Lail.

# Table of Contents

The most effective political statement I could make is in my art work....
The most radical kind of politics is language as plain truth.
— Leslie Marmon Silko, 1985

We came out of this land and we are hers.
— *Ceremony*

A'moo'ooh, my dear one
these words are bones.
— *Storyteller*

# *Preface*

For readers perusing Leslie Marmon Silko's broad canon of nativist, feminist, Southwestern, and American literature, the present work offers an initiation and guided overview. Commentary informs the reader, feminist, historian, linguist, student, researcher, teacher, reviewer, and librarian with analysis of characters, plots, humor, symbols, philosophies, and classic themes from the writings and tellings of a pace-setting native American culture keeper. The text opens with an annotated chronology of Silko's multiracial heritage and life, early works, classroom experience, public appearances, and honoraria. A family tree of the Leslie-Marmon families clarifies relationships of the people who fill her autobiographical musings. The 87 A-to-Z entries combine analysis from scholarly Americanists, literary historians and critics, and book reviewers along with generous citations from primary and secondary sources and comparisons to classic and popular literature. Commentary from Austria, Canada, England, Italy, Germany, the Netherlands, Spain, and Switzerland and from Amerindian scholars illustrates the range of scholarly interest in Silko's canon. Each entry concludes with selected source material on such subjects as adaptation, siblings, music, order, reading, food, color, writing, and achievement. Annotated charts identify interrelated casts of characters, notably, the most resilient women, both fictional and historical. In addition to substantiating dates and events, character lineages account for the relationships among fictional casts of her most celebrated works, *Ceremony, Almanac of the Dead, Gardens in the Dunes,* and "Yellow Woman." Generous cross references point to divergent strands of thought and point the reader toward peripheral territory, e.g., from vengeance to violence, from powerlessness to vulnerability, from women to wisdom, and from ritual to religion.

Back matter is designed to aid the student, reviewer, and researcher in locating and understanding specific details. A glossary of terms enables readers to understand the significance of a range of pertinent subjects, including pre–Columbian writings on *amatl,* uses for yucca, the racist intent of *sangre limpia,* variant Christian beliefs among Gnostics, methods of creating petroglyphs, and the Mayan division of time into the 7,200-day *katun.* A note on spelling contrasts alternate forms of native terms, particularly the names of deities and mythic beings and of the *hummah-hah,* Pueblo creation lore. "Appendix A: Events in Silko's History" retraces historical events with a timeline of people and movements that generate crises and opportunities in the lives of fictional and historical figures, for example, the formation of Lake Bonneville in 32,000 B.C., the flooding of Pueblo shrines by the Army Corps of Engineers in 1973, Nuño Beltrán de Guzmán's genocide of the Yaqui in 1529, and educator Richard H. Pratt's attempt in 1878 to eradicate indigenous culture via indoctrination at the Carlisle Indian School. The entries feature references to the works from which each event derives. A second appendix provides 43 topics suitable for group or individual projects, composition, analysis, background material, and literary companions. Notable themes are problem solving and community spirit; the impact of settings; contrasting parenting styles; evidence of the supernatural; and shifts in the family power structure as revealed in such notable authors as Joseph Bruchac, Amy Tan, Simon Joseph Ortiz, Isabel Allende, Mario Vargas Llosa, Barbara Kingsolver, Victor E. Villasenor, Kaye Gibbons, and Louise Erdrich.

Back matter concludes with an exhaustive alphabetic listing of primary sources followed by a general bibliography organized by each of the 14 Silko titles that the sources discuss. Many entries derive from journal and periodical articles, interviews, and critiques of Silko's essays, novels, and short fiction in major newspapers from the Americas and Europe. Secondary sources, particularly those by experienced reviewers, account for the advancement of Silko's earliest works to positions of authority in feminist, nativist, and postcolonial literature. A comprehensive index directs users of the literary companion to major and minor characters, divinities, events, historic eras, significant figures, place names, Silko's family and awards, published works, literary motifs, period terms, genres, and issues, e.g., Juana and Shush, Quetzalcoatl and Damballah, the Treaty of Guadalupe Hidalgo and the Vietnam War, the Great Depression and Indian Wars, Red Cloud and Wovoka, Jackpile mine and the Colorado River, Virginia Lee Leslie Marmon and *Chicago Review* poetry award, *Sacred Water* and *Popol Vuh*, Gothic and dystopia, Victorianism and polygamy, prophecy and parable, and prisoner of war and tribalism.

# *Introduction*

An original voice of the Native American Renaissance, Laguna author and teacher Leslie Marmon Silko retrieves from neglect and error the history of the American Southwest. A native of Laguna, New Mexico, she enriches her writings and speeches with authentic ethnomythography of her blended ancestry and with memories of her sixty-plus years as a teacher, speaker, writer, and activist. The author stokes her characters with the fervor and mindset of first peoples and with a nativist affinity for the land, water, and sky. Her stories resound with delight in community and with demands for justice to the American Indian. Silko contributes realism to themes of pueblo life — accounts of colonial witchery, dispossession, Christian proselytizing, and culture theft by anthropologists and archeologists. Avoiding sentimentality, she dramatizes the lot of the elderly grandmother, the battle-weary combat veteran, estranged husband and wife, the exiled traitor of the tribe, and children living on the edge of poverty and respectability. She reserves her most potent diatribes to counter the demeaning of natives into second-class citizens.

Inspired by a New Mexican upbringing, Silko respects the Pueblo matrilineage for producing hardy wives, mothers, daughters, elders, teachers, and the energetic clan matriarch, gardener, and culture bearer. Her stories highlight female accomplishments — Bronwyn's stewardship of terraced Celtic gardens, Ayah's insistence on respect, Grandmother Spider's advice to the unwary, Night Swan's devotion to dance, Hattie Abbott Palmer's research of female contributions to Christianity, *la professoressa* Laura's hybridizing of black gladioli, and Yoeme's guardianship of precious Mayan manuscripts, which Seese translates. Silko's sturdy female cast exerts skills at cooking, healing, weaving, art, acculturation, and socialization and prepares the young through wit and example. She excels at cautionary storytelling, a Marmon family strength modeled by Grandma A'mooh and Aunt Suzie Reyes Marmon. The allegiance of her storykeepers invests society with perspective on historic losses and hope for redress of anti–Indian atrocities that date from the arrival of Hernán de Cortés to Mexico into the 21st century. Through sisterhood and magnanimity, women oppose usurpation, rape, murder, and the ongoing trampling of the land by the greedy.

Readers and critics laud Silko as a one-of-a-kind teller of coyote tales, the disseminator of alternate Geronimo legends, and a spokeswoman for Amerindian artists. Her nurturance of first peoples' pride derives from representations of Hopi katsina dances, meals shared with outsiders, reverence for Star Beings, investiture in the priesthood, and reclamation of variant myths that date to the beginnings of native life in the Americas. Her gift for comic poses and turns of phrase presents human antics and failures as events worthy of scrutiny, as with Harley's inclusion of Tayo in drunken carousing, Delena's dressing of dogs in costume for a camp show, and Angelita's hanging of a Cuban Marxist for disloyalty. A self-confident shaper of lore, Silko rejects European literary paradigms in favor of non-linear text and a blend of photo, sketch, verse, prayer, and anecdote with traditional chronicle. From her skill at involving the audience in the recapture of native lore, she has earned an enviable place among world authors.

# Chronology of
# Silko's Life and Works

A Laguna-Cherokee-Latina-Caucasian wisewoman, scenarist, and revisionary mythographer, memoirist, and poet, Leslie Marmon Silko looks to stories as sources of the good and true. A multicultural native in a culture-blended land, she perceives universal strategies of postcolonial resistance and survival and mediates between the past and what lies ahead for Amerindians and mixed-blood peoples. Thematically, she focuses on matters of urgent concern — peace, land and water conservation, and opposition to culture theft, pollution, war, and violence against females. The first internationally acclaimed native female author, she confronts the white world with writings derived from Aztec myth and from Laguna songs and stories, the Pueblo Indian's mainstay against disease and death. Her organic style unites the everyday with the profound. Reflecting on Indian loss and outrage over a half millennium of illegitimate white sovereignty in the Western Hemisphere, she envisions herself as an ambassador for the Laguna, a harbinger of change. Her age-old instincts grace contemporary world fiction with a storehouse of matriarchal lore reasserting Indian insights. Of her choice to write stories rather than tell them, she mused, "For a woman of indigenous heritage to even be writing is political in and of itself" (Jeffries, 2010). The author's emergence as a major American literary force turned her early publications into touchstones of indigenous writings and into standards by which critics judge ethnic art.

**1851** The Rev. Samuel C. Gorman and his wife Catherine, emissaries from Cincinnati, Ohio, dispatched by the Baptist Mission Society, became the first to convert to Christianity the Laguna, a non-nomadic, agricultural tribe. Silko implied cultural disruption from proselytizing that "upset Laguna ceremonialism" (Silko, 1981, 256).

**1861** Silko's 16-year-old great-great uncle, Walter Gunn Marmon of Bellfontaine in Logan County, Ohio, claimed colonial ancestry dating to John Merrimoon (1713–1785) of London and Samuel Merrimoon of Northampton, North Carolina. Walter left his 13-year-old orphaned brother Robert Gunn Marmon and enlisted in the Second Ohio Heavy Artillery. A comic allusion to Robert and Walter Marmon enlivens "Toe'osh: A Laguna Coyote Story" (July 1973), in which Silko pictures herself and fellow poet Simon Joseph Ortiz as mixed-blood Pueblo "howling in the hills southeast of Laguna" (Silko, *Laguna Woman*, 1974, 4).

**1865**   Walter Marmon left the Union army with the rank of first lieutenant in the second regiment of the Ohio Heavy Artillery, which left Portsmouth, Ohio, on September 15, 1862, and served primarily in eastern Tennessee and North Carolina. Robert Marmon, at age 17, was a quiet, gentle Quaker who taught school in Harden County, Ohio.

**1869**   After the civil war, Walter Marmon surveyed for U.S. government contractor Ehud N. Darling along New Mexico's Pueblo boundaries. The project extended over the Colorado Plateau and the Middle Rio Grande Valley. Marmon came in contact with the Laguna Pueblo, a non-nomadic, agricultural people. The Keres-speaking tribe consisted of four tribal groups of the Pueblo, a highly conformist people. His fertile collaboration with aborigines foretokened the author's fostering of positive cultural exchange between races.

**1870**   For the Atlantic & Pacific Railroad, Walter Marmon mapped the track route from Albuquerque to Arizona. He settled in a Baptist mission at the Laguna Pueblo. The place intrigued Marmon with what historian Sharon Holm called the "geosacred"—a "landscape encompassing the animate matrix between and including land and sky and all plants and beings within" (Holm, 2008, 243). In subsequent generations, Silko returned to the 1870s to reclaim the native heritage destroyed by investors, earth-movers, and builders, a hurtful scenario that permeates *The Turquoise Ledge* (2010). In the estimation of critic Cynthia Carsten, a religion specialist at Arizona State University, the author "remythologizes the landscape, which has been desacralized by those who have reduced it to commodity: tourists, anthropologists, railroad moguls, and mining companies, among others" (Carsten, 2006, 123). The exploiters became the villains of her caustic works, particularly the dystopian novel *Almanac of the Dead* (1991).

**1871**   Walter Marmon set up a government school for Acoma Pueblo and, six years later, married Mary "Mollie" Sarracino (Gawiretsa), a priestess and the daughter of a Kurena-Shikani shaman-chief, Kwime (Luis Sarracino), educated at Durango, Mexico. Historians identify Kwime as the first Laguna and leader of the pueblo in the 1870s, when he introduced the Zuñi mask cult and kachina dances. Mollie's brother Giwire (José "Uncle Joe" Sarracino) was a priest-healer and heir to Luis's position as spiritual leader. The Sarracinos' hybridization of Caucasian, Lagunan, and Mexican ethnicities Americanized Laguna Pueblo. According to ethnologist Elsie Worthington Clews Parsons, Giwire ministered to the people until his death in June 1919. The marriage formed Silko's perspective. Of the hardships of mixed blood people, novelist Larry McMurtry stated that they "find themselves stuck between cultures, neither wholly in nor wholly out of what may be their native society: too often they are viewed suspiciously by both of the peoples whose blood they carry" (McMurtry, 2007, xxii).

**1872**   At age 24, Robert Marmon moved from Ohio to Laguna and lived across the street for his brother. Silko recalled how the brothers traveled by train during Reconstruction "when so many other young men migrated west" (Silko, "Introduction," 1996, v). Following the route of Spanish *conquistadores*, the railway made nearly as much change as the Europeans had. With rail jobs came outsiders, the U.S. mail, intrusive federal agents, missionaries, and boarding schools hundreds of miles away, where teachers trained Indian children to abandon their native heritage.

     The author confided to interviewer Laurie Mellas on the acculturation of the Marmon brothers: "They were accepted by the Laguna people because they were peaceable, polite men" (Mellas, 2006, 12). Robert and wife Marie Anaya Mormon boarded sightseers arriving by train to the Acoma-Laguna area, including ethnologist Franz Boas, photographer Edward Curtis, and entrepreneur John David Rockefeller. Robert substituted for Walter at the one-room school, where students sat on logs and shared one book. In the essay "Fences against Freedom" (1994), Silko notes that anthropologists are wrong in declaring the Marmon brothers dictators over the pueblo. In *Yellow Woman and a Beauty of the Spirit: Essays on Native American Life Today* (1996), she adds, "The minute the Marmon brothers crossed over the line, they would have been killed" (Silko, 1996, 104).

**Spring 1873**   Robert Marmon became proficient at the Keres language. In later years, Silko regretted knowing him only from photos and stories of a "Navajo sing" (Silko & Wright, 1986, 69). Of her study of her great grandfather, she asserted, "Yet *I feel* as if I was alive when he was" (*ibid.*, 62).

**1877**   Walter Marmon helped codify the Laguna constitution for the Indian Council.

**1878**   Working for the U.S. General Land Office, Robert Marmon and his Indian crews surveyed land grants and townships, including the Maxwell Grant of 1,700,000 acres.

**1880**   Robert Marmon became the first non–Indian elected to the governorship of Laguna. His brother Walter held the post six years later. The Americanization of the pueblo forced out the conservatives, who conveyed ritual objects, katsina dances, and altars to Mesita.

**March 1880**   The New Mexico Town Company, a realty commission of the Atcheson, Topeka, and Santa Fe Railroad, hired Walter Marmon to survey and name streets for Albuquerque.

**1882**   Captain Walter Marmon commanded a company of the New Mexico Militia. Within three years, he rose to cavalry colonel during the Indian campaign, a subject that Silko covers in *Storyteller* (1981).

**July 1882**   Walter Marmon aided ethnologist and author Adolph Francis Alphonse Bandelier in compiling a Laguna history. Bandelier became the leading expert on Southwestern history.

**1886**   Great-grandpa Zackary "Jack" Stagner and his brother, Bill Stagner, ran away from their home in Sweetwater, Texas. They left behind their sister, Lillie Ann, the name that Jack conferred on his daughter Francesca Stagner, Silko's Grandma Lillie Stagner Marmon, wife of Grandpa Henry C. "Hank" Marmon, the Laguna storekeeper. Hank became a skilled linguist in the early Laguna dialect as well as in Diné, Hopi, Spanish, and Zuñi.

**1890s**   Grandpa Hank Marmon took hundreds of photos, which Silko used in her third book, *Storyteller*. She explained, "[Pictures] are part of many of the stories and ... many of the stories can be traced in the photographs" (Silko, 1981, 1). The taking of photos by non–Indians required tact. In the essay "The Indian with a Camera" (1993), she observed, "The Pueblo people did not fear or hate cameras or the photographic image so much as they objected to the intrusive vulgarity of the white man who gazed through the lens" (Silko, 1993, 4).

**1892**   After the death of his first wife, Agness Anaya (Analla), Great Grandpa Robert Marmon married Agness's older sister, Marie Anaya (Analla), who reared her nephew Walter and niece Edith C. Marmon. The sisters came from a family of cattle and sheepherders. A beloved matriarch and stern Presbyterian, Marie took the name Grandma A'mooh for her gentle ways with children and for educating them with stories told in the Laguna language. Silko recalls in *The Turquoise Ledge* how Grandma, then in her 80s, ground green chili and garlic on a lava grinding stone. Great-aunt Susie Reyes (Rayos) Marmon, a Keres speaker and member of the Roadrunner Clan, entered Albuquerque Mission School and learned English. Silko recalls that Grandma A'mooh, Aunt Susie, and Aunt Alice Marmon Eckerman were "proud to be women of the book as well as women of the spoken word" (Silko, 2010, 28).

**August 1896**   For five years, Aunt Susie attended the Carlisle Indian School, an experiment in Amerindian acculturation in Carlisle, Pennsylvania, 2,000 miles from Paguate, New Mexico, her home. She stayed in the area and attended Fairleigh Dickinson College and Bloomsburg State Normal School. A skilled genealogist and archivist, she "[kept] the moving life of the people in [her] belly," an incubation suggestive of human gestation (Lincoln, 2008, 110). The choice proved propitious in later years when her eyesight failed and left her dependent on memory.

**ca. 1900**   Great-grandmother A'mooh, according to Silko, "ran the show" (Silko, 1994, 6). She quarreled with Aunt Susie about the book *Stiya, the Story of an Indian Girl* (1881), anti-native propaganda by Marion Bergess written under the pseudonym Tonka. Bergess intended the work to turn graduates of the Carlisle Indian School against native customs by declaring them dirty and shameful. The government sent a copy to each student returning from a boarding school. In deference to good manners, A'mooh gave the book to Susie, who concealed it from the children. Silko never saw Bergess's work until she happened on it in the archives of the University of New Mexico Library.

**1912**   At age 17, Grandpa Hank read automobile critiques and road tests in *Motor Trend* and *Popular Mechanics* and planned to design cars. His teachers at the Sherman Institute, the Bureau of Indian Affairs (BIA) vocational school at Riverside, California, dissuaded him from so complex a life plan for a non-white student. Instead, they prepared him to manage a trading post. He returned to Laguna to work at Abie Abraham's mercantile.

**1918**   The growth of the Marmon clan infused tribal hierarchy with a blended culture. After World War I, the pueblo need for continuity marginalized mixed-race members as outsiders. In "Fences against Freedom," Silko recalls animosity in the post-war generation: "I could sense an anger that my appearance stirred in them" (Silko, 1994, 6). She blamed the hostility on memories of the "outside world, where racism was thriving" (*ibid.*).

**1920s**   After teaching at Isleta Pueblo School, Aunt Susie taught at Laguna's one-room school. She sang songs about the ocean to her daughter Josephine and other Indian children who knew nothing of the seashore. During this same era, Grandpa Hank Marmon bought a snapshot camera and began photographing family and the landscapes around the pueblo, particularly Beacon Hill and Pa'toe'che. Grandma Lillie stored the keepsake pictures in a Hopi basket, which the family explored as a form of visual storytelling. As explained by critic Lawrence Buell, "Every place signifies; every place, every creature has a story connected with it that forms a web of significance (always in process, not a constant) within which human thought assumes form and meaning" (Buell, 1995, 289).

**1930**   Prematurely, some ethnologists announced the end of native oral tradition. Sociologist Ruth Benedict, in "Eight Stories from Acoma," an article for the *Journal of American Folklore*, proved that the Pueblo stories prevailed as antidotes to the despair that caused alcoholism, suicide, and violence.

**1947**   The author's parents, Mary Virginia Lee Marmon, of Anglo-Cherokee heritage, and photographer and tribal council treasurer Leland "Lee" Howard Marmon, a veteran of World War II, married in 1947. Lee narrated the background of his pictures and "always had a story to go with each" (Silko, 2010, 28). The couple traveled to Denver for the birth and adoption of Silko's half brother, Virginia's illegitimate child, to an unknown family. The loss of the unnamed baby boy contributed to Virginia Marmon's problem drinking. Her jobs teaching home economics at Grant High School and serving Laguna as postmaster helped her maintain sobriety.

**March 5, 1948**   An Anglo-Keresan native of Albuquerque, New Mexico, mythographer Leslie Marmon Silko was born "the year of the supernova in the Mixed Spiral galaxy" (Silko, 2010, 1). Because of their multiracial heritage, the Marmons took no part in tribal ritual and lived at the far edge of Laguna society near the San José River bordering the enclave, the ancestral dwelling of the Marmons for four generations. For her first year, she remained on the traditional cradleboard at the old stucco Santa Fe Railroad depot, the home of her paternal grandparents, Hank and Lillie Stagner Marmon. The building still held the sliding panel and ledge of the ticket window. During the infrequent derailment, the Laguna and train employers held a party. Children explored the wreckage for salvage. Once, they collected enough canned hams to supply the pueblo for five years. The author recalled, "It spoiled my appetite for fancy canned hams forever" (Silko, "Introduction," 1996, v).

The Marmon home reflected the Americanization of first peoples through intermarriage, a social shift that reflects the "melting pot" concept of diaspora. Silko dramatizes tribal intermarriage in *Gardens in the Dunes* (1999) with the twins, Maytha and Vedna, born to a Chemehuevi mother and Laguna Pueblo father and with Sister Salt's bearing of a first child to Big Candy, an Afro-Red Stick Indian from Louisiana.

**1950**  With her relatives, Silko regularly traveled eight miles of the state highway linking Laguna with Paguate, a route connected to the Laguna migration story. After the birth of sister Wendy in 1950, the Marmon girls grew up across the street from the depot in the adobe and rock house where their father was born. On the quarter-acre lot, the two stayed "corralled like goats" (Silko, 2010, 24). The Laguna neighbors disapproved of Lee Marmon's whipping of his small daughters. The siblings learned early the Laguna code of conduct and courtesies from stories, such as the injunction "It is bad manners to make comparisons that might hurt another person's feelings" (Silko, 1996, 65).

In her pre-school years, Silko viewed the Navajo and Pueblo purification rituals conducted for World War II veterans returning home from combat in Europe, Africa, and the Pacific to protect them from sickness and harm. The inefficacy of traditional chants and rituals caused her to reflect on the corrupting evil of 20th-century warfare on individuals, families, and clans. She learned that "No person suffers or grieves alone because the people in the Laguna community tell that person's story and inevitably other stories about similar incidents which have happened in the past to other people come to light," tales of victory and tragedy (Chavkin and Chavkin, 2007, 25).

Silko cultivated activities at home and in the wild alone on foot or on horseback. She owned two dogs, Blackie and Bozo, and observed Coonie, a stray mother cat with kittens. The author became more comfortable with cats, dogs, and horses than she was with people. To ease her daily life, she fantasized about having four fast legs like a deer. Her sense impressions reflected the Pueblo concerns for water. She states in *Sacred Water* (1993): "I learned to watch for the fat dark rain clouds, and I remember the excitement and the anticipation as the cool wind arrived smelling of rain" (Silko, 1993). With *Ceremony* (1977), she saluted the distant mountain that "could not be lost to them because it was in their bones ... vitality locked deep in blood memory" (Silko, 1977, 219).

The author and her sisters roamed the sandhills that called to their father in boyhood and enticed him away from regular employment to take pictures of the outdoors. Silko recalls in the essay "On Photography" (1996), "I have been around trays of developer and hypo under red safelights since I was old enough to perch on a high stool" (Silko, 1996, 180). The father-daughter experience encouraged her separation from peers and her contemplation of the outdoors. Leland Marmon's artistic standards for picture-taking influenced her view of sky and terrain: "From a really early age I was aware of looking at the land and shadows and sky and clouds, and so I think that part of my awareness and attention to [land] probably dates from my early experience with my dad" (Zax, 2007, 36). In an interview with Kim Jeffries, a journalist for the *Seattle Times*, the author pinpointed her specialty: "I like to do landscape — nothing with people in it" (Jeffries, 2010).

Silko and her sisters witnessed meetings where Lee Marmon hired an attorney for the Laguna Pueblo to assemble before the U.S. Court of Indian Claims expert witnesses—historian Dr. Myra Ellen Jenkins, archeologist David Brugge, and anthropologists Alfred E. Dittert, Warde Alan Minge, Dr. Robert Rands, and Dr. Florence H. Ellis. The Pueblo defended native rights to six million acres of land and the irrigation waters of the Upper San José River illegally seized by New Mexico after the 1848 Treaty of Guadalupe Hidalgo declared the Indians the rightful owners. One archeologist dated the Pueblo's residency to the time of Christ. Aunt Susie Reyes refined the oral stories of Kawakemeh residents of Laguna to convince a judge and court. Two decades later, after a verdict favored the pueblo, the court ignored the Treaty of Guadalupe Hidalgo and returned a cash settlement of $.25 per acre rather than ownership of the land. Silko concluded that "injustice is built into the Anglo-American legal system" that favors the rich and powerful (Silko, 1996, 19). The model of Aunt Susie as mediator between the Pueblo and white worlds infused Silko with ambition to translate oral lore into authentic written text. As novelist Larry McMurtry explained the necessary coming to knowledge, authors like Silko "not only know what their ancestors knew as tribal people, they know what our ancestors knew as dead white Europeans" (McMurtry, 2004, 45).

**October 1951**   Silko recalled how her father took her on errands in his pickup truck. He held her up to view the last steam locomotive of the Atchison, Topeka and Santa Fe freight train at New Laguna on its way to Gallup and Flagstaff, Arizona. Her eye for detail caught "traces of coal and old cinders [that] stained the sand on the dirt road in front of the house where I grew up" (Silko, "Introduction," 1996, iv). In the introduction to Linda Grant Niemann's memoir *On the Rails: A Woman's Journey* (1996), she joked that the four A. M. train awakened the locals and encouraged early morning sex, the reason that Laguna became the most populous pueblo.

**1952**   At age four, despite the supervision of Pueblo adults, Silko began venturing over the four-foot-high fence of her family's yard to engage people passing to the store and post office. In the distance she could view woodcutters and shepherds in the hills and hear drumming at ceremonial dances in the plaza. On her horse Joey, she rode southeast of the pueblo for hours and knew no fear of visitors or kidnappers because stories set in these locales made her feel safe on familiar ground. Her adventures included scaling cottonwoods and wading in the San José River in company with her dog Bulls-eye. In old settlements, she found arrowheads and studied petroglyphs on sandstone escarpments. With toy figures, she emulated Pueblo farmers and cowboys and Indians.

The author heard her father discussing with Laguna residents the murder of a white New Mexico police officer by three Acoma men. She was too young to read newspaper accounts and absorbed details from oral tellings. The story took shape in subsequent writings: Silko's "Tony's Story" (1969) and Simon Joseph Ortiz's "The Killing of a State Cop" (1974). Both set the compelling event during the corn dance, a late summer ceremony that propitiates deities to guard the Laguna food supply from drought. A report on the killing in the *Albuquerque Journal* set it on April 11, 1952, when 31-year-old William Felipe shot Nash Garcia, a New Mexico state trooper, at Black Mesa southeast of Grants on the Acoma Indian Reservation. After the trial on September 22, a federal judge, Carl Atwood Hatch, sentenced William Felipe and his brother Gabriel to execution.

Silko made contact with her Cherokee heritage. Her maternal great aunt Lucy Goddard Michael told her niece stories of Cherokee ancestors and gave her a copy of *Hiawatha* (1855), the literary epic by Henry Wadsworth Longfellow. Of the advance of early forebears over North America, Silko realized, "The spirits of all our ancestors are limitless, and they range all across the American continent regardless of the years or the boundary lines" (Silko, 1974, 43).

**May 7, 1952**   During this period of Silko's girlhood, the Laguna people relieved unemployment rates of 70 percent by working at the Jackpile uranium mine only 2,000 feet from the pueblo. The BIA helped negotiate the contracts, but failed to warn laborers of the danger. Regular paychecks increased crime and alcohol and drug abuse. No one offered miners protective gear or warned villagers of radiation poisoning. As housewives spread sliced fruits and vegetables to dry in the sun, radioactive dust settled on the harvest. Until the closing of the mine in 1981, residents experienced high rates of miscarriages, children with birth defects and mental retardation, upper respiratory distress, and lymph, skin, and stomach cancer. When operations ceased, the owners of the Anaconda Copper Mine left behind unstable mine shafts, 23,700,000 tons of tailings, sterile land, and contaminated water that leached pollutants into the San José River and 150 miles away into Elephant Butte Reservoir. In *Ceremony*, Silko revealed that datura, the hallucinogenic plant known as jimson weed, moon flower, or locoweed, was the only natural substance that could detoxify the land. She reprised the potency of locoweed in the myth of Pa'caya'nyi, the medicine man in *Storyteller*.

**1953**   Educated at the K–4 elementary school in Laguna, operated by the BIA, Silko rode the bus to kindergarten, where "talking Indian was forbidden" (Silko, 2010, 41). Because teachers whipped pupils who uttered native words, Grandma A'mooh stopped speaking Keres and addressed her grandchildren in English.

**Second week 1953**   Because the author spoke English, she advanced to first grade. During periods of loneliness and alienation, she turned to books because "there were no beloved grandmas or aunts to tell me stories" (Silko, 1996, 160). On return from school, she asked permission before visiting her grandmother next door. The author felt secure in the family homeplace, where tribe members trained her by example in etiquette codes and expectations and actively through dancing, singing, worshipping, and storytelling. She differentiated between stories as "evening entertainment" and Pueblo oral culture, which she designated as "the whole basis of community," a mix of history, philosophy, and native worldview (Zax, 2007, 36).

Acceptance of the mixed-blood child affirmed Silko's tribal identity and elevated her as an individual. In a loving extended household, she retained the companionship of deceased relatives, who "are still there … still a presence" (Seyersted, 1985, 18). Some 50 miles from Albuquerque, her father and grandfather, Lee and Hank Marmon, ran the Laguna Trading Post until 1966. Silko came in contact with the egalitarian community, where each adult helped to inculcate each reservation child through stories incorporating myth, religion, science, and technology. She commented in "Landscape, History, and the Pueblo Imagination" (1986), "The stories often contain disturbing or provocative material, but are nonetheless told in the presence of children and women. The effect of these inter-family or inter-clan exchanges is the reassurance of each person that she or he will never be separated or apart from the clan, no matter what might happen…. You are never the first to suffer a grave loss or profound humiliation" (Silko, 1986, 93). The concept of child rearing through personal contact with tribe members taught Silko to value each resident.

The dynamic conversation that swirled around her evolved into a gestalt, a significant whole. She recalled, "I could hear something else, that there was a kind of continuum" (Hirsch, 1988, 1). In a self-revising process, any listener, no matter how young, could interrupt to note variations on past tellings. Co-creative additions and deletions renewed narrations, producing literary offspring with an integrity of their own. They became part of the oral tradition, a flexible, inclusive body of lore that entertained and informed while giving identity to her homeland. Of the instructive worth of narration, she declared, "Our greatest natural resource is stories and storytelling. We have an endless, continuing, ongoing supply of stories" (Seyersted, 1985, 21).

**1954**   Grassroots activism influenced the author and her attitude toward the American court system. The launching of a lawsuit by the Pueblo against the state of New Mexico for the theft of Indian land introduced her to class action. Elderly Keres speakers gathered at her home, where Aunt Susie interpreted English for the elders as they amassed proof to present a federal judge. The weeping of older Laguna at their loss impressed Silko, producing the sorrow and anger that undergirds her fiction.

**November 1954**   Lee and Virginia Marmon took their daughter on a deer hunt on snowy terrain atop Mount Taylor in the Cebolleta Mountains. Her father demonstrated the hunter's walk "from rock to rock to avoid dry twigs" (Silko, 2010, 54). Her ability to listen and observe proved crucial to her ecological writings.

**1955**   At age seven, Silko brought in kindling and water and tended goats, horses, and pigs while her sister Wendy completed indoor chores. Their father disapproved of toy guns or BB rifles and taught the girls gun safety before letting them practice alone with a .22 rifle. Silko joined her sisters at the dump by the San José River to target practice with pickle jars. In *The Turquoise Ledge*, she acknowledges that shooting without ear protection compromised her hearing. She loved letter writing to Great Aunt Lucy Goddard Michael and her sister, Grandma Jessie Ruth Goddard Leslie, both natives of Kansas. The essay "On Nonfiction Prose" (1996) states that correspondence developed the author's skill at straightforward prose personalized with an I-thou tone.

**September 1955**  Silko's outdoor skills emboldened Lee Marmon to brag that his girls could do anything boys did. Armed with a borrowed .30-.30 rifle, she hunted deer with her father. Like her protagonist Tayo in *Ceremony*, she rode horseback over the mesas north toward Aunt Susie and Uncle Walter's Marmon Ranch to drive cattle at Mount Taylor. Silko failed to bag a deer and grieved that her parents hunted alone, leaving her behind with Aunt Alice. To relieve the sadness, Alice told the story of a Laguna girl who hunts just like males.

From outings on the plains, Silko acquired a humility and reverence for earth powers. Key to her outlook was the Laguna belief that each human life has value, a pre–Christian tenet stretching over some 18,000 years of Pueblo Indian history. At the post office and Laguna Trading Post, her father instilled awe for black and white photos of noble tribe members, whom Lee pictured as dignified preservers of the native past. He anticipated Silko's images of blended cultures with his major portrait, "White Man's Moccasins," a seated view of a Laguna elder dressed in native clothes and high-top sneakers. The image captures in a single pose the author's dedication to Amerindian pride in nationhood and to the sovereignty of indigenous people.

With their parents, Silko, Gigi, and Wendy involved themselves in Laguna tradition. Unlike the Irish bardic tradition, which turns storytelling into a performance, Keresan tellings engage everyone present. Her female relatives taught womanly strength by relating traditional Keres-language *hummah-hah* stories— a body of animal fables, trickster lore, and the goddess myths of Corn Woman (Nau'ts'ity'i) and the creator, Spider Woman (also Thought Woman or Ts'it-s'tsi'nako). Aunt Susie stressed the interpretation of gynocentric myth out of fear that white educators would eradicate Pueblo cosmology and lore through diminution and replacement with androcentric white writings and Christian scripture.

From spontaneous shared stories, Silko learned concentration in sessions where even the youngest child had to recall characters and episodes. In *Storyteller*, she explains, "I grew up at Laguna listening.... Most important, I feel the power which the stories still have, to bring us together, especially when there is loss and grief" (Silko, 1981, 7). Her people insisted that no obstacle could jeopardize the survival of Keresan lore. The stories remained fixed in her mind and heart as a direct contact with her ancestors and place of origin.

**1956**  By age eight, Silko hunted regularly with her father. She gained her Aunt Susie's full attention for answers to questions. Unlike the author's experience with white teachers who "[preserved] the form but [removed] the content," she honored her aunt as Laguna's last oral storykeeper who retained the entire culture, beginning with creation lore (Minh-ha, 2003, 152). The author realized that each person's hearing contributed to "the long story of the people" and treasured the stories as "an entire identity of a people" (Silko, 1981, 7, 6). The contrast put her at odds with standard American history, particularly Old West stories about the Indian Wars and about the Apache hero Geronimo.

**1958**  At age ten, Silko entered the fifth grade at the Manzano Day School, a Catholic academy in Albuquerque. Teachers instructed her to defend American democracy and constitutional ideals and to value the benefits of U.S. citizenship. In the urban setting she felt alien, out of place, in part because of student response to her lunch of deer jerky. To interviewer Per Seyersted, she explained how Pueblos manage the shift from reservation to metropolis: "We move through the city, we talk with the people, but there's an extreme amount of tension that one feels and it can only be described as strangeness" (Seyersted, 1985, 17).

The grade-schooler loved painting, cutting, and pasting, but received poor grounding in mathematics and science. Ironically, her understanding of local rock formations, weather, and desert animals proved formidable in *The Turquoise Ledge*. Unlike her urban classmates, she knew nothing about the "times tables," but excelled at writing stories using each of the week's spelling words (Silko, 2010, 27). A Norwegian teacher taught her to respect myth. Silko began writing her own stories. Analyst Brewster E. Fitz, a literary theorist at Yale University, surmised that she "[yearned] for something like a perfect language that would heal the cultural wounds embodied in her own mixed-blood ancestry" (Fitz, 2004, x).

**1959**   To assist her 85-year-old Grandma A'mooh, who lived next door, Silko helped water the cosmos and hollyhocks and pick cilantro, agrarian chores that recur in *Gardens in the Dunes*. Her reward was "family stories about relatives who had been killed by Apache raiders who stole the sheep our relatives had been herding near Swahnee," a desert mesa (Silko, 2007, 209). During story sessions with her Presbyterian grandmother, Silko loved bible stories and illustrations of Jonah swallowed by a whale and Daniel in the lions' den. To repay A'mooh, Silko carried in the coal bucket and stacked firewood. When her aunts Alice and Susie visited A'mooh, they turned the stories away from Protestant religion to the Laguna *hummah-hah* stories of creation, when people talked with animals. During times alone, Silko wrote her own stories, which she recited to sisters and cousins. In sixth grade, she risked writing a dirty joke circulating among students and proposed starting a humor magazine entitled *Nasty Asty*. Complaints from schoolmate Helen Grevey resulted in scolding by the principal, Mrs. Westerfield, but a student delegation defended Silko.

**May 7, 1960**   For her twelfth birthday, Robert Anaya, Grandma A'mooh's baby brother, gave Silko a turquoise ring, which she described in *The Turquoise Ledge*. The elegant semi-precious stone carried a long history with Southwest Indians, who traded their gems and quartz knives with tribes as far south as Guatemala. The blue-green turquoise bore ritual significance among the Aztec, who powdered the stones into paint for ritual masks.

**1961**   At age 13, Silko attended an off-reservation Catholic institution, Highland High School, 50 miles from the reservation. She fantasized about working for the railroad, sleeping in the caboose, and highballing in a diesel locomotive at full throttle. She later declared her attraction to diesel engines "a primal, fervent wish of us human beings, puny mortals of mere flesh and blood, overwhelmed by the Industrial Age" (Silko, "Introduction," 1996, vi). She admitted she lacked the vigor and dedication to live the railroader's life.

The author indulged her love of American fiction by reading William Faulkner, Edgar Allan Poe, and John Steinbeck. During a deer hunt with Richard H. "Uncle Polly" Marmon and cousin Richard, she spied a huge brown bear on the southern downside of Chato hill. Unable to determine whether the bear was sleeping or dead, she slipped away and concealed her epiphany from others. The vision, a key memory in her autobiographical writings and verse, suggests her initiation as a medicine woman.

**1962**   Silko began training a quarter horse filly in the corral, where she lost the setting from her turquoise ring. She shot her first kill, a mule deer, through the heart. Her anthology *Yellow Woman and a Beauty of the Spirit: Essays on Native American Life Today* reprises an introduction to the sandstone escarpments of Canyon de Chelly and Canyon del Muerto, Arizona, historic locations of Colonel Kit Carson's abduction of the Navajo on a relocation called "the Long Walk." As the immensity of racial discrimination against first peoples became a daily reality, she recognized residual sorrow in her Grandpa Hank. Because of low expectations for Indians in boarding schools, he studied merchandising and kept his own store rather than follow his ambition to design cars. He bought a 1957 Ford Thunderbird hardtop convertible and kept the car the remaining eight years of his life. Her elegy "A Hunting Story" (1981) honors his passing. After Great-Grandmother A'mooh, in her last decade, moved in with a daughter, she suffered from loneliness and longing for the pueblo's oral culture and died at age 93. In *Story-*

*teller*, Silko mourned the result of absence of the oral culture: "She did not last long without someone to talk to" (Silko, 1981, 158).

**1963**   At age 15, Silko struggled with migraine headaches and vertigo, which returned in 1973 while she lived in Ketchikan, Alaska.

**1964**   In her junior year, Silko chose as heroes transcendental philosopher Margaret Fuller and feminist diarist Alice James. Critics identify Hattie Abbott Palmer, the church historian in *Gardens in the Dunes* as a fictional version of Margaret Fuller, a risk taker who became the first woman to use the Harvard library and the first female correspondent for the Boston *Tribune*.

**February 13, 1965**   When her Grandpa Hank Marmon died at age 69, Silko attempted mouth-to-mouth resuscitation, but the elderly patriarch was not recoverable from heart attack. She realized that she lost the opportunity to learn more Keres vocabulary from him. In 1981, she published in *Storyteller* the poem "Deer Dance/For Your Return," a poignant tribute to the grandsire who had impacted her life. She regretted shifts in the Mormon extended family: "His death ended the happiness of my childhood; the family slowly unraveled after that" (Silko, 2010, 208).

**April 2, 1966**   At age 18, Silko experienced the divorce of her parents. She wed Richard C. "Dick" Chapman, a graduate student in archeology at the University of New Mexico. She considered the visual arts, but found the university art department blind to all but European perspective and realism. Dick encouraged her to take the best teachers in the English department and to study creative writing.

**Fall 1966**   During the first semester of her sophomore year, Silko experienced a life-threatening uterine hemorrhage. Son Robert William, born early and underweight, struggled to survive respiratory problems. Following the brief marriage, Silko sought a divorce. Virginia Marmon suggested that she apply for a United Daughters of the Confederacy scholarship. The money—$200—acknowledged the author's grades as well as her ancestors' role in the Confederate military.

**1967**   The author studied under Southwestern novelist Tony Hillerman, the best-selling author of Navajo police procedural mysteries. After two semesters of anthropology in her freshman year, Silko began composing short stories. She wrote a paper on race for a college honors seminar. In line with the research of anthropologist Ashley Montagu, author of *Man's Most Dangerous Myth: The Fallacy of Race* (1942), she and other Amerindians concluded that there are no distinct races. Her essay "Fences against Freedom" declares, "We are all one family—all the offspring of Mother Earth—and no one is better or worse according to skin color or origin" (Silko, 1994, 6).

**1969**   In the year that Navarre Scott Momaday won the Pulitzer Prize for *House Made of Dawn*, Silko graduated *magna cum laude* from the honors program with a B.A. in English. She developed a writing career by publishing stories and verse in anthologies and textbooks, including *The Norton Anthology of Literature by Women*. Her first success, "Tony's Story" (1969), appeared in *Thunderbird*, the student literary magazine of the University of New Mexico. It rationalizes an Acoma man's killing of a state police officer, an event much discussed by her father and others. She was surprised that a murder that happened when she was four years old crystallized in her mind, particularly Antonio "Tony" Sousea's belief that he was exorcising a witch.

**Winter 1969**   Silko followed with another real event described in a parable of first encounters, "The Man to Send Rain Clouds" (1969), a classroom assignment she submitted to the *New Mexico Quarterly*, an outlet for Southwestern artists and writers published in Albuquerque.

Drawing from the culture she knew best, she set the story of a Christian burial of Grandpa Teofilo, an elderly sheepherder and ceremonial dancer, at the Mission San José, a landmark of Laguna Pueblo. The story syncretizes the Catholic concept of holy water with the native perception of the sanctity of rain, a gift from deceased ancestors who visit earth in the form of rain clouds. The powerful ritual motif won her frequent publication in short fiction compendia and textbooks featuring women and non-white authors.

**January 20, 1969**   Soon after the inauguration of Richard Nixon to the U.S. presidency, Silko noticed that official government documents no longer noted "ancestry" or "heritage." Instead, "The fiction of 'the races' had been reestablished" (Silko, 1994, 6). As she stated in "Fences against Freedom," racial pandering once more dominated U.S. politics. A major issue of the Vietnam War, the wholesale mustering of men from black urban ghettoes for the military exploited poverty and unemployment among minorities.

**1970**   Silko returned to the University of New Mexico to enroll in the law program to seek justice for the Laguna. The coursework disciplined her speedy outlining of essays, but she feared the stern objectivity of law: "The curriculum sucked the life out of my imagination and out of my writing" (Silko, 1996, 193). During her classes, her people settled the lawsuit against the U.S. government that they had pressed in 1954. She was dismayed that the U.S. Court of Indian Claims found in favor of the Laguna, but awarded them only $.25 per acre for the six million acres of stolen land for a total of $1,500,000. Restitution failed to cover attorney fees of nearly two million dollars. From a study of the Anglo-American legal system and a reading of Charles Dickens's social novel *Bleak House* (1853), she concluded that the feudal system continued to reduce the lower classes to serfdom. The execution of a severely retarded man for strangling a white librarian in 1949 ended Silko's pursuit of a law degree. In 2010, she observed, "The law has nothing to do with justice, and injustice can't be left unchallenged. So I decided to be a writer" (Bennett, 2010).

The author enrolled in photography courses, switched majors, and pursued a graduate degree in creative writing, which introduced her to the illuminated texts of English visionary poet William Blake. She wed Alaskan hunter John R. Silko, the DNA lawyer at Chinle, Arizona. John Silko served as legal counsel to the Navajo to alert the Federal Trade Commission to the illegal practice of whites trading with the Navajo. The Silkos lived in the old Gunn house at New Laguna. They raised chickens, cats, and dogs and built a corral next to their residence for goats and for their horses, Molly and Sparkplug. She struggled to publish her writing. With women friends, she joined a female consciousness-raising group.

At the heart of Silko's loyalty to Keresan language and lore, a belief in native sovereignty compelled her to view the entire history of the aborigine long before the arrival of whites. The perception of organic connection to earth launched her ecofeminism, which she based on an awareness that all people share a finite planet and a responsibility to rise above arbitrary political boundaries to value earth. She adopted a humbling self-awareness that humanity is powerless to control nature, a perception that dominates *The Turquoise Ledge*. For her leadership, literary historians George A. Cevasco and Richard P. Harmond placed her in "the first wave of recent writers to be identified by ecocritical scholars for a focus on earth and the environment" (Cevasco & Harmond, 2009, 474).

**1971**   While beginning a two-year stint teaching at Navajo Community College (Diné College) at Chinle, Silko began submitting more short fiction and verse to anthologies and textbooks, including the story "Lullaby" (1974), issued in *Chicago Review*. The action occurs among the Navajo of Cebolleta in the 1950s during the government's attempt to relocate Indians from reservations to cities. The gynocentric story subverts the captive woman motif common to frontier autobiography by picturing a take-charge wife and mother who triumphs through endurance rather than empowerment. Silko creates a dissonance between the changing lives of Indians under white control and the stability of the Navajo world as revealed in a tender cradle song.

In the falling action, the woman outlasts her modernistic husband and presides over his death. In 1974, the story earned Silko a writing fellowship of $5,000 — a Discover Grant from the National Endowment for the Arts, a national encouragement for artists worth $15.1 million.

**Spring–Fall 1971**   During her second pregnancy, Silko wrote a short *bildungsroman*, "Humaweepi, the Warrior Priest," collected in 1975 in *The Man to Send Rain Clouds: Contemporary Stories by American Indians*. The story of a coming-of-age ritual prepares a 19-year-old apprentice for the role of shaman. His uncle and mentor introduces Humaweepi to spiritual union with nature by guiding him to a granite boulder shaped like a bear. Just as the great rock lies at the union of shore and lake, Humaweepi stands at the threshold of the priesthood. In a wordless encounter with the spirit bear, he intones a ritual song and presents gifts of red coral and turquoise, both gemstones bright with celebrational hues. Like the boy Arthur pulling the sword from the stone or Joan of Arc donning battle armor, Humaweepi's silent epiphany informs the initiate that he is now a warrior priest.

**Summer 1971**   The author taught English and creative writing for two summer sessions in 1971 and 1972 and for the full 1972-1973 school year. Three decades later, she remarked on her dislike of a campus milieu, where she labored like a migrant worker with no health insurance.

**1972**   After the author gave birth to son Cazimir Silko, she took beginning ballet under a professional dancer, Navajo performer Ben Barney, a teacher of ballet, jazz, and modern dance at Diné College. He taught the spiritual meaning of kinetics, not for entertainment, but for attunement of the performer with all life.

**1973**   Silko spent two years outside Rosewater Foundation-on-Ketchikan Creek, Alaska, while her husband, lawyer John Silko, supervised Alaska Legal Services. In the dark summer months, she fought lethargy caused by depression from a change of climate and terrain. She confessed in a letter to poet and confidant James Wright, "I was so terribly devastated by being away from Laguna country that the writing was my way of re-making that place, the Laguna country, for myself" (Silko & Wright, 1986, 27–28). Her writing gained momentum in September, after she enrolled her sons in day care. After retreating to the law library of her neighbor, attorney Richard "Dick" Whittaker, she wrote regularly at Mrs. Hirabayashi's cafe and took lunch breaks among Haida and Tlingit diners.

In vain, Silko tried to write a comic version of the post-war drunken antics of the fictional Harley, a veteran of the Pacific War, and attempted creating a female character different from herself. During bouts of migraine headaches and nausea, Grandma Lillie's heart attack, and son Caz's hospitalization with acute asthma, the author commiserated with Tayo, protagonist of *Ceremony*, a psychological fiction haunted by despair, displacement, and guilt. She began with a light-hearted unpublished short story about a carousing former GI entitled "Returning." Set in Ketchikan, the action of "Returning" features a severely depressed Indian prostitute whom a fisherman finds drowned in Thomas Basin after she leaps from a bridge over Ketchikan Creek. The victim wears a beaded garment that an elderly Nez Percé seamstress decorates to resemble the constellations of the night sky, a motif that recurs in *The Turquoise Ledge*. The suicide prefigures the character of "little sister" Laura, who fades from *Ceremony* after the dissipation of her dignity and heritage.

Because the female protagonist became too autobiographical, Silko moved on to a novel called *Hero*, the story of a shepherd named Louie, a war hero in the Philippines. He received 30 percent disability payments of $40 per month for surviving the 60-mile Bataan Death March of April 9–21, 1942. By the time he receives a silver medal in a velvet box at the Veterans Administration hospital, he weighs only 130 pounds. According to lecturer Robert Leslie Evans, she chose as a model the life of a distant cousin, Staff Sergeant Robert Leslie "Les" Evans, the great grandson of Robert Gunn Marmon. Sergeant Evans was a football hero at the University of New Mexico. After his drafting, he served in the U.S. Army artillery in Manchuria.

Silko shifted to the final form for *Ceremony*, in which Louie's disapproving mother becomes Auntie Thelma. Silko made Tayo, Thelma's nephew/foster son, a fictional representation of over 44,000 Indian combatants during World War II, a larger proportion in military service than any other ethnic American group. While involved in action on all fronts, they earned three Congressional Medals of Honor along with Air Medals, Bronze Stars, Distinguished Flying Crosses, Distinguished Service Crosses, Silver Stars, and Purple Hearts. Silko recalled growing up among dysfunctional veterans, some of them her cousins infected with "the war disease." She retreated into creating a Navajo ceremony to retrieve Tayo from battle fatigue. Her novel achieved critical acclaim as a rebellion, a speaking truth to power about white deception and coercion. As a religious text that mediates a supernatural experience through story, myth, and chant, *Ceremony* eradicates racial boundaries, legitimates Pueblo lore, and fuses characters in a ritual that confers atonement and peace.

Copies of the author's work-in-progress, archived at the Beinecke Library at Yale University, reveal her personal quest to tell a truly native American story. In reflecting on her first novel, Silko reported that she completed it during a period of depression "to save my life" from homesickness for the Laguna of New Mexico (Chavkin and Chavkin, 2007, 26). Between 1973 and 1974, composition became her solace — "my refuge, my magic vehicle back to the Southwest land of sandstone mesas, blue sky, and sun" (Silko, 1977, xv). Her text incorporates Diné and Pueblo lore to celebrate curative powers of oral telling, "the old-time stories [that] evoked a feeling of comfort I remembered from my childhood at Laguna" (*ibid.*). She concluded with a native chant to make the novel itself a healing ritual.

**1974**   Silko earned respect for being the youngest author represented in *The Norton Anthology of Women's Literature*, for publishing "A Geronimo Story," and for collecting her introsective verse in a poetry chapbook, *Laguna Woman: Poems*. The titles reflect dramatic scenarios enriched by personal experience with Pueblo lore: "When Sun Came to Riverwoman," "Indian Song: Survival," "Toe'osh: A Laguna Coyote Story," "Story from Bear Country," and "Horses at Valley Store." The 35-page anthology won a *Chicago Review* poetry award for its montage of color, terrain, weather, and animal imagery. In the commentary, she refuses to claim expertise in Indian mythos by declaring herself a mixed-blood writer, an issue that permeates her autobiography. With an insider's voice, her hearty, libidinous verse refutes white misperceptions of the American frontier by focusing on the traditional Pueblo, people whom pioneers displaced. That same year, editor Kenneth Rosen anthologized seven of Silko's stories in *The Man to Send Rain Clouds: Contemporary Stories by American Indians*, a compendium containing "Yellow Woman." Critics and analysts reviewed her position as shaman and informant of Indian culture rather than artist and ecocritic. Female literary historians lauded her insightful story of female agency as a landmark of insight into aboriginal feminism.

**February 1974**   On a National Endowment for the Arts fellowship, Silko served as artist in residence for four weeks at Bethel Middle School, which she described as "an Eskimo town of 2,500 eight miles from the Bering Sea" (Silko & Wright, 1986, 27). In temperatures ranging to fifty below, she observed Yupik culture on frozen tundra and listened to native stories. For the students, she wrote "How to Write a Poem about the Sky," a nature verse reverencing a winter scene blending earth with the horizon. In the estimation of critics Thomas S. Edwards and Elizabeth A. De Wolfe, the poem "comes as close as Silko ever does to lyricizing the process of the observing eye" (Edwards & De Wolfe, 2001, 190). On her 29th day of residency among the Yupik, she felt that she must return someday to a people she had come to love.

**September 1974**   In a letter to Lawson Inada (Oregon's poet laureate), Silko explained the impact of a rainy season on the Sedillo Grant outside Mesita, New Mexico. Reprised in *Storyteller*, the letter describes Silko's delight that, after years of drought, unusual flowers bloom in arroyos once bereft of streams. In the Laguna tradition of storytelling as instruction, she imagines leaving behind stories of earth's renewal for the enlightenment of her grandchildren.

**1975**    The Silko family returned from Alaska and lived with Leland Marmon in Grandma Lillie Stagner Marmon's house until the refurbishment of Grandma A'mooh's old house. "Lullaby," a memorial to New Mexico friends Ada and Nash Chakee, received honors as one of the best 20 short stories of the year.

**Summer 1975**    At a national poetry conference in Michigan, Silko met Chinese poet Mei-Mei Berssenbrugge, Oregon poet laureate Lawson Fusao Inada, and James Arlington Wright, a teacher at Hunter College and winner of the Pulitzer Prize for verse. As Silko developed *Ceremony*, she read from her manuscript, which allegorized white culture as European traditions invented by a witch. Wright remarked, "Your reading brought us all into the presence of something truly remarkable" (Silko & Wright, 1986, 3). He admired Silko's oneness with the desert and "having the landscape itself tell the story."

**July 1975**    The author completed the manuscript for *Ceremony*, which literary historians George A. Cevasco and Richard P. Harmond dub "one of [her] most transparently environmental works" (Cevasco & Harmond, 2009, 474). In the preface, she wished that readers be "blessed, watched over, and protected by their beloved ancestors" (Silko, 1977, xix). Richard Woodward Seaver, an editor at Viking Press, liked the novel, which reveals some of her homesickness for New Mexico in vivid scenarios of the Southwestern desert. Her work complete, in September, she embraced once more her pueblo home.

**1976**    After teaching at the Navajo Indian Reservation at Chinle, Arizona, Silko divorced John Silko and returned to Laguna. She purchased a Toyo field camera and tripod and backpacked into the hills to photograph the topography and horizon. With scenarist Frank Chin, she adapted "Lullaby" into a one-act play for performance in San Francisco for the American Bicentennial Theatre Project, sponsored by the City Arts Commissions.

**March 26–31, 1976**    For the short film *Running on the Edge of the Rainbow* (1982), which English department chair Larry Evers produced at the University of Arizona at Tucson, Silko played a Pueblo storykeeper opposite sons Cazimir and Robert, Laguna resident Sandy Johnson, Muskogee poet Joy Harjo, and Harjo's daughter, Rainy Dawn. The mythographer read from a text of four poems and three stories on March 26–31, 1976, on the porch of Silko's adobe house in Laguna. Her role reflects the Marmon family's respect for wisewomen. Within the performance, critic Roumiana Velikova isolated the dynamics of oral discourse and improvisation — the impact of words delivered with a unique vocalization, the kinesic movements and wielding of objects in the physical setting, and the appeal to touch and smell. At a climactic point in the film, Silko wags her head and stresses the words "the end" that conclude the poem "Laughing and Laughing about Something That Happened at Mesita" (1974). The pun rounds out the session with humor.

**July 4, 1976**    In reference to the nation's 200th birthday, Silko accused Americans of rhapsodizing about iconic heroes Benjamin Franklin, Paul Revere, and George Washington while ignoring the colonists' theft from first peoples of land and sovereignty.

**August 1977**    Silko won a Pushcart Prize for Poetry and issued her first novel, *Ceremony*, a masterwork. Critic Sven Birkerts declared her "one of the most gritty and imaginative Native American writers" (Birkerts, 1991, 39). Author Sherman Alexie proclaimed *Ceremony* "the greatest Native American novel" (Alexie, 2006, 32). Analyst Jean Petrolle classified the novel as "an allegory of nation infused with theological, cosmological, and salvational discourses from nondominant traditions" (Petrolle, 2007, 130). The action situates Tayo, a displaced veteran of the Pacific war, in familiar Pueblo territory. Clockwise, scenes picture Mount Taylor overlooking Gallup to the northwest, the Jackpile Mine and the Pueblo heartland at Paguate village in the north, Mesita village to the east, the southeastern sandhills, Dripping Springs in the south, the sheep camp southwest of Patoch Butte, and the Dixie Tavern and Night Swan's apartment as well as Villa Cubero to the west.

Applying motifs from medieval Grail lore, the post–World War II study of Tayo, a veteran of the Pacific theater and the Bataan Death March, describes redemption of a wounded soul from alcohol and rootlessness through myth, nature, and ritual. Invoked by the Navajo shaman Betonie, revived and modernized rituals acknowledge period threats and accommodate the yearnings and hurts of veterans like Tayo, who weather flashbacks from combat and tribal alienation. In the style of Greek, Roman, medieval, and Renaissance allegory, *Ceremony* provides the protagonist with specific remedies to allay his post-war ache, reawaken cleansing memories, and equip him with heart strength and hope. Among the cures, Silko draws on the Navajo Blessing Way and the Warrior Way, two rituals she learned from lengthy contact with the Navajo culture. In Tayo's reclamation, he climbs into the core of Laguna spirituality, the reclaimed kiva, a subterranean ceremonial chamber symbolic of the womb that nurtured the Pueblo. In its confines, he can unload wartime memories for the enlightenment of the elders and for his own rehabilitation. Similar to the protagonists' discoveries in Tim O'Brien's *The Things They Carried* (1990), Stephen Faulks's *Birdsong* (1993), Winnie Smith's *American Daughter Gone to War* (1994), and Khaled Hosseini's *The Kite Runner* (2003), the telling is itself a creative, expiatory miracle. Novelist Larry McMurtry celebrates the fact that *Ceremony* "has been startling and moving readers in their thousands for more than a quarter of a century" (McMurtry, 2007, xxi).

In this same period, Silko underwent emergency surgery for abdominal bleeding, a condition that had been disrupting her concentration. She worried, "Will I ever be anything like the former 'me' again? ... I'd like just to be less tense and a little more calm like I once was" (Silko & Wright, 1986, 35). Simultaneous with acclaim for Silko's masterwork, the news of serious pollution reached Laguna and increased her anxiety. The Rio Paguate, which waters the reservation and its wells, contained radium-226, a stable isotope that decays into radon gas, a major cause of lung cancer. Worsening the scenario for residents, evidence of contamination doomed the community center, roads, and tribal assembly hall, which were built with radioactive mining slag. Russell Charles Means, an Oglala Sioux activist and spokesman for the American Indian Movement, parried a suggestion that the U.S. government designate Laguna a wasteland and continue assaulting the groundwater with radioactive slag.

**November 2, 1976** Flu symptoms masked an ectopic pregnancy, which required blood transfusions and emergency surgery for Silko on All Souls' Day, a Catholic holiday honoring the deceased with prayer for forgiveness. She confided to Cat Johnson, an interviewer for *Santa Cruz News*, that duties to others distracted her from a major responsibility: "I realized that the only one I hadn't taken good care of was me" (Johnson, 2010). The episode altered her priorities: "The close call changed my consciousness of myself and my life in a fundamental way; it made me understand how short my time in this world might be" (Silko, 2010, 77).

**Early January 1978** At 8000 West Camino del Cerro at the end of a winding road northwest of Tucson, Arizona, Silko settled in a house constructed in 1929. Outside her property, she viewed a sandy arroyo "criss-crossed with bird and animal tracks that make the trail that humans have used for thousands of years" (Silko, 2010, 5). In her musings on paleo–Indians, she caught sight of comings and goings of spirits long dead who returned to commune with the landscape. Her friend Linda Grant Niemann, a literary critic and brakeman for the Southern Pacific Railroad, called the place "peaceful, a middle earth ... a dreamtime among rattlesnakes and saguaros" (Niemann & Jensen, 2010, 87). Silko chose to teach at the University of Arizona while rearing son Cazimir among the Papago and Yaqui, both displaced aborigines. (The Yaqui, a tribe of *mestizos* living over a 3,500-mile expanse, range from southern California to southern Mexico. The semi-nomadic Papago, ancestors of the ancient Hohokam, occupy a more circumscribed territory in the northern Sonora Desert of Arizona.) Among her pupils was Simon Joseph Ortiz, a distant relative and Acoma poet. Her home, situated on a slope in view of Wasson Peak, featured saguaro drawings on the outside and a fireplace, for which she chopped mesquite wood. With an autofocus 35mm camera, the author rode frequently on horseback and sought spontaneity in her photography. She loved the colors of volcanic rock, "melted exotic conglomerates of stone that dazzle the foothills like confetti" (Silko, 2007, 110).

**August 28, 1978**   Poet James Wright read and admired *Ceremony* during a vacation to Misquamicut, Rhode Island. He called the work "one of the four or five best books I have ever read about America and I would be speaking the truth" (Silko & Wright, 1986, 3).

**September 9, 1978**   In a reply to Wright, Silko described the importance of collegiality and friendship at a time when "so many sad things have happened with my marriage and my children" (*ibid.*, 4). She described herself as "an outsider and alien to mainstream poetic style" and later repined that she had lost contact with verse during her "emotional upheaval ... the mess — divorce, money, etc." (*ibid.*, 7). She later indicated involvement in a child custody suit, which she lost. She praised Wright's works for "simple guts and heart" and for a "leanness" similar to the speech of elderly Laguna. In thanks, Wright sent her a copy of *To a Blossoming Pear Tree* (1978), one of the five anthologies he issued after winning the Pulitzer Prize for Poetry. He asked about anthologies of her verse and offered to nominate her for a Guggenheim Fellowship, an annual award from the annual purse of some $45,000 distributed to artists by the John Simon Guggenheim Memorial Foundation. At some point, she mailed Wright an outline of a prospective novel about Geronimo.

**October 12, 1978**   While working as writer-in-residence in Newark, Delaware, Wright kept a copy of *Laguna Woman* in his briefcase and reread it over a four-day period. He praised Silko's rooster story for "its clarity and speed and force" and remarked on the author's "abundance" (*ibid.*, 22). Five days later, she wrote back explaining "abundance" as wading in the San José River and hiding with a lover in the river willows and sand. She marveled at "the things we writers think nothing of attempting with language — things which are impossible visually" (*ibid.*, 25).

**1979**   After a stone snake appeared in Laguna in 1979, Silko studied rumors that the phenomenon embodied an ancient prophecy. One predicted that the icon pointed to a mesa where uranium miners would open a new pit. In 1988, she interpreted the reptile to be a messenger of vindication for Amerindians colonized and exploited by Europeans. In "An Old-Time Indian Attack Conducted in Two Parts" published in *The Remembered Earth*, Silko characterized the *humaweepi* (artist) as limited by consciousness and experience. She made the remark in a period when superficial whites imitated the shamanic tradition, a violation of native authenticity by New Age imitators.

**February 1979**   In *Carving Hawk: New & Selected Poems, 1953–2000*, poet Maurice Kenny rewarded the author with a lyric encomium, "Listening to Leslie Silko Telling Stories: New York City, 2/8/79." The seven-line poem pictures a magic and stage presence so permeating that her performance dispels February cold during the speaker's train ride to Brooklyn. With poet Philip Levine, Silko participated in a double writer-in-residence initiative at Vassar College in Poughkeepsie, New York. The invitation was a first-time program funded by a grant from the National Endowment of the Arts for three weeks from April 9–29.

**March 23, 1979**   Silko accepted a ten-week writer-in-residency at the English department of the University of Washington in Seattle, teaching English 277, beginning short story writing, and English 425–426, advanced short story writing. She enjoyed her 51 students, who appeared "enthusiastic and ready to do much writing" (*ibid.*, 47). A campus furor accompanied her three weeks in Poughkeepsie in May from students complaining that they received less than a full semester of her teaching. By June 1979, she was looking forward to resigning from the University of New Mexico to free up time and flexibility for writing.

**Late August 1979**   Silko sat up late with her 75-year-old Grandma Lillie, who was ill with heart disease. The author enjoyed talking about her work with Lillie, who admired busy people.

**September 1, 1979**   During a semester of teaching advanced fiction long distance from Tucson, Silko made intermittent visits to her class in Albuquerque. On September 1, she spoke at Harvard University at an English Institute on Native American perceptions of language and the use of English.

**November 5, 1979**   Silko sent Wright a messy copy of "Coyote Sits with a Full House in His Hand," a Pueblo legend that she began transcribing in early August for publication in spring 1980. She regretted having to teach while squeezing in time to write short pieces. Of the uneven progress of such efforts, she averred, "I have a naive faith that somehow, at some time, all the stories in me will get told" (*ibid.*, 90).

**December 15, 1979**   To keep solvent after her teaching salary ended at the conclusion of the semester, Silko depended on income from readings and technical writing for lawyers. She also received $100 per month from her first husband and a clothing allowance from son Robert's grandparents. In her spare time, she knitted caps and mittens for her nieces.

**1980**   According to "Notes on *Almanac of the Dead*" in *Yellow Woman and a Beauty of the Spirit: Essays on Native American Life Today*, Silko absorbed herself in "ancient astronomical observatories and the astronomical knowledge that the tribal people of the Americas had possessed long before the arrival of the Europeans" (Silko, 1996, 135). She studied Mayan mathematics and calculations of planetary positions and read articles on rocks, meteorites, rain, and El Niño weather systems that generated extremes of drought and flood.

**March 25, 1980**   Following admission to Mount Sinai Hospital in mid–January, James Wright died of throat and tongue cancer after only two meetings with his epistolary correspondent. After eighteen months of a postal dialogue, Silko, in her final encounter with Wright at his hospital room, found comfort in their similarities: "No matter if written words are seldom, because we know, Jim, we know" (Silko & Wright, 1986, 105). Jim described her as "a very fine, great person — a true beautiful artist" (*ibid.*, 103). Silko had observed the previous All Souls' Day that death does not destroy emotion or personal relationships: "If a dear one passes on, the love continues and it continues in both directions" because spirits and their survivors exchange perpetual love and feelings of intimacy (*ibid.*, 28). Thus, she adds, "No person is ever truly lost or gone once they have been in our lives and loved us, as we have loved them" (*ibid.*, 29).

**Spring 1980**   With the aid of producer Dennis Carr, Silko completed a film, *Estoyehmuut and the Gunnadeyah* (Arrowboy and the Witches), an experiment in storytelling on film. The text examines the three strands of the Arrowboy story cycle she incorporated in *Storyteller*. During her search for filming locations, she visited the 30-foot stone snake that appeared at the Jackpile uranium mine, a religious site that recalled the power of medicine people to interpret symbol. Of the film script, she exulted, "I love the stories so much that just working with them gives me great pleasure" (*ibid.*, 85). She chafed at the lengthy layout process, but acknowledged, "It is the book I was worried about, the book I felt I should do" (*ibid.*, 88). She added a regret that there were other books crowding her writing agenda.

**Summer 1980**   Following Silko's absence from home, she discovered the disappearance of Baby, her pet diamondback rattler, North America's largest venomous reptile. The snake lived in her barn to kill rodents.

**Summer and Fall 1980**   With color, Polaroid, and black-and-white film, Silko began photographing rocks in the arroyo near her home. The results turned terrain into worthy representations of earth: "Stone formations with Hohokam cisterns carved in them appeared as sacred cenotes (sinkholes), and flattop boulders looked as if they were sacrificial altars" (Silko, 1996, 181). When Konomi Ara, an author, reviewer, and professor at Tokyo University of Foreign Studies, completed the Japanese translation of *Ceremony*, she photographed Silko outside her Tucson home. The author was delighted to see how Japanese her features looked in the snapshot, a subtextual element of the protagonist Tayo's inability to shoot the enemy.

**January 24, 1981**  Silko worried over the low ebb of Lee Marmon's life from joblessness and poverty in the months preceding the birth of his son Leland. For the previous 16 years, he had worked as a freelance portraitist, completed a commissioned study of tribal pottery for the Nixon White House, and served the Bob Hope Desert Classic Gold Tournament as official photographer. When his career waned in his 56th year, she mourned, "I just hurt for him" (Silko & Wright, 1986, 37).

**May 19, 1981**  In *Storyteller*, recipient of the John Donald and Catherine Terese Hyland MacArthur Foundation Prize of $176,000, Silko wove 26 of Grandpa Hank's family photographs into eight short stories and 25 poems. The anthology developed into a treasury of legend, song, genealogy, and personal experience at the Laguna Pueblo. Material extended beyond the reservation to intertribal strands from the Acoma, Apache, Hopi, Navajo, and Sioux. The text stresses the humanity of the Pueblo who, "Like all human beings ... are concerned with their continued survival as the people *they believe themselves to be*" (Silko, 1993, 7). Critic Abby H. P. Werlock applauds the author's faith in folklore and describes her as "a proponent of the need for change to keep stories and society strong" (Werlock, 2010, 594).

The themes and actions derived from the writing of Aunt Susie Reyes Marmon. Refined by Richard Woodward Seaver and Jeannette Medina Seaver of Viking Press, the manuscript required re-editing to preserve the author's order of material and her pose as ethnographer of polyphonic narratives, an innovative technique that critic Hertha Dawn Sweet Wong called "communo-bio-oratory" (Wong, 1992, 26). The work illustrates Silko's overlay of memory and imagination, which, she admitted, "are not so easily distinguished" (Hirsch, 1988, 4). One of the mythic poems, "Laguna Coyote" from *Laguna Woman: Poems* (1974), recurred in *Storyteller* as a mark of Silko's contribution to the ongoing versions of animal fables that she heard from Grandpa Hank.

The author, divorced from her second husband, attorney John Silko, singlehandedly parented both sons. Of the rarity of marital breakup, she mused, "This is my second divorce, while Laguna is just now learning about divorce at all.... It's shaping up that I am known now for my husbands" (Silko & Wright, 1986, 60). During the tense domestic situation, she avoided her family in person and letters. A decade later, Bob Edwards, narrator of National Public Radio's *Morning Edition*, complained that, in the late 1970s, Silko virtually disappeared from the literary world for a decade. While ceasing to return phone calls or letters, she began taking notes and writing sections of *Almanac of the Dead*, stressing the predations of "the Portuguese monster de Guzman, the slave catcher in the 1500s" and the "criminality that seemed to permeate Tucson" (Silko, 1996, 139). She chose the title and began writing loose sections to piece together later in a book-length prophecy.

**July 12, 1981**  A decade after the American Indian Movement seizure of Alcatraz in San Francisco Bay, the *Los Angeles Times* published on the op-ed page Silko's essay "America's Debt to the Indian Nations: Atoning for a Sordid Past." She charges white America with "simplistic and inaccurate" reporting of "the validity of Indian claims of treaty violations and the legitimacy of other Indian grievances" (Silko, 1981, 2). The essay claims that Americans still cling to dime novel and Hollywood stereotypes of rebellious Indians. To make her own inroads against injustice, she stated, "I feel it is more effective to write a story ... than to rant and rave.... It is more effective in reaching people" (Romero, 2002, 623).

**1982**  Silko made a video of *Running on the Edge of the Rainbow: Laguna Stories and Poems*. She continued writing *Almanac* in sections like fragments of ancient Maya parchments, which exist in museums in Dresden, Madrid, and Paris. For the reader's convenience, she began plotting a way of linking the stories through time.

**1983**   The author made a clay figure inspired by the 30-foot stone snake at Paguate and photographed plastic snakes floating in her pool. Her mother, Virginia Marmon, retired from the Gallup public schools and lived with the author and her sons until her move to Ketchikan, Alaska, to tutor community college students in algebra and geometry. Virginia remained in Alaska until her death in 2001.

**October 1984**   At a three-week symposium sponsored by the Chinese Writers Association and the University of California at Los Angeles, Silko joined poet Allen Ginsberg, critic Francine du Plessix Gray, travel writer William Least Heat Moon, novelist Toni Morrison, journalist Harrison Evans Salisbury, and essayist and poet Gary Snyder, all U.S. authors. Her career took on an urgency in the publication of broadsides in *After a Summer Rain in the Upper Sonoran* (1984) and a humorous essay in *Mother Jones*, "Auntie Kie Talks about U.S. Presidents and U.S. Indian Policy." With three semesters of legal training in the past, she assembled the first rough draft of *Almanac*, which she described as a "seven-hundred-and-some-odd-page indictment" of the Anglo-American legal system (Silko, 1998, 94).

   The lengthy period of composition required rental of an office space at 930 Stone Avenue near central Tucson. She later abandoned her hideaway because of commuting difficulties. In the rundown section three blocks from the Salvation Army, she observed "the United States of America that no one wants to talk about"— the homeless and unemployed, drive-by shootings, and abandoned vehicles (Silko, 1996, 141). Attorneys in the building contributed anecdotes of crimes and verdicts of court trials in Pima County and further south. According to journalist Laurie Mellas, Silko "is keenly aware that outspokenness on issues such as native exploitation, capitalism, imperialism, discrimination, poverty, and the United States/Mexico border — which she calls 'meaningless and ridiculous'— moves some to anger" (Mellas, 2006, 11).

**Fall 1985**   As characters and dialogue captivated Silko, the manuscript for *Almanac* reached 1,000 pages. It featured a sustained apocalyptic vision of spiritual crisis and cultural disaster brought on by the white interpretation of "progress." The author viewed white successes as the outgrowth of land grabs and exploitation of natural resources.

**November 11, 1985**   Following Silko's lecture at the Walker Art Center in Minneapolis, Coffee House Press issued 300 numbered copies of *Ordinary Places*, a collection of broadsides transforming mundane sites into imaginative locales.

**1986**   During the presidency of Ronald Reagan, which ended in 1989, Silko regretted the dominance of the white male in American society and the lack of opportunities for women authors, especially ethnic and lesbian writers. She won the $500 *Boston Globe* prize for nonfiction for published letters in *The Delicacy and Strength of Lace: Letters between Leslie Marmon Silko and James Wright* (1986), edited by Wright's wife, Edith Anne Runk "Annie" Wright. Silko issued a critique for the *New York Times Book Review* and two short works, "Landscape, History, and the Pueblo Imagination" in *Antaeus*, and "Here's an Odd Artifact for the Fairy-Tale Shelf," a critique of Anishinabe novelist Louise Erdrich's *The Beet Queen* for *Impact/Albuquerque Journal*. In the latter, Silko embraced Laguna-Pueblo ancestry and upbraided Erdrich for exploiting Indian themes and motifs. The rebuke, according to critic Laurie Champion, charged Erdrich with "[sanitizing] American history and [obscuring] the truth about contemporary Indian life in the Dakotas" (Champion, 2002, 335). Public reaction to the caustic book review skewed criticism of Silko's works as rigidly tribal.

**Fall 1986**   With her MacArthur fellowship already spent, Silko tried to sell the first 660 pages of *Almanac*. During an intense period of composition following the inauguration of a bigoted felon, Arizona Governor Evan Mecham, and the rise of cocaine smuggling in Tucson, she perused the history of Coronado, Portuguese enslavement, and silver mines. To get at the truth about corruption in the Southwest, she allowed an aboriginal spirit to guide her insights. Echoing her concern, historian and satirist Eduardo Galeano, the Uruguayan author of the *Memoria del fuego* (Memory of Fire, 1986) trilogy, sent her galleys of his work in progress. The parallel thoughts and concepts of European usurpation of the Western Hemisphere affirmed Silko's long incubation period of *Almanac*. She impugned Tucson, a place she dubbed "city of thieves. Third generation burglars and pimps turned politicians" (Silko, 1991, 386). She spray-painted her office wall with "Recall Mecham. Impeach him. Indict him. Eat more politicians, end war, end taxes" (Silko, 1996, 143).

In opposition to Silko's publisher, her alternative history imitated the style of the Mayan scripture *Popol Vuh* (ca. 1554) and Amerindian medicine almanacs, which native authors compiled in many short chapters. The chapter headings themselves summarized the narrative. Two casts of characters—evil sadists and noble eco-warriors—infuse the circular narrative with allusive views and mythic prophecies affecting the future of capitalism and world history. According to critic Jean Petrolle, Silko avoided the vapid tricks of such postmodern fiction as Louise Erdrich's *The Beet Queen*, which clouded commentary with variant points of view. Instead, Silko remained faithful to "ethical perspective, political commitment, historical verity, and spiritual vitality" (Petrolle, 2007, 146).

Silko also joined Helen M. Ingram and Lawrence A. Scarr in debating the allocation of water in the Southwest in "Replacing Confusion with Equity: Alternatives for Water Policy in the Colorado River Basin," an essay issued in *New Courses for the Colorado River* and reprinted in *A River Too Far: The Past and Future of the Arid West* (1991). The essay points out the fragmentation of supervision, which prevents adequate policing of violations that victimize the greater population. The article concludes that civilization depends on fair distribution of water resources, a theme that Silko stresses in *Almanac of the Dead* through the work of greedy land developers.

**1988**   Silko halted her writing to spray-paint a folk art snake in acrylic on the brick wall of her office near De Anza Park in downtown Tucson. She described the 30-foot reptile as a sacred messenger modeled on West African and Amerindian mythos. A vision of a snake compelled her to work six months on the shaping of the giant blue icon. To express menace, she drew skulls in the reptile's gut, a symbol of starvation and injustice against the peasantry. A four-line dirge in Spanish blamed the rich for stealing freedom and land. The people—cold, hungry, and demanding redress—threaten revolution against the oppressors. She exulted, "The longer I worked on the mural, the better I felt about the novel" (Silko, 1996, 143). She remarked in 2010, "I was suddenly aware that I was self-taught, that I hadn't had any classes" (Jeffries, 2010). The completed painting, measuring 12 × 40 feet, had a therapeutic effect on the writing. Silko exulted, "I went back inside and finished *Almanac of the Dead*. The whole Mexico section, it all came. It all came" (Silko & Arnold, 2000, 100). The act of painting preceded the drawing of star beings in *The Turquoise Ledge*, an act of defiance to a bulldozer of desert terrain.

Silko's folk art won recognition as one of the best pieces of outdoor art of the year. The snake carries the story as a parturient woman bears a fetus. As a comeuppance to a 1988 law making English the legal language of Arizona, the author completed the visual caution with a caption in Spanish accusing the rich of suppressing civil liberties. The graphic symbol drew the attention of homeless women and children subsisting in cars, the victims of Reagan era "trickle down" economics, until a new landlord whitewashed the work six years later. Silko delighted in the peeling whitewash, which failed to conceal the powerful reptilian icon. On April 29, 1998, a decade after the racist English-only law altered the Arizona constitution, the state supreme court declared the muzzling of Hispanics and Indians restricted their free speech in conducting government business with elected officials and public employees.

The New Mexico Humanities Council designated Silko a Living Cultural Treasure. Her alma mater awarded her a University of New Mexico Distinguished Alumnus Award. Her honoraria as a writer and speaker combine with her repute as teacher of poets Joy Harjo and Luci

Tapahonso to reward a well-rounded literary powerhouse who influences writers, readers, historians, and students. A favorite story about Silko's beneficence to the next generation of native writers describes her giving Harjo her first electric typewriter. Of her mentoring of rising talent, creative writing director Sharon Oard Warner asserted, "I can think of no finer compliment for a writer and no more sacred obligation for a university" (Mellas, 2006, 14).

**1989**   The author issued in *Artforum* "The Fourth World" (Summer 1989), which reports responses to the stone snake at Paguate, New Mexico. Of the impact of her artistry on the scholarly community, she chortled at her own audacity: "I don't want to write something that the MLA [Modern Language Association] will want. I want something that will horrify the people at the MLA" (Barnes, 1986, 83). Her sentiment hints at the stir created by *Almanac of the Dead* for violating the conventions of an historical novel.

**July 1989**   After a decade of writing, at age 41, Silko completed the manuscript for *Almanac,* her boldest confrontation of the Anglo world for its crimes against Amerindians. The daring of her charges against Tucson and the Mexican underworld attest to a mid-life shift in style and intent. By championing the victims of white bigots, she broadened her outreach to the handicapped and homeless, the throwaway people who hovered on society's outer limits and fed on economic and political neglect.

**1990**   In a fertile period, the author published "Criminal Justice in American Indian Literature" in the *Oshkaabewis Native Journal.* In a submission to *American Indian Quarterly,* Paula Gunn Allen rebuked Silko for violating Pueblo privacy by expropriating and disseminating in print intimate Laguna clan stories. Within months of Allen's publication of *Spider Woman's Granddaughters* (1989), she savaged the continuity of the action in Tayo's story in *Ceremony.* Allen declared, "I could no more do (or sanction) the kind of ceremonial investigation of *Ceremony* done by some researchers than I could slit my mother's throat. Even seeing some of it published makes my skin crawl" (Allen, 1990, 382). Critic Robert M. Nelson riposted in 2001 with admiration for Silko's embedding of her writings with native tales, which he called the backbone of Tayo's story. Nelson compared the narratives to "bits of turquoise and coral in some kinds of Zuñi jewelry." (Nelson, 2001, 47).

**January 22, 1991**   During a state hiring freeze at schools and universities, Silko had to resign her job to allow time to finish *Almanac of the Dead.* Because critics charged her with "being oh-so-angry," she later replied, "I didn't make the history that I write about. It happened! And the fact that it's so ugly, that's not my fault" (Metz, 2010).

**March 1991**   Along with Tucson poet Jane Miller, Silko received the Lila Wallace–*Reader's Digest* Writers' Award for merit and commitment. From 1990 to 2000, the Wallace fund distributed $9 million to nonfiction and fiction writers, playwrights, and poets. The prize carried a purse of $35,000 per year for three years to finance Silko's work.

**November 2, 1991**   Over a decade, Silko restructured creation myth with technical innovation to write *Almanac of the Dead,* a jarring, 763-page maelstrom that maligns the Christian-capitalist hegemony. The novel grew out of a single photograph of a spider's web that appeared to outline a shallow grave. Critic Peter Kerry Powers identifies the text as a companion work to *Ceremony* for its broadened survey of evil and conspiracy on an international scale. He characterized the author as a rejecter of "the role of gentle and noble savage" (Powers, 2001, 83). She conceded to Ruth Lopez, a reporter from the *Santa Fe New Mexican*: "It was such a powerful and dark work that I didn't want to keep it under the same roof" (Lopez, 1998, 30).

Silko took the writing task seriously as an indictment of U.S. anti–Indian policy, which she issued to coincide with the 500th anniversary of Columbus's arrival in the Caribbean. According to her friend, Creek poet Joy Harjo, Silko obeyed the spirits, which began directing her in 1980, the year the *Ejército Zapatista de Liberación Nacional* (EZLN, Zapatista Army of

National Liberation) assembled in the mountains of Chiapas. She credited the spirits with a sense of timing. Led by Emiliano Zapata, an agrarian reformer, the EZLN plotted a nonviolent assault on corporate, military, and paramilitary forces that relegated indigenous people to poverty and inequality. Simon & Schuster published the work 11 years later on November 2, the *Dia de los Muertos* (Day of the Dead), a Christian saints' day honoring the deceased. The text became "my indictment, my serving the complaint in the name of the people," a pan-tribal population whom she defended for demanding justice for their disinheritance (Lopez, 1996, D6).

Like Zora Neale Hurston's ethnographic *Tell My Horse: Voodoo and Life in Haiti and Jamaica* (1938) and Jamaica Kincaid's anti-tourist diatribe *A Small Place* (1988), Silko's *Almanac* refights colonial adversity by continuing the Indian Wars, the undercurrent of frontier myth. Critic John J. Su credited her impetus to loss, nostalgia, and yearning. *Almanac* became her "means of establishing ethical ideals that can be shared by diverse groups who have in common only a longing for a past that never was," a negated possibility that should have been, but wasn't (Su, 2005, 3). Su describes such fiction as alternative routes that history might have followed, a "sideshadowing" of past eras to erase such grim realities as dispossession and genocide. For background material, she studied Mayan cosmology and the solar observations at Chaco Canyon in northwestern New Mexico from Anthony F. Aveni's book *Skywatchers of Ancient Mexico* (1980), an introduction to Mesoamerican astrology, religion, and quantitative astronomy. To interviewer Linda Grant Niemann, she confided her intent to jolt the reader's inner thought process: "These stories work on unconscious levels that we don't have control of and access to by direct everyday means" (Niemann, 1992, 10). In the process of turning history itself into a character, she fell under a narrative spell, a supra-rational method of historiography covering "500 of the ugliest years in world history" (*ibid.*). By compiling unforgettable scenarios and dialogue, Silko anticipated a magical "after-effect in the unconscious" (*ibid.*).

During her years of writing, Silko pondered the serial killers of the 1980s, Mayan rebellion in Chiapas, and the cannibalism of sex offender Jeffrey Dahmer, murderer of 17 boys and men. Contributing dissonance to her musings was the rise of the prison and law enforcement industries and of pharmaceutical hegemony over the sick. She dedicated the moral history to Western novelist Larry McMurtry, author of *Lonesome Dove* and acknowledged the concept of philosopher Marshal McLuhan of a global village visible on satellite television. Compelling themes call for a human reconciliation with the universe, as recommended by Mayan codices inscripted in Latin or Spanish. The experimental narrative moves 70 characters from prehistory into an era of illicit revenue from drug sales. In the opening paragraphs, the author elaborates on the function of Zeta, a Yaqui crone, in preserving proud and empowering stories from pre–Columbian times that answer humanistic quandaries of the present.

The author pushed her character list toward caricature to wrest from the company extremes of depravity and criminality. To engineer the overthrow of a venal white hegemony, the author shapes what Judith Wynn, book critic for the *Boston Herald*, calls a "murky rogues' gallery" populating settings "from Tucson to Mexico, Alaska, Central America and New Jersey" (Wynn, 1991, 62). To fight the residue of white genocide left from frontier times, Silko stated with mock humor, "I'm still a believer in subversion. I don't think we're numerous enough ... to take them by storm" (Kincaid, 1992, 24). To speak from an Amerindian perspective, she chose "to approach language from the Pueblo perspective, one that embraces the whole of creation and the whole of history and time" (*ibid.*, 26). Reviewers in *Time, USA Today,* and book columns of major newspapers charged her with imprudence, recklessness, insanity, and sexual preoccupation. The hoopla over her view of global war and eco-catastrophe embarrassed the publisher, Simon & Schuster.

**July 1992**     At the Returning the Gift festival at the University of Oklahoma in Norman, Silko addressed 300 Amerindian authors and poets from Canada, Central America, Mexico, and the

United States. She repeated her jeremiad from *Almanac of the Dead* by urging listeners to look to the south for a folk resurgence that was already heading north.

**Winter 1992**   Another impromptu Border Patrol detention on I-25 in New Mexico halted Silko and her friend Gus on the way west from Albuquerque to Tucson. Because of the late hour and the remote location, the author cowered under "an awful feeling of menace and of violence straining to break loose" (Silko, 1996, 109). An Immigration and Naturalization agent forced a German shepherd to sniff the two detainees, a violation of constitutional protection against capricious search and seizure.

**1993**   The author continued publishing short reflections on reservation upbringing with "A Laguna Portfolio" (1993). Published in *Studies in American Indian Literature*, the photo-essay contains snapshots of relatives made by Lee Marmon. Silko established herself as a major feminist author with the creation of Kochininako, a liberated heroine of *Yellow Woman* (1993). She also composed a preface to a 32-page compendium of Amerindian photos, *Partial Recall: With Essays on Photographs of Native North Americans* (1993), the first essay anthology by Indians to examine photography from the perspective of aborigines. The preface praises the work of 12 Amerindian contributors for "stripping away comfortable images and cliches about photography and about Native Americans ... [to expand] the esthetic and perceptual boundaries of Western European art history" (Silko, 1993, 10). Of the "post–Indian" work of Hopi videographer Victor Masayesva, Silko admired Hopi reverence for culture from "the images they choose *not* to make" (*ibid.*). According to critics Thomas Claviez, a literary theorist at the University of Berne, and American studies specialist Maria Moss, the author acquired the Pueblo eye for illustration from her father's photos: "Their very presence, as products of a 'western' technological process, alongside myths, stories and poems that repeatedly foreground the fluidity of time, inevitably emphasizes the fractured present" (Claviez & Moss, 2000, 226). The critics conclude that, by enfolding past stories into her text, Silko depicts "an ongoing present" (*ibid.*)

Silko's own publishing house, Flood Plain Press, issued *Sacred Water: Narratives and Pictures* (1993), an 80-page work containing elemental polaroid snapshots of cloud masses, snakes and water lilies, stone formations and arroyos, which she considered pictorial versions of oral narrative. Near the conclusion of her 41 vignettes, she warned of looming disaster from destroyers of the ecosystem. She kept the balance of minimalistic pictures to limited words. Of the relationship of photo to text, she stated, "The influence ... is almost subliminal" (Silko, 1996, 169). To maintain control of bookmaking, the author copied, hand-stitched, and glued each volume personally. She reported feeling "magically transported back to the blissful consciousness of a fifth-grader" (*ibid.*). In the second printing of 2,500 copies, she took into account suggestions for correcting spelling errors identified by readers.

British critic Laurelyn Whitt notes the interconnection of Silko's storytelling to the arts and to the experiences of Indian lives. Whitt explains, "Within indigenous knowledge systems, knowledge is typically tied so intimately to experience and imagination as to be inconceivable without them" (Whitt, 2009, 35). In the essay "The Indian with a Camera," the foreword to *A Circle of Nations: Voices and Visions of American Indians* (1993), Silko lauds the "vast networks of trade and commerce" that allied desert dwellers during hard times. She accounted for Mesoamerican coalitions: "During times of famine, trade partners sent food. Guatemalan macaw feathers went to Taos, and Minnesota pipestones to Honduras" (Silko, 1993, 6). As a result, "Hopi, Aztec, Maya, Inca — these are the people who would not die" (*ibid.*, 7). To those whites who sought to obliterate the native spirit, she vilifies the removal of American children to acculturation boarding schools. The text charges educators and missionaries with stealing language and oral lore from Indians and with robbing the vulnerable young of ties to their homelands.

**February 1993**   The Women's Studies Department of the University of California at Los Angeles chose Silko as distinguished visiting lecturer. Her comment on racial profiling by the

Border Patrol drew similar accounts of capricious detainment based on racial profiling and unconstitutional search and seizure. Silko concluded, "No person, no citizen is free to travel without the scrutiny of the Border Patrol" (Silko, 1996, 111).

**November–December 1993**   Silko refreshed her folk art snake, this time painting it red. She worked alone with her own funds to escape the supervision of art committees, who preferred bland, predictable motifs and themes. The snake inspired a children's art project, a three-dimensional snake sculpted from concrete.

**1994**   Silko received the third annual Wordcraft Circle of Native Writers and Storytellers Lifetime Achievement award. In her mid–40s, she produced stronger and more varied nonfiction, including "An Expression of Profound Gratitude to the Maya Zapatistas," issued in *People's Tribune*, a national revolutionary newspaper published in Chicago. The text anticipates that rebels in Chiapas, Mexico, will continue the "same [500-year] war of resistance that the indigenous people of the Americas have never ceased to fight" (Silko, 1996, 153). She published a four-page folded broadside, *How to Hunt Buffalo*, dedicated to her friend Linda Grant Niemann, a writer, teacher at Kennesaw State University in Kentucky, and former brakeman and conductor on Amtrak, Southern Pacific, and Union Pacific Railroads. The essay offers one-on-one instruction in facing death, which Silko examines through the eyes of the buffalo chosen from the herd for sacrifice.

   Silko dedicated the second edition of *Laguna Woman: Poems* to her beloved in-laws, Carl Haley Chapman, 71, and Eleanor Finley Chapman, 70, of Columbia, Missouri, who died in a car crash in Osceola County near Kissimmee, Florida, on February 20, 1987. The Chapmans wrote *Indians and Archaeology of Missouri* (1964, 1983) for the University of Missouri Press.

**January 1, 1994**   Silko was thrilled to learn that the Mayan *Ejército Zapatista de Liberación* (Zapatista Army of Literation) invigorated a rural rebellion by readings of *Almanac* in summer 1993. George Collier, author of *Basta! Land and the Zapatista Rebellion in Chiapas* (1994), reported that the troops, envigorated by Silko's novel, launched a rebellion in Chiapas on January 1, 1994. She admired the spirit of aboriginal people still resisting usurpation. In an essay, she charged Mexican militarists with readying for all-out annihilation of Zapatistas by purchasing Black Hawk helicopters to carry out air assaults. Her diatribe blamed President Bill Clinton's immigration policy and vilified "the elected leaders of the United States and their sluttish handmaidens, the big television networks" (Silko, 1994, 6).

**Fall 1994**   After enduring an obvious example of racial profiling and intimidation by immigration officials and their dogs, Silko composed for *The Nation* a personal essay, "America's Iron Curtain: The Border Patrol State," a diatribe against Manifest Destiny. With her friend Gus, she survived a late-night road stop and the insult of identification as a foreign-looking, potentially criminal brown invader and a threat to white citizens of New Mexico. Similar in outrage to Angela Yvonne Davis in "Race, Cops, and Traffic Stops" (1997), Silko charged U.S. politicians with "trying to whip up hysteria over immigration policy in the most blatantly racist manner" (Silko, 1994, 6). Critic Elizabeth Archuleta identified the policy as "purposely [confusing] drug and immigration enforcement policy with efforts to fight terrorism in [a] quest to combat the movement of people across the border" (Archuleta, 2005, 128). Detention by the Border Patrol outside Tucson enraged Silko, who composed "Fences against Freedom" for *Hungry Mind Review* in protest of violation of citizen rights. In anger at intimidating officers, she retorted, "This is our home.... You are not wanted here" (Silko, 1996, 109). The essay interpreted the phrase "illegal aliens" to mean nonwhite people, whom the media demonized and dehumanized as a danger to the country. She charged defense contractors with creating a national enemy of undocumented Hispanics as a means of justifying defense spending.

**October 11–13, 1994**   With friend Linda Grant Niemann, Silko traveled to Chiapas, Mexico, to the *Convención Nacional Democrática* (National Democratic Convention) in San Cristobal de las Casas. They attended a town meeting led by Mexico City intellectuals and masked Zapatistas to distribute counter-information opposing official government reports and commercial mass media. Silko received a message from Subcommandante Marcos, the sobriquet of a leader of the faction. She identified with anarchists, who held a march the following day of 20,000 indigenous Mexicans.

**November 1994**   Silko submitted "Hunger Stalked the Tribal People" to the Thanksgiving edition of *People's Tribune*. The brief essay reveals a spirit of giving among the Laguna, a people least able to feed visiting Navajo. Critic Helen Jaskoski lauded the short personal essay for explaining the sharing with a fellow tribe of Pueblo. Laguna generosity spawned a "consequent tradition of friendship and exchange of gifts" (Jaskoski, 1998, 63).

**1995**   The author produced "Bingo Big" for *The Nation* and "In the Combat Zone" for *Hungry Mind Review*, a personal message to women on developing attitudes of self-protection from stalkers and rapists. In the book review "Bingo Big," Silko compared the demise of good jobs to the passing of the buffalo. The bad faith of the U.S. Housing and Urban Development Department and the Bureau of Indian Affairs reduced Indians to powdered milk, which "always came out with those lumps of coagulated powder," a common denominator of U.S. poor (Silko, 1995, 857). In place of industry and hope, native peoples chose gambling at reservation halls. After decades of interest in photography, she used her snapshots to complete "An Essay on Rocks" (1995) for *Aperture* and "Interior and Exterior Landscapes: The Pueblo Migration Stories" (1995) for *Antaeus*.

**May 5, 1995**   Silko joined novelist Dorothy Allison, short story writer Toni Cade Bambara, playwright and teacher Cherrie Moraga, and poet and reformer Grace Paley at Dartmouth College for a symposium, "The Writer as Activist."

**July 23, 1995**   The discovery of the Hale-Bopp Comet turned Silko's attention to the night sky. During the 18 months the bright phenomenon illuminated the heavens, she believed it "the single most beautiful and seductive visitor to this solar system in my lifetime" (Silko, 2010, 142). She was not surprised at the news of group suicide among the Heaven's Gate cult, which sought to travel in the comet in a giant space ship. The comet's temporary allure made her nostalgic for space travel, a topic she covers at length in *The Turquoise Ledge*.

**1996**   Silko published *Love Poem and Slim Man Canyon* and *Rain*, a collaboration with Lee Marmon for the Library Fellows of the Whitney Museum of American Art. She wrote an introduction to *On the Rails: A Woman's Journey*, Linda Niemann's memoir of her career as a "railroader," beginning in Watsonville, California, with the Southern Pacific. Silko's nonfiction anthology, *Yellow Woman and a Beauty of the Spirit: Essays on Native American Life Today* touches on the oral themes of Aztec, Inca, Maya, Mixtec, and Pueblo and focuses on ecology and a reverence for the inexorable powers of nature. The text reveals the Pueblo tradition of interring family members in collapsed rooms of a multifamily residence, where artifacts and debris are as valuable as the remains of ancestors. In terms of native ecofeminism, she notes that "corncobs and husks, the rinds and stalks and animal bones were not regarded as garbage or filth. The remains were merely resting at a midpoint in their journey back to dust ... because for the ancient people all these things had spirit and being" (Silko, 1996, 26). She summarizes that respect for life reflects love and reverence to Mother Earth, the universal creator. The repetition of myth links the current generation with all who came before: "Through the stories we hear who we are" (*ibid.*, 30). She valorized the place of oral stories as tutorials and cautionary tales: "It is the only way human culture survives, by learning from our mistakes" (Lopez, 1996, D6).

**February 1996**   To a reporter from the *Santa Fe New Mexican*, Silko groused about the marketing ploys of book tours, which kept her moving at the rate of two cities per day. She chuckled, "They kind of market writers like soap" (*ibid.*). Of her authority on native concerns, she declared herself only one of many spokespersons for Amerindians: "At this point, at the end of the millennium, it is really demeaning to imply that with all these millions of people that there can be only one speaker ... one authorized spokesperson per culture" (*ibid.*). From her perspective, justice for first peoples is the essential purpose of writing because "the U.S. legal system is designed by crooks" (*ibid.*).

**March 1997**  Downtown Tucson preservationists banded to save Silko's snake mural, an urban petroglyph depicting the sufferings of the underclass under the fist of the white capitalist. To interviewer Ellen L. Arnold, the author fulminated at a "wretched dickhead" who painted over the mural "because he hated what it stood for" (Silko & Arnold, 2000, 176). The *Arizona Daily Star* described the wall art as the source of the second half of *Almanac of the Dead*. The author painted it in 1988 as "an enigmatic bit of cosmic doodling," part of the creative process. In the endpapers, she describes Tucson from the Laguna perspective as "Home to an assortment of speculators, confidence men, embezzlers, lawyers, judges, police and other criminals, as well as addicts and pushers, since the 1880s and Apache Wars" (Silko, 1991, endpapers). The text warns that the dead refuse to be silenced: "The ghosts can't rest ... are still running away, thinking they are escaping the slaughter. They just keep traveling" (*ibid.*, 190). The novel pictures the spirits converging at Tucson, where water and arable land are disappearing. For her outspoken first person outlook, Michael Dirda, literary critic for the *Washington Post*, listed her among the era's ethnic all-star writers alongside Sherman Alexie, Isabel Allende, Sandra Cisneros, Louise Erdrich, Laura Esquivel, Oscar Hijuelos, Gish Jen, Amy Tan, and August Wilson.

**April 1997**  Silko served as a judge for the 1997 PEN/Faulkner Award for Fiction, which required the review of 300 novels and short fiction published in 1996 from 88 publishing houses. On a visit to Leipzig and Berlin, she perused the pre–Christian lore of Germany and Great Britain. She found similarities to aboriginal American culture in the closeness to land and trees, particularly the archetypal fable of the magic cow that gave enough milk to sustain the people. The rise of the Green Party and postmodern politics of conservation gave the author hope that greed can be a catastrophic force arousing rebellion.

**August 1998**  After Silko refined the manuscript for *Gardens in the Dunes* in mid–July, she began a round of festivals and public readings. The grunt work essential to writing and publishing did not surprise her. She reported to Ruth Lopez, a writer for the *Santa Fe New Mexican*: "I knew it would be all muddled up, so I am not trying to start anything new" (Lopez, 1998, 30). The mass of duties left her "on the run and discombobulated" (*ibid.*). She observed that travel disrupts creativity: "You completely lose your train of thought. The entire process is disruptive, from the time it takes to pack to how it pulls you away from the writing" (*ibid.*)

**November 1998**  The full calendar and office work left Silko empty. She stated, "This is what happens each time I finish a book," a feeling of everything spoken and nothing left to say. (*ibid.*). To revive the spark, she stayed home to read, her favorite form of refueling.

**1999**  At the beginning of an 11-year period asthma free, the author reprised her signature nature lore in *Gardens in the Dunes*, an historical novel and tribute to the psychoanalytic theories of Sigmund Freud. She intended to remain apolitical in a plot about flower and vegetable gardening, but discovered from research that "the plant collectors followed the *Conquistadores*. I realized that this was going to be a really political novel" (Li, 2009, 18). Silko based *Gardens* on allegories and tales related by Silko's grandpa, Henry C. "Hank" Marmon, which she subtly infuses with Celtic myth, early medieval scriptural interpretation, and ecofeminism as well as the resilient rebellion of Mesamerican aborigines. Scots critic Stuart Christie, an anarchist writer from Glasgow, describes the work as "an ambitious summation of many of Silko's career-long interests" (Christie, 2009, 90).

Suzanne Ruta, a reviewer for the *New York Times*, surmised that literary foils Indigo and

Hattie Abbott Palmer present two sides of the author's life, as native outdoor girl and as scholarly traveler. Significantly, Indigo, the youthful gardener of the Southwestern sandhills, has much to teach Hattie, the bookworm, an expert on early Christian church history and miserable depressive. Ruta charged the author with overloading the woven plots with too little dialogue and too many agendas, "feminist, anticlerical, millennial" (Ruta, 1999, 31). An anonymous critic for *Book Review* added complaints of overwriting and hardhandedness. *Booklist* editors chose *Gardens* as one of the year's best novels, in company with Ralph Ellison's *Juneteenth* and two feminist classics, Sena Jeter Naslund's *Ahab's Wife or the Star Gazer* and Isabel Allende's *Daughter of Fortune*.

Publication of *Gardens* coincided with a Laguna Pueblo celebration of a decade of cooperation organized by the Indigenous Environmental Network. At the assembly, 1,000 participants honored a coalition of tribes that battled multinational mining firms for inflicting ecological disasters on tribal homelands. A parallel group, the Laguna Acoma Coalition for a Safe Environment, testified at the 1992 World Uranium Hearing in Salzburg, Austria; the 1998 World Conference Against Atom and Hydrogen Bombs in Hiroshima, Japan; and at the Hague Appeal for Peace the following year. The coalition continued to defy the U.S. government and polluters at the 2001 World Conference against Racism, the 2002 World Summit on Sustainable Development in South Africa. Campaigning continued in Vancouver at the 2003 Western Mining Activists Network Conference and in Alaska at the 2003 National Environmental Conference.

In *Gardens*, Silko echoes the postcolonial concerns of Antiguan author Jamaica Kincaid, writer of *My Garden (Book)* (1999) and "Sowers and Reapers: The Unquiet World of a Flower Bed" (2001). Silko observed that she planned no polemics for her novel, but, "Oh my gosh! Right behind *conquistadores* came the plant collectors" (Saguaro, 2006, 186). In the style of a Victorian historical romance, Silko's reflections on the Colorado River Tribes demonizes the colonial era bio-pirates by having botanist Dr. Edward Palmer acquire Indigo, an Indian child kidnapped like Yellow Woman (Kochininako). Silko characterizes the Indian wisewoman, Grandma Fleet, who leads granddaughters Indigo and Sister Salt to the joyous ceremonies of Wovoka, the native evangelist. At the messianic Ghost Dance, Indigo foresees an uprooting that takes her far from home, but never shakes her faith in her grandmother's Southwest American garden. At Dr. Palmer's demise from respiratory disease, Indigo has no pity for a scholarly exploiter who literally gives his last breath for the commercialization of nature.

**2000**  The Lannan Foundation chose Silko and feminist poet Cynthia Ozick to receive the Lannan Literary Award for Fiction for writing of exceptional quality. The foundation is a family fund that fosters creativity, freedom of enquiry, and diversity in contemporary artists and writers and native activism in rural Indian communities. During the year, at presentations and interviews as part of her position as Roy F. and Joanne Cole Mitte Endowed Chair in Creative Writing at Texas State University at San Marcos, Silko revealed the origins of *Ceremony*.

**October 2002**  With donations from the Danforth Barney Fund, the Beinecke Rare Book & Manuscript Library at Yale University acquired a retrospective of *Gardens in the Dunes*. The Silko archives include first draft revisions, corrected typescripts, an untitled essay on the novel's origins, and advance proofs as well as a broadside of *How to Hunt Buffalo*, hand colored by Silko.

**2003**  The author and poets Joy Harjo and Simon Joseph Ortiz collaborated with photographer Lee Marmon on his first book, *The Pueblo Imagination: Landscape and Memory in the Photography of Lee Marmon*, a collection of photographic images similar in thrust to her storytelling about the experience of detribalization. With photos dating to 1949, the work chronicled the last generation of the Acoma and Laguna people to live by traditional ways and values. Silko also provided a foreword to the 30th anniversary edition of Vine Deloria's *God Is Red: A Native View of Religion* (1973), a courageous text reflecting the turmoil of assassinations of Dr. Martin

Luther King and Malcolm X. Her message of truth in the face of white lies charges the U.S. history of "power elites," Christianity, and the U.S. military with twisted tales "fabricated for the glory of the white man" (Silko, 2003, vii).

**2004**   For National Women's History Month, Silko shared the list of March honorees with educator Marian Wright Edelman and writers Maxine Hong Kingston and Jill Ker Conway. Selectors for the National Women's History Project in Santa Rosa, California, acknowledged the winners as "Women Inspiring Hope and Possibility" and chose Silko for her role in matriarchal storytelling. With a fierce passion for indigenous lore, she maintained, "These things will only die if we neglect to tell the stories. So I am still telling the stories" (Silko, 2000, 31). The annual selection fostered female leaders and influential forces in society and recognized their dreams and accomplishments as sources of strength and inspiration for all girls and women. That same year, *American Indian Culture and Research Journal* published a special issue on teaching *Ceremony*, a pervasive entry on high school, college, and university reading lists. The book is also available on audiotape and in German and Italian.

**March 5, 2005**   Because of Silko's nature consciousness, she received the American Indian Festival of Words Author Award from the Tulsa Library Trust. Previously bestowed on Vine Deloria, Jr., the biennial honor recognizes the literary contributions of outstanding Amerindian writers.

**April 1, 2005**   In Denver, Colorado, Silko joined her father at the Marriott Hotel to accept the Spirit of the West Award from the Mountains and Plains Booksellers Association, which chose *The Pueblo Imagination* as the year's best art book. Marmon also won the annual award from a monthly e-zine, Independent Publisher Online, for creating "a groundbreaking, multidimensional showcase of Native American culture, talent, and history" (Corbett, 2005). Lee Marmon acknowledged the honors for his family, the Laguna Pueblo, and Amerindians. He stated that, for his 55 years as a professional photographer, the ceremony instilled pride as an artist and father.

**Fall 2005**   Silko took a brief sabbatical to paint, "an illicit holiday from writing" (Silko, 2010, 129). For teaching her English classes at the University of Arizona, she favored the works of Flannery O'Connor. From faith in the power of art, Silko operated Flood Plain Press, a source of handmade books printed on North Stone Avenue in Tucson by her son Robert Chapman. For her revelations of peasant struggles, she shared the values and aims of tribal internationalists, artists who defend earth. To defeat injustice and racism, she championed aboriginal tradition and sacred ritual that realigned and healed fragmented first peoples.

**August 2006**   Silko traveled to Chihuahua, Mexico, to receive a writing award from the state governor, José Reyes Baeza Terrazas.

**2007**   Penguin released a 30th anniversary deluxe edition of *Ceremony*. In the introduction, novelist Larry McMurtry proclaimed the author "a literary star of unusual brilliance" endowed with "blazing talent" (McMurtry, 2007, xxxi). At an appearance at the National Museum of the American Indian in Washington, D.C., Silko noted the shift in American culture to embrace a psychological novel once considered suitable only for graduate courses.

**January 27, 2007**   Philip Thompson, a Maryland composer, set Silko's poem "In Cold Storm Light" (1972) to electroacoustic music as a segment of *Free Play 6: Listening Chamber*, performed on January 25, 2007, at Grand Valley State University in Allendale, Michigan.

**May 7, 2007**   After agent Jin Auh at the Wylie Agency negotiated with Stephen Morrison, acquisitions editor at Viking, Silko left Simon & Schuster and signed on for a novel, *Blue Sevens*; a novella, *Ocean Story*; and a memoir, *The Turquoise Ledge*. The latter focuses on history, landscape, and wildlife in the Sonoran Desert west of Tucson.

**June 14, 2007**    At the Native Voices Indigenous Language and Poetry Symposium, the author delivered a keynote address—"500 Years from Now Everyone in Tucson Speaks Nahuatl Not Chinese"—to the Indigenous Languages Conference in Tucson. Supported by the 28th annual American Indian Language Development Institute, local Tohono O'odham, and the University of Arizona Poetry Center, the symposium also featured poets Joy Harjo and Simon Joseph Ortiz. The purpose of the gathering was a study of bookmaking, poetry, storytelling, and writing that preserved and invigorated linguistic and cultural diversity.

**July 11, 2007**    A fall in her house caused Silko to rethink her opinions of living alone so far from Tucson. Because emergency service was slow and expensive, she asked her son Caz for immediate help and sought acupuncture treatment of her injuries.

**April 7, 2008**    Following her lecture at West Virginia University, while composing the novel *Blue Sevens*, Silko served as elder-in-residence, a staff position co-sponsored by the Carolyn Reyer Endowment for Indian Studies, the English department, and the Center for Women's Studies. As part of the Native American Studies Program, Silko taught a seminar in creative writing for graduate students and faculty.

**October 8, 2009**    At the Heard Museum in Phoenix, the author delivered the Simon Ortiz and Labriola Center Lecture on Indigenous Land, Culture, and Community. Sponsored by the American Indian Studies and Women and Gender Studies programs at Arizona State University, her presentation included a reading from *The Turquoise Ledge*.

**April 8, 2010**    The author was keynote fiction reader at the Colorado State University writing conference, the largest of its kind in the country. Some 7,000 writers assembled at the Denver convention center for a literary arts consortium sponsored by the Association of Writers and Writing Programs.

**July 30, 2010**    Silko appeared at Macondo Nuevo Mundo (Spanish for "New World"), an arts festival and writers' workshop that she and novelist Sandra Cisneros initiated in 1998. The 2010 gathering featured music, dance, and readings by Silko, Cisneros, and Elena Poniatowska. The purpose of the Macondo Foundation was to attract compassionate artist to build community and propose non-violent social change.

**September 8, 2010**    At the Watson Theater at Syracuse University, Silko presented a speech, "On Conflict: Peace and War" and a reading from *The Turquoise Ledge*. She discussed with participants the Indian Wars of the Southwest and their impetus to the Mexican slave trade in Amerindian children.

**Late October 2010**    Silko published *The Turquoise Ledge*, her first full-length non-fiction work, a clan history set on the Sonora Desert and based on her 32 years in the Tucson Mountains. She began a seven-city tour, during which she gave an interview to Kim Jeffries of the *Seattle Times*. Her commentary on the characters she derived from real acquaintances and from personal experience preceded a statement about separation: "I had to stand back or stand apart from myself to get away from self-consciousness" (Jeffries, 2010). The struggle accounted for her preference for fiction over autobiography. She added, "Real life isn't that neat at all.... There's no pure objective self that can ever be accessed" (*ibid.*).

Silko derided publishers who "want 'product' every 18 months like clockwork because they think readers have impaired memories and will forget the author if two years pass" (Bennett, 2010). She reverted to tribal elders who valued "time as space, infinite generous space on the plane of being" (*ibid.*). Like the old Laguna, she deliberately wrote and painted slowly "to counter the disproportionate value placed on speed" (*ibid.*). Her tour concluded at the Chicago Humanities Festival. The Library Foundation of Los Angeles acknowledged her worth to the area's intellectual life.

## • *Sources*

Alexie, Sherman. "Root Juice," *American Poet* 31 (Fall 2006): 32–33.

Allen, Paula Gunn. "Special Problems in Teaching Leslie Marmon Silko's Ceremony," *The American Indian Quarterly* (Fall 1990): 379–386.

Archuleta, Elizabeth. "Securing Our Nation's Roads and Borders or Re-circling the Wagons? Leslie Marmon Silko's Destabilization of 'Borders,'" *Wicazo Sa Review* 20:1 (Spring 2005): 113–137.

Armstrong, Gene. "Invigorated by Poetry: Top Native American Writers Get Together for a Three-Day UA Symposium," *Tucson Weekly* (7 June 2007).

Barnes, Kim. "A Leslie Marmon Silko Interview," *Journal of Ethnic Studies* 13:4 (1986): 83–105.

Barnett, Louise, and James Thorson, eds. *Leslie Marmon Silko: A Collection of Critical Essays*. Albuquerque: University of New Mexico Press, 1999.

Bennett, Steve. "Author Silko Isn't Concerned about Time," *Express News* (25 July 2010).

Birkerts, Sven. "Apocalypse Now," *New Republic* 205:19 (4 November 1991): 39–41.

Buell, Lawrence. "Leslie Silko: Environmental Apocalypticism," in *The Environmental Imagination: Thoreau, Nature Writing, and the Formation of American Culture*. Cambridge, MA: Harvard University Press, 1995.

Carlin, Margaret. "Apocalypse Any Day Now: Angry Indian Writer Calmly Predicts End of Rule by White Man," *Rocky Mountain News* (19 January 1992).

Carsten, Cynthia. "Storyteller: Leslie Marmon Silko's Reappropriation of Native American History and Identity," *Wicazo SA Review* 21:2 (Autumn 2006): 105–126.

Cevasco, George A., and Richard P. Harmond. *Modern American Environmentalists: A Biographical Encyclopedia*. Baltimore: Johns Hopkins University Press, 2009.

Champion, Laurie. *Contemporary American Women Fiction Writers: An A-to-Z Guide*. Westport, CT: Greenwood, 2002.

Chavkin, Allan Richard, and Nancy Feyl Chavkin. "The Origins of Leslie Marmon Silko's *Ceremony*," *Yale University Library Gazette* 82:1/2 (October 2007): 23–30.

Christie, Stuart. *Plural Sovereignties and Contemporary Indigenous Literature*. New York: Palgrave Macmillan, 2009.

Claviez, Thomas, and Maria Moss. *Mirror Writing: (Re-)Constructions of Native American Identity*. Berlin: Galda & Wilch, 2000.

Coltelli, Laura. *Winged Words: American Indian Writers Speak*. Lincoln: University of Nebraska Press, 1990, 135–153.

Corbett, Thomas. "Acclaimed Native American Artist and Author Lee H. Marmon Takes Top Honors in Regional Book Awards Competition," www.leemarmongallery.com/pressrelease_MPBA-award.html, 2005.

Dirda, Michael. "Stylists and Visionaries: 25 years of American Fiction," *Washington Post* (1 June 1997).

Donovan, Kathleen M. *Feminist Readings of Native American Literature: Coming to Voice*. Tucson: University of Arizona Press, 1998.

Edwards, Thomas S., and Elizabeth A. De Wolfe. *Such News of the Land: U.S. Women Nature Writers*. Hanover, NH: University Press of New England, 2001.

Evans, Robert Leslie. "A Real Life Model for Tayo in Silko's *Ceremony*," *American Indian Culture and Research Journal* 28:1 (2004): 15–22.

"Fatal Flaw Kills 'Dead' as It Offers Apologia for Yaqui People," *Washington* (D.C.) *Times* (19 January 1992).

Fear-Segal, Jacqueline. *White Man's Club: Schools, Race, and the Struggle of Indian Acculturation*. Lincoln: University of Nebraska Press, 2007.

Fitz, Brewster E. *Silko: Writing Storyteller and Medicine Woman*. Norman: University of Oklahoma Press, 2004.

Grobman, Laurie. "(Re)Interpreting 'Storyteller' in the Classroom: Teaching at the Crossroads," *College Literature* 27:3 (Fall 2000): 88–110.

Hirsch, Bernard A. "'The Telling Which Continues': Oral Tradition and the Written Word in Leslie Marmon Silko's 'Storyteller,'" *American Indian Quarterly* 12:1 (Winter 1988): 1–26.

Holm, Sharon. "The 'Lie' of the Land: Native Sovereignty, Indian Literary Nationalism, and Early Indigenism in Leslie Marmon Silko's Ceremony," *American Indian Quarterly* 32:3 (Summer 2008): 243–274.

Jacobs, Connie. "A Toxic Legacy: Stories of Jackpile Mine," *American Indian Culture and Research Journal* 28:1 (Winter 2004): 41–52.

Jaskoski, Helen. *Leslie Marmon Silko: A Study of the Short Fiction*. New York: Twayne, 1998.

Jeffries, Kim. "A Conversation with Leslie Marmon Silko on The Turquoise Ledge," *Seattle Times* (19 October 2010).

Johnson, Cat. "Silko Heads for Santa Cruz," *Santa Cruz News* (21 October 2010).

Karem, Jeff. *The Romance of Authenticity: The Cultural Politics of Regional and Ethnic Literatures.* Charlottesville: University of Virginia Press, 2004.

Kincaid, James R. "Who Gets to Tell Their Stories?" *New York Times* (3 May 1992): 24–29.

Lee, A. Robert. *Multicultural American Literature: Comparative Black, Native, Latino/a and Asian American Fictions.* Jackson: University Press of Mississippi, 2003.

Li, Stephanie. "Domestic Resistance Gardening, Mothering, and Storytelling in Leslie Mamon Silko's *Gardens in the Dunes,*" *Studies in American Indian Literature* 21: 1 (Spring 2009): 18–37.

Lincoln, Kenneth. *Speak Like Singing: Classics of Native American Literature.* Albuquerque: University of New Mexico Press, 2008.

Lopez, Ruth. "Exploring Passions," *Santa Fe New Mexican* (13 November 1998): 30.

_____. "Finding Justice Through Words," *Santa Fe New Mexican* (3 March 1996): D6.

Marmon, Lee. *The Pueblo Imagination: Landscape and Memory in the Photography of Lee Marmon.* Boston: Beacon, 2003.

McMurtry, Larry. "Introduction" to *Ceremony.* New York: Penguin, 2007.

_____. *Sacagawea's Nickname: Essays on the American West.* New York: New York Review of Books, 2004.

Mellas, Laurie. "Memory and Promise: Leslie Marmon Silko's Story," *Mirage* 24 (Spring 2006): 11–14.

Metz, Nina. "Author Silko Makes a Point to Tell Story," *Chicago Tribune* (16 October 2010).

Minh-ha, Trinh T. "Difference: A Special Third World Women Issue" in *The Feminism and Visual Culture Reader,* ed. Amelia Jones. New York: Routledge, 2003, 151–173.

Morgan, Thomas D. "Native Americans in World War II," *Army History* 35 (Fall 1995): 22–27.

Nelson, Elizabeth Hoffman, and Malcolm Nelson, eds. *Telling the Stories: Essays on American Indian Literatures and Cultures.* New York: Peter Lang, 2001.

Niemann, Linda. "New World Disorder," *Women's Review of Books* 9:6 (March 1992): 1–4.

_____, and Joel Jensen. *Railroad Noir: The American West at the End of the Twentieth Century.* Bloomington: Indiana University Press, 2010.

_____, and Leslie Marmon Silko. "Narratives of Survival," *Women's Review of Books* 9:10–11 (July 1992): 10.

Petrolle, Jean. *Religion without Belief: Contemporary Allegory and the Search for Postmodern Faith.* Albany: State University of New York Press, 2007.

Powers, Peter Kerry. *Recalling Religions: Resistance, Memory, and Cultural Revision in Ethnic Women's Literature.* Knoxville: University of Tennessee Press, 2001.

Roeder, Fred. "The Marmon Brothers of Laguna," *Storyteller.* New York: Arcade, 1981.

Romero, Channette. "Envisioning a 'Network of Tribal Coalitions': Leslie Marmon Silko's *Almanac of the Dead,*" *American Indian Quarterly* 26:4 (1 September 2002): 623–640.

Ruta, Suzanne. "Dances with Ghosts," *New York Times* (18 April 1999): 31.

Saguaro, Shelley. *Garden Plots: The Politics and Poetics of Gardens.* Burlington, VT: Ashgate, 2006.

"Save the Snake," *Arizona Daily Star* (23 February 1997).

Seyersted, Per. "Interview with Leslie Marmon Silko," *American Studies in Scandinavia* 13 (1985): 17–25.

Silko, Leslie Marmon. *Almanac of the Dead.* New York: Simon & Schuster, 1991.

_____. "Bingo Big," *Nation* 260:23 (12 June 1995): 856–860.

_____. "Breaking Down the Boundaries: 'Earth, Air, Water, Mind'" in *The Tales We Tell: Perspectives on the Short Story,* ed. Barbara Lounsberry. London: Greenwood, 1998.

_____. *Ceremony.* New York: Penguin, 1977.

_____. "Fences against Freedom," *Hungry Mind Review* 31 (Fall 1994): 6–20.

_____. "Foreword" to *God Is Red,* by Vine Deloria, Jr. Golden, CO: Fulcrum, 2003.

_____. *Gardens in the Dunes.* New York: Simon & Schuster, 2000.

_____. "The Indian with a Camera," foreword to *A Circle of Nations: Voices and Visions of American Indians.* Hillsboro, OR: Beyond Words Publishing, 1993.

_____. "Introduction," *On the Rails: A Woman's Journey,* by Linda Niemann. Berkeley, CA: Cleis, 1996.

_____. *Laguna Woman: Poems.* New York: Greenfield Review Press, 1974.

_____. "Landscape, History, and the Pueblo Imagination," *Antaeus* 51 (Autumn 1986): 83–94.

_____. "'Not You,' He Said" in *What Wildness Is This: Women Write about the Southwest,* eds. Susan Wittig Albert and Susan Hanson. Austin: University of Texas Press, 2007.

_____. "An Old Fashioned Indian Attack in Two Parts" in *The Remembered Earth: An Anthology of Contemporary Native American Literature,* ed. Geary Hobson. Albuquerque: University of New Mexico Press, 1979.

_____. "The People and the Land ARE Inseparable" in *What Wildness Is This: Women Write about the Southwest,* eds. Susan Wittig Albert and Susan Hanson. Austin: University of Texas Press, 2007.

_____. "Preface" to *Partial Recall: With Essays on Photographs of Native North Americans,* eds. Lucy R. Lippard and Don Desmett. Philadelphia: Temple University Press, 1993.

_____. *Sacred Water: Narratives and Pictures.* Tucson: Flood Plain, 1993.

_____. *Storyteller.* New York: Seaver, 1981.

_____. *The Turquoise Ledge: A Memoir*. New York: Viking, 2010.

_____. *Yellow Woman and a Beauty of the Spirit: Essays on Native American Life Today*. New York: Simon & Schuster, 1996.

_____, and Ellen L. Arnold. *Conversations with Leslie Marmon Silko*. Jackson: University Press of Mississippi, 2000.

_____, and James Wright. *The Delicacy and Strength of Lace Letters*. St. Paul, MN: Graywolf, 1986.

Su, John J. *Ethics and Nostalgia in the Contemporary Novel*. Cambridge: Cambridge University Press, 2005.

Tallent, Elizabeth. "Storytelling with a Vengeance," *New York Times Book Review* (22 December 1991): 6.

Thornton, Matthew. "Deals," *Publishers Weekly* 254:19 (7 May 2007): 14–15.

Van Gelder, Lawrence. "Footlights," *New York Times* (27 September 2000).

Velie, Alan R. *Four American Literary Masters*. Norman: University of Oklahoma Press, 1982.

Velikova, Roumiana. "Leslie Marmon Silko: Reading, Writing, and Storytelling," *MELUS* 27:3 (22 September 2002): 57–74.

Werlock, Abby H. P. *Facts on File Companion to the American Short Story*. New York: Facts on File, 2010.

West, Paul. "When a Myth Is as Good as a Mile," *Los Angeles Times* (2 February 1992): 8.

Whitt, Laurelyn. *Science, Colonialism, and Indigenous Peoples: The Cultural Politics of Law and Knowledge*. Cambridge: Cambridge University Press, 2009.

Wong, Hertha D. Sweet. "Native American Visual Autobiography: Figuring Place, Subjectivity, and History," *Iowa Review* 30:3 (Winter 2000-2001): 145–156.

_____. *Sending My Heart Back across the Years: Tradition and Innovation in Native American Autobiography*. New York: Oxford University Press, 1992.

Wynn, Judith. "Nightmare Vision of 'Almanac' Succeeds," *Boston Herald* (22 December 1991): 62.

Zax, David. "Q&A," *Smithsonian* 38:5 (August 2007): 36.

# Silko Genealogy

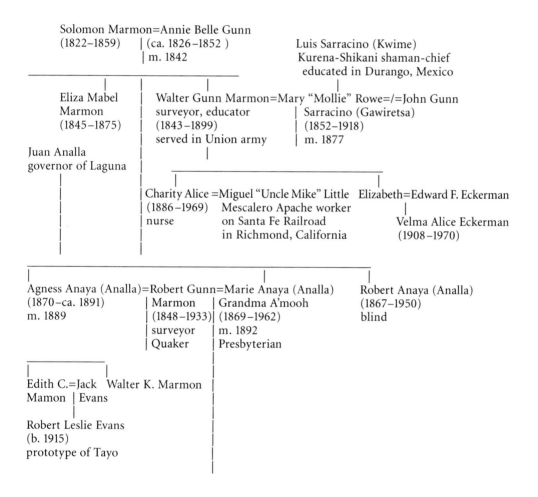

Solomon Marmon=Annie Belle Gunn
(1822–1859) | (ca. 1826–1852 )
              | m. 1842

Luis Sarracino (Kwime)
Kurena-Shikani shaman-chief
educated in Durango, Mexico

Eliza Mabel | Walter Gunn Marmon=Mary "Mollie" Rowe=/=John Gunn
Marmon      | surveyor, educator | Sarracino (Gawiretsa)
(1845–1875) | (1843–1899)        | (1852–1918)
            | served in Union army | m. 1877

Juan Analla |
governor of Laguna |

Charity Alice =Miguel "Uncle Mike" Little   Elizabeth=Edward F. Eckerman
(1886–1969)    Mescalero Apache worker
nurse          on Santa Fe Railroad                Velma Alice Eckerman
               in Richmond, California              (1908–1970)

Agness Anaya (Analla)=Robert Gunn=Marie Anaya (Analla)   Robert Anaya (Analla)
(1870–ca. 1891)       | Marmon    | Grandma A'mooh         (1867–1950)
m. 1889               | (1848–1933)| (1869–1962)           blind
                      | surveyor  | m. 1892
                      | Quaker    | Presbyterian

Edith C.=Jack   Walter K. Marmon
Mamon | Evans

Robert Leslie Evans
(b. 1915)
prototype of Tayo

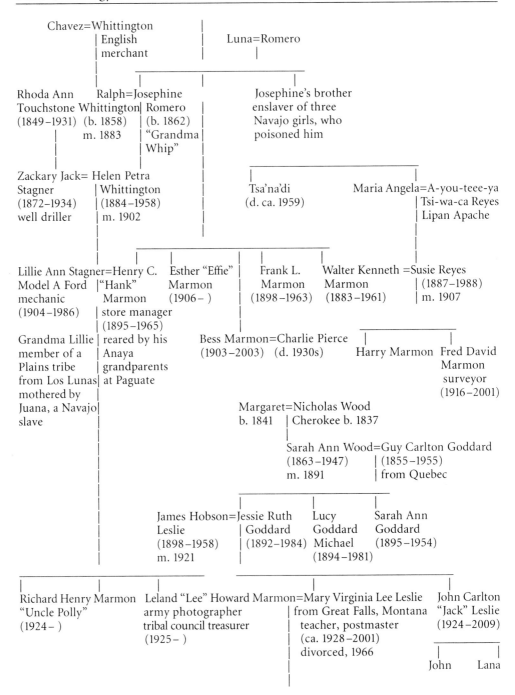

Chavez=Whittington
| English
| merchant

Luna=Romero

Rhoda Ann        Ralph=Josephine
Touchstone Whittington| Romero
(1849–1931)  (b. 1858)  | (b. 1862)
          m. 1883      | "Grandma
                       | Whip"

Josephine's brother
enslaver of three
Navajo girls, who
poisoned him

Zackary Jack= Helen Petra
Stagner       | Whittington
(1872–1934)   | (1884–1958)
well driller  | m. 1902

Tsa'na'di
(d. ca. 1959)

Maria Angela=A-you-teee-ya
            | Tsi-wa-ca Reyes
            | Lipan Apache

Lillie Ann Stagner=Henry C.     Esther "Effie"     Frank L.     Walter Kenneth =Susie Reyes
Model A Ford      |"Hank"       Marmon             Marmon       Marmon         | (1887–1988)
mechanic          | Marmon      (1906– )           (1898–1963)  (1883–1961)    | m. 1907
(1904–1986)       | store manager
                  | (1895–1965)

Grandma Lillie   | reared by his    Bess Marmon=Charlie Pierce  |
member of a      | Anaya            (1903–2003)  (d. 1930s)   Harry Marmon  Fred David
Plains tribe     | grandparents                                             Marmon
from Los Lunas   | at Paguate                                               surveyor
mothered by      |                                                          (1916–2001)
Juana, a Navajo  |
slave            |                  Margaret=Nicholas Wood
                 |                  b. 1841  | Cherokee b. 1837
                 |
                 |                           Sarah Ann Wood=Guy Carlton Goddard
                 |                           (1863–1947)   | (1855–1955)
                 |                           m. 1891       | from Quebec
                 |
                 |           James Hobson=Jessie Ruth    Lucy          Sarah Ann
                 |           Leslie       | Goddard      Goddard       Goddard
                 |           (1898–1958)  | (1892–1984)  Michael       (1895–1954)
                 |           m. 1921      |              (1894–1981)

Richard Henry Marmon  Leland "Lee" Howard Marmon=Mary Virginia Lee Leslie    John Carlton
"Uncle Polly"         army photographer          | from Great Falls, Montana   "Jack" Leslie
(1924– )              tribal council treasurer    | teacher, postmaster         (1924–2009)
                      (1925– )                    | (ca. 1928–2001)
                                                  | divorced, 1966
                                                  |                           John     Lana

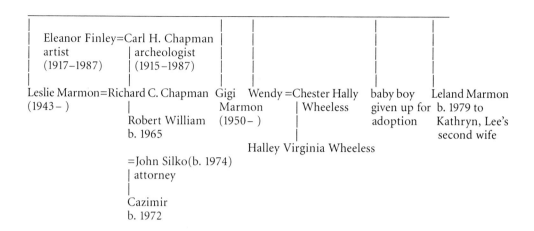

Eleanor Finley=Carl H. Chapman
artist           archeologist
(1917–1987)      (1915–1987)

Leslie Marmon=Richard C. Chapman   Gigi     Wendy =Chester Hally   baby boy      Leland Marmon
(1943– )        |                  Marmon    | Wheeless           given up for  b. 1979 to
                Robert William     (1950– )  |                    adoption      Kathryn, Lee's
                b. 1965                       |                                  second wife
                                    Halley Virginia Wheeless
                =John Silko(b. 1974)
                | attorney
                |
                Cazimir
                b. 1972

# Leslie Marmon Silko: A Literary Companion

## Abbott-Palmer genealogy

In her third novel, *Gardens in the Dunes* (1999), Leslie Marmon Silko contrasts the simple desert life of the Sand Lizard people of Arizona with the grandeur of the Abbott-Palmer genealogy, a prestigious family that produces two scholars. Hattie Abbott's New York existence, first on Fifth Avenue, then at Oyster Bay on Long Island, astounds her foster daughter Indigo, who views "grand new dwellings rising out of the meadowlands above the beach" (Silko, 1999, 155). Eight months after the Palmers' wedding, the reunion of Edward and his sister and brother-in-law, Colin and Susan Palmer James, introduces them to Indigo, who becomes "a Sand Lizard girl ... loose in the white people's world" (*ibid.*, 159). After the Palmers take Indigo to England aboard the S.S. *Pavonia*, Edward worries that passengers view the Indian child as the white family's adopted daughter.

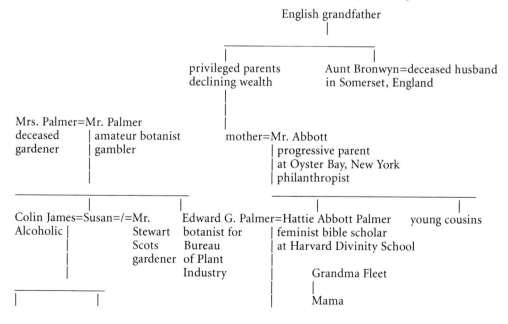

41

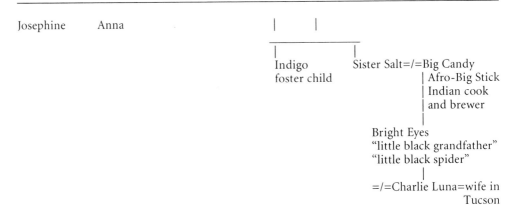

Josephine        Anna

Indigo                    Sister Salt=/=Big Candy
foster child                    | Afro-Big Stick
                                | Indian cook
                                | and brewer

                          Bright Eyes
                          "little black grandfather"
                          "little black spider"

                          =/=Charlie Luna=wife in
                                         Tucson

• *References and further reading*

Isernhagen, Hartwig. "Of Deserts and Gardens: The Southwest in Literature and Art, 'Native' and 'White'" in *Literature and Visual Arts in Twentieth-Century America*, ed. Michele Bottalico. Bari: Palomar Eupalinos, 2002, 173–187.

Silko, Leslie Marmon. *Gardens in the Dunes*. New York: Scribner, 1999.

## abortion

In matters of women's reproductive health and family planning, the feminism of Leslie Marmon Silko avoids fanatical adherence to choice. In "Poem for Myself and Mei-Mei: Concerning Abortion" (1973), the poet makes no judgment against the prospective mother. The focus of the paradoxical poem on vulnerability in tumbling butterflies and mustard flowers after snow reflects compassion for the unborn, who "die softly," like pathetic insects (Silko, 1994, 2). The image of "iridescent wings" clinging to a windshield indirectly castigates modern technology for impacting a source of life too weak, too undeveloped to shield its own destiny. The return of the motif of hopelessness in pregnant women in *Ceremony* (1977) depicts derelict women surviving along the riverbank outside Gallup from sexual commerce in exchange for wine or food. Their offspring, who sleep in holes in the clay, express sorrow at the burial of remains from self-induced abortions, the siblings whom ill fate denies a chance at life.

In the apocalyptic novel *Almanac of the Dead* (1991), abortion recurs as an adjunct to other gory motifs that vilify cruel males rather than reluctant mothers-to-be. Menardo Panson, the insurance seller in Tuxtla, Mexico, seems unaffected by his wife Iliana's multiple miscarriages, but shudders at General J.'s tales of invading soldiers who rape pregnant captives to abort their fetuses, then re-impregnate them with enemy seed. In another perverse scenario, the shock value and tissue dismemberment associated with abortion draws the interest of Beaufrey, a mentally deranged sadist. In partnership with a seedy book dealer in Buenos Aires, Brazil, Beaufrey specializes in a line of dissection videotapes of emasculation, rape, ritual circumcision, sex change operations, snuff films, sodomy, and strangulation.

Silko's *Almanac* devotes chapter one of Book Four to the pervert's fascination with the death of "it," his dehumanization of a fetus. The chapter depicts the burgeoning trade in abortion films from the religious right as evidence of deception by anti-choice fanatics, whose fascination with fetus dismemberment identifies them with extreme pornographers. Beaufrey muses that, since the U.S. Supreme Court's decision in the case of *Roe v. Wade* made abortion legal on January 22, 1973, "The biggest customers for footage was the antiabortionist lobby, which paid top dollar for the footage of the tortured tiny babies" (Silko, 1991, 102). Specialty pornographers profit more from videos of late-term procedures than for the early embryonic stage. Beaufrey enjoys details of needle probes, curettes, and crushed skulls because purveyors of sadistic film prefer atypical surgeries for the "blood and mess" (*ibid.*). Exhaling his fetid breath in the face of Seese, an unmarried parturient drug addict, he insists that she will love having her pregnancy terminated under morphine. The emphasis on deadening of nerves mirrors the death in Beaufrey, also reflected in his halitosis and his mental identity with maiming and killing.

The author views fetus harvesting through a cannibalistic image consistent with the tone and atmosphere of the entire text. From intrauterine views of the scraper at work, Beaufrey imagines late-term abortion to be "a giant dragon head opening and closing in search of a morsel" (Silko, 1991, 102). The metaphor of the dragon head parallels Beaufrey's misogynistic view of abortion as art in the experience of Seese, his rival for the affection of the artist David. A naive pawn in Beaufrey's underworld *ménage à trois*, Seese shuns the destroyer's art as loveless and barbaric. She relives the abortion of her first child in a flower nightmare. After surgery, she imagines dozens of yellow roses disbudded over the white linens of her hospital bed. Before they can open, the petals shrivel, much as her unformed embryo died in pre-infancy. Through her deciphering of Lecha's Mayan almanac, Seese "[understands] more than you think" about cruelty and the negation of normal human feeling (Silko, 1991, 24). She distances herself from Beaufrey's microcosm of torture and death and the clients who pay for his repulsive videos. Her atonement, mourning for her kidnapped baby Monte, turns her inexorably to the revolution that will cleanse North America's slimy underbelly.

*See also* mothering; social class; women

• *References and further reading*

Horvitz, Deborah M. *Literary Trauma: Sadism, Memory, and Sexual Violence in American Women's Fiction.* Albany: State University of New York Press, 2000.
Hume, Kathryn. *American Dream, American Nightmare: Fiction since 1960.* Urbana: University of Illinois Press, 2002.
St. Clair, Janet. "Death of Love/Love of Death: Leslie Marmon Silko's *Almanac of the Dead*," *MELUS* 21:2 (1996): 141–156.
Silko, Leslie Marmon. *Almanac of the Dead.* New York: Simon & Schuster, 1991.
_____. *Laguna Woman: Poems.* New York: Greenfield Review Press, 1974.

# achievement

Silko's quest stories and poems illustrate a universal truth, that the journey alters identity, a fact that marks the epic characterizations of Odysseus, Moses, Fa-Mulan, King Arthur, Arjuna, and Joan of Arc. The author's initial tribute to the searcher in the coming-of-age story "Humaweepi, the Warrior Priest" (1974) honors the humble, willing student and the aged mentor as co-achievers. Through emulation, the youthful, naive Humaweepi, at age 19, stores up songs, chants, and prayers for use in his service to the Pueblo as a holy man. On an expedition into the wild, he surprises himself at the end of his hymn to the bear of the lakeshore by proclaiming himself a warrior priest. The achievement, rather than an appointment to boast over, becomes an "aha!" experience, a viewing of his gradual evolution from apprentice to sacred servant of the mother creator.

The revelation of divine guidance dominates Silko's first novel, *Ceremony* (1977). At a test of his return to normality, the protagonist Tayo, a veteran of the 1942 Bataan Death

March, achieves wholeness in a dual reordering of self—by reclaiming nature and by rejecting white materialism. On the upswing from crushing sorrow and guilt for not saving his cousin/foster brother Rocky during the march, Tayo faces his own timidity in a confrontation with Floyd Lee's steel wire wolf-proof fence, a stark symbol of the undeniable boundary between white and Indian values. To retrieve Uncle Josiah's stolen cattle, Tayo talks himself into cutting the wire at a place where lightning marked a pine tree, a proof of divine intervention in human plans. As though striking falsehood with the blade of truth, he feels himself slashing at the lies of whites, the source of Amerindian displacement, poverty, and witchery. The fence, an emblem of "the starving against the fat, the colored against the white," demands a requital of justice against the polarization caused by wealth and privilege, "patriotic wars and ... great technology" (Silko, 1977, 191). Even the moonlight deceives him into stumbling on roots and rocks, symbols of whites and their deceptions. To complete the bold reclamation of Josiah's cattle, Tayo opens himself to the power of nature. He sprinkles yellow pollen into the tracks of a mountain lion, the embodiment of stealth and grace and a feline ideal of endurance that Silko introduces in her poem "Indian Song: Survival" (1973). Upon locating the herd in a dry lakebed, Tayo trusts the animals' instinct to return to their birthplace to the south. Significantly, the herd restores order in Tayo's world, beginning his healing from war trauma and separation from his people and their values.

In her third novel, *Gardens in the Dunes* (1999), Silko focuses on the female perspective on ambition. Unlike what critics Thomas S. Edwards and Elizabeth A. De Wolfe refer to as "European-based egocentric cultures," the Indian siblings, Indigo and Sister Salt, show no evidence of the masculine lust for power and territorial control, the longings that destroy the camp cook and gambler Big Candy and Dr. Edward Palmer, a plant smuggler and commercializer (Edwards & De Wolfe, 2001, 198). Obedient daughters of Mama and proteges of Grandma Fleet, the Sand Lizard matriarch, the girls require none of the punitive rearing methods and threats common to Christian society. Endowed with what De Wolfe and Edwards call "joyous female earth energy," the girls approach womanhood with a competence sufficient to help them survive their mother's disappearance with the Ghost Dance followers and their grandmother's death (*ibid.*). Achievement for Sister Salt hinges on her ability to adapt to life in a tent city outside the construction of an aqueduct on the Colorado River outside Parker, Arizona. In contrast to muscular men who wrench the current from its ancestral bed and leave "the earth blasted open, the soil moist and red as flesh," she earns her living as a laundress and comfort girl, standard sources of income for minority women in male-dominant settings (Silko, 1999, 213). Her outstanding accomplishment, the birthing and nurture of "little black grandfather," ties her to female strengths of patience and endurance of ill fortune (*ibid.*, 344).

Silko pursues a duality of experience and challenge in the sisters' lives. For Indigo, achievement derives from discreet sampling of white society and theological history and from constructing a more sophisticated worldview consistent with her Sand Lizard heritage. To preserve self, she escapes the Sherman Institute in Riverside, California, where educators encourage female students to develop "a docile willingness to serve" as a lady's maid (*ibid.*, 311). From her hiding place in the greenhouse of Dr. Edward and Hattie Palmer, Indigo examines a showplace of elegant and exotic flowers and fruits, but looks beyond for the functional garden, the one that feeds the household. Her perusal acknowledges years of training in survival by Mama and Grandma Fleet, the nurturers of the remains of the Sand Lizard clan who view plants as potential meals.

For Indigo, the introduction to decorative horticulture impresses her senses without distracting her from edible produce, the main purpose of gardening. During her months with the Palmers, she collects seeds and keeps notes and drawings on plant variety and propagation with the intent of rejoining the dwindling Sand Lizard people and replanting their ancestral sandhills in new species. Unlike Edward, a bio-pirate and exploiter of native flora in Guatemala, Surinam, and Corsica, Indigo respects plants as elements of the human diet. During her incarceration at the American Embassy in Livorno, Italy, and her sea voyage back to North America, she treasures a valise stocked with seeds and corms intended for a future garden. Against a backdrop of the Palmers' depression and loss, the budding botanist maintains optimism that she will reunite with her people. She repudiates "regular churchgoers," the enemies of the dispossessed Indians, who have lost ancestral land to grasping hypocrites (*ibid.*, 206). The text rewards her outlook with the return of Sister Salt and a nephew, the infant "little black grandfather," the first male to join the matriarchy. Indigo achieves status among the small clan as the teller of a new story and planter of seeds and corms, notably, the hybridized black gladiolus from Lucca, Italy, a source of exotic flowers and food.

See also *Gardens in the Dunes*; names; Palmer, Hattie Abbott; reclamation

- *References and further reading*

Edwards, Thomas S., and Elizabeth A. De Wolfe. *Such News of the Land: U.S. Women Nature Writers.* Hanover, NH: University Press of New England, 2001.
Friedman, Susan Stanford. "Bodies on the Move: A Poetics of Home and Diaspora," *Tulsa Studies in Women's Literature* 23:2 (Fall 2004): 189–212.
Silko, Leslie Marmon. *Ceremony.* New York: Viking, 1977.
_____. *Gardens in the Dunes.* New York: Scribner, 1999.

## adaptation

By extolling the human agency and adaptability of her own generation, Silko challenges *The Last of the Mohicans* (1826), the American myth of the doomed Indian created by James Fenimore Cooper, a romanticist who lived in New York City while he wrote the first of his classic Leatherstocking Tales. One of Silko's early stories, "Bravura," anthologized in *The Man to Send Rain Clouds: Contemporary Stories by American Indians* (1974), introduces the theme of the outsider acclimating to life in the desert among natives. The text implies a naivete among academics who retreat to the Southwest to "live Indian." The theme darkens in her first novel, *Ceremony* (1977), set at the Laguna Pueblo in New Mexico. She creates a hostile milieu in which Tayo, a battle-strained veteran of World War II, attempts to find peace from the horrors of soldiery. A Pueblo half-breed from Laguna, New Mexico, he journeys to California before embarking to the Philippines in the Pacific theater. In San Diego, he views a milieu in which whites live in comfort in sprawling residences. He remarks on the adaptation of the poor to an imbalance of wealth. After affluent whites leave for the garbage huge meals, the homeless scrounge to survive on "the leftover things the whites didn't want" (Silko, 1977, 127). The image returns to haunt Tayo on his entry to Gallup, where a riverbank community salvages scraps to build hovels.

The lure of materialism and white debauchery seduces Silko's protagonist. Among bumptious war buddies— Emo, Harley, Leroy Valdez, and cousin Pinkie — in spring 1948, Tayo allows himself to follow the lead of hard drinkers and boasters who glory in sexual escapades with white women. While Emo, the belligerent malcontent, grouses about fighting a white man's war and returning to drought on Indian land, Tayo drifts away to ponder the label of Coors beer. In the gushing spring on the label, he wonders if the brewery in Golden, Colorado, is too far north to experience the aridity of New Mexico's desert. Tossing back beer after beer, he identifies with the abundant flow in the picture, which he wills to slake the thirst "deep down, somewhere behind his belly, near his heart" (*ibid.*, 56). As Tayo hallucinates his grueling march to a Bataan prison camp in April 1942, the text turns the crystal stream on the beer label into a death-stained flood of the Filipino monsoon. The dual image of beer and urine in the men's toilet reveals his mental conversion of normal thoughts into flashbacks, the nightmares that "came out anytime," jerking him back and forth between the brutal past and the shapeless, hopeless present (*ibid.*).

Silko uplifts the human will as the power source for adaptation. Fully accepted as an Indian despite his mixed blood, Tayo flourishes in the resolution as a nativist hero and potential member of Laguna Pueblo's kiva society. The text notes his humility in relating his story to elders and in accepting the shaman Ku'oosh's order to fast to attain wisdom. The kiva wisemen accept the rehabilitated Anglo-Indian veteran for his potential to uplift and refresh pueblo traditions, which require a perspective on world change to give the Laguna strength to face the future. The men agree: "We will be blessed again" (*ibid.*, 257). Left in isolation underground in the adobe circle, Tayo sits, not on standard kiva benches, but on a chair purloined from St. Joseph Mission, a hint at the hybridity of influences shaping native culture in the late 1940s. The seating symbolizes his Anglo paternity and suggests the peripheral significance of the Hebrew carpenter Joseph, the biblical outsider who reared the divine child Jesus as though he were blood kin.

For *Almanac of the Dead* (1991), Silko's ghoulish meta-narrative, she creates a character list of misfits and trauma victims, all of whom must adapt to disappointment or die trying. Two characters, Max "Mr. Murder" Blue and Eddie Trigg, suffer an inability to achieve a satisfactory orgasm, a prophecy of cultural sterility. In the sex-obsessed underworld of Tucson, the two worship wealth over normal family life. Max, a murder-for-hire capo from Cherry Hill, New Jersey, loses his desire for Leah, his money-mad realtor wife. In place of marital harmony, he chooses a daily golf game shielded from potential snipers by a corps of trained security guards. In a phallic distraction, he "[savors] the single instant of perfection when the ball and the head of the club met in absolute alignment" (Silko, 1991, 356).

Ironically, Max's pseudo-orgasmic sports performances leave his wife opportunities to seek satisfaction elsewhere. While he treats business clients to a round of golf, Leah indulges in an affair with Eddie, a wheelchair-bound paraplegic and fellow entrepreneur. Incapable of physical fulfillment through ejaculation, Eddie satisfies his ego with the knowledge that he has adapted to his handicap by romancing Max's woman, a conquest over a menacing underworld figure. Critic Jane Olmstead notes the similarity in the two men's adaptation. Both extol masculinity in alternate modes from the coital norm. For Max, being a man involves playing golf on a lush course in the midst of the desert with men who admire his clout and reputation for orchestrating executions. Eddie Trigg, the owner of a blood and organ harvesting complex, adapts to paralysis by acquiring clinics and hospitals that promise a cure for paraplegia and restoration of feeling in his stunted legs and penis. Neither of Leah's lovers achieves the basics of male normality, either through murder or fantasy.

In her third novel, *Gardens in the Dunes* (1999), Silko focuses on the 1890s by picturing a vast engineering project outside Parker, Arizona, altering the bed of the Colorado

River. The violation of native plants and the Amerindians who cultivate them requires rapid adaptation to flooding and lost acreage. The allocation of Indian homelands to devout churchgoers sharpens Silko's barbed satire of Christian hypocrisy and rapacity. German analyst Hartwig Isernhagen, an American literature specialist at the University of Basel, identifies in the mass alteration of life for the indigenous Sand Lizard people a threat to "a pure source, a genius of the race" (Isernhagen, 2002, 179). An echo of the Sand Lizard predicament appears briefly on Manhasset Bay, Long Island, where the landless Matinnecock transfer garden cultivation to the reaping of kelp and oysters, the means of their survival of European invasion. Because of childhood training in adaptation passed through a sound matriarchy, the critic admires "an ineradicable essence that will survive cultural change, that will constitute a fallback position in moments or periods of crisis, and that — because crises require adaptation — will not only survive change but ultimately embody it" (*ibid.*). A symbol of the viability of Sand Lizard spirit derives from the "little old grandfather," the child of Sister Salt and Big Candy, the Afro-Red Stick Indian cook and brewer. Before birth, the baby boy speaks from the womb in the Sand Lizard language. Isernhagen identifies the child as an emblem of miscegenation and adjustment to change.

   *See also* Indigo; Sister Salt; Tayo

• *References and further reading*

Cutchins, Dennis. "'So That the Nations May Become Genuine Indian': Nativism and Leslie Marmon Silko's Ceremony," *Journal of American Culture* 22: 4 (1999): 77–89.

Hebebrand, Christina M. *Native American and Chicano/a Literature of the American Southwest*. New York: Routledge, 2004.

Isernhagen, Hartwig. "Of Deserts and Gardens: The Southwest in Literature and Art, 'Native' and 'White'" in *Literature and Visual Arts in Twentieth-Century America*, ed. Michele Bottalico. Bari: Palomar Eupalinos, 2002, 173–187.

Olmstead, Jane. "The Uses of Blood in Leslie Marmon Silko's *Almanac of the Dead*," *Contemporary Literature* 40:3 (Fall 1999): 464–490.

Silko, Leslie Marmon. *Almanac of the Dead*. New York: Simon & Schuster, 1991.

_____. *Ceremony*. New York: Viking, 1977.

## *Almanac of the Dead* (1991)

   Leslie Marmon Silko compiled abuse and genocide by a Eurocentric world into a speculative chronicle, *Almanac of the Dead*, an anti–Western, anti–Christian, anti-capitalist diatribe. Abby H. P. Werlock, a former English professor at St. Olaf College, links the novelist's rebellion to the bristly verse of the Beat generation of the 1920s. Like democracy itself, the text, divided into 208 vignettes, chronicles a span of viewpoints aquiver with brooding and rage against repression and menace resulting from what critic Jeff Berglund calls "the distorted state of human affairs during the reign of the Destroyers" (Berglund, 2006, 158). A scalding rant lacking the lyricism of *Laguna Woman* (1974) or *Ceremony* (1977), the novel begins epic style *in medias res* in a kitchen scene that resembles a *Macbeth*-like witches' sabbath of pot stirring and illicit drugs while the twin crones' foster son cleans carbines and pistols. The text follows a pattern that critic Carl Abbot calls "a dozen out-of-control life stories in parallel ... all with lives intersecting in Tucson" (Abbott, 2008, 14–15). The complex web of scenarios mimes the storytelling of Ts'its'tsi'-nako (Grandmother Spider or Thought Woman), the creator, who crisscrosses destinies through conflict and resolution. To Silko, Pueblo myth possesses more reality than the illusory domination of whites. Cherokee critic MariJo Moore explains that "While white reality may indeed be a very powerful illusion (on the order of a horrible bad dream), Native reality is fact" (Moore, 2003, 311).

Interconnections focus on the disempowerment of indigenous people during the shaping of the New World into a global power. Unlike predictable sci-fi fiction that extrapolates action from futuristic technology, in the style of the *Egyptian Book of the Dead* (1240 B.C.), Silko's developing world looks back to tribal prophecy for an explanation of what lies ahead. The allegorical apocalypse foretells an era of chaos and "the disappearance of all things European" from Amerindian homelands (Silko, 1991, 14). The question of sovereignty underlies an ongoing scramble for control. In the estimation of author and editor Sara L. Spurgeon, the struggle over borders and frontiers grows slippery and indefinite: "Dangerous, fluid, permeable, [the frontier] is a product and producer of a particular brand of myth structured ... around a privileged form of sacred violence all sides battle to claim for their own" (Spurgeon, 2005, 103). Silko validates the push from the south, which foreshadows the overthrow of white society by poor indigenous Mesoamericans reclaiming their heritage.

New from Old

Told in spiraling time rather than standard conveyor belt chronology, the layered circular narrative mirrors what Silko learned from her study of archeoastronomy, the Mayan calendar, and Central American codices. In 2010, she vindicated her discreditation of modern time constraints: "There are intervals between heartbeats, between the planting of a seed and the sprouting.... But hours and minutes and seconds? Those are man-made" (Bennett, 2010). Critical commentary validates the author's methods and themes. Seneca analyst Penelope Myrtle Kelsey describes the parchment sources as "ageless, literally undatable ... traditions of writing, record, and book fashioning" (Kelsey, 2008, 2). Eerily, the text itself is the outgrowth of Mesoamerican prophecy of what critic Paul Lauter pictures as a "cosmopolitan patriotism," another name for global community (Lauter, 2010, 632). Silko described the finished effect as a "shattered two-hour movie" that she tore, chopped, and remixed to refute the sanctioned American myths of Anglo superiority to the lifestyle of first peoples (Coltelli, 1990, 150). Vindication, the thematic focus, underlies the connections between disaffected Americans and their alliance against the white capitalist, their mutual exploiter and enslaver. In the opinion of Sanhya Rajendra Shukla and Heidi Tinsman, Silko reconfigures the standard postcolonial novel by "[imagining] a world beyond the simple dualism of colonizer and colonized" (Shukla & Tinsman, 2007, 192). The effect, according to critic Bonita Lawrence, is "dazzling, bewildering, and shocking" (Tewinkel, 2003, 23).

With gestures of respect and honor to Geronimo, Red Cloud, and Sitting Bull, heroes of the Indian Wars of the late 1800s, and to the scattered Yaqui of Mexico and the United States, Silko pictures the Western Hemisphere made whole once more by the erasure of political borders. Critic Rachel Adams accounts for the vision of a transborder Indian reunion as a narrative retort to those who would militarize North American borders, which "are failing as nation-states lose their ability to control the transnational circulation of people and goods" (Adams, 2009, 52). Silko introduces her text with a five-century, pan-historic map of peoples— African Americans, Aztec, Cubans, Guatemalans, Haitian black Indians, Hopi, Inupik, Laguna, Lakota, Mafiosi, Mexicans, Tohono O'odham, and Yaqui as well as the handicapped, homeless, and war veterans. The disaffected populations converge on Tucson, the story's geographic anchor. Myriad characters, like pilgrims to the shrine of St. Thomas à Becket in Geoffrey Chaucer's *Canterbury Tales*, bring with them their individual, socio-economic, and ethnic agendas. On a north-south continuum, the intersecting forces malign and negate the effects of America's Manifest Destiny, the gradual dislocation of first peoples, and the usurpation of western frontiers, especially those parcels containing valuable minerals, oil, timber, and waterways. Energized by bitterness and fury, the author's creolized view of anarchy in southern Arizona looks toward the Maya of Yucatan in hope for a reunion of indigenous peoples. Generating the necessary centripetal force is the transcription of ancient prophecy.

MULTICULTURAL MYTHOS

Silko's mantra of survival through storykeeping takes reverential and dynamic form in *Almanac*. According to analysts Shukla and Tinsman, Silko unites the voodoo lore of the West African with Amerindian animism to achieve a resilient truth about divinity and humanity. During the kidnap of Yoruba into bondage, their *loa* (spirits) "crossed the oceans with colonizers, workers, and slaves, and like the moving, multiracial human populations around them, they too were changed by the journey" (Shukla & Tinsman, 2007, 202). As critic Michelle Jarman points out, the author rejects the romanticism of these ethnic additives. With candor toward native faults, Silko charges Indians with allowing murderous rivalries to distract them from halting the European encroachment, which results in the lynching of Yaqui in a cottonwood arbor. The narrative salutes her Laguna and Maya ancestors for keeping the faith: "If the people had not retold the stories, or if the stories had somehow been lost, then the people were lost" (Silko, 1991, 316). She exults that, through retellings, "the ancestors' spirits were summoned by the stories" (*ibid.*). Parchments and sheets inserted in the ancient almanac derive from the "unearthing of palimpsestic records of stories from the now dead labor that has gone into the making of modern capitalism" (Shukla & Tinsman, 2007, 197). The pages—the "collective account of American Indians"—bear the marks of food stains and body effluvia, evidence of the human effort to rescue and preserve holy writ (*ibid.*).

To redeem the soul of the Western Hemisphere, Silko's mythic underpinnings support a vigorous resolution. Midway through the text, logic takes second place to diatribe after Clinton, a paranoid Afro-Cherokee watchman employed by Vietnam vet Rambo-Roy, musters an army of homeless. Like the faceless, anonymous warriors in Apollonius's tale of "Jason and the Golden Fleece" (ca. 250 B.C.), the redeemers trudge north from Chiapas, Mexico. The result is a deliberate reader onslaught enhanced by ambiguous syntax and encrypted Mayan prophecy too rambling and too pictographic to make literal sense. In the words of analyst Patrick O'Donnell, a specialist in American fiction, the book "envisages a future where ancestral ghosts and indigenous people reclaim and restore the world," a strand that Silko furthers in *Gardens in the Dunes* (1999) in the secondary plot of Delena, the dog circus Gypsy and Mexican gun runner (O'Donnell, 2010, 168).

The author draws on a long apocalyptic tradition espoused by the Aztec, Hopi, Laguna, Lakota, and Maya. Validating the overturn of white dominance, Chilam Balam's 18th-century Mayan almanac, a collection of nine sacred codices from Yucatan, verifies colonial usurpation and predicts its self-annihilating egocentrism and decadence. The dynamics of doom in Grandmother Yoeme's old notebooks, which she stores in a wooden ammunition crate, come from the giant snake Maah' shra-True'-Ee, an icon that Silko returns to in *The Turquoise Ledge* (2010). The reptile resides in the lake at Laguna Pueblo until jealous neighbors crack the lake bottom and drain the water from the reptile's lair.

In the almanac's coded message, recorded by Chilam Balam, the serpent claims to have provided names and stories from past history. His time-spanning prophecy warns of the end-time when the world will cease to exist. Yoeme's granddaughter Lecha, the seer of the dead and subsequent keeper of the almanac, respects the old parchments for predicting catastrophes—"drought or flood, plague, civil war or invasion" (Silko, 1991, 137). The storytelling of an old man, who welcomes Menardo Panson to a garden *ramada* (shelter of branches), typifies the fragility of Indian history. The only requirement for transmission is that the boy listen. The command echoes the Paiute prophet Wovoka's chant to participants in the Ghost Dance and the repeated war cry of Silko's Barefoot Hopi, who leads his New Age followers into the breach caused by social chaos.

## VILLAINS AND ANARCHY

The waves of revolt in *Almanac of the Dead* come from identifiable populations of the dispossessed:

- Clinton and Rambo-Roy lead Vietnam veterans, including the homeless in Tucson and the wannabes too young to have served in the Southeast Asian war.
- Awa Gee, the Korean-American techno-hacker, plots power outages across the United States and predicts that revolution will come spontaneously with help from electronics manipulators.
- The Mayan twins, El Feo and Tacho, lead Amerindians by spying on whites and by channeling orders from ancestral spirits, who speak through macaws.
- Green Vengeance eco-kamikazes engineer terrorist sabotage of dams, the technological obstructions of nature's waterways.
- The Marxist Mexican-Indian leader Angelita, known as La Escapía and the Meat Hook, plots execution of traitors, a partisan purge common to anarchy.
- The Barefoot Hopi, a rabble-rouser and fundraiser, orchestrates jail and prison riots and musters a multiracial coalition of rebel inmates to whom he ministers.
- Wilson Weasel Tail, a Lakota demagogue who recites the Paiute prophet Wovoka's outcry, a galvanizing call to arms.

In the description of analyst Katherine Sugg, a specialist in comparative literature of the Americas, the allegory is a biblical jeremiad—"the prophesied apocalypse [that] signals the desire for a radical cleansing, a sweeping away, of the old, corrupt social order" (Sugg, 2008, 68). Like Revelation (ca. A.D. 65), St. John's anti-oppression apocalypse of the Roman Empire, Silko's fiction tabulates the losses to genocide, persecution, and death squads and anticipates a new definition of "civilization." Balancing the radical upheaval engendered by utopists, Indian wannabes, and eco-warriors, Silko depicts a Dantean rogues' gallery—vampiric opportunists, on-the-take police, alcohol and drug addicts, sexual deviants, fetishists, and psychopaths:

- Realtor Leah Blue, who designs Venice, Arizona, a gated community and water park that wastes the area's potable groundwater for canals and fountains.
- De Guzman, a military officer married to a Yaqui wife (who tortures Indian women).
- Eddie Trigg, the paralyzed blood bank organizer who harvests skin, corneas, and organs from Tucson's homeless to merchandise at his network of medical clinics.

- Beaufrey, the homosexual pornographer who markets snuff and torture videos, including abortions and the slaying and dismemberment of the infant Monte, son of David and Seese.
- Serlo, a white supremacist who supports the creation of an AIDS virus designed to annihilate Hispanics and blacks.
- Max Blue, a Mafioso and contract killer, who poses as a harmless retiree playing golf for rehabilitation.
- Mr. B, a hush-hush CIA agent who hires second-generation felon Sonny Blue to infiltrate smuggling from Mexico.
- Bartolomeo, the arrogant Cuban Marxist who minimizes blacks and Indians as savages lacking a worthy history.
- Judge Arne, a federal jurist from Phoenix who enables the corrupt to exploit Arizona.
- Menardo Panson, an insurance dealer who promises the rich the protection of mercenary security forces to combat all eventualities, even anarchy.

Silko's sprawling chapters maintain consistency and unity through their denigration of white colonialists, whom she abases as "Eurotrash oligarchy," "sweat hogs of capitalism," "vampires and monsters," the "heartless and craven" inhabiting "cities of werewolves" (Silko, 1991, 289, 312, 488, 313). Calabazas, a Yaqui marijuana smuggler, justifies the return of stolen land to the Yaqui: "We are here thousands of years before the first whites. We are here before maps or quit claims. We know where we belong on this earth" (*ibid.*, 216). His manifesto foretells the return home of the story's moral center, Sterling, the Indian exiled for betraying the sanctity of the Laguna Pueblo to Hollywood filmmakers, who trivialize the sacred snake.

For the sake of transcultural social justice, Silko seeks to salvage the Americas from five centuries of domination by the European conqueror, who "had no future here because he had no past, no spirits of ancestors here" (*ibid.*, 313). In the characterization of Angelita, Clinton, and Sterling, Silko valorizes the peasant communism of the homeless and of mountain Indians who share space, water, and wild game to facilitate survival on a harsh landscape. Similar to her view of blended cultures in *Ceremony*, *Almanac* anticipates a coalition and mutiny of Amerindians, blacks, and other downtrodden peoples against Caucasian arrogance and rapacity: "Nothing could be black only or brown only or white only any more.... This was the last chance the people had against the Destroyers, and they would never prevail if they did not work together as a common force" (*ibid.*, 747). Zeta, the Anglo-Yaqui gold smuggler, learns subversion from her grandmother Yoeme. Zeta rationalizes her own crimes as no worse than those of Washington, D.C.: "How could one steal if the government itself was the worst thief?" (*ibid.*, 133). The inevitable downfall "would catch up with the white man whether the Indians did anything or not. History was the sacred text" (*ibid.*, 316). Silko's readings of Sigmund Freud and her understanding of the Jungian collective unconscious, a repository of human experience over time, undergird the kaleidoscopic view of rebel motivations. According to analyst Jean Petrolle, by conferring sacred power on the narrative, Silko, like the Vietnam vet protagonist of Arthur R. Flowers's *De Mojo Blue: De Quest of High John de Conqueror* (1986), hopes "to energize indigenous peoples to organize and sustain their own revolutionary political campaigns to hold or reclaim land" (Petrolle, 2007, 133). Thus, revolution evolves naturally from change rather than cataclysm.

POLITICAL PAYBACK

A latter-day Hellmouth, Silko's *Almanac of the Dead* plunges into a tumult of exploitation and evil. Analysts compare her style to that of postmodernists Don DeLillo and Thomas Pynchon in setting up a vast *dramatis personae* against a somber wasteland—"an infinite variety of greasy detritus, from sex malls to abortion movies, from organ transplants to cocaine shipments made by balloon" (West, 1992, 8). The urgent non-chronological montage immerses the reader in shifting community action, a feat that reviewer Sharon Weinstein of the *Virginian-Pilot* declared "the Great American Novel" (Weinstein, 1992, C3). Paul West, book critic for the *Los Angeles Times*, surmised that the looming text comprises "half a dozen disparate novels ... rammed together" (West, 1992, 8). The hyperbole and repetition caused Charles Larson, literary critic for the *Washington Post*, to charge Silko with overkill. Late in the assessment, critic A. Robert Lee stated, "Silko Overreaches, her novel too crowded, or hectoring, or damagingly under-edited" (Lee, 2009, 23). Intending what she jokingly called cultural terrorism, she relieved Native American ignorance of their own roots, particularly the imprisoning of the poor who take escape through drugs. Her style, as described in the *Buffalo News*, revives the formulaic proletarian novel of the 1930s—Grace Lumpkin's *To Make My Bread* (1932), Myra Page's *Moscow Yankee* (1935), Robert Cantwell's *The Land of Plenty* (1935), Meridel Le Sueur's *The Girl* (1939), John Steinbeck's *The Grapes of Wrath* (1939)—with Indians in the place of factory drones and migrant laborers.

A gnawing, arrhythmic rant, *Almanac* accounts for the residue of anger in Native Americans some five centuries after the establishment of an illegitimate Anglo government on stolen land. To expose the culpability of the Christian-capitalist society, Silko amalgamates classic epic and medieval allegory with native-style storytelling and symbolism. One of her more intriguing tales, the disappearing Geronimo, asserts the skill of the profiled Indian to recede into the background, a tactic that the old Chiricahua Apache practiced for 15 years until his surrender in 1886 at Skeleton Canyon, Arizona. In the spirit of the Indians who aided Geronimo, Silko incorporates a Marxist perspective on underclass solidarity and predicts a revolt of the powerless to transform society. For spirituality, she emulates myth and epic genres akin to the Mayan scripture in the *Popol Vuh* (ca. 1554), the Western Hemisphere's earliest codified scripture, to expose the soul killing caused by dope dealing and global aggression. For maximum revulsion of the world order, she pictures narcissistic characters who become so self-absorbed and predatory that they deserve no pity for their "necropolitics," the generation of a death-in-life existence for such social outcasts as street people, handicapped war vets, AIDS victims, and the *mestizo* servant class (Sugg, 2008, 70). For the audacity and satiric jest of Silko's charges, critic Linda Grant Niemann labeled the book a "radical, stunning manifesto on the history of the Americas since the conquest" (Niemann, 1992, 10).

THE IMPACT OF *ALMANAC*

Critical response to Silko's storied web is understandably mixed, beginning with an onslaught of puzzled and negative criticisms of her hostile tone and free-form chapter outline. Silko deliberately razzed the academic world by writing a dystopian meta-narrative, something that would outrage members of the Modern Language Association. The chutzpah of a Laguna woman taking on North American history raised questions of her objectivity from John Skow, critic for *Time*. Under the heading "People of the Monkey Wrench," he charged her with vengeance and self-righteousness in creating a list of characters who are "drunk, doped or crazy" and with declaring white culture "a sickness, bloody and metastasizing" (Skow, 1991, 86). Likewise, Malcolm Jones, Jr., of *Newsweek* found her depiction of whites unfair. Kathryn Hume, an expert on contemporary fiction, notes that Silko admits the blood thirst of Aztecs, but fails to mention the imaginative skinnings, burnings, and tortures that forest and plains Indians staged to punish white prisoners of war. On-line reviewer Steve Brock dismissed the work as depressing; *Entertainment Weekly* reduced its style to sarcasm. Alan Ryan, a reviewer for *USA Today*, impugned *Almanac*'s literary merit. Edward B. St. John, in a critique for *Library Journal*, dismissed Silko's efforts with a sneer: "The frame story of apocalyptic racial warfare is clumsy comic book fare" (St. John, 1991, 124). Sven Birkerts, reviewer for *New Republic*, entitled his critique "Apocalypse Now" and bemoaned that analysis of *Almanac* was like "describing Rodin's 'The Gates of Hell' figure by figure" (Birkerts, 1991, 40).

From a positive perspective, commentators praise Silko for the orchestration of characters and plots leading up to the 500th anniversary of Christopher Columbus's discovery of the Western Hemisphere. For the novel's excursions into character lives, Birkerts compared Silko to the Roman novelist Petronius Arbiter by calling *Almanac* "a veritable 'Satyricon' of late-century sexual and narcotic practices" (*ibid.*, 40). Western novelist Larry McMurtry found Silko's text tinged with genius. Elizabeth Tallent, in a review for the *New York Times Book Review*, admired the drama of *Almanac* for "passionate indictment, defiant augury, bravura storytelling," but declared that Silko confused random violence with acts of justice (Tallent, 1991, 6). Lakota author Richard Erdoes called the novel an epic landmark for Native American literature and compared it to Tolstoy's *War and Peace* (1869). In a review for *Women's Review of Books*, literary scholar Linda Grant Niemann elevated *Almanac* to "an ark filled with the stories and the voices and the people who will create a new world out of the destruction of the old" (Niemann, 1992, 1).

*See also* Calabazas's genealogy; Lecha and Zeta's genealogy; Max Blue's genealogy; Menardo Panson's genealogy; Seese's genealogy

• *References and further reading*

Abbott, Carl. *How Cities Won the West: Four Centuries of Urban Change in Western North America.* Albuquerque: University of New Mexico Press, 2008.
Adams, Rachel. *Continental Divides: Remapping the Cultures of North America.* Chicago: University of Chicago Press, 2009.
Bennett, Steve. "Author Silko Isn't Concerned about Time," *Express News* (25 July 2010).
Berglund, Jeff. *Cannibal Fictions: American Explorations of Colonialism, Race, Gender and Sexuality.* Madison: University of Wisconsin Press, 2006.
Birkerts, Sven. "Apocalypse Now," *New Republic* 205:19 (4 November 91): 39–41.
Cevasco, George A., and Richard P. Harmond. *Modern American Environmentalists: A Biographical Encyclopedia.* Baltimore: Johns Hopkins University Press, 2009.
Coltelli, Laura. *Winged Words: American Indian Writers Speak.* Lincoln: University of Nebraska Press, 1990, 135–153.
Hume, Kathryn. *American Dream, American Nightmare: Fiction since 1960.* Urbana: University of Illinois Press, 2002.
Jarman, Michelle. "Exploring the World of the Different in Leslie Marmon Silko's *Almanac of the Dead*," *MELUS* 31:3 (Fall 2006): 147–168.
Kelsey, Penelope Myrtle. *Tribal Theory in Native American Literature: Dakota and Haudenosaunee Writing and Indigenous Worldviews.* Lincoln: University of Nebraska Press, 2008.
Kutzbach, Konstanze, and Monika Mueller. *The Abject of Desire: The Aestheticization of the Unaesthetic in Contemporary Literature and Culture.* Amsterdam: Rodopi, 2007.
Larson, Charles. "'Almanac': Tribal Assault," *Washington Post* (26 November 1991).
Lauter, Paul. *A Companion to American Literature and Culture.* Malden, MA: Blackwell-Wiley, 2010.

Lee, A. Robert. *United States: Re-viewing American Multicultural Literature*. València: Universitat de València, 2009.

Moore, MariJo. *Genocide of the Mind: New Native American Writing*. New York: Nation Books, 2003.

Murray, David. *Matter, Magic, and Spirit: Representing Indian and African American Belief*. Philadelphia: University of Pennsylvania Press, 2007.

Niemann, Linda. "New World Disorder," *Women's Review of Books* 9:6 (March 1992): 1–4.

_____, and Leslie Marmon Silko. "Narratives of Survival," *Women's Review of Books* 9:10–11 (July 1992): 10.

O'Donnell, Patrick. *The American Novel Now: Reading Contemporary American Fiction since 1980*. Chichester, UK: Wiley-Blackwell, 2010.

Olmstead, Jane. "The Uses of Blood in Leslie Marmon Silko's *Almanac of the Dead*," *Contemporary Literature* 40:3 (Fall 1999): 464–490.

Petrolle, Jean. *Religion without Belief: Contemporary Allegory and the Search for Postmodern Faith*. Albany: State University of New York Press, 2007.

Romero, Channette. "Envisioning a 'Network of Tribal Coalitions': Leslie Marmon Silko's *Almanac of the Dead*," *American Indian Quarterly* 26:4 (1 September 2002): 623–640.

St. John, Edward B. "Review: *Almanac of the Dead*," *Library Journal* 116:17 (15 October 1991): 124.

Schueller, Malini Johar. *Locating Race: Global Sites of Post-Colonial Citizenship*. Albany: State University of New York Press, 2009.

Shukla, Sanhya Rajendra, and Heidi Tinsman. *Imagining Our Americas: Toward a Transnational Frame*. Durham, NC: Duke University Press, 2007.

Silko, Leslie Marmon. *Almanac of the Dead*. New York: Simon & Schuster, 1991.

Skow, John. "The People of the Monkey Wrench," *Time* 138:23 (9 December 1991): 86.

Smith, Carlton. *Coyote Kills John Wayne: Postmodernism and Contemporary Fictions of the Transcultural Frontier*. Hanover, NH: University Press of New England, 2000.

Spurgeon, Sara L. *Exploding the Western: Myths of Empire on the Postmodern Frontier*. College Station: Texas A&M University Press, 2005.

Sugg, Katherine. *Gender and Allegory in Transamerican Fiction and Performance*. New York: Palgrave Macmillan, 2008.

Tallent, Elizabeth. "Storytelling with a Vengeance," *New York Times Book Review* (22 December 1991): 6.

Tewinkel, Wim. "Elders' Stories Saved for Future," *Windspeaker* 21:8 (November 2003): 23.

Weinstein, Sharon. "A Radical Premise about America as a Stolen Land," *Virginian-Pilot* (12 January 1992): C3.

Werlock, Abby H. P. *Facts on File Companion to the American Short Story*. New York: Facts on File, 2010.

West, Paul. "When a Myth Is as Good as a Mile," *Los Angeles Times* (2 February 1992): 8.

## ambition

Silko valorizes native ambitions for their victory over poverty and hopelessness. In an early story, "Bravura" (1974), she generates a subtle humor at the poet deserting the university to live Indian style in a poor community, where he intends to write verse about "life." A more poignant pairing between mentor and pupil in "Humaweepi, the Warrior Priest" (1974), introduces the title figure under the tutelage of an elder uncle/foster father, a character who prefigures Betonie and Uncle Josiah in Silko's first novel, *Ceremony* (1977). In the daily discourse between Humaweepi and his uncle, according to the opening sentence, example carries more weight than precept: "The old man didn't really teach him much; mostly they just lived" (Silko, 1974, 161). The statement implies Silko's approval of hands-on pedagogy, the one-on-one method common to Pueblo people long before they entered schools and learned to read and write. The mentor compares their relationship to mother and child by observing that the two "can sleep on the ground like the doe and fawn," a pairing that suggests tender mothering to a neophyte. The title figure achieves the "aha" experience of gestalt psychology: "I have been learning all this time and I didn't even know it" (*ibid.*, 162). Thus, Humaweepi enters a tribal priesthood without realizing that the ambition shaped his coming of age.

Replicating the unstated principle of youthful readying for a career, the text of *Ceremony* hints that ambition among the Pueblo requires a long-term commitment. Uncle

Josiah saves for 20 years at the rate of $25 per year to acquire $500 so he and his brother Robert can breed cattle. In addition to ambition, Josiah displays the discipline to research breeding techniques from a Bureau of Indian Affairs (BIA) extension agent and to rule out scientific method, a white man's concept suited to agrarian conditions. Based on his experience with all forms of life in the drought-ridden New Mexican desert, Josiah trusts the wild long-horned Mexican cattle from Magdalena—a blend of Anglo Herefords and Mexican longhorns—as the most likely stock to thrive on mesquite and little water. As adaptable as bovines capable of "living off rocks," Josiah is a risk-taker (Silko, 1977, 82). His outlook on success derives from faith in the land and in the Pueblo understanding of the cycles of nature, an anchoring in Southwestern topography that Josiah gains from the native oral tradition.

The mid–20th century generation lacks Josiah's adaptive aims. While the uncle works daily at herding cattle and sheep, his nephew Rocky, "an A-student and all-state in football and track," readies himself for the university by running laps twice daily around the baseball diamond, a static running-in-circles predictive of men who came of age in the 1940s (*ibid.*, 47). For Rocky, pride in athleticism extends to being the first Laguna to gain a football scholarship without help from the BIA. His land-based cousin/foster brother Tayo perceives Rocky's distancing of self from native values: "He was already planning where he would go after high school; he was already talking about the places he would live, and the reservation wasn't one of them" (*ibid.*, 71). In contrast to Josiah's industry in summer 1940, Rocky's self-glorification through athletic preening brings no honor on the family. After his daily runs, he absorbs himself in magazines and his girlfriend in Paguate and offers no aid to his father's farming chores or to Josiah's herding. Foolishly, Rocky identifies with "the destroyers," the ones whose "highest ambition is to gut human beings while they are still breathing, to hold the heart still beating so the victim will never feel anything again" (*ibid.*, 229).

## PERVERTED AMBITIONS

The motif of necrophilia prefigures Silko's epic historical fiction *Almanac of the Dead* (1991), a cross-section of Tucson natives absorbed in illicit moneymaking schemes and sensuality. To achieve her intent, she shapes outrage at American history by telling a version that Americans don't want to hear. Of her audacity, critic Elizabeth Cook-Lynn remarks: "It is one thing to write stories suggesting that white men are outcasts from their own souls, but quite another to say that we can no longer keep under control the horrible things that result from that loss" (Cook-Lynn, 2001, 87). According to anthropologist Catherine Jane Lavender, Silko accomplishes her survey of white fault through a "tradition of comfort with gender fluidity" (Lavender, 2006, 139). The narrative of *Almanac* wrings piquant humor out of the memories of Lecha, an elderly drug addict who claims to be dying of cancer to rationalize her need for Percodan, a blend of aspirin with the painkiller oxycodone. Upon arrival at her twin sister's desert hideaway, Lecha retreats into her ambition from three decades past to open a bush plane service to villages and hamlets. She pictures herself zooming off with her nephew/foster son Ferro in his cradleboard. Her ambitions slip easily out of hand: "I would land an airplane like an angel! But all that had only been daydreams…. That's all I was—talk, hot air" (Silko, 1999, 100). Ironically, twin sister Zeta's ridicule of Lecha motivates Lecha to leave the Southwest "to explore new territory" (*ibid.*). Ferro, left behind with an unmotherly aunt, develops his own ambition for the good life financed through drug smuggling, the trade he learns from Zeta.

In the estimation of literary historian Laurie Champion, Silko is "an author with a mission ... to counter the disastrous effects of past and present 'stories' behind the violence, environmental decay, and spiritual impoverishment of the present era" (Champion, 2002, 335). Goal setting discloses the blindness of characters to normal ambition. Silko pictures Menardo Panson besotted with Algería, a woman born outside his social class. While he yearns for a mistress to replace his wife Iliana Gutiérrez, he idealizes Algería Martinez-Soto, a Venezuelan architect trained in Madrid. The narrative contrasts Menardo's erotic longings with Algería's idealization of house design: "She had a fast, breathy way of talking about her ideas and goals— the interplay of structure as sculptural form with light" (*ibid.*, 267). Farther down the monetary food chain, Silko's cast sell themselves for momentary pleasures, ignoring the undertone of revolution among the Mesoamerican dispossessed. Beaufrey, a sleazy pornographer, discounts the rumble because he "did not believe the rioting natives of the earth would have enough energy or ambition to overrun it" and exterminate the crass, power-mad authorities who care nothing about democracy or the underclass (*ibid.*, 549). Critic John Muthyala rebuts Beaufrey's dismissal of grassroots rebellion: "By going beyond tribal forms of affiliation and building an international network of supporters, the Mayans affirm nontraditional and non–Indian forms of solidarity to achieve their local, social, and political goals" (Muthyala, 2006, 184).

According to literary analysts Konstanze Kutzbach and Monika Mueller, Silko "aims at deconstructing the perverted European (American) values grounded in the Law of the Father" (Kutzbach & Mueller, 2007.13). The author places her faith in the proletariat and its syncretic resistance, a belief she affirms in the essays "An Expression of Profound Gratitude to the Maya Zapatistas" (1994), "America's Debt to the Indian Nations: Atoning for a Sordid Past" (1996), and "The People and the Land ARE Inseparable" (1996). In a personal essay, "Fences against Freedom" in *Yellow Woman and a Beauty of the Spirit: Essays on Native American Life Today* (1996), the author castigates national aims of "elected officials, blinded by greed and ambition, [who] show great disrespect to the electorate they represent" (Silko, 1996, 113). For good measure, the essay lambastes the media, "their sluttish handmaidens, the big television networks" for promoting racism as a means of dividing the U.S. citizenry (*ibid.*). Her identification with Amerindian persistence resurges in "500 Years from Now, Everyone in Tucson Speaks Nahuatl Not Chinese," the title of her speech to the 2007 Indigenous Languages Conference.

## FAMILY VS. AFFLUENCE

Ambition takes more normal routes in Silko's third novel, *Gardens in the Dunes* (1999), which contrasts the moneymaking plans of an Afro-Big Stick Indian cook and gambler with a hotel laundress eager to rear her daughters Indian style in the desert. Big Candy, reared in a Louisiana plantation kitchen, where his mother prepared dove and quail, adapts his childhood culinary skills to the needs of a workmen's camp outside Parker reservation in Arizona. While saving his wages from Mr. Wylie, Big Candy dreams of owning his own restaurant. The motivation contrasts the narcissism of botanist and photographer Dr. Edward Palmer and the greed of the bio-pirate Mr. Eliot, both of whom rob exotic locales of orchids and fruit trees to commercialize among faddish horticulturists. The narrative describes Palmer's aim as ego-based, the drive "to discover a new plant species that would bear his name, and he spent twenty years of his life in this pursuit" (Silko, 1999, 78). The push to establish himself among scholars alienates him from Hattie Abbott Palmer, his scholarly bride. A proto-feminist, she, too, seeks validation by academia, but, along with "her ambition to see her thesis completed," she pursues marriage with "a man who cared" (*ibid.*, 175). Unlike get-rich-quick entrepreneurs Eliot and Palmer, Candy maintains that "a man had to work most of his life if he wanted to have anything to call his own" (*ibid.*, 210). His yearning for a small business allies him with Sister Salt, a Sand Lizard Indian who operates her own laundry and sells sex for cash. Unlike Candy and his grandiose dreams, Sister Salt saves her earnings for a reunion with her sister Indigo and Mama. In addition to renewing the clan matriarchy, the sisters rescue Hattie from a marriage doomed from the beginning.

Gender and materialism impact the disjointed family of Big Candy, Sister Salt, and their infant son Bright Eyes, nicknamed "little black grandfather" (*ibid.*, 344). In contrast to Sister Salt's beneficent dream of a reunited family, Candy longs to "enjoy the fine food and pretty women" that come with entrepreneurial success, the kind of fantasy utopia that blinds Silko's characters in *Almanac* (*ibid.*). To the couple's benefit, both Candy and Sister Salt intend to travel north into California. To hurry the dream of independence, Candy operates a bootleg brewery and runs poker, blackjack, and dice games. His ambition grows after he moves Sister Salt into his tent, but he denies allegations that he intends to operate a bordello. Instead, he sets up more tents for gambling, drinking, and food service. By hiring Mojave women as cooks, he satisfies the dam builders' demand for meat on payday and boasts of being "this much closer to Denver" (Silko, 1999, 218). In an urban setting, he intends to direct his own rise with "an elegant dining room in a fine hotel" sheltered by "high mountains covered with snow" (*ibid.*, 360). The theft of his money in one night's rioting at the tent city leaves him "inconsolable.... Nothing else mattered," including his mate and child (*ibid.*, 388). Sister Salt regrets separation from Candy, who condemns himself to a loveless life because of his lust for money. Attuned to the needs of her infant, she scorns the cause of the couple's separation: "Money! You couldn't drink it or eat it, but people went crazy over it" (*ibid.*, 398). From a domestic perspective, her outcry discredits the human terrain of *Almanac* and, to a lesser extent, *The Turquoise Ledge* (2010), a world shattered by the scramble for power and affluence.

*See also* achievement; Betonie; materialism

- *References and further reading*

Averbach, Margara. "*Gardens in the Dunes* by Leslie Marmon Silko: Stories as Resistance" in *Raízas e rumos: perspectivas interdisciplinares em estudos americanos*, ed. Sonia Torres. Rio de Janeiro: 7Letras, 2001.

Champion, Laurie. *Contemporary American Women Fiction Writers: An A-to-Z Guide*. Westport, CT: Greenwood, 2002.

Cook-Lynn, Elizabeth. *Anti-Indianism in Modern America: A Voice from Tatekeya's Earth*. Urbana: University of Illinois Press, 2001.

Kutzbach, Konstanze, and Monika Mueller. *The Abject of Desire: The Aestheticization of the Unaesthetic in Contemporary Literature and Culture*. Amsterdam: Rodopi, 2007.

Lavender, Catherine Jane. *Scientists and Storytellers: Feminist Anthropologists and the Construction of the American Southwest*. Albuquerque: University of New Mexico Press, 2006.

Madsen, Deborah L. *Feminist Theory and Literary Practice*. London: Pluto, 2000.

Muthyala, John. *Reworlding America: Myth, History, and Narrative*. Athens: Ohio University Press, 2006.

Silko, Leslie Marmon. *Almanac of the Dead*. New York: Simon & Schuster, 1991.

_____. *Ceremony*. New York: Viking, 1977.

_____. *Gardens in the Dunes*. New York: Scribner, 1999.

_____. *The Man to Send Rain Clouds: Contemporary Stories by American Indians*, ed. Kenneth Rosen. New York: Viking, 1974.

_____. *Yellow Woman and a Beauty of the Spirit: Essays on Native American Life Today*. New York: Simon & Schuster, 1996.

## Auntie Thelma

In *Ceremony* (1977), her debut novel, Silko examines the down side of a highly conformist community that monitors member behaviors through gossip. According to Pueblo expectations, Auntie Thelma, Tayo's maternal aunt and foster mother, cares for her battle-weary nephew by default. The author implies the insidious destabilization of the family via the white man's church. Critic John Emory Dean corroborates Auntie's fear and insecurity and her need to "[buy] into Western discourse because it is the story of success" (Dean, 2009, 165). Thus, according to analyst Charles H. Lippy, the nephew/foster son matures under Christian influence, but makes no "formal affiliation" with a woman ashamed of his biracial parentage (Lippy, 2002, 83). He bears the burden of shell-shock on Iwo Jima in early 1945. Contributing to his confusion is his return to a hostile home environment comprised of Uncle Robert, Grandma, and Auntie beset by memories of Uncle Josiah and Rocky, the soldier who dies from the brutality of the Bataan Death March of April 1942.

Home warfare belittles Tayo from age four. He discerns Auntie Thelma's embitterment over shame at his illegitimacy and anger that "little sister" Laura devalues the family's prestige and dignity through public alcoholism and carousing naked with white men and Mexicans. To Uncle Josiah, Auntie demeans Tayo as "this one," a depersonalization that objectifies him as the family farmhand, the "one" to remain on the property and cultivate chili peppers and corn and to superintend herd animals while his brother Rocky cultivates urban ambitions (Silko, 1977, 73). Without words, the two—Tayo and his aunt/foster mother—read each other's attitudes and motivations in a silent guerrilla warfare carried on the presence of Grandma, Rocky, and Uncle Josiah. Through overt cruelty, like that dispensed by the dowager in Ruth Prawer Jhabvala's bicultural novel *Heat and Dust* (1983), the dismissive Mamie in Jamaica Kincaid's *Annie John* (1985), and Mama Elena, the sadistic matriarch in Lara Esquivel's magical realistic novel *Like Water for Chocolate* (1989), Auntie Thelma withholds descriptions of Laura and robs the boy of his mother's photo, his only palpable link to mothering. Auntie's self-righteousness and pernicious undertones worsen the poisonous home atmosphere, where she and Tayo "understood each other very well" (*ibid.*, 67). She wants Tayo "close enough to feel excluded, to be aware of the distance between them" (*ibid.*, 66). He perceives that she writhes under the disapproval of the clan who saw "how everything should be" (*ibid.*, 68).

Against the intrusions of external malcontent from Tayo's army buddies, Silko elevates Auntie Thelma's importance as the internal malcontent who robs the household of unity. Set during a period of flux in tribal consciousness, the narrative takes place when residents "[affirm] a way of life that is irrelevant to the modern world," especially to veterans bedazzled by urban materialism (*ibid.*, 84). Tayo's adversarial relationship with the maternal aunt accords him neither acceptance as a man or cohesion during his posttraumatic stress episodes. His daily bouts of nausea, sorrow, and nightmares derive from a homecoming burdened with battle fatigue and guilt over the death of Rocky, the favorite son. In the summation of Charles E. Wilson, Tayo needs to avoid Auntie's "eruptions" and to find "a more harmonious environment that will not disturb the peace of mind" that will make him whole again (Wilson, 2005, 77).

The dominance of Auntie Thelma and Grandma over male kin exhibits the matrilineal structure of Laguna Pueblo families and the female possession of homes, land, and stock. Short and squat, Thelma carries herself erectly as a clan shield against "worrying and wondering" over local disapproval (Silko, 1977, 88). In contrast to her blind mother, Auntie lacks the zest for life that heartens Grandma to do her own gossiping about violators of community standards, a theme that returns in *Storyteller* (1981) with the adultery of a married man with someone else's wife. Silko notes witnesses "saying all kinds of things the way they do how everyone in the village knows and that's the worst thing" (Silko, 1981, 91). In place of tale-telling, Auntie Thelma, the intrusive moralist, uses implications of disaster at the sheep camp to manipulate Uncle Josiah into spending more time with his sheep and less with Night Swan, the cat-eyed Mexican cantina dancer. Thelma's disapproval of casual coitus as a means of becalming males and restoring their self-esteem delays Tayo's eventual healing through a sexual relationship with Ts'eh Montaño, a mountain demigoddess and companion of Mountain Lion Man. Thus, Thelma's puritanic code imprisons Tayo in suffering and impedes his return to normality.

Angry and self-martyring, Auntie Thelma bears "eyes full of accusations" about family misdeeds, including Uncle Josiah's fling with Night Swan (*ibid.*, 88). Locked in the past and devoid of a forgiving spirit, Auntie views Tayo as the wages of sin, the price the family pays for "little sister's" fornication with Mexican and white men. Auntie values her son Rocky as her redemption from gossip. Paradoxically, he seems superior because he is a full-blood Laguna and because he is learning to think and act "white." Tayo knows that a perverted martyr complex is Auntie Thelma's motivation for tending him at home— spoon-feeding him blue cornmeal mush and Indian tea—rather than sending him to another veterans' hospital. By pursuing household and nursing duties as her Christian burden, Auntie Thelma believes she gains stature among the Laguna. While she uproots Tayo from his sickbed to change his sheets, Rocky's graduation picture looks down from its shrine on her bureau, a static image of the "good son." The brutal shove of Tayo into Rocky's bed vents Auntie's animosity, leaving him to cry for Grandma's help. Auntie's passive aggression takes multiple forms, notably, her *sotto voce* reminder to Grandma not to mention Josiah or Rocky, names that deepen Tayo's sadness. Ironically, it is Robert who confers parental kindness on Tayo and welcomes him home to a post-war rest and successful recovery. In similar fashion, Ku'oosh, the medicine man, conveys more compassion and tenderness than Auntie. When Auntie Thelma completes the mission of harassing Tayo into deep depression, Silko silences the character in favor of Tayo's reliance on self.

*See also* belonging; Tayo; Tayo's genealogy

• *References and further reading*

Brown, Harry John. *Injun Joe's Ghost: The Indian Mixed-Blood in American Writing*. Columbia: University of Missouri Press, 2004.

Dean, John Emory. *Travel Narratives from New Mexico: Reconstructing Identity and Truth*. Amherst, NY: Cambria, 2009.

Ganser, Alexandra. "Violence, Trauma, and Cultural Memory in Leslie Silko's *Ceremony*," *Atenea* 24:1 (June 2004): 145–149.

Lippy, Charles H. *Pluralism Comes of Age: American Religious Culture in the Twentieth Century*. Armonk, NY: M. E. Sharpe, 2002.

Silko, Leslie Marmon. *Ceremony*. New York: Viking, 1977.

_____. *Storyteller*. New York: Seaver Books, 1981.

Wilson, Charles E. *Race and Racism in Literature*. Westport, CT: Greenwood, 2005.

Winsbro, Bonnie C. *Supernatural Forces: Belief, Difference, and Power in Contemporary Works by Ethnic Women*. Amherst: University of Massachusetts Press, 1993.

# belonging

A proponent of a linguistically and culturally interlacing society, Silko maintains a uniracial, universal approach to human worth. In her philosophy, humans are clan members of *Homo sapiens*. In the essay "Fences against Freedom" (1994), she states: "Human beings need to feel as if they 'belong,'" a belief that echoes her tribal tenet that all people are the children of the "Mother Creator" Ts'its'tsi'nako (Grandmother Spider or Thought Woman) (Silko, 1994, 6). In the sprawling epic *Almanac of the Dead* (1991), the author speaks through Calabazas, a Yaqui marijuana smuggler, who states Thought Woman's maternal power over indigenous peoples: "We are here thousands of years before the first whites. We are here before maps or quit claims. We know where we belong on this earth" (Silko, 1991, 216). Reinforcing membership in the clan, native storytelling features interaction of all listeners in a living oral tradition. As analyst Gayle Elliott explains, "The principles of coherence and complemantarity are essential…. One cannot define oneself apart from community, culture, or nature — all are integrally connected" (Elliott, 2008, 178). Silko reprised the concept of belonging in nature and past history in *The Turquoise Ledge* (2010), a memoir in which she visualizes Indian spirits traversing the desert near her home, where she enjoys daily communion with insects, birds, rocks, and rattlesnakes.

The continuity of shared place and time confers what Silko identifies as cultural empowerment. In "Landscape, History, and the Pueblo Imagination" (1986), she explains, "Neither the worst blunders or disasters nor the greatest financial prosperity and joy will ever be permitted to isolate anyone from the rest of the group. In the ancient times, cohesiveness was all that stood between extinction and survival" (Silko, 1986, 93). In a personal memory, "The People and the Land ARE Inseparable" (2007), the author observes the inclusive nature of community during her drive to a Yaqui village north of Tucson. The emergence of villagers in one procession to mourn the death of a local person dramatized oneness. Her essay enlarges on "this shared consciousness of being part of a living community that continues on and on, beyond the death of one or even of many" (Silko, 2007, 113).

In the spirit of an all-inclusive Pueblo cosmology, the author accounts for the bonding of combat buddies in a first novel, *Ceremony* (1977), a dramatization of post–World War II re-entry trauma. At question is the issue of assimilation into white society versus reintegration into the pueblo. The jingoism of a white army recruiter implies that military service offers Indian males a fuller citizenship: "They were America the Beautiful too, this was the land of the free…. They got respect" (Silko, 1977, 42). Following the Japanese surrender in 1945, the letdown occurs, ironically, on native soil, where war survivors find themselves at loose ends far from the illusion of American manhood in uniform. Tayo and his army buddies miss the moment in history when "they belonged to America" because of their participation in a world war (*ibid.*, 399). To veterans who choose to boast of their prowess with prostitutes and to drink and relive the escapades of war, the expenditure of veterans' disability checks on frivolity becomes a lifestyle. Of the ephemeral membership in a past war, Tayo asserts that "Belonging was drinking and laughing with the platoon, dancing with blond women, buying drinks for buddies born in Cleveland, Ohio" (*ibid.*, 43).

The text flashes back to Tayo's need for acceptance as a festering wound inflicted before Christmas 1926. At age four, he wars against separation from his mother, "little sister" Laura, and against the impromptu pairing with Rocky, his cousin/foster brother.

With a child's intuition, Tayo knows that this parting will be his last with his mother, a promiscuous woman who drinks herself to death. Mirroring the existential displacement of True Son that Conrad Richter dramatizes in *The Light in the Forest* (1953), Silko stresses the vicissitudes of destiny. The narrative pictures Tayo's guardians, Auntie Thelma and Grandma, playing church bingo, a game of chance as unpredictable as Tayo's future. The author corroborated the needs that fill Tayo with yearning. Speaking from her own experience at Laguna with multicultural ancestry, she stressed that "we belonged there because we had been born and reared there" among Keres speakers and tellers of Pueblo stories (Silko, 1996, 41). Nonetheless, mixed-bloods like Silko and her sisters suffered "on the outer edge of the circle between the world of the Pueblo and the outside world" (*ibid.*, 102).

Silko applies clues from body language and voice tone to Tayo's imperilment as an unwanted child. Much loved by Uncle Josiah, the boy lives in a matrilineal Pueblo society where Auntie Thelma and Grandma dominate the household. Into the night, the boy lies in bed alongside Rocky and hears a hum of family conference punctuated by Auntie Thelma's clashing pots and pans, a domestic vengeance typical of women's tantrums. To Tayo, his aunt/foster mother's hostility consists of outward shows of resentment and shame, "a private understanding between the two of them" when no other adult shared their space (*ibid.*, 66). The cruelty, as obvious as the wicked stepmother's abasement of Cinderella, involves minutia — bits of leftover dough, a needle and thread to sew a scrap, all domestic playtoys — which Auntie Thelma refuses to let Rocky share with Tayo. To worsen the favoritism and exclusion, she makes Tayo stay indoors and suffer where she can enjoy his discomfort. The family dynamics shift silently back to normality when other adults join the toxic threesome. In the resolution, Tayo envisions a time in his early childhood when he rode in the back of Josiah's wagon. Wrapped in a blanket on the way home, he feels Grandma's arms about him and hears Rocky whisper "my brother" (*ibid.*, 254). The fragility of his existence grips Tayo in a glimpse of "a strength inherent in spider webs woven across paths through hills where early in the morning the sun becomes entangled in each filament, a hint at his place in Spider Woman's plan" (*ibid.*, 135). Only by reclamation of his place among fellow Pueblo through Betonie's cleansing with smudging and sand painting does Tayo embrace "the comfort of belonging with the land, and the peace of being with these hills" (*ibid.*, 108).

Silko universalizes the concept of deracination in *Almanac of the Dead* (1991), a meganovel reprising America's history from pre-colonial times. As Mesoamericans begin the northward migration to retake the land, they fight the hegemony of the Death-Eye Dog, a graphic name for the white destroyer. The marchers adhere to the tenets of Wilson Weasel Tail, a Lakota exhorter who revives native values. With the austerity of the Paiute prophet Wovoka, Weasel Tail alerts the people to a new day: "Treachery has turned back upon itself.... Step back from envy, from sorcery and poisoning. Reclaim these continents which belong to us" (Silko, 1991, 721). By extending the goal to "continents," the author broadens the reclamation process to the reestablishment of justice within global parameters.

The concept of possessions and ownership returns in *Gardens in the Dunes* (1999), Silko's paean to solid matriarchy. Sister Salt and Indigo, the children of Mama and granddaughters of Grandma Fleet, learn the Indian worldview of oneness with heritage: "Life on the high, arid plateau became viable when the human beings were able to imagine themselves as sisters and brothers to the badger, antelope, clay, yucca, and sun" (Silko,

1999, 38). The sacred snake at the spring requires reverence because the water falls under his jurisdiction. At the sandhill home in southern Arizona, "The first ripe fruit of each harvest belongs to the spirits of our beloved ancestors, who came to us as rain" (*ibid.*, 15).

The motif of cyclical separations enlarges on who belongs where. Upon Indigo's separation from family and homeland, she makes a brief acquaintance with the Matinnecock of Manhasset Bay, Long Island. Despite their hospitality, it is "clear the lost child did not belong" (*ibid.*, 167). Ironically, Indigo's foster mother, Hattie Abbott Palmer, separates from her egocentric husband Edward and commits her energies to reuniting the Sand Lizard clan. For Hattie, "The return of the child to her family had become the primary focus" (*ibid.*, 392). Silko stresses that Hattie, at odds with her birth family and husband, "was the one who no longer had a life to return to" (*ibid.*, 439). Rejoicing, Indigo can dance and sing "Over the Milky Way bridge — oh the beloved return!" (*ibid.*, 465). The restoration and enlargement of the Sand Lizard matriarchy and the continuity of land shared with past and present inhabitants never deviate from hopes that Mama will leave the Messiah's following and reunite with her girls. The narrative looks ahead to Bright Eyes, Sister Salt's infant, called the "little black grandfather," the first male to broaden the clan to two-gendered membership (*ibid.*, 344).

*See also* Betonie; nativism; Tayo.

• *References and further reading*

Eliott, Gayle. "Silko, Le Sueur, and Le Guin: Storytelling as a 'Movement Toward Wholeness'" in *Scribbling Women & the Short Story Form: Approaches by American & British Women Writers*, ed. Ellen Burton Harrington. New York: Peter Lang, 2008, 178–192.
Holm, Sharon. "The 'Lie' of the Land: Native Sovereignty, Indian Literary Nationalism, and Early Indigenism in Leslie Marmon Silko's Ceremony," *American Indian Quarterly* 32:3 (Summer 2008): 243–274.
Norman, Brian. *The American Protest Essay and National Belonging: Addressing Division.* Albany: State University of New York Press, 2007.
Silko, Leslie Marmon. *Ceremony.* New York: Viking Press, 1977.
_____. "Fences against Freedom," *Hungry Mind Review* 31 (Fall 1994): 6–20.
_____. *Gardens in the Dunes.* New York: Scribner, 1999.
_____. "Landscape, History, and the Pueblo Imagination," *Antaeus* 51 (Autumn 1986): 83–94.
_____. "The People and the Land ARE Inseparable" in *What Wildness Is This: Women Write about the Southwest,* eds. Susan Wittig Albert and Susan Hanson. Austin: University of Texas Press, 2007.
_____. *Yellow Woman and a Beauty of the Spirit: Essays on Native American Life Today.* New York: Simon & Schuster, 1996.
Stromberg, Ernest. *American Indian Rhetorics of Survivance: Word Medicine, Word Magic.* Pittsburgh: University of Pittsburgh Press, 2006.

## Betonie

The Chicano-Navajo *hataali* (healer or singer) in Silko's first novel, *Ceremony* (1977), Betonie epitomizes the eclectic harmonizer and bringer of inner peace. Silko based the healer on a man she befriended during her two years in Navajo country. She endows the fictional shaman with what critic Helen May Dennis, a specialist in native American literature at Warwick University, calls "the heart of the Navajo worldview ... the belief that thought is potent and creative," a philosophical intersection with the Laguna regard for Ts'its'tsi'nako (Spider Woman or Thought Woman), the creator who thinks the world into being (Dennis, 2007, 143). One of the author's most poignant scenarios, the meeting between healer and patient captures much of the Amerindian belief in belonging and wholeness. The venerable medicine man is a parallel of the Seneca prophet Handsome Lake, the reuniter of the Six Nations Iroquois Confederacy in 1799. Critic Winifried Siemerling places the shaman "at the crossroads between cultures, a practitioner of cultural translation and transcoding" (Siemerling, 2005, 68). Unorthodox and canny in his treatment of a reluctant trauma victim, Betonie claims kinship with blended curative traditions through his grandmother, the daughter of a Mexican curandera. In an era of what Silko calls "charlatan 'medicine people' [who] make huge profits from their chicanery," the author respects "the truth about the ways in which the spirit voices manifest themselves" (Silko, 1994, cover). Betonie applies reverse psychology in the statement, "Go ahead.... Most of the Navajos feel the same way about me. You won't be the first one to run away" (Silko, 1977, 118).

On a par with the biblical Samuel's priest Eli, Achilles's teacher Phoenix, and King Arthur's mentor Merlin, Betonie, the prototypical male sage, mentors the younger generation, a pairing that Silko introduced in "Humaweepi, the Warrior Priest" (1974). As guardian of Navajo cultural memory, Betonie derives authority from the tradition of the Ghostway story, a tale of the trickster Coyote's theft of human identity. On a slope of Chuska Mountain outside Tohatchie, New Mexico, Betonie lives above the commercialized Indian Ceremonial, a summer tourist attraction in Gallup. His residence seems "pitiful and small compared to the world [Tayo] knew the white people had" (*ibid.*, 127). In the distance, the medicine man sees "the land which was stolen, still there, within reach, its theft being flaunted" (*ibid.*). Ironically, with a Zen-like calm, he can look down on the hoop and *volantedores* (flying-pole dancers) and the traders and bootleggers who turn imported native tradition into a cheapened spectacle. A shadow figure, the acolyte Shush (Diné for "bear"), suffers incurable spiritual damage, a reminder that Betonie's medicine has its limits in engaging cosmic powers.

Silko depicts the healer as a contented peasant who nurtures a mage's respect for change. Like his great-grandfather Descheeny, Betonie feels union with his traditional homeland, which whites invaded. Critic Kenneth Lincoln remarks on the Zeitgeist or spirit of the times that calls Betonie into service "Xenophobic crisis begs cross-cultural resolution. Navajo, Hispanic, Pueblo, and Anglo are estranged cousins, indeed cousin-brothers, coming together by way of the healing powers of mothering sister-lovers" (Lincoln, 2008, 117). In his role as recycler, in late July 1948, the shaman laughs at the refuse in the dump below his hogan. In an era of advanced capitalism, garbage becomes a token of white planned obsolescence, sterility, and death. Analyst Noriko Miura blames the refuse for the "cosmic evil responsible for the physical and material incongruity" between races (Miura, 2000, 159). Despite the trash, Betonie's laughter embraces life's fullness and shuns all that is contrary to harmony. Dressed in baggy pants and sweater, he takes comfort from familiarity with rugged country, from "belonging with the land, and the peace of being with these hills" (Silko, 1977, 117). His self-approval and ease with the world precipitate in his patient a restored balance, an internal stasis that critic Jana Gohrisch magnifies to "the precondition for the successful vision-quest," a trance-like approach to divinity that rids Tayo of madness (Gohrisch, 2006, 236).

## COUNSEL WITHOUT FEAR

Silko eases Tayo's re-introduction to spirituality by presenting Betonie as an affable, non-threatening clairvoyant. Before harboring Tayo in his stone hogan to treat his shell-shock from combat on Iwo Jima in early 1945, the old man senses his patient's terror and his urge to flee. Tayo recognizes that he has reached the end of his choices, but he opts not to follow his foster father, Uncle Robert, back to Laguna. No longer welcome in home territory, Tayo must trust a new paternal figure, the shaman, who is fatherly and non-judgmental toward Tayo's inaction and shunning of responsibility. After identifying the smells of cured hides, herbs, leather pouches, and decaying paper and cardboard, Tayo senses a native element — a round, semi-subterranean room like a kiva (ceremonial chamber) attached to the western rim of Mount Taylor. Below the sky hole, Coke bottles and the stacks of trunks, footlockers, shopping bags, and boxes of rags worsen Tayo's vertigo. The tune Betonie hums to ease Tayo's misgivings reminds the patient of a butterfly's path from flower to flower, a calming image imbued with power, but devoid of menace. A mutual feature rids Tayo of unease — Betonie, a biracial Navajo, has hazel eyes inherited from a green-eyed Mexican grandmother. Within shame, he admits that his mother coupled with white men, a revelation intended to lessen Tayo's embarrassment. Essayist Gloria Bird explains Silko's address of "the Othering mechanism ... that is, that the color of his skin and eyes alone cannot determine who he is," the source of his self-hate (Bird, 2005, 101). Symbolically, the eyes of the two mixed-blood Indians look to the multiculturalism of the Amerindian future.

Silko presents Betonie to Tayo as the selective relater of truths teaching self-awareness as a benefit to the community. The old man's collection of railroad calendars, stacked out of chronological order, and in newspapers and telephone directories that help him keep track of people and places stresses a compression of time in their in-home session. The author later observed on the older generation, "who didn't look at the clock and they didn't look at the calendar; they reckoned time in a more cyclic way in which things long ago and things yesterday do link up" (Jeffries, 2010). The eccentricity of Betonie's accumulations, including stray mustache hairs, makes Tayo feel shut out, unwanted, the aura that engulfs his psyche from age four. The shaman accounts for keeping up with time and place by explaining that healing ceremonies are not static: They always reflect a changing society. Of the corrosive nature of racist hate, Betonie states, "Nothing is that simple, ... you don't write off all the white people, just like you don't trust all the Indians" (Silko, 1977, 127). The statement, a retroactive prophecy of white–Indian relations, bears the ring of Silko's own view on the racial divide.

The author generates a heroic stance for Betonie by respecting his willingness to alter tradition to rescue Indians from witchery through kinetic learning and a restored theistic consciousness. He makes a symbolic cut on Tayo's scalp to distract him from worldliness, to anticipate the head wound he receives on Mount Taylor, and to unite him with all who suffer war injuries. Through tobacco smoking, five hoops, and prayer stick ritual, the shaman is able to predict Tayo's future with the spotted Mexican cattle and a woman and to send the veteran on his way to rescue his people from white materialism. After setting Tayo in the bear's tracks and directing him to black, blue, yellow, and white mountains, the cardinal directions and seasons, the old man transfers the burden of the epic hero to the returning veteran.

## Tayo's Recovery

Silko's depiction of shamanic counseling emphasizes the role of the individual in self-cure. Foreseeing "all kinds of evil," Betonie challenges, "It's up to you" (Silko, 1977, 144, 152). The shaman initiates the repair of war-torn inner resources, which includes the Navajo red antway ceremony and the deliberately evanescent sand painting, a healing gestalt that disintegrates into separate colored grains. Critic Lawrence Buell describes the schematic drawings and cosmic metaphors as "the antithesis of 'witchery's final ceremonial sand painting,' the antiweb of 'the destroyers,' of which European conquest and technological transformation are the symptoms" (Buell, 1995, 289). A verbal obstacle, Tayo's unfamiliarity with dialect, forces him to admit shame for his childish blend of Keresan and English, emblematic of his inability to communicate with his pueblo past. More crucial to a cure, his straightforward admission of guilt for failure to save his cousin Rocky offers the shaman a window on self-persecution from survivor's guilt. Betonie condemns the white military doctors' methods of dosing mental patients with psychotropic drugs, a one-size-fits-all treatment that lacks the personal touch.

The text elevates Betonie as a purifier of the spirit. Through his gentle direction, according to critic John A. McClure, "Tayo assumes his role as an avatar of Sun Man, the hero who helps the world at times of drought" (McClure, 2007, 145). In the summation of Silko scholar Robert M. Nelson, the old Navajo relieves Tayo of the misperception that "White is right" (Nelson, 2004, 67). In place of pollutants of the spirit engendered by colonialism, materialism, and world war, the medicine man offers ritual, herbs, counsel, and a meal of grilled mutton ribs. For Tayo's enlightenment, Betonie describes the incident in the bear's den that altered Shush forever. The commentary on witchcraft and the retelling of the creation of Pollen Boy combines with the crafting of a sand painting into a powerful restorative. With Betonie's aid, Tayo sleeps and dreams of Josiah's ambition to purchase speckled Mexican cattle from Ulibarri for breeding. With straightforward advice, Betonie dispels Tayo's hopes that one ceremony can cure him of madness. The shaman's alert foreshadows Tayo's reconnection with Harley and Leroy Valdez and with Helen Jean, the Ute wanderer from the Towac reservation. Critic María Ruth Noriega Sánchez, a lecturer in Spanish at Cambridge, remarks, "The sordid reality of trucks and dirty bars contrasts greatly with the previous magic-mythical section and shows the consequences of the forces of witchery's actions" (Sánchez, 2002, 125).

In a narrative shift, Silko, like novelist Toni Morrison in *Song of Solomon* (1977), sets Tayo on a quest with himself as hero of his own adventure. Just as the jumbled leaves of the Cumaean Sibyl set Virgil's Aeneas on his way to reestablishing Trojan gods and values in Italy, the Navajo prophet foretells a magic pattern composed of a mountain, cattle, and a constellation of the night sky. Essential to the journey is a mate, who balances the predominantly male influences in Tayo's life. The composite vision sets the patient on a path toward wholeness. Sánchez notes that magical realism causes Tayo to [enter] a mythical world as if he was entering a sand painting" (Sánchez, 2002, 125). Gloria Bird comments on the completion of the counseling session, when Betonie rejects monetary payment: "In doing so, Betonie's action exemplifies an alternative value system, one in which currency has no value, and in which the act of healing is priceless" (Bird, 2005, 101).

*See also* Betonie's genealogy; madness; Tayo.

• *References and further reading*

Avila, Monica. "Leslie Marmon Silko's *Ceremony*: Witchery and Sacrifice of Self," *Explicator* 67:1 (Fall 2008): 53–55.

Bird, Gloria. "Toward a Decolonization of the Mind and Text: Leslie Marmon Silko's *Ceremony*" in *Reading Native American Women: Critical/Creative Representations*, ed. Inés Hernández-Avila. Lanham, MD: Altamira, 2005, 93–106.

Buell, Lawrence. "Leslie Silko: Environmental Apocalypticism" in *The Environmental Imagination: Thoreau, Nature Writing, and the Formation of American Culture.* Cambridge, MA: Harvard University Press, 1995.

Dennis, Helen May. *Native American Literature: Towards a Spatialized Reading.* New York: Taylor & Francis, 2007.

Ganser, Alexandra. "Violence, Trauma, and Cultural Memory in Leslie Silko's *Ceremony*," *Atenea* 24:1 (June 2004): 145–149.

Gohrisch, Jana. "Cultural Exchange and the Representation of History in Postcolonial Literature," *European Journal of English Studies* 10:3 (December 2006): 231–247.

Jeffries, Kim. "A Conversation with Leslie Marmon Silko on *The Turquoise Ledge*," *Seattle Times* (19 October 2010).

Lee, A. Robert. *Multicultural American Literature: Comparative Black, Native, Latino/a and Asian American Fictions*. Jackson: University Press of Mississippi, 2003.

Lincoln, Kenneth. *Speak Like Singing: Classics of Native American Literature*. Albuquerque: University of New Mexico Press, 2008.

Martin, Holly E. "Hybrid Landscapes as Catalysts for Cultural Reconciliation in Leslie Marmon Silko's Ceremony and Rudolfo Anaya's Bless Me, Ultima," *Atenea* 26:1 (June 2006): 131–149.

May, Janice Susan. *Healing the Necrophilia of Euro-American Society in Leslie Marmon Silko's Gardens in the Dunes*. Radford, VA: Radford University, 2000.

McClure, John. *Partial Faiths: Postsecular Fiction in the Age of Pynchon and Morrison*. Athens: University of Georgia Press, 2007.

Miura, Noriko. *Marginal Voice, Marginal Body: The Treatment of the Human Body in the Works of Nakagami Kenji, Leslie Marmon Silko, and Salman Rushdie* (Thesis, 2000), http://books.google.com, accessed July 12, 2010.

Nelson, Robert M. "Settling for Vision in Silko's *Ceremony*: Sun Man, Arrowboy, and Tayo," *American Indian Culture and Research Journal* 28:1 (2004): 67–73.

Sánchez, María Rutgh Noriega. *Challenging Realities: Magic Realism in Contemporary American Women's Fiction*. València: Universitat de València, 2002.

Siemerling, Winfried. *The New North American Studies: Culture, Writing and the Politics of Re/cognition*. New York: Routledge, 2005.

Silko, Leslie Marmon. *Ceremony*. New York: Viking Press, 1977.

_____. "Commentary" to *Mabel McKay*, by Greg Sarris. Berkeley: University of California Press, 1994.

# Betonie's genealogy

Betonie, the Chicano-Navajo shaman in *Ceremony* (1977), embodies the agency of the doer, the combater of despair and untruth. From a mixed-blood point of view, he wars against deception brought on by ethnic nationalism, the ideology of whites during their war against the Japanese in the mid–1940s. In the estimation of critic Lori Burlingame, the old Navajo clairvoyant "embodies the ideal of self-responsibility for cultural survival," which he models for Tayo (Burlingame, 2000, 10). Risking censure from his people, Betonie alters ceremonies by empowering them with updates suited to the atomic era, which has damaged World War II veterans like Tayo and his pals. Betonie's logic embraces the future, including technological advancements that heighten the risks of war.

```
Mexican grandmother=Grandfather Descheeny=three sisters
age 12 or 13        | medicine man           |
                    |                     daughters who raise Betonie
               mother
                    |
               Betonie
               Navajo shaman;
               traveler
```

### • *References and further reading*

Burlingame, Lori. "Empowerment Through 'Retroactive Prophecy' in D'Arcy McNickle's 'Runner in the Sun: A Story of Indian Maize,' James Welch's 'Fools Crow,' and Leslie Marmon Silko's 'Ceremony,'" *American Indian Quarterly* 24:1 (Winter 2000): 1–18.

Cutchins, Dennis. "'So That the Nations May Become Genuine Indian': Nativism and Leslie Marmon Silko's Ceremony," *Journal of American Culture* 22: 4 (1999): 77–89.

Silko, Leslie Marmon. *Ceremony*. New York: Viking, 1977.

# betrayal

Trust is a pillar of Silko's personal and tribal ethos. She exonerates the shiftiness of an Apache guerrilla warrior in "A Geronimo Story" (1974) and reinterprets a seduction and kidnap by Silva, the tall Navajo womanizer, in the classic story "Yellow Woman" (1974). The narrative of Yellow Woman (Kochininako), the Coyotesse, reveals a gynocentric duality of the female trickster as creator and sustainer. By profiting from an illicit encounter with Silva, she distracts him through transformative passion. On return home, she regenerates the Pueblo spirituality. Critic Carolyn Dunn explains Yellow Woman's chicanery: "She must face the wilderness and not only return a whole tribe to traditions but also trick the nontribal world into her world as well" (Dunn, 2005, 200). Through wit and wisdom, Yellow Woman's "multiplicitous nature" imports sustenance to her people (*ibid.*). Dunn concludes that Yellow Woman uses her wiles to unite the ordinary world with the spiritual domain, a magical union fraught with peril. Thus, the female culture hero "transcends both sacred and secular, becoming *both* sacred and secular" (*ibid.*, 201). From Yellow Woman's courage come hope-filled humor and stories, the foundations of Pueblo oral tradition.

In her first novel, *Ceremony* (1977), Silko turns from the tribal trickster to the white usurper. She dramatizes the cheating of Indians by exploitive whites, particularly authority figures from the Bureau of Indian Affairs and the U.S. Army. Tayo, a Laguna soldier returning from World War II, blinks back tears at the thrust of betrayal "into his throat like a fist" (Silko, 1977, 113). He expects treachery from whites, especially truck dealers, who sell worn-out hulks under suspiciously liberal conditions: "No money down! Pay at the first of the month!" (*ibid.*, 145). Taking to the road, the new owner feels the truck "vibrating hard; the steering was loose and the front end wandered across the white line" (*ibid.*, 146). A Ute woman, Helen Jean, from the Towac reservation summarizes the deceptive promises of whites with a cynical flair — "gypped again" (*ibid.*, 167). However, limiting the novel to a cynical indictment of cheating whites would have eclipsed the author's intent to warn her protagonist of a full range of evils far worse than investing in a road wreck.

## UNIVERSAL DISSEMBLANCE

To expand on the nature of fraud from everyday hoodwinking to a universal connivance, Silko interpolates the Pueblo story of the Ck'o'yo con artist and gambler Pa'-caya'nyi. The trickster entices the Pueblo from seasonal worship of the Corn Woman (Nau'ts'ity'i), a nurturing mother of humankind. Irreverence toward the earth causes an imbalance of pride over sanctity that plunges Southwestern Indians into folkloric punishments by drought and starvation. The story illustrates the author's belief that double-dealing carries a heavy price for the whole community. As Tayo learns from Betonie, the Chicano-Navajo shaman, duplicity requires knowledge of the world and of self: "As long as people believed the lies, they would never be able to see what had been done to them or what they were doing to each other" (*ibid.*, 191).

The plot escalates from white-on-Indian misrepresentation to the murderous ambush of Tayo by Harley, his Laguna army buddy, a resetting of Kochininako's betrayal of Arrow-boy in "Buffalo Story" (1981). Because Tayo outwits Harley, the traitor falls into the hands of the destroyers themselves. The author turns the conspiracy of Emo, Leroy Valdez, and cousin Pinkie into a satanic ritual of the autumn solstice, when the plotters gather around a fire and pass the bottle before torturing and murdering Harley, their former comrade. In hiding, Tayo imagines them stalking him "like a thirsty animal" across the Jackpile Mine site, a picturesque setting of white deception and exploitation of the Laguna (*ibid.*, 249). The scene concludes with the conspirators betraying each other, leaving behind "broken bottles and a black mark on the ground where the fire had been," a symbolic damnation foretelling the ignoble deaths of Leroy and Pinkie and the exile of Emo to California. For its multiple applications to betrayal, doubt, and mistrust, high school, college, and university teachers choose *Ceremony* as an intuitive text for courses in American history and literature, anthropology, religion, sociology, psychology, and criminology.

For "Lullaby" (1981), one of Silko's most anthologized stories, the author turns to a more insidious in-home betrayal. A dual deception contributes pathos to a story of loss and family dissolution. In the view of critic Deborah L. Madsen, Chato, the multilingual ranch hand, betrays his wife Ayah by siding with white officials who institutionalize their only surviving children, Danny and Ella, in a tuberculosis sanitarium. Ultimately, Chato's superiority as translator for his wife fails him after he capitulates to white promises and lies and expends his life and health to enrich a rancher. Because a horse crushes Chato's leg, the ungrateful employer evicts the couple from their boxcar, a symbol of a "boxed-in" life that recedes from regular paychecks into poverty and welfare checks. The pain of deception in "Lullaby" bites twice. Madsen concludes, "Ayah has been destroyed not only by the invasion of her life by white male culture, represented by doctors, policemen and social workers, but also by the complicity of Chato with the forces of dispossession and destruction" (Madsen, 2000, 235). Once a powerful owner of a hogan and livestock, Ayah falls victim to a male-dominated society that wrenches from her all that she holds dear. In the falling action, she summons dignity to assert her place as materfamilias. Under the silent stare of non–Indian drinkers, she strides into Azzie's Bar with the authority of a Navajo matriarch and retrieves her drunken husband. The majesty of the Navajo crone accords her a final privilege that majority males acknowledge.

## MERCILESS TREACHERY

Silko elevates treachery to the global level in *Almanac of the Dead* (1991), an indictment of Tucson's criminal element and the tentacles of evil reaching across the Western Hemisphere. Favorably compared to the complex history in Vine Deloria's *Custer Died for Your Sins: An Indian Manifesto* (1969) and *We Talk, You Listen: New Tribes, New Turn* (1970), the action takes place during the reign of the Death-Eye Dog, bringer of "plague, earthquake, drought, famine, incest, insanity, war, and betrayal" (Silko, 1991, 67). For the *dramatis personae*, Silko assembles shadowy CIA operatives, filmers of police torture chambers, cocaine runners, eugenics engineers, coyotes deceiving Mexican aliens, and human organ traders. The adulteries of Calabazos, a marijuana smuggler, with his sister-in-law Liria and of *mestizo* insurance mogul Menardo Panson with Algería Martinez-Soto, a Venezuelan architect trained in Madrid, pale beside the brazen double-crosses of hardened criminals and assassins. For redress of depravity, Mexican-Indian leader Angelita La Escapía, the Marxist ideologue known as the "meat hook," cautions: "We wait. We simply wait for the earth's natural forces already set loose, the exploding, fierce energy of all the dead slaves and dead ancestors haunting the Americas" (*ibid.*, 518). The prophecy ennobles the book title and the author's intent to examine centuries of wrongdoing through the eyes of future avengers.

Retribution takes shape on numerous levels. For her own satisfaction, Angelita retaliates against her presumptuous lover, Bartolomeo, an arrogant Cuban Marxist who repudiates blacks and Indians as savages. Critic Deborah M. Horvitz, an independent scholar, depicts Bartolomeo as the initial traitor: "He ... abandons his history, denying that anything of importance took place in Cuba prior to Castro" (Horvitz, 2000, 141). For added humor, Silko stresses the name "Angelita" (little angel) for a character capable of assassinating a trusted colleague without remorse. By arranging Bartolomeo's execution "in front of the people he betrayed," Angelita repays him for racism and elitism as well as for his sexual and social scorn of her (Silko, 1991, 518). She dismisses the scenes at the gallows and graveyard with flippancy: "Oh, well, who was Bartolomeo anyway? What did he matter? Who would remember him" (*ibid.*, 527). Her brushoff of a former lover amplifies Silko's views on shallow sexual alliances lacking in fidelity and emotional commitment.

The concept of mass betrayal outdistances Bartolomeo's hanging with the audacity of a downtrodden people seeking redress. Clinton, a paranoid Afro-Cherokee watchman employed by military veteran Rambo-Roy, views the Vietnam War during the administration of President Lyndon Johnson as a height of perfidy. More visceral than Tayo's faulting of an army recruiter in *Ceremony*, Clinton, sodden with reefers, scotch, and wine, raves at generals "smacking their lips at all the splattered brains and guts of black and brown men," whom military authorities label "expendables" (*ibid.*, 407). In sync with Clinton's rage at genocide, Rambo-Roy mulls over a list of betrayers— FBI agents who allegedly shot Martin Luther King, Jr. and warmongers who fomented the drafting of nonwhite men for the Vietnam War to forestall black riots in major U.S. cities. To assuage their animosities, Clinton and Roy ransack Tucson vacation homes and steal cars, bank accounts, and credit cards from the rich. Silko turns their felonies into black comedy after the duo plots "to reclaim democracy from corruption at all levels" (*ibid.*, 410).

TREACHERY ON THREE CONTINENTS

An insidious disloyalty swamps a marriage of scholarly horticulturists in *Gardens in the Dunes* (1999), a scramble for wealth from bio-piracy and the sale of ancient artifacts and meteorites. Dr. Edward Palmer, the solicitous groom newly married to scholar Hattie Abbott Palmer, risks life, health, and reputation through illicit scavenging for rare orchids and citron stock and for the white diamonds and precious metals extracted from fallen heavenly bodies. Because of foolish bravado, he suffers a permanent reminder of the wages of sin, a handicapped leg suffered during the burning of an Amazon jungle adorned with priceless orchids. As his accomplices depart without him up the Para River, Edward views the faithlessness of thieves. Expanding on the septic morals of disloyal comrades, Silko pictures "shattered bone [piercing] the skin" and polluted river water generating "fever and illness more grave than any broken limb," a subtle hint at Edward's self-contamination by colluding with felons (Silko, 1999, 141, 143).

In contrast to the Palmers and their enthusiasm for treasured garden plants, Silko creates Grandma Fleet, the family sage of the Sand Lizard matriarchy. An assertive crone and interim mother to Sister Salt and Indigo, Grandma Fleet knows the native stories of the trickster. When police invade her hovel near the depot, she poses as a cripple and prevents the girls from being shipped to a boarding school. Grandma "invited them to step inside, knowing they would refuse; the white man was afraid of disease and the Indian policemen feared witchcraft" (*ibid.*, 21). Her model of reverse psychology readies the girls for survival by evolving tricks of their own. After their elder's death, Sister Salt and fellow riverside launderers and comfort women fall victim to a treacherous superintendent, who has them arrested for petty theft. Significantly, the imprisonment ordered by a Yuma magistrate solidifies a female society of women who survive through deception.

Silko pairs mirrored images of betrayal in the lives of the Sand Lizard sisters. Indigo, removed from America by the Palmers, suffers a brief incarceration at the U.S. Embassy in Livorno, Italy, where she begins to view Edward's betrayal of his wife as a fatal symptom of a foundering marriage. Like the *conquistadores* who plundered the Southwest, Edward abandons morality for the sake of wealth. Typically, his only regret about his cavalier behavior is the failure to bribe Italian customs agents. After Edward's arrest in Livorno for stealing shoots from a citrus grove in Bastia, Corsica, his callous disregard for the sufferings of his wife and foster daughter Indigo amplify his greed and insensitivity to family. A downturn in his health brings Hattie back to his bedside in an Albuquerque hospital, where Edward continues to discount the value of a devoted wife: "Livorno, even Hattie and the separation, would scarcely matter beside the wall of silver and gold" (Silko, 1999, 426). Hurrying Edward's demise, the treatments of Dr. William Gates, an Australian phony and fellow hustler, deplete the plant thief, leaving unforgiven his felonious waste of her inheritance and bank overdrafts for equipment purchases.

In intercalary scenes, Silko contrasts Edward's longing to have a plant bear his name and his intent to market stolen citron shoots with the trickery of Delena, the Gypsy tarot reader and dog trainer who uses her animal act to distract the dam builders at Parker, Arizona. Foreshadowing her plot, she smirks, "A dog circus like this can make more money than you might think" (*ibid.*, 385). During the chaos of a free-for-all and camp fire, Delena robs Superintendent Wiley's strongbox and hurries south to buy guns for Mexican revolutionaries. Rather than delight in a hoax for selfish purposes, she spends the cash for repeating rifles and cartridges "no question asked" and prays to her ancestors to assist her flight through desert to Hermosillo (*ibid.*, 386). The narrative validates Delena's ethos over Edward's for her noble motives and for risking her life and those of her dogs to elevate Mesoamericans from peonage. To enhance irony, Silko pictures "Nuestra Senora de Guadalupe" instructing the rebels on which rifles to buy (*ibid.*, 354). The fervor of the Mexican trickster echoes Silko's regard for partisans in "An Expression of Profound Gratitude to the Maya Zapatistas, January 1, 1994" (1996). With pride in the Chiapas revolt, the author lauds the "same [500-year] war of resistance that the indigenous people of the Americas have never ceased to fight" (Silko, 1996, 153).

*See also* marriage; vengeance.

• *References and further reading*

Dunn, Carolyn. "The Trick Is Going Home: Secular Spiritualism in Native American Women's Literature" in *Reading Native American Women: Critical/Creative Representations*, ed. Inés Hernández-Avila. Lanham, MD: Altamira, 2005, 189–203.

Horvitz, Deborah M. *Literary Trauma: Sadism, Memory, and Sexual Violence in American Women's Fiction.* Albany: State University of New York Press, 2000.

Lee, A. Robert. *United States: Re-viewing American Multicultural Literature.* València: Universitat de València, 2009.

Madsen, Deborah L. *Feminist Theory and Literary Practice.* London: Pluto Press, 2000.

Silko, Leslie Marmon. *Ceremony.* New York: Viking, 1977.

_____. *Gardens in the Dunes.* New York: Scribner, 1999.

_____. *Storyteller.* New York: Seaver, 1981.

_____. *Yellow Woman and a Beauty of the Spirit: Essays on Native American Life Today.* New York: Simon & Schuster, 1996.

## Calabazas's genealogy

Silko depicts Calabazas, a Yaqui marijuana smuggler from Sonora in *Almanac of the Dead* (1991), in a parallel to the Genesis love triangle of Jacob, Leah, and Rebecca. Calabazas accepts a deal with Old Brito, a Tucson Yaqui, to marry his eldest, Sarita. The groom blames himself for carrying on an affair with his sister-in-law Liria while not realizing that Sarita coupled with a Catholic monsignor. Calabazas mutters, "How stupid! How blind! How arrogant! A more humble man would have seen it" (Silko, 1991, 239). The shortsightedness of the cuckolded husband places in modern setting the Laguna story cycle of Yellow Woman (Kochininako) and her seducer.

```
                         Old Brito=wife
                          gambler   |
                                    |

          _____
          |                  |                 |
monsignor=/=Sarita Brito=Calabazas=/=Liria Brito
Jesuit priest   unloved      Sonoran      saves refugees
died of heart   wife         Yaqui
attack                       smuggler
```

*See also* marriage.

- *References and further reading*

Rand, Naomi R. *Silko, Morrison, and Roth: Studies in Survival*. New York: Peter Lang, 1999.
Silko, Leslie Marmon. *Almanac of the Dead*. New York: Simon & Schuster, 1991.

## *Ceremony* (1977)

Silko's first novel, *Ceremony*, a landmark of the Native American Renaissance, authenticates the Indian worldview through ethnomythology. Living in Ketchikan, Alaska, during the composition, the author turned homesickness into nostalgic descriptions of her New Mexico homeland. She joked: "Sometimes you have to leave home to write about it" (Jeffries, 2010). Muskogee Creek critic Craig S. Womack credited her with "successfully [integrating] oral stories represented in poetic lines into the prose format of her novel..., surely another big influence on both oral expression in novels and its analysis in criticism" (Womack, 2008, 45). Creating verisimilitude are the oral stories of World War II that the author heard from childhood about her cousin, Robert Leslie Evans, a 30-year-old veteran and post-war alcoholic. The text projects a backbone of myth framed by sunrise-to-sunrise earth lore and energized by the protest of the anti–Vietnam War milieu. A character study of post-traumatic stress disorder, *Ceremony* makes accessible to the reader the death-in-life of battle fatigue and the re-integration necessary to adjustment. Similar in tone to Velma Wallis's Athabascan-centered epic *Two Old Woman: An Alaska Legend of Betrayal, Courage and Survival* (1993), the quest for wellness and forgiveness takes on epic qualities as protagonist Tayo, a survivor of the Bataan Death March of April 9–21, 1942, and shellshock on Iwo Jima in early 1945, seeks redemption for himself and all Indians from betrayal by the white world.

In Homeric style, Silko opens on a muse, Ts'its'tsi'nako, the Laguna spider deity Thought Woman. The metaphysical informer and tribal inventor dwells in the novelist's imagination and provides inspiration and guidance. For the telling of Tayo's story, the author aligns significant character types:

| | |
|---|---|
| • Rocky & Tayo, the warrior twins | apostate and loyal brother |
| • Laura & Auntie Thelma, sisters | prostitute and zealot |
| • Robert & Josiah, brothers | silent mate and mentor |
| • Night Swan & Ts'eh Montaño | maternal lover and healer divinity |
| • Ku'oosh & Betonie, healers | elderly shaman and Navajo sage |
| • Grandma & Shush | blind comforter and feral assistant |
| • Harley & Emo | harmless drunk and witch |
| • Cousin Pinkie & Leroy Valdez | clown and killer |

The pairings, according to critic Kenneth Lincoln, "represent character nodes in a series of dramatic actions— global shifts in culture and consciousness, plot points in cultural and cosmic history unfolding" (Lincoln, 2008, 114). Rather than shape interaction between "idiosyncratic individuals pitted against each other," Silko chooses kinship figures, "tracing back to petroglyphic panels before alphabetic 'writing' and paleolithic pictographs on sandstone escarpments" (*ibid.*). The central conflict, in the words of critics Joy Porter and Kenneth M. Roemer, is "the old bane known at Laguna as Ck'o'yo medicine ... made insidious by its ability to disguise itself as separate diseases" (Porter & Roemer, 2005, 250). The repetition of standard symptoms— sorrow, nausea, hallucinations, vertigo, "fever voices," and "humid dreams of black night"— and vignettes of dalliance, escapism, and drunkenness shocks the reader with the relentlessness of the protagonist's personal demons. Gnawing at Tayo are memories of orders to gun down Japanese soldiers who look like Indians (Silko, 1977, 5). He recognizes the inhumanity of war in the oneness of Americans with the enemy, whose "skin was not much different from his own" (*ibid.*, 7).

Compared thematically to John Masefield's *Gallipoli* (1917), Kenzaburo Oe's *The Silent Cry* (1974), and Sebastian Faulks's *Birdsong* (1996), Silko's novel traverses a fragmented verbal and spiritual terrain. Far worse than the demise in the Philippines of Rocky, a World War II infantryman, from a septic leg wound, Tayo envisions himself dead, but "still unburied" (*ibid.*, 28). Zombie-like with guilt and despair, he wishes for a physical death to end his terror, grief, remorse, and shame for not saving his cousin/foster brother. Through heightened sense impressions, the narrative recaptures the drumming of "unending rain," the "miles of marching," and "the Japanese grenade that was killing Rocky" (*ibid.*, 10). In retrospect, Tayo discloses to Betonie, his Chicano-Navajo counselor, the inept treatment of military psychiatrists in Los Angeles: "In that hospital they don't bury the dead, they keep them in rooms and talk to them" (*ibid.*, 114). Because of Tayo's Pueblo upbringing, psychotherapy and psychotropic drugs deepen his madness.

The Homecoming

Silko characterizes the post-war economic boom through the experiences of pueblo dwellers. Upon return to Laguna, New Mexico, in 1948, Tayo, then 26 years old, enters a depressed socio-economic climate fraught with post-war veteran unemployment of 70 percent and resultant poverty. Further depleting the community, whites scheme to generate wealth from exploitation of uranium at the Jackpile Mine, a greed that returns to Silko's apocalyptic novel *Almanac of the Dead* (1991) and *The Turquoise Ledge* (2010). As Tayo tries to direct himself toward a remedy, the feeling of slipping away like red dust in the wind replicates disturbances in nature created by the white man's atomic test at the Trinity site outside Los Alamos. The blast precedes the bombing of Hiroshima and Nagasaki, Japan, on August 6 and 8, 1945, an unprecedented double cataclysm that ends a world war. Tayo wearies of slogging through a tangle of nightmares and harrowing flashbacks to Bataan. On the back of a blind mule, he concedes his will to natural elements—his jogging mount and a southwestern wind. He admits to himself, "It took a great deal of energy to be a human being" (*ibid.*, 25). The brief respite from trauma foreshadows his eventual reunion with his homeland, the source of his rehabilitation.

Silko's text suits the settings to Tayo's mission. The milieu blends ordinary indoor sites—an upstairs apartment and Night Swan's bed, Betonie's stone hogan, a veterans' hospital, Grandma's kerosene stove, Uncle Josiah's pickup truck, and the Dixie Tavern in Budville—with battlefields in the Philippines, a San Diego bridge, the Los Angeles depot, and homier Southwestern sights—corrals, arroyos, mutton bones grilled over an outdoor fire, and fenced pastures. For cattle country, the author reprised the L Bar Ranch on Mount Taylor, where she learned in girlhood how to round up cattle for branding. Because the narrative focuses on Tayo's internal struggles, emphasis on drought and rutted roads extending over mesas and parched range mirrors Tayo's desiccated heart, dried up from anguish and self-reproach for praying for an end to rain to allow Rocky to recover. Ku'oosh, the Laguna medicine man, warns Tayo, "You know, grandson, this world is fragile," an indirect means of exonerating the veteran for emotional vulnerability (*ibid.*, 32). In contrast to their sensitive buddy, Emo, Harley, Leroy Valdez, and cousin Pinkie, Tayo's fellow veterans, escape the war memories and dreary landscape through macho rowdiness—reckless driving, exaggerated stories, womanizing, and fighting. The sterility of their gatherings further destabilizes their lives and leaves them more dependent on thrill seeking and alcohol, a self-medication that Porter and Roemer call "yet another version of Ck'o'yo medicine" (Porter & Roemer, 2005, 250).

Paralleling the epic voyages of Odysseus, Aeneas, and Bran, Tayo wanders a haunted landscape. Episodically, the action progresses from one tight spot to another. Tayo fears leaving an institutional setting to engage the outside world. His breakdown at the Los Angeles depot illustrates the inability of a rural native to find solace in an urban setting. The text stresses the kindness of Japanese American internees rather than the psychiatric ward of a veterans' hospital, where military doctors fail to exorcise nightmares with standard pharmacopoeia. Paradoxically, the rescuers have their own re-entry problems following incarceration in American concentration camps from February 19, 1942, December 18, 1944, when the U.S. Supreme Court declared the detainment unconstitutional. To avoid naming and challenging his mental torment, Tayo "had to get back [to the hospital] where he could merge with the walls and the ceiling, shimmering white," an absence of stimuli that forced him to think and feel (*ibid.*, 30). A similar emotional crisis occurs in New Laguna, where he cowers all night "against the metal wall in the men's room" rather than return to Auntie Thelma's house in shame for not saving Rocky from death in combat (*ibid.*, 27). While sitting on Rocky's bed, Tayo avoids the light that brings on nausea, a symbolic queasiness from facing too many truths. He vomits the gut-churning vortex that agitates his repose. Gradually, the settings themselves become therapy—the open sky, a spring at the base of a mesa, the apricot tree at Montaño's cabin, the range where Tayo herds cattle. By returning the herd to native soil, he requites an injustice to Uncle Josiah, the father figure who appeared to Tayo in the Philippines at the time of Josiah's death.

## A CEREMONIAL CURE

Silko proposes a remedy through prophecy and individual will, a source that critic Rinda West calls "the energies of the Self" (West, 2007, 149). The protagonist takes charge of his choices by voicing his splintered feelings to Betonie. The earnest shaman foresees a long-range cure equivalent in complexity to post-war trauma. At the end of their session of sand painting and retracing bear tracks, Tayo "stood on the edge of the rimrock and looked down below," a spiritual threshold of a peacetime topography requiring self-directed action (*ibid.*, 145). At the crux of his healing, according to critic John A. McClure, Tayo departs his inept search for meaning and his avoidance of capture by white military doctors and the Bureau of Indian affairs police. Rather than readmit himself to a hospital, he embraces improvisation and eclectic answers as well as an ecological sensibility. McClure notes, "The things Tayo does, working from his heart, may be as effective as those he would have done had he been fully initiated in his peoples' sacred practices" (McClure, 2007, 142). He flees Emo's vengeance by leaving Harley and Leroy Valdez's pickup and by walking away from the road toward open land, where Tayo reconnects with earth. Near Pa'to'ch Butte, the menace of a white rancher Floyd Lee's steel mesh, wolf-proof fence revives the threats of coercion, savagery, and confinement. Tayo confronts the man-made obstacle by working through the night to lop a 20-foot gap in the wire, a symbol of the internal barriers that prevent his recovery. In a gesture of filial love for Uncle Josiah, Tayo restores justice to his family and all Indians who have experienced the white man's rapacity.

In a self-cure similar to that of Viet Vet Tim O'Brien in *The Things They Carried* (1990), storytelling rids the protagonist of culpability while elevating him to the position of tribal storykeeper. Critic John Emory Dean explains, "Tayo has no coherent meaning outside the meanings generated for him by Pueblo stories" (Dean, 2009, 147). Wholeness lies in the veteran's remembrance and recovery of native wisdom lore, which heals him and his community. Dean explains that the star cluster that Betonie and Ts'eh Montaño describe "[weaves] Tayo into Pueblo/Navajo stories so that he may participate in and thereby add to the continuing story of native survival" (*ibid.*, 161). With renewed strength from a cosmic source, Tayo becomes Plato's ideal of the good man.

## THE WAY HOME

Freed from a mental prison foisted on him by war, Tayo experiences catharsis at the novel's climax. Arriving between Los Alamos and Trinity Site, the location of a test detonation of the atomic bomb, "He cried the relief he felt at finally seeing the pattern, the way all the stories fit together — the old stories, the war stories, their stories.... He was not crazy" (Silko, 1977, 246). He welcomes sunrise, an emblem of spiritual liberty and hope. After observing dawn at the bend of the river, a liminal spot mediating earth with the spirit world, the veteran can sit in the confines of Ku'oosh's kiva and relate his experiences to elders eager for a neophyte's view of the world situation. Porter and Roemer point out that, "like the hybrid calves of the speckled Mexican cattle," the new stories become "a part of the long story of the people," an episode of Indian history (Porter & Roemer, 2005, 255). No longer intimidated by change and modernity, in the words of John McClure, Tayo can "live now on reservations seamed with Euro-American settlers, commodities, institutions, and values, now in cities and towns that accommodate some Native American institutions" (McClure, 2007, 152). The restoration of justice to a people fits the definition of epic, the story of the people's hero who rescues his tribe from loss and hopelessness. With the wisdom of El Cid, the humility of Moses, the spirituality of Hiawatha, and the self-sacrifice of Roland, Tayo fits the description of a national or tribal savior. The epic return recurs in *Almanac of the Dead*, in which Sterling, a latter-day Tayo alienated from Laguna for betraying sanctity, survives the urban wars by retreating to the land of his ancestors. Like his predecessor, he hikes the hills, washes and drinks from local water, and weeps with joy at his homecoming.

Critical reception of Silko's maiden novel boosted her to America's first female Indian fiction maven. Analyst A. Robert Lee lauded her for restoring Tayo's troubled soul to "a sustaining myth-world, a cosmos which coheres" (Lee, 2003, 107). Essayist Sven Birkerts, writing for *New Republic*, admired the union of "naturalistic narrative modes with the more startling mythopoeia of the indigenous storytelling tradition," a blending of genres that earned the author a 1981 MacArthur Foundation fellowship (Birkerts, 1991, 39). Because Silko merges the conventions of Amerindian orality with Western written forms, her finished work, according to Silko expert Brewster E. Fitz, exhibits "a pure language ... privileged and different from Anglo-European literature" (Fitz, 2004, x). For the novel's impact on readers, critic Alan R. Velie placed Silko on a par with Kiowa writer Navarre Scott Momaday, Anishinaabe author Gerald Robert Vizenor, and Blackfeet poet James Welch as an Amerindian literary master.

*See also* Betonie; betrayal; madness; Tayo; Tayo's genealogy.

• *References and further reading*

Birkerts, Sven. "Apocalypse Now," *New Republic* 205:19 (4 November 1991): 39–41.
Dean, John Emory. *Travel Narratives from New Mexico: Reconstructing Identity and Truth*. Amherst, NY: Cambria, 2009.
Fitz, Brewster E. *Silko: Writing Storyteller and Medicine Woman*. Norman: University of Oklahoma Press, 2004.
Holm, Sharon. "The 'Lie' of the Land: Native Sovereignty, Indian Literary Nationalism, and Early Indigenism in Leslie Marmon Silko's Ceremony," *American Indian Quarterly* 32:3 (Summer 2008): 243–274.
Lee, A. Robert. *Multicultural American Literature: Comparative Black, Native, Latino/a and Asian American Fictions*. Jackson: University Press of Mississippi, 2003.
Lincoln, Kenneth. *Speak Like Singing: Classics of Native American Literature*. Albuquerque: University of New Mexico Press, 2008.
McClure, John. *Partial Faiths: Postsecular Fiction in the Age of Pynchon and Morrison*. Athens: University of Georgia Press, 2007.
Metz, Nina. "Author Silko Makes a Point to Tell Story," *Chicago Tribune* (16 October 2010).
Porter, Joy, and Kenneth M. Roemer. *The Cambridge Companion to Native American Literature*. Cambridge: Cambridge University Press, 2005.
Roberts, Kathleen Glenister. *Alterity and Narrative: Stories and the Negotiation of Western Identities*. Albany: State University of New York Press, 2008.
Silko, Leslie Marmon. *Ceremony*. New York: Viking, 1977.
Velie, Alan R. *Four American Literary Masters*. Norman: University of Oklahoma Press, 1982.
West, Rinda. *Out of the Shadow: Ecopsychology, Story, and Encounters with the Land*. Charlottesville: University of Virginia Press, 2007.
Womack, Craig S. "A Single Decade: Book-Length Native Literary Criticism between 1986 and 1997" in *Reasoning Together: The Native Critics Collective*. Norman: University of Oklahoma Press, 2008.

# color

Silko's instinct for tone and hue is both sensual and metaphoric. According to author Bruce P. Ballenger in a critique of "Lullaby" (1974), the author stresses sense impressions as a harmonic device "to make the story come alive and to further reinforce the images of nature as a benign and loving force" (Ballenger, 2005, 385). At the height of panic over social forces she can't control, Ayah, the protagonist, looks to the heavens for strength and finds "steely blue-gray horses startled across the sky ... the tail hair streaming white mist behind them," a fantasy enriched by her imagination (Silko, 1974, 15). The author's painting of a protest mural in downtown Tucson denigrated the white colonist by creating a totem snake out of bright Amerindian hues representing native vigor and innovation. Alert to varied tints, she fills her writings with chance encounters with color, the serendipity that bolsters native American legend.

A positive outlook emerges in Silko's color-saturated scenarios. In "'Not You,' He Said," anthologized in *What Wildness Is This: Women Write about the Southwest* (2007), she reflects on the glamour of the Sonoran Desert, where volcanic activity melted vivid minerals into confetti-like glints against the horizon. Her delight in the beauty emerging from a horrific eruption reflects a pervasive strand in her motifs of benefit generated by seismic clashes and disasters, the controlling theme of *Almanac of the Dead* (1991). She highlights flashes of color to mark pivotal moments, for example, the green-eyed stare of the grey mist wolf in the poem "Four Mountain Wolves" (1973), the gifts of red coral and turquoise to a spirit bear in the coming-of-age story "Humaweepi, the Warrior Priest" (1975), a foreshadowing of similar gifts to the 30-foot snake Masshastryu in *Almanac*, and the massing of thunderclouds in *Storyteller* (1981). Analyst John Emory Dean cites a reason for the meandering nature of Silko's epiphanies as "an ancient pattern of going out from a central point and then coming back with new insights," a summation of her daily walks to collect colorful stones in *The Turquoise Ledge* (2010) (Dean, 2009, 163).

LIFE HUES

Animism quickens Silko's palette. Critic Ernest Stromberg, a humanities specialist at California State University, asserts that reading her canon requires a study of "color and shape, for the aspects of the divine world alive in its images" (Stromberg, 2006, 219). The author's first story, "The Man to Send Rain Clouds" (1969), stresses the primary colors that mark a series of burial rituals—the wrapping of Grandpa Teofilo in a red blanket, blessing him with a gray feather, and the painting of his face with white, blue, yellow, and green near his death site in view of snow-capped blue mountains, a divine backdrop. The faded blue of the old man's levis connects him to standard Western dress and to the snuffing of his life, symbolized by blue, the story's dominant emblem of transcendence. Intense shades deny the finality of earthly death for a man graced by a Spanish name meaning "beloved of God." Intrinsic color symbols bind the old man's remains to an ongoing involvement in earth.

The corpse becomes a magnet to native mourners seeking outlets for their energies. More shades dominate the laying out of the deceased shepherd—red shawl, brown flannel shirt, nearby black iron stove, and the yellowing evening sky, a mellowing of hue that softens the stark edge of death. In an interview with Laura Coltelli, Silko identified yellow as a Pueblo symbol of the East, dawn, Yellow Woman (Kochininako), corn, and sacred corn pollen, a ritual offering to Mother Earth. The tints of Leon's green army jacket and Father Paul's blue eyes continue to pack the narrative with memorable particulars. Silko uses the jacket to portray Leon as an American veteran and the priest's blue eyes as a hint at the naïveté of Western religious authorities—outsiders to the Pueblo—toward centuries-old animistic ritual. The blue completes a narrative circle in Leon's lifted gaze to the snow-topped blue mountains, an icon of place and permanence as old as creation. Silko's overt addition of a red glow in the sky turns the coloring to an emblematic red, white, and blue, a coalition of flag hues suggesting the creation of a nation of blended cultures.

THE COLORS OF CEREMONY

The author's affinity for clear colors remained steady in subsequent poems, memoir, and fables. For her first novel, *Ceremony* (1977), a lyric coming-home narrative, she turns color into a kaleidoscopic symbol interlaced with glints of adventure, introspection, and duty. Against the desert backdrop, Tayo, like the amputee of Karl Shapiro's poem "The Leg" (1944), awakens sense by sense, beginning with the sound of singing in Spanish and advancing to fever and the flashing red and blue lights of a juke box. The text features him in a distinct milieu — a red plaid western shirt alongside a yellow striped cat and black goat. The stark tones set him apart, marking him as the Amerindian quest hero, a nativist variant on the frontier code heroes created by Zane Grey and Louis L'Amour. For focus, Tayo emerges from sleep and the fog of battle fatigue by concentrating on the yellow light that becomes "more yellow with the climbing sun" (Silko, 1977, 6). The dawn brightens his bedroom wall like the emergence of spring in Silko's poem "Sun Children" (1972). The glow takes the outline of the window, a square beacon on which he can watch the day progress, an indication of his loss of volition and his need to absorb the grace of sky and earth. The bold blue of the firmament and the cloud of red dust, a contrast that Silko introduced in "Hawk and Snake" (1972), jolt Tayo from his previous invisibility at the veterans' hospital in Los Angeles, where he lost himself in the shimmering institutional white of the ceiling. Like a soldier in spiritual camouflage, he had been not only colorless, but also incorporeal, a miasma without feeling or dimensions.

As Tayo abandons torpor to exert agency, blue returns to dominance in the whirling flamenco dance of Night Swan, a cat-eyed Mexican cantina dancer who lives behind a blue door. Shawled in blue, she receives Uncle Josiah in summer 1940, when he parks his blue truck outside the bar every evening and sits in her blue clawfoot armchair by wall borders painted with blue flowers. In scenes of healing, Tayo returns to blue — memories of Night Swan's sapphire cloak and bed linens, wind-swept skies, and the blue of Mount Taylor. He confesses to Night Swan that being born with hazel "Mexican" eyes causes him difficulty with pure-blood Indians. The mixed-blood dancer explains the reassurance of shared traits: "They think that if their children have the same color of skin, the same color of eyes, that nothing is changing.... They blame us, the ones who look different" (Silko, 1977, 92). Critic Gloria Bird explains that "Night Swan offers him a way out of self-inflicted metaphysical alterity," the melancholy "otherness" that alienates him from his family, army buddies, and the rest of the Laguna (Bird, 2005, 101). Night Swan's enigmatic closing remark thanks him for "bringing the message," a subtle hint at his post-war role in preparing the Laguna for change through hybridization or transnationalism of an authentic race and culture (*ibid.*).

Natural colors draw Tayo to his quest. In the second day of his residence with Betonie, the Navajo medicine man, a white corn sand painting features a blue mountain range along with yellow and white elevations. In the essay "The Indian with a Camera" (1993), Silko accounts for the shaman's abstract design: "The Pueblo people had long understood that certain man-made visual images were sacred and were necessary to Pueblo ceremony" (Silko, 1993, 4). To relieve Tayo of the coyote sickness, Shush, the medicine man's aide, adds black bear prints to the pattern while Betonie shapes blue, yellow, and white tracks. A quick slash to Tayo's head links him to all wounded soldiers of the past and readies him to walk the bear footprints, the path to home and normality. Upon encountering Ts'eh Montaño, the mountain demigoddess and consort of Mountain Lion Man, Tayo notes her yellow skirt and ocher eyes, a direct reference to the cultural hero Yellow Woman, whose sexual exploit with Silva, the tall Navajo seducer, benefits her starving people. At the novel's climax, a beneficent snow in late fall covers in white the tracks of Uncle Josiah's cattle and wipes out the scent of the mountain lion, the durable native cat that Silko introduces in "Indian Song: Survival" (1973). A divine distraction, the big cat diverts Floyd Lee's cowboys from seizing Tayo for trespass and rustling and sends them into the wild over whitened trails, a colorless terrain that deliberately thwarts their stalking.

## THE COLORS OF MYTH

As thematic handholds in a chaotic story, Silko's *Gardens in the Dunes* (1999) extends the possibilities of color. The opening palette thrusts readers into a pastoral milieu overarched by sky and horizon, a standard setting in Southwestern desert lore. So grand a heavenly vault humbles the characters, reminding the reader that cosmic forces control humankind. The flow of river water produces natural treasures—"rough granular stones of light greens and darker greens just the color of leaves" (Silko, 1999, 213). Indigo, one of the focal females, bears the name of a color in the optical spectrum and a plant that supplied the prehistoric fiber worker and worshipper with dye for cloth and skin. The runaway protagonist flees Sherman Institute in Riverside, California, and applies her survival skills to a differentiation of dawn colors, "from dark gray, then dark blue, then violet that lifted to lavender that faded to a rosy gray streaked with pale yellow ... [and] a blaze of red-yellow" (*ibid.*, 71). Just as dawning color invigorates Tayo in *Ceremony*, the progression allies Indigo naturally with the rising light, which takes on a fiery intensity. Color appreciation anticipates her sensitivity to gardens and her attempts to stuff a valise with a seed collection, the source of new hues for the dune planting beds. In a formal California garden of Dr. Edward and Hattie Abbott Palmer, Indigo deserts her search for a gourd canteen to immerse herself in unforeseen kinesthesia—the fragrances of roses, lilies, dianthus, peonies, dahlias, poppies, cosmos, wisteria, and hollyhocks. Transported by color and aroma, she palpitates to "all the red flowers" and feeds on rose hips and oranges from the citrus grove, a deviation from blue tones to a riotous panoply of the white man's decorative horticulture. (*ibid.*, 83).

For Indigo, color translates visual stimuli into the luxury of learning. As a foster child of the Palmer family, she copies plants in notebooks with her colored pencils and accesses books filled with tinted plates of "wild parrots in jungles surrounded by great trees and lovely flowering plants" (*ibid.*, 226). The opportunity to indulge her eyes in expensive texts contrasts the school she escaped, where Indian girls trained to become ladies' maids. Travel broadens her experiences with a sea voyage, when she views an ocean tone "as clear and blue as topaz" (*ibid.*, 330). During hands-on education in Aunt Bronwyn's garden in Somerset, England, Indigo absorbs a feast for the eyes—"Reds, oranges, pinks, and purples of the flowers were so saturated with color they seemed to glow above graceful narrow leaves of deep green" (*ibid.*, 245). Mother and daughter make a game of naming hues—"umber, sienna, ocher, eggshell, sage, tea, mint," a venture into earth tones reminiscent of Indigo's upbringing in the Arizona sandhills (*ibid.*, 277).

Silko advances into flower symbolism with images of black gladioli, "the color of fertility and birth, the color of the Great Mother," a binding metaphor in the gynocentric narrative (*ibid.*, 296). Critic Stuart Christie, an anarchist writer from Glasgow, Scotland, remarks on the "scatterings of mottled rose-gray and ivory-gray gladiolus [that] accented the black" (*ibid.*, 297). The up-close delineation of complex colors begs the question of race as a human demarcation. Christie surmises that *La Professoressa* "Laura's scientific savvy — with, as it seems, nature's collusion — signals Silko's careful reverse engineering of enlightenment procedural and scientific knowledge, away from colonialist exploitation, toward the purposes of refining pleasure and beauty in mixed forms" (Christie, 2009, 95). Upon return to Sand Lizard country, Indigo shares her notebooks with Sister Salt and her friends, Maytha and Vedna, to whom introduction to world gardens is an unexpected gift and impetus to renewed sisterhood and the clan.

## THE LIGHT OF LEARNING

Silko links Indigo's delight in polychromatic plantings to a similar sensuality in young Hattie Abbott, a Harvard graduate student. The alter ego of Indigo, Hattie absorbs the scent of leather bindings in Dr. Rhinehart's library. As entranced by books as Indigo stood stunned by flowers, Hattie views the shades — black, chocolate, fawn, hunter green, red, and saffron — as "a lovely strange garden," a source of ideas to invigorate her otherwise uncultivated mind (*ibid.*, 96). At moments of spiritual transport, Hattie revisits her research into early Christian worship and welcomes light in Aunt Bronwyn's garden in Somerset that is so stunning it "might have been a dream" (*ibid.*, 319). Hattie remains open to insight into divinity in her walks with *la professoressa* Laura in Lucca, Italy, a city reflecting the Latin word *lux* (light) and suggesting insight and enlightenment.

Silko uses color and light to differentiate expectations of apotheosis. The crowning of Hattie's receptivity occurs in Bastia, Corsica, where charismatic Catholics view an image of the Virgin Mary on a schoolhouse wall. More acute at fantasy than her Harvard-trained alter ego, Indigo sees glittery reflections as "flakes of snow that swirled around the dancers the last night when the Messiah appeared with his family" (*ibid.*). Hattie witnesses the transformation of color into a transcendent beam. It brightens with "a subtle iridescence that steadily intensified into a radiance of pure color that left her breathless, almost dizzy" (*ibid.*). The author depicts Hattie as ripe for ecstasy. Her failure to decode rays into a recognizable gestalt results in part from a lifetime of motherly repression and the ridicule and suspicion of orthodox faculty at the Harvard Divinity School. Their harsh slap against Hattie's open-mindedness reflects the androcentric backlash against her willingness to venture beyond the accepted. She reads Gnostic texts in search of what critic David Murray calls "an original Christianity that would share much more with 'primitive' and other religions than the present orthodoxy" (Murray, 2007, 146). The dazzling coming to knowledge rewards her at last with evidence that her thesis was correct.

## NATURE'S PALETTE

Against scenes of spiritual growth, Silko juxtaposes Hattie's sister-in-law, socialite Susan Palmer James, the Oyster Bay narcissist who labors in service to the Masque of the Blue Garden, an elaborate annual show of pretense and disguise. She demolishes and redesigns her garden so her guests can experience a new and different profusion. For impact of white against blue, she interplants cobalt blue *Delphinium belladonna*, foxglove, pansies, salvia, and violas with Asiatic lilies and lilies of the valley in shades her guests wear to the soiree. In a greenhouse chilled with ice, Susan's Scots gardener forces into bloom more blue flowers from bugloss, iris, lilac, rhododendron, and spiderwort to contrast azaleas, bellflower, bougainvillea, cornflower, datura, forget-me-not, gentian, globe thistle, lobelia, monkshood, and primula. Vying with the creator Yahweh for control, he sought "to create shimmering draperies of the pendulous blossoms," an edenic background intended for one night's service (Silko, 1999, 195). For white background, Susan mulls over an excess of blossoms from artemisia, aster, buddleia, canterbury bells, foxglove, freesia, gardenia, hollyhock, lavender, lilacs, spiky lupines and mignonettes, phlox, rambling roses, tulips, Victorian water lilies, and white and blue wisteria.

Unlike Indigo, a subsistence gardener, Susan manipulates nature for exhibitionism. While the Palmers and Abbotts assist Susan in the vast showpiece, Indigo stands aside at the pool and feeds the carp. To redirect the child toward the family endeavor, Hattie takes stock: "The child was so serious; what was she thinking?" a reference to Hattie's inability to control or even interpret the Sand Lizard understanding of nature (*ibid.*, 196). In the words of analyst Shelley Saguaro, head of humanities instruction at the University of Gloucestershire, Susan celebrates "her ability to force the natural world to fit the vision that her wealth allows— or commands" (Saguaro, 2006, 188). In contrast, Indigo possesses no control, even over her own destiny. To her, "Blue was the color of the rain clouds," a sign of moisture and relief from drought rather than the backdrop for social climbing (Silko, 1999, 177). On Indigo's way home to America, color continues to soothe her during the Atlantic crossing aboard the S.S. *Pavonia*, a ship named for the flowering mallow. Sick with the roll of the ship, she concentrates on feeding ginger cookies to her parrot Rainbow and concentrates on his brilliant shades of blue, emerald, turquoise, and golden yellow, stabilizers that reflect the desert palette she misses from childhood. On return to the desert dunes, Indigo cultivates beauty for its own sake in "silver white gladiolus with pale blues and pale lavenders [that] glowed among the great dark jade datura leaves" (*ibid.*, 476)

Indigo's love of her bright hued parrot and fragrant datura exemplifies the author's need to sketch and emulate brilliant flora and fauna. For the opening of "Chapulin's Portrait," later included in *The Turquoise Ledge* (2010), the narrative engorges the reader's eye with bold shades. Silko stresses pink and white lilies and two grasshoppers colored emerald and peacock green, yellow, orange, black, and shades of magenta, hues suiting their "great majesty" (Silko, 2010, 113). The intense tones belie the autumnal demise of one grasshopper. Another specimen appears to carry a message from Lord Chapulin, whom the poet imagines visiting her on a sandstone bench and communicating through thought transfer his specifications for a portrait. By whiting out a grasshopper image, Silko uses the absence of color to objectify the insect's death. In her typical nondirective style, she leaves to the reader to interpret Chapulin's final visit to her studio and his failure to indicate pleasure or displeasure at her attempts to reduce a wonder of nature to a drawing on paper.

*See also* symbolism.

• *References and further reading*

Ballenger, Bruce P. *The Curious Writer*. White Plains, NY: Pearson Longman, 2005.

Berglund, Jeff. *Cannibal Fictions: American Explorations of Colonialism, Race, Gender and Sexuality*. Madison: University of Wisconsin Press, 2006.

Bird, Gloria. "Toward a Decolonization of the Mind and Text: Leslie Marmon Silko's *Ceremony*" in *Reading Native American Women: Critical/Creative Representations*, ed. Inés Hernández-Avila. Lanham, MD: Altamira, 2005, 93–106.

Christie, Stuart. *Plural Sovereignties and Contemporary Indigenous Literature*. New York: Palgrave Macmillan, 2009.

Coltelli, Laura. *Winged Words: American Indian Writers Speak*. Lincoln: University of Nebraska Press, 1990, 135–153.

Dean, John Emory. *Travel Narratives from New Mexico: Reconstructing Identity and Truth*. Amherst, NY: Cambria, 2009.

Murray, David. *Matter, Magic, and Spirit: Representing Indian and African American Belief.* Philadelphia: University of Pennsylvania Press, 2007.

Saguaro, Shelley. *Garden Plots: The Politics and Poetics of Gardens.* Burlington, VT: Ashgate, 2006.

Silko, Leslie Marmon. *Ceremony.* New York: Viking, 1977.

_____. "Chapulin's Portrait," *Kenyon Review* 32:1 (1 January 2010): 109–134.

_____. *Gardens in the Dunes.* New York: Scribner, 1999.

_____. "The Indian with a Camera," foreword to *A Circle of Nations: Voices and Visions of American Indians.* Hillsboro, OR: Beyond Words, 1993.

_____. "Lullaby," *Chicago Review* 26:1 (Summer 1974): 10–17.

_____. "'Not You,' He Said" in *What Wildness Is This: Women Write about the Southwest*, eds. Susan Wittig Albert and Susan Hanson. Austin: University of Texas Press, 2007.

_____. *The Turquoise Ledge.* New York: Viking, 2010.

# coming of age

Silko views the grooming of the younger generation for adulthood as a gift and blessing for adults and tribal elders. The reciprocal nature of parenting a promising youth enhances her coming-of-age story "Humaweepi, the Warrior Priest" (1975), which involves a 19-year-old orphan with daily training by his uncle/foster father. Education seems so natural that the boy does not realize that daily stories, chants, prayers, and examples are lessons. Concluding in an outdoor initiation rite, the narrative crowns the elderly uncle's mentoring with the acceptance of holy duties by Humaweepi, an apprentice newly ushered into the priesthood. Similarly, the Yupik woman in "Interior and Exterior Landscapes" (1981) accepts an adult-sized job of requiting the murder of her parents by a member of an oil-drilling crew. By luring a potential white rapist onto an icy river, she tricks him into self-destruction in the waters below. Brewster E. Fitz, a Silko expert, pictures the woman's accomplishment as revenge for all Amerindians against white usurpers and exploiters, a "vehement bashing of Western culture" for "its mad technological arrogance" (Fitz, 2004, 70). Thus, like the culture hero Yellow Woman (Kochininako), the unnamed Yupik woman gains community esteem for using her advancing sexuality as a tool against a common enemy.

Through memoir and autobiography, Silko describes her own growing up as a community effort. She anticipates opportunity by mentioning in *The Turquoise Ledge* (2010) her birthing contemporaneous with the supernova in the Mixed Spiral galaxy, an element of the Cepheus constellation visible in 1917, 1939, 1948, 1968, 1969, and 1980 (Silko, 2010, 1). To her dismay, the celestial welcome conceals a genetic betrayal that develops along with her white facial features. An obstacle to childhood contentment, Silko's mixed blood set her and her sisters Gigi and Wendy on the outer rim of Laguna society. Unknown to her at the time, the Marmon household reflected the "melting pot" element of diaspora by which immigrant peoples intermarried with North American aborigines. Critic Andrew Jolivétte comments: "Dual bloodlines allow Indian writers to weave in threads of an almost pan–Indian tribalism, a coming together of all nations, a relationship of native writers to non-native ancestral landscape" (Jolivétte, 2006, 145).

The test of mixed nativism strengthens Silko's writing with gestures to gynocratic, matrifocal, and matrilineal tribalism. Rather than cede to public disapproval, her story "In the Combat Zone" (1995) urges the female neophyte to "learn how to take aggressive action individually" to "destroy the myth that women are born to be easy targets" (Silko, 1995, 46). The plight of the mixed blood Indian made a lasting impression and colored the author's characterization in *Ceremony* (1977), the elegies "Deer Dance/For Your Return" and "A Hunting Story" in *Storyteller* (1981), *Almanac of the Dead* (1991), and *Gardens in the Dunes* (1999). Central to her themes of miscegenation are the tribal blessings from children who revitalize a clan with blended ethnicity, particularly Sister Salt's bearing of a first child to Big Candy, an Afro-Red Stick Indian from Louisiana.

Coming of age attains critical mass in Silko's Indian characters when they reach age six and encounter the white hegemony of Christian churches and schools, a separation between the white and Indian worlds she includes in the dissolution of family in "Lullaby" (1974). Divested of her freedom in the wild alone on foot or on horseback, she suffers the loss of moral instruction in the stories of Grandma A'mooh and Aunt Susie Reyes Marmon. Upon entering Manzano Day School, a Catholic academy in Albuquerque, the author learned that discipline meant barriers, just as Aunt Susie learned that intrusive Europeans took "children away from the tellers who had in all past generations told the children an entire culture, an entire identity of a people" (Silko, 1996, 6). She gained a troubled view of a world in which her native Pueblo language and creation stories produced disapproving stares and retorts from bigots. In class, "talking Indian was forbidden" (Silko, 2010, 41). To her credit, she chose language as her métier and began translating Laguna oral tradition into written verse and narrative, an ongoing project she describes in *Storyteller* and *Yellow Woman and a Beauty of the Spirit: Essays on Native American Life Today* (1996). In "Landscape, History, and the Pueblo Imagination" (1986), she characterizes the stories and myths as "inter-family or inter-clan exchanges" that forgive human listeners of faults and encourage their tolerance of others (Silko, 1986, 93). The instructive purpose suggests her own role in guiding the next generation through maturation.

## THE FICTIONAL NEOPHYTE

For her maiden novel, *Ceremony*, Silko exemplifies Pueblo training in duty and sanctity through Tayo, a fellow horseback rider and subsistence hunter. She creates a prototype of the unwanted orphan, a motherless half-breed who hero-worships his cousin/foster brother Rocky. The author examines the pair for variant upbringings—Rocky, the self-reliant golden child and wonder worker on the football field, and Tayo, the illegitimate relative existing on crumbs of love from a blind grandmother, Uncle Robert, and Uncle Josiah. Similar in doubts and confusion to Abenaki writer Joseph Bruchac, autobiographer of *Bowman's Store* (1997), Tayo lives the daily disgrace of fatherlessness and the family embarrassment of birth to "little sister" Laura, a sexual libertine who couples with unidentified white and Mexican males and dies without accepting the role of mother.

Silko pictures episodes of growing up that predict character formation. In boyhood, Tayo wants to pet deer and "daydreamed that a deer would let him come close and touch its nose," an indication of gentle ways (Silko, 1977, 50). Significant to his emergent manhood are ceremonies of gratitude and humility to the deer spirit that brings the family venison. As he matures in body and heart, he values ritual songs of thanksgiving to the sunrise for continued life. In his mid-teens, Tayo promotes his Uncle Josiah's dream of a family herding business. The commitment of 20 years' savings spent on Ulibarri's speckled longhorns requires faith in an untried model of breeding a semi-wild Mexican strain, an image parallel to the socialization of youth.

Echoing the tone and gravity of the story of Antonio, the Chicano grandson who investigates holy power in Rudolfo Anaya's *Bless Me, Ultima* (1972), Silko's youth confront chaos, the unforeseen tests of character strength and courage. In 1940, Tayo's chat with an army recruiter fails to convince him of his obligation to fight the white man's war in Japan. Naively, he promises to sign up Rocky and to bring his brother safely back from the Pacific war, which erupts from a treacherous bombardment of Pearl Harbor, Hawaii, on December 7, 1941. Both teens experience a coming to knowledge in April and May 1942 in the Philippines during the Bataan Death March, an echo of the Civil War battles survived by 18-year-old Henry Fleming, the similarly untried protagonist of Stephen Crane's *The Red Badge of Courage* (1895). Overwhelmed by loss and struggle, Tayo commits a cosmic error in "[praying] the rain away," a sacrilege against the mythic sisters Corn Woman (Nau'ts'ity'i) and Reed Woman (Iktoa'ak'o'ya) (*ibid.*, 13). He enlarges his insult to the gods by yearning for air "dry as a hundred years squeezed out of yellow sand" (*ibid.*, 10). He worries, "Maybe the rain wouldn't come or the deer would go away" (*ibid.*, 34). The sin caps his coming of age and sends him spiraling into post-traumatic stress trauma, a man-sized madness that echoes the insanity of the bombing of Hiroshima and Nagasaki, Japan, on August 6 and 8, 1945. At age 26, he lies bedfast with a first-time knowledge of adulthood, which burdens him with fault for the death of Rocky and the drought. Worsening his remorse are flashbacks of his cowardice and disobedience in avoiding an order to shoot Japanese prisoners.

Silko reprises a formulaic frontier motif of a boy learning the adult dictum to "finish what you start," the theme of John Steinbeck's coming-of-age novella *The Red Pony* (1933). Affirmed with the wisdom of two shamans, the Laguna healer Ku'oosh and Betonie, a Chicano-Navajo healer, Tayo advances unsteadily toward his destiny because of too much alcohol and macho carousing with his war buddies, Emo, Harley, Leroy Valdez, and Cousin Pinkie. With the determination of Richard Newton Peck's boy hero in *A Day No Pigs Would Die* (1972) and the survivor of a drowning in Ron Woods's *Hero* (2002), Tayo gradually pulls away from his two-timing pals and recovers his uncle's cattle from white rustler Floyd Lee's pasture. Symbolically, during Tayo's coupling with Ts'eh Montaño, the mountain demigoddess, he dreams of reclaiming the herd: "He saw them scatter over the crest of a round bare hill, running away from him, scattering out around him like ripples in still water," a physical representation of his one-man range duties (*ibid.*, 181). Like the labors of Hercules, the multi-stage retrieval places Tayo in situations requiring prudence and expertise. Silko rewards him with the approval of his elders, who admit him to the kiva, the subterranean ceremonial chamber that serves wise men as a place of learning and tribal advancement. Grandma notes the cyclical nature of growing-up stories: "It seems like I already heard these stories before ... only thing is, the names sound different" (*ibid.*, 260). Her prophetic statement anticipates the next generation of Harleys, Rockys, and Tayos who will have their own wars to fight and promises to keep.

## LIKE PARENT, LIKE CHILD

Silko's motif of youth laden with mature responsibilities returns in her later fiction. For *Almanac of the Dead*, she glosses over the upbringing of Bingo and his older brother Sonny by their mother, Leah Blue, a self-indulgent mega-realtor, and their sociopathic father, Max "Mr. Murder" Blue, a model of the New Jersey Mafia capo. Reared in self-gratification and duplicity, the boys develop talents for betrayal and disrespect. Their mother rewards them for staying quietly in the big Chrysler during a property showing with gifts of "candy and pop," a form of bribery that teaches them to expect reimbursal in junk food for obedience (Silko, 1991, 435). The text infantilizes Bingo as an overweight sybarite whose "hairy beer-belly sat like a stuffed toy in his lap" while he reads *Penthouse* magazine (*ibid.*, 370). The siblings display their disinterest in family by indiscriminate coupling, Bingo, the cocaine snorter, with two Mexican maids, and Sonny with admiring coeds and with Algería Martinez-Soto Panson, the Venezuelan wife of a *mestizo* insurance dealer. A more detailed study of family dysfunction derives from the upbringing of Ferro, the son of Lecha, a Yaqui psychic who disdains motherhood to pursue private ambitions. Cast off on Zeta, Lecha's twin, Ferro emulates his criminal aunt/foster mother, an arms and drug smuggler, much as Sonny and Bingo copy their parents' dissolute example. None of the sons possesses the background or values to form a normal family.

A generation of young Tucson thugs and drug dealers contrasts Silko's image of matri-lineage in *Gardens in the Dunes*, in which Mama and Grandma Fleet prepare Indigo and Sister Salt for survival. Training by example rather than homily, the older women demon-strate laughter and fun as well as thrift, courtesy, and loyalty to the Sand Lizard people, a dwindling Arizona tribe. Both women "told the girls old stories about the land of per-petual summer, far to the south" (Silko, 1999, 20). Grandma sings tribal songs, tells hunt-ing tales, and alerts the girls to the sanctity of the old snake that guards the spring. Sister Salt learns to boil amaranth greens from Grandma; Indigo learns to make windbreaks for the bean seedlings from dry twigs and to prowl the arroyos to gather willow withes. From their handcrafts, Sister Salt sells homemade yucca baskets at the depot at Needles on the Arizona-California border under the surveillance of Mama. Grandma sets the example of stealth by identifying places of shelter and water locations and by escaping from soldiers and Indian police. The increments of coming of age please the older women, who expect maturity to develop in Indigo and Sister Salt day by day.

The sure test of coming of age is trust, a theme that undergirds Silko's canon. Grandma Fleet exhibits faith in informal teaching by leaving Indigo and Sister Salt unattended dur-ing the search for Mama. On return, Grandma tells them she is proud of them, a neces-sary acknowledgement of the progress the girls make toward responsible adulthood. To ensure awareness of evil, Silko notes, "Grandma Fleet taught the girls to wait and watch for the right moment to run" and to avoid alarming unfamiliar dogs and mules or attract-ing the attention of enslavers (*ibid.*, 69). During a raid on the family hovel, Grandma yells, "Run! Run get your little sister!," a command replete with motherly expectation that the two girls watch out for each other (*ibid.*, 13). The sisters, unlike the self-seeking Bingo and Sonny Blue and Ferro, contribute their adventures to the strengthening of the clan.

Silko depicts the success of coming of age in the readiness of youth to groom their own children for adulthood. With faith in the future, Sister Salt adds the first male infant, "little black grandfather," and listens to him *in utero* as he speaks a baby version of the Sand Lizard language (Silko, 1999, 344). As her grandma taught her, Sister Salt informs the unborn boy, "No place is safe," a frank acknowledgement of the fragile peace of their riverbank home and a preparation for their everyday struggle against rapid change wrought by white people (*ibid.*, 333). When the uterine contractions start too soon, Sister Salt fears for the baby's survival. Her joy in bringing the boy through a bloody and difficult birth foreshadows her success in mothering him. At the sight of his plump body, she exults, "I'm just so happy" (*ibid.*, 342). The child, whom she calls Bright Eyes, becomes a spark of hope for the sand dune family and a new duty in the ongoing process of child rearing.

*See also* mothering; parenting.

• *References and further reading*

Fitz, Brewster E. *Silko: Writing Storyteller and Medicine Woman*. Norman: University of Oklahoma Press, 2004.

Jolivétte, Andrew. *Cultural Representation in Native America*. Lanham, MD: Altamira, 2006.
Lincoln, Kenneth. *Speak Like Singing: Classics of Native American Literature*. Albuquerque: University of New Mexico Press, 2008.
Roppolo, Kimberly. "Vision, Voice, and Intertribal Metanarrative: The American Indian Visual-Rhetorical Tradition and Leslie Marmon Silko's *Almanac of the Dead*," *American Indian Quarterly* 31:4 (Fall 2007): 534–558.
Silko, Leslie Marmon. *Almanac of the Dead*. New York: Simon & Schuster, 1991.
_____. *Ceremony*. New York: Viking, 1977.
_____. *Gardens in the Dunes*. New York: Scribner, 1999.
_____. "In the Combat Zone," *Hungry Mind Review* (Fall 1995): 44, 46.
_____. "Landscape, History, and the Pueblo Imagination," *Antaeus* 51 (Autumn 1986): 83–94.

# confinement

Silko pities the victim of physical, mental, or socio-economic confinement, but confers her strongest regard on the self-liberator. As she states in *Yellow Woman and a Beauty of the Spirit: Essays on Native American Life Today* (1996), in childhood, she regretted her Aunt Susie's stories of schooling at the Indian boarding school in Carlisle, Pennsylvania. Because of social and religious strictures on dress, conduct, and language, it was "like being sent to prison for six years" (Silko, 1996, 54). Silko valued the stories of Grandma A'mooh and Aunt Susie, who taught her to value female assertiveness in real life and in stories. For her own narratives, one of the author's most satisfying characters is Ts'eh Montaño, the mysterious mountain demigoddess who rehabilitates Tayo, the traumatized war veteran in *Ceremony* (1977). Like the author herself, Ts'eh dictates her own agenda and enjoys unprecedented female freedom and control of passion, sexuality, and a personal agenda.

For Silko, assertiveness carries personal and literary rewards. Influenced by the artistic self-direction of her father, photograph Leland "Lee" Marmon, the author felt "most at home in the canyons and sandrock" of Laguna Pueblo and learned to value native freedoms from the "confinement [of] regular jobs" (Silko, 1981, 160–161). Upon establishing a writing career, like her fictional medieval scholar Hattie Abbott Palmer, the only woman attending a heresy seminar at Harvard Divinity School in *Gardens in the Dunes* (1999), Silko refused to respect the academic confines of Eurocentrism or the cultural discounting and silencing of nonwhites. Instead, she embraced the self-expression of the Native American Literary Renaissance, begun by Kiowa colleague Navarre Scott Momaday with the publication of *House Made of Dawn* (1969). The unfettered grace and personal observations of *Storyteller* (1981) and *The Turquoise Ledge* (2010) attest to the benefits of the author's lifestyle. Critic Jeff Karem, an Americanist at Cleveland State University, lauds Silko for using her freedom to express nativist truths by "[assuming] an authorial pose of almost mystical representative power, claiming for herself the role of authentic, unmediated channeler of the native spirits of the Americas" (Karem, 2004, 15).

## SILKO'S CHARACTERS

For the sake of drama, Silko extends the shadow of corralling over her characters. Custody determines the fate of the cop-killer in "Tony's Story" (1969), the abduction of a lone female in "Yellow Woman" (1974), and the lulling into death of a doomed ranch hand in "Lullaby" (1974). In a personal, essay, "Fences against Freedom" (1994), Silko's experience with the Southwestern border patrol replaces handcuffs and prison bars with the terrors of armed agents and their K-9 assistants during a post-midnight road stop that could have ended in false arrest and/or shooting. In a warning that predates the state of Arizona's 2010 war on aliens, Silko charges, "No person, no citizen is free to travel without the scrutiny of the Border Patrol" (Silko, 1994, 111). By relating the humiliating night stop from a real episode she shared with her friend Gus, she impugns a violation of the Bill of Rights that prejudices nonwhite Americans through racist intimidation and menace.

The author's first novel, *Ceremony*, a post-war reclamation of a former inmate of a Japanese prison camp, creates variant forms of constraint, from Harley's few days in a Los Lunas jail, Leroy Valdez's inability to open beers because of drunkenness, and Tayo's arrest and locking in a police car to Emo's exile to California for shooting Cousin Pinkie over the dish pan on the stove at Sarracino's sheep camp. After spending the 1940s battling Japanese soldiers in the Philippines, Iwo Jima, and Wake Island, the World War II veterans return to Laguna in various degrees of post-traumatic stress disorder. In order "to get us happy right now," they self-medicate with beer and liquor, chase women, jounce around rough roads in an unreliable pickup, and spend evenings in bars squabbling, fighting, and telling war stories (Silko, 1977, 52). Tayo, the most disturbed of the foursome, carries his prison inside, where flashbacks generate nausea and vertigo and remorse gnaws his heart. During three years of treatment at a Los Angeles military hospital, he dissociates from his role as patient and informs the new doctor, "He can't talk to you. He is invisible" (*ibid.*, 15). On Tayo's return to the hospital for slicing Emo's gut with a broken beer bottle, Harley counts his buddy lucky for being a mental patient: "If it had been me, I probably *still* been sitting in jail" (*ibid.*, 54). The self-serving remark overlooks Tayo's caging in mental agony as unstoppable as "a summer flash flood, the rumble still faint and distant, floodwater boiling down a narrow canyon" (*ibid.*, 12). Unlike his physical penning in a Japanese prison camp under armed guard, in peacetime, he carries his cage in his head.

## LOCKED IN MEMORIES

Silko interweaves the bars on Tayo's lock-up with past misery and remorse. Reprising childhood memories of losing his mother to alcohol and promiscuous sex, he relives the consolation of riding in Uncle Josiah's wagon while wrapped in Grandma's arms. More reassuring echoes Rocky's welcome to a new brother. After the long war, Tayo perceives, "They were taking him home" (*ibid.*, 254). Bedrest in Auntie Thelma's house grieves the veteran, who views his foster mother as a cunning jailer and manipulator. He sleeps in the old iron bed he once shared with Rocky, his cousin/foster brother who dies during the Bataan Death March of April 1942. Tayo's suffering takes the forms of night terrors and pain and pressure in his skull, an inescapable hell. His blind grandmother, ever his defender, cuddles his head on her lap and repeats "A'moo'oh, a'moo'ohh," an onomatopoeic solace in the Laguna language suited to the hurts of infants and children (*ibid.*, 30).

To open the gates of his pent-up psyche, Tayo must begin with outside help and progress to an inner housecleaning of regret and blame. As he begins healing through prophecy and ritual, he exerts himself from bed to wander the area around Laguna and to refamiliarize himself with home. His complete reclamation requires the cutting of rustler Floyd Lee's steel fence and the deliverance of Uncle Josiah's wild Mexican cattle, a task Tayo committed to in his teens. From an adult perspective on war and recuperation, like the spunky Yellow Woman of Laguna myth, he recognizes the crucial factor: "It was his own two feet that got him there" (*ibid.*, 254–255). For his stoic self-release, he deserves the praise and admiration of his elders, who welcome him to the kiva, a spiritual containment center wreathed in honor and community respect. Mythically, they unravel dead skin from Coyote: "Every evil which entangled him was cut to pieces" (*ibid.*, 258). The effect confers rejuvenation on the whole pueblo. Betonie, the Chicano-Navajo shaman, affirms Tayo's agency as the lifeblood of the Laguna: "Only this growth keeps the ceremonies strong" (*ibid.*, 126).

## HISTORY AS PRISON

Confinement in *Almanac of the Dead* (1991), a grueling montage of crime and recompense, takes more punitive form than that of *Ceremony*. In the collapse of five centuries of white coercion and native serfdom, according to critic Epifanio San Juan, a Filipino American essayist, Silko generates change "in trajectories of activism and imagination that span both sides of the American hemispheres and penetrate up to the continental heartlands of Europe, Asia, and Africa" (San Juan, 1999, 103). Her characters face the felonious roundup of unwary border crossers by desert coyotes, the wheelchair existence of Vietnam War amputees, and Albert Fish's jailing for eating human flesh. Silko turns image into another form of cannibalism in the draining of life from homeless drug addicts who donate blood for pay at Eddie Trigg's clinic. After crawling through bullets and poisonous snakes in Vietnam, the veterans face an ignoble future—"to starve and sleep in a ditch when you got back home" (Silko, 1991, 741).

Focal characters sort through possible methods of emancipating themselves from unjust incarceration. Clinton, the urban black vindicator and leader of a grassroots revolt, enlightens Haitian blacks about their captivity in false history, which leaves them "secretly grieved for the spirits they believed had been lost or left behind in Africa centuries before" (*ibid.*, 747). Zeta, a gun runner and drug smuggler, looks to death to liberate her from the addiction to Percodan that imprisons her in the caretaker's regimen of injections and timekeeping. For Bartolomeo, the overbearing Cuban Marxist, a flurry of handbills immures him in charges of deceiving his followers as a double agent on the CIA payroll. Awaiting court-martial, he hears Angelita La Escapía, the relentless Mexican Indian ideologue, harangue her audience with a chronology of past crimes against Indians. While their world broadens with the possibilities of revolt and reclamation, Comrade Bartolomeo advances toward his nemesis, a gallows resembling "an elevated outdoor privy without its walls, with only a simple hole in the boards for the shit to drop through" (*ibid.*, 531). Appropriately, the lessening of the Cuban's time on earth causes him to wet his pants, an infantile reaction suited to his terror of hanging. Balancing these motifs of confinement, according to critic Caren Irr, an expert in contemporary literature at Brandeis University, Silko intersperses models of flight — Seese eludes a child kidnapper, Sterling returns to his Laguna roots, Grandmother Yoeme breaks out of prison, Calabazas's wife and lover help refugees escape, and Venezuelan architect Alegría Martinez-Soto Panson survives an unforeseen border crossing threatened by coyotes. The self-liberations create temporary release. However, for a nation mired in injustice, individual victories resolve nothing permanently (Irr, 1999, 229).

## THE COMMON BOND

The cascade of actions and reactions in the novel's resolution satirizes a world gone mad with mutiny. The Korean eco-warrior Awa Gee intercepts government messages about "sweeping arrests" of environmentalists from the Audubon Society and the U.S. Forest

Service (*ibid.*, 729). One of the fallen liberators, "a gay rights activist ill with AIDS," dies in the act of exploding Glen Canyon Dam to free the water for return to its original riverbed (*ibid.*, 729). A freedom fighters' song urges the wrapping of the body in plastic explosives for the infiltration and destruction of the U.S. Supreme Court building. SWAT teams of Tucson police seize children from homeless camps to place them in the protective custody of foster homes. While veterans build firebases and dig bunkers in cities, the Barefoot Hopi's plot to lead a nationwide jail and prison uprising calls for a clever ploy. Instead of dying boxed in urban tenements, the rioters plan "to park themselves smack in the middle of the rich man's backyard" to draw police firebombs onto the heads of the wealthy (*ibid.*, 747). In a satanic voice reminiscent of English playwright Christopher Marlowe's Mephistopheles, Angelita chortles, "All hell was going to break loose. The best was yet to come" (*ibid.*, 749).

Silko's esteem for peasant revolt evolves from her veneration of group action against overarching repression of women, children, and the underclass. In an interview with Ellen L. Arnold, an expert in ethnic studies at East Carolina University, Silko corroborates Angelita's "best" of the liberated future in a personal epiphany: "This won't happen because someone preached at you, threatened you with prison, put a gun to your head. No, you'll wake up [yourself]. It will come to you through dreams!" (Silko & Arnold, 2000, 145). Analyst San Juan explains that the author's view of global dethroning of the white overlord requires unification of fragmented, subjugated peoples and groups and a subalterns' crusade for the common good. Through dissonant voices, the dispossessed rebut nihilism in "the conflicted terrains of the United States, Latin America, and the geopolitical South in general" (San Juan, 1999, 108). Because of the odds and ends of personal grudges and individualized methods of fighting back against sophisticated oppressors, the push from the south approaches the American Southwest with a hideous clangor. The innocent, including baby Monte, die in the crush, but, according to Silko, the concerted press toward justice is worth self-sacrifice and martyrdom. The vigorous, dismaying conclusion to *Almanac of the Dead* corroborates the claims of Thomas Jefferson in 1787: "The tree of liberty must be refreshed from time to time with the blood of patriots and tyrants. It is its natural manure."

ENCLOSING NATURE

Keeping the theme of historical confinement, immurement in *Gardens of the Dunes*(1999) strays to the fencing and distortion of nature. Ironically, Big Candy, an Afro-Big Stick Indian cook, brewer, and casino manager, longs for the freedom of money to invest in his own restaurant in Denver. He works toward financial independence by milking the proceeds of an engineering project that dams the Colorado River, an emblem of indigenous peoples pressed into reservations and boarding schools. To the delight of Mr. Wiley, the site superintendent, "Business was growing faster and faster as more workers arrived" to erect the monster earthwork "to feed water to Los Angeles" (Silko, 1999, 211, 394). In the background of a superproject, Candy recalls his mother's mental torment that refused to alleviate her of white bondage: she "had been born into slavery, and after the emancipation she continued to reflect on her position as a slave and then as a free woman" (*ibid.*, 217). Unlike his physically and historically corralled mother, Big Candy chains himself to greed, an enslavement to a buried strongbox. Avarice causes him to discount his pregnant common law wife, Sister Salt, a laundress of the spiritually free Sand Lizard people. By shackling himself to the strongbox like Jacob Marley in Charles Dickens's *A Christ-*

*mas Carol* (1843), Candy loses sight of an invaluable human blessing, the birth of his son, the "little old grandfather," whom Indigo calls Bright Eyes (*ibid.*, 344). Meanwhile, Indigo conceals in private thoughts her prediction that the "dam would fill up with sand some-day; then the river would spill over it, free again" (*Ibid*, 218). By extension the prophecy includes the indigenous people, who will outwit and survive white colonizers.

Although the Sand Lizard clan occupies a dugout and cave, they enjoy remarkably free movement before their retreat to the hovel near the depot in Needles, California. In contrast to the swirling bodies and elevated arms of worshippers at the dance to bring the Messiah, Indigo struggles against the confinement of Indians at the Sherman Institute in Riverside, California, where Chemehuevi and Cocopa girls must wear prim dresses, shoes, and stockings, a uniform that restrains them from the freedom of shifts and sandals or bare feet. To halt Indigo's blast of dirty words and blasphemy against her evangelical jail-ers, the janitor locks her in the mop closet amid disinfectant and mildew. Like Grandma Fleet, Indigo runs at the first opportunity and confines herself to a citrus orchard, lilac bushes, and a glass greenhouse, a shelter she shares with Linnaeus, a caged monkey that perceives her need for freedom. Her selection of a place to hide from pursuers coincides with the attempts of Dr. Edward Palmer to cache valuable meteorites for sale. His venture to the Caribbean takes place during his recovery from a permanent leg injury incurred while he attempted to impound valuable orchids growing wild in the Rio Pará valley. His failure leaves him rueful that rare orchid specimens fall into the sea and others succumb to "a damp shed in Miami," an ignoble demise for rare South American beauties (*ibid.*, 77). The multiple captivities foreshadow the Palmers' imprisonment of Indigo in tempo-rary foster care and the foundering of their own confining wedlock.

## FROM JAIL TO FREEDOM

Silko's *Gardens in the Dunes* contrasts the temporary endangerment of life through jailing with the permanent destruction of justice from falsehood. Edward's bride, Hattie Abbott Palmer, challenges the constraints of sexist orthodoxy at Harvard Divinity School, where, like Linnaeus in his cage, she matriculates as a curiosity in a man's world. Retreat-ing into celibate matrimony, she shares Edward's home and gardens in Riverside until the couple takes Indigo to Europe. Edward's concealment of a plant-hunting trek outside Bas-tia, Corsica, leaves his wife and foster daughter unprepared for his arrest at the port of Livorno, Italy, for agricultural espionage and theft. As with other disasters in Silko's fiction, the detainment becomes a serendipity. Retained at the U.S. Embassy, Hattie realizes that Edward loves fame from biopiracy more than he treasures his wife and marriage. Indigo, a veteran of police and military raids of the dancers at Needles, California, cheers her fos-ter mother with incongruous advice: "At home people got arrested for no reason all the time. There was nothing to be ashamed of; this wasn't bad at all" (*ibid.*, 322). The state-ment begs the question of who mothers whom.

In a rebuttal of white materialism, Silko concludes *Gardens in the Dunes* with a joy-ous reunion of people who live for each other rather than for wealth or power. Upon return to the Southwest, Hattie and Indigo make their way toward Sand Lizard land, where open air and sky welcome them to emancipation from a controlling male. As a satiric comeup-pance to the duplicitous husband, Silko pictures his remains in a coffin chilled in an ice-house, a token of his cold heart. Freedom from Edward comes too late to save Hattie from his squandering of her inheritance. Connecting widowhood with solitude, she confesses to herself, "She was the one who no longer had a life to return to" (*ibid.*, 429). The liberated women — Hattie and her foster daughter — enjoy release from gender and social restraints. While Hattie recuperates in England from her bad marriage, her gift of a $50 bill frees Indigo and her reformed matrilineal clan — Sister Salt, Bright Eyes, Maytha, and Vedna — of the travail of poverty and entanglements with white coercion.

*See also* Indigo; Palmer, Hattie Abbott; Tayo.

· *References and further reading*

Fitz, Brewster E. *Silko: Writing Storyteller and Medicine Woman.* Norman: University of Oklahoma Press, 2004.

Irr, Caren. "The Timelessness of *Almanac of the Dead*, or a Postmodern Rewriting of Radical Fiction" in *Leslie Marmon Silko: A Collection of Critical Essays*, eds. Louise Barnett and James Thorson. Albuquerque: University of New Mexico Press, 1999.

Karem, Jeff. *The Romance of Authenticity: The Cultural Politics of Regional and Ethnic Literatures.* Charlottesville: University of Virginia Press, 2004.

San Juan, Epifanio. *Beyond Postcolonial Theory.* New York: St. Martin, 1999.

Silko, Leslie Marmon. *Almanac of the Dead.* New York: Simon & Schuster, 1991.

\_\_\_\_\_. *Ceremony.* New York: Viking, 1977.

\_\_\_\_\_. *Gardens in the Dunes.* New York: Scribner, 1999.

\_\_\_\_\_. *Storyteller.* New York: Seaver, 1981.

\_\_\_\_\_. *Yellow Woman and a Beauty of the Spirit: Essays on Native American Life Today.* New York: Simon & Schuster, 1996.

\_\_\_\_\_, and Ellen L. Arnold. *Conversations with Leslie Marmon Silko.* Jackson: University Press of Mississippi, 2000.

Shukla, Sanhya Rajendra, and Heidi Tinsman. *Imagining Our Americas: Toward a Transnational Frame.* Durham, NC: Duke University Press, 2007.

## creation

As a Laguna and a writer, Silko connects creative energy with renewal and hope. Rather than characterize clouds, rain, gardens, edible animals, and other spiritual gifts to humanity as "magic," she prefers the word "power" and blesses the female maker, I'tcts'ity'i (Reed Woman), co-creator of the universe with her sister Nau'ts'ity'i (Corn Woman), for generosity. Because the earth-shaper — Grandmother Spider (Ts'its'tsi'nako or Thought Woman), the mother of I'tcts'ity'i and Nau'ts'ity'i — is female, the trio's mythology is potent and eternal, like that of the Greek Fates, Atropos, Clotho, and Lachesis. Silko expert Brewster E. Fitz describes the goddess-made world as a web spun centripetally by Grandmother Spider. It "gathered toward a syncretic and ancestral figure: the writing storyteller," who generates "a written web in which nature cannot be conceived without culture and the oral cannot be unraveled from the written" (Fitz, 2004, 8). Because of its source in feminine consciousness, Laguna myth places no stigmas on females and femininity as weaker, less meaningful, or less intellectual than males. In *Yellow Woman and a Beauty of the Spirit: Essays on Native American Life Today* (1996), Silko exults that "the status of women is equal with the status of men, and women appear as often as men in the old stories as hero figures," particularly the adventurer Yellow Woman (Kochininako), the redeemer of her people (Silko, 1996, 70).

Silko's repetitive imagery attests to a belief that the unity of creation allies people with animals, fish, plants, clouds, water, and rocks. A generative rather than a punitive power, the act of creation through webbing unites the Laguna world, including "all sisters and brothers because the Mother Creator made all of us — all colors and all sizes" (*ibid.*, 63). Gayle Elliott, a critic from California State University, asserts that, according to Pueblo cosmotheology, each being is "able to function meaningfully only in conscious relation to the larger systems to which the individual belongs" (Eliott, 2008, 178). Those beings out of synchrony with creation voluntarily choose a discord that punishes the malcontent. In particular, Silko ridicules the avarice of the *conquistadores*, who interpreted desert petroglyphs of snakes as markers of buried treasure rather than their true purpose — icons pointing toward fresh water, the source of life in the desert. For natives who elect spirituality over greed, reverence for the great mother figure relieves them of fear because creation is a cyclical process. Silko describes how "all originate from the depths of the earth" and, in the end, "become dust, and in this becoming they are once more joined with the Mother" (Silko, 1996, 27). The statement redefines death from nothingness to a reunion with the prime mover, the original shaping force. Thus, nothing disappears from the universe. Rather than overawe mere mortals with incalculable power, the universe becomes a living entity governed by "balances and harmonies that ebb and flow" (*ibid.*, 64).

## COMMUNICATING WITH SPIRITS

The author states the importance to humankind of internalizing divine wisdom from creation and the self. In "Fifth World: The Return of Ma Ah Shra True Ee, the Giant Serpent" (1996), she sacralizes the appearance of a 30-foot stone snake formation at the Jackpile Mine as "a messenger for the Mother Creator" warning that continued removal of uranium disturbs planetary harmony (*ibid.*, 126). To assist the creative deity in restoring order, Silko urges humankind to glean cultural meaning from their own origination myths. As she explained to interviewers Larry Evers and Denny Carr, the result of personalizing stories is self-formation: "People tell those stories about you and your family or about others and they begin to create your identity. In a sense, you are told who you are, or you know who you are by the stories that are told about you" (Evers & Carr, 1976, 29–30). A crucial example from her girlhood hunting trips in "An Essay on Rocks" (1995), the story of her viewing of a bear and the mystery of its dual appearance as sleeping and dead anticipates a mysticism that pervades her adult experience. Her oneness with creation suggests a shamanic quality that tinges her writing, especially episodes with birds and rattlesnakes in her memoir, *The Turquoise Ledge* (2010). Views of her daily interaction with desert life corroborate a statement that she made in *Yellow Woman and a Beauty of the Spirit: Essays on Native American Life Today* (1996): "The myth, the web of memories and ideas that create an identity, is a part of oneself" (Silko, 1996, 43).

In *Ceremony* (1977), the roots of earthly life impinge on the consciousness of Tayo, Silko's first fully developed protagonist. A veteran of World War II, he returns to Laguna myth to account for and cope with a traumatic reality, the death of his cousin/foster brother Rocky during the Bataan Death March of April 1942. During a respite from postcombat sorrow, Tayo recalls his Uncle Josiah's reassuring words about the source of life. At a spring in a cave, Josiah siphons icy water into a barrel while reminding his nephew that the spring gave the Laguna their beginning: "This sand, this stone, these trees, the vines, all the wildflowers. This earth keeps us going" (Silko, 1977, 45). In explanation of drought and dust, like the Dust Bowl that overwhelmed the Southwest in the 1930s, Josiah blames people who forget their moorings, the down-deep roots, the "heartrock of the earth," that stabilize and sustain (*ibid.*, 46). From Josiah's mentoring come past memories that assuage Tayo's spirit and buttress his courage to face challenges that lie ahead for himself, his family, and his people. Critic Jean Ellen Petrolle, an expert on postmodern religion, notes, "To believe that words and stories can 'change the world' is to construct a cosmology in which language wields a power that is both pragmatic and miraculous"

(Petrolle, 2007, 148). To actualize the pueblo's oral tradition, Tayo must exert himself by walking bear tracks, engaging in the hoop ritual, and interpreting the sand painting of Betonie, the Chicano-Navajo shaman. Analyst Helen May Dennis explains that "Curing ceremonies work by ritual and artistic mimesis of the creation of the world" (Dennis, 2007, 143). By reliving the primeval surge of divine powers, Tayo allies with positive forces and revitalizes his spirit to inform his contemporaries of changes in the world order.

SYNCRETIC MYTHOS

Silko looks more closely at theology and cosmology in *Almanac of the Dead* (1991). For an expanded view of Amerindian creation lore, she merges the Aztec myth of Aztlán, the home of the Nahua, with Toltec stories of the creator Quetzalcoatl's earthly return to rejoin God's kingdom. According to analyst Claudia Sadowski-Smith, a humanities professor at Arizona State University, these emergence myths, blended with the Quiche Maya creation story and the fragmented remains of the Chilam Balam "[predict] the resurgence of indigenous peoples" from colonial oppression (Sadowski-Smith, 2008, 154). Because of the diversity of perspectives about earth's provenance, Silko reverences heterogeneity as humanity's founding strength, as intended by the creator. In the resolution of *Almanac*, Calabazas, Mosca, and other rabble-rousers debate the wisdom of the Barefoot Hopi, a preacher to nonwhite inmates in prisons. To Indians and Mexicans, he declares the basics of Silko's animistic beliefs: "Earth was their mother, but her land and water could never be desecrated; blasted open and polluted by man, but never desecrated. Man only desecrated himself in such acts" (Silko, 1999, 625). The evangelist insists that attempts at earthly sacrilege do not harm earth's integrity. Mosca makes a significant assertion about the Barefoot Hopi's teaching methods: he rejected the white man's "tortured Eurocentric speculations" about "whether [god] was one spirit with many dimensions or many spirits with singular dimensions" (Petrolle, 2007, 152). Silko depicts as superior to Christian polemics the Hopi's simple embrace of earthly permanence. Because the planet is alive, she explains, it is capable of reshaping itself, replicating the cataclysms of creation with earthquakes, landslides, tidal waves, and volcanoes, the beneficent upheavals of a loving god.

In *Gardens in the Dunes* (1999), Silko again examines multiple views of godhood, creation, worship, and salvation. For Dr. Edward Palmer, the beauty of the created world exhibited at Bath, England, makes little impact on his greedy spirit. He schemes to hybridize fragrant orchids to sell to California florists and to develop "a mathematical equation to predict winning hands at twenty-one," one of several get-rich-quick strategies that isolate him from other characters (Silko, 1999, 195). His machinations distance him from Indigo and his wife, Hattie Abbott Palmer, who absorb Aunt Bronwyn's landscaping feats in honor of male and female creative spirits of the Mediterranean and Celtic worlds. In contrast to the melding of statuary with orchardry and flowerbeds, orthodox Christianity stymies Hattie, a medieval scholar at a seminar on heresy hosted by Harvard Divinity School, with its inflexibility and static logic. In her defense, Silko's narrative retorts that Western religion is "exclusionary, patriarchal, sexually and culturally repressive, primarily linear, intolerant of difference, diversity, and metamorphosis" (Fitz, 2004, 194). Hattie pictures the "Just God of the Old Testament" as a "creative power with anger, jealousy, and the urge to punish, while the God of the New Testament was a Kind God, who sent his son to rescue mankind" through crucifixion (Silko, 1999, 99). By concluding that the angry god lost out to the just god, she surmises that the orthodox church rendered itself useless and its hierarchy, tithes, and laws superfluous. To quash her dissertation on Mary Magdalene's discipleship to Jesus, the androcentric reviewing committee at Harvard presents a set-in-stone interpretation of Genesis, in which disobedience to the divine creator results in the cursing of woman and the serpent.

Shards of fearful church teachings, along with Mrs. Abbott's experiences in labor, destroy Hattie's urge to procreate and reduce her marriage to a shadow play. Silko's denunciation of paternal discounting of women occurs during an interview with Ellen L. Arnold, an expert in ethnic studies at East Carolina University. Silko corroborates variant tales of Christ as "just as valid and powerful as other sightings and versions" (Silko & Arnold, 2000, 164). As a means of self-exoneration, Hattie finds her eyes turning from stereotypical church depictions of the Virgin Mary to primitive female creators. Hattie's mind retrieves Gnostic prayers to a mystic maternal deity: "My Mother, my Spirit ... who is before all things, Grace, Mother of Mythic Eternal Silence" (Silko, 1999, 450). The prayers isolate the central strength of the generative female, whom Hattie reverences as "Incorruptible Wisdom, Sophia, ... spirit is everything" (*ibid.*). Stripped of materialism because of Edward's profligacy with her inheritance, Hattie chooses spirituality over external rewards: "She'd rather wander naked as Isaiah for years in the wilderness than go back to Oyster Bay," the story's fount of elite, banal New Yorkers (*ibid.*, 452). Although parted from Indigo during her sojourn in Bath, Hattie clings to the great mother and supports the desert matriarchy with money and long-distance love.

*See also* myth.

• *References and further reading*
Barnett, Louise, and James Thorson, eds. *Leslie Marmon Silko: A Collection of Critical Essays*. Albuquerque: University of New Mexico Press, 1999.
Dennis, Helen May. *Native American Literature: Towards a Spatialized Reading*. New York: Taylor & Francis, 2007.
Eliott, Gayle. "Silko, Le Sueur, and Le Guin: Storytelling as a 'Movement Toward Wholeness'" in *Scribbling Women & the Short Story Form: Approaches by American & British Women Writers*, ed. Ellen Burton Harrington. New York: Peter Lang, 2008, 178–192.
Evers, Larry, and Denny Carr. "A Conversation with Leslie Marmon Silko," *Sun Tracks* 3:1 (Fall 1976): 28–33.
Fitz, Brewster E. *Silko: Writing Storyteller and Medicine Woman*. Norman: University of Oklahoma Press, 2004.
Petrolle, Jean. *Religion without Belief: Contemporary Allegory and the Search for Postmodern Faith*. Albany: State University of New York Press, 2007.
Sadowski-Smith, Claudia. *Border Fictions: Globalization, Empire, and Writing at the Boundaries of the United States*. Charlottesville: University of Virginia Press, 2008.
Silko, Leslie Marmon. *Ceremony*. New York: Viking Press, 1977.
_____. *Yellow Woman and a Beauty of the Spirit: Essays on Native American Life Today*. New York: Simon & Schuster, 1996.
_____, and Ellen L. Arnold. *Conversations with Leslie Marmon Silko*. Jackson: University Press of Mississippi, 2000.
White, Daniel. "Antidote to Desecration: Leslie Marmon Silko's Nonfiction" in *Leslie Marmon Silko: A Collection of Critical Essays*, eds. Louise Barnett and James Thorson. Albuquerque: University of New Mexico Press, 1999.

# death

Images and episodes of suffering and death bind Silko's thoughts to the impermanence of earthly life, particularly for the oppressed and downtrodden. More fearful to Amerindians is the erasure of a people, a cultural demise that ends an indigenous tradition. She stresses the cyclical nature of human generations in the coming-of-age story "Humaweepi, the Warrior Priest" (1974), which prefigures the old-with-young mentorship of Grandma Fleet to indigo and Sister Salt in *Gardens in the Dunes* (1999). The title figure, a 19-year-old orphan and apprentice to his elderly uncle, recognizes advancing age in his mentor's face and skin. The change in the two men strengthens Humaweepi, who emulates his uncle's ritual songs, chants, and prayers. At a lakeside epiphany, instinctively, the youth steps into the role of Pueblo priest and lover of the mother creator. By internalizing the uncle's character and godliness, Humaweepi immortalizes the old man's good qualities, symbolized by the totemic power of the bear.

Silko's first novel, *Ceremony* (1977), shifts perspective to a child. The loss of a parent overwhelms Tayo, a fatherless illegitimate son of "little sister" Laura. In a house dominated by a religious fanatic, Auntie Thelma, an unloving aunt/foster mother, after Christmas 1926, Tayo returns from Laura's burial in a sand storm and retreats into the darkness, a symbol of survivor's despair. As though wrapping himself in a winding sheet, the four-year-old stuffs blankets around his torso to comfort his heart from "regret for things which could not be changed" (Silko, 1977, 73). The finality of orphaning introduces his immature understanding to the impermanence of earthly contentment. The search for security and belonging dominates the next two decades. While Tayo and his cousin/foster brother Rocky oil their rifles on a nameless Pacific island in spring 1942, Tayo ponders the blotching of corpses, even white infantrymen, who cease to contrast men of color. The universality of human corruption comes as a revelation: "There was no difference when they were swollen and covered with flies" (*ibid.*, 7). The statement reprises Shakespeare's comment in *King Lear*: "As flies to wanton boys are we to th' gods,/They kill us for their sport" (IV, i, 36–37).

## THE WALKING WOUNDED

The response to the threat of capture and torture and to the mangling of bodies by bombs, mortars, and grenades becomes routine to American soldiers fighting the Pacific war. As Tayo's hold on sanity slips after Rocky's death from a grenade wound to the leg during the Bataan Death March of April 1942, Tayo weeps for executed Japanese soldiers because they morph into Uncle Josiah. Fellow infantrymen dismiss Tayo's hallucination as a normal part of combat fatigue for front-line GIs, who fear what the ancient Norse called the "sleep of the sword." The concept dates to the American Civil War, when military physician Jacob Mendes Da Costa called the syndrome "effort syndrome," "nostalgia," "irritable heart," or "soldier's heart," a romanticized diagnosis of a wartime neurosis. The complex form of exhaustion, insomnia, and anxiety resulted from gross life-threatening bombardment by cannon, Gatling guns, and repeating rifles. Witnesses recoiled physically and psychologically from hideous maiming and the decapitation and dismemberment of combat casualties and civilians. Renamed "shell shock," "war neurosis," or "battle fatigue" during World War I by psychiatrist Charles Samuel Myers, the terms for stress breakdowns gave place in 1952 at the peak of the Korean War to "stress response syndrome" or "gross stress reaction," a response retiring men from close combat to behind-the-lines treatment. In 1968 at the height of the Vietnam War, military psychiatrists re-examined "transient situational disorders" and adopted the term "post–Vietnam syndrome" or "post-traumatic stress disorder" (PTSD), reduced in the vernacular to the "walking wounded." Victims like Tayo relived horrors in flashbacks and dreams. Acute PTSD dogged their consciousness for up to three months; chronic disturbance lasted longer, robbing Veterans of hopes for loving family relationships and productive lives. Helpless against the onslaught of memories, they numbed themselves to everyday stimuli by avoiding people and activities. Easily startled, Tayo becomes irritable and hypervigilant and suffers dizziness, vomiting, and ambient fevers as his mental warfare stretches into 1948.

The psychotic state, symptomized by tension, delusions, anger, and hyperawareness, can extend for life, resulting in chronic digestives ills and night sweats, alcoholism, drug addiction, accidents, bullying, spousal and child abuse, criminal assault, and suicide. For Tayo, as his mind recoils from the reality of incinerating civilian Japanese with the atomic bomb on August 6 and 8, 1945, the symptoms take the form of fog and smoke, an incorporeal state that denies him substance and color. From age 20, when he enters a Japanese prison camp, he loses identity, becoming neither Indian nor obedient American soldier. At the Los Angeles depot, the gateway to freedom from military control at a veterans' hospital, he struggles with vagueness and hollowness, fearful that he will slip into invisibility again. He anticipates that death will come "the way smoke dies, drifting away in currents of air, twisting in thin swirls" before fading into oblivion (*ibid.*, 17). Still possessed of humanity, he fights against dissolving into a state of nothingness, much as the Japanese of Hiroshima and Nagasaki burned to ash. Contributing to his confusion is the nearness of "top-secret laboratories where the bomb had been created ... on land the Government took from Cochiti Pueblo" (*ibid.*, 228). To renew life, Silko centers his struggle at the Jackpile mine, the source of uranium for weapons of mass destruction. At a satisfying "aha" moment, he weeps with catharsis and realizes, "He was not crazy; he had never been crazy" (*ibid.*, 246). The realization rids him of death in life. In the explanation of Kathleen Glenister Roberts, a specialist in rhetorical studies at Duquesne University, Tayo is able to rid himself of false notions and become "part of a collective" (Roberts, 2008, 114).

LIFE LETTERS

In subsequent works, Silko defied nihilism. To her mentor, poet James Wright, she wrote a series of letters to which he replied over an 18-month period. Collected in *The Delicacy and Strength of Lace: Letters between Leslie Marmon Silko and James Wright* (1986), the epistolary relationship captures a mutual belief that the spirit is deathless. Silko asserts that love transcends annihilation: "Love continues in both directions— it is required by the spirits of those dear ones who send blessings back to us," a concept of two-way communication with the departed that explains Tayo's hallucination of Uncle Josiah in the Philippines ("Fatal," 1992). She identifies the beneficence of spiritual visitations as a refreshing rain bearing "the feeling of continuity and closeness as well as ... past memories" (*ibid.*) The relationship of ancestral and present lives, she notes, includes the beloved as well as adversaries: "People still speak of old enemies as if the battle continues," a reference that explains Tayo's ongoing efforts to ward off Japanese captors and to retrieve Rocky from further harm (*ibid.*). With similar dedication, Silko bears the burden of uplifting Jim, her correspondent, in his final bout with throat and tongue cancer. With a flippant wit, she relates a series of close calls experienced by octogenarian Hugh Crooks, who survived tuberculosis, cirrhosis of the liver, a gunshot wound to the chest, pneumonia, and cancer of the gums. Her seriocomic example asserts the human knack for fighting cyclical threats to life.

Throughout the text of letters between Silko and Wright, the solace from both sides of an intergender relationship strengthens and heartens both writers. Jim does his part to comfort Silko from the bruising and shattering of divorce and a lost child custody battle for Robert Chapman, her elder son. For both correspondents, expressions of mortality require metaphors of advocacy and aspiration, expressed in Silko's fool tale about a Hopi bachelor posing as a medicine man. In the saga of a rooster and the stalking coyotes, she showcases the epitome of roosterhood — the "rooster out of all the rooster stories" she heard in childhood (Silko & Wright, 1986, 6). Like Geoffrey Chaucer's cocky Chauntecleer, the rooster wards off disaster with cunning: "He has all of us fooled, stepping around him softly, hesitant to turn our backs on him," a subtextual reference to the human avoidance of imminent demise (*ibid.*, 7). After Jim loses his powers of speech from surgery and cancer treatment, Silko rejects his fear that mortality has silenced him. She asserts that hearts have their own method of communicating. Analyst Caroline Joyce Simon notes the writers' even reciprocity: "Overall the friendship is (as Aristotle thinks all friendship must be) a relationship of equality in which help-giving is mutual" (Simon, 1997, 157). Within days of Jim's death, according to Silko's memoir *The Turquoise Ledge* (2010), a visit from a burrowing owl communicates the poet's nearness to his friend.

URBAN WAR

The text of Silko's *Almanac of the Dead* (1991), a doom-laden historical novel, depicts violence and murder as the expected adjuncts of career criminality, which is a form of death in life. Max "Mr. Murder" Blue, a Mafioso and contract assassin, rationalizes "Don't play if you can't pay" (Silko, 1991, 354). At murder scenes, after shooting the victim in the neck four times with a cheap .22 rifle and burning the corpse with gasoline, his subcontractor leaves a printed card as Max's token of a successful assassination. The concealment of incriminating evidence makes Mr. Murder "a scholar, an expert in a very narrow field" (*ibid.*). Silko juxtaposes harsh images of Uncle Mike Blue's hit squad murder and Max's recovery among the living dead in a veterans' hospital. For Max, death is the absolute nothingness, a dark termination of being and beginning of decay that a visit by a priest cannot allay. Two close calls — a plane crash and a bullet to the back and left shoulder — leave Max wondering, "How many chances did Death get in five years? What kind of lottery was it anyway? ... How many times, how many ways, did a man die?" (*ibid.*, 352–353). Recovery consists of drifting in and out of consciousness on painkillers and Max's meditations on violent death, including the one he orchestrated long distance from a telephone booth in Long Beach, California. The text wrests irony from the career killer's up-close confrontation with his own end-time.

Replicating the blood culture of ancient Mexico City, Silko dramatizes bloodletting as a social and religious ritual. Iliana Gutiérrez Panson, homeowner of a showy mansion facing the jungle, unconsciously choreographs self-sacrifice on the altar of money. By designing a polished marble staircase that "took no account of a person's natural stride," she mimics the ceremonial design of death altars on Mayan pyramids, modeled on the precise plazas at Palenque and Uxmal, Mexico (*ibid.*, 300). Limned in natural light, the setting, a testimonial to her self-aggrandizement, suits her fall and death, which precede her husband Menardo Panson's marriage to Alegría Martinez-Soto, Venezuelan architect educated in Madrid. Incapable of sorrow for Iliana, Menardo dismisses the foreshortened life with banality: "Everybody had to die sometime" (*ibid.*, 301). Because of the instability of his second marriage after a lengthy infidelity to his first, he enrobes himself in magic, the bulletproof vest that protects him from a crimeland execution. In an ironic self-sacrifice, he courts death from his own gun, which he places in the hand of Tacho, his Mayan driver. To Tacho's laughter, Menardo retorts, "Indians such as Tacho stayed poor because they feared progress and modern technology" (*ibid.*, 500). The shooting restores order as the Mayan chauffeur and spy extinguishes the life of the arrogant insurance broker, a *mestizo* who denies his ethnic roots and his undeniable Indian flat nose. Much as the fall from the staircase erases Iliana, Menardo's testing of the vest obliterates a man who erased himself throughout adulthood by rejecting his race and culture.

## Death and the Beyond

Silko presents a gentler view of death with the utopic plans of Laguna laborer Sterling's Aunt Marie, who relishes the thought of dying. After her sisters, Nora and Nita, depart for "Cliff House," a euphemism for residence in the afterlife, Marie looks forward to exiting the pueblo. Death offers escape from her 59-year-old nephew's shame at being exiled because he betrays his people to Hollywood filmmakers. Instead of a climate of gossip, Marie anticipates making "tamales, the first thing, because tamales require many hands" (*Almanac of the Dead*, 1991, 97). The vision of cooking in heaven allies Marie with community, the pueblo lifestyle that Sterling denigrates. In an accompanying essay, the author explains that souls like those of Nita and Nora continue their ordinary activities at Cliff House. Neither in heaven or hell in the Christian sense of death, without fear of annihilation, the departed live in an eternal present moment among friends and ancestors long gone. Critic David Mogen added a technical explanation of Pueblo cosmotheology: "Time is cyclic rather than linear, causality derives from spirit rather than mechanism, and even in apocalypse nothing is destroyed, only changed" (Mogen, 2005, 161).

Silko depicts wraiths in a variety of poses—sinister, convivial, conferring blessing, or lost in the nether world. She contributes the connection between spirits and snakes in Yoeme's conversations with a bull snake. Because of contact with the ground and hibernation in holes and crevices, the snake hears "the voices of the dead: actual conversations, and lone voices calling out to loved ones still living" (Silko, 1991, 130). Unlike Catholic priests, who kill snakes as tokens of Old Testament lore about duplicity and temptation in the Garden of Eden, Yoeme reverences reptiles for eavesdropping on adulterers and for hearing confessions from arsonists and killers. To establish trust in the living, the great bull snake coils near Yoeme to listen to the rhythm of respiration and heartbeat.

The novel discloses the joyous native afterlife in the dreams of Calabazas, a Yaqui smuggler and drug dealer. He believes that his short spans of sleep preface the soul's approach to death. Restlessness and roaming prepare him "for all eternity where the old people believed no one would rest or sleep but would range over the earth" (*ibid.*, 235). The rovings take spirits into nature's heartland, among clouds, tides, animal migrations, and heavenly bodies. The absorption of the soul into all creation comforts Calabazas, as does the prophecy that white dominion will vanish from the land. Silko explains the collapse of the white world in eco-religious terms—European Christian invaders "failed to recognize the earth was their mother" (*ibid.*, 258). The denial of the Mother Creator destabilizes their communion with nature, causing them to spread death over the land through pollution and the wasting of water and resources that sustain life.

The author returns to the topic of death as a philosophical divide between whites and Indians. In *Yellow Woman and a Beauty of the Spirit: Essays on Native American Life Today* (1996), she meditates on the custom of ancient Pueblo of burying their dead in vacant rooms in loose clay and sand. According to the essay "Interior and Exterior Landscapes," survivors express their love and respect by affixing rocks into walls with adobe mortar. She explains that "East rock had been carefully selected for size and shape, then chiseled to an even face" where the remains "[rested] at a midpoint in their journey back to dust" (Silko, 1996, 26). Literary analyst Hertha Dawn Wong explains, "Memory, of course, is crucial to the continuance of the oral tradition," which incorporates the actions of spirits among narratives of the living (Wong, 1992, 196). The reverence for earth and the nitrogen cycle exhibits the involvement of first peoples in the progressive renewal of earth through the animals, plants, and minerals that share human fate. As critic Linda Krumholz explains, the nearness of tribe members and their life stories is essential to longevity: "The real threat to Indians—and to all of us—is not physical death but spiritual and cultural death; that the stories and the shared knowledge, as well as the imaginative and ethical power they convey and continue, is the essence of Indianness" (Krumholz, 1999, 78). So long as the artifacts remain and the stories survive, the Pueblo are immortal.

In *The Turquoise Ledge* (2010), Silko maintains optimism that the earth absorbs goodness, much as Humaweepi internalizes his uncle's religiosity, Tayo acquires courage and vision from Uncle Josiah, and Indigo and Sister Salt learn from Mama and Grandma Fleet to respect the rattlesnake that rules over the Sand Lizards' spring. Indigo and her older sister learn by example the reverence necessary for beneficent forebears because "Grandma Fleet and others still visited their old houses to feed the ancestor spirits" (Silko, 1999, 15). Respect for the dead involves sensitivity to a presence of the deceased, who live on in wise mottos, dreamscapes, health directives and cures, and examples of frugality and caution. The author asserts the fusion of past and present: "We aren't dead for long before we become part of the living creatures and plants," a statement recalling Grandma Fleet's survival in instructional lessons internalized by her sorrowing granddaughters, who "do as she did" (Silko, 2010, 166, 45). The author later explains her views on the desert predator cycle: The feeding of the living on the deceased is "the only consolation the desert offers for death" (*ibid.*, 235). As moist air precedes a rainstorm, the author walks her yard and relishes the enveloping strength of nature. Without belaboring the approach of old age and death, she exults in regeneration with the lyricism of the psalmist David or naturalist Edwin Muir: "In that beauty we all will sink slowly back into the lap of the Earth" (Silko, 2010, 236).

*See also* violence.

• *References and further reading*

Beidler, Peter G. "Bloody Mud, Rifle Butts, and Barbed Wire: Transforming the Bataan Death March in Silko's *Ceremony,*" *American Indian Culture and Research Journal* 28:1 (2004): 23–33.

"Fatal Flaw Kills 'Dead' as It Offers Apologia for Yaqui People," *Washington* (D.C.) *Times* (19 January 1992).

Horvitz, Deborah M. *Literary Trauma: Sadism, Memory, and Sexual Violence in American Women's Fiction.* Albany: State University of New York Press, 2000.

Krumholz, Linda J. "Native Designs: Silko's *Storyteller* and the Reader's Initiation," *Leslie Marmon Silko: A Collection of Critical Essays,* eds. Louise Barnett and James Thorson. Albuquerque: University of New Mexico Press, 1999.

Miura, Noriko. *Marginal Voice, Marginal Body: The Treatment of the Human Body in the Works of Nakagami Kenji, Leslie Marmon Silko, and Salman Rushdie* (Thesis, 2000), http://books.google.com, accessed July 12, 2010.

Mogen, David. "Native American Vision of Apocalypse: Prophecy and Protest in the Fiction of Leslie Marmon Silko and Gerald Vizenor" in *American Mythologies: Essays in Contemporary Literature,* ed. William Blazek. Liverpool, UK: Liverpool University Press, 2005.

Roberts, Kathleen Glenister. *Alterity and Narrative: Stories and the Negotiation of Western Identities.* Albany: State University of New York Press, 2008.

Schorcht, Blanca. *Stories Voices in Native American Texts: Harry Robinson, Thomas King, James Welch, and Leslie Marmon Silko.* New York: Routledge, 2003.

Silko, Leslie Marmon. *Almanac of the Dead.* New York: Simon & Schuster, 1991.

_____. *Ceremony.* New York: Viking, 1977.

_____. *Gardens in the Dunes.* New York: Scribner, 1999.

_____. *The Turquoise Ledge: A Memoir.* New York: Viking, 2010.

_____. *Yellow Woman and a Beauty of the Spirit: Essays on Native American Life Today*. New York: Simon & Schuster, 1996.

_____, and James Wright. *The Delicacy and Strength of Lace: Letters between Leslie Marmon Silko and James Wright*. St. Paul, MN: Graywolf, 1986.

Simon, Caroline Joyce. *The Disciplined Heart: Love, Destiny, and Imagination*. Grand Rapids, MI: W. B. Eerdmans, 1997.

Wong, Hertha D. *Sending My Heart Back across the Years: Tradition and Innovation in Native American Autobiography*. New York: Oxford University Press, 1992.

# duality

Silko resurrects a pre–Columbian literary convention by double-voicing her works. Until colonization by Europeans, Indians produced no equivalent to the individual ego of Western tradition. In obedience to indigenous philosophy, they pursued a double consciousness, a rhetorical technique identified and labeled by anthropologists as a bicultural awareness of the role of self within the tribe. As Silko explains in *Yellow Woman and a Beauty of the Spirit: Essays on Native American Life Today* (1996), "Whatever the event or the subject, the ancient people perceived the world and themselves within the world as part of an ancient, continuous story composed of innumerable bundles of other stories" (Silko, 1996, 30–31). Thus, taking action involved decision-making suited to personal needs and to the welfare of the tribe. By seeing themselves as single beings and as part of a progression of indigenous people, Indians acquired a respect for the past and future in which each person played an integral part.

According to *Storyteller* (1981), for Silko and her Aunt Susie Reyes Marmon, conflicting world views began in white schools, where, according to Silko expert Brewster E. Fitz, they and other Indian girls absorbed both "Pueblo oral and Western literate" awareness (Fitz, 2004, 252). Significant to white pedagogy, lessons in Western lore superseded the lore Indians absorbed in early childhood, for example, episodes of the legendary Geronimo versus the Apache chief depicted in American history. Analyst Helen May Dennis, a literary scholar at Warwick University, remarked on the sober intent of native folktellers: "Stories are told not for amusement, but to hold the fabric of human society together and to remind us of our place in the larger landscape" (Dennis, 2007, 61). For vulnerable 20th-century children like Silko and her sisters, Gigi and Wendy Marmon, Aunt Susie became the bridge between dual global perspectives, the gifted storyteller who revered accounts of Ts'its'tsi'nako (Thought Woman) and Kochininako (Yellow Woman) and who also read world literature and history in print. Thus, in the words of analyst David Seed, people like Aunt Susie maintained a balanced perspective: "Awareness never deteriorated into Cartesian duality [of sacred versus profane], cutting off the human from the natural world" (Seed, 2010, 186). Rather, Aunt Susie and her clan respected a vast kinship among beings and species, whether human or animal, vegetable or mineral, living or dead.

## DUAL EXISTENCE

In her first novel, *Ceremony* (1977), a meta-fiction that oscillates between myth and history, Silko reveals the difficulty of existing in the "fifth world," a Laguna term for earthly reality (Silko, 1977, 68). In fealty to clan configuration and values, members abide by a tight structuring of human behavior, an obligation to rightness that casts guilt over Auntie Thelma for her "little sister" Laura's drunkenness and promiscuity with white and Mexican males. Living in the fifth world after Western colonization requires a juggling of divergent mindsets. Armed with a double list of animal, plant, and topographical terms and human surnames in English and Laguna, Indians maneuver through antipathetic philosophies—the salvation of the elect in Christian cosmogeny and the animistic belief in a loving mother creator who embraces all her children. As Laura reaches maturity in high school, she flirts with white man and discovers that their smiles conceal viciousness and lust. Ambivalence toward white and Laguna societies fills her with internal anarchy. Silko imagines the turmoil as "monstrous twins that would have to be left in the hills to die," an allusion to the fates of Greek Oedipus Rex, the Trojan prince Paris, and Romulus and Remus, the mythic founders of Rome (*ibid.*, 69). Laura's social infraction alienates her not only from her household and older sister but from the whole village. For Auntie Thelma, collecting gossip and antipathy from villagers is like gathering willow twigs for a prayer bundle. As she grasps at strands of local approbation, she finds neighborhood feelings too tangled and contorted with Caucasian taboos for her control. Bound by a duality of heart, she trudges to Catholic Mass to cleanse herself of failing a Pueblo obligation to discipline her younger sibling.

Auntie Thelma's dilemma sheds light on the struggles of the protagonist, who views his options in terms of untangling the spools of thread snarled in his grandmothers sewing basket. For Tayo, a veteran of the Pacific war, recovery from battle fatigue must cut through the complexity of native healing, which relies on primeval meanings of Laguna words. The first practitioner, the Laguna shaman Ku'oosh, fails to connect with Tayo because of the old man's dependence on ancient etymology: "The word he chose to express 'fragile' was filled with the intricacies of a continuing process, and with a strength inherent in spider webs woven across paths through sand hills where early in the morning the sun becomes entangled in each filament of web. It took a long time to explain the fragility and intricacy because no word exists alone" (*ibid.*, 35). In expressing the nature of Tayo's vulnerability, Ku'oosh loses traction because of Tayo's inadequate knowledge of Laguna language and myth. In the analysis of Winfried Siemerling, a professor of North American studies at the Université de Sherbrooke in Quebec, Tayo fails to apply communal knowledge —"a dual temporal structure in which the disturbances and imbalances in the contemporary present and immediate past [refer to] equivalent events in the 'traditional past'" (Siemerling, 2005, 74). Lacking a perception of the mythic Ts'its'tsi'nako, the Laguna spider deity who spins webs into life narratives, Tayo misunderstands the organic nature of tribal thought — how words make stories and stories make worlds.

## THE INDIAN WARRIOR AND SAVANT

Only after trial and error does Tayo rid himself of torpor and purify himself of self-blame by acting out a prophecy from the Chicano-Navajo medicine man Betonie. The healer's helter-skelter hogan bemuses the patient with its jumble of parcels, bags, hides, telephone books, and Coke bottles, a symbol of the old man's dual cultural membership and his belief that Tayo must learn to navigate the present world with wisdom from the past. Unlike military psychiatrists who force the veteran into a treatment based on medical theory, Betonie believes in reality therapy via graphic direction: "All these things have stories in them" that direct wanderers over the maze of the future (Silko, 1977, 121). Soothed by the old man's relaxed counsel, Tayo confides his hallucination of seeing Uncle Josiah die in battle in 1942 in the Pacific. According to analyst Berenice Walther of the University of Munster, Germany, the confused memory leaves Tayo "standing in the story of his life" unaware that he is "part of something larger, a piece of the ceremony," a ritual that brings forgiveness and restores well being (Walther, 2006, 13, 14).

Silko pictures Tayo as a dazed bystander pushed to the front lines. By viewing the two purposes of narrative — a relic of the past and a pattern for the future — he activates himself in his unfolding autobiography. The symbolic route of a sand painting and bear tracks takes Tayo through the four cardinal directions — north, south, east, and west — by which he eludes capture by military authorities for return to the veterans' hospital. At first, he delights in reunion with his fellow veterans, then realizes an existential truth: "He knew that they were not his friends but had turned against him" (Silko, 1977, 242). Silko embroiders the scene with a verse meditation on betrayal: "Whirling darkness/has come back on itself./It keeps all its witchery/to itself" (Silko, 1977, 261). On the autumnal equinox of September 22–23, 1948, Tayo survives the implosion of the male support group by rejecting violence as an antidote to battle fatigue. Three die — Harley, Leroy Valdez, and cousin Pinkie — and a fourth, Emo, enters exile for murder, leaving Tayo as the tribe's spokesman for a generation of veterans of World War II.

Tayo's coming to knowledge takes him from sunrise to darkness and back again to recover Uncle Josiah's wild Mexican speckled longhorns, the family's investment in the future. His muse, Ts'eh Montaño, explains the necessity of reclaiming the stolen herd: "The destroyers: they work to see how much can be lost, how much can be forgotten. They destroy the feeling people have for each other" (*ibid.*, 229). After Tayo synchronizes his consciousness with the tribal mindset, he is able to celebrate sunrise as the death of "the way of witchery" and an epiphany of the unending future (*ibid.*, 253). The narrative rewards Tayo with a dual tribal function — a veteran reporting on Indian soldiery in a world war and a storyteller imparting wisdom to tribal elders. Significant to nonlinear history, he sits alone in the kiva and surveys its geometric form, a circle with no beginning or end.

## BLENDED MYTH

The growth of the American consciousness through fusion takes on crucial meaning in *Almanac of the Dead* (1991) and *Gardens in the Dunes* (1999), in which past and present sins encroach on the survival of disparate peoples. The text of *Postcolonialisms: An Anthology of Cultural Theory and Criticism* (2005) notes that the "apparent duality of social assimilation and resistance entails a metacommunication," a talking across borders that facilitates Americans, Indians, and Mesoamericans who thrash out syncretic strategies for coexistence and change (Desai & Nair, 2005, 300). In *Almanac*, for strength, prophecy, and direction, the populace of a deteriorating milieu around Tucson, Arizona, looks to past myth from the Aztec stories of Aztlán, the home of the Nahua, Toltec episodes of the creator Quetzalcoatl's earthly return, Quiche Maya creation lore, and fragments of the Chilam Balam texts. In *Gardens*, Sister Salt profits from an alliance with a comic duo, Maytha and Vedna, Chemehuevi-Laguna laundresses and comfort girls from Winslow, Arizona, whose knowledge of other tribes and of white abuses assists Sister Salt in acclimating to a perplexing riverside culture. Vedna shares her reading skills with sexy stories from the Old Testament and the Hebrew wonder tales of "Chariots of fire! Beasts with seven heads!" (Silko, 1999, 334).

Analysts Angela L. Cotten and Christa Davis Acampora account for the vigor of multiculturalism, an elided world energy that Silko shares with authors Toni Morrison, Olaudah Equiano, and Zora Neale Hurston: "For Silko, people of African and indigenous American descent are connected, not only through a shared history of white/western oppression and cultural similarities, but also by larger, unseen forces and cosmic entities" (Cotten & Acampora, 2007, 10). Critics Tiya Miles and Sharon Patricia Holland esteem the cover of *Almanac of the Dead* by Lakota artist Francis J. Yellow, who coordinates pictographs to explain shared world views in his drawing "First They Made Prayers, and They Sang and They Danced and Then They Made Relatives" (Miles & Holland, 2006, 13). Silko creates irony out of the emergence of African lore from former slaves: "Right then the magic had happened: great American and great African tribal cultures had come together to create a powerful consciousness within all people" (Silko, 1991, 416). As the Yaqui join Mexicans in marching north to the U.S. border, authors Sandhya Rajendra Shukla, an Americanist at the University of Virginia, and Heidi Tinsman, a history professor at the University of California at Irvine, recognize the centrality of Clinton, the urban black vindicator and rebel leader who orchestrates change. Like Caliban, the primitive slave in William Shakespeare's *The Tempest* (1611), Clinton binds in resistance racial entities who reconfigure polyculturalism, a "New World as a new utopia, a place for uprooted Europeans to start over and to construct new and ideal societies" (Shukla & Tinsman, 2007, 193). The syncretism of black with Indian recurs in *Gardens in the Dunes* in the common law marriage of laundress Sister Salt with Big Candy, the Afro–Big Stick Indian cook, brewer, and casino director who fathers their biracial son, Bright Eyes, the first male born to the Sand Lizard clan.

In the 21st century, Silko continues to locate strength in the melding of entities. In her perusal of two Nahuatl dictionaries in *The Turquoise Ledge* (2010), she seeks inspiration from an unknown language that epitomizes the absorption of the tribal member into the clan. By reading alphabetically, column by column, she studies the development of complex words from morphemes (fundamental units of meaning), such as *cacahtli* (toad) and *cacacuicatl* (toad song), a signifier of seasonal change. The extension of fundamental terms through metaphoric combination echoes the Old Norse concept of kenning, which perceives "sun" as "sky-candle," "ship" as "sea-steed," "king" as "ring-giver," and "god" as "giant-slayer." She combines *mixtli* (cloud) and *coatl* (snake) into *mixcoatl*, a cloud companion who is also an ancestor or ghost warrior. The connection between *celiya* (to sprout) and the return of a ghost warrior leads her to *cempohualxochitli* (marigold or revenant warrior) as well as *calli* (house) and *mixcocacalli* (house of the cloud companions). Because of the dual meanings, she concludes that "revenants hold a central position in the Nahua cosmology" (Silko, 2010, 242–243). The observation connects her verbal exercises with Amerindian dualities of past and present.

*See also* hypocrisy; language; siblings; storytelling.

• *References and further reading*

Caton, Louis Freitas. *Reading American Novels and Multicultural Aesthetics: Romancing the Postmodern Novel.* New York: Palgrave Macmillan, 2008.

Cotten, Angela L., and Christa Davis Acampora. *Cultural Sites of Critical Insight: Philosophy, Aesthetics, and African American and Native American Women's Writings.* Albany: State University of New York Press, 2007.

Desai, Gaurav Gajanan, and Supriya Nair. *Postcolonialisms: An Anthology of Cultural Theory and Criticism.* New Brunswick, NJ: Rutgers University Press, 2005.

Dennis, Helen May. *Native American Literature; Towards a Spatialized Reading.* New York: Taylor & Francis, 2007.

Fitz, Brewster E. *Silko: Writing Storyteller and Medicine Woman.* Norman: University of Oklahoma Press, 2004.

Miles, Tiya, and Sharon Patricia Holland. *Crossing Waters, Crossing Worlds: The African Diaspora in Indian Country.* Durham, NC: Duke University Press, 2006.

Seed, David. *A Companion to Twentieth-Century United States Fiction.* Malden, MA: Wiley-Blackwell, 2010.

Shukla, Sanhya Rajendra, and Heidi Tinsman. *Imagining Our Americas: Toward a Transnational Frame.* Durham, NC: Duke University Press, 2007.

Siemerling, Winfried. *The New North American Studies: Culture, Writing and the Politics of Re/cognition.* New York: Routledge, 2005.

Silko, Leslie Marmon. *Almanac of the Dead.* New York: Simon & Schuster, 1991.

_____. *Ceremony.* New York: Viking, 1977.

_____. *Gardens in the Dunes.* New York: Scribner, 1999.

_____. *Storyteller.* New York: Seaver, 1981.

_____. *The Turquoise Ledge.* New York: Viking, 2010.

_____. *Yellow Woman and a Beauty of the Spirit: Essays on Native American Life Today.* New York: Simon & Schuster, 1996.

Stigter, Shelley. *Double-Voice and Double-Consciousness in Native American Literature* (thesis). Lethbridge, Alta.: University of Lethbridge, 2005.

Walther, Berenice. *Storytelling in Leslie Marmon Silko's Ceremony.* Munich: Ravensburg Grin Verl, 2006.

Weso, Thomas F. "From Delirium to Coherence: Shamanism and Medicine Plans in Silko's 'Ceremony,'" *American Indian Culture and Research Journal* 28:1 (Winter 2004): 53–65.

# ecofeminism

Silko fosters the preservation of life on earth through ecofeminism, an alliance of ecology and feminism for the common good. To Cat Johnson, an interviewer for *Santa Cruz News*, she confides, "I'm really blessed" in her life in the Tucson desert (Johnson, 2010). She adds, "I just write the things that make me happy" (*ibid.*). As revealed in the early verse "Prayer to the Pacific" in *Laguna Woman* (1974), the short story "Bravura" in *The Man to Send Rain Clouds* (1974), *Storyteller* (1981), *Yellow Woman and a Beauty of the Spirit: Essays on Native American Life Today* (1996), *Gardens in the Dunes* (1999), and her latest work, *The Turquoise Ledge* (2010), a sense of intimacy and belonging to terrain comes naturally to an author shaped from childhood by her regard for all creation. From her Laguna upbringing, she developed what Kiowa novelist Navarre Scott Momaday calls "a moral comprehension of the earth and air," which provides the theme for the two-page prose ode "How to Hunt Buffalo" (1994) (McClure, 2007, 145–146). In the advice to a friend facing death, Silko demystifies the end-of-life transition: "No one of us wants to die, though we all must change, and turn to mother earth" (Silko, 1994, 2).

Plainspoken, yet rhapsodic, even in the falling action of "Lullaby" (1974), Silko expresses trust in the human place in creation. Her glimpses of oneness with nature promise "We are together always/There never was a time/when this/was not so" (Silko, 1981, 51). The focus places her in the first wave of ecocritical scholars and writers alongside Margaret Atwood, Eavan Boland, Octavia Butler, Rachel Carson, Clarissa Pinkola Estes, Joy Harjo, Ursula Le Guin, and Marge Piercy, all of whom survey the human relationship to an environment badly in need of supporters. As writer Barbara Kingsolver warns in *Animal Dreams* (1990), "People can forget, and forget, and forget, but the land has a memory" (Kingsolver, 1990, 255). The statement, for Silko, is two-edged: threat to those who discount nature and joy in the promise of bounty. She explains to the buffalo in her rifle sites, "Thank you, my brother, we cherish you" (Silko, 1994, 3).

## The Indian Point of View

Silko's perspective dates before the arrival of whites in the New World. In pre–Columbian times, aboriginal values demanded the conservation of natural resources, which Amerindians considered sacred rather than exploitable. Analyst Maggie Ann Bowers, a lecturer in transnational writing at the University of Portsmouth, England, remarks that the author "[presents] a relationship of humans to the land and locality which counters the dominant Western approach of ownership and resource" (Bowers, 2004, 267). She shapes narrative to demonstrate the Pueblo interrelation with "their plant and animal clanspeople" (Silko, 1993, 52). Rather than limit herself to her Laguna homeland, Silko espouses a holistic view that prioritizes a reverence for nature and for sharing its bounty with all people. Critics George A. Cevasco and Richard P. Harmond analyze Silko's challenge to the "traditional ways in which Americans view property rights—suggesting that shared property and resources would lead to a more coherent, universal valuation of the earth and the people on it" (Cevasco & Harmond, 2009, 472). The theme of humane apportionment dominates *Ceremony* (1977) and *Almanac of the Dead* (1991) with pity for Japanese civilians of Hiroshima and Nagasaki incinerated by the atomic bomb on August 6 and 8, 1945, and with condemnation for the waste of groundwater by late 20th century land developers of the Southwest. For *The Turquoise Ledge*, Silko pictures herself an element of the terrain, as integral to the pueblo as boulders and the sky. In reference to the future, she projects a time when her ashes will become a part of the land near her house northwest of Tucson.

Silko goes to unusual lengths to attest to the human oneness with the universe. The text of *Yellow Woman* displays the requisite nature of place and word in the blue wrapper, a cover made from Albuquerque artist Stephen Watson's blue corn paper. According to analyst Hertha Dawn Wong, the cover "contains bits of blue corn (another limited edition was covered in Watson's white Volcanic Ash paper containing small amounts of fine ash obtained from the volcanoes just west of Albuquerque)" (Wong, 2000–2001, 155). The syncretism of texture, color, image, and thoughts invest what Wong calls "lushly polyphonous Native American subjectivities" (*ibid.*). In the introduction to the 30th anniversary edition of *Ceremony*, novelist Larry McMurtry honors Silko's humility before all creation: "Her 'tellings' never lose sight of the fact that the earth was here first, along with the sun and the moon and other permanent powers" (McMurtry, 2007, xxiii).

CHAMPION OF EARTH

In reference to Silko's strong sense of place, German analyst Aleida Assmann, a professor of comparative literature at the University of Konstanz, observed an irony: "The distribution between rich or fertile White land and poor or dry Indian land is strikingly unjust" (Assmann, 1999, 63). Despite the scarcity of water and arable land, Silko venerates the Laguna complex for its role in the history and ongoing saga of its people. In *The Turquoise Ledge*, she berates enforcers who neglect ecology laws and complains of a prevailing attitude of exploiters to destroy "willy-nilly no matter the impact on others or himself—that's the credo of southern Arizona, and much of the West" (Silko, 2010, 170). On January 2, 2008, when she reports intentional damage to the flood plain, the hydrologist dismisses it as insignificant. In anger at bureaucratic ineptitude, the author charges county government with failure "at everything except collecting taxes and bribes" (*ibid.*, 207). She credits willful damage for the trashing of Tucson. In homage to Edward Paul Abbey, an environmental advocate and author of *Desert Solitaire: A Season in the Wilderness* (1968), she extols him for endorsing monkey-wrenching, the deliberate sabotage of bulldozers and power poles to stop intrusion on natural beauty and to rein in the technology that crushes animals, hills, and rock "without a second thought" (*ibid.*, 177). Her words take on desperation as land defilement within walking distance of her home in the Sonoran Desert continues at an alarming pace.

From her childhood, as she stated in *Sacred Water: Narratives and Pictures* (1993), Silko reverenced lakes and rain because of her Grandmother A'mooh's membership in the water clan. Ethicist Vernon Ruland admires *Sacred Water* for its intrinsic value: "Here it is possible to gather the ingredients for an ethics of environmental affinity, wonder, and responsibility," an apt summation of the author's response to moisture in a dry land (Ruland, 2002, 53). Barbara Cook, the author of *Women Writing Nature: A Feminist View* (2008), prizes Silko's "indigenous perspective that understands all subterranean water as connected, that understands human action having moral ramifications upon a landscape" (Cook, 2008, 19). The link between water and reptiles, especially snakes and toads, became part of the author's conscious cataloguing of changes in weather. In Amerindian style, her stories and verse depict the Earth Mother as a living, eternal parent, an entity demanding homage and protection. Silko's Laguna mythos anthropomorphizes ecology as a tight family network of related species: "This system of cooperation extends to all living things, even plants and insects, which Laguna Pueblo elders refer to as sisters and brothers, because none can survive unless all survive" (Silko, 1996, 130). She insists that even the trees in the Brazilian rain forest impact the lives of Manhattanites.

## WOMAN AS EARTH-TENDER

Silko's stories extol female agency. She honors the mythic savior Kochininako (Yellow Woman) as a virgin hunter, mother, game protector, and the solitary moon goddess who shields creation. The author exemplifies the regard of the Pueblo for Yellow Woman's resourcefulness and divergent thinking in unusual situations, such as her role in the verse tale "Cottonwood" (1981) in halting the advance of perpetual winter. In the second stave, "Buffalo Story," Kochininako enables the starving Pueblo to reconfigure their hunting to include stalking the buffalo over the eastern plains. To complete her exploit, she must violate the sexual proprieties for married women by becoming a nonconforming wife and mother and by sacrificing her reputation for the greater good of the pueblo. As a result of her martyrdom, "They would bring home all that good meat. Nobody would be hungry then" (Silko, 1981, 76).

The author claims that ecological, economic, and socio-economic disasters such as the Dust Bowl and the Great Depression of the 1930s are the price of the Western concept of progress. In the summation of Amanda Porterfield, a specialist in American religion at Florida State University and the author of *American Religious History* (2002), Silko values Pueblo lore as tutorials of nature stewardship—"guides to the well-being of individuals, communities, and the earth" (Porterfield, 2002, 305). In *Storyteller* (1981), Silko explains the urgency of stories "about drastic things which must be done for the world to continue out of love for this earth" (Silko, 1981, 65). The author mourns the destruction of apricot orchards and melon gardens following the atomic blast in New Mexico's desert at the Trinity site outside the Los Alamos laboratory on July 16, 1945. The casual sacrilege by white loggers, miners, and physicists generated "a growing identification in women's writing with the earth itself, an increasingly intimate engagement with the natural world" called ecofeminism (Anderson & Edwards, 2002, 8). For her leadership in an evolving field, environmental humanists Joni Adamson and Scott Slovic salute Silko's canon as "the vanguard of environmental thought" (Adamson & Slovic, 2009, 13).

## AMERINDIAN STEWARDSHIP

The author came of age in what Kathryn Hume, a professor of comparative literature at the Pennsylvania State, typified as "a low-tech mode of living that demands little petroleum-derived fuel, electricity, water, and fertilizer" (Hume, 2002, 205). Silko acknowledged from a reading of Sigmund Freud's *Interpretation of Dreams* (1899) that folkloric wisdom demands regard for the pueblo's earth-bound truth and immediacy. The coming-home narrative *Ceremony* returns to peasant lore in depicting the power of the female to restore life and well being. In the protagonist Tayo's vision of a spider and her egg sac at dawn, he takes comfort from Pueblo images of the mothering of Spider Woman (Ts'its'tsi'nako), the rescuer: "She alone had known how to outsmart the malicious mountain Ka't'sina who imprisoned the rain clouds in the northwest room of his magical house" (Silko, 1977, 94). An early story of the Ck'o'yo scammer Pa'caya'nyi, a double-talking deceiver, reminds listeners of trickery that lures Pueblo workers from devotion to the corn mother Nau't-s'ity'i. By enticing the Laguna from hard farm labor, the gambler causes tribe members to abandon the deity's altar and to stop tending the cornrows. The fable warns Tayo of the danger of drought and famine and of the deeper hazard of human frailty. Out of harmony with the natural world, the corn growers learn through hunger to study their inner weaknesses and to avoid the delusion that survival is easy.

The concept of planetary stewardship undergirds the insights of *Ceremony*, which portrays a war veteran out of balance with earth. By moving the action closer to her own time, Silko discounts the white boast of 500 years of conquest on a continent where aborigines have lived for 18,000 years. Her protagonist comes to near disaster in his travels by pickup trucks, which disorient him with speed, sound, and blurred vision. Only by walking and riding horseback does he repossess what critic John A. McClure terms a "sense of visceral relatedness to an ordered, beautiful and benignant cosmos" (McClure, 2007, 148). Tayo reverences the order of nature in the track of a mountain lion, which he traces along "the delicate edges of dust the paw prints had made, deep round imprints, each toe a distinctive swirl" (Silko, 1977, 196). He cleanses himself of white debauchery and world war by witnessing a pivotal scene of hypnotic song, prayer, drumming with a tire iron, fire ritual, and human sacrifice, the vengeful slaughter of Harley by his crazed war buddies Emo, Leroy Valdez, and Cousin Pinkie. On the autumnal solstice, the battle between good and evil occurs amid chiaroscuro as the wind blows clouds over moonlight, a metaphoric blurring of the outlines of evil.

The possibilities of planetary destruction grip the characters in *Ceremony*, where Tayo discovers catch basin contamination in bitter water. The text repines, "There is no end to it; it knew no boundaries ... a circle of death that devoured people in cities" (Silko, 1977, 246). By restraining himself from intervening in human assault and by leaving Harley to suffer for his betrayal, Tayo envisions himself in boyhood innocence returning home in Uncle Josiah's wagon. Like heroes of Grail narratives, Tayo elevates himself from fighting and torture to a higher plane of oneness with the stars, a dependable celestial pattern that unites him with his ancestors, who "had come down from White House in the north" (*ibid.*, 254). Recalling tales of historic disasters, he acknowledges the wrenching choice between good and evil: "It has never been easy" (*ibid.*). His statement resonates beyond the self-destruction of war veterans to the cosmic sin of dropping atomic bombs on civilians to end the Pacific war. Critic Sara L. Spurgeon stresses that Tayo arrives at "the geographic and spiritual center of a cosmic illness" near the Los Alamos site and reveals the American west as "the nexus of all modern history" (Spurgeon, 2005, 98).

THE COMING APOCALYPSE

Through Tayo's life-journey, Silko incorporates the lives of the Pueblo in the self-destructive weaponry of world war, a white man's folly that betokens the depredations of the Columbian era on first peoples unfamiliar with metallurgy and firearms. In defiance of the exploiters, the text declares, "We came out of this land and we are hers" (*ibid.*, 255). Stressing the femininity of guardians, Silko creates Ts'eh Montaño, the mythic mountain demigoddess who goes about her replenishment and restocking of plants as a seasonal duty. Like the color logic of the blanket weaver, Ts'eh's reasoning about the morning glory vine is transcendent: "This [flower] contains the color of the sky after a summer rainstorm. I'll take it from here and plant it in another place, a canyon where it hasn't rained for a while" (*ibid.*, 224). In 1981, Silko, like her mountain spirit Ts'eh, mused on the resilience of the creator's wisdom. The author concluded, "Now that we've used up most of the sources of energy, you think perhaps the old people were right" that the white destroyers will eventually lose power and depart, just as the *conquistadores* once did (Silko, 1981, 67).

Because of the open-pit mining north of Laguna at the Jackpile uranium mine, Silko responded to apocalyptic alerts, which she repeated in *Almanac of the Dead*, *Sacred Water*, and *Gardens in the Dune*. Silko's essay "Landscape, History, and the Pueblo Imagination" (1986) for *Antaeus* regrets, "I have lived long enough to begin hearing the stories [of the Rio Paguate contamination] which verify the earlier warnings.... By its very ugliness and by the violence it does to the land, the Jackpile Mine insures that from now on it, too, will be included in the vast body of narratives which make up the history of the Laguna people" (Silko, 1986, 510–511). Because of the usurpers' profligacy, life "changed forever" (Silko, 1991, 35). In the *Gardens of the Dunes*, she replicates the destruction at Paguate, New Mexico, of serenity and fecundity in the fragile squash and bean patches and apricot and peach trees. Set in southwestern Arizona, the narrative develops an ecofeminist alliance of gardeners who value vegetable patches, vines, and orchards as survivors of white havoc to Indians and the land. The author speaks through the Mojave their sorrow that the rechanneling of the Colorado River outside Needles, Arizona, uproots "beloved ancestors and dead relatives," who dwell under the water (Silko, 1999, 212). Critic Stuart Christie, a Scots anarchist from Glasgow, identifies the villain in the piece — builders of a dam and aqueduct — as "Anglo-European capitalism ... and toxic intruders upon natural places" (Christie, 2009, 90).

## A WORLD RIPE FOR DESTRUCTION

Silko's apocalyptic novel *Almanac of the Dead* employs the conventions of postmodern surrealism to add human drama to prophecy of widespread upheaval. She adopts an unsettling tone of lost hope, decenters heroics, details consumer frenzies and resultant toxins, enjambs time, relishes multiplicity, and brings into collision the holy and the profane (Ammons, 2010, 149). Old Yoeme, the self-sufficient grandmother of twins, relates her chopping of a cottonwood tree. Analysts Thomas S. Edwards and Elizabeth A. De Wolfe clarify "a haunting awareness ... of human smallness in relation to the earth's ecological being" (Edwards & De Wolfe, 2001, 197). Because white men lynched and displayed the corpses of brown people on its limbs, the tree defiled native land, much as a Hollywood film crew dishonors the Laguna Pueblo by treating sacred space near the uranium mine as rental property, where crewmembers snort cocaine. In an epiphany of recompense for evil, Sterling, the novel's moral center, realizes, "Humans had desecrated only themselves with the mine, not the earth. Burned and radioactive, with all humans dead, the earth would still be sacred" (Silko, 1991, 762). Silko repeats the epiphany in *Sacred Water: Narratives and Pictures*: "Human beings desecrate only themselves: The Mother Earth is inviolable" (Silko, 1993, 76).

To contrast earth's profanation with edenic plenty, the Yaqui drug dealer Calabazas recalls the memories of the elders of clean water and deer thick in the high grass. In view of rapid despoliation, he fears the future holds "more endings than beginnings" (Silko, 1991, 222). He pictures his people and the refugee Apache they shelter retreating to the high country of "sheer basalt ridges and thorny brush" to escape "the blood-drinking Beast," the elders' term for white conquerors (*ibid.*, 223). In contrast to the lovers of the terrain, whites view the canyons and hills as all the same, just as they recognize Geronimo's likeness in multiple Apache warriors. Until the revolution and establishment of an equitable global community, outcasts can only cling to each other, share, and survive.

The author's stern disapproval of earthly befouling extends to all violators, whatever their race. In "Tribal Councils: Puppets of the U.S. Government," an essay in *Yellow Woman and a Beauty of the Spirit: Essays on Native American Life Today* (1996), she excoriates Amerindians who taint the holiness of nature. In reference to the Navajo's deforestation of the Chuska Mountains on the northwestern border of New Mexico, the author fulminates about a host of "serial killers of life on earth"—"strip mines, clear-cut logging, hydroelectric dams, and radioactive waste" (Silko, 1996, 95, 92). She blames the Indian Reorganization Act of 1941 for forcing communities to adopt a tribal council comprised of Bureau of Indian Affairs puppets, mouthpieces for politicians. With the gravity of a former law student, the author declares the congressional act unconstitutional and coercive for forcing tribes to abandon traditional governments. With the lucidity of a prophet, she declares: "All places and all beings of the earth are sacred" and warns of a time when "hundreds of years of infamy will be redressed" (*ibid.*, 94). The author reassures readers of earth's resilience in "Fifth World: The Return of Ma ah shra true ee, the Giant Serpent" (1996). Echoing elders who laugh at European predations against natural resources, Silko contends, "Blast it open, dig it up, or cook it with nuclear explosions: the earth remains" (*ibid.*, 125). In the essay "Breaking Down the Boundaries: 'Earth, Air, Water, Mind'" (1998), she predicts the end of "European behavior, values, and attitudes toward the land" in the coming apocalypse: "Those ways and those days are numbered" (Silko, 1998, 94).

A RETURN TO COEXISTENCE

With *Gardens in the Dunes*, Silko shapes a native Eden in a canyon south of the Colorado River. The last of the Sand Lizard people — Indigo, her older sibling Sister Salt, and their grandmother, Grandma Fleet — conceal their three-woman clan among the amaranth and pumpkins growing on the Arizona-California border. With the naïveté and vulnerability of the Paiute mystic Wovoka, the three live in accord with the old rattlesnake, shielder of their desert spring, in a worshipful attitude they share with the title characters in Rudolfo Anaya's *Bless Me, Ultima* (1972) and Laurel Thatcher Ulrich's Pulitzer Prize–winning history *A Midwife's Tale: The Life of Martha Ballard* (1991). Encroaching from the north, the white destroyers of the frontier build a dam and aqueduct to direct water to Los Angeles. Simultaneous with the draining of the original riverbed, the text depicts an intentional fire in the Amazon jungle to control ownership of hybrid rubber plants; the bulldozing of an Italian garden to suit an annual costume ball, the Masque of the Blue Garden; and the imprisonment of a monkey and parrot for pleasure. Tayari Jones, a reviewer for *The Progressive*, depicts the number one plant pirate, Dr. Edward Palmer, as a "capitalist eco-menace," an apt description of his pseudo-scientific field scavenging for the sake of marketable plants and botanic immortality (Jones, 2000, 44). Suzanne Ruta, in a critique for the *New York Times*, notes that Palmer's eco-pillaging suggests "the tainted genesis of our great natural history museums, only now de-accessioning their vast collections of Indian bones" (Ruta, 1999, 31).

Critic Margara Averbach reads into Silko's eco-fiction a subtext of hope for minorities. Averbach summarizes the plunder in *Gardens* as "a globalization of disaster whose root is always a fear of the different" (Averbach, 2001, 558). She adds that objectification of plants and animals ignores an ecological truth: "What is done to the Other is ultimately done to the self," a proverb reminiscent of the Golden Rule (*ibid.*). In Indigo's collection and planting of seeds and corms, Averbach locates metaphors of "seeds of rebellion and resistance," the rumblings that stir the Yaqui to action in *Almanac of the Dead* (*ibid.*, 562). Indigo exalts the waxed paper packets of plant life from her journey as "the greatest travelers of all!" (Silko, 1999, 293). Circling back to the opening setting, the narrative pictures a gendered blessing on the Sand Lizard clan in the establishment of "Old Snake's beautiful daughter" as the guardian of the clan's water supply, a symbol of the eternal feminine creative spirit (*ibid.*, 479).

In *The Turquoise Ledge* (2010), a memoir, Silko revisits the despoliation of the Southwest by cactus thieves and developers. The spread of suburbs from Tucson into the mountains threatens "pristine desert habitat and [leaves] the desert tortoises in danger of extinction along with the monster lizards and spotted owls" (Silko, 2010, 82). In contrast to wasteful acts, the author ennobles a low-impact residence that recycles gray water from showers to flush the toilet. According to an unsigned critique from *Kirkus Reviews*, the author "invites readers to reflect on their own trespasses against nature" ("Review," 2010, 336). She sides with the boulders "slashed and shattered by the steel claw" of the bulldozer and refers to the freebooter as "dickhead" (Silko, 2010, 269). From preschool days, she recalls the Cold War era's mania for uranium to build atomic bombs. After dynamiting the outskirts of Paguate, the Anaconda mining authorities conducted open-pit ore removal. Because Indians deified the earth and refused to dig in the tunnels, only whites and Hispanics molested the underground. In the early 1950s, the company tested explosives at Jackass Flats in south central Nevada. Maps of fallout indicate that "the U.S. Government managed to nuke this country more completely than the USSR ever dreamed" (*ibid.*, 69). The worst of the contamination struck Arizona, Colorado, Nevada, New Mexico, and Utah. In a terse charge of federal malfeasance in stockpiling radioactive tailings, Silko asserted that the Laguna and neighboring "down-winders" joined "other 'expendable' people who became human guinea pigs" (*ibid.*, 70). Ironically, the government excused its base treatment of citizens as a necessary part of "national security," an excuse for infractions against democracy that is still a favorite of willful politicians.

*See also* Grandma Fleet; Indigo; Montaño; Ts'eh.

• *References and further reading*
Adamson, Joni, and Scott Slovic. "The Shoulders We Stand On: An Introduction to Ethnicity and Ecocriticism," *MELUS* 34:2 (1 June 2009): 5–24.
Ammons, Elizabeth. *Brave New Words: How Literature Will Save the Planet*. Iowa City: University of Iowa Press, 2010.
Anderson, Lorraine, and Thomas S. Edwards. *At Home on This Earth: Two Centuries of U.S. Women's Nature Writing*. Hanover, NH: University Press of New England, 2002.
Assmann, Aleida. "Space, Place, Land—Changing Concepts of Territory in English and American Fiction" in *Borderlands: Negotiating Boundaries in Post-Colonial Writing*. Amsterdam: Rodopi, 1999.
Averbach, Margara. "*Gardens in the Dunes* by Leslie Marmon Silko: Stories as Resistance" in *Raízas e rumos: perspectivas interdisciplinares em estudos americanos*, ed. Sonia Torres. Rio de Janeiro: 7Letras, 2001.
Blazek, William, and Michael K. Glenday. *American Mythologies: Essays in Contemporary Literature*. Liverpool, UK: Liverpool University Press, 2005.

Bowers, Maggie Ann. "Eco-Criticism in a (Post-)Colonial Contest and Leslie Marmon Silko's *Almanac of the Dead*" in *Towards a Transcultural Future: Literature and Human Rights in a "Post"-Colonial World*, ed. Peter H. Marsden. Amsterdam: Rodopi, 2004.

Cevasco, George A., and Richard P. Harmond. *Modern American Environmentalists: A Biographical Encyclopedia*. Baltimore: Johns Hopkins University Press, 2009.

Christie, Stuart. *Plural Sovereignties and Contemporary Indigenous Literature*. New York: Palgrave Macmillan, 2009.

Cook, Barbara. *Women Writing Nature: A Feminist View*. Lanham, MD: Rowman & Littlefield, 2008.

Cutchins, Dennis. "'So That the Nations May Become Genuine Indian': Nativism and Leslie Marmon Silko's *Ceremony*," *Journal of American Culture* 22: 4 (1999): 77–89.

Edwards, Thomas S., and Elizabeth A. De Wolfe. *Such News of the Land: U.S. Women Nature Writers*. Hanover, NH: University Press of New England, 2001.

Goldstein, Coleman. "Silko's *Ceremony*." *The Explicator* 61:4 (Summer 2003): 245–248.

Hume, Kathryn. *American Dream, American Nightmare: Fiction since 1960*. Urbana: University of Illinois Press, 2002.

Johnson, Cat. "Silko Heads for Santa Cruz," *Santa Cruz News* (21 October 2010).

Jones, Tayari. "Folk Tale of Survival," *The Progressive* 64:2 (February 2000): 43–44.

Kingsolver, Barbara. *Animal Dreams*. New York: HarperCollins, 1990.

McClure, John. *Partial Faiths: Postsecular Fiction in the Age of Pynchon and Morrison*. Athens: University of Georgia Press, 2007.

McMurtry, Larry. "Introduction" to *Ceremony*. New York: Penguin, 2007.

Piper, Karen. "Police Zones: Territory and Identity in Leslie Marmon Silko's *Ceremony*," *American Indian Quarterly* (22 June 1997): 483–501.

Porterfield, Amanda. *American Religious History*. Malden, MA: Blackwell, 2002.

"Review: *The Turquoise Ledge*," *Kirkus Reviews* 78:13 (1 July 2010): 336.

Ruland, Vernon. *Conscience across Borders: An Ethics of Global Rights and Religious Pluralism*. San Francisco: University of San Francisco, 2002.

Ruta, Suzanne, "Dances with Ghosts," *New York Times* (18 April 1999).

Silko, Leslie Marmon. *Almanac of the Dead*. New York: Simon & Schuster, 1991.

_____. "Breaking Down the Boundaries: 'Earth, Air, Water, Mind'" in *The Tales We Tell: Perspectives on the Short Story*, ed. Barbara Lounsberry. London: Greenwood, 1998.

_____. "How to Hunt Buffalo" (1994), unpublished fourfold housed in the Bienecke archives at Yale University Library, New Haven, Connecticut.

_____. "Landscape, History, and the Pueblo Imagination," *Antaeus* 51 (1986): 83–94.

_____. *Ceremony*. New York: Viking, 1977.

_____. *Gardens in the Dunes*. New York: Scribner, 1999.

_____. "Language and Literature from the Pueblo Indian Perspective" in *English Literature: Opening Up the Canon*, eds. Leslie Fiedler and Houston Baker, Jr. Baltimore: Johns Hopkins University Press, 1981.

_____. *Sacred Water: Narratives and Pictures*. Tucson: Flood Plain Press, 1993.

_____. *Storyteller*. New York: Seaver Books, 1981.

_____. *The Turquoise Ledge: A Memoir*. New York: Viking Adult, 2010.

_____. *Yellow Woman and a Beauty of the Spirit: Essays on Native American Life Today*. New York: Simon & Schuster, 1996.

_____. "Yellow Woman and A Beauty of the Spirit," *Los Angeles Times* (19 December 1993): 52.

Thompson, Joan. "Yellow Woman, Old and New: Oral Tradition and Leslie Marmon Silko's *Storyteller*," *Wicazo SA Review* 5:2 (Autumn 1989): 22–25.

Wong, Hertha D. Sweet. "Native American Visual Autobiography: Figuring Place, Subjectivity, and History," *Iowa Review* 30:3 (Winter 2000–2001): 145–156.

# Emo

A satanic figure, Emo, the U.S. Army buddy of Harley and Leroy Valdez on Wake Island in Silko's first novel, *Ceremony* (1977), shares the Pacific war horrors that infect returning Laguna soldiers with alcoholism, aggression, and aimlessness. An Iago to the protagonist Tayo's Othello, Emo struts like Kaup'a'ta the Gambler, a snazzily dressed trickster from Reedleaf Town equipped with a bag of stars. Kenneth Lincoln, a specialist in native American literature at the University of California at Los Angeles, describes Emo's milieu as a rat-hole near the reservation where "bar jives and rez riffs stud the dialogue with machismo, purple hearts, and stale beer — the street chaff of cheap shots, thought-less angers, and bad jokes" (Lincoln, 2008, 112). As evidence of Emo's pollution by white ideals, he admires San Diego, bright city lights, and technology, a welcoming port of embarkation that causes an elderly woman to admire uniforms and to utter "God bless you" twice from the window of her big Chrysler (Silko, 1977, 112). Emo mistakes adula-tion for the warrior as praise for the man. His GI haircut betokens an identity locked in the past beyond the reach of change and growth. Critic Alexandra Ganser, a German Silko expert at the University of Oklahoma, connects Emo with a frontier stereotype, the crazy Indian, who retreats to the bottle. A classic malcontent, Emo complains that he fought the white man's war for no payoff. He licks his wounds in a welter of self-pity that "us Indians deserve something better than this goddamn dried-up country around here" (ibid., 55). The denigration of his homeland anticipates his ouster from the Laguna complex.

A cynic twisted by mid-twentieth century witchery, the folk term for manipulation, like the young soldiers in Peruvian novelist Mario Vargas Llosa's The Time of the Hero (1962), Emo commits iniquities and displays war trophies that Silko equates with sacri-lege. Michael D. Wilson, a literature teacher at the University of Wisconsin, categorizes the sinner among other World War II veterans who "abjure the traditions of the commu-nity" because battlefield conquests "cause them to devalue their homelands in relation to the material wealth of Americans" (Wilson, 2008, 27). As explained by AnaLouise Keat-ing, a specialist in women's studies at Texas Woman's University, the author demonizes the drifter's yen for whiteness by "associating it with greed, restrictive boundaries, destruc-tion, emptiness, absence, and death," a punishment Emo escapes through banishment (Keating, 2007, 68). Lacking respect for his Laguna upbringing, Emo avoids his native legacy, a responsibility toward earth and community. As the author explained to inter-viewer Ellen L. Arnold, "There is always this double image of the American Indian, the noble savage and the mysterious evil" (Silko & Arnold, 2000, 151). Thus, Emo retains the tribal lore of his ancestry, but alters the content to reflect the barbarity of white warriors, who enjoy the suffering of dying victims. Despite earning a Purple Heart, by regressing to barbarism, Emo fosters the white world's denigration of Amerindians. He courts dis-aster by practicing "Ck'o'yo magic," the Laguna term for destructive power (Silko, 1977, 85). Silko expert Robert M. Nelson deflates Emo's menace by dismissing him as "only a watered-down agent of the Ck'o'yo way" (Nelson, 2008, 130).

RECKLESS TALK

To undermine ethnic tradition, Emo commits the classic Greek sin of hubris (pride) by desecrating nature. He tramples ants under his boots and stomps melons for fun. While his pals focus on city escapades and sexual adventuring with blondes, Emo boasts of his belonging to the U.S. Army: "We butchered every Jap we found" (Silko, 1977, 138). His loss of respect for humanity extends to denigration of the land. During the drought of spring 1948, he horrifies Tayo with blasphemy: "Here's the Indians' mother earth! Old dried-up thing!" a dual aspersion of his homeland and of sacred womanhood (ibid., 25). At the Dixie Tavern in Budville with Harley, Leroy Valdez, cousin Pinkie, and Tayo, Emo besots himself on whiskey, pulling slugs straight from the bottle and stoking his mean streak. His churlish boast about posing as a "Wop" and calling himself Mattuci to score with a large-breasted white blonde enlivens the evening with the kind of man-talk that entertains fellow GIs (ibid., 53). Subtextually, he disguises himself as Christopher Colum-bus, the Italian navigator from Genoa who sailed to the New World under a Spanish flag.

Only Tayo withholds his approval of sexual and military conquests, which tag Emo as a dishonored warrior and apostate.

The episode reveals contrasting perspectives on the "boys' night out." Displaying the atavism of a witch, Emo takes pride in his wartime motto "Make them talk fast, die slow," a suggestion of native American torture methods exploited in Dorothy M. Johnson's short story "A Man Called Horse" (1950) (*ibid.*, 61). He loosens up by tossing his Bull Durham tobacco sack filled with teeth that he knocked from the jaws of a Japanese colonel. Critic John Lloyd Purdy, a professor of English at Western Washington University, interprets the scene as a Faustian wager on Tayo's vulnerability: Emo "rolls them like dice; he's quite literally gambling for Tayo's life, and he nearly wins" (Purdy, 2009, 36). To the native reader, the sack is a bag of bad medicine to generate evil. The contamination of holy tobacco with parts of a corpse exacerbates Emo's sacrilege, a taboo that Silko develops in "A Geronimo Story" (1981). At the rattle of teeth in the bag, Tayo, the mythic redeemer, tamps down nausea. Emo beams a hateful look at Tayo for ruining an evening of boozing and war stories, a foreshadowing of Emo's orchestration of ritual torture and murder. The power game between the peace-bringer and the agitator continues until the novel's resolution.

THE UNIVERSAL STRUGGLE FOR THE SOUL

In a subsequent power play, Silko showcases the outcome of the standoff — Tayo's near murder of his war buddy by shoving a broken beer bottle into Emo's gut. Symbolically, she charges alcohol with fueling Emo's disgruntlement. Indirectly, the text satirizes the infantile nature of the blood feud as the result of a childhood rock fight, the residue of grade school vengeance. A later revelation, Emo's envy of Tayo's white paternity, explains the sour mood that Leroy dismisses as drunkenness. Emo aggravates the quarrel by baiting Tayo, calling him "white trash," a lacklogic aspersion that devalues Tayo's superiority from white blood to inferiority for mixed blood (Silko, 1977, 63). To Tayo, an evil aura surrounds the bar fight, a hovering negativity from Emo, the wartime barbarian, who was "asking for it" (*ibid.*, 53). Silko inserts intertextual hints that Emo's war glorification borders on vampirism, a form of sadism that she explores in *Almanac of the Dead* (1991). Tayo redeems Emo from total damnation by classing him with Harley and Helen Jean, "people [who] had been taught to despise themselves" (*ibid.*, 204).

Emo's treacherous nature reemerges in the falling action, where, in company with his Ck'o'yo brotherhood, he yields his humanity to sorcery. Silko laments that the veteran "grew from each killing" (*ibid.*, 138). Analyst Ole Wagner connects Emo with "people who have lost their respect for their mother nature and turned to playing around with bad magic" (Wagner, 2004, 6). In mid–September 1949, the Laguna believe Emo's lies about Tayo's residency at the ranch and about his hallucination that he is a Jap soldier living in a cave. Literature expert John Emory Dean interprets the rumor campaign in terms of Plato's cave myth in the *Republic* (ca. 380 B.C.): "Emo is stoking the fire that helps create the shadows on the cave wall ... but [Tayo] does not buy into the wisdom of the cave" (Dean, 2009, 170, 171). Rather, he turns from deep, dark caves of subjective confusion to Enchanted Mesa, where "all things seemed to converge" from the stores of wisdom that survived in Tayo from birth (Silko, 1977, 237). Remaining *hors de combat*, he rejects a white stereotype, "another victim, a drunk Indian war veteran settling an old feud" (Silko, 1977, 253). By rejecting the hypothesis of witchery, Tayo avoids being Emo's sacrificial beast.

ONE ON ONE

Emo chips away at Tayo's belief in the curative power of ceremony. Of Tayo's vision quest with the mountain demigoddess Ts'eh Montaño, Emo diminishes its majesty as "bullshit about caves and animals," another blasphemy against animism (*ibid.*, 228). On the run from betrayal by Harley and Leroy Valdez, Tayo hides at the uranium mine, a flight from Emo's evil to deep-earth mysticism. During the autumn solstice, Tayo watches the drunken orgy of Emo, Leroy, and Pinkie. Kurt Caswell, a literature professor at Texas Tech University, describes the demonic ritual as a "totem meal ceremony [by which] forces of witchery feed on the ritual killing" that could doom the Laguna people (Caswell, 2008, 175). As Betonie, the Chicano-Navajo shaman, predicts, the "contest/in dark things" derives, not from white witches, but from the Indians themselves (Silko, 1977, 133).

Silko manages to mitigate Emo's sins. He and his pals become the sorcerer's tools— "Objects to work for us/objects to act for us/Performing the witchery/for suffering/for torment.... It can't be called back" (*ibid.*, 137–138). Tayo cringes at Pinkie's hammering on the car hood, a mockery of holy drumming. The emblematic witchery of three native rebels defiling tradition enlightens Tayo to the source of loss, drought, and Indian vulnerability to bootleg wine, rumors, womanizing, and materialism. While the trio crucify Harley in barbed wire for failing to lure Tayo out of hiding, Tayo sees Emo's ritual barbarity morphing into universal evil — the deaths of Japanese civilians from the atomic bomb and the poverty of homeless children outside Gallup. The plot exiles Emo to California, a banishment that Grandma approves for Emo's murder of Pinkie. A merciful punishment, expulsion returns Emo to the beguiling West Coast milieu that launched his corruption.

*See also Ceremony*; Tayo; vengeance; violence.

- *References and further reading*

Avila, Monica. "Leslie Marmon Silko's *Ceremony*: Witchery and Sacrifice of Self," *Explicator* 67:1 (Fall 2008): 53–55.
Bird, Gloria. "Toward a Decolonization of the Mind and Text: Leslie Marmon Silko's *Ceremony*" in *Reading Native American Women: Critical/Creative Representations*, ed. Inés Hernández-Avila. Lanham, MD: Altamira, 2005, 93–106.
Caswell, Kurt. "The Totem Meal in Leslie Marmon Silko's *Ceremony*," *ISLE* 15:2 (2008): 175–183.
Cutchins, Dennis. "'So That the Nations May Become Genuine Indian': Nativism and Leslie Marmon Silko's *Ceremony*," *Journal of American Culture* 22:4 (1999): 77–89.
Dean, John Emory. *Travel Narratives from New Mexico: Reconstructing Identity and Truth*. Amherst, NY: Cambria, 2009.
Ganser, Alexandra. "Violence, Trauma, and Cultural Memory in Leslie Silko's *Ceremony*," *Atenea* 24:1 (June 2004): 145–149.
Keating, AnaLouise. *Teaching Transformation Transcultural Classroom Dialogues*. New York: Palgrave Macmillan, 2007.
Lincoln, Kenneth. *Speak Like Singing: Classics of Native American Literature*. Albuquerque: University of New Mexico Press, 2008.
Nelson, Robert M. *Leslie Marmon Silko's Ceremony: The Recovery of Tradition*. New York: Peter Lang, 2008.
Olsen, Erica. "Silko's *Ceremony*," *Explicator* 64:3 (Spring 2006): 190–192.
Purdy, John Lloyd. *Writing Indian, Native Conversations*. Lincoln: University of Nebraska Press, 2009.
Roberts, Kathleen Glenister. *Alterity and Narrative: Stories and the Negotiation of Western Identities*. Albany: State University of New York Press, 2008.
Silko, Leslie Marmon. *Ceremony*. New York: Viking, 1977.
_____, and Ellen L. Arnold. *Conversations with Leslie Marmon Silko*. Jackson: University Press of Mississippi, 2000.
Wagner, Ole. *The Stolen Land Will Eat Their Hearts — Leslie Marmon Silko's Ceremony from an Environmentalist Perspective*. Norderstedt, Ger.: GRIN Verlag, 2004.

Wilson, Michael D. *Writing Home: Indigenous Narratives of Resistance.* East Lansing: Michigan State University Press, 2008.

## evil

Leslie Marmon Silko excels at repudiation of cruelty, sin, wrongs against nature, and betrayal of ancestry and self. From early in her career, the author maintained belief in the creation myth of good and evil by which relentless forces of witchery challenge the concepts of birth and vitality. Clara Sue Kidwell and Alan R. Velie account for the author's rejection of a "universal contract" of behavior equivalent to that of Christianity and Islam (Kidwell & Velie, 2005, 32). The analysts note the absence of a legalistic "concept of good and evil" in Silko's canon and stress a central difference: "Christians are more likely than believers in traditional Indian religions to think of people as either righteous or depraved" (*ibid.*). White sermonizers favor the thundering admonition from Numbers 32:23, "Be sure your sins will find you out." In *Other Destinies: Understanding the American Indian Novel* (1994), Cherokee-Choctaw author Louis Owens satirizes the prototypical evildoer as "the malignant Moby-Dick of the heartland," an allusion to the Cartesian concept of good and evil that dominates American literature (Owens, 1994, 236).

With a gesture toward native grace, Silko's "Fences against Freedom" (1994) validates the generosity and tolerance of the Laguna, who welcome strangers and share food with them, even when drought prevails and supplies are scare. Because of a tolerant worldview, the tribe delights in human idiosyncrasies and in "learning odd facts and strange but true stories" from outsiders (Silko, 1996, 103). At the core of their open-door policy lies a belief that no one is completely evil: "Some of them had evil hearts, but many were good human beings" (*ibid.*, 103). The statement suggests a naiveté in Pueblo tribes and implies the author's wish to excuse them for an ingenuous hospitality to newcomers, one of the ethical obligations they share with the ancient Mediterranean world. Conversely, her redactions of the myths of the Evil Gambler Kaup'a'ta and of Yellow Woman (Kochininako) reassure the reader that the Laguna are anything but naive. They recognize in evil-doers like the Navajo abductor Silva two threats toward survival — a limitation of Yellow Woman's freedom of movement and a possible truncation of the tribe's sources of food.

Unlike writers of color who fulminate against all whites, Silko eviscerates the notion of race. Instead, she pictures willful destruction as a socialized cultural value that occurs in all ethnicities, including the hospitable ancient Greeks (Teuton, 2008, 140). In the essay "Tribal Prophecies" in *Yellow Woman and a Beauty of the Spirit: Essays on Native American Life Today* (1996), she describes the ruthlessness of Hernán de Cortés, a mercenary dispatched by the Spanish crown ostensibly to civilize Mesoamericans. He begins exterminating the Aztec empire by setting fire to groves and roasting alive sacred macaws and parrots of Tenochtitlán as icons of pagan idolatry. Under the aegis of the Inquisition and Pope Clement VII, the head of the Roman Catholic Church, the conqueror's followers exonerate wholesale torture and death, an institutionalized genocide that sets in motion five centuries of carnage against indigenous Americans. For blame, the author turns to Amerindian sorcerers: "Already familiar with evil themselves, [they] had conjured up more evil by calling out these white men from Europe, their spiritual brethren in destruction and suffering" (Silko, 1996, 146–147). A startling shift for Indian narrative, the sharing of guilt identifies evil as a burden borne by all humankind.

## Dramatizing Evil

In *Ceremony* (1977), the author introduces the aboriginal concept of primordial evil, a form of sorcery that overruns the earth with rampant bloodlust and ruin. Through the ritual of the Chicano-Navajo shaman Betonie, Silko identifies the source of global wickedness. Destroyers aspire "to gut human beings while they are still breathing, to hold the heart still beating so the victim will never feel anything again," an allusion to Aztec ritual sacrifice and cannibalism witnessed by Bernal Díaz, author of *The Conquest of New Spain* (1576) (Silko, 1977, 229). Rather than blame whites for the world's soulless zombies, Silko's medicine man categorizes evil as witchery fomented by people with "slanty eyes" and "black skin," including Pueblo Indians, Eskimo, and Sioux (*ibid.*, 133). In rebuttal of critics who charge Silko with racial favoritism, Cherokee critic Betty Louise Bell, a teacher of American culture at the University Michigan, exonerates Amerindians of fostering insidious destruction because of "the failure of Euroamerican history to empower native peoples in the production of the New World" (Bell, 2005, 22). Because Silko's aborigines have no voice in governing the Western Hemisphere, according to Bell, they bear no blame for global evil, such as the execution of Japanese prisoners that Tayo views in the Philippines.

In verbal 3-D, Silko enlarges on ritual evil. With a mythic poem, she mimics a witches' sabbath, a consortium of enchanters who stir up cauldrons of death — empty skulls and dead infants simmered in blood. In the style of William Shakespeare's cave scenes in *Macbeth* (1606), the devilish soup distorts human propagation by cooking among flint and cinders fragments of clitoris and penis, the essentials of human reproduction. More powerful than the perverted stew is the story related by an unknown witch, who sets the mass "Whirling/whirling/whirling/whirling," a rhythm that echoes the swirling primordial liquids of the *Kojiki* (712), the Japanese creation myth (*ibid.*, 138). Like the atomic weaponry that ends World War II on August 6 and 8, 1945, the cannibalistic spell is intractable, a ceaseless menace that spreads as more nations acquire "the bomb." The culinary myth explains Silko's belief that "If the white people never looked beyond the lie (sorcery) ... then they would never be able to understand how they had been used by the witchery" (*ibid.*, 191).

## Silko and the Amerindian Perspective

Silko's premiere novel, which grew organically from a single character, followed Kiowa author Navarre Scott Momaday's introduction of the Indian point of view to mainstream fiction in his Pulitzer Prize-winning classic *House Made of Dawn* (1968). Mirroring Momaday's war veteran Abel, Silko's narrative pictures Tayo, the protagonist, at the Jackpile uranium mine in New Mexico, where he realizes that all people labor under the possibility of an apocalyptic end engineered by nameless, faceless destroyers. To account for betrayal of earth's promise, Silko incorporates the myth of the Ck'o'yo con artist and gambler Pa'caya'nyi, a trickster who lures the Pueblo away from revering Corn Woman (Nau't-s'ity'i), a maternal nature deity. Disrespect for the land causes an imbalance engendered by the Greek sin of *hubris* (pride), which overshadows reverence. Blasphemy by both Tayo and Emo, his nemesis, leads to drought and famine, an ecofeminist punishment for corrupting the Laguna Pueblo's sources of food and groundwater. In the estimation of Jesús Benito Sánchez, Ana Ma Manzanas Calvo, and Begoña Simal González, literary specialists at the universities of Valladolid, Salamanca, and La Coruña, respectively, the novel posits Silko's vision of human fallibility, "an example of tragic ecoapocalypse truncated by a utopian ending" (Sánchez, Calvo, & González, 2009, 218). The trio declare that "what is required is salvation, not merely emendation" (*ibid.*). Thus, after Tayo's purification of self-hatred and vengeance, he assumes the role of savior.

To rescind desecration of the Mother Creator, Tayo must freelance a modern ceremony to absolve himself of sin. According to Sara L. Spurgeon, a specialist in frontier mythos, Tayo "engages in neither passive resignation nor violent retribution when he identifies the witches who are working to bring about his own death and the worldwide destruction promised by their acts at Trinity Site and Los Alamos, nor does he succumb to a blind hatred of whites" (Spurgeon, 2005, 97). Implementing the wisdom he gains from two sages, Ku'oosh and Betonie, Tayo subverts the aim of evil by refusing to stab his enemy Emo with the sharpened screwdriver and redeems himself from wrong by allying with Ts'eh Montaño, an avatar of Ts'its'tsi'nako (Thought Woman), the Mother Creator. In her honor, Tayo leaves Harley to his own destruction and returns to the propagation and collection of Ts'eh's healing plants. Implicit in the protagonist's escape lies Ts'eh's warning: "They have their stories about us— Indian people who are only making time and waiting for the end" (Silko, 1977, 232). A hero over sorcery, Tayo negotiates his own release: "Every evil which entangled him was cut to pieces" (*ibid.*, 240). Critic John Emory Dean warns that, for Tayo, "It will not be easy exposing the lie of the shadow discourse" (Dean, 2009, 170). For his integrity and his rational control of instinct, Tayo accepts a signal reward from Laguna elders, an invitation to the kiva to prepare himself for a Pueblo priesthood and share his story. As the novel predicts from the beginning, "Evil is mighty but it can't stand up to our stories" (Silko, 1977, 2).

## SILKO'S CHALLENGE

The original manuscript of *Ceremony* teetered on the edge of too much candor. Richard Seaver, Silko's editor at Viking Press, feared that the racial depiction of evil as white witchery too strongly berated white Americans for subverting good, specifically, President Harry Truman for ending World War II by dropping the atomic bomb on unsuspecting Japanese civilians. Retreating from the role of a Cassandra, Silko moderated the image of the demonized white by incriminating military leaders and scientists for rushing into bomb making without perceiving its cataclysmic power and the danger it poses to nature. Silko's cautionary tale warns that, once evil breaks loose, "it isn't very easy to fix up things again," an understatement of the desecration of Laguna land by uranium mining and of the threat of nuclear warfare among nations (*ibid.*, 256). Critic Spurgeon enhances the face-off at the Jackpile mine to "a profound change in the narrative trajectory of captivity myths, which have traditionally been constructed around the idea of separation and the mortal dangers of contact with the Other" (Spurgeon, 2005, 98). Unlike the standard frontier captivity episode, temporarily, Silko's novel spins evil away from the control of the wicked. The narratives declares, "It is dead for now," a statement repeated four times to encompass the four cardinal directions that Tayo traverses in restoring wholeness and health to himself and the Laguna (*ibid.*, 261).

Despite Tayo's pious greeting to the sunrise, Silko indicates that a deadly power still stalks the land. John Emory Dean surmises that, by recognizing "that evil cannot be destroyed because it is an integral part of the cosmic balance," Tayo becomes the messenger to the kiva, the platonic quester who has tracked yin and yang to their source, much as Fly and Hummingbird trail Ck'o'yo magic into the netherworld to restore the rainclouds (Dean,

2009, 15). For the author's humanistic evaluation of evil, critical evaluations boost the novel to classic status among high school, college, and university teachers of American literature, anthropology, sociology, women's studies, psychology, religion, and criminology. For the global impact of *Ceremony*, critic Alan Velie named the author a native literary master in company with Momaday, Anishinaabe author Gerald Robert Vizenor, and Blackfeet poet James Welch. According to Frank MacShane, a critic for the *New York Times*, the folkloric quality and the concluding benediction to dawn earn Silko acclaim as her era's most accomplished native writer.

## A SUPERSATURATED EVIL

By ramping up the volume of vicious deeds in *Almanac of the Dead* (1991), an allegory of universal strife between good and evil, Silko shocked readers and critics with the boldness of her indictments against white capitalism and Christianity. She chooses Tucson as a locus of manipulation, crazed materialism, and self-gratification. Polluted by its modern sewage system and cynical coyote deliveries and land deals, the city becomes a nexus of alcohol, marijuana, cocaine, arms and drug trafficking, medical malpractice, and sexual depravity. Lacking a model of stable marriage and family life, the action spreads across the land like a reeking stain from the residue of murder for hire, decaying corpses, organ harvesting, trafficking in illegal Mesoamerican aliens, and casual snuff-outs of children, prisoners, and Viet vets recorded for sale on video. Beaufrey, a clinically detached photographer, profits from stills of the suicide of his lover Eric; in Colombia, Beaufrey kidnaps and dismembers Monte, Seese and David's six-month-old son, and offers the baby's body parts for sale. Meanwhile, developer Leah Blue plots with paraplegic Eddie Trigg to drain Tucson's water reserves to plan an aqua-themed city named Venice, Arizona, adorned with nonnative water plants and trees. Silko turns to caricature "the architect's scale models of the canals and lakes and golf courses," where "quaint gondolas" ferry players to the tee (Silko, 1991, 378, 652). Silko sparks satire in a comparison of the fantasy city with Venice, Italy, an ancient urban settlement once decimated by the Black Death and permanently weakened by its gradual sinking into the Mediterranean Sea. In Mexico, evil takes the form of newborn infants tossed into trashcans and the decapitation of the U.S. legate to Mexico and his aide, whose skulls pollute the Xochimilco gardens. The outrageous iniquity of *Almanac* leaves no out for earth's destroyers, whom Silko depicts as so haunted by the cries of wraiths that they develop a restless urge to quit earth and travel Mars and Saturn.

*Almanac*'s degenerates are icons of white materialism, which objectifies nature as a commodity rather than earth's life-support system. To interviewer Ellen L. Arnold, the author justified the cast of dissolute characters: "I had to look for what was good and positive, because I saw political evil going on — the way the Tucson police killed people and beat them up" (Silko & Arnold, 2000, 100). The novelist extended the range of malignancy by declaring, "Evil is everywhere just like the dry heat that parches the landscape" (*ibid.*, 130). In particular, she vilified "the use of economics to terrorize and coerce" the underclass (*ibid.*, 132). A prime example of criminality in dissolute authority figures, Judge Arne metes out verdicts in the Phoenix federal district court that favor his perverted notion of right. Favoring the white rationale for repression of the poor, he "was sophisticated enough to understand the strategy for national security: cocaine smuggling was a lesser evil than communism. Cocaine smuggling could be tolerated for the greater good" (*ibid.*, 648).

## PLOTTING AN APOCALYPSE

The novel spins out Silko's hatred of whites for arming themselves to slaughter animals and redistribute confiscated cocaine, poisoning water and causing drought and famine, engineering a form of AIDS to kill off minorities, and spreading despair among the dwindling population of Indians who survive racial profiling by military and undercover cops. Of the wrongs committed against the powerless, Silko explained, "Injustice I pretty much equate with evil, an imbalance and un-wellness" (Silko & Arnold, 2000, 105). The exploitation of uranium ores and the disconnect of humankind from the Earth Mother's discipline whirl into motion global doom. In the falling action, Montaño describes the witchery of whites as a form of Aztec sacrifice, the evisceration of a living being and the removal of a beating heart. Given full rein, the murderous bent gradually thickens whites' scars and rids them of feeling while enlarging their hunger for butchery.

For metaphoric shape, Silko chooses the webbed circle. The matrix functions as both an interlocking of heinous schemes and a tribute to Grandmother Spider (Ts'its'tsi'nako or Thought Woman), the maternal creator voice, and to the sacred wheel radiating from Tucson. In the estimation of Ann Folwell Stanford, an expert on literature and healing at the University of North Carolina at Chapel Hill, *Almanac* challenges readers to ponder not only individual faults "but also the role of institutional blindness, complicity, and neglect as factors contributing to oppression and disease" (Stanford, 1997, 28). The evil generated by technocracy and by corrupt police, CIA, border patrols, and federal courts derives from a nation trying to live out its rosy myths of Manifest Destiny while camouflaging generations of conquest, bondage, and dispossession.

In the finale, redress erupts into a cacophony of strategies. New Age medicine applies snake-oil treatments, sorcery, chants, meditation, and crystals to combat "dark nights of the soul on the continents where Christianity had repeatedly violated its own canons" (Silko, 1991, 478). A ragtag assembly at the International Holistic Healer's Convention musters pan-American rescuers, shamans, mountebanks, and prophets who propose to cleanse the planet of its malefactors. The collection of Asians, blacks, Cubans, Indians, *mestizos,* and down-on-their-luck whites merges because of a mutual political expediency, a need to relieve the anguish of the doomed and economically fettered have-nots. Silko pictures the behind-the-scenes labors of eco-terrorists, who blow up Glen Canyon Dam, and antagonized fomenters who "burned with the blue flame of bitterness and outrage" (*ibid.,* 690). Awa Gee, a Korean techno-wizard, plants computer viruses and sabotages electrical grids so "Earth that was bare and empty ... that had been seized and torn open, would be allowed to heal and to rest in the darkness after the lights were turned out" (*ibid.,* 683). The prophecy suggests a return to the basic circle of communities gathered around a restorative fire.

## EVIL AND WOMANHOOD

In *Gardens in the Dunes* (1999), Silko focuses on females caught in a vortex of evil just as insidious as that of *Almanac of the Dead.* Her white protagonist, Hattie Abbott Palmer, muddles through the Cartesian paradigm of evil that Puritanic teachers inflict on children in Sunday school. From her humanistic father, Hattie trusts a loving, merciful god: "No devil could harm Hattie — she was confident God loved her too much to allow evil to touch her" (Silko, 1999, 94). Taboos against masturbation and recreational sex confuse her understanding of femininity and destroy her natural urge for coitus with her husband, Dr. Edward Palmer, and a willingness to bear children. Complicating her consciousness of self and career, the all-male reviewing committee at Harvard Divinity School castigates Hattie for impiety in researching Gnostic church authors Basilides, Carpocrates, Cerinthus, Marcion, Simon Magus, and Valentinus and for postulating a discipleship of Mary Magdalene to Jesus. Hattie's critics declare her reasoning "impetuous and unsound ... heresy, pure and simple" (*ibid.*, 98). Because of the shunning by male prelates, Hattie recognizes the ongoing power struggle between vulnerable women and arrogant men, the omnipotent rulers of state, the economy, and theology. Rather than kowtow to ecclesiastical tyrants, Hattie chooses the way of Sophia (wisdom), a contemplation of truth outside the dogma of orthodoxy. A one-on-one confrontation with evil proves more destructive than Hattie's grilling by misogynistic scholars. Like the serpent in Eden, Mr. Hyslop, Hattie's classmate, worms his way into her confidence and attempts a carriage rape by which "confidence in her entire life and her very being were changed forever" (*ibid.*, 103. Sexual battery distorts Hattie's rationality, plunging her into a cycle of psychosomatic ills, a Freudian response to evil.

Silko segues immediately to Indigo, her Sand Lizard heroine, who flees confinement at the Sherman Institute in Riverside, California, a source of brainwashing of Indian girls to ready them for domestic service to white women. Ironically, the institute bears much in common with the pompous Harvard Divinity School. Upon arrival at the Palmers' glass greenhouse, Indigo struggles with white duplicity, symbolized by a cunning door latch — "press down, lift up, twist left, twist right," a physical barrier to female freedom that echoes Hattie's attempts to refute male doctrinal theology. The bonding of the two — Hattie with foster daughter Indigo — creates a womanly force against a shared evil, the greed of Edward, a bio-pirate. Following Edward's coma and death from the malpractice of Dr. William Gates and the return of the Abbotts and a hovering lawyer to reclaim their daughter from Indians, Hattie turns her back on white authority figures. By torching the town of Needles, California, she ignites "little wings of flame [that] gave off a lemon yellow glow ... reds as rich as blood, the blues and whites luminous," a madwoman scene suggesting the torching of Thornfield Hall by Bertha Mason, the suppressed wife in Charlotte Bronte's *Jane Eyre* (1847) (*ibid.*, 472). Significantly, the fire at Needles centers on the train depot, the arrival point for destructive engineers and dam builders and the place of degradation for women, who hawk woven baskets to tourists to save their families from starvation. Hattie's sacramental arson retaliates against evil by destroying the commercial mechanism that males flaunt over women and children in the Southwest.

   *See also* Betonie; Emo; genocide; Hattie; Indigo; Tayo; vengeance; Yellow Woman.

• *References and further reading*

Baringer, Sandra. *The Metanarrative of Suspicion in Late Twentieth Century America.* New York: Routledge, 2004.
Bell, Betty Louise. "Indians with Voices: Revisiting *Savagism and Civilization*" in *American Mythologies: Essays in Contemporary Literature*, eds. William Blazek and Michael K. Glenday. Liverpool, UK: Liverpool University Press, 2005, 15–28.
Dean, John Emory. *Travel Narratives from New Mexico: Reconstructing Identity and Truth.* Amherst, NY: Cambria, 2009.
Kidwell, Clara Sue, and Alan R. Velie. *Native American Studies.* Lincoln: University of Nebraska Press, 2005.
Lauter, Paul. *A Companion to American Literature and Culture.* Malden, MA: Blackwell-Wiley, 2010.
MacShane, Frank. "Review: *Ceremony*," *New York Times Book Review* (12 June 1977): 15.
Martin, Holly E. "Hybrid Landscapes as Catalysts for Cultural Reconciliation in Leslie Marmon Silko's *Ceremony* and Rudolfo Anaya's *Bless Me, Ultima*," *Atenea* 26:1 (June 2006): 131–149.
Owens, Louis. *Other Destinies: Understanding the American Indian Novel.* Norman: University of Oklahoma Press, 1994.

Sánchez, Jesús Benito, Ana Ma Manzanas Calvo, and Begoña Simal González. *Uncertain Mirrors: Magical Realisms in US Ethnic Literatures*. New York: Rodopi, 2009.

Silko, Leslie Marmon. *Almanac of the Dead*. New York: Simon & Schuster, 1991.

_____. *Ceremony*. New York: Viking, 1977.

_____. *Gardens in the Dunes*. New York: Scribner, 1999.

_____. *Yellow Woman and a Beauty of the Spirit: Essays on Native American Life Today*. New York: Simon & Schuster, 1996.

_____, and Ellen L. Arnold. *Conversations with Leslie Marmon Silko*. Jackson: University Press of Mississippi, 2000.

Spurgeon, Sara L. *Exploding the Western: Myths of Empire on the Postmodern Frontier*. College Station: Texas A&M University Press, 2005.

Stanford, Ann Folwell. "'Human Debris': Border Politics, Body Parts, and the Reclamation of the Americas in Leslie Marmon Silko's *Almanac of the Dead*," *Literature and Medicine* 16:1 (Spring 1997): 23–42.

Teuton, Sean Kicummah. *Red Land, Red Power: Grounding Knowledge in the American Indian Novel*. Durham, NC: Duke University Press, 2008.

Velie, Alan R. *Four American Literary Masters*. Norman: University of Oklahoma Press, 1982.

# feminism

Silko characterizes a native woman's view of the Women's Movement, a stance she evolves from her gynocratic Laguna birthright rather than from her blood kinship to Mexicans and whites. A focus of feminist narrative by such experts as Isabel Allende, Laura Esquivel, Maxine Hong Kingston, Toni Morrison, Fae Myenne Ng, and Amy Tan, woman-to-woman talk-story, such as episodes involving Yellow Woman, convey female experience on the innocent. Silko's wisewoman tales reclaim the maternal tradition of teaching and alerting girls through confessional, exemplum, fable, folklore, genealogy, legend, morality tale, and therapeutic anecdote, such as the author's unpublished tutorial "How to Hunt Buffalo" (1994). The testimonial of a life passage addresses the teller's violation of good sense or of sexual or social infractions, the focus of "Laughing and Laughing about Something That Happened at Mesita" (1974). Wendy Ho, author of *In Her Mother's House* (1999), describes the rhythm of womanly tales as "a complicated vocabulary of rupture"—downcast gaze, handwringing, sighing, silences, quivering lips, and sobs (Ho, 1999, 19).

The author grounds her perspective on creation in the web spun by Grandmother Spider (Ts'its'tsi'nako or Thought Woman), a Pueblo image replete with connections and possibilities of extension. Unlike Judaeo-Christian philosophy, which limits Eve, the Hebrew prototype, with transgression and damnation, Pueblo cosmology reveres the female as generator of the "motherworld," the universal feminine, which knows no limitations. Silko, a 21st-century granddaughter of the spider-creator, explained in an interview why she follows the example of the spinner of webs: "I feel it is more effective to write a story ... than to rant and rave. I think it is more effective in reaching people" (Seyersted, 1985, 24). Critic Gayle Elliott explains that, by spinning a circular matrix, Silko, the present-day equivalent of Grandmother Spider, avoids the legalistic and deterministic mindset of the West. Instead, she views the tensions between opposites as "interactive and dynamic, part of a process that establishes continuity and relation, even within areas of difference" (Elliott, 2008, 181). Consequently, Silko's feminist stories maintain a freshness and renewed applicability to a variety of human situations.

The author's early verse probes the motivation of female self-starters. In the poem "Si'ahh aash" (1972), the speaker contrasts the anti-woman gossip about adulteresses in the first stave with the subjective self-analysis of a Pueblo woman in the second stave. A 17-syllable haiku, the second half mocks the arrogant man who can number his conquests like horses in a corral. In the female perspective, the addition of one more woman to his stable acknowledges the fertility and beauty in all the married women he preys on. The author credits possessors of a healthy libido and intellectual curiosity as females capable of embracing human sexuality in all its forms, including self-expression and pleasure. The poem corroborates Silko's admiration for assertive characters such as Yellow Woman (Kochininako), the mountain demigoddess Ts'eh Montaño, and Helen Jean, the Ute wanderer from the Towac reservation in *Ceremony* (1977); Aunt Susie Reyes Marmon and Grandma A'mooh in *Storyteller* (1981); Seese and Yoeme in *Almanac of the Dead* (1991); Sister Salt, Grandma Fleet, and Mama, the brave foragers for love in *Gardens in the Dunes* (1999); and the author herself in *The Turquoise Ledge* (2010). These free-spirited characters embody the erotics of nature, where rainclouds distribute droplets (sperm) on the receptive womb of the terrain, a womanly metaphor that Silko celebrates in words and photos in *Sacred Water: Narratives and Pictures* (1993).

In a paired poem, "Mesita Men" (fall 1972), Silko stresses the female need to evaluate choices to ensure self-regard. She shifts the tone of the previous poem from encouragement of hasty coupling to an examination of male motives. The satire skewers womanizers who consider a meal of chili stew an appropriate introit to a hasty fling. The rhymes make short work of identifying the stew with "you," the momentary *desiderata* whom the seducer devours like a snack (*ibid.*, 21). The comment reminds females of the first order of feminism: determine, validate, and nurture woman's worth. If a rendezvous with Mesita men honors that worth, then Silko fosters a conjugal episode for its value to both parties. Carolyn Dunn, a Cherokee/Muskogee/Seminole scholar at the University of Southern California, explains the author's depiction of female passion: "While modern middle-class academic feminists try to regather and remember the power they once had, we women of color never forgot our power" (Dunn, 2005, 197). Unlike the white captivity narratives of frontier literature featuring fear of cross-cultural sexual escapades, Silko places her assertive women in tales that prioritize the relation of tribes to the Coyotesse, the sacred storyteller and bringer of nourishment and vision. Without misgivings or shame, the female buccaneer celebrates life and regeneration as the core of tribal beliefs.

## AYAH, THE MERCIFUL

Silko's most famous story, "Lullaby" (1981), a selection in *The Best American Short Stories of 1975*, depicts an imposing womanly empowerment. At the height of personal loss, the elderly protagonist, Ayah, copes by displaying dignity and perseverance. In early womanhood, she goes into labor "learning the rhythms of the pains," which "merged into the births of the other children and to her it became all the same birth" (Silko 1974, 13). Her welcome of motherhood as a life pattern derives from a serene harmony with the elements and from receptivity to the inborn fertility that grants her babies. In the face of unspeakable poverty, the combat death of Jimmie, Grandma's loss to tuberculosis, the detribalization of her children, Danny and Ella, and the diminished manhood of her husband Chato, Ayah maintains vigor and patience unlike that found in white feminist literature. Her attitude toward change epitomizes the Navajo goddess Changing Woman (Asdz a nádleehé), the mystic deity of nature and birth. For her position over earth events—the changing of the seasons and the life cycle, birth, maturity, old age, and death—Changing Woman serves as guardian of *hozho*, the Navajo ideal of order, balance, and beauty.

A model of the unassimilated Indian woman in a land dominated by hostile whites,

Ayah witnesses attrition in a native culture that traditionally valued female solidarity in birthing, mothering, and domestic work in the family hogan. She internalizes the handicap to Chato's crushed leg, which reduces him from cowboy to sheepherder: "She knew he did not like walking behind old ewes when for so many years he rode big quarter horses and worked with cattle" (*ibid.*, 12). The image of the macho rider following female sheep epitomizes Chato's ignominy in a lusty male milieu. At the height of her resolve to exert her role as wife and helpmeet, Ayah, an ordinary Navajo matriarch at Cebolleta Creek outside Cañoncito, New Mexico, takes on the form of the Pueblo goddess Ts'its'tsi'nako. In interloper among white males, Ayah achieves status for autonomy, persistence, and an endurance that repudiates victimhood. Silko ennobles Ayah's stride into Azzie's Bar, where Chato turns to wine as an antidote to pain and humiliation. The drinkers view her as "a spider crawling slowly across the room. They were afraid; she could feel the fear" (*ibid.*, 16). On the couple's return home, lacking Chato's bilingual methods of engaging with the outside world, Ayah retreats to Yeibechei (spirit) song, a matriarch's ideal stated in pastoral verse. From an animistic perspective, she solaces their pain by acquiescing to the spirit world. Her benediction retains the dignity of husband and wife as they lapse into a graceful, naturalistic death from exposure to cold. Her choice presents a model of mercy toward Chato and cooperation with nature that refutes Darwin's belief that life equates with struggle. Critic Patrice E. M. Hollrah, a specialist in native American literature at the University of Nevada, summarizes: "The story ends on a dual note, one that implies death, but more importantly one that signifies continuity, survival, and hope" (Hollrah, 2004, 54).

## FEMINISM IN GIRL AND WOMAN

In a similar spirit of cohesion, Silko's most effective comparison of "womanthought" occurs in *Gardens in the Dunes* (1999), an intercalary study of two women seeking self-regard and purpose. According to Silko expert Brewster E. Fitz, the author creates "tension between writing, embodied in the thesis project Hattie never completes, and the 'language of love' that Silko depicts spoken at the Ghost Dance," where the Messiah and Holy Mother address all participants in their own languages (Fitz, 2004, 193). The epiphany of universal love as a communicator returns to Hattie in the vision of the Virgin Mary in Bastia, Corsica, above the door on a schoolhouse wall, a Pentecostal event that engages the spirit rather than the intellect. The press of peasants and their awe at the appearance nudges Hattie toward a new level of sanctity: "So this was what was called a miracle — she felt wonder and excitement, though she saw the glow of colored light on the wall for only an instant" (Silko, 1999, 320). Beside her, Indigo, a runaway from Sherman Institute in Riverside, California, welcomes an otherworldly message: "All who are lost will be found, a voice inside her said" (*ibid.*). Indigo accepts the statement as the Messiah's promise. In the background, Hattie's husband, Dr. Edward Palmer, "wisecracked about 'religious hysteria,'" his explanation of a visitation by the Blessed Mother (*ibid.*). The contrast explains why Hattie finds joy in foster motherhood rather than in wedlock to a pedant.

While fostering and educating Indigo, Hattie ignores Edward's cynicism and evolves a syncretic, universal belief in goddess worship. She reveres snake images, a mystic, primal force in paleolithic religion that connects the sinuous reptilian body with the meandering of flowing waters, which have their source underground in the unseen realm of the gods. Brewster Fitz notes that the libraries and gardens in Somerset, England, and Lucca, Italy, form a web that rescues Hattie from the grip of an androcentric scholarly world that is intolerant, repressive, straitlaced, and exclusionary. In place of male dominance, she achieves "endless transition ... in a world in which spatial and temporal boundaries and inequality are erased in an embrace that is earthly, maternal, spiritual, and writerly" (*ibid.*, 200). Significant to Hattie's liberation is the storage of the remains of her unfeeling husband, in an ice locker, a suitable repository for a man devoted to the patronizing of his wife and the financial exploitation of natural beauty and of her bank account. Renewed by her experiences in the gardens of Aunt Bronwyn and *la professoressa* Laura and by her transcendent experience in Corsica, Hattie embraces her abandoned academic heresy as a source of social equality and openness to diversity, qualities that dominate Silko's canon.

See also abortion; food; Indigo; Montaño, Ts'eh; Palmer, Hattie Abbott; sex; women; Yellow Woman.

• *References and further reading*

Cook, Barbara. *Women Writing Nature: A Feminist View.* Lanham, MD: Rowman & Littlefield, 2008.

Danielson, Linda L. "Storyteller: Grandmother Spider's Web," *Journal of the Southwest* 30:3 (Autumn 1988): 325–355.

Dunn, Carolyn. "The Trick Is Going Home: Secular Spiritualism in Native American Women's Literature" in *Reading Native American Women: Critical/Creative Representations*, ed. Inés Hernández-Avila. Lanham, MD: Altamira, 2005, 189–203.

Elliott, Gayle. "Silko, Le Sueur, and Le Guin: Storytelling as a 'Movement Toward Wholeness'" in *Scribbling Women & the Short Story Form: Approaches by American & British Women Writers*, ed. Ellen Burton Harrington. New York: Peter Lang, 2008, 178–192.

Fitz, Brewster E. *Silko: Writing Storyteller and Medicine Woman.* Norman: University of Oklahoma Press, 2004.

Ho, Wendy. *In Her Mother's House: The Politics of Asian American Mother-Daughter Writing.* Blue Ridge Summit, PA: AltaMira, 1999.

Hollrah, Patrice E. M. *"The Old Lady Trill, the Victory Yell": The Power of Women in Native American Literature.* New York: Routledge, 2004.

Seyersted, Per. "Interview with Leslie Marmon Silko," *American Studies in Scandinavia* 13 (1985): 17–25.

Silko, Leslie Marmon. *Gardens in the Dunes.* New York: Scribner, 1999.

_____. *Laguna Woman: Poems.* New York: Greenfield Review, 1974.

_____. "Lullaby," *Chicago Review* 26:1 (Summer 1974): 10–17.

# food

The feeding of the clan holds a prime position in Silko's ordering of native priorities, which includes shielding the family and feeding hungry visitors, a Laguna tradition. Kenneth Lincoln, an English professor at the University of California at Los Angeles, characterizes her pueblo story-poems as embodiments of nourishment in all nature — "family quests, trysts and heartbreaks, daily food-and-shelter needs and fears, seasonal observances to petition natural spirits of place and time, muses and mythological advisories, the rocks and soil and foliage and streams and animals of a given place known as home or village" (Lincoln, 2008, 90). Silko stresses in *Yellow Woman and a Beauty of the Spirit: Essays on Native American Life Today* (1996) that, in her childhood, food introduced an evening of storytelling, where sharing was communal — "past, present, and future, in a never-ending story": "No person, no stranger who arrived at mealtime was ever refused, even if everyone else had a bit less on the plate, because the sharing of food is a fundamental expression of humanity" (Silko, 1996, 97). Even the Navajo, known for raiding pueblos for foodstuffs and women, received welcome. For everyday sharing, the Laguna meted out all resources "so that no one person or group had more than another," a concept contrary to the materialism of the white world (*ibid.*, 65). Adults scolded children who wasted their portions and insisted that each diner observe mealtime thanks "to all of the animal and plant being that had given themselves to human beings to stop hunger" (*ibid.*, 96–97). The ritual concludes with a gesture of thanks to past lives, which the Laguna honor with pinches of food, an act that Silko reiterates to James Wright, her correspondent in *The Delicacy and Strength of Lace* (1986), and in *Sacred Water: Narratives and Pictures* (1993).

For an early coming-of-age story, "Humaweepi, the Warrior Priest" (1974), the author depicts the title character and his elderly uncle/mentor making simple preparations for a camp-out with the packing of trail food — dried apples, venison jerky, and piki bread — in a cotton sack. On ventures into thickets to sleep on the ground, sometimes they pack nothing and rely on foraging — wild grapes dried into raisins, iris roots, wild tulip bulbs, tumbleweed sprouts, and grass roots washed in rainwater. The lesson from mentor to neophyte elicits sympathy for all creation: "All the animals are hungry — not just you" (Silko, 1974, 163). The elderly uncle's trust translates into humility and gratitude in Humaweepi, who applies the moral to his emergence into full priesthood.

FOOD AND RITUAL

In *Ceremony* (1977), her premiere novel, Silko depicts the healing quality of food and food ritual, especially the local commodities found at Laguna. Symbolically, according to frontier expert Sara L. Spurgeon, the world's pain begins with "the coming of white people who bring with them disease, starvation, and massacres, and for whom the natural world, the rocks, plants, and animals are dead things" (Spurgeon, 2005, 96). For 26-year-old Tayo, the battle-fatigued veteran of the Pacific war, the nothingness of medical treatment at a veterans' hospital in Los Angeles includes "outlines of gray steel tables, outlines of the food they pushed into his mouth" (Silko, 1977, 13). Because of his affliction with post-traumatic stress disorder, his stomach cramps from swallowing these meaningless meals. He recalls in his teens hunting deer with his Uncle Josiah and cousin/foster brother Rocky. At the end of a kill, Josiah and Tayo perform ceremonial thanksgiving over the carcass and thank the deer for giving its life to provide the family with venison. Rocky expresses his contempt for nativism by refusing to take part in glorifying an animal carcass. The image foreshadows his own death in the Philippines, where the desecration of life plunges Tayo into despair.

On Tayo's return to the care of Auntie Thelma, native food is both restorative and curative. A spoon-feeding of mush made from blue cornmeal (*Zea mays*) and sips of Indian tea (*Ephedra fasciculata*), an alkaloid stimulant also called Mormon tea, calms his chronic nausea and heaving. On a long ride to the Dixie Tavern with Harley, a gift of small wild grapes (*Vitis vinifera*) "not much bigger than blueberries" confers the strength of the vine, which grows from sand in the fissure of a boulder, a symbol of native hardihood (*ibid.*, 41). Harley crunches seeds while Tayo, fearful of the sound, chooses a sip of spring water as a deterrent to war memories of Japanese rifle butts crushing skulls. Silko confers restorative power to the water, which flows during the drought to nourish the cottonwoods, yucca, rabbit brush, and yellow daisies. The flow refreshes Tayo with a childhood memory of siphoning water from the cave in boyhood from a cascade "always cold icy cold, even in the summer" (*ibid.*, 45).

The commitment to Uncle Josiah's spotted Mexican cattle anchors the resolution of *Ceremony* to the hardscrabble desert and the frequent scarcity of food and water for Laguna. Contrasting his return to pueblo bounty, Silko depicts Tayo on a bridge at Gallup gazing down at shanties on the riverbank, where Hopi, Laguna, Navajo, and Zuni derelicts live on wine and liquor. He observes children who "learned to stand at a distance and see if [their mothers] would throw them food" (*ibid.*, 108). Out of pity, especially for the innocent, Tayo tosses coins to the poor. He continues his search for wellness by reenacting the journey of Fly and Hummingbird to the fourth world to seek rain and sustenance from the Mother Creator. To accomplish the task, he follows a spiritual map that removes obstacles between humankind and animals. In thanks for Tayo's recovery, his cousins repay Ku'oosh with lard buckets filled with home-cooked food—chili, oven bread, and fry bread, a native delicacy.

BOLSTERING THE POOR

Silko's *Almanac of the Dead* (1991), an excoriation of widespread iniquity radiating from Tucson, Arizona, poses a more lacerating condemnation of hunger. Katherine Sugg, an English expert at Central Connecticut State University, depicts the work as Gothic allegory: "The apocalypse that is recorded in the notebooks is thinly veiled to suggest a period after the colonial conquest of the Americas, after 'the Butcher' and 'the aliens' have exploited and devastated the land and the people" (Sugg, 2008, 90). The narrative begins with the needs of the have-nots, who cluster in homeless urban shelters and along the Arizona-Mexico border. In the glimpses of starvation that Calabazas views in Mexico, he flinches from Guatemalan and Salvadorian refugees contributing to daily human collapse throughout Sonora. Amid the struggle for sustenance, "The children poked around in the dirt looking for coins that might have been lost in the confusion," a pathetic reminder that even loose change can mean the difference between starving and surviving (Silko, 1991, 477). As the situation worsens, drought and heat "trigger famines that sent refugees north faster and faster," a steady flow of needy that escalates hunger to catastrophe (*ibid.*, 756). The Mexican air force, lacking any means of rescuing people from want, turns them into corpses at the city dump, where army bulldozers level lean-tos and shanties amid human remains, "broken glass, rusted tin cans and rotting dog carcasses" (*ibid.*, 583). Those who survive roast rats at the risk of contracting bubonic plague and cholera. The revolting ingestion of vermin shames Americans for such third world conditions.

At a turning point in her fiction of a spontaneous revolt, Silko must admit that food staples are essential to a revolution: "A people's army needed food" (*ibid.*, 710). She turns human need into further demonizing of the U.S., where the "government might have no money for the starving, but there was always government money for weapons and death" (*ibid.*, 711). Channeling the sermons of Wovoka, the Paiute evangelist of the previous century, at the International Holistic Healers Convention in Tucson, Lakota poet and visionary Wilson Weasel Tail meets need with fantasy by foreseeing the return of the buffalo, the Amerindian version of manna from heaven. Clinton, the cynical black–Cherokee teacher of Afro-American history, manages to dismiss as minimal the 200 to 300 casualties of police firefights: "Hundreds more of them died every year from starvation and its complications, which were slow and painful" (*ibid.*, 747). Silko predicts that, "Like little seeds, the [outrage] would grow, and the police violence that had rained down on the people would only nurture the growing bitterness" (*ibid.*, 741). As usual in global strife, "women and children, the old and the sick, the innocent and the weak, would die first" (*ibid.*, 753). In Silko's merciless urban anarchy, no one has the time or resources to minister to those most in danger of dying.

To repudiate Marxism as an answer to global poverty and oppression, the author declares the unforgivable sin of Mao and Stalin, Chinese and Russian Communist patriarchs, for uneven food distribution during famines: "No crime was worse than to allow some human beings to starve while others ate, especially not one's own sisters and brothers" (*ibid.*, 316). In Silko's lengthy exoneration of Geronimo's renegade Apache band in the previous century, she pictures the more beneficent Amerindian guerrilla warriors climbing to the high country to share mutton ribs with hungry Yaqui, a people separated by the American boundary with Mexico. In contrast to Indian generosity, the text pictures "bankers and Christians of the capitalist industrial world" as guilty of the mass starvation of "*many many millions*" (*ibid.*). The statement conveys Silko's pervasive curse of Christians for violating the basic ideals of Christ, who fed the multitudes on five loaves and two fish. Rather than carry her prophecy to its inevitable conclusion, she closes the curtains on the suffering masses to picture Sterling returning to the Laguna to make peace Indian style with past sins.

HORTICULTURE AND FOOD GROWING

In the dry desert sandhills featured in *Gardens in the Dunes* (1999), Silko attempted to write an apolitical story about flowers and food plants, but found she "had stumbled into the most political thing of all—how you grow your food, whether you eat, the fact that the plant collectors followed the Conquistadors" (Silko & Arnold, 2000, 164). In the text, lessons in survival begin early for protagonists Indigo and Sister Salt, members of the last Sand Lizard matriarchy. The uniqueness of "sand food" has its own appeal, a "mild salty green tastes better than cucumbers" (Silko, 1999, 244). Indigo especially loves yellow squash stewed with sweet red peppers, a vegetable meal devoid of the grease that white gluttons prefer. The Sand Lizard matriarch, Grandma Fleet, teaches the sisters to raid a squirrel cache of acorns (*Quercus fagaceae*) and piñons (*Pinus cembroides*). Rather than live at a reservation and eat processed "white food—white bread and white sugar and white lard," Grandma chooses to subsist on meager desert fare (Silko, 1999, 17). She sets the tone of frugality with rationing, which the girls violate. The sisters fear she "would be furious when she found out the two of them had eaten enough food in one evening to last three people for a week," a profligacy that threatens the tribe's survival (*ibid.*, 40). The girls accept her wisdom and apply it to future situations. When food supplies dwindle at the people's campsite along the big river, Sister Salt returns to the abandoned gardens in the sandhills to gather amaranth (*Amaranthus arenicola*, called pigweed) "just like Grandma Fleet taught her" (*ibid.*, 14). The lesson illustrates the female ideal of training children in survival within the constraints of their own milieu.

In adulthood, Sister Salt and Indigo associate food with planting and harvesting. In observations of white gluttony, they wonder, "Where did white people get their food if they didn't plant these fields" (*ibid.*, 165). The question posits the difference in background between urban whites and native hunter-gatherers. For the sisters and their value system, amaranth, a common herb, supplies leafy greens as well as seeds for cereal and flour. They kneel over their grinding stone to crush the seeds into meal for tortillas, which they eat with wild honeycomb. Other backup dishes come from sunflowers (*Helianthus annuus*), prickly pear fruit (*Opuntia ficus-indica*, called tuna), and roots; the high country offers acorns and piñons. In spring, gatherers locate shoots and sprouts; from mesquite (*Prosopis glandulosa*) come beans for flour, which Indians harvest and cache in August. During the incarceration of the sisters on reservations, they lack the freedom to collect nature's bounty while the Indian agent and his staff gobble the cattle and sheep intended to feed captives. The depiction of greed substantiates Silko's claims in *Almanac of the Dead* that oppression begins and ends with control of the food supply.

## DESERT BOUNTY

According to myth, the metaphysical beginning of the gardens preceded the migrant Indians, who profited from the agrarian skills of the "Sand Lizard, a relative of Grandfather Snake" (*ibid.*, 14). When the dune garden flourishes, the sisters look forward to food from the floodplain terraces—black-eyed peas, black corn, chiles, coriander, muskmelons, pumpkins and pumpkin blossoms, speckled beans, squash, white tepary beans (*Phaseolus acutifolius*), and bush beans, which grow under shady pumpkin leaves. During hand watering, the people honor plants by giving them nicknames "Bushy, Fatty, Skinny, Shorty, Mother, and Baby," an anthropomorphism of flora that evidences a familial love of nature (*ibid.*, 16). Upon the return of Mama from kidnap by Indian police and soldiers at Parker, Arizona, a flood of survivors straggles back to the old gardens to dig roots and succulents and gather amaranth. The overflow uses up staples and demands the consumption of sprouted seeds and wild gourd vines. In winter at the depot in Needles, California, Grandma gathers nuts for flour and wildflowers for tea while Mama returns from the hotel with wood scraps and vegetable crates to burn in their cook-fire.

Silko details meals for a family in constant search of nourishment. During the four-day Ghost Dance at Parker, the sisters, Indigo and Sister Salt, partake of water and holy piñon nuts. On the fifth day of their migration south to the dunes, they feed themselves on the roots of cattail (*Typha latifolia*) and fill wild gourds (*Cucurbita pepo*) with water. At Grandma Fleet's house of mesquite poles and willow boughs, they find no cache of kitchen supplies, but her appearance on the sixth day introduces them to canning and preserving by Mrs. Van Wagnen, the historic name of a family of Mormon pioneers. From her shelves and crockery jars, Grandma receives gifts of dried apples and apricots, dried venison, and beans. Silko explains the bounty in terms of location: "Mrs. Van Wagnen had great success growing beans because her garden was near the river" (*ibid.*, 38). She returns the gesture with gifts of leaves, roots, and seeds for Mrs. Van Wagnen's use as curatives and spices. In Grandma's absence, the sisters slither down the canyon into the palm grove to taste sweet dates (*Phoenix dactylifera*). Because the summer heat dries up succulent desert plants, Grandma teaches the girls to listen for roosting birds and to rob the coyote of their prey. From a swift gallop into the night toward sounds of struggle, the girls return with baby rabbits for a stew seasoned with moss and roots. Even when staples seem plentiful, Grandma insists on continued foraging of moss, roots, seeds, and watercress (*Nasturtium officinale*) as well as bird trapping with snares made from human hair and the robbing of the pack rat's nest just in case of a drought. During the mourning period that follows Grandma's death, the sisters remain faithful to growing, drying, and storing food, a rhythm of life in the Southwest that derives from the first desert dwellers.

## FOOD IN THE WHITE WORLD

Silko uses variant meals to stress the abrupt changes in the plot, such as pomegranate trees in the Palmer's garden, mangoes and fish soup aboard the *Louis XIV*, tea in the garden at Somerset, and cactus wine and weekly rations of cornmeal, lard, salt, and sugar at the Parker, Arizona, reservation. After an Apache police officer takes charge of the sisters, food shifts from garden vegetables and fruits to a desert official's stock of canned beans and hardtack. Upon escape from Sherman Institute, in Riverside, California, Indigo encounters a tray topped with bread and strawberry jam, processed foods that seem overly lavish. On her own, she reverts to rose hips and oranges from the citrus grove while, indoors, Dr. Edward and Hattie Palmer dine on lamb chops, mint jelly, green beans, raisin-stuffed potatoes, and mincemeat pie. The complicated recipes contrast the basic Sand Lizard diet, which blends available flavorings such as coriander with desert staples. Silko hints at Hattie's affinity for a simpler diet by picturing her ridding the potato of raisins and avoiding rich lamb and mince pie. To Edward, healing blossoms and roots, seeds, and a red-fleshed melon in Tampico, Mexico, suggest the possibility of unidentified foods and plants for his botanical research. On his return to Riverside, Hattie exhibits less expansive interests than her husband by plotting a domestic garden scented with basil, catmint, coriander, geraniums, rosemary, and wild sage, a domestic array more suited to home than laboratory.

The surprises of a journey from Arizona to Corsica touch frequently on dining. For Indigo, meals take on the strangeness she associates with Atlantic Coast culture. During her travels to Oyster Bay, she encounters fried chicken and roast beef with apple pie for dessert, typical American fare on the train from the Southwest. She relishes fresh mushrooms devoured with dew still on them, wild purple pea blossoms, and green corn and roasted clams eaten along the beach at Oyster Bay. In her ignorance of shore food, she imagines the clams to be little animals living in flat gray stones. The careful recycling of the Matinnecock Indians turns out clam shell buttons. At the going rate of 50 for a quarter, the shore tribe uses the proceeds to buy flour, lard, and salt to expand their diet of dried kelp, fish, and shellfish. Indigo expresses her thanks for dinner by taking decorated gingerbread men to the Indian village and enjoys playing with tame goats by feeding their orphaned kids warm milk from baby bottles. At the Abbott house, Hattie's father delights in a philanthropy project of supplying dwarf milk goats and pigs to feed poor urban families and of raising vegetables around the animal pens. The constant references to feeding and eating undergird Silko's controlling motif of the role of food in economic and political history.

The author speaks through the Afro–Red Stick Indian cook and brewer Big Candy his rise in status among whites. The giver of licorice drops and maker of home brew and grand entrees, he knows that "The person who prepares the food has more power than most people think" (*ibid.*, 217). His interest in beer derives from greed. As a casino manager, he knows that "without beer, the gamblers couldn't hear those voices that urged them to roll the dice again to see how lucky they were" (*ibid.*, 215). For 15 years, he exercises his power over superintendent Wylie by cooking exotic entrees— pheasant in raspberry preserves, deep-fried clam croquettes, pork ribs and barbecue, scallops poached in white wine, venison in wild cranberry sauce, catfish baked in wild plums, and abalone braised in butter. His reflection on his mother, a plantation kitchen slave in Louisiana, leads him to respect females for their skills, including laundresses and sex workers like Chemehuevi-Laguna twins Maytha and Vedna, and Sister Salt. He exhibits his concern for poor women by distributing chicken and turkey skin and carcasses, stale bread, and clean rags to the female beggars in Kingman, Needles, Prescott, and Yuma. His sympathies illustrate a humanistic principle, that people who share labor regard each other's lifestyles and values.

Agrarian Gifts

When the setting of *Gardens in the Dunes* shifts to Europe, Silko dramatizes bounty at a reclaimed cloister garden once cultivated by Norman nuns outside Bath, England. The vegetable parterres offer a cultural mélange — baby peas, carrots, and spinach from the

British Isles; pear trees and peppers from Africa and Asia; asparagus, broad beans, chickpeas, garlic, and onions from Italy; Norman-French cucumbers, dandelion, eggplant, grapevine, and kale; and contributions from the Americas: corn, potatoes, pumpkins, squash, and tomatoes. At *la professoressa* Laura's villa at Lucca, Italy, Indigo loves the texture of fig bread, with its sweetness and tiny seeds. Tuscan vegetable dishes of red peppers and yellow squash return Indigo's thoughts to the travels of seeds from nation to nation, making them "among the greatest travelers of all!" (*ibid.*, 291). Caren Irr, a professor of American literature at Duke University, explains, "In Indigo's plot line, utility, free circulation, and gifts all make the mobility of seeds desirable" (Irr, Caren, 2010, 143). From a feminist perspective, the child's introduction to new lands and peoples arouses her curiosity and inspires her to collect seeds as souvenirs, a pragmatic hobby grounded in her home training in survival and respect for earth. Upon return to Arizona, she eagerly shares her plants, especially the gladiolus corm, which she values for striking beauty and as a vegetable.

Silko's gynocentric perceptions turn inward in her memoir *The Turquoise Ledge* (2010). Daily, like Indigo, she characterizes her walks in the arroyos near her house as a treasure hunt and outdoor classroom. To ensure a good crop, farmers arrange stones in a half circle to form a catch-dam for the runoff from spare rain showers. In an annual ritual, Tohono O'Odom women harvest saguaro fruit (*Cereus giganteus*), a red-hearted treat similar to the pomegranate that they dislodge from the cactus with long poles. They boil the pulp and ferment it into holy wine to encourage summer visits from the ancestors and from the newly deceased in the form of rain clouds. In addition to surveys of desert bounty, Silko ponders a quartzite stone, which appeals because it is the right size for corn grinding, the basic chore of females in the maize-centric Pueblo culture.

One surprising desert find is a concave grinding stone to accommodate the hard dry beans of the mesquite and paloverde (*Cercidium microphyllum*), which ripen in June. Because the beans are useless without pulverization, kitchen stones became the paleolithic housewife's "partners in feeding and caring for her family," which she wielded with a rhythmic song mimicking her grinding action (Silko, 2010, 12). From their centrality to everyday meals, the stones develop into family heirlooms, symbols of women's domestic arts and toils. Because the stones are heavy, they remain under the bean trees, where they are most useful to preparers of blue corn flour for flavorful thick tortillas. In reflections on the kindness of her mother, Virginia Leslie Marmon, in helping Laguna residents read and fill out government forms and write letters, Silko describes homemade gifts to Virginia of bread, blue corn enchiladas, and tamales. Like the food gifts in *Ceremony* and *Gardens of the Dunes*, the reciprocity of kitchen garden and culinary items suggests the dominance of sustenance in the female world, where female specialties become both expressions of artistry and thanks.

- *References and further reading*

Dean, John Emory. *Travel Narratives from New Mexico: Reconstructing Identity and Truth*. Amherst, NY: Cambria, 2009.

Irr, Caren. *Pink Pirates: Contemporary American Women Writers and Copyright*. Iowa City: University of Iowa Press, 2010.

Lincoln, Kenneth. *Speak Like Singing: Classics of Native American Literature*. Albuquerque: University of New Mexico Press, 2008.

Silko, Leslie Marmon. *Almanac of the Dead*. New York: Simon & Schuster, 1991.

_____. *Ceremony*. New York: Viking, 1977.

_____. *Gardens in the Dunes*. New York: Scribner, 1999.

_____. "Humaweepi, the Warrior Priest" in *The Man to Send Rain Clouds: Contemporary Stories by American Indians*, ed. Kenneth Rosen. New York: Viking, 1974.

_____. *The Turquoise Ledge: A Memoir.* New York: Viking Adult, 2010.

_____. *Yellow Woman and a Beauty of the Spirit: Essays on Native American Life Today.* New York: Simon & Schuster, 1996.

_____, and Ellen L. Arnold. *Conversations with Leslie Marmon Silko.* Jackson: University Press of Mississippi, 2000.

Spurgeon, Sara L. *Exploding the Western: Myths of Empire on the Postmodern Frontier.* College Station: Texas A&M University Press, 2005.

Sugg, Katherine. *Gender and Allegory in Transamerican Fiction and Performance.* New York: Palgrave Macmillan, 2008.

## Gardens in the Dunes (1999)

An elegiac *tour de force* set in the 1890s, *Gardens in the Dunes* is both historical novel and a reverse of the captivity narrative and assimilation fiction of the American West. German critic Hartwig Isernhagen, a specialist in American Indian literature at the University of Basel, typifies the genre as "a semantic geography that converts the moral story of the Fall of Man into the binary moral topography of culture vs. nature, history vs. prehistory, progress vs. stagnation (or even degeneration), salvation vs. eternal darkness" (Isernhagen, 2002, 174). Fleshed out in the style of Victorian allegory, the story fictionalizes the survival of the Sand Lizard, modeled on the Sand Papago living south of the Colorado River tribes in a period of Anglo-European nationalism. The narrative of the Gilded Age focuses on the building of a dam, aqueduct, and canal, a European engineering feat that Indians view as sacrilege against the Mother Creator. Scots critic Stuart Christie, an anarchist writer from Glasgow, summarizes the novelist's intent "to cultivate the diversity present in all forms of creation; to assert the essential connectedness of all women (as creators of life) to indigenous places; and, finally, to reject nationalism as an artificial abstraction dividing nature from civilization" (Christie, 2009, 90). Silko moves surefootedly over events, balancing character emotions and motivations with the logic of residents who use nature to their advantage for sustenance and in resistance against clan separation, militarization, and violations of earth. The fictional account hints at the propagation of citriculturist Eliza Tibbets's navel oranges, which she grafted in 1870 from rootstock smuggled by missionaries from São Salvador de Bahia, Brazil.

Silko posits a small closed agrarian culture secure in its identity as Amerindian. In an interview with Ellen L. Arnold, she explained that she created the clan from "one of those remnant, destroyed, extinct groups" (Silko & Arnold, 2000, 164). According to a book review by Karenne Wood in *American Indian Quarterly*, the author invented the Sand Lizard clan "to commemorate the hundreds of small tribes that were annihilated" in the late 19th century (Wood, 1999, 71). The text focuses on a sparse, eccentric family — a grandmother, mother, and two daughters — that refutes the frontier myth of the Southwestern savage. The Sand Lizards earn native American regard for hiding refugees from trouble and for avoiding capturing prisoners or fighting to the death. Essential to the action, the patience of desert dwellers indicates an inbred practicality, evidenced by the protagonist Indigo's return from Europe with corms of rare black gladioli, an emblem of fertility and a symbol of racial and cultural cross-breeding that is both beautiful and edible. Significant to the Indian Wars, the flower name derives from the Latin for "little sword," a token of warfare reduced in threat and hybridized for its rare color.

## THE MALE DESTROYER

The controlling theme relates the destruction of nature and other types of conquest, particularly the redirection of waters at Parker, Arizona, to supply water to Los Angeles. In the construction of a dam at Parker Canyon, engineers, workers, and profiteers ravage the Sonora Desert while wresting the Colorado River from its bed, destroying centuries of riverbank ecology, deliberately chopping fruit trees, and displacing first peoples by a giant man-made lake. Silko stresses the triviality of white egos, particularly the reservation superintendent at Parker Canyon, who thrives on attention from dignitaries from Washington, D.C.: "All winter he had important visitors in suits who patted him on the back and shook his hand" (Silko, 1999, 205). British critic David Murray, an American studies specialist at the University of Nottingham, characterizes the milieu as a "heartless and reductively rationalist masculine world of science and commerce," which Silko develops in detail (Murray, 2007, 141).

The project becomes the historical flash point, involving state militias and the U.S. Army in furthering white efforts to rape and plunder the Southwest for the sake of profit. In contrast to the gratification of pompous government inspectors and engineers by the rapidly mounting earthwork, Sister Salt, a Sand Lizard laundress and comfort girl, regrets the disruption of land by a great soil rampart that "towered above them in a sinister hump," a hint at bestial menace (*ibid.*, 339). Progress on the digging and ground reshaping "resembled more and more one of the monster stories.... This monster ate up all living things up and down the poor river" (*ibid.*, 364). She mourns the drowning of watercress and moss and the disappearance of minnows, all models of vulnerability. At the felling of trees by bulldozer, the author embroiders the image with Gothic details by viewing destruction to cottonwood and willow roots that "reached out plaintively like giant skeleton hands" (*ibid.*, 216). Sister Salt mourns, "Oh poor trees! I'm sad for you. Poor river! What have they done to you?" (*ibid.*). With native wisdom, she looks forward to the silting in of the dam, a reclamation allowing the river to "spill over it, free again" (*ibid.*, 218). Her prophecy echoes the author's predictions in *Almanac of the Dead* (1991) of the collapse of the European hegemony and the return of Amerindians to traditional homelands.

## THE FEMALE GARDENER

Through the unifying metaphor of gardening, an emblem of native writing and art, the text surveys colonial expansionism by displacing characters from the Sonora Desert to Surinam, Mexico, Long Island, Somerset, Tuscany, and Corsica. Analyst Isernhagen describes the contrasting styles of gardening as "a pervasive gendering that associates the 'good' garden with female principle" (Isernhagen, 2002, 178). The text directs its literary outrage at female bondage, assault on women, and forced acculturation. Silko fosters the retreat of the scholar Hattie Abbott Palmer and her foster daughter Indigo, a remnant of the languishing Sand Lizard tribe, into unique orchards and garden spots as sources of recuperation and healing. Scriptural in tone, the action contrasts Genesis and Adam's receipt and naming of Eden's flora and fauna with the recovery of historic plantings and garden statuary by worshipful women. Hattie learns from research the Gnostic account of the allegorical Sophia (Greek for "wisdom"), the mother of Eve: "It is she who is the Physician, and the Woman and She who has given birth" (Silko, 1999, 100). The narrative reveals shared instincts in female Indians, Mormon housewife Mrs. Van Wagnen, expatriate American proto-environmentalist Aunt Bronwyn in Somerset, England, and Italian gardener *la professoressa* Laura, whom the author models on Laura Coltelli, an Italian translator and professor at the Institute d'Inglese of the University of Pisa. Reverence for garden divinity unites the women in a global sisterhood whose values diverge from those of bio-pirates and land despoilers like Edward Palmer, Wiley, and Susan James's Scots landscaper.

Silko introduces the two main Indian characters rolling on sand dunes to celebrate rain. Like singers in Scandic literature honoring the end of winter and the return of warm weather, the sisters rejoice in cooling showers. A timeless mythos instructs the younger generation in their people's migration to the gardens of the Sand Lizard people and of the famine and bloodletting that followed the long anticipated arrival of aliens. The unidentified usurpers, a "dirty people who carried disease and fever," take native food and leave the people starving and fever-ridden (*ibid.*, 15). During an anti–Indian backlash against invasion, some 30 campfires cluster around the spring in the sandhills. Silko develops conflict from Indian police and soldiers who eventually seize the protagonists and transport them south to Yuma for the inevitable split-up of tribes. Part Two introduces the infamous government assimilation plan to educate Indian children "away from their blankets," a cynical dismissal of native roots that simultaneously calls up the image of unsuspecting swaddlings (*ibid.*, 67). The author uses the diabolic acculturation plot to extol first peoples for their refusal to be tricked by educators, Indian agents, merchants, and Christian missionaries. The integrity of clan, family, and self survives a litany of threats—death, dispersal, the military, and thievery—to prove the prophecy of Wovoka's Ghost Dance, a Utopian revelation that restores hope.

## DERACINATION AND DISPLACEMENT

The novel attacks an illogical worldview: the marginalization of females under a false patriarchal domination of three monolithic institutions, government, scholarship, and religion. Upon Indigo's escape from the Sherman Institute in Riverside, California, the pre-teen encounters a sensory overload in fragrant exotica—groves of lemons and oranges, white lilies, bougainvillea, and a climbing arch of red roses. The plantings grouped by color, texture, and aroma contrast first people's adaptation to the sandhills and its indigenous flora. Imported blossoms mirror Indigo's fostering by the Palmers, who enjoy the pleasures of a formal garden that Edward's mother once propagated with eucalyptus, roses, spring bulbs, fruit trees, and lilacs. The addition of Indigo to the household suits the lifestyle of a collector of living curios. Edward, the amoral photographer, botanist, and commodifier of nature, represents the recorder of natural beauty whom greed entices from empirical science to the underworld of ecological imperialism. In the view of critic Amelia V. Katanski, "for Edward, the apex of civilization remains the domain of the white man" (Katanski, 2005, 206). His father-in-law, Mr. Abbott, notices the strangeness of the newlywed groom, who "sailed away almost immediately after a brief honeymoon, to collect algae and mosses in the Caribbean" (*ibid.*, 154). With a quaint gentility, the text explains Edward's inclination toward bio-piracy: "Business was conducted discreetly; buyers or their agents made their requests, and Albert Lowe & Company contracted with independent plant hunters like himself to go into the field to obtain the specimens" (*ibid.*, 128). His losses and impaired mobility incurred during an orchid-scavenging trip upriver from Portal, Surinam, into the Amazon jungle suggest the risk of snatching rare plants from the wild to market to wealthy flora fanciers. On another level, he snatches from defeat and melancholia his Long Island bride, Hattie Abbott, a well-dowryed mate whom he adds to his assortment of treasures.

Silko creates satire out of the native girl on a standard Continental tour that elite Northeastern girls enjoy upon their coming out into society. Critic Elvira Pulitano, an expert in indigenous and diaspora literature at California Polytechnic State University, locates humor in the reversal of Christopher Columbus's discovery of the East Indies in Indigo's discovery of Europe, a motif James Welch employed in *The Heartsong of Charging Elk* (2000). Upon the Palmer family's arrival at Oyster Bay, New York, Edward's sister, Susan James, demonstrates material extremes in bulldozing her Italian garden, linden and plane trees, topiaries, and circular herb bed to create an English design for a one-night costume ball, the Masque of the Blue Garden. Silko puns on "blue," the organizing hue of the evening as well as the slang term for "cheerless and depressing." To achieve Susan's ends of stunning her guests with a complete overhaul of the yard, she orders two 60-foot copper beeches hauled through town for the event. An echo of the uprooting of Indian children like Indigo for training as servants to whites, one tree lies "helpless, its leaves shocked limp ... the stain of damp earth like dark blood seeped through the canvas" (*ibid.*, 183). Indigo interprets the wagon groans and creaks as cries from the exiled trees, an example of destruction replicated in Bath, England, by saboteurs of standing stones and ancient oak groves originally cultivated by the aboriginal Celts. The repeated themes of conquest and ruin link subsequent passages with Indigo's past and the New World conquerors' preoccupation with violence and greed.

## WOMEN AS CULTURE BEARERS

Botanic scholarship and ancient lore vie for dominance throughout the novel. As a contrast in motive and method, Silko describes the marriage of gentleman naturalist and photographer Dr. Edward Potter to researcher Hattie Abbott, a graduate of Vassar and scholar in early church history at a graduate seminar on heresy at Harvard Divinity School. She reads in medieval texts that redemption lies within the individual spirit: "Abandon the search for God.... Learn who is within you who makes everything his own and says: My God, my mind, my thoughts, my soul, my body. Learn the sources of sorrow, joy, love, hate. If you carefully investigate these matters you will find him in yourself" (*ibid.*, 99–100). In the appraisal of Brewster E. Fitz, a Silko specialist, the reading initiates Hattie's "'conversion' to a syncretic culture in which pre–Christian and so-called heretical Christian beliefs coexist" (Fitz, 2004, 192). From her studies comes a thesis, "The Female Principle in the Early Church," a feminist topic ahead of its time. At the reviewing committee's condemnation of her work as apostasy and a subsequent rape attempt by a classmate, Hattie falls back on two female retreats from vanquishment—bouts of the vapors and marriage. Complicating her choice, her fears of pregnancy and childbearing stymie a major purpose of matrimony, the production of offspring.

In Hattie's appraisal, Edward accepts a platonic relationship and childlessness in their union because he possesses "only a modest appetite for female anatomy," an indication of his lack of passion and zest for life and a contrast to his yearning for money and fame (*ibid.*, 274). In Bath, England, Edward absorbs himself in recovered artifacts from Aquae Sulis, the Latin name for the waters of the Celto-Roman mother goddess Sulis Minerva. In his private thoughts, he examines his knife and wonders if it is suited to his planned bio-piracy of shoots of citron (*Citrus medica*) from Bastia on the northern coast Corsica. His ambition to have a species named for him rather than children from his marriage places him in company with Mr. Eliot, a fellow conspirator and representative of Albert Lowe & Company, another pun on the evil scientist as "low-life" for setting fire to rubber trees in the Amazon jungle. Like engineers who resituate the Colorado River, the novel's male characters share a rapacity that sets them apart from the nurturing sisterhood in the female cast that uplifts and redeems Hattie from cyclical depression.

In a feminized garden setting, Silko expresses overarching views on womanly accomplishment. The plant variety in European gardens illustrates the colonization of many lands by usurpers and invaders, from the Romans in Celtic Britannia to the dam builders in Parker, Arizona, as well as the devotion of female curators to surviving trees and flowers. Simultaneously, the success of the messianic movement begun by the Paiute visionary Wovoka proves that utopian evangelism speaks across cultures and continents in a mystic meta-language understood by faithful women and children. He degenders the search for earthly happiness in a call-and-response exercise: "To the Universe belongs the dancer."—"Amen" (*ibid.*, 74). After Hattie gathers her notes on church history, she turns her attention away from her daring thesis on Mary Magdalene and female spirituality revealed in the Gnostic gospels to listen to Aunt Bronwyn, a savant and expert on Celtic and Roman superstitions, magic wells and springs, brownies, fairies, and Arthurian lore. Enhancing the atmosphere of timeless wonder at the Knights of the Round Table, Silko sets the storytelling session during an atmospheric rainstorm, a reflection of turmoil and threat in the male-dominated centers of power. The eventful visit to Bath concludes with joyous news in the London *Times*, the authentication of the Coptic scrolls and vindication for Dr. Rhinehart and Hattie. She exults "True words were beautiful words!" (*ibid.*, 266). Edward's faint praise declares that science has rescued "muddled humanists," an offhand insult to Aunt Bronwyn, his wife, and her research (*ibid.*). His mutterings preface a falling action that lauds the rise of his wife and foster daughter above serious examples of disempowerment. Suitably, in widowhood, Hattie returns to her aunt—the preserver of ancient feminine strengths—for comfort and guidance.

## A GENDERED PERSPECTIVE

Silko contrasts men and women in the role of solacers and healers. David Murray asserts that "*Gardens in the Dunes* revolves largely around women and their sensibilities and vulnerabilities in their society" (Murray, 2007, 145). For Hattie, a visit with Aunt Bronwyn, an anti-urban recluse who studies prehistoric archeology of the British Isles and Europe, introduces a non-directive docent alive to the spirits in nature. As an introduction to the gentle hostess, Silko presents Bronwyn guiding a wayward bull by scratching his forehead while leading him home. Amid picnics and meal hampers, gifts of prize pea seeds, and sprightly talk of sacred wraiths and serpents, Bronwyn relaxes the women in the garden while Edward journeys to London for another polite male conspiracy—a visit England's Royal Botanic Gardens at Kew to plot with the director the sale of *Citrus medica* cuttings. The contrast deepens in the falling action after Edward falls ill with respiratory distress. Although Hattie has severed emotional ties to her husband, she dutifully attends him at St. Joseph's Hospital, a tuberculosis treatment center in Albuquerque. Dr. William Gates of Melbourne, an Australian bounder and groper of women, ends Edward's struggle with a leg injury and pneumonia through an experimental treatment involving camphor inhalation. Rather than hearten Hattie, Gates's nearness is "almost intolerable" (*ibid.*, 423). As a priest administers extreme unction to Edward, Gates slithers down the hall to conceal his criminality and quackery from the hospital staff. Silko dramatizes Gates's fraud as another example of the male scholarly humbuggery that ruined Hattie's research at Harvard Divinity School and destroyed her self-esteem and health.

In the resolution of *Gardens in the Dunes*, Silko contrasts Edward's shallow horizons with the breadth of hope and vivacity in Indigo and Hattie. His failure at the union of American and European biota parallels his defeat at wedlock and foster parenting. A suitable irony to his demise arises from his loveless death witnessed by the woman he devalued. In his final reveries, he regrets failing to steal citron slips from Bastia and dreams of returning to Tampico to "acquire" meteor irons, an indication of his rationalization of international thievery. Critic Douglas Cazaux Sackman, a history professor at the University of Puget Sound, notes that "Edward's mind and body come apart as if some Cartesian curse had been put upon him: poisoned by his will to plunder earth, the rational man of science descends into madness, losing the power to think and therefore be" (Sackman, 2005, 23). Silko uses Edward less as a villain than as a model of male acquisitiveness. In the words of critic Janice Susan May, Edward "exposes the possessive, manipulation of all life for the purposes of capital investment; [the female gardener] portrays a regard for plant life as one of preserving life" via life-affirming gardening, meals, and stories (May, 2000, 14). To Edward, such a valorization of garden beauty is a silly pursuit appropriate for women, whom he dismisses as too superficial to attain greatness. Her duty as helpmeet completed, Hattie leaves Edward's remains in the icehouse for his frivolous sister to deal with. The reference to ice captures the atmosphere of a marriage to a cold-hearted man that is doomed from the start. In the joyous reunion of Indigo, Hattie, Sister Salt, Bright Eyes, and the Chemehuevi twins Maytha and Vedna, the gathering celebrates their survival of male pillage. Critic Amelia V. Katanski exalts above all Indigo, a "boarding-school student as a moral victor, one who was able to taste the fruit of knowledge, hybridize it to grow in her own climate, and then tend her gardens on her ancestral lands" (Katanski, 2005, 214).

*See also* Abbott-Palmer genealogy; Grandma Fleet; Indigo; Indigo and Sister Salt's genealogy; Palmer, Hattie Abbott; Sister Salt.

· *References and further reading*

Christie, Stuart. *Plural Sovereignties and Contemporary Indigenous Literature.* New York: Palgrave Macmillan, 2009.

Fitz, Brewster E. *Silko: Writing Storyteller and Medicine Woman.* Norman: University of Oklahoma Press, 2004.

"Gathering the Gardens in the Dunes: Leslie Marmon Silko Makes the Flora Central to Her Latest Fiction," *Kansas City Star* (20 June 1999): K5.

Isernhagen, Hartwig. "Of Deserts and Gardens: The Southwest in Literature and Art, 'Native' and 'White'" in *Literature and Visual Arts in Twentieth-Century America*, ed. Michele Bottalico. Bari: Palomar Eupalinos, 2002.

Katanski, Amelia V. *Learning to Write "Indian": The Boarding-School Experience and American Indian Literature.* Norman: University of Oklahoma Press, 2005.

Krupat, Arnold, and Michael A. Elliott. "American Indian Fiction and Anticolonial Resistance" in *The Columbia Guide to American Indian Literatures of the United States since 1945.* New York: Columbia University Press, 2006.

May, Janice Susan. *Healing the Necrophilia of Euro-American Society in Leslie Marmon Silko's Gardens in the Dunes.* Radford, VA: Radford University, 2000.

Morisco, Gabriella. "Contrasting Gardens and Worlds: America and Europe in the Long Journey of Indigo, a Young Native American Girl" in *Nations, Traditions and Cross-Cultural Identities: Women's Writing in English in a European Context*, eds. Annamaria Lamarra and Eleonora Federici. Bern: Peter Lang, 2010.

Murray, David. *Matter, Magic, and Spirit: Representing Indian and African American Belief.* Philadelphia: University of Pennsylvania Press, 2007.

Pulitano, Elvira. *Transatlantic Voices: Interpretations of Native North American Literatures.* Lincoln: University of Nebraska Press, 2007.

Sackman, Douglas C. *Orange Empire: California and the Fruits of Eden.* Berkeley: University of California Press, 2005.

Seaman, Donna. "Earthwork a Rich, Panoramic Tale about the Relationship between People and the Natural World around Them," *Chicago Tribune* (8 August 1999): 5.

Silko, Leslie Marmon. *Gardens in the Dunes*. New York: Scribner, 1999.

_____, and Ellen L. Arnold. *Conversations with Leslie Marmon Silko*. Jackson: University Press of Mississippi, 2000.

Summers, Wynne L. *Women Elders' Life Stories of the Omaha Tribe: Macy, Nebraska, 2004–2005*. Lincoln: University of Nebraska Press, 2009.

Wood, Karenne. "Review: *Gardens in the Dunes*," *American Indian Quarterly* 23:2 (1999): 71–72.

# genocide

The shadow of New World depopulation, deliberate pox infections, scalp-taking, and mass murder hovers over much of Leslie Marmon Silko's historical ruminations. Author Paula Gunn Allen justifies Silko's obsession with killing of aborigines as a pervasive inheritance of Amerindians that lodges like a projectile in their consciousness. In an interview with Jane B. Katz, Silko explained her belief that creation established a yin and yang of forces, by which witchery perpetually counters birth and vitality. The sources of racial annihilation begin in "Toe'osh: A Laguna Coyote Story" (1974) with the white men who ravage Acoma and Laguna pueblos for their land and women. In "A Geronimo Story" (1974), the author pictures the satirically named Major Littlecock as the balding veteran Indian hunter who has already damaged the Crow and Sioux and who takes a new assignment to wipe out Geronimo's Apache resisters. Silko subverts the strength of the U.S. Army by depicting Siteye, Captain Pratt, and the Laguna Regulars searching for renegades at Pie Town, even though they know "the Apaches were long gone" to White Mountain. A wicked humor undergirds her ridicule of the white military under General George R. Crook, who stalked Indians from 1870 to 1885 until the elderly Geronimo surrendered in 1886. Of the perversion of power in military authorities like Crook, critic Cathy Moses accounts for their obsession as an absence of moral anchors: "They had no tribe, no village, no family, and no community to censure their behavior" (Moses, 2000, 99).

Silko extends the sources of tribal decimation to include medical and economic threats. For "Lullaby" (1974), an elegiac story of family dissolution, the culprits that erode a Navajo clan include world war, tuberculosis, cultural erasure, and poverty. Despite the loss of Danny and Ella to white institutions, Ayah, their mother, rejects annihilation by singing a lullaby, which critic Jordana Finnegan depicts as an "[assertion of] the survival of indigenous cultural forms" (Finnegan, 2008, 115). The lyrics declare, "We are together always/ There never was a time/When this/was not so" (Silko, 1974, 17). The author develops the concept of survival through native lore in "The Storyteller's Escape" (1981), a poem reverencing the storykeeper for amassing escape stories and for accompanying the people "on every journey" as a dynamic form of collective memory (Silko, 1981, 247). Like food and water packed for travel, the stories retain tribal history and genealogy by reinterpreting narratives of "the dear ones who do not come back so that we may remember them and cry for them with the stories" (*ibid.*). The old teller justifies his keeping of the dead with the living, blurring the boundaries that separate worlds at the same time that he rids death of its terrors. He concludes that, from stories comes courage: "In this way we continue" (*ibid.*).

## Counteracting Erasure

Resembling the tone of Simon Joseph Ortiz's *Fight Back: For the Sake of the People, For the Sake of the Land* (1980), Silko's outrage takes the form of direct indictment of colonialism along with dates and details of events. In her essay "Fences against Freedom"

(1994), published in *Hungry Mind Review*, she charges whites and *mestizos* in El Salvador and Guatemala with warring against indigenous people to steal their land. Of her own post-midnight experience with the border patrol along Arizona's shared boundary with Mexico, she predicts "the inexorable slide into further government-mandated 'race policies' that can only end in madness and genocide" (Silko, 1994, 19). By enlarging the menace from her personal endangerment to that of all brown-skinned people, she envisions an explosion of socially acceptable persecution of non-whites, which occurred in Arizona in 2010. Finnegan comments on Silko's sense of shared threat: "The fact that the 'I' is subsumed in collective experience can thereby be read as the survival of a Native sense of self," the communal identity that informs all of Silko's canon (Finnegan, 2008, 69).

As a model of the insidious nature of white dissolution of tribalism, in *Ceremony* (1977), Silko pictures Pueblo veterans of World War II searching for purpose and meaning. Critic Jonathan Brennan, a specialist in minority literature at Mission College in Santa Clara, California, categorizes Tayo, Silko's protagonist, as the prototypical orphan/wild boy. Brennan pictures each of the returnees stumbling through a shadowland "through his personal darkness, feeding on beer and twisted memories of wartime mutilations and liaisons with uniform-enamored blondes who do not want them anymore" (Brennan, 2002, 64–65). Silko's narrative pictures the destabilized egos as victims of Pueblo institutions. She charges that Christianity "separated the people from themselves; it tried to crush the single clan name, encouraging each person to stand alone, because Jesus Christ would save only the individual soul" (Silko, 1977, 68). Lacking cohesion, the war buddies cope with the ending of the Pacific war in the dropping of atomic bombs on August 6 and 8, 1945. The explanation derives from myth. At a sorcerers' conference, the witchery that unleashes slaughter extends "from ocean to ocean" as people "destroy each other" by turning native rocks into the source of atomic annihilation (*ibid.*, 136–137). The author foresees Amerindian sympathy for the Japanese of Hiroshima and Nagasaki, who died from the grotesque powers of Laguna uranium from the Jackpile mine, "rocks which boiled up their slaughter" (*ibid.*). The enormity of sin against humanity generates self-rescuing pantribalism: "From that time on, human beings were one clan again, united by the fate the destroyers had planned for all of them, for all living things" (*ibid.*).

## URBAN CHAOS

In the apocalyptic saga *Almanac of the Dead* (1991), Silko reprises images of famine, death, revolution, and bloodlust, the precedents to near genocide on the American frontier. After five centuries of life-and-death struggle, a grassroots revolt challenges the "Reign of the Death-Eye Dog" (Silko, 1991, 257). To combat violence, for a pragmatic reason, the author presents fragmented stories such as the Afro-American history expounded by Clinton and translations of Mayan prophecies as political activism at the peasant level. The tribal approach to starvation, joblessness, and police tyranny strikes the enemy's Achilles heel: "The white man hated to hear anything about spirits because spirits were already dead and could not be tortured and butchered or shot" (*ibid.*, 581). Critic Lidia Yuknavitch, a literature professor at Mt. Hood Community College, refutes charges of vengefulness from critics of *Almanac* with socialist reasoning. She ripostes that "Silko relentlessly represents capitalism as economic violence, and in particular, her insistence that economic violence against displaced indigenous peoples is always war ... drug wars, race wars, sex wars, wars on crime, wars on poverty, wars on homelessness, even psychic warfare" (Yuknavitch, 2001, 100).

Silko begins the peasant revolt with an informational campaign. She alerted interviewer Donna Perry to a national tragedy — the ongoing amnesia that suppresses the truths of U.S. history. Silko compared the erasure of genocide of the Indian Wars from the collective memory to the apathy of Germans to the Jewish Holocaust. To arouse terror from the past and launch it as future weaponry, the author overturns definitions of primitivism and civilization in *Almanac* by creating a cast of ghoulish killers. Goaded by greed and sexual depravity, the destroyers seek to expunge indigenous peoples as well as their memories and customs. Critic Sharon Patricia Holland, a specialist in minority literature at the University of Illinois, credits the author with an even-handed distribution of vilification: "Silko meticulously depicts characters from *all* ethnic backgrounds as caught up in the pursuit of whiteness.... This configuration challenges the 'othering' generally associated with theories of the grotesque — as grotesque others are most often outside of normative whiteness" (Holland, 2000, 69–70). Just as all races share iniquities, so too do they share the job of rebellion. Tacho, the Yaqui spy on dissolute insurance magnate Menardo Panson, interprets the sacred Mayan macaws as predicting a pan-tribal revolt: "The battle would be won or lost in the realm of dreams, not with airplanes or weapons" (Silko, 1991, 475). In the fighting, whites will erase themselves from the inside out. Tacho observes, "The disappearance had already begun at the spiritual level," a comment on white soullessness (*ibid.*, 511).

PAYBACK TO THE WICKED

Silko pursues evildoers with psychological urgency, shifting unexpectedly from past to present tense to enhance immediacy. At the head of her list of multicultural Southwestern villains, de Guzman, the husband of Yoeme Guzman, resembles conquistador and colonial administrator Nuño Beltrán de Guzmán in savagery. In the planting of cottonwoods in the desert, the latter-day Guzman forces his Yaqui slaves to irrigate the grove: "All water went to the mules or to the saplings. The slaves were only allowed to press their lips to the wet rags around the tree roots" (*ibid.*, 116). Brewster E. Fitz, a Silko expert, comments, "Guzman's aqueous parsimony places the Indians below beasts of burden and suggests that they might even be considered inferior to the uprooted trees whose rag-wrapped roots they must nurse for water" (Fitz, 2004, 164). Like the devalued black laborers in Joseph Conrad's *Heart of Darkness* (1899) and Peter Carey's *Oscar and Lucinda* (1988), the transplanted cottonwoods symbolize the deracinated Yaqui, who "are forced to suck justice and life from the fabric of a desiccating legal system" (*ibid.*). Legends of Guzman invigorate the Yaqui resistance, turning Spanish wickedness into a rallying cry.

Silko's symbolic tome takes up the task of avenging the massive mortality figures of post–Columbian North America — only ten million surviving the epidemics and slaughter that killed off over 86 percent of the 72 million alive in the Americas in 1500. Clinton predicts, "Maybe not tomorrow or next week, but someday ... the other homeless people would remember the defiance of the homeless vets; the dumpy, pale women and their skinny, pale men would remember the absolute surge of pride and power the veterans' defiance had given them" (Silko, 1991, 741). Lecha, the Yaqui visionary and translator, also recognizes the human penchant for violence, but she foresees the likelihood of collateral damage to the vulnerable from the clash, a proof of the Darwinian principle of survival of the fittest. Although the novel concludes with the bumbling rhetoric of Wilson Weasel Tail, a drumhead court and public hanging in Cuba, and a seriocomic International Holistic Healers Convention in Tucson, critic Jane Olmstead asserts that Silko promises triumph "for those who see the connection between reclaiming the land and the histories stolen by military force or eclipsed by oppressor-histories that glorify leaders whose agendas often demanded genocide" (Olmstead, 1999, 480).

## DEFIANCE OF THE STATUS QUO

In *Yellow Woman and a Beauty of the Spirit: Essays on Native American Life Today* (1996), Silko steps up her charges against U.S. repression of non-whites. Recalling her Aunt Susie Reyes Marmon's experience 2,000 miles from home at the Indian school in Carlisle, Pennsylvania, the author states, "The U.S. government used books in their campaign of cultural genocide. Thus, the representation or portrayal of Native Americans was politicized from the very beginning and, to this day, remains an explosive political issue" (Silko, 1996, 22). The author compares the removal of Amerindian children to boarding schools and the disruption of the diet, hairstyle and dress, religion, language, and customs as "a calculated act of cultural genocide" (*ibid.*, 179). In "An Expression of Profound Gratitude to the Maya Zapatistas, January 1, 1994" (1996), Silko credits the rebel irregulars in Chiapas, Mexico, with fighting the "same [500-year] war of resistance that the indigenous people of the Americas have never ceased to fight" (*ibid.*, 153). Of late 20th-century slaughter, she foresees no change in the immediate future. She warns that "Rwanda and Bosnia did not occur spontaneously — with neighbor butchering neighbor out of the blue; no, politicians and government officials called down these maelstroms of blood on their people by unleashing the terrible irrational force that racism is" (*ibid.*, 114).

A digression in *The Turquoise Ledge* (2010) examines the era of genocide through commentary on the *corrido*, a north Mexican folksong written about crime and public outrages. Silko focuses on border violence at Cubero, New Mexico, in 1882 when Apache raiders kill a ranch hand and abduct his wife, Placida Romero, and her infant. Symbolically, the kidnappers choose the site of an old slave market. The author marvels over the Apache women who comfort Placida and offer her clothing, provisions, and a burro for an escape seven weeks later. The collaboration of women from two cultures occurs at a time when Americans and Mexicans earn bounties for scalps of murdered Apaches. Nonetheless, the text adds, the female Apaches "did not let the genocide destroy their human decency" (Silko, 2010, 33). To refute the notion that whites retain power by exterminating non-white aliens, Silko cites ways in which immigrants flourish despite an ongoing attempt to crush illegal aliens at the U.S. border with Mexico. For Silko's reclamation of humanity in Arizona, Finnegan compares the author to Chicana writer Sandra Cisneros in "[contesting] white 'ownership' of the West by depicting displacement, loss, and cultural suppression on 'storied' landscapes" (Finnegan, 2008, 152). Finnegan explains that, by defeating genocide with pluralism, newcomers demonstrate how Mesomericans "transform the national narrative while challenging — by expanding — dominant conceptions of the category of 'American'" (Finnegan, 2008, 145).

*See also Almanac of the Dead*; violence; vulnerability.

• *References and further reading*

Brennan, Jonathan. *Mixed Race Literature.* Stanford, CA: Stanford University Press, 2002.
Carter, Nancy Corson. "Apocalypse Imminent Series," *St. Petersburg Times* (24 November 1993): 6D.
Domina, Lynn. "'The Way I Heard It': Autobiography, Tricksters, and Leslie Marmon Silko's Storyteller," *Studies in American Indian Literatures* 19:3 (Fall 2007): 45–67.
Finnegan, Jordana. *Narrating the American West.* Amherst, NY: Cambria Press, 2008.
Fitz, Brewster E. *Silko: Writing Storyteller and Medicine Woman.* Norman: University of Oklahoma Press, 2004.

Katz, Jane B., ed. *This Song Remembers: Self Portraits of Native Americans in the Arts.* Boston: Houghton Mifflin, 1980.

Moses, Cathy. *Dissenting Fictions: Identity and Resistance in the Contemporary American Novel.* New York: Routledge, 2000.

Olmstead, Jane. "The Uses of Blood in Leslie Marmon Silko's *Almanac of the Dead*," *Contemporary Literature* 40:3 (Fall 1999): 464–490.

Perry, Donna. *Backtalk: Women Writers Speak Out.* New Brunswick, NJ: Rutgers University Press, 1993.

Silko, Leslie Marmon. *Almanac of the Dead.* New York: Simon & Schuster, 1991.

_____. *Ceremony.* New York: Viking, 1977.

_____. "Fences against Freedom," *Hungry Mind Review* 31 (Fall 1994): 6–20.

_____. "A Geronimo Story" in *Come to Power: Eleven Contemporary American Indian Poets*, ed. Dick Lourie. New York: Crossing, 1974.

_____. "Lullaby," *Chicago Review* 26:1 (Summer 1974): 10–17.

_____. *Storyteller.* New York: Seaver, 1981.

_____. *The Turquoise Ledge: A Memoir.* New York: Viking Adult, 2010.

_____. *Yellow Woman and a Beauty of the Spirit: Essays on Native American Life Today.* New York: Simon & Schuster, 1996.

Yuknavitch, Lidia. *Allegories of Violence: Tracing the Writing of War in Late Twentieth Century Fiction.* New York: Routledge, 2001.

## Geronimo

The example of Geronimo, perhaps America's wiliest guerilla warrior, permeates Silko's writings with images of resistance and betrayal. Critic Claudia Sadowski-Smith identifies him as "a communal sign for the dissolution of national borders," over which the Apache operated in defiance of Mexican and U.S. troops (Sadowski-Smith, 2008, 80). A wry initiation narrative of a lad named Andy, "A Geronimo Story," first published in 1974, outlines a passive aggressive method of contesting oppression. The Amerindian method of insurgency makes the most of a small band that regularly outsmarts whole army regiments. The narrative focuses on the younger Indian generation, the ones who have no memory of communal life before incarceration on reservations and forced peonage in Mexican haciendas. The story discloses Andy's coming-of-age during the ride southwest of Laguna scouts to capture a renegade Apache. Doubling as both cautionary tale and satire, the account becomes just "a story" in a sizeable and growing body of Geronimo lore, filled with inaccuracies, conflations, even photos that may or may not feature the real historical Apache legend. The famed escape artist remained at large from 1875 to 1886 and evaded 5,000 U.S. cavalrymen. He chose to surrender on September 4, 1886, to General Nelson Appleton Miles for incarceration in a prison camp at Fort Pickens, Florida. His capture cost the U.S. government $20 million plus the humiliation of mounted soldiers.

Silko creates a fictional episode from the perspective of Geronimo hunters and sets it in late April in the black lava malpais (badlands), a treacherous expanse of volcanic rock sparsely covered with soil. With the same firmness as Uncle Josiah to Tayo and Rocky in *Ceremony* (1977) and of elders to the three Marmon sisters in Silko's *Storyteller* (1981), Siteye, a Laguna Regular, instructs his nephew Andy through memories of his own first ride to the Zuni Mountains. During a rite of passage, the boy proves that he already knows how to corral, feed, saddle, and ride a horse, but he has yet to learn why taking care of mounts is crucial to an overland expedition. Siteye explains why horses need hobbling for the night to keep them from returning home. He orders Andy to build a trench to fill with hot coals under a layer of dirt for a warm bed and cautions the boy about stuffing his rolling papers with enough tobacco to make a tamale. Snatches of story alert the nephew to secret caves that Indians once stocked with corn and water for the sustenance of hunters and travelers. Pointedly instructive, the silences in Siteye's stories inform the boy about absences, a subtle reminder that Geronimo is not only not in Pie Town, he never has been. The ambiguity of Geronimo's whereabouts creates an aura of the ghost rider, a Western staple in the works of frontier novelists Zane Grey and Louis L'Amour.

## Subversion from Within

In remembrance of the shadowy Geronimo and his followers, Silko subverts the standard conquest narrative with hints that Indian guides and scouts deliberately mislead the U.S. Cavalry. In the style of witty coyote fables, her tale of a field search depicts man and horse in daily motion broken only for food, limited conversation, sleep, and hunting. In contrast to the elusive Apache, she creates Major Littlecock, a snide pejorative surname for a cocky white leader. A native version of the classic *miles gloriosus* (soldierly glory-hound) of the Roman stage, like the real army climbers General Dreedle and Colonel Cathcart in Joseph Heller's anti-war satire *Catch-22* (1961) and the strutting legionnaire in Stephen Sondheim's musical *A Funny Thing Happened on the Way to the Forum* (1962), Littlecock is foolish enough to expect his company to wear wool uniforms in summer. Self-important to a fault, he hires Laguna scouts as guides, then belittles their expertise and abases their humanity by forcing them to eat in the kitchen at a separate table. Short, pale, and balding, Littlecock patronizes Indians who lack his access to "sophisticated communications" (Silko, 1981, 220). To the white major's fear that Indians sleeping in the kitchen might harm white women, Siteye sets an example of non-confrontational resistance by accusing the major of a need to be near horses in the night, an unstated charge of bestial sexuality. Captain Pratt, a white among the scouts, refrains from translating the charge of equine copulation against Littlecock. From the episode, Andy learns a valuable tool of minorities— to "destroy his enemy with words," a nonviolent method of retaining dignity (*ibid.*, 222). Even more illustrative of non-violent tactics is the continued roaming of the Apache out of reach of the army. Critic John Muthyala, an English professor at the University of Southern Maine, explains, "The power of Geronimo lies precisely in his absence, in the traces and tracks he leaves behind ... [a] strategic contestation" of the U.S. military and their genocidal methods (Muthyala, 2006, 130).

The text admires the Laguna attitude toward getting paid for pretending to scout another Indian. Analyst Eric Gary Anderson, a specialist in native American and indigenous studies at George Mason University, summarizes the historical subtext as "inter-tribal resistance that successfully counters threats of Indian removal and assimilation," the punishments that await Geronimo and his renegade band (Anderson, 1999, 63). Critic Ellen L. Arnold chortles at white ineptitude in a chapter entitled "The Battle of Pie Town or Littlecock's Last Stand," a sneering comparison of Littlecock's tactical blunder to the lethal miscalculation of Lieutenant Colonel George Armstrong Custer at the Little Big Horn on June 25, 1876. Siteye comments to Andy that, so long as the Apache elude army custody, "I like to think that it's us who get away" (*ibid.*). Osage critic Robert Allen Warrior interprets the line to mean escape from the Apache as well as venturing from home to view "an earlier Laguna geography that had become circumscribed by settlement" (Warrior, 2005, 133). Eric Anderson proposes another perspective, a question about the antecedent of "us," an ambiguous pronoun that could refer to the party of scouts, of all Laguna, or of all native Americans. Anderson assumes that the story is "not simply unpredictable but actively and productively evasive" (Anderson, 1999, 64). From the experience, Andy gains traditional education in horsemanship, scouting, deer hunting, and co-existing with and outsmarting pompous whites.

## THE GROWTH OF A LEGEND

In *Almanac of the Dead* (1991), a brutal survey of corruption in Southwestern America, Silko relates variant episodes of Geronimo's flight from the cavalry as models of resistance. In reference to his advancement from renegade to outlaw, the author exonerates the Apache leader, who "had turned to crime only as a last resort, after Mexican army troops had slaughtered his wife and three children on U.S. territory in southern Arizona" (Silko, 1991, 39). The author builds on Yaqui legends that there was no actual Geronimo, rather, the combined trickery of four men, Big Pine, Red Clay, Sleet, and Wide Ledge. The text recounts the use of "Geronimo" by Mexican troops as a call on St. Jerome (Sophronius Eusebius Hieronymus), translator of the Vulgate, during a retaliatory raid by Apache. By shapeshifting, the Apache legend, originally named Goyathlay (or Yawner), becomes the storyteller's canny coyote trickster. As Calabazas learns from his aunt Old Mahalawas, Grandmother Yoeme instructs twins Lecha and Zeta on Yaqui accounts of concealing Geronimo in the Sierra Madre in Sonora, Mexico, to keep him out of the hands of Mexican and U.S. Army forces. John Muthyala explains that the breach of national boundaries evidences "the growing intertribal coalitions formed in the borderlands to oppose Mexican and American policies designed to drive the Indians further into the land and eventually dispossess them" (Muthyala, 2006, 127). The alliance supports Silko's overarching theme of cooperation among members of the underclass of all races and socio-economic classes to restore justice.

The episode "Mistaken Identity" opens on a startling statement that a substitute entered custody while the real Apache leader remained at large. Silko enhances her satire of gullible whites by pointing out that at least four men bore the name Geronimo. Reflecting on the naiveté of young cavalrymen, she charges, "Europeans suffered a sort of blindness to the world. To them, a 'rock' was just a 'rock' wherever they found it despite obvious differences in shape, density, color, or the position of the rock relative to all things around it" (Silko, 1991, 224). As proof of the mounted soldiers' limited visual acuity, she pictures the Apache retreating to crevices in the rocks, where they conceal themselves like scorpions. With "Old Pancakes," a story of the elderly joker who poses as Geronimo, Silko twists the tone from humor to peril by picturing Pancakes in danger of imprisonment, torture, or execution because he willingly assumes the identity of a folk hero.

## A HERO IN CHAINS

Silko perpetuates her defense of the wily Apache in "On Photography" (1996) by finding metaphysical residue in natural energy: "'Murder, murder,' sings the wind over the rocks in a remote Arizona canyon where they betrayed Geronimo" (Silko, 1996, 182). The essay recreates his attitude at the time of his arrest in Skeleton Canyon on the extreme southeastern tip of Arizona. Looking like a "passive beggar," Geronimo retorts to his captors that the Mexicans would have executed him, a subtle boast of his reputation south of the border. In his pose for a photo, he projects "resistance" in an unflickering gaze (*ibid.*). Writer Jimmie Durham, a Cherokee political organizer for the American Indian Movement in 1973, admired the septuagenarian's formidable defiance: "No matter what had been taken from him, he had given up nothing" (Silko, 1996, 182). Without comment, Silko juxtaposes a photo of 12 Laguna Regulars taken in 1924, nearly four decades after the Apache campaign of 1885. The pose suggests that Pueblo volunteers maintain their deception of the regular military and continue to take government money for wild goose chases.

When Silko returns to the Geronimo story in *The Turquoise Ledge* (2010), she avoids Western polemical lore about savage warriors and vulnerable white settlements. Instead, she recalls "his ragged band of women and children in their final years of resisting the U.S. troops" (Silko, 2010, 186). On the trails over Chihuahua and Sonora, Mexico, the cavalrymen outnumber Apaches 100 to one. By sticking to rocky trails, Geronimo's pedestrian followers outsmart army horsemen, whose mounts go lame in the sharp debris. Those animals abandoned or shot become valuable food for the Apache, who dry the meat in the sun. Thus, guerrilla warfare weakens the army while supplying women and children with jerky. The pragmatic solution to struggle for the displaced Apache imparts both the pathos of women and children on the run and the smug satisfaction of Geronimo in turning the sacrificed horses into food. His success at power games accounts for the longevity of his legend.

• *References and further reading*

Anderson, Eric Gary. *American Indian Literature and the Southwest: Contexts and Dispositions.* Austin: University of Texas Press, 1999.

Arnold, Ellen L. "Silko: Writing Storyteller and Medicine Woman," *Modern Fiction Studies* 51:1 (Spring 2005): 194–197.

Bentley, Nancy. *Frantic Panoramas: American Literature and Mass Culture, 1870–1920.* Philadelphia: University of Pennsylvania Press, 2009.

Cherniavsky, Eva. *Incorporations: Race, Nation, and the Body Politics of Capital.* Minneapolis: University of Minnesota Press, 2006.

Finnegan, Jordana. *Narrating the American West.* Amherst, NY: Cambria, 2008.

Krumholz, Linda J. "Reading and Subversion in Leslie Marmon Silko's 'Storyteller,'" *Ariel* 25 (January 1994): 89–113.

Muthyala, John. *Reworlding America: Myth, History, and Narrative.* Athens: Ohio University Press, 2006.

Sadowski-Smith, Claudia. *Border Fictions: Globalization, Empire, and Writing at the Boundaries of the United States.* Charlottesville: University of Virginia Press, 2008.

Silko, Leslie Marmon. *Almanac of the Dead.* New York: Simon & Schuster, 1991.

_____. *Ceremony.* New York: Viking, 1977.

_____. *Storyteller.* New York: Seaver, 1981.

_____. *The Turquoise Ledge.* New York: Viking, 2010.

Stout, Janis P. *Picturing a Different West: Vision, Illustration, and the Tradition of Cather and Austin.* Lubbock: Texas Tech University Press, 2007.

Stromberg, Ernest. *American Indian Rhetorics of Survivance: Word Medicine, Word Magic.* Pittsburgh: University of Pittsburgh Press, 2006.

Warrior, Robert Allen. *The People and the Word: Reading Native Nonfiction.* Minneapolis: University of Minnesota Press, 2005.

# Gothic

Silko earned a place among the 20th-century's facile Gothicists by compiling *Almanac of the Dead* (1991), a macabre vilification of Tucson society and its demonic economy. It flourishes from what S. T. Joshi, an expert on world Gothic, calls "a backhanded kind of psychological realism" (Joshi, 2011, xii). Wraiths haunt her fictional landscape, directing mothers to drive their cars over a precipice or into a river and instructing mad loners to fire automatic weapons on schoolyards and shopping malls. A pioneer exploiter, "old Guzman," Yoeme's husband, fails at silver mining and shrivels like a shrunken head "crackled, full of dry molts of insects" (Silko, 1991, 120). In the 1970s, his granddaughter Lecha uses clairvoyance to locate a serial killer in the sand dunes of San Diego, where he buries remains of his prey. Sterling, a Laguna native, profanes a stone snake by allowing the filming of sacred precincts near the Jackpile Mine, producer of uranium for the atomic bombs that ended World War II. Across America, federal forces battle corruption, bankruptcy, and citizen riots. In Mexico, robber barons enjoy their spoils while the dispossessed collapse in the streets. Silko pummels the reader with a Gothic aggregate as dismaying as Dante's hell. Novelist Graham Joyce justifies the rogues' gallery of Silko's terror extravaganza: "The Gothic must have its grotesques.... The secret sins naturally follow, but meanwhile these devices lend verisimilitude to the act of exploring the family tree as at the same time they fatten the ancestral history" (Joyce, 2011, 448).

In the undertow of five centuries of ghoulish crimes, normality appears to flicker out like a taper on a windy night. The disintegration of the nuclear family results in a generation of self-indulgent brats like Bingo and Sonny Blue, sons of Max "Mr. Murder" Blue. In an interview with journalist Laurie Mellas, Silko accounted for teens who grow up emotionally twisted: "Cheap labor and capitalism destroy families and now we have the turnkey children and kids that identify with gothic things. Who else and what else do they have?" (Mellas, 2006, 14). Italian critics Romana Cortese and James Cortese account for the "fundamental lack of wholeness, of personal and cultural dysfunction" as "the standard Gothic absence of the mother, physically or psychologically" (Cortese & Cortese, 2011, 533). As a token of the author's distaste for urban corruption in the "epoch of Death-Eye Dog," she pictures Tucson's construction of its largest sewage facility adjacent to the Santa Cruz River, a waterway revered by the early Papago and named in Spanish "holy cross" (*ibid.*, 251). British critic A. Robert Lee, a specialist in American literature at Nihon University in Tokyo, summarizes, "This is the Americas as broken history, dysfunctions of caste and family, modernity as glut" (Lee, 2009, 219).

## A REIGN OF EVIL

*Almanac* connects the diseases carried by Europeans to North America with the modern-day contagion of unspeakable wickedness. Adam L. G. Nevill, a specialist in supernatural horror in London, typifies past evils as "tendrils of madness and dysfunction ... fed from what refuses to be forgotten" (Nevill, 2011, 155). Symbolically, insurance magnate Menardo Panson designs and builds a lavish house featuring a conservatory looking out on jungle, a reflection of his membership in El Grupo, an unprincipled men's club that wallows in ill-gotten power and privilege. Sharon Patricia Holland, an expert in minority literature at the University of Illinois, reads the characterization of Caucasians as "grotesques, as absolute disfigurations of white people" but concedes that Silko pictures all ethnic groups as "caught up in the pursuit of whiteness" through mayhem that threatens to engulf the Americas in meaninglessness and death (Holland, 2000, 69). *Almanac*'s only salvation is the realization of a prophecy from nine Mayan codices that prefigure a reversal of imperialism. The prediction unfolds as first peoples from north to south along the Western Hemisphere ally to expunge all evidence of European conquest, hypocrisy, betrayal, and genocide. With the words of Lecha, the clairvoyant translator of the almanacs, Silko depicts the army like a Hollywood phalanx of the un-dead: "Millions will move instinctively; unarmed and unguarded they will begin walking steadily north, following the twin brothers" El Feo and Tacho, the fomenters of the diaspora who take their orders from spirits speaking through sacred macaws (Silko, 1991, 735).

In an evaluation of *Almanac*, analyst Dan Cryer, book critic for the Long Island *News-*

*day*, grappled with a welter of the grisly — gay porn, a regiment of homeless, junkies, Indian guerrillas, and a Cuban revolutionary hanged without a trial. Silko showcases dope-doing, vampirism, a federal judge's bestiality with basset hounds, snuff flicks, whoring, and homosexual acts, an emblem of sterility, overloading her text with age-old spite toward the subjugator. In Book Four, the perverse triangle of David, Eric, and Beaufrey turns on off-kilter love and voyeurism enhanced by the East Coast tabloids. Critic Jane Olmstead characterizes the need to view sufferings as "scopophilia [voyeurism] ... where the eye can go anywhere, see into any life, and alter any reality" (Olmstead, 1999, 474). In one example, David's rapid arrival after Eric shoots himself in the head with a .44 permits the snapping of glossy photos of the suicide's remains sprawled on a white chenille bedspread before the blood congeals. In a commentary on extreme pornography, the text notes how "critics dwelled on the richness and intensity of the colors"—cherry red, livid purple, ruby, black (Silko, 1991, 108). A public showing of the photos attests that David finds a suitable subject for "his style of clinical detachment and relentless exposure" of the grotesque (*ibid.*). Increasing the value of the exhibit is the court injunction that Eric's family seeks, which heightens the public's hunger for lurid details. Gothic specialist Danel Olson justifies the hunger for shock in a culture saturated with mayhem and longing for more: "We want the riddles of Thanatos and Eros that the Gothic summons" (Olson, 2011 xxiv).

The author specializes in scenarios of shock-horror that reverberate in individual lives. To express the terrors of silence in the upbringing of Ferro, the unwanted son of Lecha, Silko pictures the child opposite the forbidden door, a common motif in such fairy tales as "Bluebeard" and "The Three Bears." When the child falls prey to his curiosity, he glimpses "two glittering black eyes" of a yellow-toothed monster in a baby crib (*ibid.*, 183). Paralyzed by fears of sleeping in the room of the ghost nun Sister Mary José, Ferro is at first unable to flee the call of the skeleton man. The terror remains unaddressed as Ferro reunites with his aunt/foster mother Zeta, who asks nothing about the boy's fears. Unrequited terror turns inward, causing Ferro a lifetime of distrust and suspicion of people and power structures. Silko accounts for Ferro's syndrome by describing the Mayan concept of simultaneity: a day was "a kind of being and it had ... a personality ... it would appear again," a prediction of cyclical horror for Ferro (*ibid.*, 35). Sharon Patricia Holland explains that "No amount of personal recollection or acts of the imagination can prevent the story from repeating itself, from remaining stubbornly consistent in every life that unravels according to its logic" (Holland, 2000, 75).

## THE GOTHIC AS REVELATION

In a subsequent twisted fictional landscape in *Gardens in the Dunes* (1999), the author calls on Gothic conventions to set atmosphere and tone — visions of Jesus and the Holy Mother, an Afro-Mayan witchwoman, stalking through the desert, a fetish stone wrapped in cotton and feathers, a Gypsy interpreting tarot cards, Mormon arsonists, and inexplicable auras and lights. As in *Almanac of the Dead*, Silko pictures evil overwhelming the innocent in nonwhite children shackled by corrupt missionaries and a fire singeing screaming parrots in the Amazon jungle. She allies historical rape of the landscape with the physical subjugation of women. Hattie Abbott Palmer, an intellectual educated at Vassar and at a graduate seminar on heresy at Harvard Divinity School, fights the Victorian proprieties of the 1890s, which leave her unprepared for male predations on women. After her venture into the world of graduate studies in church history, a seduction scene introduces her to a stereotypical despoiler, Mr. Hyslop. He poses as a classmate and after-seminar ruminator until he confines her in a closed carriage, a standard confinement in Victorian women's Gothic fiction. With prim malevolence, she charges that "he was not the gentleman or Christian he appeared to be," an epiphany of the womanizer that echoes the coming to knowledge of Catherine Sloper, protagonist of Henry James's novel of disillusionment *Washington Square* (1880), and of Lily Bart, the suicidal spinster in Edith Wharton's social novel *The House of Mirth* (1905) (Silko, 1999, 101).

Silko extends the range of the female plunderer by connecting rape with unethical empirical research. More insidious than the rapists who rob and ravish Hattie and leave her naked in the desert, the text vilifies Hattie's husband, Dr. Edward Palmer, the biopirate, profiteer, and mad scientist who contributes to Anglo control of world resources. His cavalier devaluation of his wife and foster daughter Indigo congeals Hattie's distaste for marriage into a bitter abandonment of mate and home. On the train ride home to Riverside, California, "The time seemed interminable to Hattie, and she was reminded of descriptions of purgatory and hell" (*ibid.*, 374). Symbolically, Linnaeus the monkey escapes caging at the same time that Hattie plots her departure from a restrictive, unfulfilling marriage. For healing, she turns to a welcoming phantasmagoria — a profusion of bloom at the Anglo-Norman cloister of Aunt Bronwyn, the novel's endearingly eccentric post–Druidic gardener. The healing quality of fragrances, shapes, and colors of blossoms extends to Indigo, a female self-rescuer who cleanses herself of the distortions of white society and male-centered religion by creating her own seedbeds, where "in the morning sky blue morning glories wreathed the edges of the terraces like necklaces" (Silko, 1999, 478). Silko rounds out the matriarchal finale by picturing a female snake, the new divinity of the spring, a reign of femininity that counteracts the ravages the women have survived.

*See also* abortion; homosexuality; sex; Wovoka.

• *References and further reading*

Christie, Stuart. *Plural Sovereignties and Contemporary Indigenous Literature*. New York: Palgrave Macmillan, 2009.
Cortese, Romana, and James Cortese. "A Labyrinth of Mirrors: Carlos Ruiz Zafón's *The Shadow of the Wind*" in *21st-Century Gothic: Great Gothic Novels since 2000*, ed. Danel Olson. Lanham, MD: Scarecrow, 2011, 527–538.
Cryer, Dan. "Native Uprising," [Long Island] *Newsday* (17 November 1991): 35.
Holland, Sharon Patricia. *Raising the Dead: Readings of Death and (Black) Subjectivity*. Durham, NC: Duke University Press, 2000.
Joshi, S. T. "Foreword" to *21st-Century Gothic: Great Gothic Novels since 2000*, ed. Danel Olson. Lanham, MD: Scarecrow, 2011, xi–xviii.
Joyce, Graham. "Narrative and Regeneration: *The Monsters of Templeton* by Lauren Groff" in *21st-Century Gothic: Great Gothic Novels since 2000*, ed. Danel Olson. Lanham, MD: Scarecrow, 2011, 445–452.
Lee, A. Robert. *Gothic to Multicultural: Idioms of Imagining in American Literary Fiction*. Amsterdam: Rodopi, 2009.
Mellas, Laurie. "Memory and Promise: Leslie Marmon Silko's Story," *Mirage* 24 (Spring 2006): 11–14.
Murray, David. *Matter, Magic, and Spirit: Representing Indian and African American Belief*. Philadelphia: University of Pennsylvania Press, 2007.
Nevill, Adam L. G. "Wonder and Awe: Mysticism, Poetry, and Perception in Ramsey Campbell's *The Darkest Par of the Woods*" in *21st-Century Gothic: Great Gothic Novels since 2000*, ed. Danel Olson. Lanham, MD: Scarecrow, 2011, 149–157.
Olmstead, Jane. "The Uses of Blood in Leslie Marmon Silko's *Almanac of the Dead*," *Contemporary Literature* 40:3 (Fall 1999): 464–490.
Olson, Danel, ed. "Introduction" to *21st-Century Gothic: Great Gothic Novels since 2000*, ed. Danel Olson. Lanham, MD: Scarecrow, 2011, xxi–xxxiii.
Porter, Joy. *Place and Native American Indian History and Culture*. New York: Peter Lang, 2007.
Silko, Leslie Marmon. *Almanac of the Dead*. New York: Simon & Schuster, 1991.

_____. *Gardens in the Dunes*. New York: Scribner, 1999.

Smith, Carlton. *Coyote Kills John Wayne: Postmodernism and Contemporary Fictions of the Transcultural Frontier*. Hanover, NH: University Press of New England, 2000.

# Grandma Fleet

A tough ecologist and matriarch of the dwindling Sand Lizard clan in *Gardens in the Dunes* (1999), Grandma Fleet maintains her devotion to the sandhills, her people's ancestral sanctuary. At a pivotal point in the clan matrilineage, she refuses an easy death from blood loss after her first child and drinks juniper berry tea to stop the hemorrhage. Widowhood burdens her with memories of her young husband's shooting death by gold prospectors and the incarceration of women and children at Fort Yuma. Endowed with resolve, while puffing on her little clay pipe, she declares "she would die before she would live on a reservation," the epitome of death-in-life for a woman who coexists with nature (Silko, 1999, 17). She respects the tradition that "Sand Lizards ... never found a plant they couldn't use for some purpose" (*ibid.*, 84). At her dugout roofed in layered palm fronds, she twice awaits the return of her daughter, once from capture and once from kidnap. At Mama's disappearance with the Messiah's followers, Grandma states a fundamental truth of desert survival: The family "would just have to learn to get along without her" (*ibid.*, 45). The sum of Grandma's experiences with ill fate explains her importance to the family as an example of clear thinking in times of danger and loss.

After the birthing of granddaughters Sister Salt and Indigo, Grandma Fleet models the custodial techniques of gathering seeds and roots from the desert while propagating future growth. She explains why desert dwellers live at peace with coyotes, eagles, snakes, and pack rats and why the women leave fallen beans in the garden to reseed. She demonstrates how to weave bird snares from human hair, how to terrace a floodplain, and how to store staples for winter in jars buried in sand. During cold weather, she snuggles her family and tells them "old stories about the land of perpetual summer," a utopian myth that provides the warmth of narrative to repel chilling winds (*ibid.*, 22). Along with myth and legend, she informs her granddaughters of Indian enslavement and the sale of captive children in Tucson and Yuma, an aspect of American bondage typically omitted from textbooks. Forced to live among whites at a rail depot in Needles, California, on Arizona's far west border to prevent starvation, she observes the daily arrival of a sisterhood of "weary and frightened women" and avoids victimhood by remaining proactive (*ibid.*, 18).

SOUTHWESTERN ECOFEMINISM

Silko's Grandma Fleet demonstrates the Amerindian concept of recycling. She builds a new homestead by scavenging the town dump for seeds and apricot and peach pits to enclose in glass jars, dried willow limbs for baskets, and willow lattice, tamarisk branches, and scrap lumber to cobble together a lean-to for her family. The text depicts Grandma as a fierce amazon after a white women tries to barter cash for Indigo. In a flash of female energy, Grandma's brisk "No!" and her grasp on the toddler illustrates the adamancy of the head of the four-member matriarchal household (*ibid.*, 19). Critic Karen E. Waldron, a specialist on feminist literature and ecology at College of the Atlantic, explains why Grandma, "profoundly connected to the people's history with the land," returns the girls to the old gardens to "establish the alternate and egoless ground of the novel in tribal experience" (Waldron, 2001, 198). Separation from white communities shields the girls from the poisonous atmosphere of "egocentric individualism and cultural appropriation while creating land as consciousness" (*ibid.*, 180–181).

The matriarch's skill at entertaining while educating her granddaughters results in saleable goods, dog-, turtle-, and frog-shaped baskets woven from devil's claw and yucca. Silko draws on Laguna memories of tourists stopping at the Laguna station, where children sold pottery and beaded pine. Memories of clan celebrations and songs and storytelling in the Sand Lizard language fill in bitter evenings during a blizzard, when Grandma swallows homesickness for the south and beds down her family over hot coals that radiate warmth through a covering of river sand. When government agents take a shack-to-shack census of unschooled children, she hides her granddaughters from judgmental white educators and mimics a physical handicap while claiming she has no children. Pretending to cry before the Indian police, "Oohhh, she moaned, she was all alone now, an old woman alone" (*ibid.*, 21). The performance convinces the men of a folk stereotype — that an old woman is helpless in the face of age and adversity. Cagey about white attitudes, Grandma protects her family during the migration of the Paiute Ghost Dancers to Needles and anticipates a backlash by whites, who fear Indians in large numbers. In her instructions to the granddaughters, she takes pride in being "contrary" and refusing to take Apache slaves, to adopt Christianity, or to live where whites stalk Indians (Silko, 1999, 48). She reminds the girls that rain comes from deceased ancestors: "We are the last remnants of the Sand Lizard clan.... It's no wonder clusters of rain clouds gather over the old gardens" (*ibid.*, 48). Essential to her example are visits to old houses to feed ancestral spirits and cultivation of old gardens, which are both legacies and retreats for the four women in times of emergency.

## GRANDMA IN RETROSPECT

By continuing to reveal the grandmother's character long after her death, Silko dramatizes the importance of the dead to the living through the granddaughters' memories of Grandma Fleet, the saver of seeds and dispenser of love. Just as Grandma once "[greeted] the clouds with tears in her eyes" thinking of "their beloved ancestors [returning] to them as precious rain," the granddaughters perpetuate the Southwestern tradition of holding the dead in their hearts and minds (*ibid.*, 47–48). Sister Salt treasures both Mama and Grandma by kindling cook-fires over the family hearth stones, the granddaughters' inheritance from their matrilineage. Echoing in the minds of Indigo and Sister Salt are homilies on survival: "too much clothing wasn't healthy," "no one must speak even one word," "wait and watch," and "they should keep to themselves if they encountered strangers" or "unfamiliar dogs or mules" (*ibid.*, 83, 33, 69, 35, 174). Details of not eating too much or too fast, avoiding long exposure on open riverbanks, packing food for journeys, and traveling in cool weather shield the granddaughters from unnecessary hardship. More significant than warnings is Grandma's wiliness. The girls recall: "Grandma Fleet got away. We'll get away too" (*ibid.*, 64).

Silko's belief in the supernatural subverts white versions of ghost visitations. Analyst Annie Merrill Ingram, a professor of environmental studies at Davidson College, explains the connection between old tribal lore and reunions with the departed: "Inherited knowledge inspires the dreams that sustain them despite displacement" (Ingram, 2007, 136). At a difficult pass in Indigo's fostering by Edward and Hattie Abbott Palmer, a spiritual reunion promotes confidence: "Grandma Fleet came to her and she loved Indigo as much as ever; death didn't change love" (*ibid.*, 176). More important to Indigo than self-satisfaction is her need not to disappoint Grandma, whose spirit hovers in the background in the ripe fruit produced by apricot trees. The small grove illustrates the Sand Lizard concept of ecology and the nitrogen cycle in the pits salvaged from the Needles town dump and nourished by Grandma Fleet's remains, which lie buried at their roots. Rounding out the novel, Grandma's injunction to honor grandfather snake at the spring foreshadows both the worst of senseless pillage and the hope of reclamation. After the granddaughters discover the old rattler's skeleton and the ruin of their dugout, a sign of Grandma's beneficence appears in the female snake that guards their water supply. Silko implies a new strength in divine protection, which takes a feminine form.

See also *Gardens in the Dunes*; Indigo; Indigo and Sister Salt's genealogy; Sister Salt.

- *References and further reading*

Christie, Stuart. *Plural Sovereignties and Contemporary Indigenous Literature*. New York: Palgrave Macmillan, 2009.
Ingram, Annie Merrill. *Coming into Contact: Explorations in Ecocritical Theory and Practice*. Athens: University of Georgia Press, 2007.
Li, Stephanie. "Domestic Resistance Gardening, Mothering, and Storytelling in Leslie Marmon Silko's *Gardens in the Dunes*," *Studies in American Indian Literature* 21: 1 (Spring 2009): 18–37.
Silko, Leslie Marmon. *Gardens in the Dunes*. New York: Scribner, 1999.
_____. "Introduction," *On the Rails: A Woman's Journey*, by Linda Niemann. Berkeley, CA: Cleis, 1996.
Waldron, Karen E. "The Land as Consciousness: Ecological Being and the Movement of Words in the Works of Leslie Marmon Silko" in *Such News of the Land: U.S. Women Nature Writers*, eds. Thomas S. Edwards and Elizabeth A. De Wolfe. Hanover, NH: University Press of New England, 2001, 178–203.

# Harley

In Silko's premiere novel, *Ceremony* (1977), Harley represents the victimhood of men caught up in world war. A fellow soldier with "MacArthur's boys"— Emo, Leroy Valdez, cousin Pinkie, Rocky, and Tayo— Harley first appears in the story in a metaphoric funk representing the men's collective trauma in the Pacific theater (Silko, 1977, 42). The reference to MacArthur's troops both honors them as neophytes mentored by General Douglas MacArthur, one of the era's great military leaders, and demeans them as perpetual babes in combat, like Boy Scouts following a den leader. Silko pictures Harley's black burro twisting north while his body and legs sidle to the east, a contortion replicating the return home of veterans of the Pacific war whose minds and spirits reach back toward grim memories of fighting the Japanese for the U.S. Army. In a preface, the author explains that Harley began as a comic character in a short story, "But as I wrote about Harley's desperate thirst for alcohol, it didn't seem so funny after all" (Silko, 1977, xvi). For material on the Harleys of the war, she studied "survivors of the Bataan Death March, cousins and relatives of mine who returned from the war and stayed drunk the rest of their lives" (*ibid.*).

A restless jokester and hell-raiser, Harley adopts white ways and swaggers under a name implying the masculine panache of the Harley-Davidson motorcycle. Analyst Deborah Clarke, an English professor at Pennsylvania State University, commented: "Harley's name reminds us that macho masculinity and macho cars, aligned with white dominance, are equally out of place in this Native American community" (Clarke, 2007, 176). She adds that "White masculinity does not extend to Native Americans, regardless of whether they carry names of white male sexual symbols such as the Harley" (*ibid.*, 177). The failure of the disguise forces Harley and his pals into the role of poseurs. An acknowledged blusterer, in May 1948, Harley occupies what analyst Noriko Miura calls "outlaw space," a free-wheeling expanse of time and place that allows the veterans to retain the privileges of GIs long after the soldiering has stopped (Miura, 2000, 198). Like his buddy Emo, Harley has lost his respect for animals, an allegorical detachment from nature that leaves him adrift in the Indian milieu. As though plotting a new start to his life, he "kept wiping away the outlines he drew in the dirt and starting over again," a symbolic shaping and reshaping of his future and a foreshadowing of his ignoble "rubbing out" by Emo and Leroy Valdez (Silko, 1977, 22).

## A LIFE OF SUBSTANCE ABUSE

Escapism fails Harley. He prefers morning beer to coffee, an indication of his reliance on alcohol to alleviate memories of Wake Island, where he, Emo, and Leroy Valdez each earned a Purple Heart. Harley jokes about setting "an Indian world's record ... longest donkey ride ever made for a cold beer," an indication of his acquiescence to white stereotyping of the drunken Indian (*ibid.*, 24). Tayo, a fellow sufferer of battle fatigue, recognizes Harley's masking of the past with "smart talk and laughter"—"good times ... courtesy of the U.S." (*ibid.*, 23, 40). Edgy repartee attests to the wisdom of the Roman poet Horace's adage "Laughter hides the truth," an aphorism that the author repeats in *Gardens in the Dunes* as "truth in the joke" (Silko, 1999, 415). The smirking brags about outsmarting Harley's brothers and parents in "going up the line" of bars on Route 66, a cross-country migration path, suggest a veteran's desperation for an alcoholic respite from internal hurts (Silko, 1977, 24). To banish melancholy from their bar-hopping, he demands jukebox music, "Something to get us happy right now" (*ibid.*, 52). Silko interposes an outsider's opinion of long-term roistering in the nervous looks of Mannie, the fat Mexican bartender. The backward glance echoes the author's belief that honky-tonks and booze dig deeper the hole in which Harley thrusts himself.

During the men's Tuesday trek to get beer, Silko characterizes the prototypical postbattle buddy by turning Harley into Tayo's caregiver, a mirror image of the cheery soldier in Stephen Crane's *The Red Badge of Courage* (1895) and Stanislaus "Kat" Katczinsky in Erich Maria Remarque's *All Quiet on the Western Front* (1928). A flood of weeping at memories of a Filipino monsoon and blood dried on bandages forces Tayo to slide off his mule and onto the rutted ground. Harley's tender wiping of the tears precedes his convenient lie about sunstroke, a macho cover for embarrassment at Tayo's weeping. At the Dixie Tavern in Budville, Harley reminds Tayo of his share of the cost of beer. In a gesture of acquiescence to fate, Harley flips a coin with Leroy Valdez to determine who pays for the next round. Harley's casual amiability dismisses as luck Tayo's freeing from the police after the near murder of Emo after Tayo thrusts a jagged beer bottle into Emo's gut. "Breathing wine fumes," Harley flourishes at man-talk about women and war, but the subconscious self emerges along with drunkenness, which causes him to slide back into the Laguna language he learned in childhood (*ibid.*, 147).

## RETURNING HOME

Silko sets up contrast in the veterans' methods of coping with reintegration into normal adult life. In mid–August 1948 on Tayo's return from Mount Taylor for a curative ritual conducted by Chicano-Navajo shaman Betonie, he admits that Harley's camaraderie "had come and got him moving again" (*ibid.*, 232). The euphoria of healing attunes Tayo to grasshoppers and the smell of sage and juniper while Harley interrupts with laughter and teasing, his shallow substitute for introspection. Critic John Emory Dean explains the ongoing foolery in terms of Plato's cave myth: "Those in the cave [Harley] distrust anyone who leaves the cave [Tayo] to travel to the world of forms" (Dean, 2009, 169). Armed with two bottles of tokay wine and two six-packs on his way from a night-time bender in Gallup, Harley introduces a good time with Helen Jean by a wink and grin, elements of his debauched methods of recovering from war. Past Mesita, he prances in mimicry of stereotypical gay behavior and enters the Y bar to polka alone to Mexican music. His gestures emphasize his alienation from self and his pathetic efforts to mask painful memories with false merriment.

At the novel's high point, Silko separates the men into those who continue to "despise themselves" and Tayo, the loner who realizes how war has skewed Indian thinking about self-esteem and about human worth (Silko, 1977, 204). Analyst Conrad Shumaker, an expert in American culture at the University of Central Arkansas, states that the danger lies in what Silko calls "the dissolution of their consciousness into dead objects: the plastic and neon, the concrete and steel" (*ibid.*, 204). Harley and others "who participate in this attempt to gain power through separation, are equally in danger of becoming witches themselves" (Shumaker, 2008, 28). Unlike Tayo and Leroy Valdez, Harley ignores the possibility of self-endangerment and makes a joke about his beer belly. He feeds the jukebox to play tunes by Hank Williams, the country-western star who popularized his first hit, "Lovesick Blues," in 1948. Harley's boast about cheating a dealer out of a truck accompanies a brief reflection on anti-colonialism: "They owed it to us—we traded for some of the land they stole from us!" (*ibid.*, 157).

Harley's torture and death in barbed wire outside the Jackpile uranium mine links him to white materialism, the enticement that invigorates his search for sexual exploits, tippling, and thrills, motifs that the author reprises in *Almanac of the Dead* (1991). With the guile of Yellow Woman (Kochininako), betrayer of Arrowboy (Estoy-eh-muut) in Laguna myth, Harley sells out his friend Tayo to the murder-mad Emo, the most seriously deranged war veteran. Sad at his comrade Harley's suffering under Ck'o'yo witchery, Tayo must admit, "Harley had bargained for it; he realized that Harley knew how it would end if he failed to get the victim he named" (*ibid.*, 252). Dismembered in death with Leroy, Harley represents the waste of war survivors through the witchery of easy government money, substance abuse, and a loss of earth reverence.

*See also Ceremony*; names; substance abuse; Tayo.

• *References and further reading*
Clarke, Deborah. *Driving Women: Fiction and Automobile Culture in Twentieth-Century America*. Baltimore: Johns Hopkins University Press, 2007.
Dean, John Emory. *Travel Narratives from New Mexico: Reconstructing Identity and Truth*. Amherst, NY: Cambria, 2009.
Ganser, Alexandra. "Violence, Trauma, and Cultural Memory in Leslie Silko's *Ceremony*," *Atenea* 24:1 (June 2004): 145–149.
Miura, Noriko. *Marginal Voice, Marginal Body: The Treatment of the Human Body in the Works of Nakagami Kenji, Leslie Marmon Silko, and Salman Rushdie* (Thesis, 2000), http://books.google.com, accessed July 12, 2010.
Shumaker, Conrad. *Southwestern American Indian Literature: In the Classroom and Beyond*. New York: Peter Lang, 2008.
Silko, Leslie Marmon. *Ceremony*. New York: Viking, 1977.
_____. *Gardens in the Dunes*. New York: Scribner, 1999.
Spurgeon, Sara L. *Exploding the Western: Myths of Empire on the Postmodern Frontier*. College Station: Texas A&M University Press, 2005.

## healing and health

Silko's native background fosters a reverence for inner peace, which derives from a healthy mind and body. Silko interviewer Ellen L. Arnold explains that the author wraps Southwestern history in cyclical patterns that "hold out possibilities for human survival and healing" (Silko & Arnold, 2000, x). Silko's *Yellow Woman and a Beauty of the Spirit: Essays on Native American Life Today* (1996) characterizes health as "foremost in achieving [a] sense of well-being and harmony" (Silko, 1996, 65). Unlike the white world's obsession with aging, she explains that "the traditional Pueblo people did not worry about aging or about looking old because there were no social boundaries drawn by the passage of years" (*ibid.*, 66). Plastic surgical enhancements are unthinkable because the clan values uniqueness and blesses all divergent individuals as mediators between spirits and humankind. Speaking through Grandma Fleet, the weathered matriarch of the Sand Lizard people in *Garden in the Dunes* (1999), the author remarks on the hardships of staying alive: "Dying is easy — it's living that is painful" (Silko, 1999, 51). Part Two amplifies the difficulty of enduring adversity by picturing the deaths of three Alaskan girls at the Sherman Institute in Riverside, California, where dry air taxes their lungs and kills them. The image of the listless girls relieved of captivity in the afterlife inspires Indigo, the protagonist, to "get away or she would die as they had" (*ibid.*, 68). Crucial to her survival is the wisdom of Grandma Fleet, who urges patience "for the right moment to run" (*ibid.*).

In Silko's first novel, *Ceremony* (1977), healing derives from trust in words and herbal medicines that restore human identity with life forces. For Tayo, an uprooted veteran of the Pacific war, combat leaves him sickened, shivering and sweating from malaria and embroiled in anomie, a "dissolution that had taken everything from him" (Silko, 1977, 31). Critics Alan R. Velie, a specialist in Amerindian literature at the University of Oklahoma, and Shamoon Zamir, an expert in American studies at King's College London, compare Tayo's deep-gutted malaise to bodily and spiritual wounding in European grail lore. Tayo envisions himself engulfed in a Filipino monsoon, which clouds his nightmares in humidity. To the Laguna, Tayo's malady, Harley's alcoholism, and cousin Pinkie's blackout spells are new forms of Ck'o'yo medicine, an insidious alienation worsened by alcohol. Like the coma that obliterates manhood in Root after a motorcycle collision in *Almanac of the Dead* (1991) and the loss of two children in Ilie Ruby's Seneca-based novel *The Language of Trees* (2010), the nothingness seems worse than death for prolonging agony and leaving doubts of any form of rehabilitation strong enough to restore humanity. Worsening the situation are flashbacks to Tayo's childhood and his abandonment at the home of Auntie Thelma, where he lives "close enough to feel excluded" in a residence devoid of welcome and intimacy (*ibid.*, 67). Critic Kenneth R. Lincoln, a humanities professor at the University of California at Los Angeles, defines Tayo's journey to wellness in terms of catharsis: "If the world sickens or dries up or dies, the stories internalize the imbalancing affliction (lying, shame, pettiness, racism, violence, poison, alcoholism, war), and characters must vomit up the bad story to cleanse themselves internally before they can be restored to natural balance and shared health" (Lincoln, 2008, 115).

An Emotional Cleansing

In a veterans' hospital in Los Angeles, Silko presents the drug-addled Tayo fogged in and invisible. Incorporeality strips Tayo of self and allows him to "merge with the walls and the ceiling" like a psychotic invisible man (Silko, 1977, 32). A military doctor violates native logic by blocking the memories that torment Tayo. The psychiatrist forces his way into Tayo's cloud shield and provokes a patient voice-over in the third person. With the depersonalization of a sympathetic consultant, Tayo refuses a return home and asserts, "He can't go. He cries all the time" (*ibid.*, 16). The hallucination displays the veteran at the extremes of personality dissociation. Evidence of his rejection of reality, his constant vomiting represents the gut's attempt to disburden itself without help from the soul. At a turning point in his treatment, Tayo examines the nametag on his suitcase and recognizes himself from the name and serial number, superficial identifiers for a spirit still mired in a Philippine prison camp. Silko stresses the severity of Tayo's mental disintegration by the shifting image at the Los Angeles depot, where the face of a Japanese boy gives place to memories of Tayo's cousin Rocky in boyhood. Lacking medical terms to name his malady, Tayo weeps "at how the world had come undone," a multilayered metaphor of war, battle fatigue, and loss (*ibid.*, 18).

Tayo's first effort at ridding himself of sorrow and regret works through Ku'oosh, a tedious old Laguna medicine man who believes that the future of the pueblo depends on the healing of war veterans. The old man repeats dialect origin stories, but their ancient terminology has no meaning for Tayo, whose white teachers drummed them out of his head in boyhood as mere superstition. Ku'oosh accepts Tayo as "grandson," an elder-to-youth relationship meant to ease the anguish with paternal concern (Silko, 1977, 35). The healer treats Tayo with the Scalp Ceremony, an ancient purification rite that cleanses returning warriors from contact with enemies and their blood. For dosing, the shaman relies on traditional dried Indian tea and blue cornmeal. Indian tea, a common name for *Ephedra nevadensis*, derives from fresh and dry twigs or leafless needles of a gray-green broomlike plant that grows in the desert and in the mountains as high as 6,000 feet. The fibers, related to pine, produce a bracing stimulant when boiled in water, as Silko demonstrates in the beverages served by Captain Pratt in "A Geronimo Story" (1974). Herbalists refer to the decoction as Brigham tea or Mormon tea, cowboy tea, settler's tea, and squaw tea. Despite the army doctor's dismissal of indigenous medicine as a "bag of weeds and dust," the stomach soother slows Tayo's ongoing vomiting (*ibid.*, 34). Westerners consume the decoction as a tonic and blood purifier, a stimulant for the elderly, and a cure for asthma, colds, and kidney disorders. For all the good it does Tayo, the tea lacks the power to obliterate the spiritual decimation of World War II and its hellish weapons— mortar shells, flame throwers, and atomic bombs, the long-distance assault artillery that exceeds the imagination of ancient warriors. For a deep soul sickness, Tayo must look elsewhere for antidotes.

## A ONE-ON-ONE EXAMINATION

Silko depicts Tayo's inside-out self-destruction as fragmented dreams of Spanish and Japanese voices, an unintelligible language, and juke box music. In the Pacific, indications of distress begin with progressive shivering and a grief that swells his belly up toward his throat, a gastro-esophageal rejection of the army execution of Japanese captives. In his waking hours after he returns to Laguna, he combats vomiting, a form of internal disencumberment of wartime evils that leaves him weak and defenseless. In a subsequent try at self-integration and recovery, Tayo accepts his Uncle Robert's suggestion to follow the elders' advice and seek more potent healing from beyond the pueblo. The text indicates that men of experience foresee a need for strong medicine to absolve Amerindian war veterans of horror and guilt. To express the extent of war sickness among Indians, Silko pictures rootless Hopi, Navajo, and Zuni along with Laguna outside Gallup bars. Significantly, the combat-damaged men turn from the sky to crouch and gaze into mud as though war has permanently sullied their hearts.

After walking down Route 66 to the Gallup bus station, Tayo takes a Trailways to the hogan of Chicano-Navajo shaman Betonie. The cross-country bus route implies the national outbreak of war sickness by passing south and west from Chicago to Springfield, St. Louis, Tulsa, Oklahoma City, Amarillo, Santa Fe, Albuquerque, Gallup, and Flagstaff before ending at Los Angeles. In the individualistic style of Navajo medicine, the shaman begins diagnosing the source and depth of his patient's trauma through unassuming conversation embedded with gems of wisdom. Tayo's corruption by envy of whites causes him to doubt that verbal ceremonies can combat white evils—"the sickness which comes from their wars, their bombs, their lies" (*ibid.*, 132). Betonie begins with Ku'oosh's treatment by dosing his patient with Indian tea and insisting on sleep. On the second day, the old man performs a chantway, prayer, and passage through five hoops and over bear footprints. Key to patterning, a sand painting reconnects the patient organically to the community and environment, both stabilizers of order and wellness. The painting, as described by British analyst Helen May Dennis, a specialist in native American literature at Warwick University, is an "eclectic and synthetic" ritual shaped from "many elements gathered from many different locations and cultural traditions," an allusion at Tayo's personal development from shamed mixed-blood bastard to savior of his people (Dennis, 2007, 49).

Through the healing ceremony, Silko, a mixed-blood storyteller, states her faith in hybridity and syncretism. Betonie legitimates ritual alternatives because "only this growth keeps the ceremonies strong" (Silko, 1977, 126). He declares change an essential to cultural growth: "Otherwise we won't make it. We won't survive" (*ibid.*) His prediction encompasses both a generation of war-sick veterans and a world poised to spread nuclear weaponry. Drawn away from the disharmony of battle fatigue back to his homeland, Tayo returns to health and hope and stands on "the edge of the rimrock," a threshold to full involvement in his recovery (*ibid.*, 145). In an out-of-body experience, he finds the strength to retreat from his physical ache, a "molten pain" (*ibid.*, 202). The participle suggests the suffering of creation, a reflection of the Greek myth of Prometheus and Epimetheus, who mold creatures for life on earth. At the culmination of Tayo's cure, he "cried with the relief he felt at finally seeing the pattern, the way all the stories fit together — the old stories, the war stories, their stories — to become the story that was still being told" (*ibid.*, 246). His recovery allows him to shed the stereotype of "crazy Indian" and to move, like the epic hero, through "the world as it always was: no boundaries, only transitions through all distances and time" (*ibid.*).

CEREMONIAL HEALING

Silko demonstrates the cogency of words in the healing process. Tayo faces what Anishinaabe analyst Gerald Robert Vizenor describes as the adversities of "alcohol, uncouth missionaries, wicked debaucheries, avarice, fraud, corruption, violence, and colonial melancholy," a New World version of Joseph Conrad's "heart of darkness" (Vizenor, 1994, 169). Betonie guides Tayo through the story that Ts'its'tsi'nako (Spider Woman or Thought Woman) provides. The three-stage restorative process is a native convention comprised of involvement techniques— repeated language and dialogue, varying tempo and vocal pitch, melodic utterance, and kinesic stress, gesture, and mimicry. The totality, called meta-communication, amplifies and clarifies the sufferer's struggling voice. The I-thou relationship between shaman and listener restores wholeness, peace, and individuality. The constellation that Betonie draws reconfigures Tayo's relationship with self, land, endurance, and tribe. Tayo grasps a new opportunity to re-collect his fragmented ego, to see himself engaged with the world, and to glimpse what he might become rather than to reinforce the failure that he thinks he should be. The telling requires Tayo to absorb Betonie's counsel, to join the visionary ritual ceremony and the visionary telling of stories, and to frame and perform stories to aid others. By revising the oral tradition, Tayo learns to re-examine, perceive, and interpret a foreign world, a coming to knowledge prefigured in Navarre Scott Momaday's *The Way to Rainy Mountain* (1969). With a centripetal rush, Tayo comes home.

The object of Betonie's method is an interactive transformation, an "aha" moment that Jewish storyteller Peninnah Schram describes as integral to the perpetuation of ethnic lore. Through participation, like Jewish seder celebrants re-experiencing the suffering of Hebrews enslaved in pharaonic Egypt or black slaves singing spirituals about bondage and liberation, Tayo claims his entitlement to the native mindset. He actively rids himself of despair and relives the narrative as though he were the first witness of history. Silko's legitimation of oral therapy acknowledges that other traditions have no equal to tribal speech, ancient language and text, ritual, and narrative performance. She establishes the power of Betonie's storytelling as a testimonial of belonging — a legacy steeped in Navajo longevity, a verbal magic that weaves a safety net to rescue Tayo. As a result, according to Helen May Dennis, Tayo "[finds] himself promoted to central protagonist in a much larger ceremony to combat witchery" (Dennis, 2007, 47). Thus, the call to action transforms Tayo to the healer of his own malaise and the hero of his own story.

Silko's blend of memory, dreams, visions, and myth mimics the complexity of the human spirit. Critic Gay Alden Wilentz summarizes the author's methods of solace by comparing them to "Jewish acts of remembrance": "Remembering includes taking her place as storyteller to retell both painful and healing stories of survival for the next generation" (Wilentz, 2000, 86). By a variety of stimuli, she implies that Tayo's healing is an ongoing process that may continue throughout his life. Analyst John A. McClure, a specialist in contemporary literature and religion at Rutgers University, explains the internal struggle in terms of physics: "The force fields of secularism and the sacred are too strong for either one to drive the other entirely from [Tayo's] mind" (McClure, 2007, 140). Instead, the process of rehabilitation pairs yin with yang in a dynamic duality, revealing Tayo as "a newborn medicine man, for the moment at least, both the healed and healer" (Lee, 2009, 506). Vague recall of life on the range and of his assistance to Uncle Josiah's ranch breeding of spotted Mexican longhorns stirs surges of hope at the same time that it arouses grievous flashbacks of war and loss. The forces that Betonie unleashes through ceremony appear ineffective until all falls into place from Tayo's health-affirming coitus with Ts'eh Montaño, the mountain demigoddess and grower of health-restoring plants. Without revealing how sexual congress hastens recuperation, Silko turns Tayo toward the dawn, a mystic phenomenon that promises a cyclic restoration of sanity one day at a time. Sitting alone in the kiva, Tayo realizes that he is capable of personal harmony, piety, and civic duty. In a later revelation, the author explained that she composed the novel as a treatment of her own psychological unease while living on the foreign landscape of Alaska and while pondering her own mixed-blood ancestry, a hybridity she shares with Tayo. Like her protagonist, Silko comes to grips with transition and with patterns of Yupik life far from the Laguna she grew up with in the Southwest.

A Sick Generation

In telling the stories of pessimists and exploiters in *Almanac of the Dead* (1991), Silko concentrates on various forms of morbidity, from parental grief for lost children on talk shows to Root's brain damage, Amalia's coughing up blood, Rose's parents' need for bootleg whiskey, Eddie Trigg's fantasies about a cure for paraplegia, and Yoeme's untroubled death in her sleep. The author explained her unsettling historical fiction as a gift of healing and consolation to the world. Jean Ellen Petrolle, an English professor at Columbia College, observes that "the author's belief in the salvific properties of literary activity makes *Almanac* an exercise in allegory as religious ritual," much as *Ceremony* involves readers in self-cure (Petrolle, 2007, 142). The text develops in detail Root's car accident at age 19, when he sees his youth and freedom limited by a plate on his damaged brain and a limp that makes him drag his right leg. Silko extends the dependence of Root on an uncaring mother after she notices tears soaking his hospital gown as she pushes him in a wheelchair. Mosca, Root's fellow cocaine addict, develops the notion that a witch caused the traffic mishap. Mosca's antipathy toward whites turns from taunting and beleaguering Root about the site and events surrounding the smash-up to local civil disobedience. Turning his name "Mosca" (the fly) to realistic behavior, he flits to the "firebase camp" that Vietnam War veterans build off Silverbell Road in northwestern Tucson, Arizona, along the Santa Cruz River (Silko, 1991, 210). The shift in focus to veterans mentally deranged by war allows Mosca to abandon questions about Root's coma and to move illogically toward the Nazi plot to exterminate all Europeans unfit for Hitler's master race. Root's dissociation from humanity saps him because he lacks kinship with "'something larger,' ... a restored relationship of the individual to humanity and the world" (Silko & Arnold, 2000, xi).

The intertwined scenarios of *Almanac* move relentlessly toward anarchy in a world too spiritually septic to save. As a model of pockets of resistance, the author creates a desert outpost managed by Lecha and Zeta, aging twins who hole up at a Tucson ranch along with a collection of misfits—the blonde translator Seese, the disaffected nephew Ferro, homosexual hangers-on Jamey and Paulie, Laguna exile and yardman Sterling, and a canine foursome of Dobermans capable of ripping apart any single member of the compound. The shadow world of Tucson gangsters involves the Blue family—Max "Mr. Murder," his adulterous wife Leah, and their dissolute sons Sonny and Bingo—who complicate the confused scramble for wealth with Mafia style murder for hire. Broadening the illicit plottings of criminals are two contrasting sets of parasites—El Grupo, the collusion of the Tucson police chief and Judge Arne; and the Cuban Marxist Bartolomeo. The female power broker, Angelita, the "little angel" of pure Communism who bears the contrasting sobriquets of La Escapía and the "meat hook," speaks the author's belief that histories are sacred tomes embracing the potent vengeance of justice-seeking spirits.

Critics Konstanze Kutzbach and Monika Mueller explain the cathartic effect of Silko's sadistic montage as the beginning of healing: "Images are the fragments of the deeper truth and lead to the source of illness and ultimately to recovery.... We, her readers, are part of this success" (Kutzbach & Mueller, 2007, 125). Angelita states that storykeepers can "cure the suffering and evils of the world by the retelling of stories. Stories of depravity and cruelty were the driving force of the revolution, not the other way around," a gesture of respect to Karl Marx for his tribal Jewish faith in the momentum and uplift of rhetoric (Silko, 1991, 316). Silko musters her assemblage to amplify what British critic A.

Robert Lee, a specialist in American literature at Nihon University in Tokyo, terms her glimpse of the end-time — a "hemispheric vision, mythic while would-be actual, ecological while sedimented in the humanity of its indigenous peoples, the Americas in their entirety as first and last landscape" (Lee, 2009, 222).

Instead of armament and war for empowering the underdogs, Silko orchestrates the International Holistic Healers Convention in Tucson, an assembly of disaffected peoples — Indians, "peasants without land, *mestizos*, the homeless from the cities and even a busload of Europeans, had come to hear the spirit macaws speak through Wacah" (Silko, 1991, 710). Among New Age leech handlers, Siberian and African shamans, colonic irrigators, and root doctors come the hungry and weak, eco-terrorists known as Green Vengeance who trained under 110-year-old Huichol elders, AIDS patients who become suicidal walking bombs, Mexican Indians with painted faces, Marxist agitators, and ghost dancers, 20th-century followers of the 19th-century Paiute prophet Wovoka, choreographer of the Ghost Dance. The alliance of so varied a host of constituencies is a long shot, even with the aid of global media coverage. Silko turns to satire the use of cable talk shows by New Age agitators and the juxtaposition of consumer frenzy over crystal sellers, a Tibetan chanter, an experiential medicine man, a performer on Himalayan bells, and feminist spiritualists chanting "I am goddess, I am goddess" (*ibid.*, 719). In the babble, Inca and Maya translators squabble over the translation of a term while Rose, the Yupik medicine woman, offers white and gray stones for sale in room twelve twelve. Amid a post–Woodstockian collection of exhibitionists and misfits, Lakota poet and visionary Wilson Weasel Tail discloses fractures in the overlords, who suffer increasing nervous collapse and psychotic episodes. He works the magic of cross-cultural syncretism, a demagoguery tinged with charisma and urgency summoning the defenseless to band against white capitalism. Silko calls the movement "Medicine Makers — Cures of All Kinds" (*ibid.*, 716). In contrast to the charlatanry of the conference, Sterling, the Laguna outcast, abandons escapist crime stories of Geronimo, John Dillinger, Ma Barker, and Pretty Boy Floyd in *Police Gazette, True Detective*, and *Reader's Digest* and returns to the pueblo to absorb the healing stories of elders he heard in childhood.

NATURE CURES

Unlike the male-dominant evils of *Almanac of the Dead*, the matriarchal strengths that undergird *Gardens in the Dunes* (1999) value age-old Sand Lizard methods of staving off hunger, sickness, and hurt, such as healing plants smoked in a clay pipe for headache or nausea, juniper berry tea for postpartum hemorrhage, sleeping in the heat of day and working at night to avoid overheating, and cold cloths, sips of lemon water, and paregoric for seasickness. Grandma Fleet refuses to live along the riverbank because of ambient fevers. When siblings Indigo and Sister Salt collect wild honeycomb to eat with tortillas made from crushed amaranth seeds, the elder rubs Indigo's bee stings. She explains that bee venom is "good medicine — a good cure for anything that might ail you," a reference to apitherapy, which combats arthritis by reducing inflammation with the swelling of bee stings (Silko, 1999, 14). Illustrative stories of European invaders remind the girls that aliens once attacked and killed, stole food, and left the Sand Lizard people sick with white diseases and fever. The virgin soil population makes a wise decision — to distance themselves from whites who carried with them an unknown and terrifying contagion.

Silko immerses her characters in vivid outdoor scenes. She rewards the respecters of tradition by picturing the survivors of a fever approaching the highest dunes and finding the sand laced with fields of sunflowers, vegetable vines, and orange, white, and yellow blossoms. The curative power of sunny-colored plants and of clan unity returns after the fourth night of the Ghost Dance. In a final ritual, the spirit of Wovoka leads participants in clapping, shaking, and waving shawls "to repel diseases and sickness, especially the influenza" (*ibid.*, 32). In a later scene, when Sister Salt grieves for her kidnapped sibling Indigo, by rubbing roots of the fragrant datura (*Datura stramonium*) against her cheeks and forehead, Sister Salt asks nature to alleviate the numbness. By opening her own laundry business outside Parker reservation, she lets hard work distract her from loneliness "for the touch of someone who loved her" (*ibid.*, 207).

## FEMALE HEALING

The author's juxtaposition of Indian and white womanhood pictures both helpful and harmful examples of wholeness. The text contrasts the nativism and courage of the Sand Lizard women and the conventional social climbing of Mrs. Abbott, a matriarch of Oyster Bay on Long Island, New York. Indigo retrieves internalized instruction from Grandma Fleet that too much clothing is unhealthful. Wellness information centers the runaway in sensible concerns for the individual. From a white perspective, amid the press of socially prominent people, Hattie Abbott endangers herself emotionally by ignoring her mother's advice and by venturing beyond acceptable womanly behavior and opinions. In the view of critic Stephanie Li, an English professor at Cornell University, Mrs. Abbott views her daughter as "a type of commodity to be traded in marriage for added material gain" (Li, 2009, 30). Rather than lure suitors, Hattie commits the error of pursuing a graduate degree from a heresy seminar at Harvard Divinity School by writing a thesis on Mary Magdalene's discipleship to Jesus and her gospel as revealed in Coptic scrolls. Because a reviewing committee reproaches Hattie for researching female spirituality, Hattie requires medical care under a male physician for the resulting anxiety, hopelessness, inertia, melancholia, and nervous collapse. After diagnosing her with "female hysteria, precipitated by overstimulation," like the quack who treats plantation mistress Alice Tate in Kaye Gibbons's *On the Occasion of My Last afternoon* (1998), the physician offers the standard advice of the late Victorian–early Edwardian era: ladies should relax, breathe deeply, and avoid fatigue (Silko, 1999, 229). The treatment suits a period when women avoided physical strain and exercise, dressed in lung-compressing corsets, and viewed themselves as fragile china dolls valuable only for their looks, grace, and charm.

Key to Hattie's recovery is the avoidance of academic study, which university experts limit to male scholars. The return of her faintness at a formal welcome to a church bishop explains Hattie's melancholia — the thought of kissing a bishop's ring brings on syncope and forces her outdoors for a whiff of fresh air, a symbol of unfettered thought. On her way to the door, scissors slip from her lap and impale one blade vertically in parquet flooring, an emblem of the disapproval Hattie weathers after composing a thesis on female empowerment in the early Christian church. In a subsequent dream, she envisions the bishop surrounded by sycophants in a room of empty bookshelves, a symbolic lack of scholarship amid religious posturing of androcentric clergy. An episode of sleepwalking in Aunt Bronwyn's cloister gardens outside Bath, England, overwhelms Hattie with a torrent of troubling thoughts—"poor judgment, bad timing, late marriage, premature marriage, dread of childbirth, sexual dysfunction" (*ibid.*, 249). Silko contrasts late Victorian medical knowledge with Aunt Bronwyn's tattered stories of healing stones, cursing stones, and praying stones and of curative spring water and mud, and the use of hog lice, burnt coke, red coral, crab claws, earthworms, and aqua vitae, (Latin for "water of life," or distilled wine) turned into restoratives of vigor.

In contrast to Hattie's genteel sufferings, Silko dramatizes the threats of an active male life invigorated by intellectual curiosity. Dr. Edward Palmer loses hearing in his right ear in childhood from swimming in the sea. Subsequent ventures into botanic field study threaten him with an unbearable headache during collection of seaweed and kelp samples at Campeche Bay, Mexico, and a broken left leg on the Pará River in north central Brazil. Expeditions leave him with a limp, but fail to dampen his zest for searching for the unknown, perhaps a new food plant or medical panacea. Worries about a frivolous lawsuit return the headache during a long train ride, when Edward dismisses the pain as "too much reading and writing in a jolting coach for an old man" (*ibid.*, 123). In his thoughts, he relives the broken leg he suffered during a jungle fire upriver from Portal, Surinam, where *mestizos* treat his injury with kerosene and a round of rum. Edward's six-day recuperation begins with splinting and rest in a hammock, while his rescuers offer tincture of Merthiolate, aspirin, belladonna, tea, and hot fish soup. When pain in the recovered leg persists in Genoa, Italy, and a fluttery stomach disturbs his composure before his arrival in Bastia, Corsica, Edward's reliance on morphine and paregoric parallels Hattie's need for laudanum for headache, a pairing of painkillers that suggests misallied marriage partners facing stress and uncertainty in a foreign land. For Hattie, the cleansing of self from wedlock and of the town of Needles, California, by arson precedes her return to the King's Bath in England, where Aunt Bronwyn dispenses serenity and wellness in her healing garden.

*See also* Betonie; homosexuality; Tayo.

• *References and further reading*

Davidson, Michael. *Concerto for the Left Hand: Disability and the Defamiliar Body.* Ann Arbor: University of Michigan Press, 2008.

Dennis, Helen May. *Native American Literature: Towards a Spatialized Reading.* New York: Taylor & Francis, 2007.

Kutzbach, Konstanze, and Monika Mueller. *The Abject of Desire: The Aestheticization of the Unaesthetic in Contemporary Literature and Culture.* Amsterdam: Rodopi, 2007.

Lee, A. Robert. *Gothic to Multicultural: Idioms of imagining in American Literary Fiction.* Amsterdam: Rodopi, 2009.

Li, Stephanie. "Domestic Resistance Gardening, Mothering, and Storytelling in Leslie Mamon Silko's *Gardens in the Dunes*," *Studies in American Indian Literature* 21: 1 (Spring 2009): 18–37.

Lincoln, Kenneth. *Speak Like Singing: Classics of Native American Literature.* Albuquerque: University of New Mexico Press, 2008.

McClure, John A. *Partial Faiths: Postsecular Fiction in the Age of Pynchon and Morrison.* Athens: University of Georgia Press, 2007.

Petrolle, Jean. *Religion without Belief: Contemporary Allegory and the Search for Postmodern Faith.* Albany: State University of New York Press, 2007.

Ramirez, Susan Berry Brill. "Storytellers and Their Listener — Readers in Silko's 'Storytelling' and 'Storyteller,'" *American Indian Quarterly* 21:3 (22 June 1997): 333–357.

Shanley, Kathryn W. "The Indians America Loves to Love and Read: American Indian Identity and Cultural Appropriation," *American Indian Quarterly* 21:4 (22 September 1997): 675–702.

Silko, Leslie Marmon. *Almanac of the Dead.* New York: Simon & Schuster, 1991.

_____. *Ceremony.* New York: Viking, 1977.

_____. *Gardens in the Dunes.* New York: Scribner, 1999.

_____. *Yellow Woman and a Beauty of the Spirit: Essays on Native American Life Today.* New York: Simon & Schuster, 1996.

_____, and Ellen L. Arnold. *Conversations with Leslie Marmon Silko.* Jackson: University Press of Mississippi, 2000.

Stanford, Ann Folwell. "'Human Debris': Border Politics, Body Parts, and the Reclamation of the Americas in Leslie Marmon Silko's *Almanac of the Dead*," *Literature and Medicine* 16:1 (Spring 1997): 23–42.

Teuton, Sean Kicummah. *Red Land, Red Power: Grounding Knowledge in the American Indian Novel.* Durham, NC: Duke University Press, 2008.

Vizenor, Gerald Robert. *Shadow Distance: A Gerald Vizenor Reader.* Hanover, NH: Wesleyan University Press, 1994.

Wilentz, Gay Alden. *Healing Narratives: Women Writers Curing Cultural Dis-ease.* New Brunswick, NJ: Rutgers University Press, 2000.

## homosexuality

Silko internalized in childhood the live-and-let-live attitude of the Pueblo toward individual differences. Her tolerance of alternative sexuality includes acceptance of adulterers in wanton Yellow Woman (Kochininako) episodes and of her Aunt Charity Alice Marmon Little, who dislikes marital sex and prefers living apart from husband Miguel "Uncle Mike" Little, a Mescalero Apache worker on the Santa Fe Railroad in Richmond, California. The author explains in *Yellow Woman and a Beauty of the Spirit: Essays on Native American Life Today* (1996) that humankind is "a mixture of male and female, and this sexual identity is changing constantly, sexual inhibitions did not begin until the Christian missionaries arrived" (Silko, 1996, 67). Out of respect for the *berdache* (a North American-French term for a homosexual or two-spirit person), she makes no distinction toward a young cross-dresser from nearby "who wore nail polish and women's blouses and permed his hair" (*ibid.*). Open-minded villagers refrain from mockery of femininity in a male. Rather, they overlook eccentricities and physical deformities "because survival of the group means everyone has to cooperate," regardless of their sexual orientation (*ibid.*). Carrying the Pueblo attitude into the religious realm, elders honor exceptional sexual identities and bless the unique person for mediating between the spirits and humankind.

Some book reviewers find *Almanac of the Dead* (1991) too pernicious, too anti–Caucasian to exonerate for its unconventional scenes of non-standard carnality. More troubling to critics is the straight female's depiction of bisexuals and homosexuals as hedonists, narcissists, and sadists. Early on in the text, the author states the forbearance of Indians who are "very secure in themselves and their identity; and thus they were able to appreciate differences and to even marvel at personal idiosyncrasies so long as no one and nothing was being harmed" (Silko, 1991, 9). Critic Sandra Baringer, a lecturer in English at the University of California at Riverside, rebuts critical charges against Silko of anti-gayness. Baringer claims that the outré characters—some celibate, some autoerotic, some bestial, and some bisexual or gay—serve Silko's refutation of "the abuse of power and phallocentric race privilege [derived from] the sense of masculinity" (Baringer, 2004, 113). Reigning over the disintegrating social scene is the Death-Eye Dog, a European symbol of faithful companionship that the text describes as male and "somewhat weak and very cruel" (Silko, 1991, 251). Critic Cathy Moses envisions homosexual sadism as an embodiment of "the colonial mentality and ... witchery," a demonization of the feminine to elevate the traditional Western notion of white masculinity and dominance (Moses, 2000, 115).

### PHALLOCENTRISM

The psychopathological focus on men and male genitalia turns characterization into caricature and transforms the evidence and source of manhood into a bizarre fetish. Critic Janet St. Clair, an English professor at Regis University, admits that the text is full of stalking, symbolic cannibalism, bestiality, egomania, and voracious appetites of "savage white homosexual men who prey on weak and unsuspecting victims to feed their insatiable lusts for sex, money, and power" (St. Clair, 1999, 207). Of the effect, she concedes, "Mired in negative stereotypes [of homosexuality], it offends. On the other hand, the metaphor works" (*ibid.*, 208). She defends Silko against charges of homophobia and gay bashing by viewing brutal homosexuality as examples of abuses of power: "The equation of carnal gratification with viciousness and their gynephobic sexual self-absorption emblematize the egocentric, phallocentric, and misogynistic savagery that Silko sees as endemic to Western culture" (*ibid.*). Sandra Baringer concurs and notes, "It is not homosexuality which is under fire, but rather the abuse of power and phallocentric race privilege" as proofs of maleness (Baringer, 2004, 113). She links the "hyperbolic excess" of Silko's characters to humor "in the spirit of Juvenalian satire" (*ibid.*). For the governor, a member of the exclusive El Grupo along with the police chief and Judge Arne, the expanse of his erection horizontally rather than vertically turns a normal response to desire into an awkward penis. Silko comments that the "long, thick erect organ ... might be mistaken for a loaf of bread," a subtextual commentary on the reign of the powerful over the starving subclass (*ibid.*, 273). Serlo, the neo–Nazi white supremacist, fantasizes about *sangre pura*, the empirical proof of Hitler's *Lebensborn* (German for "fount of life") project and the production of a master race of supermen. Serlo masturbates to collect his ejaculate in a sperm bank "where a superior human being would be developed" (*ibid.*, 547). Feminist critic Jane Olmstead interprets Serlo's sexual distancing from a love object as proof of his "spiritual and emotional death," an overarching theme in *Almanac* that dooms Serlo's dream of supermen (Olmstead, 1999, 473).

Another of Silko's perverts views homosexual acts as a means to a cure. The obsession of wealthy bisexual Eddie Trigg with full manhood turns him toward blood as a pathological fetish and a source of repair for his paraplegia. He supersedes other perverts and voyeurs in believing that "the sight and smell of blood naturally excited human sex organs" (Silko, 1991, 337). Olmstead surmises that, rather than lust for other males, "For Trigg, sexual desire is tied up with fantasies about power, wholeness, and defiance of death through risk and danger" (Olmstead, 1999, 473). Because Eddie can maintain a useless erection, he delights in sexual romps with Leah, wife of Max "Mr. Murder" Blue, and in congratulating himself on cuckolding a legendary Mafioso. For male-to-male manipulation, Eddie's choice of fellatio as a means of soothing potential blood and organ donors precedes the complete drainage of the victim's vascular system. Unlike fulltime homosexuals, Eddie uses oral sex as an introit to the harvesting of body parts from derelicts and homeless men to stock his refrigerated basement vault. Jane Olmstead notes that "the erotic thrill is certainly present: it is the idea of killing during a sexual act that eroticizes an otherwise merely callous murder" (*ibid.*, 472).

HOMOSEXUALITY AND FEMININITY

Silko connects the psychopathology of sexual perversion with absent sires, inadequate mothering, and resultant mother-hate in men. Konstanze Kutzbach, an English professor at the University of Cologne, and Monika Mueller, a lecturer in American literature at the University of Stuttgart, explain the twisted logic of vicious gays as "the product of their own civilization, the rejection by their mothers and the total absence of their fathers" (Kutzbach & Mueller, 2007, 113). Thus, Silko's generation of merciless homosexuals derives from "aggressive vampire mothers who abort or abandon their progeny" (*ibid.*). The result of disunion of male from female is the denigration of women as "cunts" and "receptacles" and the devaluation of the nuclear family and community (Silko, 1991, 536, 657). Without respect for dynasty and ancestry, the disaffected retreat to an infantile pleasuring of the senses to assuage emptiness and spiritual drift. Ferro, the abandoned son, retreats from Lecha, his birth mother, to a choice between two gay partners—Paulie, the attendant of guard dogs, and Jamey, an undercover cop. Choosing the latter for "all the pleasure he got with Jamey," Ferro fantasizes about being sodomized and abandoned and "waited for the kiss-off" (*ibid.*, 455). By allying with a virile male, Ferro "wanted to escape the stink of women," whom he associates with betrayal (*ibid.*, 692).

A more complicated triangle—the photo artist David, Eric the model, and Beaufrey, the techno-vampire who sells snuff videos and films of torture, abortion, and ritual circumcision of virgins—reveals Beaufrey also as a mom-hater. He extends his hostility from his dismissive parent to all women: "Hating the rest of them was easy" (*ibid.*, 102). Kutzbach and Mueller interpret anti-mom malice as the source of Silko's virulent fiction: "She rejects the strong gynophobia that determines so much of European American culture" (Kutzbach & Mueller, 2007, 118). Speaking for the aggressive female, Lecha, guardian and translator of the title almanacs ridicules pedophiles like Beaufrey who reject women in favor of young boys: "The white men kept their women small and weak so the women could not fight back when the men beat them or pushed them around" (Silko, 1991, 597). The paradox of tough men who prefer cowering women reveals the cowardly nature of bullying and victimizing the vulnerable.

## KILLING CHILD AND MOTHER

Silko carries her most disgusting homosexual triangle to a direct attack on mother and child. The three-way tangle—Beaufrey/David/Eric—perverts the basis of family through David's impregnation of Seese and Beaufrey's theft of the infant Monte, the mystery boy of the novel. Eric's suicide leaves evidence of disharmony of mind and spirit: "The clenched muscles guarded divisions and secrets locked within him until one day the gridwork of lies had exploded bright, wet red all over," a visual amalgamation of ejaculation and expulsion of the menses (*ibid.*, 106). In contrast to Eric's search for peace, Silko dramatizes Beaufrey's murder and dismemberment of Monte for the boy's organs. In Seese's tortured memories of Beaufrey, he is a coke-head standing outside the family circle and displaying a "Smirking, sucking mouth," an emblem of cannibalism (*ibid.*, 112–113). With a woman's chutzpah, she spits Vodka on him and David and mocks, "You can't have babies. You can't do that, can you?" (*ibid.*, 113). Because of her own substance abuse, she fails to recognize Beaufrey's malignity. The paired deaths—a suicide and infanticide—result in two film records of white society at its most despicable low. Beaufrey's merchandising of beauty, innocence, and slaughter leaves no doubt of androcentric rottenness at the core of civilization.

Analyst Tara Prince-Hughes, a specialist in gender studies and native American literature at Whatcom Community College, presents an alternate view of Silko's intent. She pictures the self-damning of gay men as the result of crimes against holy Mother Earth. The sacrilege is an outgrowth of New World male domination, atrocities, and acquisitiveness introduced to Mexico by Spanish conquistadors. David, once shielded from a drunken father by a loving mother, loses his ability to enjoy male-female relationships. He loves seeing his own features mirrored in his son Monte, but recoils from Monte's mother Seese after birthing releases uterine effluvia and breast milk. In the triangle with Eric and the reptilian Beaufrey, David despises feminine emotions in Eric, who can relate to the feminine in Seese as a result of what Prince-Hughes calls "two-spirit mediative skills," a reference to the Indian concept of gayness (Prince-Hughes, 2000, 6). The victim of a father who called him "queer and swish and fairy. 'Faggot.' Never just 'fag,'" Eric values his sensitivity to others (Silko, 1991, 59). At his most womanly, he can weep like a girl. The tears "nearly drive David insane with the compulsion to smash the crybaby's face to bloody pulp" (*ibid.*). Ironically, David's emotionless snapping of glossy photos of Eric's corpse foreshadows a subsequent photo shoot of David's mangling when a horse rolls over him. Beaufrey, the least humane of the gay trio, casually photographs David for the sake of the cash he will earn from art purveyors of the grotesque. Prince-Hughes concludes that scorn of the feminine side of the personality leaves "no place for the balance and harmony represented by the two-spirit" (Prince-Hughes, 2000, 6).

See also Gothic.

• *References and further reading*

Baringer, Sandra. *The Metanarrative of Suspicion in Late Twentieth Century America.* New York: Routledge, 2004.
Kutzbach, Konstanze, and Monika Mueller. *The Abject of Desire: The Aestheticization of the Unaesthetic in Contemporary Literature and Culture.* Amsterdam: Rodopi, 2007.
Moses, Cathy. *Dissenting Fictions: Identity and Resistance in the Contemporary American Novel.* New York: Routledge, 2000.
Olmstead, Jane. "The Uses of Blood in Leslie Marmon Silko's *Almanac of the Dead*," *Contemporary Literature* 40:3 (Fall 1999): 464–490.
Prince-Hughes, Tara. "Worlds In and Out of Balance: Alternative Genders and Gayness in the *Almanac of the Dead* and *The Beet Queen*" in *Literature and Homosexuality*, ed. Michael J. Meyer. Amsterdam: Rodopi, 2000.
St. Clair, Janet. "Cannibal Queers: The Problematics of Metaphor in *Almanac of the Dead*" in *Leslie Marmon Silko: A Collection of Critical Essays*, eds. Louise Barnett and James Thorson. Albuquerque: University of New Mexico Press, 1999, 207–222.
Silko, Leslie Marmon. *Almanac of the Dead.* New York: Simon & Schuster, 1991.
_____. *Yellow Woman and a Beauty of the Spirit: Essays on Native American Life Today.* New York: Simon & Schuster, 1996.

# humor

Humor shaped from varying degrees of wit and acerbity serve Silko as touches of humanity and sources of derision of white dominance. She began writing short stories early in her career and tinged them with subtle snickers, such as the ebullience of "Laughing and Laughing about Something That Happened at Mesita" (1974), the folk playfulness of "Uncle Tony's Goat" (1974), the whimsy of "From a Novel Not Yet Titled" (1975), and the bittersweet comeuppance in "An Old-Time Indian Attack Conducted in Two Parts" (1976). In "Bravura" (1974), a snidely titled vignette, she mocks the naïveté of the white poet who deserts the university to live native style, a direct reference to the Indian wannabe common to celebrity, fiction, and film. Standard native chuckles derive from the sisterly squabbles of Iktoa'ak'o'ya (Reed Woman) and Nau'ts'ity'i (Corn Woman) and from bamboozling of husband Al by Yellow Woman (Kochininako). Her audiotape "The Laguna Regulars and Geronimo" (1977) taps the pervasive legend of an Apache leader who befuddles the U.S. cavalry with now-you-see-him, now-you-don't sightings of the Southwest's most wanted renegade.

Overall, the author's stories exhibit a sassy resilience that honors Amerindians for their endurance. According to critic Patrice E. M. Hollrah, survival humor illustrates a rejection of despair, for example, Ayah, the protagonist of "Lullaby" (1974), who laughs at her husband Chato's wrapped feet, which "look like little animals up to their ears in snow" (Silko, 1974, 16). The anecdotal humor offers a clue to Ayah's empowerment as a wife and clan matriarch. In "Language and Literature from the Pueblo Indian Perspective" (1981), Silko exonerated the Hopi for punning in English as their sacred duty to get a laugh, even in a ceremony. To interviewer Laura Coltelli, the author explains that Indian stories rely on humor "especially areas in justice, loss of land, discrimination, racism, and so on, ... there's a way of saying it so people can kind of laugh or smile ... so you can keep their interest" (Coltelli, 1990, 146).

## TALES AND JOKES

Silko is a facile teller of animal jokes. In *Conversations with Leslie Marmon Silko* (2000), she elicits coarse belly laughs from the coyote fable, "Toe'osh: A Laguna Coyote Story" (1973), collected in *Storyteller* (1981). The laugh hinges on the string of coyotes, all cousins linked mouth to tail over a precipice. They fall down to the mesa below after one animal farts in another's face. Her moral for the writer is to follow the coyote and "keep trying and trying" (Silko & Arnold, 2000, 38). For another beast fable in *The Turquoise Ledge* (2010), she pictures Coyote coated in pine pitch and feathers and flapping around in circles to allow him to follow the female cedarbirds to a mesa top to learn their grinding song. The tale takes a second humorous turn as Coyote climbs into the sewing basket of Old Spider Woman (Ts'its'tsi'nako or Thought Woman). Against her instructions, Coyote looks up and falls, landing in a heap of smashed basket withes on the rocks below. The feminist humor depicts the nosy male as the victim of his own plots to steal ritual music from females.

The author varies comedy to suit situation and tone. In less bumptious scenes than coyote stories, in her first novel, *Ceremony* (1977), puns and incongruity invigorate the text, such as the prostitute Helen Jean cruising for war veterans in the El Fidel bar, a name suggesting fidelity. Soldiers attempt to unwind from war trauma in the Philippines by telling raucous battle stories laden with bloodletting and sexual conquest. On a peasant level, Tayo, the protagonist, recalls how Uncle Josiah gently ridicules a Bureau of Indian Affairs agricultural handbook for the absence of details on raising wild Mexican longhorns. Turning mockery to pride, he plans to create his own livestock advice after breeding a tough strain of spotted cattle capable of surviving on drought and desert fare around Laguna Pueblo. A standard tale of cuckoldry and mutual lust in a version of the Yellow Woman cycle concludes with Al, an annoyed husband, demanding a "damned good story" explaining where his wife went the previous evening (Silko, 1981, 95). Before the abduction tale reaches its end, Silko acknowledges that "tragic encounters between Pueblo people and Apache raiders were no more and no less important than stories about the biggest mule deer ever taken or adulterous couples surprised in cornfields and chicken coops" (Silko, 1993, 31). An example of humor by juxtaposition derives from Silko's use of the outhouse as a common place holder in folk stories of pranks and of late-night adultery. In a twist on poverty, Indians fail to notice the Great Depression because of an unusually bountiful harvest. Storytellers chuckle, "They remembered 'The Crash' as a year of bounty and plenty" (Silko, 1991, 41).

## THE COMIC BACKDROP FOR HORROR

Silko's most Gothic writing manages to balance humor with grotesquerie. Punctuating *Almanac of the Dead* (1991) with cathartic chuckles, she relieves a horrorscape rife with paranoia and slaughter. Occasional incongruencies, both personal and dramatic, alleviate the author's battery of the reader with evil, for example, the old maids who stalk a lone bachelor, Popa chasing Lecha's taxi the day after old Guzman's funeral, the Barefoot Hopi's prison break plot, Korean computer whiz Awa Gee's selection of false identities from tombstones, and the Tucson "copcake" calendar of scantily clad police officers. The resolution focuses on motley eco-defenders who assemble at the International Holistic Healers Convention and who buy pebbles from Rose, the Yupik hawker of amulets in room twelve twelve. In a macabre death scene, Seese, the transcriber of Mayan codices, wets her pants while chuckling over the squirt of Tiny's blood that titillates police officers. In the opening vignette, Ferro accuses his mother Lecha of enjoying a "junky orgasm" from a shot of dope in the arm (Silko, 1991, 2). Subtextually, the coital reference recalls her rejection of her son by overlayering the whiteness of the drug with the whiteness of ejaculate and with mother's milk, the tenderness she refused him within days of his birth. At a serio-comic epiphany, Lecha, a psychic and finder of the dead, performs at cable talk shows before a studio audience desperate for magic. The shared desperation encourages her dedication to transcribing ancient Mayan parchments, the codices of the novel's title.

In the same vein as the parody of T. Coraghessan Boyle's *East Is East* (1990) and Kathryn Stockett's *The Help* (2009), Silko allies humor with felony and death. She is particularly caustic in characterizing conceited, over-dressed social matrons who lunch at the country club while their husbands, members of El Grupo, plot corrupt deals. In an ironic twist redolent with black humor, Iliana Gutierréz, the elitist wife of *mestizo* insurance magnate Menardo Panson, designs and builds a bleak mansion with a focal adornment, a polished marble staircase overlooking the jungle. After Iliana falls down the stairs and breaks her neck, Menardo, a fellow elitist and denier of his jungle origins, marries his Venezuelan mistress, Alegría Martinez-Soto, the two-timing architect of the mansion. At Menardo's shooting death, a demonstration of the efficacy of a bullet-proof vest by his chauffeur Tacho, the second wife and current widow snaps off her classy high heels to enable her to flee coyotes who abandon her in the desert as though she were a peasant alien sneaking into the American Southwest. Dickensian in its comeuppance to a social climber, the desert scenario implies that, for humble crossers of national boundaries, obstacles are more lethal than a broken shoe.

Silko's ability to dot melodrama with macabre sight gags and irony relieves her jeremiad of one-dimensional tone and atmosphere, for instance, the image of real estate developer Leah Blue, one of the "greedy hagglers of the world" (Silko, 1991, 576). To lure self-important investors, she designs a desert water community complete with Venetian canals and gondolas that float golfers directly to their tees. Another example of Silko's deft handling of tone shift occurs on live cable TV, where Lecha goes into a trance that bores the host with its mundane description of the gardens of Xochimilco, a tourist delight. To a nervous titter from the audience, Lecha intones her discovery of death — two human heads enclosed in a red and yellow net shopping bag, "their blue eyes open wide, staring at the sky" (*ibid.*, 164). The swift segue to horror explains how the author enhances excesses of violence with the absurd events that precede it.

Key to the author's incidental comedy is the universal trickster, such as Rambo-Roy's indoctrination of an army of homeless and the *mestizos* who wheedle foreign governments to underwrite dynamite and uniforms for a peasant army by concealing their need as the outfitting of a baseball team and the clearing of land for a sports field. Silko creates comic book fun out of old Mosca, who suffers from an evil spirit that settles in his shoulder. To his pal Root, Mosca relates a host of Gothic tales of "zombies, open graves, and ghost armies traveling in green fireballs" (*ibid.*, 605). Mosca's tormented imagination contrasts the novel's greater evil — the primal terrors of the Tucson underworld. Critic Sandra Baringer, a lecturer in English at the University of California at Riverside, accounts for the use of such finaglers, who "are always testing themselves against an Other, defining their boundaries" (Baringer, 2004, 15). Another relief valve, invective, opens Arne, the corrupt federal judge, to ridicule for his sexual relations with a basset hound stud and bitches. Baringer explains that "making fun of the enemy's sexual proclivities is one of the oldest forms of rhetorical excoriation," dating to Greek and Roman stage comedies of Aristophanes and Plautus (*ibid.*, 105).

In *Gardens in the Dunes* (1999), Silko creates drollery out of the disparities between Hattie and Indigo, co-protagonists. The text uses paradox and incongruity to illustrate the absurdity of a Victorian upbringing for girls. Hattie Abbott, a scholar trained at Vassar and in a seminar on heresy hosted by Harvard Divinity School, marries a passive botanist, Dr. Edward Palmer, and lives in chaste brother-sister arrangement. Even at naptime, Edward locks the bedroom door to conceal any evidence of their platonic intimacies. In California, New York, Bath, and Genoa, Hattie peruses gardens before arriving at the plantings and voluptuous statuary of *la professoressa* Laura in Lucca, Italy. Skilled in mythic iconography, Hattie recognizes phallic symbols and fertility icons and suffers an anxiety attack upon encountering an egg-shaped vulva. Further wanderings in a garden of rare black gladioli leads Hattie to wonder if she should send Indigo upstairs lest she see "other figures ... unfit for a young girl" (Silko, 1999, 296). Unknown to the Palmers, Indigo has already witnessed a passionate tryst between Edward's married sister Susan and Mr. Stewart, her Scots gardener. Laura, reared without the Puritanism of Hattie's childhood, openly discusses with Edward the symbolism of black, "the color of fertility and birth, the color of the Great Mother," patron of blackbirds and water birds, "the nourishment givers" of water and milk (*ibid.*). Upon viewing a stone phallus atop oversized gonads, Edward sends Indigo away from the garden tour. Indigo chuckles at American prudery and sings, "See you can't see what you see" (*ibid.*, 302).

*See also* Harley; irony.

• *References and further reading*

Baringer, Sandra. *The Metanarrative of Suspicion in Late Twentieth Century America*. New York: Routledge, 2004.
Birkerts, Sven. "Apocalypse Now," *New Republic* 205:19 (4 November 91): 39–41.
Coltelli, Laura. *Winged Words: American Indian Writers Speak*. Lincoln: University of Nebraska Press, 1990, 135–153.
Hollrah, Patrice E. M. *"The Old Lady Trill, the Victory Yell": The Power of Women in Native American Literature*. New York: Routledge, 2004.
Olmstead, Jane. "The Uses of Blood in Leslie Marmon Silko's *Almanac of the Dead*," *Contemporary Literature* 40:3 (Fall 1999): 464–490.
Sadowski-Smith, Claudia. *Border Fictions: Globalization, Empire, and Writing at the Boundaries of the United States*. Charlottesville: University of Virginia Press, 2008.
Silko, Leslie Marmon. *Almanac of the Dead*. New York: Simon & Schuster, 1991.
_____. *Gardens in the Dunes*. New York: Scribner, 1999.
_____. "Language and Literature from the Pueblo Indian Perspective" in *English Literature: Opening Up the Canon*, eds. Leslie Fiedler and Houston Baker, Jr. Baltimore: Johns Hopkins University Press, 1981.
_____. "Lullaby," *Chicago Review* 26:1 (Summer 1974): 10–17.
_____. *Storyteller*. New York: Seaver, 1981.
_____. *The Turquoise Ledge: A Memoir*. New York: Viking Adult, 2010.
_____. *Yellow Woman*. New Brunswick, NJ: Rutgers University Press, 1993.

_____, and Ellen L. Arnold. *Conversations with Leslie Marmon Silko*. Jackson: University Press of Mississippi, 2000.

Tallent, Elizabeth. "Storytelling with a Vengeance," *New York Times Book Review* (22 December 1991): 6.

# hypocrisy

Silko recognizes the duality of the Americanized Laguna in emulating two gestalts—white Christianity and the Pueblo clan tradition. Conflicting worldviews strain individuals caught in the acculturation process, which involves syncretism of diet, behaviors, governance, and worship. In "Auntie Kie Talks about U.S. Presidents and U.S. Indian Policy," an essay in *Yellow Woman and a Beauty of the Spirit: Essays on Native American Life Today* (1996), Auntie Kie lashes out at white hypocrisy in "a nation that claims to value 'liberty and justice for all,' while practicing 'fraud, armed robbery, and murder' to appease its appetite for exploitable land" (Silko, 1996, 81–82). In "Fences against Freedom" (1994), Silko experiences a close-up view of governmental hypocrisy in the late-night roadblocks intended to trap nonwhite undocumented aliens. The author pictures her response as "an awful feeling of menace and of violence straining to break loose" (*ibid.*, 109). In the midst of the police grilling and intimidation, she pities the drug-sniffing dog, which must obey the commands of men who trounce with impunity the human rights guaranteed in the Constitution.

In the author's first novel *Ceremony* (1977), a post–World War II elegy, Silko champions Laguna tradition by describing white teachers, police, and missionaries as judgmental intruders on the pueblo and its values. In home economics classes, girls like Laura learn that proper dressing demands the costume and grooming favored by white society. The text creates irony from Laura's return home from a night of sexual carousing wearing no clothing, but carrying a lipstick in her purse. For acceptance as Christians, the obedient, including the older sister Thelma, must shame those like Laura and Night Swan, who follow "the deplorable ways of the Indian people" (Silko, 1977, 68). Rather than accept Indian parishioners for themselves, priests urge the abandonment of nativism as though animistic customs are as iniquitous as sin. Thelma bolsters her place among Christians by speaking "with an edge of accusation about to surface between her words," a rejection of Christian love in favor of self-righteous judgments of others (*ibid.*, 240).

Silko's characters engage Laguna values in constant combat with the white beliefs of priests, psychiatrists, recruiting officers, and science teachers. Auntie Thelma looks for a reason to dissuade her husband Robert and his brother Josiah from collaborating on cattle breeding. Her absurd rationalization invalidates the cattle as the property of Ulibarri of Magdalena, the cousin of the whore Night Swan, Josiah's mistress. In token of Auntie's outward show of piety, she dusts her black church shoes and attends mass alone. Ostensibly, she bases devotion to the Catholic Church on hopes of having her son Rocky and nephew/foster son Tayo baptized. Tayo, who absorbs her words and interprets her expressions and attitudes, knows that the martyred pose of loyal Catholic is Auntie Thelma's antidote to family disgrace and local gossip.

## CITIZEN MANIPULATION

Compared to Auntie Thelma's double life as pious Catholic and belittler of her foster son/nephew, the U.S. military poses a more pernicious threat to Tayo and Rocky. More threatening to the self-image of volunteers, whites treat Indians like Tayo, Rocky, and their war buddies as a ready source of cannon fodder for the Pacific war. Admirers gravitate to GI uniforms, not the men inside them. At war's end, whites strip nonwhite veterans of their heroism. Critic Charles E. Wilson declares the pride in voluntary service to the beleaguered country a dilemma: "Patriotism is at once seductive and lethal" (Wilson, 2005, 84). Tayo realizes that the returning GIs "never saw that it was the white people who took [honor] away again when the war was over" (Silko, 1977, 43). Looking around at the pueblo, "from horizon to horizon ... every day the loss was with them; it was the dead unburied, and the mourning of the lost going on forever" (*ibid.*, 169). Only after Tayo begins herding Uncle Josiah's cattle from white rustler Floyd Lee back to Laguna land does he "better [understand] such propaganda and the hypocrisy that upholds it" (Wilson, 2005, 84). Like the goats weaning their kids in the corral, Tayo must wean himself from political indoctrination to discover the deceit of economic, racial, and social boundaries.

Wartime perils serve Silko's text by creating a contrast between a Filipino prisoner of war camp and a censorious, unloving home environment. Hypocrisy dominates the household, giving Auntie opportunities to backhand Tayo with cruel words and gestures. In a voice meant to resonate to his bed, she "warned them to be careful to make no mention of Rocky or Josiah," but her transparent methods of deepening Tayo's sorrow are obvious to him and to Grandma (*ibid.*, 31). To demean the combat-wracked veteran, Auntie demonstrates that "She could hold her head up ... because of Rocky," her "special one," who dies in Japanese custody (*ibid.*, 91, 85). Tayo recalls that, while pretending to rear him as her own, Auntie limits his ambitions with a cruel dig: "This one, he's supposed to stay here" (*ibid.*, 67). At Grandma's suggestion that they summon a shaman to treat Tayo's post-war flashbacks, weeping, and vomiting, Auntie declares the consultation worthless because "[Tayo's] not full blood anyway," a vicious gibe at the veteran to punish him for the sins of his mother, "little sister" Laura, who coupled with Mexicans and whites (*ibid.*, 33). A second proposal to take Tayo to Betonie at Gallup reaps another outburst from Auntie, who demeans the Chicano-Navajo medicine man for his humble home. She sneers, "What kind of medicine man lives in a place like that, in the foothills north of the Ceremonial Grounds?" (*ibid.*, 107). Her *non sequitur* attacks expose a cruel streak that belies her religiosity and pairs her with Japanese guards who torment American captives. Sweating and shivering from her barbed words, Tayo "expected a rifle barrel to be shoved into his face when he opened his eyes" (*ibid.*, 17). Silko enhances the irony of torment at home with the contrast between an armed enemy and an aunt/foster mother who only pretends to care for her troubled nephew for the sake of her reputation in the pueblo.

HYPOCRISY AND REBELLION

Silko's loathing of self-righteous posturing reaches extremes in *Almanac of the Dead* (1991), an historical apocalypse. The author develops her diatribe against intrusive, duplicitous sanctimony, which she pictures as "rotted with hypocrisy" (Silko, 1991, 212). In one scenario, the hundreds of Yaqui who grow up in the *mestizo* and Jesuit and Franciscan traditions attempt to visit family cemeteries every November 2 on All Souls' Day. Calabazas rationalizes the right of tribe members to unite for a religious holiday: "We don't believe in boundaries. Borders. Nothing like that. We are here thousands of years before the first whites.... We have always moved freely" (*ibid.*, 216). During border crossings south, the visitors have no problem with Mexican security forces. On the return through Sasabe on the Arizona-Mexico border, U.S. guards at the two-man desert station hassle the celebrants and remain "on the alert for brothers and uncles hiding under firewood" (*ibid.*, 217). Thus, extreme right-wing Americans, on the lookout for brown-skinned intruders, disrupt the very faith that Europeans claimed to have dispensed among first peoples. Silko's shaming of white Christians predates by 19 years Arizona's aggressive attempts in summer 2010 to rid the state of undocumented Hispanics.

Silko's denunciation of Christian hypocrisy pinpoints the hypocrisy of the church-supported invasion of Santo Domingo, Hispaniola, by Hernán de Cortés on April 7, 1504. Critic Rauna Johannan Kuokkanen, an expert educated at the University of British Columbia in native American studies, notes the duality inherent in the Roman Catholic colonialist. She declares that, according to Silko, human intermingling and migration are unstoppable: "Like rivers and winds, human beings are also natural forces of the earth" (Kuokkanen, 2007, xiii). For latter-day analysis of Indian behavior, the author turns to Sterling, the outcast Laguna, one of the characters in *Almanac* who recognizes racial hypocrisy. He spends his free time reading *Police Gazette* and *True Detective* and concludes that outlaw heroes tend to be Indians. He surmises that history and dime novel writers "preferred that Indians got left out of that part of American history too, since their only other appearances had been at so-called massacres of white settlers" (Silko, 1991, 40). One mythic hero to survive white libel and culture theft, Geronimo lives on in Silko's recreations as an Apache guerrilla warrior who realizes that the U.S. cavalry must inflate his menace to secure their reputation as warriors and trackers. Thus, accounts of his treachery against mounted regiments extend his elusive powers to the near-magic. His standing among late twentieth-century Amerindians approaches the legendary for its ability to unite rebels in a war against white supremacy. In the fictional army of Indian prophets, transcribers of almanacs, and leaders of the underclass, according to American philosopher Richard Rorty, a specialist in human rights and irony, Silko anticipates a grassroots overthrow of hypocrisy and self-deception: "Something we must hope will be replaced, as soon as possible, by something utterly different" (Rorty, 198, 7).

In *Gardens in the Dunes* (1999), Silko vents her distaste for church hypocrisy, including the public piety of Mrs. Abbott and Susan Palmer James, who "organized charity events to raise money for the Catholic bishop's aid society" (Silko, 1999, 158). From the Amerindian perspective on "aid," the Sand Lizard clan refuses to allow the lying clergy to touch their children. At the height of their double-dealing, missionaries insist that "Jesus didn't want to see women's bare breasts no matter how hot the summer day" (*ibid.*, 49). After Sister Salt takes the job of camp follower and comfort girl to laborers on the Colorado River dam project, she pictures disapproving Christians "[pursing] their lips anus-like to spit insults at her" (*ibid.*, 220). She blames prudes for costing her the patronage of Charlie Luna, a married man, and charges hypocrites with forgetting Jesus' love of the prostitute Mary Magdalene. Sister Salt mulls over the mixed message about charity: "Jesus knew there could be no peace without love — why didn't the churchgoers remember that?" (*ibid.*). The open-ended question depicts Silko at her most adamant about two-faced piety.

*See also Almanac of the Dead*; Auntie Thelma; duality; social class; Tayo.

• *References and further reading*

Kuokkanen, Rauna Johanna. *Reshaping the University: Responsibility, Indigenous Epistemes, and the Logic of the Gift*. Vancouver: University of British Columbia Press, 2007.

Rorty, Richard. *Achieving Our Country: Leftist Thought in Twentieth-Century America*. Cambridge, MA: Harvard University Press, 1998.

Sadowski-Smith, Claudia. *Border Fictions: Globalization, Empire, and Writing at the Boundaries of the United States*. Charlottesville: University of Virginia Press, 2008.

Silko, Leslie Marmon. *Almanac of the Dead*. New York: Simon & Schuster, 1991.
_____. *Ceremony*. New York: Viking Press, 1977.
_____. *Gardens in the Dunes*. New York: Scribner, 1999.
_____. *Yellow Woman and a Beauty of the Spirit: Essays on Native American Life Today*. New York: Simon & Schuster, 1996, 80–84.
Wilson, Charles E. *Race and Racism in Literature*. Westport, CT: Greenwood, 2005.

## Indigo

The vector and cultural mediator of Silko's *Gardens in the Dunes* (1999), a *bildungsroman* featuring an 11-year-old orphan and runaway from an Indian school, Indigo bears in mind and heart the true north of home. An analog of Yellow Woman (Kochininako), a recurrent female icon in the author's mythography, Indigo incurs abduction, incarceration at a pan–Indian boarding academy called the Sherman Institute, and escape from the white world's "education for extinction," the subject of Sherman Alexie's *Indian Killer* (1996) (Cheyfitz, 2006, 140). Scots critic Stuart Christie, an anarchist writer from Glasgow, states that she "transcends nationalist captivity through picaresque exposure to a universalizing gynocentrism that, as in *Ceremony*, fuses the regional and global" (Christie, 2009, 94). He compares the novel's "global arc" to Grand Tour novels, such as Madame de Staël's *Corinne* (1807) and Patricia C. Wrede's *The Grand Tour* (2006), which detail the socialization of young bourgeois women in European styles and mores (*ibid.*). The irony of a grand tour for an Indian girl offers Silko myriad opportunities for humor and satire.

Silko introduces her character in a fragile sandhill garden, a fictionalized version of the Paguate vegetable beds and orchards ruined by the opening of the Jackpile uranium mine in 1949. From conception by an unidentified light-skinned father, Indigo conciliates between her clan and the outside world. At her birth, the Sand Lizard maiden receives the name for desert indigo (*Salvia arizonica*), a powerful herb bundled into cigar-shaped clumps for smudging or purification ceremonies, a subtextual hint at her naiveté, sincerity, and natural rectitude. The name foretells her value to the fictional Sand Lizard people, whom she helps to resurrect from near extinction. Critic Elvira Pulitano spotlights seeds as Indigo's regenerative tool: "Plants, Silko suggests, are *the* universal, transcultural elements defining a global web of cultures ... unifying forces in world history (underlying migrations, colonizations, and conflicts)" (Pulitano, 2007, 95). Indigo refuels her clan with new stories and exotic seeds, including the corm of the rare black gladiolus, a hybrid of African and European cultivars. The hybrid symbolizes her vigor and uniqueness as well as her willingness to incorporate outside knowledge and outside alliances into the clan's environment.

Indigo embodies the author's native alliance with earth. She comes of age in what critic Gabriella Morisco calls "an ecological niche," a timeless edenic garden (Morisco, 2010, 140). A delicate balance of nature and desert climate instills a pastoral respect for plants, mammals, reptiles, birds, and insects, including an accommodating pack rat who stores usable foodstuffs in a nest. Grandma Fleet retrieves Indigo from a white traveler, a foreshadowing of Hattie Abbott Palmer and her acquisitive husband, and sequesters her in the sandhills. In the clan sanctuary, Grandma introduces the child to earthly coexistence with the warnings, "Don't argue or fight around the plants— hard feelings cause the plants to wither" and "Old Ratty does all the work for you, so don't harm her!" (Silko, 1999, 14, 47). Coexistence with nature involves sharing an eagle's kill and fresh meat seized by a coyote. At age six, the protagonist dances with her older sibling, Sister Salt, and with

Mama and Grandma Fleet and other Ghost Dancers outside Needles, California, at a firepit on a sandy riverbank, a fecund setting abundant with life. Because her sister experiences a trance of light and love on the first night of a four-night dance, Indigo feels cheated that no ancestral spirits reunite with her. On the fourth night of the ritual dance, she witnesses weird shadows that coalesce into Jesus, Wovoka the Prophet, Jesus' mother, and his wife and 11 children. The holy family feeds the people on squash blossoms, a tender snack that Indigo treasures. The delicate treat foretells more nourishing rewards that alleviate Indigo's meager experience with the world.

A FEMININE ENVIRONMENT

The author places her protagonist among influential females who build strength of character and nurture an instinct for creativity. After Mama's disappearance in the uproar caused by soldiers breaking up the Ghost Dance, Indigo models the dependence of orphaned children in transferring her mother hunger into love for Sister Salt. As a younger sibling, Indigo follows her sister's example and treasures the old ways of robbing nature for enough sustenance to live and of planting seeds and fruit trees in the dunes to keep the family larder supplied. In the warm sand, Indigo emancipates her imagination with fantasy: "She watched the water bugs scurry.... The big bugs moved with dignity, but the smaller bugs darted about as if they were playing chase" (*ibid.*, 35). The childish interpretation of insect movement affirms the artlessness that sustains Indigo in a predatory milieu.

Silko illustrates the means by which adults introduce ingenuous children to potential danger. From Grandma Fleet, Indigo learns the cycles of death and rebirth that turn carrion into a part of the nitrogen cycle: "Some hungry animal will eat what's left of you and off you'll go again, alive as ever, now part of the creature who ate you" (*ibid.*, 51). After Grandma's death from old age and exhaustion, Indigo learns the lesson firsthand. She is too overcome with sorrow to help Sister Salt with the burial and adult chores. Unlike her more mature, more pragmatic sibling, Indigo lapses into a malaise of grief and loneliness and imagines conversations with her mother and grandmother, the voices who began her education. At night, she relies on Grandma's spirit to guard and defend her. Indigo indulges in fantasies of Mama traveling with the Messiah and his family, a utopian vision that heartens and encourages the pre-teen during the months ahead.

Curiosity and sophistication alter the Sand Lizard girl intellectually, but not spiritually. On Indigo's odyssey from the Colorado River Valley to a Dickensian Indian acculturation school at the Sherman Institute in Riverside, California, she views the deaths of three Alaskan girls as a warning of the dangers of despair: They "stop eating, lie listlessly in their beds, then die, coughing blood," a reflection both of the virulence of tuberculosis in virgin soil populations and of the retreat into the spirit world from white domination observed in the writings of Iowa-Omaha physician Susan La Flesche Picotte (*ibid.*, 70). Indigo, a more vigorous survivor than the Alaskans, resolves, "She had to get away or she would die as they had" (*ibid.*). She displays spunk among the docile Chemehuevi and Cocopa girls and a wiliness in fleeing barefoot through lemon and orange groves and in outfoxing pursuers, a skill she learned from Grandma Fleet. On the run, she finds her way through a tidy hedge to a lilac bush and on to a glass home, the greenhouse of the gentleman botanist and photographer Dr. Edward Palmer and his bride, Hattie Abbott Palmer, a specialist in medieval church history educated at Vassar and at the Harvard Divinity School. Edward values the child as a scientific examination of what "might be the last remnant of a tribe now extinct, perhaps a tribe never before studied by anthropologists" (*ibid.*, 113). Ironically, the couple, who become Indigo's foster parents, have much to learn from her.

## INDIGO'S EDUCATION

The text introduces opposing Amerindian and Western education models through Christian proselytizers, who condemn and suppress native instincts and interests. After her rescue from pursuers and introduction to the Palmer household, Indigo enters what critic Christie describes as a "period formula from the mid– to late–Victorian novel: bourgeois entrapment within the family drama of Hattie and Edward Palmer" (Christie, 2009, 90). The advance of the captive from boarding school to out-family fostering combines two of the era's solutions to the "Indian problem," both insidious methods of erasing tribalism. She experiences her first view of gardening by unnatural artistic arrangement for the purpose of visual delight and sensual groupings and fragrances. Roses entice her senses, turning her thoughts to a snack of rose hips. Pragmatically, she uses her meanderings in citrus groves, orchards, and a lily bed as opportunities to gather seeds for later planting. Poised in an alien setting, Indigo laughs at Edward's attempt to speak Indian languages. She is a worthy match for Edward, who views her as a pagan native needing "a docile willingness to serve" (*ibid.*, 311). Her affinity for nature enables her to mother Linnaeus, a pet monkey who serves as the mediator between the Sand Lizard runaway and white adults. Like Linnaeus, Indigo allows herself to become a kept darling, caged in love and materialism. Dressed in sashed frocks, kidskin slippers, and straw hats, she fills notebooks with plant sketches and becomes a willing surrogate for the children that Hattie and Edward choose not to conceive. Perceptive in her observations of white people, Indigo notes a peculiarity of urban citizens: "They did not look at one another or greet one another as they passed," a deliberate rejection of human contact that is foreign to native custom (*ibid.*, 154). Her surmise, devoid of fear or intimidation, illustrates her penchant for studying other cultures and for musing on social differences.

In a reversal of the "training the savage" motif found in Daniel Defoe's *Robinson Crusoe* (1719) and Helen Hunt Jackson's *Ramona* (1884), Indigo becomes the household teacher. She instructs her foster parents on such simple expediencies as removing superfluous clothing in hot weather, sleeping on the cool floor on hot nights, and eluding slave catchers. At the extravagant garden of Susan Palmer James, an Oyster Bay socialite and pseudo-aunt obsessed with social climbing, Indigo encounters materialism on a grand scale. She witnesses creation of a garden that Swiss critic Hartwig Isernhagan, an expert in American studies at the University of Basel, calls "a mere object of display and ... the extreme transience of forced or otherwise manipulated natural products" (Isernhagen, 2002, 180). At a sumptuous soirée, no space calls to Indigo, who reverts to her childhood perception of planting and harvesting as elemental rather than decorative. In contrast with the lack of welcome at the James home, in a brief encounter with the Matinnecock on Manhasset Bay, New York, Indigo experiences a pan–Indian kinship with a landless East Coast tribe that adapts indigenous horticulture to production of kelp and oysters. During a brief meeting with a Matinnecock woman, Indigo recognizes Amerindian sorrow at the loss of homelands to whites. A single souvenir — a button carved from a clamshell — introduces the child to her cultural link to all first peoples. Subtextually, the button represents native adaptation to colonialism by producing closures for the garments of whites.

Indigo believes that travel with the Palmers from Long Island, New York, to Bath,

England; Lucca and Livorno, Italy; and Bastia, Corsica, constitutes a religious pilgrimage. She puts her journey to good use in the collection of seeds, a reversal of colonial rapacity. Indigo's harmless version of plant theft parallels the energy of Delena, the gypsy thief who initiates recompense for Amerindians against the engineers who distort the path of the Colorado River to speed water to Los Angeles. Along the way to England and Europe, Indigo fantasizes a reunion with Mama: "The farther east they traveled, the closer they came to the place the Messiah and his family and followers traveled when they left the mountains beyond Paiute country" (Silko, 1999, 320–321). Even separated from her childhood matrilineage, Indigo relies on women and dreams of matriarchs to solace her during months in Great Britain and the Continent. Unlike the pretense of Susan Palmer James's soirée, walks with Aunt Bronwyn in a cloistered Celtic retreat relax and educate Indigo naturally. Female principles of sacred gardening introduce the child to European concepts that duplicate and reconstitute those of Mama and Grandma Fleet. Traces of communal ritual in England and Italy confirm the universality of the Ghost Dance. Echoing the thoughts of Sister Salt, Indigo focuses on returning to Arizona to her dugout home — to the bones of Grandma Fleet — to practice new visions of beauty and sustenance.

## MATURITY AND SYNCRETISM

Experiences in white gardens inform Indigo of cultural pluralism comprised of indoctrination in Western culture, which she compares to Sand Lizard tradition. Unlike puritanical whites, the child exhibits an uninhibited socialization toward sexuality and the artistic recreation of genitalia. Swiss critic Elvira Pulitano, a specialist in postcolonial Indian studies at the University of Geneva, observes that Indigo's "reaction to some of the Old European stone figures (snakes and bears) suggest an affinity between the sensibilities of pre–Christian Europe and Native America, an affinity that eludes Hattie and Edward" (Pulitano, 2007, 97). Usurpation of the British Isles by enemies of King Arthur's Camelot and by Roman legionaries teaches Indigo more about the blending of cultures following conquest. She obtains rich rewards in European travel from observation of pagan Celtic ritual sites and the Roman veneration of Minerva, the goddess of wisdom, a version of Sophia, the divinity who inspires and guides Hattie. According to Silko expert Brewster E. Fitz, Indigo "reads stones as glyphs of pagan European spirituality ... the space of heresy in which Hattie has placed herself by writing a protofeminist thesis on an allegedly apocryphal gospel" (Fitz, 2004, 50). From a rebel perspective, critic Christie views the trek from New York to Europe as Silko's refutation of white superiority: "Oases of imagined difference, these gardens seek to subvert the positivist, Anglo-European construction of nation and science rising triumphantly throughout the world" (Christie, 2009, 90).

Secretly, Indigo taps a store of images and visions of female inviolability. She nurses a lingering grief that she fails to escape white kidnappers as proficiently as Grandma Fleet could have. Dreams bring comfort in the form of love from Mama and Sister Salt, a conscious embrace of the ephemeral to ease the distress of overseas travel far from familiar topography and climate. Indigo struggles with astounding anomalies on her journey, such as la professoressa Laura's garden with its huge Medusa head and the centaur, a mythic beast produced from the sexual union of a human male with a mare. Critic Amelia V. Katanski, an English teacher at Kalamazoo College, stresses that Indigo "reaffirms her tribal identity and develops strategic pan-tribal alliances as she gathers seeds from across the United States and Europe" and becomes "an active agent of hybridity" (Katanski, 2005, 202). The seeds that Indigo secures in wax paper represent physical evidence of Europe's garden riches as well as her willingness to introduce new sources of sustenance to the sandhills.

Silko reveals her protagonist's heroism in a face-off with what critic David Murray, a professor of American studies at the University of Nottingham, calls " a heartless and reductively rationalist masculine world of science and commerce" (Murray, 2007, 142). The role reversal that turns Sister Salt into a mother figure prefigures Indigo's new relationship with Hattie, who requires maternal comfort after Edward's arrest for stealing citron cuttings from an orchard in Bastia, Corsica. In the hands of authorities, Indigo is the expert on avoiding police brutality. She recognizes that, in Livorno, "the police here did not shove or kick them," a hopeful sign to a Sand Lizard girl educated in avoiding captivity and harm by white soldiers and Indian police (Silko, 1999, 322). In Indigo's care, Hattie abandons the world view of the late nineteenth-century bourgeoisie and begins to heal a bruised heart and ego: "She scarcely thought of her thesis now; it was already part of another life, and another person, not herself" (*ibid.*, 370). Silko accentuates the irony of a transformation that flourishes under the compassion and understanding of an 11-year-old Sand Lizard girl.

The story resolves itself harmoniously with Silko's sense of belonging to a place. As she explains in *Yellow Woman and a Beauty of the Spirit: Essays on Native American Life Today* (1996), "We have always been able to stay with the land. Our stories cannot be separated from their geographical locations, from actual physical places on the land" (Silko, 1996, 58). On return to Arizona, Indigo is indifferent to the death of Edward, her fusty white father, but exultant to reunite with Hattie, his widow. Indigo puts her education in horticulture to use in the sandhill gardens, which she plants according to Aunt Bronwyn's principles of diversification. The addition of gladiolus corms for food and color corroborates Grandma Fleet's teaching that "Sand Lizards ... never found a plant they couldn't use for some purpose" (Silko, 1999, 84). Critic Caren Irr, an English professor at Brandeis University, observes an obvious global reciprocity: "Indigo's cultivation of a lovely new food crop comes as a fair exchange for the prior gift of squash to the Old World" (Irr, 2010, 143). The reunion with land and family precedes a restoration of order, a confirmation of nativism, a redressing of injustice, and Indigo's bestowal of the traveler's gifts. Like the Magi and Marco Polo, Indigo presents gleanings from exotic locales as well as a story that broadens the Sand Lizards' horizons.

*See also* Grandma Fleet; Indigo and Sister Salt's genealogy; Palmer, Hattie Abbott; Sister Salt; women.

• *References and further reading*

Cheyfitz, Eric. *The Columbia Guide to American Indian Literatures of the United States since 1945.* New York: Columbia University Press, 2006.

Christie, Stuart. *Plural Sovereignties and Contemporary Indigenous Literature.* New York: Palgrave Macmillan, 2009.

Colwell-Chanthaphonh, Chip. "Portraits of a Stories Land: An Experiment in Writing the Landscapes of History," *Anthropological Quarterly* 78:1 (January 2005): 151–177.

Fauntleroy, Gussie. "In Silko's Garden," *Santa Fe New Mexican* (23 May 1999): 2.

Fitz, Brewster E. *Silko: Writing Storyteller and Medicine Woman.* Norman: University of Oklahoma Press, 2004.

Irr, Caren. *Pink Pirates: Contemporary American Women Writers and Copyright.* Iowa City: University of Iowa Press, 2010.

Isernhagen, Hartwig. "Of Deserts and Gardens: The Southwest in Literature and Art, 'Native' and 'White'" in *Literature and Visual Arts in Twentieth-Century America*, ed. Michele Bottalico. Bari: Palomar Eupalinos, 2002, 173–187.

Karem, Jeff. *The Romance of Authenticity: The Cultural Politics of Regional and Ethnic Literatures*. Charlottesville: University of Virginia Press, 2004.

Katanski, Amelia V. *Learning to Write "Indian": The Boarding-School Experience and American Indian Literature*. Norman: University of Oklahoma Press, 2005.

Marsden, Peter H. *Towards a Transcultural Future: Literature and Human Rights in a "Post"-colonial World*. Amsterdam: Rodopi, 2004.

Morisco, Gabriella. "Contrasting Gardens and Worlds: America and Europe in the Long Journey of Indigo, a Young Native American Girl" in *Nations, Traditions and Cross-Cultural Identities: Women's Writing in English in a European Context*, eds. Annamaria Lamarra and Eleonora Federici. Bern: Peter Lang, 2010, 137–148.

Murray, David. *Matter, Magic, and Spirit: Representing Indian and African American Belief*. Philadelphia: University of Pennsylvania Press, 2007.

Pulitano, Elvira. *Transatlantic Voices: Interpretations of Native North American Literatures*. Lincoln: University of Nebraska Press, 2007.

Silko, Leslie Marmon. *Gardens in the Dunes*. New York: Scribner, 1999.

_____. *Yellow Woman and a Beauty of the Spirit: Essays on Native American Life Today*. New York: Simon & Schuster, 1996.

## Indigo and Sister Salt's genealogy

Silko's union of the animal and human worlds in *Gardens in the Dunes* (1999) takes palpable shape in the emergence of the fictional Sand Lizard clan of southern Arizona from a rattlesnake, the sire and guardian who guards the clan's spring. In the final years of the Indian Wars, the growth of the family tree allies Mama with a white Presbyterian minister, evidence of the immorality and predatory nature of white conquerors. The author presages a flourishing history of surviving Sand Lizards in the union of Sister Salt with Big Candy, an Afro–Red Stick Indian cook and brewer from Louisiana. (Additional commentary on Sister Salt's male clientele suggests that Charlie Luna, a construction worker from Tucson, may have sired her baby.)

The birth of a son, Bright Eyes, introduces a male figure to the matrilineage, a hopeful sign of vigor and regenerative power. The male infant, the first to survive in three generations, carries the name of Dr. Susan "Bright Eyes" La Flesche Picotte, an Iowa-Omaha from Nebraska who became the nation's first female Indian physician. The nickname "little grandfather" completes connection to the Sand Lizard beginnings from Grandfather Snake, the uncle of the original Sand Lizard.

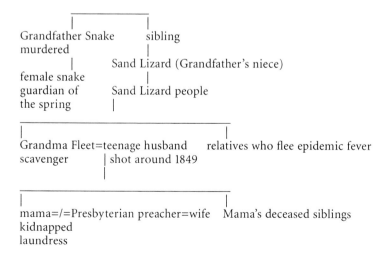

```
at Needles,
California
|
|                                                                    |           |
|          grandma, a Baton Rouge Indian            Indigo    dead baby
|              |
|          mother a cook in Baton Rouge
|              |
Sister Salt=/=Big Candy the cook
light-skinned | ex-army Indian fighter
              |
              | =/=Charlie Luna=wife in Tucson
              |    construction
              |    worker
              |
         baby Bright Eyes
         "little black grandfather"
         "little black spider"
```

*See also* Abbott-Palmer genealogy; *Gardens in the Dunes*; Grandma Fleet; Indigo; siblings; Sister Salt.

• *References and further reading*

Silko, Leslie Marmon. *Gardens in the Dunes*. New York: Scribner, 1999.


## injustice

Silko's views on anti–Indian measures echo the plaintive outcry of native writers of the Native American Renaissance, initiated in 1969 by Navarre Scott Momaday, winner of the Pulitzer Prize for *House Made of Dawn*. Environmentalists George A. Cevasco and Richard P. Harmond characterize her intent to clarify "environmental justice, gender roles, political and physical borders, and even the accuracy of the historical record," a redress of wrong against truth (Cevasco & Harmond, 2009, 47). Her themes denounce illegalities and promote self-determination by the scions of tribes that survive displacement, attempted genocide, and indoctrination of Indian children in government boarding schools such as the Carlisle Indian School in Carlisle, Pennsylvania. To interviewer Ellen L. Arnold, the author stated her credo concerning discrimination by white colonialism: "Injustice I pretty much equate with evil, an imbalance and un-wellness," a fundamental disorder that transgresses the Amerindian notion of fairness (Silko & Arnold, 2000, 105). In an interview with Laurie Mellas, the author fostered the importance of oral storytelling as a source of might and direction for Southwestern aborigines. During the Indian wars and Christian proselytizing of the late nineteenth and early twentieth century, the Laguna prized their collective memory of past injustices. Silko maintains, "It goes way back, farther than western Europeans would like to admit" (Mellas, 2006, 12). In early childhood, Silko admired her Aunt Susie Reyes Marmon for translating testimony by Laguna elders of their loss of tribal land to white usurpers. Because of the longevity of native residency and the prominence of tribal and clan histories, Indians rebutted white property boundaries and corrupt laws and reclaimed their homeland.

In *The Turquoise Ledge* (2010), the author recalls from childhood the Marmon family's tensions. She misunderstood "the injustice that fueled the undercurrents" in pueblo politics (Silko, 2010, 25). In the essay "An Expression of Profound Gratitude," anthologized in *Yellow Woman and a Beauty of the Spirit: Essays on Native American Life Today* (1996), she revisits yearnings for the primordial utopia. A beginning for Laguna myth, the ancient Eden produced the clan of Mother Earth, whose equality ruled relationships. Key to the family concord of "birds, lizards, bugs, plants, and human beings" was the sharing of water and sustenance and the creation of an amicable, just world (Silko, 1996, 152). During story time, the Laguna return to the pre–Columbian haven, which thrived before April 7, 1504, when the Spanish conquistador Hernán de Cortés, brought greed and destruction to the New World. Silko contributed to the pueblo tradition of oral instruction an early model, "Tony's Story" (1969), a cop-killer tale of a misguided idealist striking out at age-old kachina witchery, a menace to the Pueblo. Brewster E. Fitz, a Silko expert, defines her concept of fairness as "perspicuous, loving, holistic, nonlinear, maternal, life-affirming, and open ended," a perplexing style that leaves loose ends (Fitz, 2004, 256). Left unstated at the end of "Tony's Story" is the punishment the white world will inflict on the protagonist for murdering a corrupt policeman and sacrificing himself to the needs of his people.

## VIOLENCE AS INJUSTICE

Throughout her life, Silko witnessed world cataclysm in a series of wars. The Marmons lived amid the Los Alamos Jackpile uranium mines and the Trinity atomic bomb test site, an exploitation of natural minerals that exposed uninformed miners to uranium poisoning. The ore armed the atomic bombs that ended World War II. A mile from Paguate Village and 159 miles from Laguna, a test blast wrecked melon beds and apricot trees. Silko used the issue of exploitation of the uninitiated in the short story "Lullaby" (1974), in which white legalism entangles Ayah, the non–English-speaking protagonist and victim of dispossession and loss. Without an interpreter, she witnesses the arrival of a telegram announcing her son Jimmie's death in combat — possibly the Vietnam War — and the permission form that transports his younger siblings, Danny and Ella, to a tuberculosis sanitarium. Lacking the semantic tools to defend herself, Ayah asserts the might of the Navajo matriarch by reclaiming her dignity and control of a dwindling family. Often interpreted as a tragedy, the story honors Ayah for applying limited powers to a social system stacked in favor of white English speakers.

The author's nonfiction retained its zeal for restoring lawfulness and due process to aborigines. On New Year's Day 1994 in the essay "An Expression of Profound Gratitude to the Maya Zapatistas," she exults in retaliation for the slaughter of Montezuma's people — the uprising of "the intrepid Maya people of Chiapas," Mexican rebels who championed peasant rights (*ibid.*, 153). She describes the infractions as cosmic sacrilege. The essay avenged centuries of injustice by "those destroyers who delight in the suffering and destruction of Mother Earth and her children," including the pillagers of Mesoamerican libraries (*ibid.*). In a personal essay, "America's Iron Curtain: The Border Patrol State" (1994), Silko stresses the patriotism of Indians who believed that freedom of travel was an "inalienable right" (Silko, 1994, 412). In "Auntie Kie Talks about U.S. Presidents and U.S. Indian Policy," an essay in *Yellow Woman and a Beauty of the Spirit: Essays on Native American Life Today* (1996), Auntie Kie lambastes white duplicity in "a nation that claims to value 'liberty and justice for all,' while practicing 'fraud, armed robbery, and murder' to appease its appetite for exploitable land" (Silko, 1996, 81–82). To hearten those yearning for a return to peace and sovereignty, Silko asserts the rejuvenation generated by early stories that "don't ever end; they continue on" (*ibid.*, 153). With a fury directed at ecological terrorism, her nonfiction predicts post-apocalyptic doom: "When humans have blasted and burned the last bit of life from the earth, an immeasurable freezing will descend with a darkness that obliterates the sun" (*ibid.*, 47). Analyst Cevasco and Harmond applaud these texts as "an alternative version of events where justice is found" (Cevasco & Harmond, 2009, 473).

## LAW AND INDIVIDUAL REDRESS

During three semesters of law school, Silko developed a loathing for the Anglo-American foundations of American law during the reign of England's King John over a feudal system favoring hereditary fiefs over serfs. Of the ongoing struggle for right, the essay "America's Debt to the Indian Nations: Atoning for a Sordid Past" (1996) addresses the wrongdoing that continues to cheat native Americans of full citizenship. Comparing the illegalities to the situations that tormented Rhodesians and South Africans, Silko charges that the institutionalization of conquest in education, government, and religion, and the romantic and sentimental attitudes toward Indians fostered by dime novels and Hollywood fiction perpetuate suppression of native rights. To interviewer Steve Bennett, a journalist for the San Antonio *Express News*, she stated, "The law has nothing to do with justice, and injustice can't be left unchallenged" (Bennett, 2010, 1K). To direct her outrage at a real target, she became a writer. Concerning her attack on usurpation, she stated, "I feel it is more effective to write a story ... than to rant and rave.... It is more effective in reaching people" (Romero, 2002, 623). To interviewer Laura Coltelli, the author explained that, rather than inveigh against conquest, Laguna stories depend on mirth and optimism, "especially areas in justice, loss of land, discrimination, racism, and so on" (Coltelli, 1990, 146). By remaining upbeat, Pueblo lore subverts terror tactics with satire and invective.

Silko's first novel, *Ceremony* (1977), a post-war elegy, builds on the author's young adulthood, when global protests of the drafting of poor and nonwhite American GIs demanded an end to the Vietnam War (1965–1975). As a model of post-traumatic stress disorder, she dramatizes the sufferings of Tayo, the Anglo-Laguna survivor of the Bataan Death March of April 9–21, 1942. At the acme of conflict, military orders to shoot Japanese prisoners of war drives him to a battlefield breakdown. During treatment by Betonie, a Chicano-Navajo shaman, the old man explains that Indians share a 30,000-year kinship with the Japanese. Tayo's recoil from the shooting of enemy soldiers who share his features and coloring precipitates a more troubling event, the hallucination of Uncle Josiah on the battlefield. Silko's depiction of psychological trauma deepens during Tayo's interaction with civilians after he realizes that citizens maintain no regard for veterans after they abandon their uniforms. In civilian clothes, Tayo is just an Indian.

In a symbolic thrust against American displacement, Tayo takes action. He cuts white rustler Floyd Lee's boundary, 20 feet of steel mesh, wolf-proof fence, a token of "thievery and injustice boiling up the anger and hatred that would finally destroy the world: the starving against the fat, the colored against the white" (Silko, 1977, 191). The steel fence becomes a symbol of wealth and privilege that undergirds "patriotic wars and ... great technology," a reference to the unleashing of the atomic bomb against Hiroshima and Nagasaki on August 6 and 8, 1945 (*ibid.*). By thwarting the white man Floyd Lee's rustling, Tayo rehabilitates himself while enriching his family with restoration of their herd. Of the universality of Tayo's heroism, critic Conrad Shumaker, an English professor at the University of Central Arkansas, warns whites that we "must understand our culture's role in the injustices that have happened, not because American Indians want us to feel guilty, but because otherwise we will fail to see that they have happened and are happening to us too" (Shumaker, 2008, 40).

## MYTHIC REDRESS

To involve all cultures and classics in redressing wrongs, the novelist's mega-saga *Almanac of the Dead* (1991) empowers the underclass, living and dead, to contest law that is more punitive than fair, a situation that cows peasant in Mario Vargas Llosa's *Conversation in the Cathedral* (1969). Critic Sara L. Spurgeon describes the mounting clash as "righteous violence and a seemingly justified war" (Spurgeon, 2005, 109). The novelist pictures the influence of Marxist doctrine in the demand for the empowerment of the bottom echelon of society for border-crossing rights: "This man Marx had understood that the stories or 'histories' are sacred; that within 'history' reside relentless forces, powerful spirits, vengeful, relentlessly seeking justice" (Silko, 1991, 316). In the gathering storm of rebellion, the dead return to bolster the forces of the living: "Now the ghosts have come, and they want to know where the lake they were always hearing about has gone" (*ibid.*, 140). By fostering trans-cultural social justice for past and present, the author exhibits belief that histories alluded to in the title comprise a sacred touchstone unleashing metaphysical vengeance. She amasses evidence of injustice from the past, including the persecution of John Dillinger for being part Indian and the theft of holy stone figures—the "little grandparents"—for exhibit in a museum, an injustice that Silko characterizes as "a glimpse of what was yet to come" (*ibid.*, 33).

Silko pictures a milieu out of control in a welter of "speculators, confidence men, embezzlers, lawyers, judges, police and other criminals, as well as addicts and pushers, since the 1880s and the Apache Wars" (*ibid.*, endpapers). Felony runs rampant over the dispossessed, handicapped, nonwhite peasantry, and survivors of war. Sara Spurgeon notes that Indians and Mexicans "freely cross and re-cross the international border, ignoring both the U.S. and Mexican governments' insistence on their national sovereignty and security. They engage gleefully in smuggling drugs and archeological antiquities" (Spurgeon, 2005, 110). Governments on both sides of the divide are pointless because "no legal government could be established on stolen land" (*Silko*, 1991, 133). Main characters sort through possible means of liberating themselves from generations of disservice. Muttering over results of the "Native American holocaust," Zeta, a drug smuggler, spends "every waking hour ... scheming and planning to break as many of their laws as she could" (*ibid.*, 133). Calabazas, a Yaqui marijuana smuggler, legitimates the reclamation of stolen property: "We are here thousands of years before the first whites. We are here before maps or quit claims. We know where we belong on this earth" (*ibid.*, 216). His claim exonerates the story's moral center, Sterling, an outcast Laguna who must atone for desecrating pueblo land. Commentator Katherine Sugg, an English professor at Central Connecticut State University, states the subverted logic: "Using the empirical logic of Western thought itself, Silko exposes the ruses of discourses of Euro-American modernity that rely on notions of property rights and the sacred sovereignty of the individual" (Sugg, 2008, 85). The novelist's plan of attack begins with a few peasants and increases to a groundswell of rebellion. In the resolution, she states her credo of reclamation: "All their lives they had witnessed their people's suffering and genocide; it only took a few, the merest handful of such people, to lay the groundwork for the changes" (Silko, 1991, 742).

Calabazas's manifesto foretells Sterling's redemption. In thinking over readings about

Indian and half-breed outlaws—Geronimo, Red Cloud, Jesse James, Cole Younger, John Dillinger, Billy the Kid, the Starr family, Ma Barker, and Pretty Boy Floyd—in *Police Gazette, True Detective,* and *Reader's Digest,* Sterling notes the respect of sheriffs for legendary lawbreakers. He believes that "there was no excuse for crime," but he draws a conclusion about legality from "instances when the law has nothing to do with fairness or justice" (*ibid.,* 40, 79). Tucson's high-toned main street, the result of white exploitation and enrichment from stolen property, offers "the best proof that murderers of innocent Apache women and children had prospered," producing a hierarchy of "fine old families" (*ibid.,* 80). From Sterling's self-education from pop culture, he surmises that revolution in Mexico generates a standard injustice of war—the arrest and execution of "the losers for being 'criminals,'" his explanation of the demise of Dillinger, Floyd, and Geronimo (*ibid.,* 89). From Sterling's firsthand experience with gunrunners, drug dealers, and assassins, he resolves to withdraw from "people who got rich off the suffering of Geronimo and his people" and to reclaim old Laguna stories (Silko, 1991, 81). Meanwhile, Silko enacts the turmoil of comeuppance, a revolt that includes the murder and dismemberment of baby Monte. She states that the surge toward redress is worth self-sacrifice and martyrdom. For a nation bogged down in criminality, individual victories prove ephemeral.

FUNDAMENTAL FAIRNESS

Similar in scope to *Almanac of the Dead,* the global intrigue of *Gardens in the Dunes* (1999) tracks the injustices of the Indian Wars and of dam building and bio-theft, both violations of Mother Earth. The U.S. Cavalry exonerates military genocide as suppression of murderous renegade Indians and legitimizes attacks on Mormons as a method of halting Utah settlers from allying with Indians against the government. The impetus to diverting the Colorado River from its banks to an aqueduct and canal answers the demands of Californians for fresh water supplies in Los Angeles. On a scientific level, the greed of orchid hybridizer Dr. Edward Palmer, a gentleman naturalist, derives from profit motives from hybridizing "a fragrant bright red orchid to rival the English rose" (Silko, 1999, 139). Critic Douglas Cazaux Sackman, a history professor at the University of Puget Sound, characterizes the pillaging of biota as "a system of capitalism whose agents penetrate every corner of the globe, seeking plants that, as if by bio-alchemical magic, may be turned into gold" (Sackman, 2005, 23). An innocent abettor of Mr. Eliot, a rubber tree pirate dispatched by Albert Lowe & Company, Palmer travels to Portal, Surinam, to hunt contraband specimens of the rare *Laelia cinnabarina* orchid. Because white brokers lash and maim Indians to coerce their labor, the natives flee to a French boat captain for protection. Simultaneously, rival rubber firms torture and kill black and Indian slaves. The underworld business supports the sale of women in cantinas "by the dance or by the night" (*ibid.,* 134). The proliferation of evil results in Eliot's torching of a floating village, a cleansing by arson that Silko repeats in Hattie Abbott Palmer's burning of the seedy town of Needles, California, as payback to a rapist and to an androcentric society that tyrannizes women and children.

In contrast to Edward's collaboration with plant pilferage, Silko depicts the suppression of female intellect by orthodox Christianity, a crime against gender. Janis P. Stout, an English teacher at Texas A&M University, explains the inclusion of the female perspective as abandonment of "masculine [stories] of conquest, violence, and ruggedness" in favor of "stories about justice and injustice, preservation of a valued tradition even as that tradition changes, and sexual liberality ... an opening for escape from stifling conventionality and a place for living" (Stout, 2007, 225). Edward's wife Hattie, a scholar at a heresy seminar hosted by Harvard Divinity School, compiles a thesis on the female element of the medieval church. To examine the contribution of early female Christians, she depicts the "Just God of the Old Testament" as a "creative power with anger, jealousy, and the urge to punish, while the God of the New Testament was a Kind God, who sent his son to rescue mankind" through crucifixion (*ibid.*, 99). By concluding that the angry father deity lost out to the compassionate son, she concludes that the orthodox church negated its premise and rendered its patriarchal hierarchy, treasuries, and laws superfluous. With thesis in hand, she confronts a review panel that is "exclusionary, patriarchal, sexually and culturally repressive, primarily linear, intolerant of difference, diversity, and metamorphosis" (Fitz, 2004, 194). To nullify her theory on Jesus' acceptance of Mary Magdalene as a disciple, the all-male arbiters dictate a conformist interpretation of Genesis, in which disobedience results in the cursing of woman and the serpent that lures her into sin against the divine creator. By taking Hattie's side and authenticating alternate tales of Christ as "just as valid and powerful as other sightings and versions," the novelist demands justice for women (Silko & Arnold, 2000, 164).

See also abortion; order; racism; social class; vengeance; violence.

• *References and further reading*

Abbott, Carl. *How Cities Won the West: Four Centuries of Urban Change in Western North America.* Albuquerque: University of New Mexico Press, 2008.
Bennett, Steve. "Author Silko Isn't Concerned about Time," (San Antonio) *Express News* (25 July 2010): 1K, 4K.
Cevasco, George A., and Richard P. Harmond. *Modern American Environmentalists: A Biographical Encyclopedia.* Baltimore: Johns Hopkins University Press, 2009.
Coltelli, Laura. *Winged Words: American Indian Writers Speak.* Lincoln: University of Nebraska Press, 1990, 135–153.
Fitz, Brewster E. *Silko: Writing Storyteller and Medicine Woman.* Norman: University of Oklahoma Press, 2004.
Mellas, Laurie. "Memory and Promise: Leslie Marmon Silko's Story," *Mirage* 24 (Spring 2006): 11–14.
Romero, Channette. "Envisioning a 'Network of Tribal Coalitions': Leslie Marmon Silko's *Almanac of the Dead,*" *American Indian Quarterly* 26:4 (1 September 2002): 623–640.
Sackman, Douglas C. *Orange Empire: California and the Fruits of Eden.* Berkeley: University of California Press, 2005.
Shumaker, Conrad. *Southwestern American Indian Literature: In the Classroom and Beyond.* New York: Peter Lang, 2008.
Silko, Leslie Marmon. *Almanac of the Dead.* New York: Simon & Schuster, 1991.
_____. "America's Iron Curtain: The Border Patrol State," *Nation* 259:12 (17 October 1994): 412–416.
_____. *Ceremony.* New York: Viking, 1977.
_____. *The Turquoise Ledge: A Memoir.* New York: Viking Adult, 2010.
_____. *Yellow Woman and a Beauty of the Spirit: Essays on Native American Life Today.* New York: Simon & Schuster, 1996.
_____, and Ellen L. Arnold. *Conversations with Leslie Marmon Silko.* Jackson: University Press of Mississippi, 2000.
Sol, Adam. "The Story as It's Told: Prodigious Revisions in Leslie Marmon Silko's 'Almanac of the Dead,'" *American Indian Quarterly* 23:3–4 (Summer-Autumn 1999): 24–48.
Spurgeon, Sara L. *Exploding the Western: Myths of Empire on the Postmodern Frontier.* College Station: Texas A&M University Press, 2005.
Stout, Janis P. *Picturing a Different West: Vision, Illustration, and the Tradition of Cather and Austin.* Lubbock: Texas Tech University Press, 2007.
Sugg, Katherine. *Gender and Allegory in Transamerican Fiction and Performance.* New York: Palgrave Macmillan, 2008.
Tallent, Elizabeth. "Storytelling with a Vengeance," *New York Times Book Review* (22 December 1991): 6.

# irony

Silko wields sustained, mordant irony with a steady synthesis of the pagan and the urbane. Her early works prosper from paradox, for example, the complicity of a Catholic priest in grave ritual for Teofilo, a Pueblo elder in "The Man to Send Rain Clouds" (1969). More succinctly, she juxtaposes the strutting of male womanizers and the comeuppance of savvy women in a pair of poems, "Si'ahh aash" (1972) and "Mesita Men" (1972), highlights of her first verse anthology, *Laguna Woman: Poems*. Her autobiographical musings contribute a significant irony in her alienation in childhood for being a mixed breed Laguna and her development into a spokesperson for her people as novelist, essayist, and storyteller. She explains, "I suppose at the core of my writing is the attempt to identify what it is to be a half-breed or mixed blooded person; what it is to grow up neither white nor fully traditional Indian" (Silko, 1975, 35). In "Toe'osh: A Laguna Coyote Story" (1974), she alludes to her herself as the speaker "howling in the hills southeast of Laguna," a direct connection with the trickster tradition (*ibid.*, 4).

The author typically spotlights the inconsistencies in law and government that demean Indians. In the book review "Here's an Odd Artifact for the Fairy-Tale Shelf" (1986), the author makes a sardonic comment about lies from the United States Civil Rights Commission in 1986, which belongs on "the same shelf that holds The Collected Thoughts of Edwin Meese on First Amendment Rights and Grimm's Fairy Tales" (Silko, 1986, 179). Central to her feminist themes is the unorthodox heroism of Yellow Woman (Kochininako), a mythic Coyotesse, wise and witty, who dominates three episodes from *Yellow Woman and a Beauty of the Spirit: Essays on Native American Life Today* (1996)—"Buffalo Story," "Cottonwood," and "Estoy-eh-muut and the Kunideeyahs." In one episode, she blesses her people with nourishment by allying with a kidnapper named Silva and returning to her husband Al to explain her overnight absence from home. Empowered by assertiveness and sexuality, Yellow Woman epitomizes the strength of the Amerindian female, whose equality perplexes white readers. Cherokee/Creek/Seminole critic Carolyn Dunn, a director of Red Nation Celebration, applauds the Coyotesse as a regenerator and sustainer of culture through ironic stories because she "takes the language of colonization and makes it her own" (Dunn, 2005, 201).

In a more touching story, "Lullaby" (1974), Silko develops incongruity in the socioeconomic ruin of Ayah, a Navajo matron who loses her home and family one by one. The paradox of Ayah's strength at the family's nadir uplifts the theme from tragedy to resilience in the face of overwhelming white forces that destroy Indian sovereignty. Ironically, she takes pride in her only accomplishment in English: Chato had taught her to sign her name. With her signature, she hopes to achieve autonomy, for "She only wanted [whites] to go, and to take their eyes away from her children" (Silko, 1974, 11). The author achieves optimism in Ayah's defiance of the white male hegemony by breaching the men-only sanctum of a bar to fetch her husband Chato. At the height of female self-empowerment, the protagonist takes on the majesty of Spider Woman (Ts'its'tsi'nako or Thought Woman). A face-off against white drinkers at Azzie's Bar awes them with Ayah's impertinent stare. In the falling action, she sings a lullaby to reassure and calm Chato from alcoholism and a crushed leg as he slowly freezes to death in the snow. With the drama of George Orwell's anti-authoritarian essay "Shooting an Elephant" (1936), Ayah becomes the awe-inspiring heroine, the defender and rescuer of home.

EXISTING IN TWO WORLDS

In *Ceremony* (1977), her first novel, Silko dramatizes incongruity in the exclusion of first peoples from shaping the New World. The text generates dramatic Irony in Laura's classroom experience, where she "hated the people at home when white people talked about their peculiarities; but she always hated herself more because she still thought about them" (Silko, 1977, 69). The novelist creates scenes of "little sister" Laura's training in ladylike behavior and her return home at daylight unclothed and drunk, but bearing the requisite lipstick in her purse. From the muddle of ideologies comes profligacy, the opposite of intent in a Pueblo school operated by Christian pietists. At the story's beginning, the author builds contrast between Rocky, the full-blood Laguna who avoids nativism, and Tayo, a half-breed who pities Indians who have left the reservation to join Gallup's homeless winos and prostitutes who live like his mother Laura. Tayo respects old traditions, particularly the covering of the eyes of a dying deer and the sprinkling of cornmeal to nourish the animal's spirit. The honor to an animal prefigures Tayo's burden in letting go of his cousin Rocky's spirit and in choosing life over a permeating sorrow that robs Tayo of identity and volition. A subsequent dramatic irony at the Los Angeles train station befuddles Tayo's brain with the sounds of Japanese words. Expecting a pummeling from prison camp guards in the Philippines, he encounters a rescuer, a Japanese mother and her small children. The meeting attests to goodness from the race that killed Rocky and dehumanized captives. The social situation of Japanese-Americans reminds Tayo, subliminally, that U.S. internment mirrored the Indian Wars and the forcible dispossession and containment of tribes on reservations in the mid–1800s.

As the internal conflict worsens for the protagonist, Silko broadens incongruities. During the curing of Tayo from weeping, flashbacks, hallucinations, and nightmares, he comes under the safekeeping of his hostile foster mother, Auntie Thelma, a self-righteous Catholic who baits him with *sotto voce* comments about his being mixed blood and illegitimate. At one point, he awakens from her ongoing harping expecting a Japanese rifle in the face rather than the resentful care of his aunt. A contrasting caregiver, Betonie, the Chicano-Navajo shaman at an untidy hogan north of Gallup, recognizes Tayo's burdening by war trauma as part of the witchery that paralyzes Amerindians, a twist on the Puritan charge that Amerindians were hellish demons. Rather than yield to emotional immobility, Betonie urges Tayo to take action against injustice and to ensure the Laguna pueblo's endurance of new kinds of wickedness. Silko's remobilization of a veteran implies that war in the Philippines was nothing compared to the battles that lie ahead.

The text fosters incongruities in Tayo's preparation for the fight. To ready himself for a challenge, the traumatized veteran must acknowledge a lie that teachers thrust on him in public school: "Only brown-skinned people were thieves; white people didn't steal" (Silko, 1977, 191). Tayo becomes the champion for "Indians like Harley and Helen Jean and Emo ... [who] had been taught to despise themselves" (*ibid.*, 204). His heroism focuses on events at the Jackpile mine, a towering irony that places a uranium extraction operation and the source of the atomic bomb at his Laguna home. Viewing the shafts from which Indians dig ore sharpens Tayo's perspective on the bombing of noncombatants on August 6 and 8, 1945, in Hiroshima and Nagasaki. The author returns to the abomination of atomic weapons in *The Turquoise Ledge* (2010), in which she demonizes the U.S. government for authorizing the production of weapons of mass destruction, ostensibly in the interest of national security. Critic John Muthyala, an English professor at the University of Southern Maine, can't resist an aside that "the Laguna were the first of the Pueblo tribes to benefit, in some measure and ironically, from the devastation of native land" (Muthyala, 2006, 142).

## THE ENIGMA OF THE UNDERCLASS REVOLT

In *Almanac of the Dead* (1991), Silko wrests from incongruity, inversion, social satire, and comic exaggeration the themes that express her denunciation of an unjust and racist world. Her method, as described by analyst David Mogen, a specialist in American literature at the University of Colorado, lies in "[reshaping] traditional American mythologies of apocalypse" by "[evoking] underlying patterns of Indian prophecy to project apocalyptic images of cultural and spiritual crisis" (Mogen, 2005, 157). She pictures the photographer David taking glossy shots of his lover Eric's corpse shortly before David himself lies maimed and gory after a horse crushes him, leaving remains for the lens of Beaufrey, the most diabolical of a gay triad. She reprises the ironies of the criminal capture of John Dillinger and Geronimo. Seese, a blond touring the historical highlights of Tucson with Sterling, a Laguna gardener, realizes the incongruities of frontier history. She exults, "All these Tucson family fortunes made off war — the way all money is made!" (Silko, 1991, 80). She views the scenery as "proof that murderers of innocent Apache women and children had prospered," producing "Tucson's 'fine old families'" (*ibid.*). Commentator Sara L. Spurgeon, a specialist in women's studies at Texas Tech University, observed that Silko's subversion of frontier legend "Built ... on the blood money of arms and whiskey traders who willingly supplied both the U.S. Army and the Indians they fought, Tucson is the ugly, postmodern reality of the mythic 'Wild West town' brought glaringly into the present without the rose-colored glasses of colonial nostalgia that so often shade such sites in traditional westerns.... Instead of a paradise successfully carved from the wilderness ... Tucson is hell on earth" (Spurgeon, 2005, 109).

The issue of social prominence in *Almanac of the Dead* hinges on variant views of dynasty and affluence. Commentator Katherine Sugg, an English professor at Central Connecticut State University, applauds the role of irony in Silko's grand plan: "Because Silko writes so clearly against the expectations and comfort zones of all its readers — both minority identified and cosmopolitan, white, U.S.-oriented — *Almanac* illustrates the ability of particular narratives to use allegory 'with a vengeance'" (Sugg, 2008, 32). In a twist of black humor, Iliana Gutiérrez, the social climbing wife of *mestizo* magnate Menardo Panson, owner of Universal Insurance, designs a bleak showy residence featuring a polished marble staircase overlooking the jungle. Iliana's death in a tumble down the stairs leaves Menardo, a fellow elitist and concealer of his *mestizo* lineage, free to wed his Venezuelan mistress, Alegría Martinez-Soto, the two-timing architect of the building project. As poetic justice advances to the widower, the text pictures a macabre sight gag — Menardo foolishly wearing a bulletproof vest while commanding his chauffeur Tacho, a Mayan spy, to fire at his chest. Because of a flaw in the fabrication, Menardo falls dead, still wrapped in the vest he believed would save him from harm. The irony of his fail-safe heightens the tension of the allegory, illustrating the absence of security in Tucson's underworld.

More unsettling than the collapse of the Panson *ménage à trois* and the insurance dealer's downfall is the pervasive cannibalism among Silko's cast of rogues. She dramatizes the paradox of street addicts who allow Eddie Trigg to dupe them into blood donation centers with fellatio generates a ghoulish dichotomy of blood extraction and oral sex. Katherine Sugg explains, "Nearly all of the characters are marked linguistically and affectively by death and violence and have developed an apparent numbness to both" (Sugg, 2008, 71). With sadistic necropolitics, Trigg drains dry hapless volunteers in a Dracula-esque act, then sells their life force for profit. Abetting Trigg are respectable co-conspirators, West German buyers and U.S. medical colleges that legitimate the depersonalizing of the subclass by commercializing biomaterials, detox centers, and rehab clinics. As the underdogs band — Maya and Yaqui with black, Pueblo with derelict Viet vet — they resurrect ancient Mesoamerican, African, and Caribbean prophecies and follow deities — Damballah and Quetzalcoatl — that Christianity claimed long before to have suppressed.

## GENDERED IRONIES

In the same ironic vein as Isabel Allende's *Daughter of Fortune* (1999) and Michel Faber's *The Crimson Petal and the White* (2002), the novelist pursues incongruity in *Gardens in the Dunes* (1999), historical fiction that draws disparities and humor from the conventions of the Victorian social novel. Contrast enhances Silko's condemnation of the displacement of tribes and indigenous plants. Critic Annie Merrill Ingram, an Americanist at Davidson College, observes: "Silko uses the seed to highlight the irony of non-native people concerned about the impact of exotic, invasive plants on the landscapes they themselves have invaded" (Ingram, 2007, 138). While the Sand Lizard people, a matriarchal clan, nourishes roots, berries, and grains in the sandhills of southern Arizona, Dr. Edward Palmer, a gentleman naturalist, stocks his garden in Riverside, California, with exotic vines, citrus trees, and aromatic lilacs and roses. To increase his wealth, he travels Guatemala, Surinam, Brazil, Mexico, and Corsica in search of saleable plants that he steals with the backing of Albert Lowe & Company and its attorney, Mr. Grabb. Naive to a fault, Palmer puts his faith in a shifty operation and assumes that "surely they had no idea of the true nature of Mr. Eliot's mission" to steal rubber plants from Brazil (Silko, 1999, 141). The insatiable drive to pirate more stock for sale to plant collectors and commodifiers rapidly depletes Palmer's credibility with scientists and with his wife, Hattie Abbott Palmer, whose inheritance he squanders. In the end, his health, career, and marriage wrecked, he dies under the watchfulness of his devalued mate while fostering dreams of enrichment through bio-piracy. Safe from his ruinous greed, Indigo, his foster daughter and literary foil, returns to the Sand Lizard clan to share seeds and corms collected legally in England and Italy and to flourish with her reconstituted family, a beloved stronghold that Palmer could not begin to understand.

Silko undermines Edward Palmer's authority for its androcentric character flaws. The source of Indigo's education in European horticulture derives from foster mothering by Edward's estranged wife, an altruistic scholar who also fails to achieve renown in her research field. Illogically, Hattie's education in medieval religious studies at a seminar on heresy sponsored by Harvard Divinity School's anti-woman clerics parallels Indigo's preparation for domestic service to white households at the authoritarian Sherman Institute in Riverside, California. Both receive indoctrination in androcentric thinking rather than an egalitarian freeing of the mind to explore ideas. A female frustrated by misperceptions of birthing and parenthood, Hattie encourages Indigo to simulate procreation by drawing plants in her notebooks and by mothering two pets, Linnaeus the monkey and Rainbow the parrot. While Hattie retreats from overt genitalia on statuary in the gardens of Aunt Bronwyn in Bath, England, and of *la professoressa* Laura in Lucca, Italy, her foster child, soundly educated in anatomy, shows no aversion to human sexuality. The novelist extends the absurdity of an Oyster Bay darling's embarrassment at genitals and an Indian girl's straightforward training in life science by picturing Hattie "[stepping] back so suddenly she bumped into Indigo" (*ibid.*, 290). The incident sets the tone of Indigo's rise from foster daughter to savior and reclaimer of Hattie from emotional distress.

In an inversion of history, unlike Christopher Columbus, who discovers the New World, Indigo rediscovers the Old World. She flourishes at age 11, weathers a long separation from home, and reclaims Hattie from bankruptcy and the trauma of a brutal rape. Ironically, Indigo becomes the maternal figure and bolsterer of a needy female seeking safe harborage. The bonding between females echoes a similar situation faced by Indigo's sister, who generates commerce from an engineering project on the Colorado River at Needles, California, by taking in laundry and offering workers sexual services. A crackdown by a Yuma magistrate not only sequesters Sister Salt and her women co-laborers in prison, but also gives them an opportunity to refine their underground commerce and strengthen their female society. The women liberate themselves through the intervention of another female entrepreneur, Delena, a gypsy Yaqui who operates a dog show as a pretext to setting fire to the men's camp and robbing them of the proceeds of gambling and home brew. To enhance irony, Silko pictures Delena furthering the cabal of revolutionaries by funding their weapons and ammunition with stolen cash. For a witty fillip, Silko describes "Nuestra Señora de Guadalupe" (Our Lady of Guadalupe, an avatar of the Virgin Mary) as abetting the conspiracy by instructing the rebels on which rifles to buy (*ibid.*, 354). The snide image of Our Lady dealing with gunrunners is consistent with the author's disdain for Christianity.

*See also* humor.

• *References and further reading*

Dunn, Carolyn. "The Trick Is Going Home: Secular Spiritualism in Native American Women's Literature" in *Reading Native American Women: Critical/Creative Representations*, ed. Inés Hernández-Avila. Lanham, MD: Altamira, 2005, 189–203.

Ingram, Annie Merrill. *Coming into Contact: Explorations in Ecocritical Theory and Practice*. Athens: University of Georgia Press, 2007.

Mogen, David. "Native American Vision of Apocalypse: Prophecy and Protest in the Fiction of Leslie Marmon Silko and Gerald Vizenor" in *American Mythologies: Essays in Contemporary Literature*, ed. William Blazek. Liverpool, UK: Liverpool University Press, 2005.

Muthyala, John. *Reworlding America: Myth, History, and Narrative*. Athens: Ohio University Press, 2006.

Silko, Leslie Marmon. *Almanac of the Dead*. New York: Simon & Schuster, 1991.

_____. *Ceremony*. New York: Viking, 1977.

_____. *Gardens in the Dunes*. New York: Scribner, 1999.

_____. "Here's an Odd Artifact for the Fairy-Tale Shelf," *Studies in American Indian Literatures* 10:4 (Fall 1986): 177–184.

_____. *Laguna Woman: Poems*. New York: Greenfield Review Press, 1974.

_____. "Lullaby," *Chicago Review* 26:1 (Summer 1974): 10–17.

_____. *Yellow Woman and a Beauty of the Spirit: Essays on Native American Life Today*. New York: Simon & Schuster, 1996.

Spurgeon, Sara L. *Exploding the Western: Myths of Empire on the Postmodern Frontier*. College Station: Texas A&M University Press, 2005.

Sugg, Katherine. *Gender and Allegory in Transamerican Fiction and Performance*. New York: Palgrave Macmillan, 2008.

West, Paul. "When a Myth Is as Good as a Mile," *Los Angeles Times* (2 February 1992): 8.

## *Laguna Woman: Poems*

Silko's first verse collection, *Laguna Woman: Poems* (1974), mimics native storytelling in its polyphonic energy and verbal acuity. By fusing perspectives in "Hawk and Snake"

(1973), first published in *Chicago Review*, she glimpses Chinle, Arizona, as a human visitor, a reptile, and a raptor. The fusion of the viewer with outdoor elements begins with a departure from buildings, which elicit two backward gazes. Passing fences, the speaker, no longer a human traveler, becomes both snake curled on a rock and the hawk that patrols the blue air above, an allusion to Quetzalcoatl, the feathered serpent deity of Aztec cosmology. Reviewer Thomas C. Gannon, a specialist in native American literature at the University of Nebraska, marvels at the "cross-species merger" and states that "Such an intimate union of bird and reptile, of spirit and earth…, and of human narrator seems nearly unimaginable in the canon of Western literature" (Gannon, 2009, 231).

The paired images in the title "Hawk and Snake" introduce the author's focus on equilibrium. No longer psychologically fenced in by human habitation, the speaker experiences the balance of nature, which is both earthbound and free to the sky. In union with "Hawk and Snake," the adjacent poem, "The Time We Climbed Snake Mountain" (1973), presents the speaker as tour leader, a disseminator of wisdom gained from traversing the countryside. The guide respects the uniquely colored snake, a sacred Laguna divinity, for its merger with its habitat and uses "spotted yellow snake" as its rightful name rather than a descriptor (Silko, 1974, 35). The speaker alludes to an acceptance of atavism by reaching hands to the cliff above, a fearless touching of the snake's resting place. Like the gentle sheltering of amphibians in Joseph Bruchac's classic poem "Birdfoot's Grampa" (1987), Silko's verse acknowledges that lowly beings have the same right to life as humankind.

For "Sun Children" (1972), first published in *Quetzel*, a Latino literary journal, Silko discloses a scenario from two perspectives, winter and summer. Seemingly serene, the book-ended views contrast the extremes of seasons. In winter, before the snow flies, wild ducks migrating south devour water spiders while dried cattails rattle like ritual rhythm instruments, the type that the poet heard at ceremonial dances in the Laguna plaza. On the return north, the ducks sing their way over the water scene, missing the spiders lurking in river moss. Like a fetus in a parturient woman, the joy of the season grows inside the viewers, who journey with the sun east to west at dawn like fawns nibbling spring shoots. Repetition of the title in the final line stresses the childlike trust of humans in a setting that faithfully repeats its cycle. The poem illustrates a fundamental belief of Amerindian verse in the predictability of Mother Earth.

Epiphanies

Silko's command of outdoor imagery isolates in time and nature the psychic gestalt, the "aha" pattern that coalesces around a single perception. The wonder lyric "In Cold Storm Light" (1972), first published in *Quetzel* when the poet was 24 years old, coalesces a mystic vision, an emergence of a snow elk through the wet cold of a canyon rim, a distinct shape that marks place and time. Contributing energy, synesthesia — the mingling of sense impressions— turns wet wind fragrant with piñon and audible in the movement of juniper. Unlike static earth, the beast pounds the ground with its hooves and swirls in a dramatic leap over trees, a dynamic burst of natural brio that dispels winter's inactivity. The momentum of Silko's elk churns up crystals that sparkle in the ground mist. To create a sense of union with the terrain, the poet allies sibilance with soft "w" sounds. Consonance introduces mist, which takes the form of strands tangled at ground level. In 2006, Philip Thompson, a Maryland composer, set the poem to electro-acoustic music as a segment of *Free Play 6: Listening Chamber*, performed on January 25, 2007, at Grand Valley State University in Allendale, Michigan.

The poet's skill at orality and tone enhances a text echoing with native vigor and tinged with the elegiac call of Riverwoman for her lover, a direct evocation of Yellow Woman (Kochininako), a pervasive female symbol in the author's mythography. For "When Sun Came to Riverwoman" (June 10, 1973), the poet builds momentum from rustling willows and an intense brown current, which yields a warm penetration, a nature-spun tale of outdoor coupling between the disparate elements of sunlight and water. Crucial to the fragments of an intimate encounter, an elegiac memory ties Riverwoman to the place to relive her rapture and to sing the rejuvenating rainsong, a motif that recurs in the last stave of "Prayer to the Pacific" (1973), first published in *Chicago Review*. Silko juxtaposes "Poem for Ben Barney" (spring 1973), a paean to the end of winter, announced by the arrival of rhythmic wind and birdsong. The sounds harmonize to welcome "sunshine not yet ended" for two Pueblo cultures, Laguna and Navajo (Silko, 1974, 9). A subsequent verse, "Love Poem" (1972), affirms the feminine nature of rain, which awakens hibernating toads from the fecund earth and recalls an erotic ecstasy from the female perspective, a motif that informs the falling action of *Ceremony* (1977) and the rescue of Tayo by Ts'eh Montaño, a semi-divine lover.

The anthology opens and closes with poems encompassing the Laguna concept of the life cycle. In "Poem for Myself and Mei-Mei" (April 1973) and "Preparations," color and light unify vibrant elements that demystify death. Fragile images of iridescent yellow butterflies, an icy stream, and mustard grass look to the creator for delight and subsistence. The resilience of dying butterflies on a windshield offers a visual benediction for the universal journey "all the way home" (*ibid.*, 2). A more formal benediction honors the carrion crows' reduction of a dead sheep to polished bones, a desert-style return to the earth that the text celebrates for its thoroughness. In both poems, Silko stresses the natural order of the cycle in which life remains unfinished without the closure of death, a concept honored by Ayah in the short story "Lullaby" (1974), by the speaker of "How to Hunt Buffalo" (1994), by Grandma Fleet in the novel *Gardens in the Dunes* (1999), and by the poet herself in *The Turquoise Ledge* (2010).

A subsequent verse, "Slim Man Canyon" (summer 1972), retreats from the specter of mortality to the continuum of Navajo residence in a canyon adorned with ancient petroglyphs illustrating native songs and tales. A contrast to delicate pumpkin flowers, the permanence of place and seven centuries of Indian residence uplift and reassure. Similarly overlaying human responses to those in the outdoors, "Horses at Valley Store" pictures the instinct of horses for self-preservation. Decking them with the cosmic power of the steeds in the Greek myth of Phaethon and the chariot of the sun, Silko pictures the hooves dragging the day along as the steeds approach a concrete trough. Separated by instinct from human water seekers, the horses wait their turn at a refreshing drink. Silko deliberately graces the poem with respect between species, a motif that returns in the release of Uncle Josiah's speckled Mexican cattle from a fence in *Ceremony* and in the author's coexistence with rattlesnakes in *The Turquoise Ledge*.

VERSE MYTHOGRAPHY

The anthology features one of Silko's archetypal Laguna fables, "Toe'osh: A Laguna Coyote Story" (July 1973), which she dedicated to Simon Joseph Ortiz, a fellow Keresan speaker and major figure in the Native American Renaissance. The narrative verse illustrates the continuum allying traditional wisdom and cautionary tales with everyday pueblo life. Critic Jeff Karem notes that the poet "does depict the vitality of Laguna ways, but she offers an even deeper challenge to her nonnative readers: an indigenous reinterpretation" of native myth and legend (Karem, 2004, 181). To the story of Coyote's deception of badger, chipmunk, and squirrel, the third stanza acknowledges the arrival of white men of the previous century and their marriage with local women, a wry allusion to the mixed-blood Marmon clan and the poet herself, "howling in the hills southeast of Laguna" (Silko, 1974, 4). Although the author admits in *Yellow Woman and a Beauty of the Spirit: Essays on Native American Life Today* (1996), "It was not so easy for me to learn where we Marmons belonged," she absorbed the social undercurrent like a full-blood Laguna (Silko, 1996, 102). The passive aggression of pueblo people outfoxes the candidates buying votes with hams and turkeys and the pompous vice president of the Transwestern oil pipeline, whom Lagunans keep waiting as a chastening for his arrogance. The bumptious nature of Coyote and his pals produces a coarse fart joke in stanza seven, but returns to serious business in the final stave. Silko's manipulation of tone and atmosphere valorizes native guile and wit, two coping mechanisms that bolster native outlook for five centuries, from the arrival of Columbus to her own time.

Alongside the celebration of the cycles of nature, Silko's verse captures the nostalgia of change that affects pueblo life over a millennium. In "Where Mountainlion Lay Down with Deer" (February 1973), she outlines an Indian view of the Peaceable Kingdom, a pervasive motif in Christian imagery of Eden, an earthly utopia. With the skill of a watercolorist picturing an ascent to the homeland of her ancestors before A.D. 1000, she dramatizes a time when the mountain lion and deer coexist against the stark background of black stone. The indistinct forebear, hearty and attuned to constellations and a mountain cataract, swims from a canyon into later eras, a memory of an amorphous timeline that flows with the vigorous current parallel to the passage of centuries. Graceful and wistful like the wonder incorporated in "How to Hunt Buffalo" (1994), *The Turquoise Ledge*, and "Chapulin's Portrait" (2010), the poem characterizes a fragment of history reborn in narrative, a life force too primal, too buoyant to die.

In contrast to her image of the cohabitation of deer with mountain lion, Silko's "Four Mountain Wolves" (winter 1973) illustrates a free verse setting of native chant replicating bestial instinct. The four-stage text separates into four views the nature of the wolf, an icon of primitive ferocity and an analog of human need. Following the northeastern wind over snowy terrain, gray mist evokes the austerity and cry of the hungry wolf, the last animal to depart high country in winter. With inchoate insistence, it howls its need for prey. The second stave releases the wolf's violence. Like Orion, the cosmic hunter, and Saturn, the Greek titan, the wolf tears and rips into the silence with an utterance meant to terrify, like Alfred Lord Tennyson's description of "red in tooth and claw/with ravine" (1849). Never sated, the lean canid lopes toward the she-elk, intent on a satisfaction that refuels and empowers survival, an amoral force of nature. The mountain lion returns in "Indian Song: Survival" (1973), a poem rich in sense impressions initially published in *Chicago Review*. In a first-person "desperation journey" of endurance, the speaker, a feathered spirit, flees endangerment, which smells like winter, a connection the author makes in the resolution of the short story "Lullaby" (Silko, 1974, 26). The speaker recedes into a spider web and trusts her guide, which grasps at hummingbirds and wildflower petals and pollen. Paradoxically, the web, birds, petals, and pollen are symbols of fragility as well as tokens of Spider Woman (Ts'its'tsi'nako or Thought Woman), the creator mother. Sure-footed on slopes, the mountain lion leads the way up Cloudy Mountain. The occluded view suggests the confusion of a lifeway that moves constantly ahead of havoc to a cosmic goal, the rainbow. The two-dimensional arc supports the lean gray deer, which balances as light as the wind on the multicolored rim. Silko's early verse, published when she was 26 years old, anticipates images and themes of her more mature work, particularly the balance that Tayo restores in *Ceremony* and that the two Sand Lizard matrons, Indigo and Sister Salt, reestablish in *Gardens in the Dunes*. The concept of oneness in nature and the balance of life forces also infuses the poet's revelations to another writer, collected in *The Delicacy and Strength of Lace: Letters between Leslie Marmon Silko and James Wright* (1986).

See also religion; writing.

• *References and further reading*

Gannon, Thomas C. *Skylark Meets Meadowlark: Reimagining the Bird in British Romantic and Contemporary Native American Literature*. Lincoln: University of Nebraska Press, 2009.

Hollrah, Patrice E. M. *"The Old Lady Trill, the Victory Yell": The Power of Women in Native American Literature*. New York: Routledge, 2004.

Jolivétte, Andrew. *Cultural Representation in Native America*. Lanham, MD: Altamira, 2006.

Karem, Jeff. *The Romance of Authenticity: The Cultural Politics of Regional and Ethnic Literatures*. Charlottesville: University of Virginia Press, 2004.

Lincoln, Kenneth. *Speak Like Singing: Classics of Native American Literature*. Albuquerque: University of New Mexico Press, 2008.

Silko, Leslie Marmon. *Laguna Woman: Poems*. New York: Greenfield Review Press, 1974.

_____. *Yellow Woman and a Beauty of the Spirit: Essays on Native American Life Today*. New York: Simon & Schuster, 1996.

## language

Silko recognizes that there is no standard language, no single lexicon that translates human attitudes and principles. In *The Turquoise Ledge* (2010), she demonstrates her willingness to explore petroglyphs and other forms of communication dating into prehistory. She retreats into two Nahuatl dictionaries in hopes of inspiration from the unknown: "It is possible to do a great deal with a language we don't speak or understand, as long as we freely employ our imaginations and have access to good dictionaries" (Silko, 2010, 241–242). In a letter of poet James Wright in September 1979, compiled in *The Delicacy and Strength of Lace: Letters between Leslie Marmon Silko and James Wright* (1986), she remarks on the fastidious sneers of the English Institute at Harvard University at the thought of native versions of English. In a comment on the exclusivity and elitism of syntactical correctness, she cites as an example of vigor the street language of dramatist William Shakespeare, the writer of "puns and jokes and political jokes" (Silko & Wright, 1986, 82). She reflects on the past: "Pre-Columbian America had hundreds and hundreds—maybe thousands—of completely distinct language groups," each with variances (*ibid.*). Her exuberance accounts for her constant winnowing of words and terms to explain human thoughts and needs.

Coming from one of 20 pueblos in the Southwest that speak six or seven disparate languages, the author esteems language as an introit to multiculturalism — the acceptance of all beings into the family of Mother Earth. Brewster E. Fitz, a Silko specialist, declares Silko a part of "a tradition in which the oral and the written are already linguistically and culturally irrevocably interwoven" like the strands of the Navajo blanket in "Lullaby" (1974) (Fitz, 2004, 18). Rather than pursue standardization, Silko celebrates the strands of language needed for "a land as big and as geographically diverse as this" (*ibid.*). Mormon critic Joanna Brooks, a resident at the Hedgebrook women's writers' retreat at Whidbey Island, Washington, explains the importance of language as a conduit: "Stories have the power to enact new realities, create communities, and effect new power relationships," a truth reflected in the Hispanic Catholic fear of the Mesoamerican archives, which the Spanish bishop of Yucatán Diego de Landa Calderón burned in 1540 (Brooks, 2008, 221).

Silko recognizes how language figures in the conquest and alienation of peoples via arbitrary boundaries. Concurring with the biblical account of the Tower of Babel in Genesis 11:5–8, her writings warn of allowing language variation to disunite and foster suspicion and dissension. She creates a feeling of unease in the home of the Navajo weaver Ayah in "Lullaby" by dramatizing a visit by a white social worker. Shut out of the conversation by her lack of familiarity with Diné, the agent fears "the children jabbering excitedly in a language she did not know," an innocent exchange not meant to imply threat or harm (Silko, 1974, 49). As an antidote to "othering," Silko validates the transcoding and transmigration of one body of native lore to others in a cross-pollination. Martha J. Cutter, a specialist in multi-ethnic literature at the Institute for African American Studies of the University of Connecticut, identifies the meeting places of diverse tongues as other "discursive landscapes" and contact zones (Cutter, 2005, 111).

## Words into Narrative

In *Yellow Woman and a Beauty of the Spirit: Essays on Native American Life Today* (1996), Silko declares that "language is story" and that the nested episodes within stories, like mirrors facing mirrors, "never truly end" (Silko, 1996, 50). The perpetual churning of episodes into tales impacts her short anti-colonial writings "Tony's Story" (1969) and "Lullaby," the allegorical novel *Almanac of the Dead* (1991), and the diatribe "America's Iron Curtain: The Border Patrol State" (1994). Key to her dedication to honest portrayal is the Pueblo use of words to perpetuate culture and the white perversion of words to exonerate land theft. As a tool of U.S. imperialism, white legalese entangles Ayah, the protagonist of "Lullaby," in a web of dispossession and loss. Knowing only her signature in English, Ayah witnesses the injustice of a telegram announcing her son Jimmie's death in combat — possibly the Vietnam War — and the permission form that quarantines his younger siblings, Danny and Ella, in a tuberculosis clinic.

The issue of how and by whom interpretation occurs impacts home environments and marriages as well as interaction with social institutions. In the analysis of Suzanne Evertsen Lundquist, an English teacher at Brigham Young University, Ayah depends on her husband Chato "to translate between her traditional world and the encroaching Anglo Society" (Lundquist, 2005, 239). Ironically, Ayah's singing of a reassuring lullaby to Chato translates for him the fearful passage from alcoholic numbing to death by freezing under a blanket of snow. In the U.S. military hunt for the renegade Apache in "A Geronimo Story" (1974), Silko's version features another example of impending capture and death, but fosters drollery rather than the subtlety and poignance that dominates "Lullaby." The Geronimo tale illustrates to Andy, the *naïf*, what John Muthyala, an English professor at the University of Southern Maine, calls "the power of language, how it functions as a fluid, open-ended, and paradoxical process of representation" (Muthyala, 2006, 130). By adding to a body of Apache lore, she produces "a" story, rather than "the" story, thereby honoring and empowering the famed guerrilla warrior for his wiliness, a controlling character trait of Southwestern coyote stories.

In *Almanac of the Dead*, an alternative history to European mythos, Silko legitimates a Mesoamerican communication style, the Maya and Mixtec amalgamation of painting with writing. The creators of codices, called painter-scribes for their shaping of pictoglyphs, complemented oral story transmission with icon and symbol. After Catholic priests forced Mayan children to study Latin and Spanish in the sixteenth century, Mayan elders realized that written texts offered a tool to combat grand scale genocide. In assessing the worth of Chilam Balam's ancient texts drawn and written on horse gut, Zeta speaks for all first peoples a charge of colonial theft — Whites "came in, and where the Spanish-speaking people had courts and elected officials, the *americanos* came in and set up their own courts — all in English" (Silko, 1991, 213). The damning factor in interracial negotiations, a one-sided legitimation of language shut out the non–English speakers and tipped sovereignty and recompense in the favor of usurping whites, who took "all the best land and ... the good water" (*Ibid*). Critic Elizabeth Archuleta, a humanist at Arizona State University, further condemns "Janus-faced" whites for demeaning "the stories that reflect [Pueblo] reality and their experience" (Archuleta, 2005, 124, 122). She extols Silko for protesting historical land grabs and massacres that U.S. law refuses to acknowledge, investigate, and/or rectify.

## Language Mediators

Silko's works reflect Amerindian suspicions of translation and translators. Of the transformation of Keres into English, she warns that English lacks the ability to restate "language from the Pueblo perspective, one that embraces the whole of creation and the whole of history and time," a definition that journalist John R. Kincaid repeated in "Who Gets to Tell Their Stories?" an article for the *New York Times* (Kincaid, 1992, 27). Because words themselves have their own stories, the effect of narrative within narrative invites listeners to examine a whole cosmology of Indian experience. In *Ceremony* (1977), the novelist treats words and narrative as thought they were magical or sacramental for their creation of a world capable of intervening in ruinous acts and murderous attitudes. In homage to the sacred potency of words, she views them as salvific and transformative. In flashbacks to childhood, Tayo, the protagonist remembers his mother in terms of the language she used when she talked to him. Her syntax, as dear to him as her photo or her fragrance, clings to memory as unique and motherly. After undergoing what Spokane Indian critic Gloria Bird calls "colonialist indoctrination" at high school, he loses the mother-son intimacy he remembers from age four (Bird, 2005, 102). The loss fictionalizes an event in the author's childhood mentions in *Storyteller* (1981), when demands for English only at Silko's Christian elementary school causes Grandma A'mooh to stop using Keres for conversation and storytelling. The author lives to regret her lack of fluency in the Laguna language.

Silko envisions the inexact verbal training of the mixed breed Indian as a deterrent to full participation in Amerindian healing ceremonies. The text recognizes the tradition-rich language of the Laguna medicine man Ku'oosh, who speaks dialect sentences "involuted with explanations of their own origins" (Silko, 1977, 34). His method of clarification, for example, of the word "fragility," is tedious and counterproductive. He infers that "the reason for choosing each word had to be explained with a story about why it must be said this certain way ... because no word exists alone" (*ibid.*, 35). Because of their longevity, the phrases take the form of a healing chant, a blending with rhythm for the sake of heightening and stylizing a memorable thought. From reference to a deep lava cave to the northeast, Tayo recalls a recuperative place for hibernating snakes in spring, a menacing tangle that Ku'oosh connects with the "white people's big war," a simplification of American involvement in a world clash that began in Germany and spread to Italy and Japan (*ibid.*,

35). By explaining diction with stories amplifying each term, Ku'oosh aims for verbal integrity, the root of healing.

Because the shamanic encounter with Ku'oosh fails to counter the harm that war has done to Tayo's spirit, the veteran must migrate beyond the pueblo to another tradition practiced north of Gallup. At first, he has difficulty understanding the ritual because "his language was childish, interspersed with English," an infantilization of Tayo that deprives him of adult communication skills (*ibid.*, 31). To engage with a healing spell, he joins the story and becomes part of its telling, an action that occurs in the hogan of Chicano-Navajo shaman Betonie. In the analysis of John Emory Dean, an English professor at Texas A&M International University, Tayo "comes into being by engaging in the dialectic," an absorption of words and meanings that establishes a gestalt or pattern essential to wholeness (Dean, 2009, 164). Because he is born of native and non-native parentage, Silko pictures him as a suitable hybridizer and bringer of change, contingent upon his understanding of the elements of his post-war syndrome. Dean compares Tayo's initial subjectivity in terms of Plato's cave myth: in the cave, the veteran interprets experience through emotions of anger and humiliation. Unchained from the cave wall by Betonie's sand painting, hoop ritual, and bear tracks, Tayo frees himself of hurt and guilt and directs his thoughts and actions away from past regrets toward intellectual problem solving.

In Tayo's private battle with 20 feet of steel mesh, wolf-proof fence, he loses himself in the language of his people. Without past, present, or future tense, he resurrects Rocky and Uncle Josiah as a cosmic night engulfs him —"a single night; and there has never been any other" (Silko, 1977, 192). In Silko's literary *tour de force*, timelessness rids him of combat residue and cleanses him of regret and sorrow that he couldn't save Rocky, his cousin/foster brother and combat buddy. The psychological depth of Silko's description won her credibility with language arts teachers as well as ministers, psychologists, and humanists. During an interview in 1999 with journalist Philip Connors for *Newsday* about the novel, Silko expressed humility that a university humanities class studied *Ceremony* along with the fiction of Franz Kafka, Karl Marx's treatises, and the poems of William Wordsworth. She observed, "That's kind of overwhelming. I've always felt that I was blessed or watched over by the old spirits or the old ancestors. I think for all writers language is a great ocean or river. Our stories flow into the river, and each story adds to the whole. They mingle and swirl together" (Connors, 1999, B11).

## LANGUAGE AND REBELLION

The novelist's next project, *Almanac of the Dead*, attempted such a broad examination of the role of language in North American history that it generated an array of critical response, from commendation to outright damnation. Tol Foster, a Muskogee Creek expert on Indian and American literature at the University of North Carolina at Chapel Hill, claimed that "the text brings crucial discussions and relations to the fore like none other in Native American Literary Studies" (Foster, 2008, 297). During the fictional transcription and publication of Mesoamerican texts, Silko accords sanctity to a tattered and pillaged codex, which the preserver Yoeme, a Yaqui savant, personalizes as "mouths and tongues" (Silko, 1991, 142). The Yaqui revere the original almanac because it identifies them as a nation from earliest times—"who they were and where they had come from ... all the days of their people" (*ibid.*, 246, 247). The value to the 20th-century generation is profound. As the author explains in *Storyteller* (1981), "It will take a long time, but the story must be told. There must not be any lies" (Silko, 1981, 26). She enhances her original comments in the essay "Language and Literature from the Pueblo Indian Perspective" (1996) by reminding the reader that even a single word can generate narratives that range outward like a web of living language, an allusion to Spider Woman (Ts'its'tsi'nako or Thought Woman), the creator mother and spinner of tales. Much as Adam and Eve shoulder the job of naming items in Eden in the first chapters of Genesis, Spider Woman both begets and identifies the world. Critic Ellen Burton Harrington, an English professor at the University of South Alabama, marvels at the scope of the mythic spider's powers: "Everything exists as a result of Thought Woman's naming" (Harrington, 2008, 182).

Silko encases the history of the ancient manuscripts in a Gothic fable. The transport of fragile coded texts in the clothing of three children requires a night pilgrimage from Sonora north to the Arizona clan. The youngest child becomes so hungry that she chews the parchment; the eldest adds a page to a vegetable stew, literally feeding the siblings on Yaqui history. To preserve precious lore orally, the eldest relates the contents of the page to the other three. Crucial to the future of the people's history is the "epoch of Death-Eye Dog," epitomized by the crippled crone who cannibalizes a child, a chilling episode resembling Jacob and Wilhelm Grimm's fairy tale "Hansel and Gretel" (1812) (*ibid.*, 251). As described by critic Martha Cutter, the almanac is no longer original, authentic, static, or uncontaminated but a fluid work in progress, an evolving narrative. Only through a generative decoding of arcane glyphs and ancient chants and prophecy does Silko make the earliest staves accessible to the late 20th century as history and revelation. Cutter concludes that the transcription reveals connection and reciprocity: "Truth is multifaceted and multilingual ... [it] exists only in the web and tangle of discourse, of contradictory narratives and languages" (Cutter, 2005, 114). The inconsistencies reflect the fates of divergent tribes and peoples who overcome differences to forge a single assault against the white usurper.

Threatening the integrity of the text is the commitment of centuries of lore to "bundle of pages and scraps of paper with notes in Latin and Spanish" and "loose notebook pages and scraps of paper with drawings of snakes" (Silko, 1991, 134). Lecha, a clairvoyant and the official storykeeper, fears that the gradual drying and curling of the parchment will make the words illegible. She learns from Yoeme, her grandmother, that eyewitnesses to conquest of the Yaqui feared that the history would disappear with their deaths. Thus, Yoeme warns, "you must understand how carefully the old manuscript and its notebooks must be kept" to ensure the preservation of the Yaqui past (*ibid.*, 129). The old woman maintains that the task is exacting. It allows for repairs and requires a "suitable code," the Rosetta Stone that Yoeme never locates (*ibid.*). The transcriber of the almanac recognizes the problem of lacunae or gaps in the body and the significance of a lost section. She admits, "One naturally reflects upon one's own experiences and feelings throughout one's life," a subjectivity that threatens the original intent of ancient scribes (*ibid.*, 129). Lecha's introspection implies a holy office that demands strict tending and upkeep of the manuscript and notebooks without distortion or misrepresentation of the original.

The work of the linguist bears rewards at the same time that it sustains memories, faith, and hope. In translated form, the almanac changes worlds with miraculous rhetorical power. After Lecha records one of Yoeme's stories in English on a blank page, she recognizes a transcendent event — the transference of ancient lore to a new generation, "the sign the keepers of the notebooks had always prayed for" (*ibid.*, 130). Lecha herself joins the lineage of Yaqui scribes. In terms of the wrongs that await righting in the coming political apocalypse, Silko refers to episodes of language trickery that *americanos* perpetrate on Spanish speakers during the settlement of Arizona and New Mexico. By manipulating deeds and quitclaims in English, whites discredited the land grants and hereditary titles bestowed by the Spanish king. Over the centuries, spirits agitate for justice: "No excuses, no postponements, not even for one day, must be tolerated by the people" (*ibid.*, 524). They anticipation that "True leaders of the revolution would deed back thousands of millions of acres of land" (*ibid.*). Thus, manipulation of language becomes the only recourse open to five centuries of victims for requital of their dispossession.

## LANGUAGE IN GLOBAL SETTINGS

For *Garden in the Dunes* (1999), a neo–Victorian novel featuring the language of flowers, Silko intended to abandon the grim trudge of rebels that marked *Almanac*. In an edenic setting, she invents the Sand Lizard language, which exists contemporaneously with the talk of desert animals, particularly the coyote. However, postcolonial issues refused to cooperate with her peaceful endeavor. Her visionary four-night Ghost Dance returns to the concept of Babel in the languages spoken by Havasupai, Mormons, Paiute, and Walapai. After episodes of spiritual ecstasy and glossolalia, dancers witness the return of Jesus and his family. In greetings from the Messiah, language presents no problem because "there was only one language spoken — the language of love — which all people understand ... because we are all the children of Mother Earth," a pure and mystic form of communication that transcends common discourse (Silko, 1999, 32). British critic David Murray, an expert on American studies at the University of Nottingham, notes that, "The crucial thing about it is not that everyone shares a metalanguage, but that each person hears the message in his or her own language," an internalizing of godhood that bypasses the meticulous work of the translator (Murray, 2007, 147). Silko contrasts the gentle inclusion of all dancers to the circle with the vocabulary that Indigo learns from whites: "Jesus Christ, Mother of God, Father God, Holy Ghost, hallelujah, savior, sinners, sins, crucify, whore, damned to hell, bastard, bitch, fuck," an indication of the hypocritical, coarse, punitive attitudes conveyed by the proselytizers (*ibid.*, 68).

Indigo's pinpointing of the conqueror's faults equips her for thwarting the enemy. Skill at English facilitates her coping with orphaning and living among whites. To the pompous Dr. Edward Palmer, a gentleman naturalist, Indigo contends, "I talk English way better than you talk Indian," a retort replete with the global perception of Americans as too self-involved to learn the languages of others (*ibid.*, 108). On her train ride from Needles to Riverside, California, she rhymes with the song of the rails "Clackety-clack! Never get back, never get back, get back, get back" (*ibid.*, 121). In the loving company of Aunt Bronwyn, an eccentric neo–Druid in Bath, England, Indigo is able to link Celtic ritual to the coming of the Messiah at the Ghost Dance and a reunion with Mama, whom soldiers rout on the fourth night of the dance. Like Grandma Fleet and Sister Salt, Indigo and Bronwyn share a common embrace of spirituality and ancestry, much of which they absorb through walks among iconic statuary in terraced gardens and orchards. Silko adds a literary encore by pairing Indigo with *la professoressa* Laura, a horticulturist in Lucca, Italy, who values the same serpent lore that Grandma Fleet taught at the sand dunes.

Indigo's flexibility, developed like that of Silko during the early years of language learning, is startlingly effective in bracing her for varied changes in lifestyle and experience. Because of the child's open-minded tribal upbringing, she outpaces Edward and his scholarly wife, Hattie Abbott Palmer, both self-important cosmopolites who find snake icons grotesque and shockingly carnal. In contrast to Hattie, the spurned wife, and to Edward, the broker of exotic plants who suffers arrest and humiliation, confiscation of specimens, and jailing for theft of citrus cuttings from Bastia, Corsica, Indigo returns home with a variety of seeds collected legally from Bronwyn and Laura. A source of optimism abides in her faith that sightings of the Ghost Dancers in Europe prove that the Messiah may be making his way home, as his words promised. Upon reunion with Sister Salt and Bright Eyes, the "little black grandfather," and with the Chemehuevi twins Maytha and Vedna, Indigo bubbles with episodes of her journey, a new strand of Sand Lizard lore.

See also "Lullaby"; writing.

• *References and further reading*

Archuleta, Elizabeth. "Securing Our Nation's Roads and Borders or Re-circling the Wagons? Leslie Marmon Silko's Destabilization of 'Borders,'" *Wicazo Sa Review* 20:1 (Spring 2005): 113–137.
Bird, Gloria. "Toward a Decolonization of the Mind and Text: Leslie Marmon Silko's *Ceremony*" in *Reading Native American Women: Critical/Creative Representations*, ed. Inés Hernández-Avila. Lanham, MD: Altamira, 2005, 93–106.
Blackmarr, Amy. *Above the Fall Line: The Trail from White Pine Cabin*. Macon, GA: Mercer University Press, 2003.
Brooks, Joanna. "'This Indian World': A Petition/Original Story from Samson Occom (Mohegan) and the Montaukett Tribe" in *Early Native Literacies in New England: A Documentary and Critical Anthology*, eds. Kristina Bross and Hilary E. Wyss. Amherst: University of Massachusetts Press, 2008.
Brooks, Lisa Tanya. *The Common Pot: The Recovery of Native Space in the Northeast*. Minneapolis: University of Minnesota Press, 2008.
Connors, Philip, "Talking with Leslie Marmon Silko," *Newsday* (4 April 1999): B11.
Cutter, Martha J. *Lost and Found in Translation: Contemporary Ethnic American Writing and the Politics of Language Diversity*. Chapel Hill: University of North Carolina Press, 2005.
Dean, John Emory. *Travel Narratives from New Mexico: Reconstructing Identity and Truth*. Amherst, NY: Cambria, 2009.
Fitz, Brewster E. *Silko: Writing Storyteller and Medicine Woman*. Norman: University of Oklahoma Press, 2004.
Foster, Tol. "Of One Blood: An Argument for Relations and Regionality in Native American Literary Studies" in *Reasoning Together: The Native Critics Collective*. Norman: University of Oklahoma Press, 2008.
Harrington, Ellen Burton. *Scribbling Women & the Short Story Form: Approaches by American & British Women Writers*. New York: Peter Lang, 2008.
Kincaid, James R. "Who Gets to Tell Their Stories?" *New York Times* (3 May 1992): 24–29.
Lundquist, Suzanne Evertsen. *Native American Literatures: An Introduction*. New York: Continuum, 2005.
Murray, David. *Matter, Magic, and Spirit: Representing Indian and African American Belief*. Philadelphia: University of Pennsylvania Press, 2007.
Muthyala, John. *Reworlding America: Myth, History, and Narrative*. Athens: Ohio University Press, 2006.
Petrolle, Jean. *Religion without Belief: Contemporary Allegory and the Search for Postmodern Faith*. Albany: State University of New York Press, 2007.
Silko, Leslie Marmon. *Almanac of the Dead*. New York: Simon & Schuster, 1991.
_____. *Ceremony*. New York: Viking, 1977.
_____. *Gardens in the Dunes*. New York: Scribner, 1999.
_____. "Lullaby," *Chicago Review* 26:1 (Summer 1974): 10–17.
_____. *Storyteller*. New York: Seaver, 1981.
_____. *The Turquoise Ledge*. New York: Viking, 2010.
_____. *Yellow Woman and a Beauty of the Spirit: Essays on Native American Life Today*. New York: Simon & Schuster, 1996.
_____, and James Wright. *The Delicacy and Strength of Lace: Letters between Leslie Marmon Silko and James Wright*. St. Paul, MN: Graywolf, 1986.

# Lecha and Zeta's genealogy

A hybridized link to Yaqui prophecy and history, the sexagenarian twins Lecha and Zeta bear contrasting traits, a reflection of their mixed Anglo-Indian background and contrasting character. In similar fashion to that Henry C. "Hank" Marmon, Silko's white grandsire, the twins' grandfather, old Guzman, marries the Yaqui Yoeme, but Guzman continues to exploit and murder Indians. As story transcriber, Lecha bears a cultural and tribal responsibility, which analyst Kimberly Roppolo calls "the visual/holistic receiving of and the visual/holistic recording of knowledge" (Roppolo, 2007, 543).

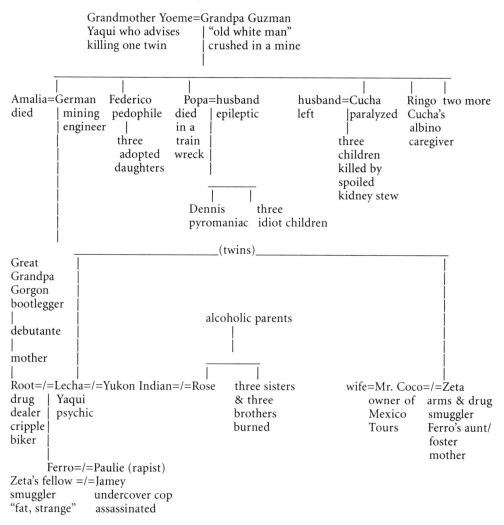

*See also Almanac of the Dead*; siblings.

## • *References and further reading*

Roppolo, Kimberly. "Vision, Voice, and Intertribal Metanarrative: The American Indian Visual-Rhetorical Tradition and Leslie Marmon Silko's *Almanac of the Dead*," *American Indian Quarterly* 31:4 (Fall 2007): 534–558.

Silko, Leslie Marmon. *Almanac of the Dead*. New York: Simon & Schuster, 1991.

## "Lullaby" (1974)

One of Silko's most haunting postcolonial stories, "Lullaby" speaks the joy of mothering and the harsh truth of a native mother's life in a milieu damaged by white ways. Whites marginalize women like Ayah, the protagonist, for their color, race, language, socio-economic class, and advanced age. Her own culture, according to critic Patrice E. M. Hollrah, an English professor at the University of Nevada, epitomizes Ayah as a Navajo deity, Changing Woman (Asdz nádleehé), the icon of cyclical nature and birth. In the traditional matriarchy of Cebolleta, a border town west of Albuquerque, New Mexico, Ayah owns her own hogan and livestock and complements her husband Chato's role by rearing children and attending to domestic duties. Although anchored to a world of female collaborative work separate from Chato's paid job as a fence rider, Ayah receives an equal share of dignity and authority from her traditional position as wife and mother in a four-generation matriarchy. Silko, a Laguna, sympathizes with the Navajo matron as a means of searching for her identity. Hollrah surmises that "Silko's project when writing about another culture ... [explores] issues that will contribute to a fuller understanding of her own personhood and perhaps gender" (Hollrah, 2003, 59).

Opening on snowflakes, a symbol of womanly purity and uniqueness, Silko introduces an intra-familial, intra-cultural Navajo matrilineage in a fiberwork image of wooly white tufts, the craft element that Spider Woman (Ts'its'tsi'nako or Thought Woman), the creator mother, gave to the tribe's women. In girlhood, Ayah combs burs and twigs from fleece, a task that foreshadows the thorny obstacles that lie ahead in the lengthy stages of female life from child to elder. Ayah's grandmother turns wool into yarn on a cedar spindle; Ayah's mother dyes the threads gold, red, and yellow and weaves them at the loom, an allusion to the role of Grandma A'mooh, Aunt Susie Reyes Marmon, and Silko herself as storyweavers for the Laguna. The mother produces soft, tightly woven blankets that repel rain "like birds' feathers," a sensual image of warmth and bright color as well as fragility and replication of natural protection (Silko, 1974, 10). According to Navajo custom, women owned their crafts and the proceeds from selling them, a source of self-expression and empowerment.

WOMAN AS PROTECTOR

Cherokee critic Rayna Green, the curator of the Amerindian division of the National Museum of American History, surveys Ayah's role as an autonomous adult and agent of change. In the Navajo culture, the wife displays a womanly persistence, endurance, valor, and resolve in the face of hardship. Unlike white feminist literature, the story depicts Ayah combating racial bias and allying with her husband to seek economic and social justice. Nostalgia for the tribal past stalks her old age to the last. Among her memories are the standard buckskin leggings and elk-hide moccasins that preceded black rubber overshoes, the white world's invention that separates Ayah from Southwestern nativism. Wrapped in Jimmie's olive drab army blanket, she becomes an icon of the unassimilated Indian woman in a depressing culture dominated by whites.

Silko makes literacy the focal issue in Ayah's assimilation. The author noted that Pueblo people learned early in their relationship with the Spanish the value of words and signatures on royal land grants. The older generation urged youth to become fluent in reading and writing to protect themselves from the self-serving laws of Europeans. The protagonist can scribble her name, but can't interpret the words and legalism of the white world that impact her family's lives and hopes. Critic Jordana Finnegan, an English professor at Foothill College in Los Altos, California, interprets the value of a signature in English as evoking "historic manipulations of the treaty-signing process that resulted in the involuntary dispossession of Native peoples from their lands," an expulsion that eventually wrecks the security of Ayah and Chato (Finnegan, 2008, 114). Because white doctors take the couple's youngest, Danny and Ella, to a tuberculosis treatment center, fragmentation of the household infects Ayah with "pain in her belly [that] was fed by everything she saw," a reverse image of labor pains (Silko, 1974, 11). Significant to the human situation, Jimmie's military blanket, which Ayah wears like a shawl, ravels about the edges, a fraying symbolic of the attrition of Amerindian customs and security under white domination. Finnegan adds a hopeful interpretation: "Ayah's association with the spider figure, even in the midst of painful losses, offers a source of empowerment," but not a solution to household collapse (Finnegan, 208, 114).

## A Study of a Marriage

Parallel to the theme of family unity, Silko particularizes the role of trust between husband and wife. Contrary to the couple's commitment to each other lies what Jeff Karem, a humanities professor at Cleveland State University, claims is a "disappearing culture," a bold description of threat to Navajo beliefs and practices (Karem, 2004, 186). Unlike the female solidarity that joins women in birthing, mothering, and fiber work, Ayah's relationship with her husband withers as the couple suffers the loss of their children and home. The fatal barrier is language, which allows Chato to join Spanish-speaking drinkers at Azzie's Bar and to negotiate for his family with white authority figures because he speaks English. Just as Chato rides the boundaries of the white rancher's land and repairs fences, he occupies a position of authority on the outer rim of the Navajo community. However, knowing the ciphers of the white world does not save Chato from suffering what critic Erin Fallon, editor of *A Reader's Companion to the Short Story in English* (2001), characterizes as "transcendent grief," an incomparable sorrow over the downward spiral of family fortunes (Fallon, 2001, 394). To Ayah, her husband is gullible in believing white promises and lies. Swiss critic Deborah L. Madsen, an American literature expert at the University of Geneva, sees through Ayah's perspective a husband "who accepts the assumption of the supremacy of white men, which his wife does not. And so she has no sympathy for him" (Madsen, 2000, 233). The breach contributes to Ayah's burdens and inspires a majesty in her refusal to cower before adversity.

Silko segues to family bereavement at the arrival of the military vehicle marked with indecipherable white writing on the doors. A military death notification team delivers a yellow telegram rather than the remains of Jimmie, the healthy firstborn son, who left home to fight in a war. Losing the family's other adult male forebodes economic and marital hardship for Ayah and Chato. For her, Chato's multilingual communication with outsiders turns him into an outsider who allies via language with the enemy. After the deaths of Ayah's grandmother and at least three babies in infancy, son Jimmie dies burned beyond recognition in a helicopter crash in war, leaving Ayah to internalize her grief. Because she signs a paper, her youngest, Danny and Ella, follow white doctors to a hospital in Denver where, according to critic Laurie Champion, a humanities professor at South Dakota State University, "their Indian identity, as well as their disease, [is] the target of the white man's 'rehabilitative' efforts" (Champion, 2002, 334). Ostensibly a period of cure and well being, the absence of tribal language and customs in the children's lives alienates them permanently from their family, creating another amputation of loved ones for Ayah to weather. Again, she has no words to express her hurt and disappointment or to fight for custody of Danny and Ella, whom the hospital staff estranges from their mother's ways and language.

## TRIAL AS CHALLENGE

After a horse crushes Chato's leg, Silko pictures Ayah as bereft of family and the boxcar home on the ranch, but still possessing Navajo womanhood and her hogan. The preliterate wife avoids a conjugal relationship with Chato, yet, typical of matriarchy, she retains agency and decision-making powers. Like a parent trailing a straying child, Ayah follows her handicapped husband to a bar, where he cashes a government disability check and drinks up his money. By urinating on himself, he infantilizes himself and demeans his role as husband and provider. A parallel to Spider Woman, Ayah, white-haired and webbed with wrinkles, maintains dignity and a mythic privilege as she surveys the white tavern for Chato. The story marginalizes the drinkers at the bar, who acknowledge the authority of the resilient Navajo crone by remaining silent. Escorted by his wife, Chato stumbles home undone at losing his respectability as a mounted ranch hand repairing barbed wire fences and recovering stray cattle for an ungrateful white employer. Critic Janet Zandy, an expert in working-class studies at the Rochester Institute of Technology, laments Chato's diminution into "a ghosted worker, discarded by the rancher as too old to work," a prophecy of postindustrial laborers in America's factory cities (Zandy, 2004, 149).

The mothering image deepens in the final scene, in which Silko depicts the circular nature of maternal demands that confer harmony and identity. Ayah lets Chato freeze to death in a snowstorm symbolic of the slow stifling of the Indian lifestyle in a cultural landscape that changes and evolves under cultural genocide. One view of Chato pictures his "limited lifetime options and powerlessness" in old age, a devaluation rooted in white capitalism (Stoller and Gibson, 2000, 71). Much as she covered her infants' corpses in dust and rubble, she wraps Chato in a blanket. Under her care, he rolls to one side like a child at rest. As though comforting her little one, in elegiac mode, Ayah sings to Chato a mother's ideals in a nature-centered lullaby that promises eternal togetherness. With pastoral grace, Silko turns the lullaby into a benediction as the couple recede into the landscape, which blankets them with snow.

The poignant death scene depicts family unity in ecological terms, a harmony with their Indian homeland. The courageous mother figure, as purposeful as Indigo and Sister Salt in Silko's *Gardens in the Dunes* (1999) and as enduring as mythic Yellow Woman (Kochininako), watches over her drunken husband as she, too, becomes one with nature in sleep. Janis P. Stout, an English professor emerita at Texas A&M University, lauds the wife as the "more [courageous] of the two because in his stupor he 'would not feel it'" (Stout, 2007, 220–221; Silko, 1974, 17). From a Eurocentric perspective, the story concludes in tragedy and defeat. From an Amerindian point of view, in the words of critic Julie Bird, the resolution "[reflects] the interrelatedness of man and nature that permeates Native American literature" by picturing Ayah "[walking] into the sky, stepping through clouds endlessly" (Bird, 2005, 383; Silko, 1974, 17). Silko succeeds at the eternal paradox of continuity in mortality — death becomes a healing of Ayah's pain and a release from circumstances that trammel the true Navajo lifestyle.

*See also* feminism; genocide; Spider Woman; women.

• *References and further reading*

Barnett, Louise, and James Thorson, eds. *Leslie Marmon Silko: A Collection of Critical Essays*. Albuquerque: University of New Mexico Press, 1999.

Champion, Laurie. *Contemporary American Women Fiction Writers: An A-to-Z Guide*. Westport, CT: Greenwood Press, 2002.

Fallon, Erin. *A Reader's Companion to the Short Story in English*. Westport, CT: Greenwood, 2001.

Finnegan, Jordana. *Narrating the American West*. Amherst, NY: Cambria Press, 2008.

Grobman, Laurie. "(Re)Interpreting 'Storyteller' in the Classroom: Teaching at the Crossroads," *College Literature* 27:3 (Fall 2000): 88–110.

Hollrah, Patrice E. M. *"The Old Lady Trill, the Victory Yell": The Power of Women in Native American Literature*. New York: Routledge, 2003.

Karem, Jeff. *The Romance of Authenticity: The Cultural Politics of Regional and Ethnic Literatures*. Charlottesville: University of Virginia Press, 2004.

Madsen, Deborah L. *Feminist Theory and Literary Practice*. London: Pluto Press, 2000.

Silko, Leslie Marmon. "Lullaby," *Chicago Review* 26:1 (Summer 1974): 10–17.

Stoller, Eleanor Palo, and Rose Campbell Gibson. *Worlds of Difference: Inequality in the Aging Experience*. Thousand Oaks, CA: Pine Forge Press, 2000.

Stout, Janis P. *Picturing a Different West: Vision, Illustration, and the Tradition of Cather and Austin*. Lubbock: Texas Tech University Press, 2007.

Van Dyke, Annette. "Silko, Writing Storyteller and Medicine Woman," *Studies in American Indian Literatures* 21:3 (Fall 2009): 102–104.

Zandy, Janet. *Hands: Physical Labor, Class, and Cultural Work*. New Brunswick, NJ: Rutgers University Press, 2004.

# madness

Silko surveys the mental landscape of disturbed people to isolate the cause and nature of their distress. In *The Turquoise Ledge* (2010), an undercurrent of suspicion accumulates around Aunt Margaret, an unfaithful wife who becomes unhinged because of her extramarital affairs around the Acoma-Laguna area. The response to inappropriate words and behaviors illustrates how observers contribute to neurosis, a motif of Silko's first novel, *Ceremony* (1977). The author, in a conversation with editor Dexter Fisher, claimed that the writing had a therapeutic effect on her: "Writing the novel was a ceremony for me to stay sane" while she coped with a lengthy sojourn in Alaska far from her Southwestern homeland (Fisher, 1980, 20). The text focuses on a mixed-blood Laguna native like Silko, the war casualty Tayo, son of "little sister" Laura, an outcast for drunken carousing and for copulating with whites and Mexicans. An abandoned illegitimate, he grows up in New Mexico near the Jackpile mine, source of uranium for the atomic bombs that level Hiroshima and Nagasaki on August 6 and 8, 1945. Unable to rescue his cousin/foster brother Rocky, Tayo breaks down from emotional trauma in a world war too terrible to contemplate.

The problem of treating battle-fatigued soldiers extends beyond the years of combat. After World War II ends in the Pacific on September 2, 1945, Tayo enters a military mental hospital in Los Angeles. Under the care of a white psychiatrist who, according to Brewster E. Fitz, a Silko specialist, "tends to deny the sacred interconnectedness of life," Tayo shields himself in a foggy dissociation from reality (Fitz, 2004, 52). His volunteering for the military places him in the Pacific at the time of the explosion of the world's first atomic weapons, "the alleged crowning achievement of twentieth-century Western science ... the harness of atomic energy, the use of which some white Americans judged appropriate to end the imperialistic dreams of the Land of the Rising Sun" (*ibid.*). In the diagnosis of Holly E. Martin, a literature specialist and assistant dean of Notre Dame University, in reliving combat, Tayo suffers the incongruity of being "both a destroyer and a person who hates destruction," especially of lives, memories, and stories (Martin, 2006, 139). Because he loses the power to process individual memories and to sort out past from present, in May 1948, his thoughts become demons that stalk his consciousness and sleep in Gothic hallucinations and flashbacks. Critic Lawrence Buell, the Powell M. Cabot Professor of American Literature at Harvard University, acknowledges the rightness of the collapse as a psychological stumble under overwhelming stimuli: "What he had experienced as insanity, as the uncontrollable montaging of impressions (seeing the face of his Japanese 'enemy' as the face of his Uncle Josiah, for instance), is sanity" (Buell, 1995, 288).

RESTORING THE PSYCHE

Silko identifies the veteran's internal torment as survivor's guilt (or survivor syndrome), a self-blame for the deaths of others that generates depression, anxiety, withdrawal, harried sleep, and malaise marked by emotional incontinence. The return to Laguna exacerbates Tayo's symptoms with ongoing weeping and vomiting. Rather than inhabit his own mental landscape, Tayo experiences a haunting that alienates him from self. At the height of violence, he "went crazy in the bar and almost killed Emo" by thrusting a jagged beer bottle into his comrade's gut (Silko, 1977, 48). Outside of Gallup, a healer, the Chicano-Navajo shaman Betonie, names Tayo's syndrome as the work of white witchery, which destroys and kills derelicts who cluster around the riverbank. Tayo must reconcile the warring white and native halves of his identity to suppress the phantasms and his reliving of capture on the Bataan Death March, which began in the Philippines on April 9, 1942. Wrenched back to combat again and again, he becomes unhinged from place and purpose. At an extreme of hallucination, he views the enemy Japanese as his Uncle Josiah, a foster father and "old Laguna man, thousands of miles from the Philippine jungles and Japanese armies" (*ibid.*, 8). Through a precognitive inkling, Tayo intuits the death of Josiah back home in New Mexico and experiences the helplessness of mortality worsened by distance and war. Brewster Fitz explains Tayo's Jungian moment: "In a sense, the vision that brings Tayo to the verge of madness is a photo-mytho-graphic total perspective ... the state of affairs as it was thirty thousand years ago" (Fitz, 2004, 41).

In the estimation of Lawrence Buell, Silko has a reason for packaging her novel as ecological ethnopoetics. The text indicates that mental derangement requires a physical reunion with the Southwestern desert to recover "a sense of [Tayo's] reciprocity with the land" (Buell, 1995, 289). The veteran bears a load of regret and shame for his poor wartime performance, primarily for not saving his cousin/foster brother Rocky from death. In the drumming, corrupting Pacific monsoon, rain delays the evacuation of Rocky, who dies of a septic grenade wound to the leg and a captor's thrust of a rifle butt to the skull. In ineluctable circumstances, Tayo can only damn the rain, a misaimed curse that violates his holistic upbringing that honors Mother Earth as the source and nurturer of all. He forgets the Pueblo myth of rain as the blessing of departed spirits on native soil. Silko declares white psychiatrists at the veterans' hospital in Los Angeles incapable of understanding Tayo's self-recrimination for killing his uncle and bringing drought on the Laguna Pueblo. Even the Laguna medicine man Ku'oosh has no weapons strong enough to restore sanity to battle-crazed veterans exposed to "the cities, the tall buildings, the noise and the lights, the power of their weapons and machines," particularly the bombing of noncombatant Japanese with ore mined at Laguna (Silko, 1977, 169).

Silko depicts recovery in the form of the universal quest for an apotheosis, which takes shape in a healing gestalt, "the pattern, the way all the stories fit together" (*ibid.*, 246). At a crisis in his therapy, he experiences a breakdown, "a sudden overwhelming fatigue took hold, and his heart pounded furiously" (*ibid.*, 195). Accompanying the physical discomposure, panting precedes the buckling of his knees and collapse under a pine tree, where "his body became insubstantial" (*ibid.*). By riding and walking the wilderness around Tse'pi'na (Mount Taylor) in his central New Mexican homeland and eluding the distractions of dissolute military veterans Emo, Harley, Leroy Valdez, and Cousin Pinkie, Tayo simultaneously observes native reverence for earth and the white world's mining of uranium to make bombs. At a vulnerable moment in his search for Uncle Josiah's wild Mexican cattle, Tayo encounters Ts'eh Montaño, a desert spirit who re-introduces him to love and spiritual peace. Their coupling reinstates a rightness of self and a oneness with the cyclical seasons. Siding with his Laguna ancestry, Tayo rids himself of perpetual mourning and mental fragmentation, symbolized by a VA hospital ward, Los Angeles train depot, a logging site and uranium mine, Rocky's iron bed, Lalo's bar, and the fences imposed on New Mexico by white ranchers. At a pivotal moment, Tayo cuts 20 feet of the white rustler's steel mesh, wolf-proof fence and allows Uncle Josiah's speckled longhorns to migrate south, their instinctive search for oneness with their natal origins. The release prefigures his own unshackling from anguish.

## Social Lunacy

Just as the aberration of war besets *Ceremony*, the psychopathology of avarice and competition haunts characters in *Almanac of the Dead* (1991) and *Gardens in the Dunes* (1999). The frontier curse of Eldorado, the search for a legendary city of gold, overarches the scramble for money and power in *Almanac*, an apocalyptic grabbing at water, land, and human resources to create an Italianate planned community, sex mall, outlets for LSD and snuff movies, federal courts presided over by a devotee of sex with basset hounds, murder for hire, and clinics enriched by the sale of human blood and organs. The Yaqui dismiss European nuttiness as the result of being "the orphan people," a mob of anchorless newcomers who lack fundamental respect for earth or themselves (Silko, 1991, 258). First peoples retell "stories of colonials sunk into deepest depravity — Europeans who went mad while their Indian slaves looked on" (*ibid.*, 531). At a height of irony, the novelist introduces sanity from a crazy Hopi prophet. Her logic reflects the lunacy of Joseph Heller's *Catch-22* (1961) and Richard Hooker's *M\*A\*S\*H* (1968): "A crazy man can get things done" (*ibid.*, 732).

In *Gardens in the Dunes*, Silko turns the Western notion of progress into a prowling monster as indescribable as Grendel. Fueling its lurk over the land are opportunities at rapid affluence that thrust the gold rush prospectors, railroad builders, cattle barons, and oil drillers into the Gilded Age. The novelist speaks through a new mother, Sister Salt, the diagnosis of another instance of mass hysteria over money: "You couldn't drink it or eat it, but people went crazy over it" (Silko, 1999, 398). She denounces her lover, Big Candy, an Afro–Red Stick Indian cook and brewer from Louisiana and the father of their son Bright Eyes, for abandoning them during a fire and robbery of his gambling and beer proceeds. With no preparation for a pursuit over the desert, he flees "half crazy, frantic to recover the money" (*ibid.*, 385). Silko forgives, in part, his monomania, the outgrowth of slave times, which drives him toward independence as owner of a restaurant in Denver. Toward other money-obsessed frauds, adventurers, and cheats — Hattie's rapist, Mr. Hyslop, Mr. Maxwell, Dr. Edward Palmer, thesis reviewers at the Harvard Divinity School, Mr. Eliot, Dr. William Gates — Silko is less forgiving.

The novelist grounds the breakdown in Edward Palmer, an egocentric photographer and gentleman naturalist, in lust for money and scholarly prestige. He obsesses over the naming privilege accorded the scientist who discovers a new botanic species. In his plant scavenging foray into the Amazonian jungles of Surinam and Brazil, he comes close to death after bio-piratical scoundrels dispatched by Albert Lowe & Company leave him in the burning countryside while they heist "*Hevea brasiliensis*, the most important source of natural rubber in the world" (Silko, 1991, 130). Creeping to the Pará River on a compound fracture of the leg, he manages to flag a pair of rescuers, but never reclaims his health, mobility, or objectivity. In the estimation of analyst Douglas C. Sackman, an historian at the University of Puget Sound, Edward's "mind and body come apart in a fulfillment of a kind of Cartesian curse. Madness descends, and the cogito [Latin for "I think"] becomes a pathetic scramble" (Sackman, 2005, 246).

Palmer's loss of detachment and order precipitate his end. In a descent into greed and connivance against border guards, he falls into the hands of Italian shore agents at Livorno and declines rapidly into a soulless miser incapable of relating to his wife Hattie or to Indigo, their Sand Lizard foster daughter. Under the medical care of the heinous Dr. William Gates from Melbourne, Edward experiences out-of-body hallucinations. From the quack's regular morphine injections as the botanist sinks toward death, Edward "experienced agitation from disquieting thoughts laced with regrets," a double whammy of cognitive confusion and amorality (Silko, 1999, 426). Like Marley's ghost grasping at ledgers and cashboxes, Edward carries into his dreams disappointment at his first attempt to acquire iron meteorites from an Afro-Mayan seer in Tampico, Mexico, the source of an implied curse. Silko leaves unresolved the nature of the hex, which implies both supernatural payback as well as natural disintegration of the mind.

*See also* Betonie; *Ceremony*; Tayo.

• *References and further reading*

Beidler, Peter G. "'The Earth Itself Was Sobbing': Madness and the Environment in Novels by Leslie Marmon Silko and Louise Erdrich," *American Indian Culture & Research Journal* 26:3 (2002): 113–124.

_____, and Robert M. Nelson. "Grandma's Wicker Sewing Basket: Untangling the Narrative Threads in Silko's *Ceremony*," *American Indian Culture and Research Journal* 28:1 (2004): 5–13.

Buell, Lawrence. "Leslie Silko: Environmental Apocalypticism" in *The Environmental Imagination: Thoreau, Nature Writing, and the Formation of American Culture*. Cambridge, MA: Harvard University Press, 1995.

Fisher, Dexter. "Stories and Their Tellers— A Conversation with Leslie Marmon Silko" in *The Third Woman: Minority Women Writers of the United States*. Boston: Houghton Mifflin, 1980.

Fitz, Brewster E. *Silko: Writing Storyteller and Medicine Woman*. Norman: University of Oklahoma Press, 2004.

Ganser, Alexandra. "Violence, Trauma, and Cultural Memory in Leslie Silko's *Ceremony*," *Atenea* 24:1 (June 2004): 145–149.

Martin, Holly E. "Hybrid Landscapes as Catalysts for Cultural Reconciliation in Leslie Marmon Silko's *Ceremony* and Rudolfo Anaya's *Bless Me, Ultima*," *Atenea* 26:1 (June 2006): 131–149.

Sackman, Douglas C. "A Garden of Worldly Delights" in *Land of Sunshine: An Environmental History of Metropolitan Los Angeles*, ed. William Deverell. Pittsburgh: University of Pittsburgh Press, 2005.

Silko, Leslie Marmon. *Almanac of the Dead*. New York: Simon & Schuster, 1991.

_____. *Ceremony*. New York: Viking Press, 1977.

_____. *Gardens in the Dunes*. New York: Scribner, 1999.

_____. *The Turquoise Ledge: A Memoir*. New York: Viking Adult, 2010.

# marriage

From a Pueblo perspective, Silko muses on her perception of the rocky state of American monogamy. In an interview with Ellen L. Arnold, the author admitted her admiration for transcendental philosopher Margaret Fuller, the Boston proto-feminist: "What a woman! What a hero! Free love, so brave, goes to Italy, has a baby out of wedlock" (Silko, 2000, 179). Hero worship suits Silko's upbringing, which lacks the idealistic Christian notion of "till death do us part." Pueblo author Paula Gunn Allen explains that "marriage among traditional Keres is not particularly related to marriage among Anglo-European Americans" (Allen, 1993, 101). Silko enlarges in *The Turquoise Ledge* (2010) that "Marital infidelity was not a crime among the Pueblos" (Silko, 2010, 50). She explains, "It was not remarkable for young men to marry women as old as their mothers," in part because the Laguna are matrilineal (*ibid.*, 66). The author cites as an example her great-grandfather, Robert Gunn Marmon, "a white man, married into the Anaya family, [who] was adopted into the community by his wife's family and clans" (*ibid.*, 103). As the result of allying with a matriarchy, he "became a part of the political intrigues at Laguna" through his association with powerful female Indians (*ibid.*).

Silko stresses the gender equality of Indians, a balance of power lacking in white Puritanic society. Both genders have affairs with whites and Hispanics, including promiscuous youth and Catholic priests. As she explains in *Yellow Woman and a Beauty of the Spirit: Essays on Native American Life Today* (1996), the elder Pueblo view of wedlock values "teamwork and social relationships, not about sexual excitement" or loyalty to one sex partner (*ibid.*, 67). As demonstrated by the sexual union of Tayo with Ts'eh Montaño, the mystic demigoddess and consort of Mountain Lion Man, no one expects husband or wife to give up attractions to lovers; no one holds a grudge over sexual peccadilloes or extended adulteries. Pregnancy is a positive sign for the clan, who value children whatever their paternity. Open adoptions between unmarried mothers and childless parents encourage the clan-wide system of parenting all children within the community. The open-mindedness of Amerindians, according to Sara L. Spurgeon, a specialist in women's studies at the University of Arizona, is the antithesis of the Western concept of sexual virtue: "Once a border has been penetrated, there can be no return to purity, no final or complete separation" (Spurgeon, 2005, 101). Christian absolutism about breach of female purity explains the white world's shudder at reclaimed white captives, who leave with their Indian captors their value as women and sex objects.

## MARRIAGE IN STORY AND VERSE

After relating variations of the Yellow Woman (Kochininako) and Buffalo Man paradigm, in the elegy "Out of the Works No Good Comes From" in *Storyteller* (1981), the poet presents gendered sides of a lament for a dwindling relationship. From the male perspective in the poem "Possession," the lapse of attraction and love feels like "something no longer with you," like an item that should lie apart from the body with pocket change and keys (Silko, 1981, 103). The woman's riposte, "Incantation," takes a less objective view by imagining her straying bedmate driving over the Sierras to the Pacific Coast. In the gray light of a television screen, she ponders a statement in her notebook that frightens her husband away, a mathematical equation characterizing the stages of marriage and parenthood and the restlessness that comes from the gradual loss of zing in a mature relationship. Silko concludes with a coda, a note warning of the cliff that lies ahead for the marital partner who allows fantasy to lead to the rim of oblivion. The speaker warns her wandering mate, "Don't go looking," a reference to the male predilection for sexual adventuring (*ibid.*, 108).

The author's interest in wilting marital unions returns in film, *Estoyehmuut and the*

*Gunnadeyah* (Arrowboy and the Witches), a 1980 experiment in storytelling on film. Just as she reveals in "Possession," the husband has an inkling of dissatisfaction, but no name for his restlessness. In *Almanac of the Dead* (1991), she passes lightly over Seese's mother, who "had always known how to spend the salary a lieutenant commander flying combat received" (Silko, 1991, 57). After a divorce and second marriage to an air force officer, Seese charges her mother with choosing absent men: "What's the point in being married to him? He's not even as good as Daddy!" (*ibid.*). The text enlarges on the domestic *ménage à trois* of Calabazas, a Yaqui marijuana smuggler, who rationalizes his arranged marriage to Sarita and his adultery with Liria, Sarita's sister. As comic recompense to the cheated wife, a parallel to the matriarch Leah undervalued by the patriarch Jacob in Genesis, the novelist pictures Liria taking her comfort with a Catholic monsignor, much to Calabazas's chagrin. At the prelate's death, Sarita moves on "to radical young priests smuggling political refugees across the border," an indication of the wife's daring and a subtextual hint that Calabazas may not know the real Sarita (*ibid.*, 245).

A subsequent character, Sterling, the exiled Laguna gardener, avoids matrimony because he prefers experienced Winslow whores to wives. His sexual escapades reduce his idea of intimacy to anatomical mechanics. He justifies his life as the favored nephew of aunts Marie, Nita, and Nora and the frequenter of prostitutes because "he was not used to telling anyone else what to do," his summation of a husband's duty (Silko, 1991, 86). To escape complexity in his simply life, he eludes the widows his aunts set up for him and retreats to fantasies of his three trips to Janey, a blonde who performs "the deluxe" in the backseat of her plush Cadillac, Silko's satiric take on carnal materialism (*ibid.*, 84–85). The self-centered notion of sexual release contrasts a revelation of true partnership in *The Delicacy and Strength of Lace: Letters between Leslie Marmon Silko and James Wright* (1986) in which Wright divulges to Silko his happiness with wife Annie and a sudden "deeper and clearer understanding of how very strong this marriage is" (Silko & Wright, 1986, 96). Wright's revelation suggests a maturity lacking in Silko, who has not experienced the onset of cancer and the devotion of a mate to the beloved's welfare.

Wedlock in Long Fiction

Silko's *Gardens in the Dunes* (1999) explores the expansion of nationalism across the Americas through Christian proselytizing, entrepreneurial investment, and claustrophobic monogamy. The text covers a variety of male-female relationships, beginning with Grandma Fleet's widowhood from a man shot in his youth and with Mama, the victim of rape by a Presbyterian minister, who produces a second child after an informal coupling. For Big Candy, an Afro–Red Stick Creek cook from Louisiana, and Sister Salt, a mixed-race Sand Lizard, monogamy does not carry the demands it places on Christian society. After she develops a sideline sex trade with her laundry clients, Big Candy exhibits no possessiveness or jealousy. Her pregnancy, possibly by Mexican client Charlie Luna or by Big Candy, leaves her musing on the merger of racial traits in the unborn child, who could be either Hispano-Indian or Afro-Indian. Silko creates a tender drollery out of Sister Salt's belief that intercourse with an assortment of men throughout her pregnancy enhances the number and variety of ethnic traits in the baby, whom she names Bright Eyes. Scots critic Stuart Christie, an anarchist from Glasgow, describes the embrace of hybrid offspring as a refutation of ethnic purity, the "effective instrument of genocide" he compares to smallpox-infested blankets Colonel Henry Bouquet used to kill off the Iroquois on June 29, 1763, outside Fort Pitt, Pennsylvania (Christie, 2009, 94).

Among the novelist's white cast of characters, couples appear misaligned under the aegis of holy wedlock. Edward Palmer's mother and father enjoy gambling, but not community property because the wealthy mother refuses to allow her mate to squander her inheritance. Money welds the bond between Edward's sister Susan and Colin James, who indulges his wife in frivolous spending and social posturing. She returns the pampering by coupling in the greenhouse with the family's Scots gardener. On the other side of the family tree, Hattie Abbott's parents express divergent aims and philosophies of parenting. To Mrs. Abbott's social climbing and grooming of Hattie for marriage to a likely New York aristocrat, Mr. Abbott encourages his only child's studies at Vassar and Harvard Divinity School and applauds her risky thesis topic, which embarrasses Mrs. Abbott with its apostasy toward orthodox church beliefs about women. It is perhaps predictable that the marriage of Hattie to Edward, an amoral botanic thief and plant broker, perpetuates risk and compromise, particularly after he woos her with deceptive stories of "his adventures, in which he portrayed himself humorously, as the innocent tourist hell-bent on disaster" (Silko, 1999, 79). In contrast to his scholarship and dreams of moneymaking off bio-piracy and resale of meteorites, rare orchids, *Citrus medica* cuttings, and Celtic artifacts from Bath, England, Hattie retreats into pure medieval scriptural research and pride in her groundbreaking religious thesis on the "female spiritual principle in the earthly church" (*ibid.*, 100). Among the iconoclastic writers she admires, Valentinus, a Gnostic theologian in second-century Rome, introduces the anti-monogamy beliefs that "there are no sins of the flesh, and no sacrament of marriage is necessary either, since the spirit was everything" (*ibid.*, 99). By indulging in recovery from hysteria at near-rape by Mr. Hyslop in a carriage, she overlooks an opportunity to weigh her father's opinion that Edward is "too old and he travels too much" (*ibid.*). Neither Abbott perceives the real threat to marriage, Edward's duplicity and obsessions with money and fame.

## MISMATCHED PAIRING

Silko satirizes the naïveté of the unwary in an unassuming statement about the Abbott-Palmer union: "Their marriage fit their needs perfectly" (*ibid.*, 175). The lack of intimacy in their home life and Edward's evenings apart from his wife in explorations and during their lengthy journey indicate that marriage leaves them free to investigate their singular aims and pleasures, including Edward's study of leaves and blossoms and Hattie's rearing and education of a foster daughter. Silko stresses Hattie's surprise that *la professoressa* Laura, an Italian horticulturist, is separated from her wandering mate, who travels to Cairo ostensibly in search of stone statuary and remains gone from their villa. Laura later discloses that he divorced her to marry the daughter of a multimillionaire arms dealer in Egypt, a consistent pattern in Silko's self-indulgent, money-mad males. Although Hattie generously adapts to Edward's globe trotting, she realizes that Laura's husband has "gone astray" during his military posting to Eritrea (Silko, 1999, 287). Rather than grieve over the rupture, Laura takes the view of the sophisticated European — she celebrates the breach for ridding her of a coward.

In contrast to the worldly Laura, the novel hints at serious faults in Victorian Americans who grow up sheltered from human sexuality. For all her education and experience, Hattie sabotages her own happiness via "poor judgment, bad timing, late marriage, premature marriage, dread of childbirth, sexual dysfunction" (*ibid.*, 249). She prefers solitude, husbandly respect, or platonic companionship to romance and coitus and warns her parents not to expect the Palmer marriage to produce children. She suffers an anxiety attack in a stone grotto upon reaching her hand toward a giant stone vulva. The stark symbol of femininity interests both Edward and Laura, but sends Hattie fleeing into the sunlight away from the dark powers of prehistoric femininity. More shocking, Edward's refusal to apologize for his arrest at Livorno and for Hattie and Indigo's detention at the consulate leads Hattie to a cruel awakening: "She and the child were his dupes—his decoys!" while he pilfered a citrus grove of valuable citron cuttings (*ibid.*, 329). At a defining moment, she realizes that she, too, has been plundered.

At the collapse of the marriage, Silko ridicules Edward's response, "a loud sigh," then silence (*ibid.*, 329). An insidious memory haunts Hattie that Edward exonerates Dr. William Gates for groping Hattie during a medical examination, a devaluation of her modesty and womanhood that opens his loyalty to question. Too late, Edward's realization that their union has crumbled leaves him wondering if "they were better suited to each other than to marriage itself" (*ibid.*, 401). Hattie takes the pragmatic approach: "If it was money Edward wanted for the mine venture, then she would arrange a letter of credit for him" (*ibid.*, 377). Previous to widowhood, Hattie carries out her responsibilities as dutiful comforter and nursemaid. In an era when divorce brought shame to the wife and her extended family, Hattie accepts separation "because it was the right thing," a liberating thought to a woman who values justice (*ibid.*, 409). She concludes, "She wasn't suited to marriage," a statement that seems to apply to the twice-divorced novelist as well (*ibid.*, 423). Afterward, Hattie treats herself to wanderings in European gardens and orchards, a freedom missing in her brief union with Edward.

*See also* Palmer, Hattie Abbott; women.

• *References and further reading*

Allen, Paula Gunn. "Kochinnenako in Academe: Three Approaches to Interpreting a Keres Indian Tale," *Yellow Woman*, eds. Leslie Marmon Silko and Melody Graulich. New Brunswick, NJ: Rutgers University Press, 1993.
Christie, Stuart. *Plural Sovereignties and Contemporary Indigenous Literature*. New York: Palgrave Macmillan, 2009.
Karem, Jeff. *The Romance of Authenticity: The Cultural Politics of Regional and Ethnic Literatures*. Charlottesville: University of Virginia Press, 2004.
Silko, Leslie Marmon. *Almanac of the Dead*. New York: Simon & Schuster, 1991.
_____. *Storyteller*. New York: Seaver Books, 1981.
_____. *The Turquoise Ledge: A Memoir*. New York: Viking Adult, 2010.
_____. *Yellow Woman and a Beauty of the Spirit: Essays on Native American Life Today*. New York: Simon & Schuster, 1996.
_____, and Ellen L. Arnold. *Conversations with Leslie Marmon Silko*. Jackson: University Press of Mississippi, 2000.
_____, and James Wright. *The Delicacy and Strength of Lace: Letters between Leslie Marmon Silko and James Wright*, St. Paul, MN: Graywolf, 1986.
Spurgeon, Sara L. *Exploding the Western: Myths of Empire on the Postmodern Frontier*. College Station: Texas A&M University Press, 2005.

## materialism

In her catalogue of human faults, Silko tenders no mercy toward money grubbers. Her early verse and stories, particularly "Lullaby" (1974) and "Humaweepi, the Warrior Priest" (1974)—illustrate the contentment of the simple life. For Ayah, the Navajo protagonist of "Lullaby," material gain for her family results in heartache after Chato, her husband, loses his job and retreats into drinking at Azzie's Bar as a solace. In contrast to Chato, Humaweepi learns to live in the wild and to dine on nature's bounty while building riches from the mentorship of an elderly uncle. The two stories conclude in opposing scenarios—Ayah preparing Chato for death in the snow and Humaweepi claiming the sanctity that his training bestows. Both Ayah and Humaweepi embrace nature as the sum of earthly goodness, the gift of Spider Woman (Ts'its'tsi'nako or Thought Woman), the creator mother. In "An Old-Time Indian Attack Conducted in Two Parts" (1976), the author lashes out at scholars who appropriate Amerindian lore for profit, particularly the "prayers, chants, and stories weaseled out by the white ethnographers" who view the myths of Spider Woman as ready grist for the publisher's mill (Silko 1976, 78). To interviewer Ellen L. Arnold, the author declared such amoral moneymaking a sin: "Big capitalism is evil. It's flat out evil" (Silko & Arnold, 2000, 186). As an example, in "Interior and Exterior Landscapes: The Pueblo Migration Stories," Silko asserts that "Great abundances of material things, even food ... tend to lure human attention away from what is most valuable and important," an allusion toward her own devotion to storykeeping as a holy duty (Silko, 1996, 40).

In addition to poems and stories of greed and sacrilege, Silko's novels dramatize the personal and social disruption of amassing wealth. Insidious in her writings in *Ceremony* (1977), *Almanac of the Dead* (1991), and *The Turquoise Ledge* (2010), the rapacity of Southwestern miners continues to undermine health and safety at the Laguna Pueblo, the location of the Jackpile Mine. Helen May Dennis explains: "In fictional form Silko depicts strikingly the disruptive effects of advanced industrial capitalism on a community whose land is rich in uranium" (Dennis, 2007, 55). From stories passed on by Grandpa Henry C. "Hank" Marmon and Aunt Susie Reyes Marmon, Silko demonizes the windfall that enriched the pueblo. The assurance of full employment for Indian workers failed to prepare them for threats to their health from radiation sickness or from the spiritual dysfunction of soldiers witnessing the attack of noncombatants at Hiroshima and Nagasaki, Japan, on August 6 and 8, 1945, with atomic bombs made from Laguna ore.

The author denounces envy of wealth and power as a corrosion of the soul. Tayo, the protagonist of *Ceremony*, Silko's first novel, suffers from colonization of the psyche by white values. The native philosophy comes under direct attack in churches and classrooms. In school, the staff abases Tayo's spirituality as "the deplorable ways of the Indian people," an overt shaming that dooms his mother, "little sister" Laura, to self-hatred (Silko, 1977, 68). More destructive to his spirit is Auntie Thelma's pride in pure blood and her son Rocky, a conceit that shuts out the half-breed nephew/foster son as "other." Tayo and Rocky buy into the stereotypes and exploitation wrought by the white world through liquor, promiscuous sex, land defilement, and war. Lured by a recruiter flaunting "a gold eagle with its wings spread across an American flag," the two men enlist in the military (Silko, 1977, 59). Upon return home to Laguna Pueblo in 1948 after three months in a veterans' hospital in Los Angeles, Tayo lies in his bed picturing himself not as a war hero, but as the white world's detritus, "like debris caught in a flood" (*ibid.*, 5). Emo, a war buddy, heightens the insult: "You aren't shit, white trash. You love Japs the way your mother loved to screw white men" (*ibid.*, 63). The image of drifting garbage returns in the childhood of neglected children whom Tayo views on a riverbank north of Gallup, where prostitutes snatch at alcohol and brief comforts to relieve their destitution. Their escapism offers no lasting solution to a manipulated, demoralized culture.

WANTING AND HAVING

The author attacks acquisitiveness for creeping into the Amerindian mindset, replacing generosity with greed. In the words of analyst Jean Petrolle, an English professor at

Columbia College, Silko exposes white ethnocentrism and devalues the materialism "that has so infiltrated European-descended cultures" that they accept it as reality (Petrolle, 2007, 131). Like the stacks of boxes, bundles, and bags that Betonie, the Chicano-Navajo medicine man and packrat, stores in his stone hogan north of Gallup, Tayo harbors false perceptions gained from education biased by white notions of the good life. He gazes at Betonie's poverty: "All of it seemed suddenly so pitiful and small compared to the world he knew the white people had" (Silko, 1977, 127). After Tayo offers money for the medicine man's ceremony, the old man rejects cash. Cherokee critic Gloria Bird explains: "Betonie's action exemplifies an alternative value system, one in which currency has no value, and in which the act of healing is priceless" (Bird, 2005, 101).

Critic Catherine Rainwater, an English professor at St. Edward's University, notes the multiple meanings of the eagle — a token of gold coins, of the American war effort, and of majesty in nature. She explains the duality of the symbol to Indian GIs like Rocky and Tayo: "Silko iconizes this debilitating cultural contact between Indians and whites ... through references to the golden eagle, an emblem of America for the U.S. Army and an embodiment of sacred medicine for the Navajo" (Rainwater, 1992, 238). Treatment by Betonie redirects Tayo from the distortion of Pueblo values by his battlefield experience to a shamanic purpose by employing holy tools of the healer's office — a yellow gourd rattle and an eagle's claw. Betonie declares that, by applying sacred signs to newer, more power ceremonies, Tayo can halt the evildoers who would "take this world from ocean to ocean ... [and] explode everything" (Silko, 1977, 137). The statement links war to material gain, a subversion of the public perception of volunteering for the military as a model of self-sacrificing patriotism.

RESTORING BALANCE

For Tayo's recovery, Betonie instructs him on the elements of a mystic pattern that shines from the sky in a constellation, a guidepost that requires no monetary investment. In his trek to retrieve Uncle Josiah's spotted Mexican cattle from a white rustler, Tayo quests for a tough, bred-in-the-wild survivor like himself. The rejected longhorns symbolize the dedication of Pueblo Indians to recycle native stock by herding them on dry, unpromising desert land. On the journey, Tayo encounters the waste of white materialism, from the homeless drunks slumped in alleyways in Gallup, rusted-out cars in ravines, and the promiscuity of Helen Jean, a Ute from the Towac reservation, to the bull with the broken left front leg that Romero rescues from the discards of a rodeo. In reference to the disservice wrought by white avarice, Gloria Bird, associate editor of the *Wicazo Sa Review*, characterizes the Amerindians— Tayo, Helen Jean, and the GIs, Emo, Harley, Leroy Valdez, and cousin Pinkie — as "inheritors all of a legacy of pain and disinheritance" (Bird, 2005, 103).

Silko dramatizes Tayo's conflicted value system by picturing vignettes of possessions. In flashbacks of his journey to the Philippines from San Diego, he tosses coins in a pool, a white good luck ritual devoid of meaning for a Laguna. Lashing out illogically at all Caucasians, including those who shoot Japanese captives, Tayo stokes his hatred of white destroyers, who use brutal roping techniques on animals and who track for sport the mountain lion, a symbol of endurance that Silko introduces in "Indian Song: Survival" (1973). Tayo longs to decolonize Emo, Harley, and Helen Jean by informing them that their obsession with the music, food, and excitement of white cities is a form of thievery from their native culture. To retrieve themselves from white pride in stolen land and technology, Tayo and his fellow Indians need to recognize the death icons—concrete, neon, plastic, and steel—and the fences that indicate fanatic attempts to possess nature. He deepens his curse on white materialism by charging them with cultivating sterile art "which continued to feed off the vitality of other cultures," a kind of vampirism that Silko explores in her allegorical novel *Almanac of the Dead* (1991) (Silko, 1977, 204).

GREED AS SELF-DESTRUCTION

Silko's survey of materialism in Tucson, Arizona, fills *Almanac*, a saga of greed carried to murderous extremes. Dorothea Fischer-Hornung, a lecturer at the University of Heidelberg, lauds the text for "exploring the psychological and material abjection of the European American tradition" (Fischer-Hornung, 2007, 125). The novelist outfits her Gothic cast of characters with showy comforts and baubles—gondolas on the canals designed by Leah Blue, drugs and willing college coeds for her sons Bingo and Sonny, a marble staircase in the showy mansion of Iliana Gutierréz Panson, a choice of homosexual targets for filmmaker Beaufrey, Winslow whores for gardener Sterling, a phalanx of bodyguards for Max "Mr. Murder" Blue, and a round of drugs injected into Zeta, the Arizona smuggler. Jean Petrolle characterizes the delusions of white conquerors that acquired wealth is the only reality, a focus that leaves them depthless, self-absorbed, and nihilistic. Critic Malini Johar Schueller, an expert on race at the University of Florida, maintains that the novelist deliberately juxtaposes Western and Indian values, thus nullifying materialism and reifying "a redemptive world of 'Indian' values such as oneness with the land, harmony, and so on" (Schueller, 2009, 155). The reclamation of values underlies the homecoming of Sterling, the exiled Laguna, who abandons steady pay as Zeta's gardener to reunite with the pueblo. His punishment ended for sacrilege against Laguna terrain, he looks back on Tucson's craziness—"Rambo of the Homeless," "Poor People's Army," the Barefoot Hopi and Wilson Weasel Tail"—as a "bad dream" (Silko, 1991, 762).

Materialism retains its hold on Silko's later works, but her survey lacks the ferocity of *Almanac of the Dead*. The non-fiction in *Yellow Woman and a Beauty of the Spirit: Essays on Native American Life Today* (1996) retreats from overt censure of Western values and actions. In an understated account of the rejection of Silko by white tourists seeking to photograph "real" Indian children in the schoolyard, the author refrains from disparagement of rude adults. In *Gardens of the Dunes* (1999), the author highlights materialism as a prime source of human anguish and marital discord. Mr. Abbott, father of Hattie Abbott Palmer, glories in his only child's bookishness, which begins at age four when she learns to read. Throughout Hattie's education at Vassar and Harvard Divinity School and during her writing of a thesis on Mary Magdalene's position as Jesus' apostle, Mrs. Abbott mutters maternal worries about her daughter's dowry and chances of marrying well. Hattie recalls her mother's obsession with affluence—"who had money, how they got the money, and who lost their money" (Silko, 1999, 79). Gnawing at Mrs. Abbott's contentment is the memory of declining household wealth since Hattie's childhood. From her readings in the Gnostic gospels, Hattie pursues a less material future: "Incorruptible Wisdom, Sophia, the material world and the flesh are only temporary ... spirit is everything!" (*ibid.*, 450). The mantra consoles Hattie during the vicissitudes of her marriage to Dr. Edward Palmer, a bio-pillager who loses his scientific objectivity in the search for riches.

Silko enlarges on money hunger in the portrayal of Susan Palmer James, Hattie's sister-in-law. Like her brother, Susan values botany as a source of prestige among shallow social climbers. She uproots an Italian garden to plant a fairyland of white and blue flowers for a single evening's costume ball, the Masque of the Blue Garden, her annual bid for social approval at which she dresses in matching hues to blend with the display. Critic Gabriella Morisco, a literature expert at the University of Urbino, describes Susan's manipulation of gardening as "a total detachment from it, a lack of respect and an uninhibited consumer mentality typical of certain aggressive American female social climbers … a sort of sick symbiosis" and a "caricature of the inclusive nature of the American melting pot" (Morisco, 2010, 142).

The author builds droll satire on perverted values in the siblings' critiques of each other's aims. Edward, himself an exploiter of decorative plants, charges Susan with enslavement to "fickle garden fashion" and sniffs, "the so-called English garden was already passé" (Silko, 1999, 190). Susan and her husband James consider funding Edward's investment in a commercial citron orchard in Riverside, California, but only after he rids himself of the stigma of a lawsuit involving him with Albert Lowe & Company, plunderers of rare orchids. To achieve his orchard, Edward must complete an expedition to a citron grove at Bastia, "an ember of hope [that] glowed on the shores of Corsica" (*ibid.*, 177). Even on his deathbed from respiratory failure, the glittering dreams haunt Edward's rest, goading him for failure to bribe enough border guards at Livorno, Italy, to achieve his botanic piracy. By describing Edward's wife paying the hospital bill and leaving his remains in an icehouse for Susan to deal with, Silko compounds the irony of ill-gotten gain. Indigo rounds out the satire in her study of Edward's orchids: "How strange to think these small plants traveled so far with so many hazards, yet still thrived while Edward died' (*ibid.*, 447).

*See also* achievement; ambition; irony; self-esteem.

• *References and further reading*

Bird, Gloria. "Toward a Decolonization of the Mind and Text: Leslie Marmon Silko's *Ceremony*" in *Reading Native American Women: Critical/Creative Representations*, ed. Inés Hernández-Avila. Lanham, MD: Altamira, 2005, 93–106.

Dennis, Helen May. *Native American Literature: Towards a Spatialized Reading*. New York: Taylor & Francis, 2007.

Fischer-Hornung, Dorothea. "'Now we know that gay men are just men after all': Abject Sexualities in Leslie Marmon Silko's *Almanac of the Dead*" in *The Abject of Desire: The Aestheticization of the Unaesthetic in Contemporary Literature and Culture*, eds. Konstanze Kutzbach and Monika Mueller. Amsterdam: Rodopi, 2007.

Kennedy, Virginia. "Unlearning the Legacy of Conquest: Possibilities for 'Ceremony' in the Non-Native Classroom," *American Indian Culture and Research Journal* 28:1 (Winter 2004): 75–82.

Morisco, Gabriella. "Contrasting Gardens and Worlds: America and Europe in the Long Journey of Indigo, a Young Native American Girl" in *Nations, Traditions and Cross-Cultural Identities: Women's Writing in English in a European Context*, eds. Annamaria Lamarra and Eleonora Federici. Bern: Peter Lang, 2010, 137–148.

Petrolle, Jean. *Religion without Belief: Contemporary Allegory and the Search for Postmodern Faith*. Albany: State University of New York Press, 2007.

Rainwater, Catherine. "The Semiotics of Dwelling in Leslie Marmon Silko's *Ceremony*," *American Journal of Semiotics* 9:2/3 (1992): 219–240.

Schueller, Malini Johar. *Locating Race: Global Sites of Post-Colonial Citizenship*. Albany: State University of New York Press, 2009.

Silko, Leslie Marmon. *Ceremony*. New York: Viking Press, 1977.

_____. *Gardens in the Dunes*. New York: Scribner, 1999.

_____. "An Old-Time Indian Attack Conducted in Two Parts," *Yardbird Reader* 5 (1976): 77–84.

_____. *Yellow Woman and a Beauty of the Spirit: Essays on Native American Life Today*. New York: Simon & Schuster, 1996.

_____, and Ellen L. Arnold. *Conversations with Leslie Marmon Silko*. Jackson: University Press of Mississippi, 2000.

## Max Blue's genealogy

A witty stereotype of the Italo-American mafioso and professional hit man, Max "Mr. Murder" Blue lives a life of golf and contract killing. His management of what critic Elizabeth Tallent, a reviewer for the *New York Times*, calls an "assassination franchise" replaces the sensuality he enjoyed before lightning struck him (Tallent, 1991, 6). His sons, Bingo and Sonny, reared by a sybaritic, money-grubbing mother, realtor Leah Blue, carry on the family tradition of criminality and self-indulgence by treating themselves to sex and cocaine.

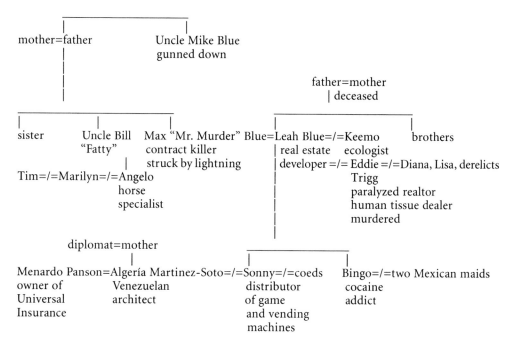

See also Menardo Panson's genealogy.

• *References and further reading*
Silko, Leslie Marmon. *Almanac of the Dead*. New York: Simon & Schuster, 1991.
Tallent, Elizabeth. "Storytelling with a Vengeance," *New York Times Book Review* (22 December 1991): 6.

## Menardo Panson's genealogy

A victim of class snobbery and self-hatred for his *mestizo* blood, Menardo Panson escapes his upbringing in Chiapas, but can't outrun his nose, the telltale proof of his mixed parentage. Foolishly, he chooses a lucrative career in selling insurance to cover accidents, wars, and natural cataclysms, such as the death of his first wife, Iliana Gutiérrez, in a fall down marble stairs. As his business grows with the addition of a professional security army, air force, and arsenal to protect his clients, he marries his paramour, the Venezuelan architect Alegría Martinez-Soto, and falls in love with a new mistress, a bulletproof vest. In a darkly ironic end, he orders his own execution by having Tacho, his Mayan driver, shoot him in the chest. The bullet strikes an unprotected spot on the vest and kills

Menardo instantly, leaving Alegría to drive away from a failed marriage and impromptu widowhood.

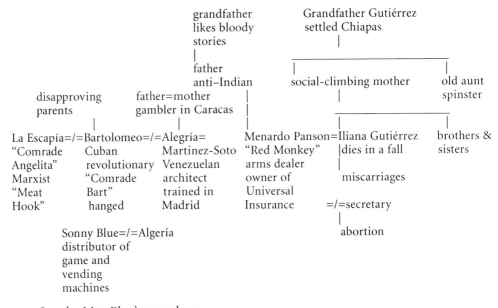

                                grandfather            Grandfather Gutiérrez
                                likes bloody            settled Chiapas
                                stories                        |
                                   |                           |
                                father                  _____
                                anti–Indian                |                    |
         disapproving      father=mother      social-climbing mother      old aunt
         parents          gambler in Caracas       |                      spinster
              |                  |             |         _____           |
    La Escapía=/=Bartolomeo=/=Alegría=   Menardo Panson=Iliana Gutiérrez   brothers &
    "Comrade      Cuban      Martinez-Soto  "Red Monkey" |dies in a fall    sisters
    Angelita"   revolutionary Venezuelan   arms dealer   |
    Marxist     "Comrade      architect    owner of       miscarriages
    "Meat        Bart"        trained in   Universal
    Hook"        hanged       Madrid       Insurance   =/=secretary
                                                            |
         Sonny Blue=/=Algería                            abortion
         distributor of
         game and
         vending
         machines

*See also* Max Blue's genealogy.

• *References and further reading*

Birkerts, Sven. "Apocalypse Now," *New Republic* 205:19 (4 November 91): 39–41.
Silko, Leslie Marmon. *Almanac of the Dead*. New York: Simon & Schuster, 1991.

## Montaño, Ts'eh

In Silko's skillfully gendered text of *Ceremony* (1977), the sexuality of native women releases and directs power, a replication of the dynamism of the female deity Spider Woman (Ts'its'tsi'nako or Thought Woman), the creator mother who nurtures and superintends the universe. Ts'eh Montaño, a surreal, semi-divine life force and consort of Mountain Lion Man, joins Night Swan, the Mexican cantina dancer, to form a significant dyad, "the two Marys of legendary resurrection, mother-lover twin-sister goddesses essential to the hero's salvation and his culture's regeneration" (Lincoln, 2008, 114). Ts'eh derives validity from universal reverence for the female hunter, as depicted in classic myths of Artemis/ Diana, sister of Hera/Minerva (wisdom) and Hestia/Vesta (home). Ts'eh bears a given name meaning "rock" in Navajo, an echo of "Rocky," the nickname of Tayo's cousin/foster brother. The spelling of "Ts'eh" suggests a shortened given name for Tse'pi'na (Mount Taylor) or Ts'its'tsi'nako, both female forms of divinity, a metaphor for the land itself. In an animistic theology that has no separate word for religion, Silko connects Ts'eh with Spider Woman by picturing her rolling twine into a tight ball and using cotton string to bundle willow twigs, domestic chores that restore household order. Gayle Elliott, a specialist in myth at California State University, honors the character as "the singer of the song, and, ultimately, the creative force at the center of the novel and the source from which all stories are born" (Elliott, 2008, 182).

A respecter of nature, Ts'eh contrasts the destructive females in *Ceremony*—Auntie

Thelma, the blonde flirt, "little sister" Laura — with her womanly generosity and whole-some sensuality. John Emory Dean, author of *Travel Narratives from New Mexico* (2009), pictures her as Tayo's mythic constant: "She had encircled him long ago as she had always been in his and his people's collective memory" (Dean, 2009, 159). A visual implication, her appearance west of the Rio Puerco Valley under an apricot tree reminds the reader that stone fruit on the inside mirrors the outline of the female vulva and vagina. Dressed Indian style in shin-high buckskin moccasins, the demigoddess wears her hair long and knotted, an indication of nativist order and self-discipline. Pollen-hazel eyes, yellow skirt, a clay-washed adobe home, and chili made from dried corn and venison suggest her one-ness with the earth as an avatar of the cultural hero Yellow Woman. Silko graces the cou-ple's meal with a fall sky spangled by the constellation that Betonie predicts, an ancient form of calendar that heralds the end of Tayo's wanderings and his turn to regular life rhythms. Like Grandmother Spider's web, the star pattern links Ts'eh to the totality of Tayo's recovery, which requires his return of his uncle's rustled longhorns from Floyd Lee and the reestablishment of normality for Tayo's family and clan.

An avatar of Corn Woman (Nau'ts'ity'i), a source of sustenance, Ts'eh begins heal-ing Tayo, the spiritually maimed veteran of World War II. She first makes contact with him at a sheltering cliff by the Dripping Spring near Pa'to'ch, a holy plain south of Laguna. The setting, which David S. Whitley, the chief archeologist at the University of Califor-nia at Los Angeles, describes as the portal to a holy realm, a version of the Sibyl's cave in Virgil's *Aeneid* (19 B. D.) or of Avalon in Arthurian lore, places Tayo at the boundary between the real and spiritual worlds. The site incorporates Ts'eh's body in a merger with "iron deposits [streaking] the yellow sandstone cliffs," as though she camouflages her humanity with facets of the terrain (Silko, 1977, 221). The serendipity on Tayo's path to wellness, Ts'eh symbolizes libido, the procreative force that ensures the continuation of *Homo sapiens.* Conveying both strength and the rejuvenation of fresh water, Ts'eh, "the woman veiled in clouds," guides the seeker on a vision quest through a trancelike coital union (*ibid.*, 20).

## Sacred Sex

In mystic holy union in the style of tantric yoga and the sacred prostitutes of Greek and Roman temples, Tayo finds balance and order. Kenneth Lincoln, an English profes-sor at the University of California at Los Angeles, explains the acceptance of hybridity — "the mixed blessings of sex and the sacred, Corn Mother and Water Sister, male rain and female rain, the procreative energies that exorcise poison and regenerate the living" (Lin-coln, 2008, 123). The war veteran reconnects intimately with earth, specifically, the centuries-old homeplace of the Laguna people. The coital act takes on elements of the Greek concept of *agape*, a giving without assurance of reciprocity. Unlike the insubstantial and unblessed love of "little sister" Laura, who abandons her four-year-old to Auntie Thelma, the anti-nurturer, an unloving aunt/foster mother, Ts'eh's affection confers stability. Critic Helen May Dennis, a specialist in native American literature at Warwick University, explains that Ts'eh makes Tayo "comfortable with separations and endings, because he learns from her that the larger pattern is one of healing and renewal ... that transitions are a necessary part of the process of survival" (Dennis, 2007, 67). In the spirit of the Amerindian concept of the "giveaway," a sharing ceremony among tribe members, Tayo bestows his passion and affection generously and without expectation of possessing or controlling his sex partner. Unlike Greek myth, in which copulation with the divine or semi-divine, such as Zeus's coupling with Leda and Hephaestus's marriage to Aphrodite, bestows harmful burdens and penalties, lovemaking between Tayo and Ts'eh furthers the healing and spiritual redemption begun by Betonie, the Chicano-Navajo medicine man.

The lustiness of a normal female becomes the antidote to Tayo's restlessness and guilt. Foretokened by the Mexican cantina dancer Night Swan, in late September 1948, Ts'eh's mystic allure re-energizes and strengthens her mate as though he penetrates her body to the depth of sacred water (*tsits*). Inside her vagina, he fears losing his way, but finds his path back to wellness through earthly trail markers. Employing magical realism, Silko alludes to a hallucinogenic experience like a peyote ritual by picturing Ts'eh alongside a moonflower, the *Datura stramonium* (jimson weed or locoweed) plant that peyote cultists and healers sometimes substitute for the button of *Lophophora wukkuansuu*, the divine peyote. As though infused with potent charm, the kind displayed in the myth of Pa'-caya'nyi's magic medicine, Ts'eh's effects on Tayo leave him "shaky inside," a post-sacramental response akin to Moses's obeisance to the burning bush and young Arthur Pendragon's amazement at the wonder-working sword in the stone (*ibid.*, 222).

## A PROPHECY OF RENEWAL

After Tayo's night of passion and sleep, a whiff of fresh winter air, snow, and ponderosa pine and a welcoming sunrise restore his joy in life. A touch of blessing derives from blue morning glories (*Ipomoea nil*), which climb strings to the window frames, a fragile variant of Grandmother Spider's web. More reassurance rains down from a blue autumn sky and blue-gray clouds. The terrain is devoid of signs that "white people had ever come to this land" (*ibid.*, 184). When Tayo reunites with Montaño in May 1949, the two discuss the curative powers of plants and the symbolic grandeur of a she-elk petroglyph. He fears that attrition will wear away the mythic shape, but Montaño reminds him, "As long as you remember what you have seen, then nothing is gone" (*ibid.*, 231). With Betonie's confidence in clairvoyance, she visualizes threats of white witchery against Tayo: "The violence of the struggle excites them, and the killing soothes them" (*ibid.*, 232). She pictures false rumors circulated by the army psychiatrists, other GIs, and the Bureau of Indian Affairs police about madness in Tayo as a trap "encircling slowly to choke the life away," the antithesis of Spider Woman's life web (*ibid.*).

Silko describes Ts'eh's magic as a geo-spiritual inscription and sacred logo on Tayo's consciousness, much like the extensive female icons and runes that Indigo encounters in Bath, England, and Lucca, Italy, in *Gardens in the Dunes* (1999). Tayo adheres to Ts'eh's other-worldly potency by following her tracks, a repetition of his following of ritual bear tracks at Betonie's hogan. Tayo clings to the heritage of the desert rock people by grasping at "niches for toes and fingers ... worn into the yellow sandrock" (*ibid.*, 222–223). Blessing the couple's union, the she-elk pictograph, chipped into a boulder, confers dynamism and shamanic healing. In retrospect after Emo plots a ritual assassination, Tayo relives the brief coupling with his spirit mate as a hallowed vision — "memories and shifting sounds heard in the night, diamond patterns, black on white; the energy of the designs spiraled deep, then protruded suddenly into three-dimensional summits, their depth and height dizzy and shifting with the eye" (*ibid.*, 228–229). Critic David Whitley characterizes the configuration of sight and sound into black diamonds as an image of the rattlesnake, the spiritual guardian of female genitals and of portals to the spirit world, through which snakes carry the guardianship of departed spirits.

The incorporeality of the sacred instills in Tayo a glimpse of his mission to his people. Critic Monica Avila notes the crucial role of his "sacrifice of self and complete surrender to vulnerability," a release of ego that Jesus called "becoming a little child again" (Avila, 2008, 53; Matthew 18:3). With Ts'eh, the veteran refoliates earth by gathering and planting seeds in the sand: "The plants would grow there like the story, strong and translucent as the stars" (Silko, 1977, 266). Through spiritual communion with Ts'eh throughout the spring and summer of 1949, the ailing GI reclaims the land and reunites with his lapsed respect for heritage. Fearful that Ts'eh is slipping from his physical embrace, he merges her image with the iconography of the sacred she-elk. Just as rain, sun, and wind erase the pictograph from the rock, the priestess Ts'eh begins to fade from his vision. More voice than body, she promises that, even though the paint will disappear from the elk image, the power remains so long as he remembers his holy trance. Thus, ritual intercourse with Ts'eh infuses Tayo's spirit with a holy mantle of agency to erase the hurt of world war from his people by the "renewal, rebalancing, and remaking of Laguna traditions" (Lincoln, 2008, 111).

See also Betonie; religion; ritual; Tayo; Tayo's genealogy; women.

• *References and further reading*

Avila, Monica. "Leslie Marmon Silko's *Ceremony*: Witchery and Sacrifice of Self," *Explicator* 67:1 (Fall 2008): 53–55.

Dean, John Emory. *Travel Narratives from New Mexico: Reconstructing Identity and Truth.* Amherst, NY: Cambria, 2009.

Dennis, Helen May. *Native American Literature: Towards a Spatialized Reading.* New York: Taylor & Francis, 2007.

Elliott, Gayle. "Silko, Le Sueur, and Le Guin: Storytelling as a 'Movement Toward Wholeness'" in *Scribbling Women & the Short Story Form: Approaches by American & British Women Writers*, ed. Ellen Burton Harrington. New York: Peter Lang, 2008, 178–192.

Gohrisch, Jana. "Cultural Exchange and the Representation of History in Postcolonial Literature," *European Journal of English Studies* 10:3 (December 2006): 231–247.

Lincoln, Kenneth. *Speak Like Singing: Classics of Native American Literature.* Albuquerque: University of New Mexico Press, 2008.

Martin, Holly E. "Hybrid Landscapes as Catalysts for Cultural Reconciliation in Leslie Marmon Silko's *Ceremony* and Rudolfo Anaya's *Bless Me, Ultima*," *Atenea* 26:1 (June 2006): 131–149.

May, Janice Susan. *Healing the Necrophilia of Euro-American Society in Leslie Marmon Silko's Gardens in the Dunes.* Radford, VA: Radford University, 2000.

Olsen, Erica. "Silko's Ceremony," *Explicator* 64:3 (Spring 2006): 190–192.

Powers, Peter Kerry. *Recalling Religions: Resistance, Memory, and Cultural Revision in Ethnic Women's Literature.* Knoxville: University of Tennessee Press, 2001.

Silko, Leslie Marmon. *Ceremony.* New York: Viking, 1977.

Spurgeon, Sara L. *Exploding the Western: Myths of Empire on the Postmodern Frontier.* College Station: Texas A&M University Press, 2005.

Whitley, David S. *Cave Paintings and the Human Spirit.* Amherst, NY: Prometheus Books, 2009.

# mothering

Silko's vignettes of Laguna matriarchy reveal a culture in which the woman is the source and matrix of life, the transmitter of culture through storytelling, and the solace and buffer against an unstable world. Kenneth Lincoln, an English professor at the University of California at Los Angeles, summarizes the multiphasic mothering role as "mother, lover, girlfriend, wife, flirt, witness, confessor, poet-singer, and storyteller" (Lincoln, 2008, 106). In the early story "Humaweepi, the Warrior Priest" (1974), the elderly mentor addresses the neophyte priest with assurance that the two can exist on the land like doe and fawn, a gendered image that dramatizes the nurturing bond between the old man or his pupil. More pairings of mother and child enhance the author's presentation of the Amerindian mother, including the mother's mourning of a drowned little girl in *Storyteller* (1981), a mythic tragedy that ends with the emergence of colored butterflies.

For the reflective story "Lullaby" (1974), Silko captures the strands of female life in a fiberwork image. The small girl Ayah combs burs and twigs from wool while the grandmother spins yarn on a cedar spindle and the mother dyes the threads gold, red, and yellow and weaves them at the loom. Unlike the ties that bind the women, Ayah's relationship with her husband Chato, a ranch hand, loses passion as the couple suffer the loss of their children and Chato retreats to Azzie's Bar and turns to alcohol for comfort. At least three children die in infancy, son Jimmie dies in a helicopter crash in war, and Danny and Ella separate from their parents after years in a tuberculosis hospital in Denver. The mothering image returns along with fiber in the final scene, in which Ayah lets her drunken husband freeze to death. Wrapped in their shared blanket, he smells of wine and urine, marks of his shame after an injury crushes his leg and ends his ranch employment. While tucking the blanket around him, "she felt the rush so big inside her heart for the babies," a maternal surge that extends to her adult husband (Silko, 1974, 17). As though comforting a little one, Ayah returns to the mothering role and sings a reassuring lullaby promising immortality.

## MOTHER AND WEAVER

Silko's pervasive references to the weaver Spider Woman (Ts'its'tsi'nako or Thought Woman), the web-spinning creator, relate the myth that becomes the fount of Pueblo maternalism. In *Sacred Water: Narratives and Pictures* (1993), the author pictures the four worlds of the Laguna ethos in a natural state of feminine loveliness: "Down there, clear streams run all year round, and flowers are everywhere because the Mother Creator is there" (Silko, 1993, 23). The author adds that, "whatever may become of us human beings," Mother Earth continues to bless all with purple hyacinth and white datura (*ibid.*). The connection of the female creator with maternal instincts corroborates the ethos of the Pueblo, who avoid the Old Testament damning of snakes and beasts and the pain of parturient women as God's punishments of humankind for disobedience. In a beatific vision, the Laguna honor the web-maker, who receives earth messages and prayers through the service of the snake Ma'shra'true'ee.

The antithesis of the Christian Virgin Mary, the mother of God, Spider Woman, the Pueblo primal mother, IS God. Through the beneficence of creation, she blesses humankind by instinctively softening the hurts of the world. The author exemplifies maternal solace in her memories of schoolyard rejection and of comforting stories told by Grandmother A'mooh and Aunt Susie Reyes Marmon. Silko refigures the loving, accepting elderly female in the fictional blind grandmother of Tayo, protagonist of *Ceremony* (1977). Without direct confrontation of the ogrous Auntie Thelma, her unnamed mother relays love and welcome to Tayo, the illegitimate mixed-blood son of Thelma's little sister Laura, a sullied unwed mother who "went with white men" (Silko, 1977, 128). Twisted by Catholic misogyny, Auntie, a regular Mass-goer, charges Tayo with humiliating the family. Kenneth Lincoln typifies the inter-pueblo method of repaying the unintentional bringer of dishonor to the group: "Family shame and tribal gossip keep the orphan distinct from his 'twin brother' Rocky, a full-blood inversely acculturated to White sports, schooling, and nationalistic war" (Lincoln, 2008, 116). Fortunately for the bastard nephew, a double layer of mothering, like Silko's Grandma A'mooh, lessens the sting of blame. Symbolic of a radiant, intrinsic relationship, the small space heater takes on the task of warming both Grandmother and Tayo during bleak cold days when combat memories pummel him toward madness.

The novelist dramatizes obsessive behavior in a kid that tries to nurse from a nanny goat weeks after the weaning process. The scenario suggests Tayo's return to Grandma's mothering, a redemptive force that fails to assuage the combat hurts that refuse Tayo any relief. The nanny's shoving of the kid from a feeding of cracked corn replicates the perverted mothering of Tayo's Auntie Thelma, who shuns the motherless nephew and denies him alleviation from weeping and vomiting in punishment of his illegitimate birth. In his reclamation, Silko mirrors the grandmother's affection and the brief sexual episode with Night Swan, the Mexican cantina dancer. In a setting rich with images of the weaver goddess—wicker chair, spiral stairs, blue dress and shawl, curtains—the dancer lightens the earth-bound Tayo. The one-night tryst prefaces Tayo's encounter with Ts'eh Montaño, a blend of mother and lover. As prophesied by the Chicano-Navajo shaman, the mountain demigoddess spreads her blanket on the stone floor and shares a mature conjugal love with Tayo, wooing him into sleep and peace. The text depicts a gentle wafting from white androcentric culture back to native matriarchy.

## THE ANTI-MOTHER

As described in *Almanac of the Dead* (1991), the arrival of white men to Indian land discounts the sacred womanly touch, which elevates the female and the domestic sphere to the divine. Above cooking, pottery making, and basket weaving, the height of housewifely duty—childcare—requires tact and nuance. Through everyday interaction, the mother conveys sources of character and resilience. To the child falls the responsibilities of memory and obedience, a pattern similar to the centrality of the African griot. Sullied and discredited by the anti-woman, anti-family cant of Catholic *conquistadores* and resultant Western materialism, women sink from queens of the family and clan to declassé drudges. Critic Jane Olmstead describes the ruin caused by a loss of mothering: "Love is nonexistent in the face of avarice, or the capacity for it has been destroyed or limited by the effects of personal trauma.... Sex is exalted as a commodity, the ultimate generalized fetish" (Olmstead, 1999, 471).

Without positive models, Silko's female characters turn to evil, the equivalent of Lilith, the Assyrian anti–Eve described in the Talmud. The denigration of maternity and housewifery fosters a generation of North American witchwomen — Leah Blue, the money-mad realtor and land developer; Iliana Gutierréz Panson, the house-proud victim of a polished marble staircase; Yoeme, the cynical wife; and Root's racist mother, who doesn't want her son to be extra work. Lecha, a clairvoyant who abandons son Ferro to Zeta, her drugged-out twin, infuses the boy with disillusions. From early childhood, he concludes that "his aunt did not raise him out of maternal love but out of duty" (Silko, 1999, 183). From the quandary of night terrors and neglect, he learns to "[hate] her, with all his being" (*ibid.*). In the post–Columbian revolution, atonement plunges the novel's most devoted mother into tragedy. Seese, the parent of doomed toddler Monte, pays a grievous penalty for her association with David, a homosexual who uses her as a cover for his preference for male sex partners. The worst of David's lovers, the filmmaker Beaufrey, murders and dismembers Monte in a cannibalistic attack on maternity and family. At the end of an epoch of decadence and family dissolution, aggressive women, led by the amazon Angelita, known as La Escapía and the Meat Hook, redirect tribes to a spirit-centered and humane culture.

## The Mothering Culture

Variant styles of mothering contrast women in *Gardens in the Dunes* (1999), an historical novel set in the Gilded Age and enriched with images of gardening, cooking, teaching, dressing, and feeding. Indigo and Sister Salt profit from a matriarchy headed by Grandma Fleet and Mama, her daughter. The foursome works at domestic chores while the elder pair instructs the girls on survival, gardening, tribal tradition, and wellness. The disruption of the Ghost Dance leaves the girls motherless, but well parented by their grandmother, who increases her emphasis on recycling trash, saving seeds, cultivating the Arizona sand dunes, and preserving food for hard times. As the grandmother slips away into decrepitude and death, Sister Salt moves easily into the parenting role and disciplines her younger sister.

As the action finishes the job of sundering the family, Indigo begins her own period of mothering by sheltering in a greenhouse and tending Linnaeus, the pet monkey of Dr. Edward and Hattie Abbott Palmer. The substitution of a maid as the monkey's mother during the family's absence requires the domestic's training in feeding and cleaning the cage, but Indigo doubts that Linnaeus will survive in a loveless household. As a literary foil to Dr. Edward Palmer, a passive, disinterested father figure, Indigo embraces nature. Critic Stephanie Li, an English teachers at the University of Rochester, describes the affinity for all living things as a "nurturing force rather than as a resource to be exploited and abused for capitalistic profit and personal gain," the aim of Edward and Mr. Eliot, both amoral bio-pirates for Albert Lowe & Company (Li, 2009, 19). While Edward plots to steal potentially lucrative citrus grafts from Bastia, Corsica, Indigo acquires experiences and seeds with which to upgrade and expand the Sand Lizard heritage to combat cultural erasure.

Silko's interwoven plot makes clear parallels between mothering, caretaking, and storytelling, all of which impact personal and collective identity. The Palmer family's visits to gardens and orchards in Bath, England, and Lucca, Italy, turn the subject matter from flowers and trees to ancient stone icons. The phallic icons, grotesque snake Madonnas, and vulvar representations concern Hattie, who worries that such "vulgar marble" might upset Indigo (Silko, 1999, 290). After encountering a particularly graphic stone figure of a "waterbird goddess" with women's breasts, the "owner and guardian of life water and life milk," Hattie proposes shielding Indigo from more blatant anatomical images (*ibid.*, 298). In the next scene, the concern proves unfounded after Indigo encounters the likeness of a seated mother bear cradling a cub. Memories of Mama and Grandma Fleet give Indigo the feeling of being loved and nestled, a soothing memory so far from home. Hattie responds to the Madonna-and-child pose with tears for her maternal emotions. For the sake of dramatic irony, Silko emphasizes the natural tenderness welling up in a woman who chooses not to conceive or give birth.

With the same fervor of other couples, the Palmers debate appropriate upbringing for Indigo. After Indigo's tantrum over the loss of her parrot, on the departure from Livorno, Italy, for Bastia, Corsica, Hattie is inclined to let the child sleep on the cool hotel floor and grieve for Rainbow. Edward, who wants Indigo to display "a docile willingness to serve," charges Hattie with soft-heartedness and an inability to discipline the child (*ibid.*, 309). His short-tempered scoldings illustrate a common parental fault, the transfer of time constraints and concerns to children, who become obstacles to adult expedience. Silko counters his illogic with frequent scenarios of patience and understanding, even from Delena's mama dog called Bear, leader of the Gypsy dog circus, "who led the troop despite her lameness" (*ibid.*, 381). After the dissolution of Hattie's marriage and Indigo's reunion with Sister Salt, Hattie realizes, "Without the girl she didn't know what she would do" (*ibid.*, 409). Ironically, the empty nest syndrome strikes hard at a woman who wanted no children in the first place.

In *The Turquoise Ledge* (2010), the author honors her own mother, Virginia Lee Marmon. Of the parental introduction to nature, Silko thanks Virginia for removing fear of the wild: "My mother taught us not to be afraid of snakes, so I started out my life with a pretty good attitude toward them" (Johnson, 2010). During walks in the arroyo, the author reveres rattlesnakes as "very peaceful beings with a generosity of spirit" (*ibid.*). One unusual anecdote reveals how she calms a diamondback rattler caught in bird netting and frees it before the heat kills it. From an animistic perspective, she intuits that the snake cooperates and poses no threat.

Silko's text revisits the subject of foster parenting, a standard among first peoples, especially after the decimation of a tribe. The memoir lauds the generosity of childless couples from the time of the Anasazi in rescuing children endangered by drought and resultant famine. The Anasazi combed the desert plateau of north central New Mexico for berries, roots, seeds, bird eggs, rodents, and birds and hunted the mountains and plains for antelope, bison, deer, and elk. Hunting and gathering brought tribe members in contact with orphans. Volunteer mothers also adopted infants and small children from starving villages of Hopi and Western Pueblo "so the babies might survive" (Silko, 2010, 20). The depiction illustrates the devotion of natives to survival via the fostering of subsequent generations of Indians.

*See also* abortion; Lecha and Zeta's genealogy; Seese's genealogy; women.

- *References and further reading*

Johnson, Cat. "Silko Heads for Santa Cruz," *Santa Cruz News* (21 October 2010).
Li, Stephanie. "Domestic Resistance Gardening, Mothering, and Storytelling in Leslie Mamon Silko's *Gardens in the Dunes*," *Studies in American Indian Literature* 21:1 (Spring 2009): 18–37.
Lincoln, Kenneth. *Speak Like Singing: Classics of Native American Literature.* Albuquerque: University of New Mexico Press, 2008.
Lippy, Charles H. *Pluralism Comes of Age: American Religious Culture in the Twentieth Century.* Armonk, NY: M. E. Sharpe, 2002.
Olmstead, Jane. "The Uses of Blood in Leslie Marmon Silko's *Almanac of the Dead*," *Contemporary Literature* 40:3 (Fall 1999): 464–490.
Shumaker, Conrad. *Southwestern American Indian Literature: In the Classroom and Beyond.* New York: Peter Lang, 2008.
Silko, Leslie Marmon. *Almanac of the Dead.* New York: Simon & Schuster, 1991.
_____. *Ceremony.* New York: Viking, 1977.
_____. *Gardens in the Dunes.* New York: Scribner, 1999.
_____. "Lullaby," *Chicago Review* 26:1 (Summer 1974): 10–17.
_____. *Sacred Water: Narratives and Pictures.* Tucson: Flood Plain Press, 1993.
_____. *The Turquoise Ledge: A Memoir.* New York: Viking Adult, 2010.

# music

As with word, rhythm, and image, sounds in the works of Leslie Marmon Silko derive from natural sources and wonders, such as the Jamaican poesy she admires in *The Delicacy and Strength of Lace: Letters between Leslie Marmon Silko and James Wright* (1986). Caribbean verse, emerging from the experience of black people, "loves the music of the language so much as it loves the people and the life which speak the language" (Silko &

Wright, 81–82). When applied to Amerindian storytelling, the concept of lyric melody-story embraces the uniqueness of each performance. As though honoring individual lives, the author recognizes the worth of variation. She values each occasion for telling and singing a narrative because "the story ... will never again be told in quite the same way with quite the same context" (*ibid.*, 86). Her statement enwraps a paradox—the stability of oral tradition and the revival of native beliefs in each new version.

In *The Turquoise Ledge* (2010), the author extols the indigenous nature of a grinding song that Indian women sing while pulverizing mesquite and palo verde beans into flour for tortillas. Aunt Susie Reyes Marmon recalls women singing work songs that "changed their task from hard work to pleasure as they lost themselves in the sounds and the words," a source of comfort in an oral culture (Silko, 2010, 18). The concept of solacing tunes dominates an early story, "Lullaby" (1974), in which the pacifying of babies prepares a Navajo crone for death. Ayah, an aged weaver of blankets and householder of a hogan, awaits death in the snow for herself and her defeated husband Chato. A natural urge to mother and comfort elicits a Yeibechei (spirit) song, a matriarchal ideal stated in pastoral verse that dates back to Ayah's mother and grandmother. By acquiescing to the spirit world, the song embraces the eternal in nature in the words "The earth is your mother,/she holds you" (Silko, 1974, 17). By singing the familiar stanzas, Ayah alleviates the fear of imminent death.

SONGS AS BEGINNINGS

In a setting where Meadowlark chirps the exploits of Coyote and where "in the night/I hear music/song of branches ... green spotted frogs sing to the river," nature and song undergird the sanctity of Silko's narratives about the Amerindian animistic faith and their survival songs (Silko, 1981, 37). In "Humaweepi, Warrior Priest," a coming-of-age story published in 1974, she sets the title figure, a 19-year-old initiate, in the outdoors, where his uncle readies him for priestly service. She states the gradual acquisition of wisdom in a description of incremental native education by example: "All your life ... every day I have been teaching you" (Silko, 1974, 164). Humaweepi realizes that "after all these years of sitting beside his uncle in the evenings, he knew the songs and chants for all the seasons and he was beginning to learn the prayers for the trees" (*ibid.*, 162). Unlike the force-feeding of didactic lessons in government boarding schools, the melodic instruction begun in childhood, like that exemplified by Marion Zimmer Bradley's *The Mists of Avalon* (1982), fits daily events as instinctively as words, facial expressions, and ritual gestures. The teaching method illustrates John Dewey's philosophy of instrumentalism, a theory that learning should predict and mirror reality.

Song moves to a central point of pedagogy as the novice Humaweepi enters the last phase of training. On the day of the initiation, the elderly mentor takes the boy to the shore of a mountain lake, a liminal spot between land and water that symbolizes Humaweepi's investiture, a sacred ordination that echoes the enlightenment of Arjuna in the *Bhagavad-Gita* (ca. 200 ) and of young Arthur Pendragon, soon-to-be king of Camelot in T. H. White's epic *The Once and Future King* (1958) and Mary Stewart's *The Hollow Hills* (1973). Like Moses before the burning bush in Exodus 3:2–5, Humaweepi removes his cowboy boots, a demonstration of humility and trust as well as respect for the earth that he has celebrated in song. The uncle sets the tone of the induction by singing to the wind and scattering corn pollen, a sanctifier of Humaweepi's vision that calls on Corn Woman (Nau'ts'ity'i), the nurturer and bringer of goodness. Silko applies a lyric tenderness to the onomatopoeia: "The songs were snowstorms with sounds as soft and cold as snowflakes; the songs were spring rain and wild ducks returning," harbingers of plenty (*ibid.*, 165). Humaweepi adds his own praise anthem along with gifts to propitiate a granite rock shaped like a bear. The invocation takes on new significance after the novice realizes that he honors his own installation as priest.

Silko depicts a lyric invocation as the appropriate address to the spirit world. The music of the ritual comes instinctively to Humaweepi, like night wind through trees. The preparation concludes with his song to the bear-shaped granite boulder asking for the powers of manhood and the sanctity of the warrior shaman. He intones: "Bear resting in the mountains sleeping by the lake," an amalgam of ferocious beast and a torpid state (*ibid.*, 166). Along with coral and turquoise beads from his medicine bundle, the song courts the bear spirit, a patron of Keres, Tewa, and Zuni healing societies. The old man replicates the internalization of animal power by howling like a wolf. Thus, beast songs and seasonal chants and prayers celebrate a continuum of natural powers that the new priest and his uncle share with the animal kingdom.

## Music and Healing

For her first novel, *Ceremony* (1977), the author incorporates variant sounds suited to dramatic contrasts of violence and restoration. To introduce the vortex of madness in Tayo, a troubled veteran of World War II, the story opens on his night-time torment, which takes the form of loud Japanese voices and of a "man singing in Spanish the melody of a familiar love song," a ballad that recalls Tayo's initiatory sexual experience (Silko, 1977, 5–6). The jumble signifies a mind trapped in reliving combat and captivity, a hellish polyglot set in counterpoint to technological cacophony—"loud, loud music from a big juke box, its flashing red and blue lights pulling the darkness closer" (*ibid.*, 6). Among army buddies Emo, Harley, Leroy Valdez, and cousin Pinkie, Tayo takes no comfort from demands for honky-tonk music "to get us happy right now" (*ibid.*, 48). Rather than enjoy the raucous sounds of the white world at Lalo's bar, Tayo combats rage that sends him crashing into Emo to plunge a jagged beer bottle into his gut.

In the reclamation of Tayo from the witchery that gives him no peace, the novelist juxtaposes music with therapy. In the room of Night Swan, the Mexican cantina dancer, a scratchy flamenco tune and exotic heel-tapping dance prefaces promiscuous lovemaking with Uncle Josiah and, later, with Tayo. On a rainy night, "the songs were soft and slow, without voices," as thunder cracks from the cliffs to the canyons in a paradoxical fusion of passion and loosened tension (*ibid.*, 98). A more therapeutic music emerges from the humming of Betonie, the Chicano-Navajo shaman who begins Tayo's recuperation from captivity by the Japanese during the Bataan Death March. In a clutch at empowerment from nature, Tayo chants to the mountain lion, a symbol of shapeshifting that prefigures the GI's advance from sickness to wellbeing. Accepting the challenge of recovery, he concludes, "It was up to him" (*ibid.*, 202). Silko blesses his soundness of body and mind in a lyric benediction, "Sunrise,/accept this offering,/Sunrise" (*ibid.*, 262).

## Song in Story

Adaptation of ritual and custom to the times dominates the author's later writings on religion and tradition. In *Storyteller* (1981), songs wind in and out of narratives. During a military expedition by Pueblo volunteers in "A Geronimo Story," the outrider Siteye sings "a spring song to the stars; it was an old song with words about rivers and oceans in the sky," a comfort to the initiate he teaches about tracking and caring for horses (Silko, 1981, 217). In similar style to the chant-songs of Ayah, Humaweepi, and Siteye, Silko's *Sacred Water: Narratives and Pictures* (1993) savors the rain music of the red-spotted toad. After a shower, "Hundreds of toads used to sing all night in a magnificent chorus with complex harmonies," a commentary on the demands of life for fauna (Silko, 1993, 63). Because of the destruction of the toads by two boys and a dog, symbols of New World conquest, she mourns the red algae that clouds the water and misses "the night-long choirs of multitudes of toads" (*ibid.*, 66). Recognizing nature's regenerative powers, she welcomes pollywogs in the pond and regrets that "the toads need a few years more to recover," a subtextual reference to Amerindian recuperative powers (*ibid.*).

A similar connection between revival and music fills the hopes of the Paiute in *Gardens in the Dunes* (1999). In a time of military coercion, imprisonment, and starvation, the people join in visions of a messiah: "As Jesus sang, hundreds and hundreds of people began to dance in a circle around him" (Silko, 1999, 23). Under a buffalo horn moon, the musical gathering propitiates the almighty to restore an idyllic haven — a peaceful age and the reclamation of earth by the buffalo and by the resurrected souls of the dead. In anticipation of the prophet Wovoka, Jesus, the Holy Mother, and Jesus' 11 children, the singing speaks of natural elements—clear water flowing from black rock, wind in the willows and grass, cottonwood groves, and green leaves. A crescendo intones "Dust of the whirlwind, dust of the mountains in the whirlwind, even the rocks are ringing!" (*ibid.*, 30). The epiphany of the messiah suggests Mother Earth in labor for a metaphysical birthing welcomed by the people's hosannas.

DOMESTIC MUSIC

Silko connects the Sand Lizard matriarchy with the natural music of their surroundings. Although the Ghost Dance erupts in violence, the escape of Indigo and Sister Salt results in a reunion six days later with Grandma Fleet, who announces her arrival with song. The girls identify their grandparent with music, such as a tune she made up the previous summer about a baby tarantula and her anthem greeting the rain. In childhood, Indigo naps after Grandma cajoles that "the bees sang a lullaby ... so she must not disappoint them" (*ibid.*, 69). In the absence of their guardian, the siblings absorb night music — "slithering, rustling, rattling, stirring, chirping, whistling, barking, all the sounds descended" (*ibid.*, 42). After the initial mourning for Grandma's death, Sister Salt takes up the domestic tune, a hum that indicates contentment from food grown, dried, and stored in the dugout. In hiding from searchers under bushes, Indigo consoles herself with the sound of crickets: "Desert singers like them knew the night was made for music and love," a linkage of lyricism and procreation (*ibid.*, 71). By connecting music with mothering and security, the text rids the desert compound of fears and comforts the girls during their period of mourning and mother hunger.

In a subsequent scene of smuggling and duplicity in the Surinam jungle, sound foregrounds theme. Silko describes how "the screeching and calling of the parrots and macaws rose to a crescendo" after the arsonist Mr. Eliot, an agent of Albert Lowe & Company, sets fire to the natural habitat of a rare orchid (*ibid.*, 142). She contrasts the squawks to the exuberance of *mestizos* who rescue Dr. Edward Palmer after the fire. Because a trained monkey locates the botanist, the natives compose a victory song, which they sing with drunken enthusiasm. The words celebrate retrieval of the white man: "We saved the white man ... we saved him with the help of the good luck monkey" (*ibid.*, 146). The jolly tune makes no secret of the fact that Palmer might have died. During his recovery in the boat *Louis XIV*, he listens to the hurdy-gurdy in the cantina, where the monkey turns the crank in exchange for gifts of dry bread, a subtle indictment of men like Eliot and Palmer, who "turn the crank" of bio-piracy in exchange for money.

After the formation of the Palmer foster family, the author turns Indigo's experiences and nostalgia into indulgences for the senses, including memories of Grandma Fleet telling stories or singing softly in a darkened room to comfort the sick. For Indigo, Oyster Bay, New York, swirls with delights—blue satin slippers, a meal of raw green corn eaten in the field, and the chorus of birdsong in Susan Palmer James's garden. Upon hearing Chinese thrushes in the glass aviary, Indigo interprets their "sunrise songs" as "tragic, maybe because they were born in cages," a doleful parallel of her own sadness during incarceration at the Sherman Institute in Riverside, California (*ibid.*, 193). At a cloister outside Bath, England, Indigo thrills to Aunt Bronwyn's singsong calls to her cattle, a link with nature that reminds the child of her former home in the Arizona sandhills. In an impromptu anthem to godhood, Indigo rushes into a stone circle above Bath to sing the black rock song and to rejoice that the Messiah passed through the area on his way east. Music fades from the falling action, where Hattie hears only chanted strains from Hispanic women attending Mass in Albuquerque, where the ritual seems "quite remote and strange to her now," evidence of Hattie's disconnection from rote Christian liturgy and her preference for the instinctive joy and melody of liberation (*ibid.*, 425).

*See also* religion; ritual.

• *References and further reading*

Brown, Julie. *American Women Short Story Writers: A Collection of Critical Essays.* New York: Routledge, 2000.
Iftekharrudin, Farhat. *The Postmodern Short Story: Forms and Issues.* Westport, CT: Praeger, 2003.
Ridington, Robin, and Jillian Ridington. *When You Sing It Now, Just Like New: First Nations Poetics, Voices, and Representations.* Lincoln: University of Nebraska Press, 2006.
Silko, Leslie Marmon. *Ceremony.* New York: Viking, 1977.
_____. *Gardens in the Dunes.* New York: Scribner, 1999.
_____. "Humaweepi, Warrior Priest" in *The Man to Send Rain Clouds: Contemporary Stories by American Indians*, ed. Kenneth Rosen. New York: Viking, 1974.
_____. "Lullaby," *Chicago Review* 26:1 (Summer 1974): 10–17.
_____. *Sacred Water: Narratives and Pictures.* Tucson: Flood Plain Press, 1993.
_____. *Storyteller.* New York: Seaver, 1981.
_____. *The Turquoise Ledge: A Memoir.* New York: Viking Adult, 2010.
_____, and James Wright. *The Delicacy and Strength of Lace: Letters between Leslie Marmon Silko and James Wright*, St. Paul, MN: Graywolf, 1986.

# myth

Silko's literary starting points derive from Aztec, Laguna, and Mayan prophecy, ritual, creation and migration lore, folk tales, and numinous historiography. The validation of lore in everyday places instills in Pueblo natives a regard for sandstone petroglyphs, cattails, and clouds. Springs offer the possibility of "the one and only true Emergence Place," the birthing canal through which first peoples pushed from the nether world onto earth. (Silko, 1996, 36). In "Humaweepi, Warrior Priest," a coming-of-age story published in 1974, the mythic quality of seemingly straightforward stories takes on a mysticism that grows out of normal human sense impressions of forest and stream. In the teaching of the 19-year-old title figure in preparation for shamanic duties, the elderly mentor speaks, sings, chants, prays, and models appropriate priestly behaviors through humility and perceptions of the outdoors. On the day that Humaweepi crosses the divide between ordinary man and spiritual leader, the old man communicates silently, a clairvoyance that marks their relationship as above the ordinary, the stuff of myth. At the right moment, a lakeside initiation advances to Pueblo lore as a timeless tale of induction into medicine rites, an adaptive, syncretic story empowered by the dynamics of spirituality. For this reason, as the author explains in "Cottonwood" in *Storyteller* (1981), the storyteller performs an act of continuity in relating episodes with episodes—"stories/about drastic things which/must be done/for the world to continue" (Silko, 1981, 65).

The author justifies her immersion in myth in the essay "Interior and Exterior Landscapes: The Pueblo Migration Stories" (1996) by echoing the Jungian concept of the collective unconscious: "The myth, the web of memories and ideas that create an identity, is a part of oneself" (*ibid.*, 43). In "Estoy-eh-muut and the Kunideeyahs" in *Storyteller*, she echoes the wisdom of the Greek fabulist Aesop by depicting Spider Woman as a tiny arachnid in a hole under a snakeweed plant and by picturing chipmunks carrying water in acorn shell cups to revive from thirst the hero Estoy-eh-muut. In the style of Aesop's mouse chewing the lion free of a captor's net, the small mammals elevate themselves in importance despite their small size and limited strength by liberating the great Pueblo hunter. The combined narrative elements embody the destruction of evil through the reemergence of humankind in newer worlds purified through cataclysm.

Unique to myth is the manipulation of time. According to humanist Ernest Stromberg, a specialist in Indian oral tradition, "Myths of ongoing creation also enfold historical development within the patterns of mythic timelessness," a unity of time that compresses the past with the present and future (Stromberg, 2006, 220). To account for Silko's *tour de force* ethnomythography in "Yellow Woman" and *Almanac of the Dead* (1991), Stromberg enhances his definition of layered time as "a 'timefulness,' in which all times are present at once" (*ibid.*, 222). By envisioning a "concentric unfolding and cyclic emergences," the author assumes the role of shaman/storyteller. She pushes the bounds of past tellings to reveal upheavals that precede "new levels of complexity and consciousness," a cosmic form of redemption and release from threats embedded in contemporary events, such as the twentieth-century Indian's confrontation with drugs, automatic weapons and gang wars, sexual permissiveness, and AIDS (*ibid.*, 220). Both cathartic and therapeutic, the eternal compression of time readies humankind to accept and profit from change, the task of Ayah, Betonie, Geronimo, Humaweepi, Indigo, Lecha, Maytha and Vedna, Sister Salt, Sterling, Tayo and his grandma, and Yellow Woman, Silko's Amerindian survivors.

With the skill of the 1,000 life-sparing stories told by the Arabic raconteur Scheherazade in *The Thousand and One Nights* (ca. A.D. 942), Silko's metafictional novel *Ceremony* (1977) expresses Keresan cosmology, which subverts the Western hero tale and its vindication of the genocide of first peoples. As described by Sara L. Spurgeon, a specialist in women's studies at the University of Arizona, myth, by its nature, "[compels] belief in itself and its narrative" (Spurgeon, 2005, 96). Influenced by Pueblo *hummah-hah* (long ago stories) as she reexamines American history, the novelist inserts mythic reality in her text by omitting chapter breaks as boundaries of chronology. Critic James Ruppert, English department chair at the University of New Mexico, described the absence of boundaries as a form of simultaneity—a unified telling of events mimicking concentric waves fanning out from a pool where a rock disturbs the surface. The circularity of storytelling enhances the myth of Spider Woman (Tsi'its'tsi'nako or Thought-Woman), the arachnid generator of all and the fount of imagination. Like the mad Cumaean Sibyl who swirls her leaf pages in Virgil's *Aeneid* (19 B.C.), Spider Woman, a parallel prophet and female agent, commands order out of chaos. According to Robin Ridington, professor of mythology at the University of British Columbia, and Jillian Ridington, an expert in the lore of first peoples, Silko invokes Spider Woman to establish the Laguna concept of creativity as the bedrock of spirituality: "The idea that thought and substance combine in the creation of storied lives is central to Native American spirituality" (Ridington & Ridington, 2006, 163). Spider Woman reshapes stories into new transmissions and perceptions as though spinning a web with delicate strands forming sturdy geometric connections. In the style of a cosmic divinity, she produces disembodied voices and personalities, shards of imagery and light, dabs of color, and realities lopped into pieces. By juxtaposing these myths, Silko establishes themes and tone modifications that reconfigure Spider Woman's inklings.

SALVATION THROUGH STORIES

To counter the evil of 50-foot wolf-proof steel mesh fences, Lalo's bar, white man's psychiatry at a veteran's hospital in Los Angeles, imprisonment in a Japanese war camp in the Philippines, and the atomic bombs that rain death on noncombatants at Hiroshima and Nagasaki on August 6 and 8, 1945, Silko relies on good earth magic, the health-restoring sun, clouds, corn, Indian tea, and spring water. A examples of opposing forces, she presents Spider Woman's sisters, Corn Woman (Nau'ts'ity'i) and Reed Woman (I'tcts'ity'i), as a separate yin and yang, the sweating planter and the self-indulgent river soaker. A quarrel results in a power struggle, which sends Reed Woman "down below" to the four levels of the underworld and leaves earth to a rainless planting season that dries up beans and corn, the staffs of life (Silko, 1977, 12). In the style of myth, the loss of sibling harmony explains the dry weather that starves the Laguna. In boyhood, Tayo learns the connection between the sins that bring drought and the intervention of the greenbottle fly, the humble intermediary who negotiates forgiveness for the Laguna to restore rainfall. Uncle Josiah narrates the story of the fly to remind Tayo that flies, though seemingly unimportant insects, "[ask] forgiveness for the people" to relieve humanity of the punishment for sin (*ibid.*, 93). Redemption in the brief episode foreshadows the massive burdens of guilt and shame that the adult Tayo, the sacred hunter, brings home from war.

To express the anguish of the war survivor, Silko relies on beast fable, a standard genre in native American literature. A telling bear story explains Tayo's fault in volunteering for the U.S. Marines and in fighting the Japanese in the Philippines during World War II. The story of the boy who strays into bear country predicts a potent bestiality that subsumes his consciousness, turning his humanity into atavistic behavior. Like the battle fatigue that imprisons Tayo's spirit, a bear sickness overwhelms the boy. Retrieving him from the mountains rescues him bodily from bears, but leaves his soul suspended between bestial and human consciousness. Only "step by step" ritual can retrieve his spirit (*ibid.*, 130). The story implies that departure from home can bedazzle and doom the mind to doubt everyday reality, the tragedy of "little sister" Laura, Rocky, the acolyte Shush, and the prostitutes and winos trapped on a riverbank dump in Gallup. Critic John A. McClure, an English professor at Rutgers, connects the abduction of wits to "colonial cultural kidnapping," which "requires complex acts of 'calling' and recalling, acts that can be initiated by spiritual adepts and the ceremonies they have devised" (McClure, 2007, 142). The calling retrieves the *naïf* whom war strands in "intolerable in-betweenness, or negative hybridity" (*ibid.*). Betonie, the Chicano-Navajo shaman, describes Tayo's quandary as assuming an alien identity, a dead Coyote pelt that cloaks GIs and creates a scary appearance to friends, family, and community. The myth explains the craziness of post-traumatic stress disorder as "the dry skin ... still stuck to his body," a psychic pollutant that takes the form of alcoholism, bar brawling, and uncontrollable vomiting, weeping, flashbacks, and retreat from light (Silko, 1977, 153).

## MYTHIC QUALITIES OF HEROES

To indicate epic strengths similar to those of Samson, Joshua, Achilles, and Hiawatha, Silko endows Tayo with a messianic gift. It is up to him to dispel what analyst Jana Gohrisch, a literature expert at the University of Leibnitz, calls "Native American witchcraft gone wild," the cause of white sorcery (Gohrisch, 2006, 238). To rip off the clinging coyote fur, particularly hallucinations, distorted logic, and tendencies toward violence, the war veteran must identify with all Indians and with the history of colonization of the Western Hemisphere by European usurpers. By broadening his worldview through experience and struggle, he empowers himself as a "special breed," the epic savior, the Odysseus, El Cid, and Moses of North America's first peoples. At the face-off at the Jackpile uranium mine during the autumnal solstice, Tayo stands at a cosmic divide and wrestles with rage that goads him to stab the skull of Emo, his enemy, with a screwdriver. Like the myth of Sun Man gambling with Kaup'a'ta, the immortal high-stepper from Reedleaf town, Tayo evades either-or thinking and opts for an end to vengeance. Much as Sun Man has no hope of killing the divine trickster, Tayo stands no chance of rescuing Harley from torture or of eradicating the post-war venom of veterans like Emo, the collector of enemy teeth. Sun Man chooses to use the flint knife to lop out Kaup'a'ta's eyes and hoist them into the heavens as stars; Tayo resolves to leave Emo and his bewitched war buddies to their own internal extinction. In the format of the myth, Kaup'a'ta can't be killed by a human. Similarly untouchable, Emo enters banishment from the pueblo to California, the white man's fantasyland and source of his hyped-up ego and dreams of sexual and material bliss.

To restate myth for her own times, Silko draws on a fascination with oral and plastic arts, including the drawings of a galloping herd in "How to Hunt Buffalo" (1994), an unpublished fourfold that honors the mystic union between the hunter and the self-sacrificing "chosen one" and the petroglyphs of a she-elk in *Ceremony* (Silko, 1994, 3). To interviewer Ellen L. Arnold, the author acknowledged herself a devotee of nature — a "stone-worshipper" who reveres the inexplicable spirit of rocks (Silko, 2000, 166). She enlarged on the powers of a mineral: "A rock has being and spirit, although we may not understand it.... In the end we all originate from the depths of the earth" (*ibid.*).

## MYTH AS ECSTASY AND REALITY

To syncretize earth forms and cultures in the quest novel *Gardens in the Dunes* (1999), the author reduces the perception of harmony to a child's vision of dancing, singing, and awaiting a visit from the Messiah. The gynocentric assembly of worshippers harmonizes women in face painting, dance, chant, and food sharing. Indigo, still impressionable and reliant on female instruction from Mama and Grandma Fleet, continues her learning during a journey to Oyster Bay, New York; Bath, England; and Lucca, Italy. Enhancing her intellectual curiosity is a receptivity toward miracle and salvation, which she learns from the readings of her foster mother, Hattie Abbott Palmer. The text pictures Hattie's eagerness to absorb world mythos: "When she finished with Greek, Roman, and Norse mythology, she began to read about the Egyptians," the source of details about "hidden tombs and mummies," symbolic inquiries into the nature of death and the afterlife (Silko, 1999, 95). Silko bombards Hattie with divinity from varied sources. While studying medieval church history and heresy at a seminar hosted by Harvard Divinity School, Hattie turns to Valentinus, "who prayed to the Mother as the mythic eternal Silence," an iconic female who buttresses Hattie's consciousness during her recuperation from separation, widowhood, and rape (*ibid.*, 98). Critic David Murray, a specialist in American studies at the University of Nottingham, lists the sources of enlightenment for both Indigo and her foster mother — "Tarot cards and Ezekiel ... Celtic and Arthurian Grail legends, and sacred groves and circles" along with plant myths and statuary dramatizing the sacred genitals of male and female (Murray, 2007, 145). Rather than confuse Indigo or dash her hopes that Mama is dancing her way across Europe with Wovoka cultists, the multiple images of divinity reassure the child, relieving her vulnerability in a strange land. At the same time, the mythic strands enfold Hattie in a self-study that relieves her ignorance of marriage, sexuality, and womanhood.

Silko's stories retain the vigor and cunning of age-old narratives explaining the way of things on earth. She exemplifies the sanctity of snakes, birds, and turtles and the process by which turquoise forms in hardened lava, the focuses of the memoir *The Turquoise Ledge* (2010), her most recent work. She graces the text with a myth about wind from a cave announcing the arrival of bison on earth, the beginning of an indigenous golden age. The narrative endows an owl with its mythic title, "Owl the Warrior Scalp-taker, the Sacrificer," a gesture of respect to the hunting style of an avian predator (Silko, 2010, 258). A similar respect for the hummingbird elevates it to the level of the owl and eagle, both great warriors and hunters. Critic MariJo Moore characterizes the palpability of Silko's mythic lore as a quality found in all Amerindian literature: "To Native thinkers, the mythic is not a trick of the human mind but a pulsating fact of existence as real as a village, a trailer court, a horse, a spouse, or a tradition is real" (Moore, 2003, 311).

*See also* creation; Spider Woman; storytelling; Tayo.

• *References and further reading*

Chabram, Angie, and Rosa Linda Fregoso. "Decolonizing Imperialism: Captivity Myths and the Postmodern World in Leslie Marmon Silko's *Ceremony*" in *Exploding the Western: Myths of Empire on the Postmodern Frontier*, ed. Sara L. Spurgeon. College Station: Texas A&M University Press, 2005.

Gohrisch, Jana. "Cultural Exchange and the Representation of History in Postcolonial Literature," *European Journal of English Studies* 10:3 (December 2006): 231–247.

Hailey, David E., Jr. "The Visual Elegance of Ts'its'tsi'nako and the Other Invisible Characters in *Ceremony*," *Wicazo Sa Review* 6:2 (Autumn 1990): 1–6.

Lee, A. Robert. *Multicultural American Literature: Comparative Black, Native, Latino/a and Asian American Fictions.* Jackson: University Press of Mississippi, 2003.

McClure, John. *Partial Faiths: Postsecular Fiction in the Age of Pynchon and Morrison.* Athens: University of Georgia Press, 2007.

Moore, MariJo. *Genocide of the Mind: New Native American Writing.* New York: Nation Books, 2003.

Morel, Pauline. "Counter-Stories and Border Identities: Storytelling and Myth as a Means of Identification, Subversion, and Survival in Leslie Marmon Silko's 'Yellow Woman' and 'Tony's Story'" in *Interdisciplinary and Cross-cultural Narratives in North America*, eds. Mark Cronlund Anderson and Irene Maria Blayer. New York: Peter Lang, 2005.

Murray, David. *Matter, Magic, and Spirit: Representing Indian and African American Belief.* Philadelphia: University of Pennsylvania Press, 2007.

Porter, Joy, and Kenneth M. Roemer. *The Cambridge Companion to Native American Literature.* Cambridge: Cambridge University Press, 2005.

Ridington, Robin, and Jillian Ridington. *When You Sing It Now, Just Like New: First Nations Poetics, Voices, and Representations.* Lincoln: University of Nebraska Press, 2006.

Ruppert, James. "Dialogism and Mediation in Leslie Silko's *Ceremony*," *Explicator* 51:2 (Winter 1993): 129–134.

Silko, Leslie Marmon. *Gardens in the Dunes*. New York: Scribner, 1999.
_____. "How to Hunt Buffalo" (1994), unpublished fourfold housed in the Bienecke archives at Yale University Library, New Haven, CT.
_____. *Storyteller*. New York: Seaver, 1981.
_____. *The Turquoise Ledge*. New York: Viking, 2010.
_____. *Yellow Woman and a Beauty of the Spirit: Essays on Native American Life Today*. New York: Simon & Schuster, 1996.
_____, and Ellen L. Arnold. *Conversations with Leslie Marmon Silko*. Jackson: University Press of Mississippi, 2000.
Spurgeon, Sara L. *Exploding the Western: Myths of Empire on the Postmodern Frontier*. College Station: Texas A&M University Press, 2005.
Stromberg, Ernest. *American Indian Rhetorics of Survivance: Word Medicine, Word Magic*. Pittsburgh: University of Pittsburgh Press, 2006.
Winsbro, Bonnie C. *Supernatural Forces: Belief, Difference, and Power in Contemporary Works by Ethnic Women*. Amherst: University of Massachusetts Press, 1993.

## names

Silko's intuitive selection of character and place names invokes reader perceptions of nuance and theme, such as the solacing euphony in "A'mooh" in her grandma's name. One evocative example, "Bravura" (1974), takes shape in a vignette bearing the snide name of the protagonist, a starry-eyed poet who leaves academe to emulate the life of a poor Southwestern Indian. For her first story, "The Man to Send Rain Clouds" (1969), she names a deceased sheepherder Teofilo, Spanish for "beloved of God," a version of the Greek "Theophilus," an honorary title once conferred on Jesus' apostles. The name rounds out an animistic burial rite by which Ken and Leon honor Teofilo's corpse with a gray feather, red blanket, face paint, and a sprinkling of corn meal and pollen, natural elements that accentuate the title image of rain and survival. To enhance the divide between animism and Christianity, Silko creates confusion in the dialogue with Father Paul, bearer of the name of St. Paul, the letter writer to new Christians and instigator of orthodox Christian worship. A Franciscan parish priest viewing a death notice from Western tradition, Paul misinterprets the arrival as good news that Teofilo is alive. The priest misunderstands that the shepherd is "O. K. now" because the native men have accorded it an earth-based blessing that links the departed spirit with the ancestral tradition of watching over their progeny and sending rain for their crops. The storytelling of Teofilo returns to "Tony's Story" (1969) with a reminder that native lore has power in situations of postcolonial menace.

In *Ceremony* (1977), Silko's quest novel, she chooses evocative names to create subtextual commentary, such as the humor of the prostitute Helen Jean's searching for war veterans at the El Fidel bar, a title suggesting fidelity. Rocky bears a nickname reminiscent of the Laguna boulders. His real name — Augustine — derives from the obsessive Catholicism of Auntie Thelma. Shush, the shaman's apprentice, carries the Diné name for "bear," the source of his feral characterization. For the restless, beer-swilling Harley, a returnee from World War II with a Purple Heart, she selects a macho symbol, the Harley-Davidson motorcycle, which American riders embraced in 1903 as a symbol of virility. Critic Deborah Clarke, a professor of English and Women's Studies at Pennsylvania State University, explains how the name reverses the car industry's commercialization of Indian names — Cherokee, Dakota, Pontiac — for vehicles. By giving the GI the name Harley, "Silko subtly challenges both the symbolic appropriation of Indian culture by car manufacturers and the implied masculinity of such culture" (Clarke, 176). A typical good-timer in his mid-twenties, Harley slumps sideways on a burro, a posture reminiscent of the casual hog rider. He exults in "good times ... courtesy of the U.S. government," a reference to disability checks from the army (Silko, 1977, 36).

In the same novel, Silko uses implication to connect human healers with nature's powers. Ts'eh Montaño, a surreal life force whose given name means "rock" in Navajo, suggests a shortening of Tse'pi'na (Mount Taylor) and of Ts'its'tsi'nako (Spider Woman or Thought Woman), both female forms of divinity. The Chicano-Navajo shaman Betonie bears the name of *Stachys officinalis*, a medicinal herb valued as a cure for cranial disease, an appropriate curative for Tayo's mental torments. Dispensed thrice daily in the proportion of a half-ounce of dried leaves to a cup of boiling water, betony is a gentle curative for convulsion, epilepsy, and respiratory difficulties. Spicy and sweet, dried betony leaves are effective as a nervine or tonic to treat fever, headache, hysteria, palpitation, neuralgia, and other autonomic disorders, the maladies that leave Tayo suddenly weak and sweating with terror.

For *Storyteller* (1981), Silko chooses emblematic names for characters, particularly Silva, the tall Navajo rustler-seducer whose name means "river." An icon of untamed freedom and unpredictable behavior, he represents unbounded undertow and wanderlust, two aspects of his character that prefigure a conflict and shooting involving a pudgy white rancher. Like Coyote, the classic trickster of Amerindian cautionary tales, Silva represents the uncontrolled ego, an unprincipled despoiler and a delightful individual whose antics provide listeners with vicarious fun. Unlike Yellow Woman (Kochininako), the assertive wife of Whirlwind Man and mother and symbol of yellow corn, Silva is a transitory figure whose residence whittles down to bare necessities for the seduction of women. Silva's fate, like a roiling current in flood, remains troubled and ambiguous, a state left unresolved as Yellow Woman flees the sound of gunfire in the background to return home to husband Al.

## Naming as Caricature

*Almanac of the Dead* (1991), Silko's complex allegorical novel, perpetuates the choice of comic designations (Rambo-Roy, Eddie Trigg, Bingo, Wilson Weasel Tail, Awa Gee, and Keemo "chemo" the ecologist) and enigmatic names to impact atmosphere and motif, for example:

- Tacho (Greek for "Speed"), the spy who hastens the revolution by conveying prophecies from sacred macaws
- Iliana (Greek for "Trojan woman") Gutiérrez, the doomed wife who fosters her own death from a broken neck by building a slick marble staircase into her ornate mansion
- Alegría (Spanish for quick; also the name of a type of candy) Martinez-Soto, the alluring, but duplicitous Venezuelan lover/second wife of insurance mogul Menardo Panson who conducts an affair with Sonny Blue, the privileged son of Max "Mr. Murder" Blue
- Max (Latin for "the greatest") Blue (American slang for "lewd and risqué"), the retired New Jersey mafioso who orchestrates murders long distance while he plays golf under armed guard
- Leah (Hebrew for "weary") Blue, Max's unloved wife who bears the name of the first mate of the biblical patriarch Jacob, who preferred Leah's beautiful sister Rachel

- Liria (Hebrew for "harp") Brito, the sister of Sarita and lover of brother-in-law Calabazas
- El Feo (the ugly), leader of a raw peasant revolt.

A prime mover in the action, Angelita (Spanish for "little angel") answers to a satiric name for the executioner of Bartolomeo, a Cuban devotee of Marx who bears the Hispanic version of Bartholomew, an apostle of Christ martyred by flaying, upside down crucifixion, and decapitation. Yoeme bears the Yaqui word for "person," a synonym for Yaqui, the natives occupying Sonora, Mexico, as far north as Arizona. Calabazas, a *mestizo* white-hater and drug smuggler, names himself "pumpkins" for the pumpkins and squash his family grows at San Rafael. Upon his transport of produce into Tucson on All Souls' Day, he congratulates himself: "What I sold that load for was a great deal of money. My wife's family had to take notice" (Silko, 1991, 218). Mosca (housefly) and Lecha (milk) needle Root, the scion of Grandpa Gorgon, a white bloodsucker who makes his fortune during the Indian Wars by cutting bootleg whiskey with river water and formaldehyde. The choice of "gorgon" for a name connects the act of hooking Indians on rotgut with the Greek snake-headed mesmerizer Medusa, a gorgon who kills her prey by paralyzing them with a single glance. In reference to the passage of supernatural powers through the family genealogy, Lecha asks Root "if the sins of the great-grandfather bash in the head of the great-grandson" (*ibid.*, 214).

In the midst of vicious character duplicity, the protagonist Sterling, the dependable Laguna yardman and moral center of the novel, learns early to avoid Cy, Mag, Nitro, and Stray, four snarling guard Dobermans named for cyanide, magnum, nitroglycerin, and stray bullets, emblems of varied forms of death that stalk the text. The most pitiable character, the blonde transcriber Seese (cease) bears a name that cries for the cessation of torment to her six-month-old son Monte, named for a game of chance that reflects his ill fate. After abductors steal Monte from his crib, they transport him to a *finca* (plantation) in Colombia and murder him to obtain his blood and organs for sale. The atrocity epitomizes the novel's plunge into the extremes of decadence and cannibalism. In the falling action, it is Sterling (English for "genuine and reliable") who completes a pilgrimage home to Laguna to reinstate himself after betraying the tribe by allowing Hollywood filmmakers to desecrate the holy stone serpent. When Sterling focuses on the messenger snake, he sees that it looks south for a pan–Indian reconciliation. Like the novelist herself, Sterling violates clan taboos to bring change to the pueblo.

## PARODY AND SYMBOLISM

For *Gardens in the Dunes* (1999), Silko chooses meaningful names for places and characters, such as Mr. Grabb, the corporate attorney for Albert Lowe & Company, and Mr. Wiley, the conniver in bootlegging, gambling, and whoring. The monkey Linnaeus bears a suitable name for the pet of a botanist — the primate studied by Darwin and bearing the surname of the Swedish scientist who created the binomial naming system for living things, a token of the crusade to name and control all earthly organisms. Indigo names the parrot Rainbow for his brilliant feathers. "Abbott" identifies a prominent, lineage-conscious family at Oyster Bay on Long Island, whose cook Lucille (Latin for "little light") introduces young Hattie to the bible. Indigo, child of the Sand Lizard family in Arizona, carries the common designation of the *Baptisia tinctoria*, a bright blue annual flower that Indians tie into bundles for smudging or burning to purify the air before rituals. She receives mothering from Hattie Abbott Palmer, whose surname suggests a Christian leader, and from Aunt Bronwyn, whose Welsh genealogy derives from "fair breast," a suitable identification of a maternal rescuer of needy women.

Reflecting on her years in Needles, California, and the racism of whites, Indigo thinks the town deserves to be called by the word for "sharp-pointed objects" (Silko, 1999, 120). The concept of sharpness recurs in her collection of the *la professoressa* Laura's black glad-ioli, flamboyant cutting flowers bearing the Latin name "little swords." Silko links the unusual species to the glamour and fertility of the female. Typical of Indigo's adaptation of her travel souvenirs to desert nurturing, she realizes that the gladiolus corms produce both flowers and a tasty new food. Thus, in an everyday horticultural epiphany on "little swords," she reduces the piercing weapons of the New World conquerors to an aesthetic utility. In the restoration of the Sand Lizard clan, the author honors the birth of Bright Eyes, the Afro-Indian son of Sister Salt and Big Candy, the Afro–Big Stick Indian cook and brewer at a construction project. The baby, nicknamed the "little grandfather," bears the name of Dr. Susan "Bright Eyes" La Flesche Picotte, an Iowa-Omaha from Nebraska who became the nation's first female Indian physician. The nickname completes connection to the Sand Lizard beginnings from Grandfather Snake, the uncle of the original Sand Lizard.

*See also* Geronimo; Seese's genealogy; Sister Salt; symbolism.

• *References and further reading*

Clarke, Deborah. *Driving Women: Fiction and Automobile Culture in Twentieth-Century America*. Baltimore: Johns Hopkins University Press, 2007.
Dunn, Carolyn. "The Trick Is Going Home: Secular Spiritualism in Native American Women's Literature" in *Reading Native American Women: Critical/Creative Representations*, ed. Inés Hernández-Avila. Lanham, MD: Altamira, 2005.
Sackman, Douglas C. "A Garden of Worldly Delights" in *Land of Sunshine: An Environmental History of Metropolitan Los Angeles*, ed. William Deverell. Pittsburgh: University of Pittsburgh Press, 2005.
Schorcht, Blanca. *Stories Voices in Native American Texts: Harry Robinson, Thomas King, James Welch, and Leslie Marmon Silko*. New York: Routledge, 2003.
Silko, Leslie Marmon. *Almanac of the Dead*. New York: Simon & Schuster, 1991.
_____. *Ceremony*. New York: Viking, 1977.
_____. *Gardens in the Dunes*. New York: Scribner, 1999.
_____. "The Man to Send Rain Clouds," *New Mexico Quarterly* 38:4/39:1 (Winter-Spring 1969): 133–136.
_____. *Storyteller*. New York: Seaver, 1981.
Tallent, Elizabeth. "Storytelling with a Vengeance," *New York Times Book Review* (22 December 1991): 6.

# nativism

Silko's personal and literary worlds converge on native tribalism in a geomythic place, a grounding for her verse, essays, myths, and stories. Author Simon Joseph Ortiz depicts the concept as "[relying] on the multifaceted, lived experience of families who gather in particular places" (Ortiz, 2006, 244). Silko describes the native cosmology as an outgrowth of the spinning of Spider Woman (Ts'its'tsi'nako or Thought Woman), the creator mother who nurtures and superintends the universe. She generates "a spider's web — with many little threads radiating from a center, crisscrossing each other. As with the web, the structure will emerge as it is made and you must simply listen and trust ... that meaning will be made" (Silko, 1981, 54). Her coming-of-age story "Humaweepi, the Warrior Priest" (1974), depicts the centrality of reverence and obedience in the title character, an orphan who grows up under the care and tutelage of an elderly Indian. Learning the philosophy and rituals of the Pueblo requires Humaweepi to follow native traditions of sleeping and eating in the wild and walking barefoot in the snow, a closeness to earth that toughens the spirit for endurance and sacred service. When he advances from novice to shaman, Humaweepi sings instinctively the bear song, a native gesture of reverence to a dominant animal spirit. Analyst Christopher Douglas, a literature expert at the University of Victoria in British Columbia, refers to the inner resources as "memory in the blood," which "describes learned things—acquired things—as both inherited and natural" (Douglas, 2009, 248).

Silko respects and safeguards Laguna lore. In the satiric story "Bravura" (1974), the author challenges the Indian wannabe for violating the outsider's understanding of native life and thought. Her essay "An Old Fashioned Indian Attack in Two Parts," anthologized in *The Remembered Earth* (1979), vilifies fiction that profits from publishing native legend as original writing. In the opening line, she calls anthropologist Franz Boas, writer William Eastlake, anthropologist-author Oliver La Farge, and ethnologist John Reed Swanton intruders who purloined prayers, songs, and stories from American communities for literary exploitation. She vilified extra-tribal "Indian experts" for violating truth and their own history and origins. Of La Farge's Pulitzer Prize–winning novel *Laughing Boy* (1929), the story of a bereaved Southwestern Indian, Silko accused the author of "[falling] victim to the assumption that he could write a novel centered in the consciousness of a Navajo man" (Silko, 1979, 211). More damning of La Farge's effort at recreating native sensibility was the selection of a protagonist who had "almost no contact with white people" (*ibid.*). Silko seethes at writers who pretend to know Indian culture and thought and who reduce aborigines to a literary device, "the grossest stereotype of all" (*ibid.*, 213).

## Belonging vs. Materialism

In the post–World War II milieu of Silko's generation, her characters retreat into native mysticism to shuck off the materialism and chaos of the American social fabric. A variety of intrusions jeopardize their native integrity, from Bureau of Indian Affairs boarding schools and barbed wire fences around ranches to the World War II draft, the retrieval of uranium from the Jackpile mine adjacent to the Laguna Pueblo, and the testing of atomic destruction at Trinity site outside the Los Alamos laboratory in central New Mexico. In *Almanac of the Dead* (1991), the author speaks through Calabazas, a Yaqui smuggler, a pervasive belief in the inseparability of the Amerindian and the outdoors: "It was the land itself that protected native people" (Silko, 1991, 222). In the evaluation of critic Holly E. Martin, a literature specialist and assistant dean at Notre Dame University, the dynamic landscape screens the acculturated native from the falsehoods of the white world and "jolts the character into a heightened state of his own cultural hybridity" (Martin, 2006, 131). The relationship between people and events depends so completely on the Pueblo settlements of the American Southwest that they produce a psychic positioning—a verifiable source of stability and ego defense. Her themes work toward restoring justice and self-determination to the exploited Pueblo while maintaining the integrity and purity of their homeland.

The author epitomizes an approach-avoidance dilemma, the nonwhite ambivalence toward patriotism in a white-dominated nation. According to critic Elizabeth Archuleta, an expert on Amerindian studies and women's studies at Pennsylvania State University, Silko's personal essay "America's Iron Curtain: The Border Patrol State" (1994), like the writings of Angela Yvonne Davis and Sherman Alexie, reveals the "colonialist tendency to identify non-white citizens as perpetually foreign and to use legal means as a way to reinforce racial hierarchies" (Archuleta, 2005, 115). In support of people of color, Archuleta denounces "White fear of an alien nation [that] undeniably fortifies public support for the perpetuation of race-based laws as an exercise of power" (*ibid.*). In defense of the rights of first peoples, Silko's canon discloses the shared components of native life that build community among Indians, whether full- or mixed-blood. In one scenario—the Hopi, Laguna, Navajo, and Zuni warning in *Ceremony* (1977) that the Gallup ghetto is not safe for Indians after dark—disparate tribes disseminate a common cache of information about intertribal concerns.

During visits to European capitals, Silko admired the resilience of paganism. Concerning her own people's experience with proselytizers, she remarked, "As hard as Christianity tried to wipe it out, and tried to break that connection between the Europeans and the earth, and the plants and the animals—even though they've been broken from it longer than the indigenous people of the Americas or Africa—that connection won't break completely" (Arnold, 1998, 6). In her description of cattle breeding in *Ceremony*, she speaks through Uncle Josiah a rebuttal of the Caucasian point of view. Basing his philosophy on Pueblo Indian experience, Josiah closes the husbandry texts that the Bureau of Indian Affairs extension agent supplies and jokes that he will raise longhorns "that don't eat grass or drink water," an indirect metaphor for the toughness and adaptability of desert Indians (Silko, 1977, 75). In a riposte, his nephew Rocky, the anti-nativist, trusts only scientific methods that refute the experience-based outlook of the Laguna.

THE NATIVE MINDSET

The character Betonie, one of Silko's hybrids, epitomizes native strengths. She depicts him as elderly, but hardy and proud of his Chicano-Navajo ancestry. In a stone hogan attached to the side of Mount Taylor, he lives in the style of his grandmother and forebears. He describes belonging as stewardship of the earth, which owns its inhabitants. While living uphill from the Gallup city dump, he surrounds himself with found objects, including the grille from a junked car, which he uses as a barbecue grill. Jovial and upbeat, he admits to Tayo, the battle-weary veteran, the misery of looking out on stolen Indian land, which whites defile with industrial waste. Betonie's respect for human variance exonerates Shush, the emotionally impaired bear boy, for being different. The aged medicine man fights back against loss by discounting deeds and official documents and by remaining realistic about the good and bad traits of whites and Indians. Critic John Emory Dean concludes that the open-minded survey of humanity and "the weaving in of the platonic travel pattern with Tayo's ceremonial Pueblo and Navajo patterns adds new vitality to Tayo's and his people's stories" (Dean, 2009, 163).

Of the authenticity of non–Indian writers creating a native consciousness, Silko doubted the ability of outsiders to navigate "very uncertain, unsteady ground," such as Tayo's inability to think as "I" rather than "we" (Seyersted, 1985, 19). Citing ethnologist Oliver LaFarge as an example of a failed novelist, Silko asserted that the effort of thinking like another race violates the writer's dictum of truth to self and to experience, particularly Tayo's search for an inclusive cure for pervasive Indian sickness. Silko's work contrasts the phoniness of outsiders by speaking directly of experience amid natural phenomena. In "The Time We Climbed Snake Mountain" (1981), she characterizes the ascent of a cliff as a tactile touch of "good places" on warm rock (Silko, 1981, 76). The sunbathing of a yellow spotted snake echoes her depiction of daylight as a divine blessing, a common element in native American imagery. She revisits the beneficent symbol in *Ceremony*, where Tayo views the yellow spotted reptile as a harbinger from the underworld returned to alert his people to spring and the coming of rain. Another given, the sanctity of corn meal, permeates the story of Hummingbird, the messenger to the rain spirits, who knows the ritual and chant for reviving the dead. The author's most intense submergence in nature, the memoir *The Turquoise Ledge* (2010), plunges her into daily walks in the Sonora Desert, where her native consciousness views both the 21st century changes to the land and the relics of the Anasazi, an ancient Pueblo culture some 3,200 years in the past. The unity of desert dwellers resonates in her reverence for land that perpetuates a welcome and challenge to first peoples.

NATIVE EMPOWERMENT

Nearly 14 years after the issuance of *Ceremony*, Silko staggered her readership with a transnational saga, *Almanac of the Dead* (1991). The stark accusation of white capitalism and Christianity for sharply reducing Amerindian tribes through disease, starvation, war, and genocide raised cries of "tribalism" from book reviewers. Surface scans of the novel failed to grasp the significance of a coalition of have-nots comprised of *mestizos*, Indians, derelicts and homeless, Vietnam War veterans, abused females, abandoned children, and the handicapped. Scots critic John Beck, an American literature specialist at Newcastle University, typified the ragtag assembly as "the abjected multitude from the South ... an awakened underworld power capable of dismantling the Anglo social order" (Beck, 2009, 194). Their common interest, in the words of Linda Martín Alcoff, a philosopher at Hunter College, is a revolt against "xenophobia directed within" (Alcoff, 2005, 260). The 208 vignettes account for a criminal entourage assailing Tucson. Their zeal points not to tribal purity but to a convergence of the American underdogs of many castes, all chained to the socioeconomic bottom. The transcription of coded Mayan parchments becomes an imperfect guide to a hemispheric purge of elitism and exclusivity. Calabazas admits that corruption in Mesoamerica predates the arrival of Europeans, the native American holocaust, and the Indian diaspora: "The tribes in Mexico had been drifting toward political disaster for hundreds of years before the Europeans had ever appeared" (Silko, 1991, 220). Silko asserts that the Mayan and Aztec bloodletting cult allied with the savagery of the Spanish *conquistadores* to initiate the "epoch of Death-Eye Dog," the mythic prophecy of five centuries of white misrule of the New World (*ibid.*, 251).

To overthrow the destroyers, an army of the poor and disadvantaged affiliates for good and for a true democracy engineered by the Mayan Marxist Angelita, the Korean-American saboteur Awa Gee, the Lakota demagogue Wilson Weasel Tail, Vietnam War veteran Roy-Rambo, prisoners liberated by the Barefoot Hopi, and terrorist eco-warriors who explode the Glen Canyon Dam. In the lead is the Afro-Cherokee organizer Clinton, who brandishes a history of 66 black and Indian acts of resistance spanning 336 years from 1526 to 1862. The coalition is a necessary connection of people whom critic Jane Olmstead describes as "hopelessly marginal, homeless, unrelated, and without ties and their (as yet unrealized) power to coordinate efforts to undermine the status quo" (Olmstead, 1999, 488). Among them, Sterling, the Laguna gardener, recognizes in Mexicans "remnants of different kinds of Indians [who] had lost contact with their tribes and their ancestors' worlds" (Silko, 1991, 88). Of the ominous march on Tucson, Silko gleefully exults, "All hell was going to break loose. The best was yet to come" (*ibid.*, 749). The unifying factor of the revolutionary web is nativist resolve to facilitate land restitution and a righting of historic wrongs.

*See also* genocide; racism; reclamation.

• *References and further reading*

Alcoff, Linda. *Visible Identities: Race, Gender, and the Self.* New York: Oxford University Press, 2005.

Archuleta, Elizabeth. "Securing Our Nation's Roads and Borders or Re-circling the Wagons? Leslie Marmon Silko's Destabilization of 'Borders,'" *Wicazo Sa Review* 20:1 (Spring 2005): 113–137.

Arnold, Ellen. "Listening to the Spirits: An Interview with Leslie Marmon Silko." *Studies in American Indian Literature* 10:3 (Fall 1998): 1–33.

Beck, John. *Dirty Wars: Landscape, Power, and Waste in Western American Literature.* Lincoln: University of Nebraska Press, 2009.

Cutchins, Dennis. "'So That the Nations May Become Genuine Indian': Nativism and Leslie Marmon Silko's Ceremony," *Journal of American Culture* 22: 4 (1999): 77–89.

Douglas, Christopher. *A Genealogy of Literary Multiculturalism.* Ithaca: Cornell University Press, 2009.

Dean, John Emory. *Travel Narratives from New Mexico: Reconstructing Identity and Truth.* Amherst, NY: Cambria, 2009.

Grobman, Laurie. "(Re)Interpreting 'Storyteller' in the Classroom: Teaching at the Crossroads," *College Literature* 27:3 (Fall 2000): 88–110.

Martin, Holly E. "Hybrid Landscapes as Catalysts for Cultural Reconciliation in Leslie Marmon Silko's Ceremony and Rudolfo Anaya's Bless Me, Ultima," *Atenea* 26:1 (June 2006): 131–149.

Olmstead, Jane. "The Uses of Blood in Leslie Marmon Silko's *Almanac of the Dead*," *Contemporary Literature* 40:3 (Fall 1999): 464–490.

Ortiz, Simon J. "Towards a National Indian Literature: Cultural Authenticity in Nationalism" in *American Indian Literary Nationalism*, eds. Jace Weaver, Craig S. Womack, and Robert Allen Warrior. Albuquerque: University of New Mexico Press, 2006.

Seyersted, Per. "Interview with Leslie Marmon Silko," *American Studies in Scandinavia* 13 (1985): 17–25.

Silko, Leslie Marmon. *Almanac of the Dead.* New York: Simon & Schuster, 1991.

_____. *Ceremony.* New York: Viking, 1977.

_____. "Language and Literature from the Pueblo Indian Perspective" in *English Literature: Opening Up the Canon*, eds. Leslie Fiedler and Houston Baker, Jr. Baltimore: Johns Hopkins University Press, 1981.

_____. "An Old Fashioned Indian Attack in Two Parts" in *The Remembered Earth: An Anthology of Contemporary Native American Literature*, ed. Geary Hobson. Albuquerque: University of New Mexico Press, 1979.

_____. *Storyteller.* New York: Seaver, 1981.

# order

The interplay of order and disorder permeates Silko's canon. In her meditations on human frailty and injustice, she equates derangement with "an imbalance and unwellness," a situation calling for healing or restructuring (Silko & Arnold, 2000, 105). Her early poems from *Laguna Woman: Poems* (1974) idealize instinctive responses in "Four Mountain Wolves" and "Horses at Valley Store," seasonal rhythms in "Poem for Ben Barney" and "Sun Children," and coexistence with all living things in "Hawk and Snake" and "Indian Song: Survival." In "Where Mountainlion Lay Down with Deer," she visualizes an Amerindian view of the Peaceable Kingdom, a utopian motif in Christian imagery of Eden. Her later works survey the complexities of reordering world chaos, for example, the author's recovery from divorce and a lost custody battle for her son in *The Delicacy and Strength of Lace: Letters between Leslie Marmon Silko and James Wright* (1986) and the reclamation of Arizona peasant life from white engineers who dislodge and redirect the Colorado River in *Gardens in the Dunes* (1999). In both cases, the impossibility of complete victory over upheaval requires trade-offs and concessions to a less-than-perfect recovery. In reference to her loss of elder son Robert to his father, Richard Chapman, Silko speaks the wisdom of the experienced woman: "How deep and painful the bruises are. Well, ... we must persist, and take heart" (Silko & Wright, 1986, 22).

The author exemplifies Amerindian contentment in nature with the status quo. She explains in *Yellow Woman and a Beauty of the Spirit: Essays on Native American Life Today* (1996) the essential harmony between health and beauty: "The whole person had to be beautiful, not just the face or the body; faces and bodies could not be separated from hearts and souls" (Silko, 1996, 65). Her canon employs disarray to highlight the disruption caused by a married Laguna man visiting his lover near the outhouse, by the theft of Indian land and labor from Mexico, and by a curious mourner touching the dead wrist of the Tuxtla banker's daughter killed in a bomb explosion. In "Fifth World: The Return of Ma Ah Shra True Ee, the Giant Serpent" (1996), the author urges jangled survivors to trust divine spirits in restoring order. A believer in therapy through narrative, she advocates locating cultural direction from tribal origination myths, the source of beginnings and endings and all that lies in between.

## WAR DAMAGE

The disorder of combat fatigue in *Ceremony* (1977), the author's first novel, captures the native perception of disharmony and of a life out of sync with nature, self, and community. Tayo, a GI returning to Laguna from the Pacific war in 1945, bears a spirit disoriented by war and a heart burdened with grief for his fallen cousin/foster brother Rocky. The veteran seeks therapies for reordering his psyche and outlook. In the past loom memories of "killing across great distances without knowing who or how many had died ... the mortars and big guns," a combined artillery gouging a monstrous wound in his conscience (Silko, 1977, 36). In the fog of battle fatigue, he perceives a vulnerability shared by humankind — the powerlessness to control history. To grasp a future, he must break free of similarly disquieted comrades Emo, Harley, Leroy Valdez, and cousin Pinkie and must purify himself of sorrow and self-blame to achieve serenity.

*Ceremony* pictures Tayo as a young man who expects too much of himself. His disordered logic forces him to blame himself for enlisting in the military and for leaving Uncle Josiah with "no one to help him search for the cattle after they were stolen," a theft that replicates the injustices of the white world against first peoples (*ibid.*, 114). At war's end, Tayo bears another infraction against his family, the failure to keep Rocky safe from "those yellow Jap bastards" during the Bataan Death March of April 1942 in the Philippines (*ibid.*, 39). The unpredictability of "miles of marching or the Japanese grenade that was killing Rocky" disprove Rocky's rosy view of soldiery and his belief that "We can do real good, Tayo" (*ibid.*, 66). Silko presents military medicine at a Los Angeles veterans' hospital as a numbing of the very senses that Tayo needs to cleanse his war-polluted spirit and reshape his adult life. After three years of confinement to a ward, he makes his way to the Laguna Pueblo to seek shamanic healing. A metonym for all first peoples, Tayo needs to shed the corruption of white materialism and self-gratification through alcoholism, lawlessness, whoring, self-endangerment, and out-of-control behaviors. Gazing into the label on a bottle of Coors, Tayo surveys clear, tumbling cascades for the perfect world.

## THE WILL TO CHANGE

Betonie, the Chicano-Navajo medicine man at Gallup, pits his healing skills against a hate "located deep inside, below [Tayo's] lungs and behind his belly" (*ibid.*, 58). The old man recognizes the GI's struggle with oversized burdens as part of the witchery that paralyzes indigenous people, an ironic twist on the Puritan charge that Amerindians were iniquitous tools of Satan. Key to patterning, a hoop ceremony, sky watching, and sand painting reconnect the patient organically to the community and environment, both stabilizers of order and wellness. Silko symbolizes Tayo's redemption as the molting of skin he once observed in snakes in a deep cave. To roust the victim from his psychic paralysis, Betonie "[prays] him through each" ritual (*ibid.*, 132). Of the sufferings of battle-weary returnees, the shaman counsels, "This has been going on for a long long time now. It's up to you," a reassurance that Tayo is not the first veteran to wrestle with post-traumatic stress disorder (*ibid.*, 141). Betonie urges acceptance of "transitions that had to be made in order to become whole again, in order to be the people our Mother would remember" (*ibid.*, 157). During the recuperative period, the shaman requires accountability for subsequent personal actions as the basis for the pueblo's survival.

The reordering of a shattered life is both physically and emotionally rigorous. To redress injustice against his deceased Uncle Josiah, Tayo releases the family's herd of wild Mexican longhorns from 50 feet of steel wolf-proof fence and barbed wire erected by white rustler Floyd Lee. Only by complying with native priorities— hiking the hills, riding horseback, tracking a mountain lion, lovemaking with a mountain demigoddess, and reuniting with prayers, songs, and Pueblo food, medicines, and lore — does Tayo reclaim what critic John A. McClure calls a "sense of visceral relatedness to an ordered, beautiful and benignant cosmos" (McClure, 2007, 148). With the fervor of ancient warriors who redeemed themselves of blood crimes by abandoning scalps in a post-war ritual, Tayo gains forgiveness for failing his uncle in time of need and achieves spiritual wholeness, his only escape from K'oo'ko, the fanged nightmare that haunts his rest. His rehabilitation derives from what novelist Larry McMurtry calls a "faithful story.... The stories help the people move from imbalance and disorder back to a kind of balance, the balance that comes from the accuracy and depth and beauty of the stories" to "recover their primal strength" (McMurtry, 2007, xxii).

## GEOMETRIC ORDER

In *Storyteller* (1981), the author advances from the disorder of world war and approaches narrative conflict from the perspective of a homegrown rumpus within the pueblo. In "Estoy-eh-muut and the Kunideeyahs," the befuddled title husband experiences vertigo and malaise from an unknown source. Through Spider Woman (Ts'its'tsi'nako or Thought Woman), he discovers that his agitation derives from the witchery of his wife Kochininako, the mythic Yellow Woman. In a parallel to his suspicion that all is not well at the couple's home and in their marriage, the Gunideeyahs also experience a disturbance of their midnight coven meeting. Because Estoy-eh-muut lurks outside the witches' cave, their spells fail to turn participants into animals after they pass through the magic cottonwood bow. The removal of the spying husband relieves the disorder of their sorcery and allows each evildoer to take a bestial shape for the commission of the night's wickedness. Their first hexes involve "[stampeding] the deer from the hunting places/so the village people would go hungry," a form of disorder that threatens survival (Silko, 1981, 148).

Much as Betonie redeems Tayo from mental chaos through geometric ceremonies and sky patterns, Estoy-eh-muut employs universal shapes depicting the cycles of nature. The action returns cosmic order to the family and community through the weaving of a circle from yucca, an essential desert plant that once supplied the Pueblo with coarse strands for shoes and rope, edible fruits and seeds, roots for soap and shampoo, and hardened leaf tips for projectiles. Rather than confront Kochininako for her witchery, Estoy-eh-muut rolls the powerful circlet toward her and watches her fall dead after "the coiled ring of woven yucca fiber" turns into a rattlesnake and rolls downhill straight at the wayward wife (*ibid.*, 154). Once again, the eternal circle, a native American icon of stability and longevity that Betonie uses in his sand painting, proves more lethal than erratic sorcery.

## DISORDER ON A GRAND SCALE

In 1991, Silko attacked world disorder in *Almanac of the Dead* (1991), an apocalyptic jeremiad against European elitism and misappropriation of native lands. The text pictures Caucasians as abandoners of their religion and ancestry. Through acts of sacrilege, they engineer their own damnation. By setting Lecha, an Anglo-Yaqui psychic, the task of transcribing ancient Maya codices, the text turns smudged, disorderly parchments and interpolated pages and marginalia into symbols of unrefined prophecy similar to the scattered leaves containing predictions of the Cumaean Sybil in Virgil's *Aeneid* (19 B.C.). Like the gradual focusing of a lens on its subject, the author brings to the forefront an astounding encyclopedia of historic crimes, from conquest and bondage to cannibalism and genocide. By connecting the slaughter of Maya by Spanish conquistador Hernán de Cortés with late 20th-century amorality and commercialized depravity, Silko impugns her own times with crimes far more insidious and lucrative than the post–Columbian usurpation of the Western Hemisphere. Drifting from assassination to the harvesting of human plasma and organs, she foresees a collapse of humanity.

Restoration of normal human conduct comes at a price. Analyst Katherine Sugg, a specialist in comparative literature of the Americas, describes the apocalypse as "a radical cleansing, a sweeping away, of the old, corrupt social order," including casual killings, the assassination of CIA agent and two U.S. ambassadors, and the kidnap, murder, and dismemberment of six-month-old Monte, a symbol of innocence (Sugg, 2008, 68). Critic Jeff Berglund, an English professor at Northern Arizona University, states, "The epoch finally arrives when the cannibals' destructive behavior will be turned back, when the cannibals will devour themselves. The earth is out of balance, but it will be renewed" (Berglund, 2006, 159). Through the power of treasured manuscripts and the guidance of sacred macaws, Silko pictures the renewal as the work of Indian spirits and enslaved Africans collaborating with white derelicts to cleanse and purify the race. In the future looms the establishment of a Utopia where "the Spirits of the Night and the Spirits of the Day would take care of the people" (Silko, 1991, 524).

*See also* injustice; Montaño, Ts'eh; vengeance.

• *References and further reading*

Berglund, Jeff. *Cannibal Fictions: American Explorations of Colonialism, Race, Gender and Sexuality* Madison: University of Wisconsin Press, 2006.
Burlingame, Lori. "Empowerment Through 'Retroactive Prophecy' in D'Arcy McNickle's 'Runner in the Sun: A Story of Indian Maize,' James Welch's 'Fools Crow,' and Leslie Marmon Silko's 'Ceremony,'" *American Indian Quarterly* 24:1 (Winter 2000): 1–18.
Langen, T. C. S. ""Estoy-eh-muut and the Morphologists," *Studies in American Indian Literatures* 1:1 (Summer 1989): 1–12.
McClure, John. *Partial Faiths: Postsecular Fiction in the Age of Pynchon and Morrison.* Athens: University of Georgia Press, 2007.
McMurtry, Larry. "Introduction" to *Ceremony*. New York: Penguin, 2007.
Prince-Hughes, Tara. "Worlds In and Out of Balance: Alternative Genders and Gayness in the *Almanac of the Dead* and *The Beet Queen*" in *Literature and Homosexuality*, ed. Michael J. Meyer. Amsterdam: Rodopi, 2000.
Silko, Leslie Marmon. *Almanac of the Dead.* New York: Simon & Schuster, 1991.
_____. *Ceremony.* New York: Viking Press, 1977.
_____. *Laguna Woman: Poems.* New York: Greenfield Review Press, 1974.

_____. *Yellow Woman and a Beauty of the Spirit: Essays on Native American Life Today.* New York: Simon & Schuster, 1996.

_____, and Ellen L. Arnold. *Conversations with Leslie Marmon Silko.* Jackson: University Press of Mississippi, 2000.

_____, and James Wright. *The Delicacy and Strength of Lace: Letters between Leslie Marmon Silko and James Wright,* St. Paul, MN: Graywolf, 1986.

Sugg, Katherine. *Gender and Allegory in Transamerican Fiction and Performance.* New York: Palgrave Macmillan, 2008.

## Palmer, Hattie Abbott

A model of the protofeminist of the Gilded Age trapped in Victorian fastidiousness, Hattie Abbott Palmer, a protagonist of *Gardens in the Dunes* (1999), draws strength from a reconnection with nature and its female earth-keepers. In the anti-bourgeois style of novelists Henry James, Kate Chopin, and Edith Wharton, Silko depicts Hattie in a Pyrrhic struggle against a battery of obstacles to happiness—a social-climbing bourgeois mother, gender-prejudiced Ivy League educators, discounting and silencing by a misogynistic review panel, naïveté, bankruptcy, rape, neurasthenia, and sexual dysfunction. A daddy's girl in childhood, she anticipates wooing for her sizeable dowry, but shows little interest in girlish training in rhyming books, begowned dolls, and china tea sets, the requisites of the Victorian education system for wives-to-be. As a model "new woman" reared under the liberal philosophies of John Stuart Mill, she cleanses Needles, California, of white oppressors and herself of a sterile, tyrannic marriage.

Hattie's precocity takes shape in girlhood in the form of skepticism toward the Cartesian paradigm of good and evil. During catechism classes, she thrills to the stories related by a Jesuit priest of "the old struggle between God and the devil played out in endless new situations," a foreshadowing of her adult deviations from rote dogma (Silko, 1999, 94). After earning a degree from Vassar, she delights in becoming an iconoclast by researching assumptions from Dr. Rhinehart's Coptic scrolls at Cambridge about Jesus' female disciples and Mary Magdalene's gospel. David Murray, professor of American studies at the University of Nottingham, describes her research as an exposure of "the exclusion of many disparate texts and divergent ideas" and a questioning of religious claims to authenticity (Murray, 2007, 146). Because of the Ivy League reviewing panel's rejection of her thesis, "The Female Principle in the Early Church," Hattie laughs with suitor Edward Palmer over "My heresy ... a lively topic of dinner party conversations on Long Island for months!" (*ibid.*, 77). She sees in her potential mate "a man who cared" (*ibid.*, 175).

### Mother and Child

Ironically, eight months into her marriage, Hattie, in terror that marital intimacy may lead to pregnancy and painful birthing like her own mother experienced, unearths unforeseen resources through surrogate motherhood. To assuage her subconscious yearning for female wholeness, she rescues a runaway Indian, an example of extra-tribal adoption common to white solvers of the late nineteenth-century "Indian problem." Whereas Edward, the rationalist male, views the child as a curio, Hattie embraces Indigo as her foster daughter and values the child's intellectual curiosity and instinctive spirituality. Mr. Abbott approves the pairing and concludes: "It was clear the Indian child was just what Hattie needed after her disappointments" (*ibid.*, 179). Paradoxically, the comment foretells the eventual breakdown of the Palmer marriage after motherhood replaces marital intimacy and tenderness as Hattie's refuge.

The Palmer family's grand tour of Europe discloses significant character traits in mother and child. Unlike Indigo, a devoted seed collector and sexually liberated observer of phantasmagoric nude statuary, Hattie recoils from phallic and full-busted pagan fertility icons and carnal Indo-Mediterranean runes shaped like vulvas, prepatriarchal artifacts of spiritual motherhood. An upbringing of propriety, refinement, and suppression of outré opinions and observations turns Hattie into the similar type of parent she experienced, an indulgent father and a stifling mother incapable of all-encompassing nurturing. While Hattie stands on the sidelines of joy, Indigo instinctively cradles fat baby squashes, runs barefoot through vines and vegetable rows, and treats her parrot Linnaeus and monkey Rainbow as beloved children. Paradoxically, Indigo's spunk retrains Hattie in misconceptions about life and love that she learned in girlhood.

## A MYSTIC EPIPHANY

In the same spirit as Mama and her Amerindian companions on the fourth night of the Ghost Dance, at Bastia, Corsica, Hattie experiences a transcendent religious conversion that legitimizes metaphysical claims. In the estimation of David Murray, she responds to "a religion based on unmediated vision rather than dogma," the rigid orthodoxy that precipitated psychosomatic ills after her fiasco at Harvard (Murray, 2007, 147). Because she encounters a mystic luminosity and iridescence in the "Blessed Mother," an ethereal aura that Edward deflates as "religious hysteria," she exudes "wonder and excitement" and embraces reclaimed gardens and orchards as balms to a bruised soul (Silko, 1999, 320). During a stay with Aunt Bronwyn, a cloister keeper of Anglo-Norman plantings at Somerset, England, Hattie glimpses Celtic wells and Roman springs that convey curses to thieves and villains, a form of justice that eventually chastens Edward for his faults as a husband, foster father, and profiteering scientist. Hattie next enjoys a visit with *la professoressa* Laura, a hybridizer of black gladioli and disciple of pagan Madonnas in Lucca, Italy. The visitors enjoy aromas of blossoms and luscious meals in a fairyland similar to that of William Shakespeare's *A Midsummer Night's Dream*. After the drubbing to her ego at the heresy seminar at Harvard Divinity School, the horticultural haven begins restoring Hattie's outlook and self-esteem.

In contrast to Edward, who believes that stone and terra cotta icons belong on shelves under the care of scientists and curators, Hattie agrees with Laura that religious statuary "must have fresh air and sunshine, not burial in a museum," a *sotto voce* commentary on the unconsummated Palmer marriage (Silko, 1999, 294). Among Mediterranean peasants, Hattie reflects on her apotheosis at a schoolhouse wall, where she, Indigo, and some peasants witness an apparition of the Holy Mother on a wall. As a token of syncretic culture, Silko affirms individual claims to miracles while negating the power of Christian missionaries to indoctrinate all believers under a single catechism. According to analyst Brewster E. Fitz, a Silko specialist, the vision redirects Hattie from her graduate studies of the patristic writings of the early church to "the matriarchal spiritual principle," the intended subject of "The Female Principle in the Early Church," her thesis on medieval orthodoxy (Fitz, 2004, xii). The reclamation of Hattie's belief in the sacred female suits the Zeitgeist — the era's spirit of women's rights to birth control, the vote, and equitable divorce and the dropping of barriers to females in education, scholarship, research, the professions, business, and religion.

To depict variant opinions in husband and wife, the novelist contrasts opposing views of flora and fauna. To Dr. Edward Palmer, biota are exploitable resources to be turned to financial profit; to Hattie and her foster daughter, nature makes plants and animals interdependent on humankind. From the Amerindian view, the author notes the link between the land and its inhabitants: "Not until they could find a viable relationship to the terrain — the physical landscape they found themselves in — could they *emerge*" (Silko, 1999, 38). In Hattie's case, suppression takes the form of cyclic "female complaints"— nausea, headaches, palpitations, fatigue, and anxiety attacks— which suggest a Freudian interpretation of illness generated by her distaste for patriarchal Puritanism. The long days of communion with ancient European orchards and stone icons steady her for a test of mental and spiritual wholeness and of her devotion to motherhood. Only in the midst of phantasmic ancient fertility icons does she witness a mystic glow and experience serenity. In contrast to her attention to travel details and to her foster daughter Indigo's education and socialization, her husband combines the worst of late 19th-century colonialism and capitalism — greed and competition to be the first merchant collector to "discover" rare orchid species and to profit from theft of the *Citrus medica* and from mining a meteorite crater pocked with diamonds and precious metals.

## Male Treachery

Silko stokes a blistering epiphany in Hattie by which she discerns Edward's violation of their marriage vows to make her and Indigo "his dupes— his decoys!" (*ibid.*, 329). He gladly sacrifices her safety, inheritance, and reputation for his professional schemes, a self-aggrandizement he shares with Silko's eco-villains in *Almanac of the Dead* (1991). Critic Fitz comments that "Edward's greed blinds him not only to the apparition that his spouse, the Corsican villagers, and Indigo have 'seen,' but also to the arrest that awaits him in Livorno and to Dr. William Gates's mining scam that will lead him like a credulous fool to bankruptcy, illness, and death in the desert" (Fitz, 2004, 228). At St. Joseph's Hospital, a tuberculosis treatment center in Albuquerque, Hattie attends Edward in his final days out of duty, but not wifely devotion.

The text amplifies Hattie's imperilment in the savage rape and battery by unidentified assailants, as faceless and mercenary as Edward and his cohorts, Mr. Eliot and Dr. Gates. The author describes the scenario as bleak: "She'd been found wandering naked and dazed beside the road near Topock, at the northern edge of the Chemehuevi reservation" (Silko, 1999, 456). After Hattie sets fire to a barn in Needles, she unleases the millennial change prophesied by the Ghost Dance. Arson dramatizes the failure of sexism, patriarchal religion, and aggression to cow her. As fire spreads to haystack, Hattie experiences her third luminous glow: "What a lovely light the fire gave off as she warmed her hands over it," a transcendent enlightenment that completes her empowerment (*ibid.*, 473). Critic Caren Irr, an English professor at Brandeis University, validates the liberating nature of revenge as "cosmic retribution ... setting fire to the town where she became the robbed rather than the robber" (Irr, 2010, 142). Irr pictures Hattie fully transformed from the would-be academic to the devotee of the allegorical Sophia (Greek for "wisdom"), the mother of Eve — "a goddess-worshipping heretic dressed in a native woman's blue gingham" (*ibid.*).

Cataclysm, the rejuvenating crisis that Silko acclaims in *Almanac of the Dead*, proves cleansing and emotionally purifying. Only after her trial by fire does Hattie reunite with her foster daughter in the Edenic sandhills garden. Because the leap to full sisterhood with Maytha, Vedna, and Sister Salt is too much to ask of an urbanite like Hattie, she exits the desert in search of the gynocentrism of Old Europe. Scots critic Stuart Christie, an anarchist from Glasgow, explains, "Indigenous gardens prophesy the failure of late-comer, patriarchal nationality as an alien weed" (Christie, 2009, 97). To situate themselves on familiar turf, mother and daughter repatriate to their individual founts. Hattie writes Indigo of her return to Somerset to Aunt Bronwyn's garden, a passive residency where Celtic serpentine mothers and Roman Minervas soothe the miseries of Hattie's depression and unfulfilling years with Edward.

See also Abbott-Palmer genealogy; feminism; *Gardens in the Dunes*; Indigo; women.

• *References and further reading*

Christie, Stuart. *Plural Sovereignties and Contemporary Indigenous Literature*. New York: Palgrave Macmillan, 2009.

Fitz, Brewster E. *Silko: Writing Storyteller and Medicine Woman*. Norman: University of Oklahoma Press, 2004.

Flint, Kate. *The Transatlantic Indian, 1776–1930*. Princeton, NJ: Princeton University Press, 2008.

Hamilton, Patrick Lawrence. *Reading Space: Narratives of Persistence and Transformation in Contemporary Chicana/o Fiction*. Denver: University of Colorado Press, 2006.

Irr, Caren. *Pink Pirates: Contemporary American Women Writers and Copyright*. Iowa City: University of Iowa Press, 2010.

Li, Stephanie. "Domestic Resistance Gardening, Mothering, and Storytelling in Leslie Mamon Silko's *Gardens in the Dunes*," *Studies in American Indian Literature* 21: 1 (Spring 2009): 18–37.

Morisco, Gabriella. "Contrasting Gardens and Worlds: America and Europe in the Long Journey of Indigo, a Young Native American Girl" in *Nations, Traditions and Cross-Cultural Identities: Women's Writing in English in a European Context*, eds. Annamaria Lamarra and Eleonora Federici. Bern: Peter Lang, 2010, 137–148.

Murray, David. *Matter, Magic, and Spirit: Representing Indian and African American Belief*. Philadelphia: University of Pennsylvania Press, 2007.

Saguaro, Shelley. *Garden Plots: The Politics and Poetics of Gardens*. Burlington, VT: Ashgate, 2006.

Silko, Leslie Marmon. *Gardens in the Dunes*. New York: Scribner, 1999.

## powerlessness

Through the native worldview of history, Leslie Marmon Silko surveys the difficulties of her own time as they relate to the pre–Columbian era and colonialism and to the future. Rather than deflate her canon with character victimization, according to critic Lori Burlingame, a specialist in native American literature at Eastern Michigan University, Silko empowers "through self-responsibility and cultural awareness and reconnection" (Burlingame, 2000, 1). Although Caucasians slaughter the buffalo and elk, spread European disease, pollute waters, clear-cut forests and strip mine for ore, and invent nuclear bombs, Silko avoids self-pity by looking to the future and the resurgence of Amerindian values. AnaLouise Keating, an expert in women's studies at Texas Woman's University, echoes the author's belief that, "once we begin recognizing this previously invisible 'whiteness,' we can — if we so desire — resist it" (Keating, 2007, 102).

Silko's early verse and stories depict Amerindians as an indigenous culture that draws resilience from oneness with the land. Her scenarios refute both the Hollywood "vanishing Indian" and literary stereotypes of the squaw man — Captain Pratt in "The Geronimo Story" (1981) and Great-Grandfather Robert Gunn Marmon in *Yellow Woman and a Beauty of the Spirit: Essays on Native American Life Today* (1996) — as well as the female Indian drudge and the derelict warrior trapped by a 70 percent rate of unemployment and alcohol. Not only does the author upend preconceived notions of the helpless Indian as an endangered species, she toughens the women for endurance, a characteristic shared by Ayah in "Lullaby" (1974) and the mythic heroine Yellow Woman. In her own life, as she describes in *The Turquoise Ledge* (2010), Silko banishes fragility by bonding with desert biota as a source of everyday beauty and hope, which she symbolizes with fragments of turquoise glittering in her path.

## REAL CHALLENGE

Silko's native world meets its challenges in daily confrontations with hurt and despair. *Ceremony* (1977), her first novel, pictures a variety of weaknesses, including the blindness and chill of Tayo's grandmother, the neglect of children along the riverbank outside of Gallup, and the inability of the Ute Helen Jean to escape reservation squalor and prostitution at Towac. Like Okonkwo in Chinua Achebe's Nigerian saga *Things Fall Apart* (1958) and Cormac McCarthy's apocalyptic novel *The Road* (2006), Southwestern people feel inundated by change. By rescripting history and myth, Silko resets the coming of whites to the mid–1900s, when guns "can shoot death farther than the eye can see," a reference to the dropping of the atom bomb on August 6, 1945, from the *Enola Gay* (Silko, 1977, 21). In the late 1940s, a drunken scene at the Dixie Tavern in Budville strips veterans of the Pacific war of their bravado and returns them to historic victimhood. After Emo and Harley observe Tayo's blowup over the loss of stature as war heroes, the two grab Tayo's arms and settle him back into his chair. Emo immediately parallels their fractiousness with the prejudicial treatment by clerks in Albuquerque and Gallup and with "losing the land the white people took" (Silko, 1977, 43). The history is so palpable three-quarters of a century after the Indian Wars that Emo still blames himself as though he made no effort to defend the Laguna homeland. In the preface to the 30th anniversary edition, novelist Larry McMurtry explains the perils of the post–World War II era: "Evils have been unleashed, witches have increased in power, and the indigenous people are more vulnerable than ever to spiritual and physical defilement" (McMurtry, 2007, xxii).

Silko enhances vulnerability in the novel's resolution by picturing violence and frustration turned inward. While Tayo observes from hiding near the Jackpile mine, Emo, the drunk and raging GI, tortures Harley, whom he trusses in barbed wire, the same threat that Tayo recalls from his incarceration in a Japanese prison camp. In the moonlight of the autumn solstice, the protagonist views both the belly hair of deer and "gathering tumbleweed tangled in the bottom wire," a symbol of the fragility of human life when trapped by cruel technology (*ibid.*, 231). Unlike his out-of-control war buddies, Tayo relies on the advice of Betonie, the Chicano-Navajo shaman at Gallup, who warns that witches "want us to separate ourselves from white people, to be ignorant and helpless as we watch our own destruction" (*ibid.*, 122). From his Mexican grandmother, the medicine man learns that self-empowerment requires cooperation: "We must have power from everywhere. Even the power we can get from the whites" (*ibid.*, 150).

Tayo returns to Amerindian lore and ritual to strengthen him for the test of manhood, which the author symbolizes in a one-on-one encounter with a cougar. Rather than rely on the technological education of a white-run high school, Tayo reintroduces himself to Laguna cosmology, which refutes white lies and deceptions. He uses a small weapon—a rusty screwdriver—to disable Leroy Valdez's truck, but quells the urge to shove the blade into Emo's skull, a yielding to savagery that would do nothing to save himself from more treatment in a military veteran's hospital or to help the Laguna people. McMurtry explains, "Tayo, like the wisest of his people, turns for protection to the tribe's saving stories," the narrative webs that begin with the story-spinning of Spider Woman (Ts'its'tsi'nako or Thought Woman) (McMurtry, 2007, xxii). By merging his own story with that of his people, Tayo releases dynamics of personal excellence and attainment. John J. Su, an English professor at Marquette University, summarizes Silko's themes of self-empowerment: "Only narrative refigurations of experience that use the past to envision some degree of agency rather than victimization can enable a community to move beyond its traumatic history and to imagine a more satisfying future" (Su, 2005, 148).

## APOCALYPSE AND THE INDIVIDUAL

A saga of social chaos, Silko's *Almanac of the Dead* (1991) opens on a witches' den, a kitchen cluttered with pistols and rifles, cartridges, needles, pills, and a refrigerator stocked with Demerol. Mexican tiles depicting "parrot-beaked snakes and jaguar-headed men" adorn the riotous atmosphere and its tense emotional backdrop (Silko, 1991, 21). Amid the clutter, Lecha, a sexagenarian smuggler, pulls together the threads of her life before cancer kills her. A series of memories fills the first chapters with serious disorder against the individual—the persecution of bank robber John Dillinger for being part Indian and the theft of the stone icons called the "little grandparents" for display in a museum, an injustice that Silko characterizes as "a glimpse of what was yet to come" (*ibid.*, 33). The reference introduces the discovery of uranium at Paguate in 1949 and the first time that Pueblo workers earn cash for destroying the earth, a mistake that the old ones condemn as a "crime against all living things" (*ibid.*, 35).

The novelist carries the plot to the upsurge of manipulated people who reject helplessness. A version of the *fasces* (axe-bladed bundle of sticks) borne by Roman *lictors* (bodyguards), individuals band into a single force. At the International Holistic Healers Convention in Tucson, they respond to the rabble-rouser Wilson Weasel Tail, a Lakota attorney, who reads from Pontiac's manuscript: "Where were you when the people first discussed the Europeans? Tell the truth" (*ibid.*, 721). Wilson harangues his listeners with blame for giving in to white materialism, which "swells up your belly and chest to your head" (*ibid.*). To shock the audience into fighting back against white insurgents, Wilson quotes Wovoka, the Paiute prophet of the previous century, and challenges the weak for "wringing your hands and whimpering while the invaders committed outrages against the forest and the mountains" (*ibid.*, 723). By summoning ancient spirits, the orator infuses 20th-century victims with the rage of their ancestors, who died fighting back rather than be forced to live in chains.

## FEMALE EMPOWERMENT

In the opening chapter of *Gardens in the Dunes* (1999), Silko revisits the early encounters with Europeans when "the white armies came and robbed the people of their fall harvests to starve them," the beginnings of genocide known as the Indian holocaust (Silko, 1999, 204). According to Sara L. Spurgeon, a specialist in women's studies at the University of Arizona, Western lore "preferred to see whites as vulnerable but brave pioneers beset by wild savages, and this original Puritan blueprint followed Anglo settlement westward through the eighteenth and nineteenth centuries, adapting itself to the changing social, political, and cultural realities" (Spurgeon, 2005, 75). The text diminishes powerlessness of the dwindling Sand Lizard clan in the presence of alien usurpers. An obvious allusion to the first meetings between the Pueblo and *conquistadores* in the 1540s, the text describes the wisdom of the outnumbered. Because of initial violence and pillage, the Sand Lizard clan retreats from certain death. A subsequent outbreak of fever among whites sends natives from their riverbank residence into the sandhills, where a perpetual garden of sunflowers, beans, squash, and pumpkins welcomes them from the low country. In the face of further terror, they stand "always ready to flee" higher into the mountains, a vantage point from which they can observe the strangers' movements and defend themselves from predations (Silko, 1999, 16).

Silko's *Gardens in the Dunes* subverts the frontier captivity paradigm established by *The True Story of the Captivity of Mrs. Mary Rowlandson among the Indians* (1682), *An Account of the Captivity of Elizabeth Hanson* (1796), *A Narrative of the Captivity of Mrs. Johnson* (1796), *The Life and Times of Mrs. Mary Jemison* (1824), *Narrative of the Capture and Subsequent Sufferings of Mrs. Rachel Plummer* (1839), and *Captivity of the Oatman Girls* (1859). The theme of hybridity resets the image of the stranger in a strange land by ferrying Indigo, the protagonist, to Europe to learn about paganism. Scots critic Stuart Christie, an anarchist from Glasgow, exalts the 11-year-old for "[transcending] nationalist captivity through picaresque exposure to a universalizing gynocentrism" (Christie, 2009, 94). Buttressed by memories of Mama and by teachings in survival and spirituality from Grandma Fleet, Indigo returns from the east with treasure — seeds from Aunt Bronwyn's garden in Somerset, corms of the black gladiolus hybridized by *la professoressa* Laura in Lucca, Italy, and adventures to expand Sand Lizard lore far beyond the sandhills. Christie pictures the repatriated traveler like Marco Polo, bringing home the wanderer's lore and "introducing new strains, new species, into the sovereign garden" (*ibid.*, 96).

*See also* injustice; "Lullaby"; Tayo; violence; vulnerability.

- *References and further reading*

Burlingame, Lori. "Empowerment Through 'Retroactive Prophecy' in D'Arcy McNickle's 'Runner in the Sun: A Story of Indian Maize,' James Welch's 'Fools Crow,' and Leslie Marmon Silko's 'Ceremony,'" *American Indian Quarterly* 24:1 (Winter 2000): 1–18.
Christie, Stuart. *Plural Sovereignties and Contemporary Indigenous Literature.* New York: Palgrave Macmillan, 2009.
Keating, AnaLouise. *Teaching Transformation Transcultural Classroom Dialogues.* New York: Palgrave Macmillan, 2007.
McMurtry, Larry. "Introduction" to *Ceremony.* New York: Penguin, 2007.
Silko, Leslie Marmon. *Almanac of the Dead.* New York: Simon & Schuster, 1991.
_____. *Ceremony.* New York: Viking, 1977.
_____. *Gardens in the Dunes.* New York: Scribner, 1999.
Spurgeon, Sara L. *Exploding the Western: Myths of Empire on the Postmodern Frontier.* College Station: Texas A&M University Press, 2005.
Su, John J. *Ethics and Nostalgia in the Contemporary Novel.* Cambridge: Cambridge University Press, 2005.

# racism

Silko personalizes attacks on skin color and ethnic ancestry. Of her own lineage — Cherokee, English, German, Laguna, Mexican, and Plains Indian — she joked to interviewer Laurie Mellas, a staff member of the University of New Mexico: "Through both sides, it's very mixed, literally a diaspora" (Mellas, 2006, 12). Echoing the angst of ethnographer Zora Neale Hurston in "How It Feels to Be Colored Me" (1928) and of poet Misuye Yamada in *Camp Notes* (1976), Silko states her personal confrontations with racism in "Fences against Freedom," an essay in *Yellow Woman and a Beauty of the Spirit: Essays on Native American Life Today* (1996). Etched in her memory of growing up in the late 1950s is the name-calling that victimized and bullied mixed race children like herself on the schoolyard. From Laguna elders, she learned that being herself was her only choice.

She stressed to interviewer Ellen L. Arnold, "That's the only way that it can be, including everybody" (Silko & Arnold, 2000, 172).

Carl H. Klaus, author of *The Made-Up Self* (2010), accounts for a shift in the author's presentation of personal evaluations: "Silko avoids a sustained attack on Western values and behavior, projecting herself as more tolerant by far than the white tourist who asked her to step away from her classmates" out of range of a photo of "real" Indian children (Klaus, 2010, 101). The sharing of taunts with other bicultural children gives her solace that she and the rest of the Marmons endure — "feelings of unease, of not quite belonging to the group that clearly mattered most in the United States" (Silko, 1996, 102). Glimpses of her memories color her fiction, particularly terrors of arrest in "Tony's Story" (1969), the suspicions of the white social worker in "Lullaby" (1974), and the exclusion of Indians from cafes and hotels in *Gardens in the Dunes* (1999). She substantiates her career as the proper method of defeating bigotry: "Books were and still are weapons in the ongoing struggle for the Americas" to defeat the white stereotype that "these Indians are in no condition to have such precious possessions" as land and children (Silko, 1996, 155).

To the author's benefit, the Laguna accept all people on the basis of behavior rather than external differences and idiosyncrasies. She values her Great Grandmother A'mooh for being "concerned less with a person's ancestry than with a person's integrity. Generosity and honesty were always more important than skin color in the old days" (*ibid.*, 183). Silko's essay "Fences against Freedom" accounts for variances in humans as the work of "the Mother Creator [who] had many children in faraway places" (*ibid.*, 103). The author lambastes the Immigration and Naturalization Border Patrol for brutal racial profiling and unlawful interrogation and search of citizens based on their skin color. The text blames a "terrible irrational force" for the rise in impromptu search and seizure, the "racist immigration policies, which are broadcast every day, teaching racism, demonizing all people of color, labeling indigenous people from Mexico as 'aliens'—creatures not quite human" (*ibid.*, 114, 112). The text foretells a worsening situation for nonwhite people in the Southwest during the summer and fall of 2010, when the state of Arizona crusaded against undocumented aliens.

In the memoir "The Indian with a Camera" (1993), Silko declares that "Euro-Americans desperately need to believe that the indigenous people and cultures which were destroyed were somehow less than human" (Silko, 1993, 6). Her writings battle the racist political strategies that keep dissimilar constituencies in constant states of animosity, which critic Trinh T. Minh-ha, a professor at the University of California at Berkeley, describes as "the dehumanization of forced removal-relocation-reeducation-redefinition" (Minh-ha, 2003, 152). In a discussion of "America's Iron Curtain: The Border Patrol State" (1994), critic Elizabeth Archuleta, an expert in native American and women's studies at Pennsylvania State University, defends the author's opposition to "racial laws [that] have been an important tool for the preservation and legitimation of the established order ... the benefits and privileges of an 'American' identity for whites" (Archuleta, 2005, 115). Of the creation of a steel wall on the southwestern border with Mexico, Silko depicts the grand irrationality of race policies against undesirables, the unassimilable savages whom the U.S. government perceives as dangerous, disloyal, and criminal. In the future, she asserts, such meticulous exclusion "can only end in madness and genocide," the same kind of slaughter that decimated Bosnia and Rwanda (Silko, 1994, 6).

MIXED BLOOD

In *Ceremony* (1977), bias encroaches on everyday encounters, from the ridicule of a Laguna woman who returns home naked from a date with whites to looks of white drinkers at Indian bar patrons and teasing about Tayo's "Mexican eyes" (Silko, 1977, 99). Rather than value Tayo as a hybrid like Betonie, Betonie's grandmother, Ts'eh, and the author herself, the Indian milieu marginalizes the protagonist from two perspectives—as not pure Laguna and as an Indian blend with the genes of the arrogant white. The cantina dancer Night Swan, a similar ethnic mix with Mexican ancestry, dismisses reservation favoritism toward pure heritage as misplaced pride in conformity and a mask for fear about changes in the familiar. In their late teens, Tayo and his foster brother Rocky encounter a condescending U.S. Army recruiter who accepts "even you boys" into the ranks (*ibid.*, 64). For atmosphere, Silko pictures Rocky and Tayo studying military pamphlets outside the post office. The harsh swirl of a dust storm along with the folding table and chair create a feeling of impermanence, a parallel to the fleeting detente of Plains Indians and U.S. Cavalry during the Indian Wars of the 1870s. The brochures scatter like dried leaves, recalling the confused prophecy the hero confronts in the Cumaean Sybil's cave in Virgil's *Aeneid*. The fluttering papers echo Night Swan's understanding of change, both in Laguna milieu and "inside themselves," where it counted most (*ibid.*, 100).

Silko charges racism for generating the immediate letdown following wartime euphoria. When Tayo and Rocky spend their shore leave in Oakland and San Diego, California, in 1941, they experience the gratitude of an elderly white woman and the willingness of bartenders to serve Indians. The mask of a U.S. Marine uniform draws willing dance partners and prostitutes, including a blonde who lets Tayo drive her home in her '38 Buick. Silko turns the ride into *double entendre* by picturing Tayo driving "all the way," a sexual adventure that relieves his fantasies of intimacy with non–Indian women (*ibid.*, 41). On return to Albuquerque and Gallup in 1948, Tayo, the half-breed, reconnects with Southwestern racism, an antipathy that builds a momentum "like the words were all going to explode" (*ibid.*, 42). The body language of a white female cashier who declines to touch an Indian's hand and the rude store clerk who serves Tayo last speak volumes to natives who grew up among bigots.

Racial blending turns Tayo into a failed military veteran. Surprisingly, he feels no animosity toward the Japanese, who also endure fatigue through a Filipino monsoon during the Bataan Death March of April 9–21, 1942. Upon staring into the face of an executed Japanese, Tayo suffers a double vision of the enemy and of his Uncle Josiah. The hallucination suggests the commonality of people and history that storytelling embeds in Tayo. In the essay "On Photography" (1996), Silko experiences her own double vision years later when a Japanese photographer takes the author's picture that reveals Asian features in her face. As danger pursues Tayo into the mountains, the blurring of strict ethnic boundaries works to his advantage. According to the mountain demigoddess Ts'eh Montaño, Laguna elders and veterans' affairs authorities quibble over who has jurisdiction over Tayo's bizarre behaviors. Ts'eh confides, "They haven't been able to agree.... They are trying to decide who you are" (*ibid.*, 232–233). Ironically, her statement summarizes Tayo's internal quandary—his indistinct identities as an illegitimate half-breed and mentally traumatized war veteran.

## GLOBAL RACISM

Silko attacks racial boundaries in *Almanac of the Dead* (1991), a hellish apocalypse vindicating five centuries of European colonialism and the enslavement and denigration of black Africans. Silko states in "The People and the Land ARE Inseparable" (1997) that Mexican militia threatened the survival of the Yaqui by forcing individuals to dig their own graves: "Anticipating Hitler's Third Reich by many years, the Mexican Army, under orders, attempted to eradicate the Yaquis" (Silko, 1996, 87). Racism among *mestizos* becomes a self-castigation that imprisons mixed-blood Indians in identifiable physical features. A virulent self-hater, Menardo Panson, the rising mogul of Universal Insurance, uses money and business acumen to sway the elitist mother of Iliana Gutiérrez of his worth. Mocking his effort to prove worthy of Iliana, granddaughter of the settler of Chiapas, is Menardo's flat nose, an undeniable feature of the Yaqui. Contributing to the complex relationship of husband, wife, and in-laws is the Gutiérrez contention that the family is "set on the brink of ruin by dirty, stupid Indians who had no understanding of how much they needed their *patróns* to keep the world running productively" (Silko, 1991, 270). Menardo's alter ego Sterling, the exiled Laguna gardener, recognizes the change in Yaqui hybrids from their lack of contact with tribes and ancestry. He states, "The people he had been used to calling 'Mexicans' were really remnants of different kinds of Indians. But what had remained of what was Indian was in appearance only," the physical attributes that mark Menardo's family tree (*ibid.*, 88).

Silko's spokesman for racial purity, Serlo, an aristocratic white supremacist living in Argentina, exalts *sangre pura* (Spanish for "pure blood"), an allusion to Nazis who sought asylum in Argentina after World War II. Serlo fantasizes eugenics technology that ends the dependence on the female uterus for production of the species. In a male-to-male reproductive center, he envisions himself reviving nobility in a new pure white generation as an antidote to "swarms of brown and yellow human larvae called natives" (*ibid.*, 546). His diabolic plan to engineer a virus to target and kill blacks and Hispanics echoes period conspiracy theories that AIDS is a new genocidal weapon against non-white people. Thus, Serlo intends to rejuvenate the Nordic warrior race proposed by Nazi theorist Alfred Rosenberg by harnessing technology to serve racial elitism. Critics William Blazek, a specialist in American literature, and Michael K. Glenday, senior lecturer in English at Liverpool Hope University, perceive the resultant anarchy as "the destructive, political, social and ecological costs of Western ideas of progress" (Blazek & Glenday, 2005, 10). As feminist critic Rachel Stein, an English professor at Siena College, insists, Silko has no intent of inciting an interracial war. Rather, she combats sanctioned ignorance of governmental violation of native rights, whom conservatives abase as a special interests group seeking race-based preferential treatment (Kuokkanen, 2007, 68).

In contrast to Serlo's individual arrogance and superiority, Silko looks to an inevitable synergy of underdogs to redress longstanding injustice. Speaking through Wilson Weasel Tail, the Lakota attorney and orator, the author accounts for Indian patience: "It was the Europeans, and not the Native Americans, who had expected results overnight" (Silko, 1991, 723). For contrast, she creates Bartolomeo, a Cuban Marxist whose dogmatic denial of Indian history costs him his life. He impugns himself with the sneer, "Jungle monkeys and savages have no history!" (*ibid.*, 525). His insistence that land ownership is the key issue of a people's revolution discounts the Native American holocaust as a model of "crimes against history" (*ibid.*, 528). By demeaning tribalism as primitive and by forcing revolutionaries to vindicate suppression in to the underclass, Bartolomeo inadvertently dooms himself to the gallows. In the resolution of *Almanac*, Clinton, a black–Cherokee and Vietnam War vet, refutes Bartolomeo's false ideology by informing the unenlightened of the kinship between black refugees and Indians. Upon their union, "Right then the magic had happened: great American and great African tribal cultures had come together to create a powerful consciousness within all people" (*ibid.*, 416).

For Silko, Bartolomeo's crime of disavowing racial history is worse than the slaughters perpetrated in 1519 by Hernán de Cortés against the Aztec kingdom of Montezuma II. Literary theorist Walter Benn Michaels, a teacher at the University of Illinois, explains that denial of or indifference to Indian genocide and land usurpation "are the worst crimes of all ... worse than capitalist exploitation because the capitalist steals the worker's labor, not his identity" (Michaels, 2003, 132). According to historian Arthur Schlesinger, Jr.'s *The Disuniting of America* (1992), for a people, loss of identity, is equivalent to individual amnesia, an erasure of being. The dispossessed lose their ability to fit themselves into events and to the political discourse that shapes their future. To shake off the curse of colonization, Indians follow their sacred storytelling and their mimetic ritual and dance, ways "to remember all our beloved ones" (Silko, 1991, 722). Through rhythm, chant, and historic gestures individuals recall and honor with their senses and bodies past beings and prepare for the children who will make up the tribe's future generation. Elizabeth Ammons, the Harriet H. Fay Professor of Literature at Tufts University, sums up Silko's vision: "Commitment to multiculturalism as a national and global principle is about the health and survival of the world" (Ammons, 2010, 91).

*See also* injustice; self-esteem.

## • *References and further reading*

Ammons, Elizabeth. *Brave New Words: How Literature Will Save the Planet.* Iowa City: University of Iowa Press, 2010.

Archuleta, Elizabeth. "Securing Our Nation's Roads and Borders or Re-circling the Wagons? Leslie Marmon Silko's Destabilization of 'Borders,'" *Wicazo Sa Review* 20:1 (Spring 2005): 113–137.

Berglund, Jeff. *Cannibal Fictions: American Explorations of Colonialism, Race, Gender and Sexuality.* Madison: University of Wisconsin Press, 2006.

Blazek, William, and Michael K. Glenday. *American Mythologies: Essays in Contemporary Literature.* Liverpool, UK: Liverpool University Press, 2005.

Karem, Jeff. *The Romance of Authenticity: The Cultural Politics of Regional and Ethnic Literatures.* Charlottesville: University of Virginia Press, 2004.

Klaus, Carl H. *The Made-Up Self: Impersonation in the Personal Essay.* Iowa City: University of Iowa Press, 2010.

Kuokkanen, Rauna Johanna. *Reshaping the University: Responsibility, Indigenous Epistemes, and the Logic of the Gift.* Vancouver: University of British Columbia Press, 2007.

Mellas, Laurie. "Memory and Promise: Leslie Marmon Silko's Story," *Mirage* 24 (Spring 2006): 11–14.

Michaels, Walter Benn. *The Shape of the Signifier: 1967 to the End of History.* Princeton, NJ: Princeton University Press, 2006.

Minh-ha, Trinh T. "Difference: A Special Third World Women Issue" in *The Feminism and Visual Culture Reader*, ed. Amelia Jones. New York: Routledge, 2003, 151–173.

Murphy, Jacqueline Shea. *The People Have Never Stopped Dancing: Native American Modern Dance Histories.* Minneapolis: University of Minnesota Press, 2007.

Silko, Leslie Marmon. *Almanac of the Dead.* New York: Simon & Schuster, 1991.

_____. *Ceremony.* New York: Viking Press, 1977.

_____. "Fences against Freedom," *Hungry Mind Review* 31 (Fall 1994): 6, 20, 58–59.

_____. *Gardens in the Dunes.* New York: Scribner, 1999.

_____. "The Indian with a Camera," foreword to *A Circle of Nations: Voices and Visions of American Indians.* Hillsboro, OR: Beyond Words Publishing, 1993.

_____. *Yellow Woman and a Beauty of the Spirit: Essays on Native American Life Today.* New York: Simon & Schuster, 1996.

_____, and Ellen L. Arnold. *Conversations with Leslie Marmon Silko.* Jackson: University Press of Mississippi, 2000.

Stein, Rachel. *Shifting the Ground: American Women Writers' Revisions of Nature, Gender, and Race.* Charlottesville: University Press of Virginia, 1997.

## reading

Silko speaks lovingly of her romance with books. In the introduction to Linda "Gypsy" Niemann's *On the Rails: A Woman's Journey* (1996), Silko acknowledges that "the best books change our consciousness as we read them and they free us to imagine then pursue our own vision of our destiny" (Silko, "Introduction," 1996, vi). Her list of favorite authors extends from William Shakespeare and William Blake to Dorothy Allison, Jorge Luis Borges, Isak Dinesen, William Faulkner, Henry James, Maxine Hong Kingston, D. H Lawrence, Toni Morrison, Flannery O'Connor, Edgar Allan Poe, and Gertrude Stein. Her reading plunges into heavy nonfiction, including history, economics, botany, physics, psychology, and theology, notably, the ancient codices of the Maya and Mixtec. Her people take pride in the residence of Lew Wallace at the San José Mission in Laguna while he wrote *Ben-Hur* (1880). Her essay "Fences against Freedom" in *Yellow Woman and a Beauty of the Spirit: Essays on Native American Life Today* (1996) explains the reverence for education found in Laguna elders who "believe that we must keep learning as much as we can all of our lives" (Silko, 1996, 103).

In *Storyteller* (1981), the author recalls from childhood the coverless text of *Brownie the Bear*, a favorite with children since its publication in 1939 by American commercial artist Corinne Malvern. Silko's Grandma A'mooh reads aloud to the three Marmon sisters much as she once read to their father, Lee Marmon, and his brothers. The unity of family storytime reassures the children that they follow the example of their elders. Because of the reader's skill at voice inflection and tone, she energizes the text "each time one of the bears spoke" (Silko, 1981, 93). Silko's phrasing accords the fictional bear a presence requiring the agency of the teller and her skill at animation and expression, an interpretive performance that lifts the hearer from sterile words on a page. Grandma also reads from the bible, providing what Silko expert Brewster E. Fitz calls "a space where Presbyterian Laguna progressives can reside with their syncretic Catholic and non–Christian Laguna kith and kin" (Fitz, 2004, 50). Liberal parents allowed the Marmon girls to read at will from their father's copies of D. H. Lawrence's *Lady Chatterley's Lover* (1928), Henry Miller's *Tropic of Cancer* (1934), and Vladimir Nabokov's *Lolita* (1955) and from his *Playboy* subscription, all of which tested the limits of first amendment rights. To ensure gender balance Virginia Leslie Marmon derided the white obsession with full breasts, thus preventing her three daughters from turning female anatomy into a fetish.

BOOKS AND JUSTICE

Just as Silko lauds the place of reading in childhood socialization, she values books for their role in the power struggles of nations. In the essay "Books: Notes on Mixtec and Maya Screenfolds, Picture Books of Preconquest Mexico" (1996), the author explains how Mexican painter-scribes of the classical era drew abstract and concrete ideas in picture writing on a mural that covered a screenfold. Thus, reading from the books included two interpretive skills—listening and viewing. Concerning the power of the narratives to create change, Silko rejoices that "Books were and still are weapons in the ongoing struggle for the Americas" (Silko, 1996, 155). For their integral part in human history, the Maya and Mixtec fed the books sacrificial blood offerings. Because of the link between blood-letting and reading, fastidious Spanish missionaries and repressive colonial authorities at Mexico City began burning the codices as early as 1520. First peoples revolted against European overlords by refusing to study the printed words from popes and kings. She concludes, "So illiteracy and the aversion to books that is found through the Americas descends from colonial times" as a form of resistance to Catholic brainwashing and conquerors' lies (*ibid.*, 159). The attitude shifted as reading became necessary to survival. After the Anglo-American land grab in 1848, the Pueblo people began to value literacy as a means of restoring international law and respect for historic Spanish land grants.

Silko takes as her task what independent scholar Deborah M. Horvitz calls the "harmonious blending and coexisting of disparate and discordant ideas" (Horvitz, 2000, 26). In reference to Amerindian history, the novelist recounts in *Almanac of the Dead* (1991) a series of dismemberments of bodies and of history. Rather than mourn the dead in Christian style, she validates communion with spirits, a host of specters waiting to reconnect with the living and to unify history into a truthful whole. She identifies the destruction of Mesoamerican libraries in 1540 as the work of Spanish *conquistadores* and Catholic prelates fearful of the political and religious potency of texts predating European invasion. To save indigenous stories from loss, the Yaqui organize a children's crusade by dispatching a handful of children on a long walk north through the Sonora Desert to safety in the American Southwest. So hungry are the naive for physical and spiritual nurturance that they add pages of horse-gut parchment to the soup kettle: "Outlines of the letters smeared and they floated up and away like flocks of small birds.... Well, it was a wonderful stew. They lived on it for days" (Silko, 1991, 248). The respite from hunger prefigures the subsequent feeding of America's dispossessed on native survival lore, both written and oral.

In its present-day state, Silko's fragmented collage of history requires transcription of Mayan calendars from coded pictographs. Yoeme, the fictional concealer of the sacred almanac, spots a mistranslation wrought by sorcery. Because of a miscalculation of dates, Indians, anticipating the return of Quetzalcoatl, responded inappropriately to prophecy by greeting Cortés on his arrival in Mexico. The welcome to a destroyer initiated five centuries of "plague, earthquake, drought, famine, incest, insanity, war, and betrayal" (*ibid.*, 572). The symbol-by-symbol task of decoding contributes to the understanding of Yoeme's granddaughter Lecha, the Anglo-Yaqui keeper of the Mayan codices rescued and transported from danger over the centuries. Her readings of Freud alert her to "the Western European appetite for the sadistic eroticism and masochism of modern war" (*ibid.*, 174). Lecha's perceptions parallel the enlightenment of communist agitator Angelita through straightforward readings in Karl Marx's populist stories that resurrect "the suffering of sisters and brothers long past" (*ibid.*, 632). From his skillful narrative, Angelita sympathizes with indigenous people "ground into bloody pulp under the steel wheels of ore cars in crumbling tunnels of gold mines," an historical testimonial of white rapacity and savagery (*ibid.*, 312). She accepts the proletarian sympathies of Marx despite the fact that he was a European who never saw an Indian.

Silko exonerates Indians for their confusion and naïveté about evil. The Laguna gardener Sterling, the novel's moral center, regrets that government boarding schools limited history classes to the events leading up to the American Civil War. Omitted from classroom texts are the Indian Wars, the decimation of plains renegades, and the forced relocation of non-hostiles to reservations. To fill in his truncated school experience, Sterling relies on old issues of *True Detective, Police Gazette,* and *Reader's Digest.* From these sources, he idolizes Montezuma, Geronimo, Pretty Boy Floyd, Ma Barker, the Starr family, and John Dillinger and concludes, "No wonder Cortés and Montezuma had hit it off together when they met; both had been members of the same secret clan" of destroyers (*ibid.,* 760). From Sterling's makeshift education, he deduces that revolutionary turmoil in Mexico perpetuates a standard of world injustice — the jailing and execution of "the losers for being 'criminals'" (*ibid.,* 89). From his own experience with smugglers, drug dealers, and killers, he resolves to withdraw from "people who got rich off the suffering of Geronimo and his people" and to reclaim old Laguna stories (*ibid.,* 81).

## A DOMINANT THEME

Silko's interest in the right to literature and history continues to invest her themes and motifs. In "Bingo Big" (1995), she regrets the arson committed by "Bishop Landa and his thugs," a reference to Spanish bishop of Yucatán Diego de Landa Calderón, who waged war against American libraries in the 1540s. She details how arson destroyed the Aztec and Mayan codices or folding books, bark cloth lengths inscribed like murals with scenes from Mesoamerican history. The loss robbed world readership of early American literature and of the scribes who mastered bookmaking. In the seventh decades of the Spanish Inquisition, the absence of a national literature enabled Europeans to convince the Roman Catholic Pope Paul III "that these indigenous inhabitants were not fully human and that Europeans were therefore free to do with them and their land as they pleased" (Silko, 1996, 21). The ascendance of books written from the white bias enabled the U.S. government to justify native genocide. In the second half of the 20th century, the yearning of indigenous people for past literary accomplishments pressed into service writers of the Native American Literary Renaissance, led by Sherman Alexie (Spokane–Coeur d'Alene), Linda Hogan (Chickasaw), Navarre Scott Momaday (Kiowa), and Silko herself.

The creation of a scholarly household in Riverside, California, for the neo–Victorian novel *Gardens in the Dunes* (1999) reasserts the author's love of reading. Protagonist Hattie Abbott Palmer, the newlywed scholar, meditates on her discovery of books at age four and on early bible readings by the cook Lucille, a Latinate name meaning "little light." Through a see-and-say method, the preschooler learns to read and delights her father, who showers her with alphabet and rhyming books. Transformed by words on paper, she becomes "a different person, thousands of miles away, in the middle of the action" (Silko, 1999, 73). Escapism through books separates her from the dolls and tea sets common to a little girl's playthings. To Mrs. Abbott's fears that literature ruins females, the father cites John Stuart Mill, a progressive English philosopher who championed female liberation in *The Subjection of Women* (1869), an essay Mill composed in collaboration with his egalitarian wife, Harriet Taylor Miller.

## LITERACY AND ENLIGHTENMENT

Silko makes direct reference to freedom of the mind as an introduction to the body and the pleasures of sexuality. During lectures at the convent by a dull Jesuit, Hattie ignores Catholic cant and warnings of damnation by referring to medical texts to study masturbation and sexual intimacy. During the lengthy study of ecclesiastical history, she prefers lurid saints' lives to dry orthodoxy and thrills to "the drama of the old struggle between God and the devil played out in endless new situations" (*ibid.,* 94). Private readings of Greek, Roman, and Norse mythology and Egyptian archeology precede perusals of Shakespeare's history plays and John Milton's *Paradise Lost* (1667), a literary epic that dramatizes the struggle for human enlightenment. At Vassar, Hattie retreats from Catholic, prohibitionist, and suffragist students to a library carrel and to Dr. Rhinehart's library of Coptic scrolls. Her completion of a B. A. in three years warms the enthusiasm of her father, but not of Mrs. Abbott, who fears that a study of heretics will make Hattie unsuitable for courtship by an appropriate eligible male.

   The suitability of Hattie's marriage to Dr. Edward G. Palmer takes physical shape in her survey of his upstairs, three interconnecting rooms "lined with oak bookshelves booked solid from floor to ceiling" (*ibid.*, 75). She recalls a nervous breakdown when she retreated from gossip about her thesis for a seminar on heresy sponsored by Harvard Divinity School to the safety of books. As foster mother to Indigo, the orphaned 11-year-old Indian girl, Hattie soothes the child's grief at abandoning the monkey Linnaeus to the house staff and distributes books on flowers, an atlas of Europe, and a collection of Chinese stories about a monkey. For herself, Hattie continues her perusal of church development by reading a volume by Eusebius, the father of ecclesiastical history. During the train ride from California to Long Island, she introduces a book on sunflowers and an archeological guide to stone shrines and Celtic legends, which seem suitable for an Indian child for their primitive simplicity. Upon arrival at the home of Colin and Susan Abbott James, as a preface to a social function known as the Masque of the Blue Garden, Indigo and Hattie study books of Renaissance costume and French and Italian gardens. The shift from intense study of early church history makes Hattie realize that her interest in mothering Indigo has alleviated past frustrations and stresses.

• *References and further reading*

Fitz, Brewster E. *Silko: Writing Storyteller and Medicine Woman*. Norman: University of Oklahoma Press, 2004.

Horvitz, Deborah M. *Literary Trauma: Sadism, Memory, and Sexual Violence in American Women's Fiction*. Albany: State University of New York Press, 2000.

Petrolle, Jean. *Religion without Belief: Contemporary Allegory and the Search for Postmodern Faith*. Albany: State University of New York Press, 2007.

Schorcht, Blanca. *Stories Voices in Native American Texts: Harry Robinson, Thomas King, James Welch, and Leslie Marmon Silko*. New York: Routledge, 2003.

Silko, Leslie Marmon. *Almanac of the Dead*. New York: Simon & Schuster, 1991.

_____. "Bingo Big," *Nation* 260:23 (12 June 1995): 856–860.

_____. *Gardens in the Dunes*. New York: Scribner, 1999.

_____. "Introduction," *On the Rails: A Woman's Journey*, by Linda Niemann. Berkeley, CA: Cleis, 1996.

_____. *Storyteller*. New York: Seaver, 1981.

_____. *Yellow Woman and a Beauty of the Spirit: Essays on Native American Life Today*. New York: Simon & Schuster, 1996.

Smith, Carlton. *Coyote Kills John Wayne: Postmodernism and Contemporary Fictions of the Transcultural Frontier*. Hanover, NH: University Press of New England, 2000.

## reclamation

   Integral to Silko's canon, the theme of retrieval derives from her native American heritage and from expectations that each individual will contribute to the tribe. For the uniqueness of contemporary Amerindian writing, Abby H. P. Werlock, a former literary professor at St. Olaf College, dubs Silko an autoethnographer, a "remembrancer" and revamper of ethnic heritage through imaginative stories. Out of respect for community, Silko extols nativism as the glue that gives hope and oneness to the Pueblo. In "Language and Literature from a Pueblo Indian Perspective" (1996), she states: "Separation not only endangers the group but the individual as well — one does not recover by oneself" (Silko, 1996, 52). To reassemble the pre–Columbian array of tribes over the land and the inter-tribal connections or tribal internationalism, she uses narrative as a means of revaluing the Americas before their invasion by Europeans. John J. Su, an English professor at Marquette University, explains: "The future is imagined in terms of a 'restoration' of a nostalgic past. Hence, every effort ... to reclaim place depends on a prior act of recalling its loss," the literary purpose of "Tony's Story" (1969) and, more specifically, of "A Geronimo Story" (1974) (Su, 2005, 116).

From her childhood memories of the bend of the Rio San José, Silko pictures repatriation and survival in a place on the southeastern rim of Laguna Pueblo. The banks represent the outer limits where the mixed-blood Marmon family has flourished since the assimilation of the Marmon brothers, Robert and Walter, after the Civil War. A liminal juncture between a serene flow and Route 66, the spot dominates dynamic moments in the author's writing. For Yellow Woman, the mythic heroine in *Storyteller* (1981), the river is the divide between tribal safety and Silva, the tall Navajo seducer who represents an alien culture and mindset as well as an opportunity for adventure. The region supplies the Laguna with variants of the Geronimo legend, which they treasure for its resilience and witty putdowns of the white despoilers of the frontier. For the Navajo heroine Ayah in "Lullaby" (1974), reestablishment of dignity and control of her family enables her to die peacefully and with honor. In token of the author's faith in the power of such narratives, novelist Larry McMurtry commented: "She knows that the stories won't save everyone; but, if they are faithfully kept and honored, the people will survive and perhaps in time recover their primal strength" (McMurtry, 20007, xxii).

For *Ceremony* (1977), a novel of repossession and healing set after World War II, Silko speaks firsthand of "the cycle of restoration" (Silko, 1977, 182). She introduces Katsina spirits, who arrive in Laguna each November for the masked dance by crossing the river at dawn. Countering the positive image, Auntie Thelma recalls the shame of "little sister" Laura returning naked at sunrise with only a pocketbook and lipstick, evidence of her promiscuity with Hispanic and white men. The novelist proffers two views of worries about her profligacy: "The Catholic priest shook his finger at the drunkenness and lust, but the people felt something deeper: they were losing her, they were losing part of themselves" (*ibid.*, 68). At the novel's resolution, Tayo, the ailing veteran of the Pacific war, returns home at sunrise following the autumnal equinox and the martyrdom of Harley by Emo, a war-crazed torturer and assassin, one of the witches who "destroy the feeling people have for each other" (*ibid.*, 229). After recouping Uncle Josiah's herd of wild Mexican longhorns from the white rustler Floyd Lee, Tayo enters the remodeled Laguna kiva, an underground ceremonial womb that nurtures the pueblo "and the peace of being with these hills" (*ibid.*, 108). In each example, the magic of place transforms characters — Yellow Woman into an adventurer, Laura into a pariah, Auntie Thelma into a religious fanatic, and Tayo into a cultural definer and savior.

## GLOBAL RECOVERY

In *Almanac of the Dead* (1991), the novelist writes "about the whole Earth trying to save herself" (Silko & Arnold, 2000, 131). She repudiates white concepts of land ownership and boundaries, a political situation she turns into an animal fable of red-spotted toads and pollywogs in *Sacred Water* (1993). The plot of *Almanac* sides with the Yaqui, a tribe sliced in half by the U.S.-Mexico border that President Franklin Pierce extended on

June 24, 1853. Out of respect for the people whose unity depends on visits and holidays, she exonerates illicit border crossings by poor indigenous Mesoamericans reclaiming their patrimony. A mass migration from the south threatens the pre-eminence of whites anchored at Tucson, a nexus of corruption and felony deriving from greed for property and water rights. The city becomes a hub of criminality exemplified by Lecha's drug cartel, Max Blue's murder for hire, insurance magnate Menardo Panson's private militias, Beaufrey's films of abortion and ritual circumcision, and Eddie Trigg's sex malls, blood donation sites, and organ transplant clinics—Alpha-Bio Products, Alpha-Hemo-Science Limited, Bio Mart, symbols of the decadence that consumes society. The gardener Sterling, the moral center of the cast of 77 characters, chooses to abandon the "bad dream" of drugs, guns, and easy money by salvaging his Laguna heritage, ethos, and stories (*ibid.*, 762). Calabazas, a Yaqui marijuana smuggler, fosters the rights of Sterling and other dispossessed to their homeland: "We are here thousands of years before the first whites.... We know where we belong on this earth" (*ibid.*, 216). Walter Benn Michaels, a literary theorist at the University of Illinois, summarizes the overturn of the status quo—"to replace the differences between what people think (ideology) and the differences between what people own (class) with the differences between what people are (identity)" (Michaels, 2006, 24).

In the analysis of Ernest Stromberg, a humanities professor at California State University, Silko generates a "complex web of energy and interrelationship in which nothing is ever lost" (Stromberg, 2006, 232). In honor of first peoples, *Almanac* anticipates through the prophecies of Mexican twins El Feo and Tacho the downfall of white evils because the European invader "had no future here because he had no past, no spirits of ancestors here" (Silko, 1991, 313). In a racial swap, the people's army offers white deserters from the U.S. military a cultural repatriation through "safe conduct to Oslo or Stockholm," a reunion of white with white (*ibid.*, 590–591). For the mass of revolutionaries, the Lakota attorney Wilson Weasel Tail exhorts followers in the style of Wovoka, the Paiute prophet, to retake the Southwest. His strategy is simple. The dispossessed must abandon betrayal and greed and reconcile their differences: "Step back from envy, from sorcery and poisoning. Reclaim these continents which belong to us" (*ibid.*, 721). Silko exonerates the roomful of idealists for their yearnings: "All their lives they had witnessed their people's suffering and genocide; it only took a few, the merest handful of such people, to lay the groundwork for the changes" (*ibid.*, 742). Only through revolution do the displaced peoples organize a sustainable hold on the land, cleanse it of white materialism, and recapture "democracy from corruption at all levels," (*ibid.*, 410). In reference to literature stolen and libraries burned by *conquistadores* and their followers as a means of setting in motion the Indian holocaust, analyst Jane Olmstead connects the urge to resettle stolen Indian lands with the subtextual need to redeem native histories, the touchstones of Amerindian identity.

## Seeds of Renewal

For *Gardens in the Dunes* (1999), Silko applies ecofeminism as an antidote to land theft. She chooses settings pillaged and flooded by an androcentric engineering project near Needles, California, that relocates the Colorado River to provide water for Las Vegas. The picaresque journey of Indigo, a Sand Lizard and resident of the Sonora Desert, prepare her for a radical change in lifestyle and traditional agriculture. In Somerset outside Bath, England, she views reclaimed Old World artifacts and cloister beds that Norman nuns once tended, where workers "discovered the intricate river pebble borders and carefully unearthed and repaired them" (Silko, 1999, 243). Setting a custodial example, Aunt Bron-wyn tends terraced gardens and orchards and reclaims the "stone [that] used to move and to talk until the churchgoers smashed them" (*ibid.*, 454). After collecting seeds and glad-iolus corms along her way—from Riverside, California, to Oyster Bay, Long Island; Som-erset, England; Lucca, Italy; and Bastia, Corsica—she treks back to her homeland to restore the neglected gardens of the deceased clan matriarch, Grandma Fleet.

Reseeding for Indigo parallels the reinvasion of indigenous peoples in *Almanac of the Dead*. By replanting vegetables, fruit trees, and flowers, she resows the land and initiates a hybrid agrarianism she learns from Aunt Bronwyn, a neo–Druid outside Bath, and from *la professoressa* Laura, a hybridizer of black gladioli in Lucca. Critic Annie Merrill Ingram, an Americanist at Davidson College, characterizes Indigo's new garden as an act of resist-ance, "a ritualized reenactment of communal knowledge that contests or subsumes colo-nizing claims to the same terrain" (Ingram, 2007, 138). As proof of rebirth, the dunes acquire rows of gladioli, a new snake to inhabit holy space around the garden spring, a reunion with Hattie and the Sand Lizard matriarchy, and a new member in Bright Eyes, Sister Salt and Big Candy's son. The non-native plants create a paradox of the outsider who brings good to the battered land. More significant to the area's mythos, it reintegrates a new set of episodes to bolster clan lore.

For *The Turquoise Ledge* (2010), the author's oneness with the Sonora Desert reveres the native legacy, symbolized by a grinding stone left under a tree by Indian women of ancient times. Annie Merrill Ingram lauds Silko as a model of rebalancing terrain, of "how ... ecological restoration, as a ritualized form of ecological redress, [can] deal with the ques-tions of indigenous history and sovereignty and become a framework of restitution for rights denied and peoples displaced" (Ingram, 2007, 129). The author recoups the sanc-tity of lava, bits of turquoise, raptors, and the rattlesnakes that inhabit her property. Critic Cynthia Carsten, a religion specialist at Arizona State University, celebrates how Silko's canon "remythologizes the landscape," which developers, anthropologists, prospectors, railroads, and tourists have desecrated (Carsten, 2006, 123).

*See also* Indigo; nativism; Wovoka.

• *References and further reading*

Carsten, Cynthia. "Storyteller: Leslie Marmon Silko's Reappropriation of Native American History and Iden-tity," *Wicazo SA Review* 21:2 (Autumn 2006): 105–126.

Ingram, Annie Merrill. *Coming into Contact: Explorations in Ecocritical Theory and Practice*. Athens: Uni-versity of Georgia Press, 2007.

McMurtry, Larry. "Introduction" to *Ceremony*. New York: Penguin, 2007.

Michaels, Walter Benn. *The Shape of the Signifier: 1967 to the End of History*. Princeton, NJ: Princeton Uni-versity Press, 2006.

Olmstead, Jane. "The Uses of Blood in Leslie Marmon Silko's *Almanac of the Dead*," *Contemporary Litera-ture* 40:3 (Fall 1999): 464–490.

Petrolle, Jean. *Religion without Belief: Contemporary Allegory and the Search for Postmodern Faith*. Albany: State University of New York Press, 2007.

Silko, Leslie Marmon. *Almanac of the Dead*. New York: Simon & Schuster, 1991.

_____. *Ceremony*. New York: Viking, 1977.

_____. *Gardens in the Dunes*. New York: Scribner, 1999.

_____. *Yellow Woman and a Beauty of the Spirit: Essays on Native American Life Today*. New York: Simon & Schuster, 1996.

_____, and Ellen L. Arnold. *Conversations with Leslie Marmon Silko*. Jackson: University Press of Mississippi, 2000.

Stromberg, Ernest. *American Indian Rhetorics of Survivance: Word Medicine, Word Magic*. Pittsburgh: Uni-versity of Pittsburgh Press, 2006.

Su, John J. *Ethics and Nostalgia in the Contemporary Novel.* Cambridge: Cambridge University Press, 2005.

Werlock, Abby H. P. *Facts on File Companion to the American Short Story.* New York: Facts on File, 2010.

# religion

In fond glimpses of the Laguna Pueblo and its environs, Silko stresses the continuity of place as an element of animistic spirituality. From girlhood, she learned to leave evidence of past lives untouched. As she explains in her memoir, *The Turquoise Ledge* (2010): "Human things had to be respected too and the special places where the ancestor spirits resided" (Silko, 2010, 144). She remarks on the permeation of daily activities with reverence: "Thoughtful action of any sort becomes worship; devoted attentiveness becomes worship" (Silko, 1996, 184). In her early writing, she characterized the coming of age and initiation of a Pueblo teenager in "Humaweepi, Warrior Priest," which she published in *The Man to Send Rain Clouds: Contemporary Stories by American Indians* (1974). The preparation of a young man by his uncle outlines the cyclical nature of the priestly apprenticeship, which passes down the generations. The uncle emphasizes, "Human beings are special.... They can do anything" (Silko, 1974, 162). Essential to Humaweepi's initiation into the priesthood, in addition to chants, dances, songs, and prayers, is unity with animals, plants, and the terrain. By allying with the outdoors, the 19-year-old learns to survive and to appreciate sleeping in a deer nest and subsisting on wild grapes dried into raisins, wild tulip bulbs, tumbleweed sprouts, and grass and iris roots, the gifts of the Mother Creator. By the time that Humaweepi chants reverently at the lakeshore his thanks to nature, he realizes that priesthood descends naturally on him.

Silko learned early the conflicts between Amerindian animism and orthodox Christianity. In a discussion of religious elements in the novels of native authors—Navarre Scott Momaday's *House Made of Dawn* (1969), Silko's *Ceremony* (1977), and Louise Erdrich's *Love Medicine* (1984) and *The Bingo Palace* (1994), John A. McClure, an English professor at Rutgers, acknowledged that Amerindians impacted the white world as more spiritual, more related to the planet, and closer to native gods than Euro-Americans. In each novel, characters grow disenchanted with the materialistic society and grope toward polytheism, spirituality, unity with Earth, and "a distrust at once of sweeping claims for salvation and dogmatic rigidities" (McClure, 2007, 133). Destabilizing the demands of orthodoxy is the history of conquest and punitive assimilation in locales distinct for their geographic and cultural uniqueness. McClure asserts the delicacy of psychosocial situations for native seekers: "The cosmos that sustains and heals their protagonists is intricately made, precariously balanced, full of risk, and subject to shifts and mortal disruptions" (*ibid.,* 135–136). The safety zone lies in the cultural inclusion of tribes that welcome minority opinions, struggle, reciprocal liturgies, and orderly change within the society.

## THE LAGUNA FAITH

The author's rants against the faith introduced by Christian missionaries derive from her reverence for the pueblo. In childhood, she listened to Grandma A'mooh's bible readings, but rejected Christianity "because the Christians made up such terrible lies about Indian people that it was clear to me they would lie about other matters also" (Silko, 1996, 17). As the author explains in the introduction to *Yellow Woman and a Beauty of the Spirit: Essays on Native American Life Today* (1996), the devout Presbyterianism of Grandma

A'mooh generated family conflict. Silko listened to her bible stories, but refused to believe them, a scenario she turns to fiction in the catechism classes of Sister Conrad and boarding school curriculum at the Sherman Institute in *Gardens in the Dunes* (1999). The exploitation and suppression of first peoples reveals too much racism, too much white superiority to endear Christian teachings to Silko.

To avoid punitive scripture, the author sought the love of the Laguna terrain and the companionship of her horse Joey and dog Bulls-eye. She concluded that seeing is believing — that "the squash blossom, grasshopper, or rabbit itself could never be created by the human hand" (*ibid.*, 28). She refuted the determinism of orthodox religion by recognizing random beauty — the gift of a rainstorm, humble insects and reptiles, and the destruction of a lightning strike in a single bolt from the sky. In *Sacred Water* (1993), she charges white Christian polluters with sacrilege for the threat to groundwater and natural springs and lakes from overpopulation and from toxic nuclear waste runoff, a constant menace from the Jackpile uranium mine abandoned at Paguate in 1981. The essay "Fifth World: The Return of Ma ah shra true ee" (1996) indicts religious seekers for finding miracles in places outside Indian land, but not among the Yaqui poor of New Mexico or "in the midst of a strip-mining operation" (*ibid.*, 133). Thus, her worship of creation became a response to the organic interconnection of earth dwellers, whether animal, plant, mineral, or the blessing conferred by deceased spirits.

In *Yellow Woman and a Beauty of the Spirit: Essays on Native American Life Today*, Silko's essay "Hunger Stalked the Tribal People" describes a touching solemnity to table blessings. During a period of crop failure and starvation, families scolded children for wasting food. To establish the sanctity of meals from Laguna's plants and animals, diners place pinches of servings in a small pottery bowl as a gift to the family's ancestral spirits, a ritual similar to those observed by the ancient Chinese and Romans. A common humanity required the sharing with strangers of limited foodstuffs, even with Apache and Navajo raiders who rustled sheep. The author concludes, "Each meal at Laguna was an occasion for thanksgiving" (Silko, 1996, 97). She adds a rational argument for sharing with the have-nots — hungry people are restless and dangerous. Thus, sharing promotes peace and security, two qualities missing from the cant of Christian missionaries.

A FUSION OF FAITHS

As explained by critic Charles H. Lippy, the LeRoy A. Martin Distinguished Professor of Religious Studies at the University of Tennessee at Chattanooga, Silko avoids setting tribal religiosity above Christianity. Instead, she looks to a fusion of faiths "along with a vibrant substratum of indigenous religiosity that may have defied or minimized syncretism with Christianity" (Lippy, 2002, 83). According to the author's essay "The Indian with a Camera" (1993), at the outset, Amerindians welcomed "Jesus, Mary, Joseph, and the saints" and "set the Christian gods on their altars to join the legions of old American spirits and gods," including Quetzalcoatl, the feathered serpent deity of the Olmec and Aztec who "[shared] the altar with Jesus" (Silko, 1993, 6). Inclusivity shocked whites for the syncretism of the old with the new. From childhood, she recalls that her people allowed white photographers to view kiva ritual and katchina dances. The openness to visitors ended after the Hopi and Pueblo realized that white camera bugs "were cheap voyeurs who had no reverence for the spiritual" (Silko, 1993, 5). Intruders created antipathy by testifying in court against caciques and kiva elders. Prosecutors charged native priests for violating white statutes outlawing indigenous religion, which whites replaced with Christianity.

In accordance with Amerindian theology, Silko's works perpetuate Laguna open-mindedness. She extols an ungendered belief system unsullied by the Judeo-Christian, Buddhist, and Islamic reverence for male deities only. In a preface to Vine Deloria's *God Is Red* (2003), she asserted, "God has always been red on these continents called the Americas. And God — Mother Earth God — and the religions of the indigenous communities of the Americas are alive and thriving" (Silko, 2003, viii). Critics Bridget Keegan, an English professor at Creighton University, and James C. McKusick, dean of the honors program and the University of Montana, state that the author "sees nature as inseparable from divinity," a union that garnishes her verse and prose with luminosity (Keegan and McKusick, 2000, 1081). In a celebratory verse, "Slim Man Canyon" (1972), she creates serenity from acclimation of desert people to terrain and climate. Gracing the setting, petroglyphs recall seven centuries of Navajo songs and tales that unify Pueblo people and perpetuate their longevity and lore. Her "Prayer to the Pacific" (1973), a ritual poem and commentary on the rain myth first published in *Chicago Review*, pictures Laguna origination from the sea. Dated 30,000 years earlier, the arrival of giant sea turtles, led by Grandfather Turtle, requires the phalanx of swimmers to cross the ocean from China and lumber up on shore. In native style, the scenario carries the blessing of the sun, a constant in Silko's devotional imagery and a reminder that life on earth is an ongoing gift. The flow of phrases and typography that lavishes the words wave-style across the page connects the Indian diaspora and survival in a new land with water, a necessary focus of the literature of desert peoples. In an allusion to the flow of breast milk from the mother, the third stave depicts the selection of four shore stones that revive the speaker after an encounter with the Pacific coast.

## Spiritual Fiction

Silko's skill at metafiction in *Ceremony* (1977), a novel of reclamation, reveals native imagination and the merger of vital faiths as antidotes to world cataclysm, injustice, and despair. The hypocrisy introduced by Spanish *conquistadores*, Roman Catholicism equates with the theft of the sacred, a destabilization of native belief systems that leaves Tayo with no weapons to counter his aunt's stiff-necked cruelty. The text pictures the humiliation of a worthy man, Uncle Josiah, the whipping boy of his mother and sister and the victim of a Puritanic church. In the bed of Night Swan, the Mexican cantina dancer, he rails against a sexual attraction that turns him into a fornicator. In the presence of his own weakness, he turns his self-loathing into accusations of witchery against Night Swan, whom he threatens to run out of town. Josiah's innate compassion for others grates on his pious sister, an orthodox Roman Catholic, whose fear of criticism turns her against Tayo, her mixed-blood nephew/foster son. Like Josiah, Tayo gropes his way home through muddled values toward Pueblo spirituality, a polytheism that exposes the overt racism and elitism in Auntie Thelma's piety. In place of "white man talk" about deity, Silko substitutes the simplicity and wonder of animism.

To face challenges of the atomic age, Silko's Laguna characters adapt beliefs to counter incomprehensible threats to human survival, symbolized by the detonation of atomic bombs over Hiroshima and Nagasaki, Japan, on August 6 and 8, 1945. Critic Brenda J. Powell, a professor at the University of St. Thomas in Minnesota, describes the atmosphere of Silko's first novel as "fundamentally in tension with and often destructive of indigenous culture and myths," a necessary adaptation to the dilemmas introduced by World War II (Powell, 2010, 481). To retain power over evil, according to analyst Amanda

Porterfield, a religion professor at Florida State University, the people's lore needs "to be continually relived, reimagined, and represented in new ways," such as Tayo's hallucinogenic coitus with the earth priestess Ts'eh Montaño and the markers and guides in old Betonie's heap of telephone directories and out-of-date calendars, the clutter evidences his attempt to restore order to a perplexing world beset by falsehood (Porterfield, 2002, 306).

Silko's evocative passages, like those of Louise Erdrich's *Tracks* (1988), describe the disjointed thoughts and emotions of Tayo, a victim of monstrous war trauma. At the depth of despair, he longs to dematerialize, "to fade until he was as flat as his own hand looked, flat like a drawing in the sand which did not speak or move, waiting for the wind to come swirling along the ground and blow the lines away" (Silko, 1977, 106). In the description of analyst Jean Ellen Petrolle, an English professor at Columbia College, the novelist "[perceives] salvific potential in the rewriting of history" to show "how indigenous peoples might respond creatively and powerfully to the challenge of surviving colonization and genocide" (Petrolle, 2007, 130). While Tayo weeps helplessly after his return from a Japanese prison camp in the Philippines, Silko strips him of the sturdy U.S. military bravado capable of exterminating the enemy. Sorrowing for his near-brother Rocky, Tayo regresses to the abandoned illegitimate son of Laura and blames himself for praying away the rain that plunges Laguna into a drought. As childhood stories and memories of family relations swirl in his mind, he reaches for handholds on stability. The reclamation of Laguna ceremony promises healing through traditional oneness with divinity on the sacred land.

## Pragmatic Religion

Silko's theology vibrates with complex, often disturbing conjecture. Her abhorrence of missionary interference re-emerges in "Grace Abounding in Botswana" (1986), a critique for the *New York Times Book Review*. She concurs with the Chinese that, where peasants starve, dogs are a viable option for fresh meat. The concept survived among Plains Indians "until Christian missionaries arrived with their sentimentality for their pets" (Silko, 1986, 7). With *Ceremony* and *Almanac of the Dead* (1991), Silko refutes the Cartesian concept of the dualism of good and evil. In conversation with interviewer Ellen L. Arnold, Silko reasoned, "Just because somebody like Nietzsche says God is dead doesn't mean that evil left, too" (Silko & Arnold, 2000, 111). Speaking through Uncle Josiah, she states a native truism: "Nothing was all good or all bad either; it all depended," a flexible ethos that dominates her views of humankind and the ramifications of survival (Silko, 1977, 11).

Silko pictures evil as too much of a good thing, such as rain on young corn seedlings or an adobe roof. In a chaotic resolution to *Almanac of the Dead*, she dramatizes Clinton, the Afro-Cherokee historian and liberator, charging "Jesus junkies" with making religion into a drug much like the substances that addict dope takers and winos (Silko, 1991, 742). In an interview with critic Linda G. Niemann, an English professor at Kennesaw Sate University, Silko put a human face on too much of a good thing by characterizing the voting process as a formalized exclusion of the homeless and alienated, members of the American Third World. After a groundswell of rebellion, idealists picture the yin of electoral yang stripping professional politicians of authority and placing in positions of power ordinary people, including women and people of color. Silko's faith in natural change asserts itself in her belief that the birth rate, immigration, and threats to women's reproductive rights pose the strongest antidote to the swaggering white male conqueror and his materialistic haven.

## SALVAGING THE PAST

From an emphasis on patriarchal conquest, homosexual bloodlust, and carnal gratifi-cation, Silko's *Almanac of the Dead* makes a wrenching departure from her lyric ecofem-inist verse and stories and the gentle spiritual awakening in *Ceremony*. The corruption of a lustful monsignor and a priest's complicity with a pedophile in the rape of a young girl strengthen the anti–Western, anti-patriarchal, anti–Christian tone and atmosphere of her allegorical apocalypse. Zeta, an Anglo-Yaqui smuggler, fumes over the Catholic teaching that smuggling is a sin "because smuggling was stealing from the government" (*ibid.*, 133). Critic Claudia Sadowski-Smith, a humanities specialist at Arizona State University, inter-poses a rhetorical question: "Where were the priest and his Catholic church when the fed-eral soldiers used Yaqui babies for target practice? Stealing from the government?" (Sadowski-Smith, 2008, 78). In a dystopia destabilized by morbid voyeurism, lust, and greed, a delegation of Laguna elders visits a Santa Fe museum to identify and repatriate ancestral stone icons of "Little Grandmother" and "Little Grandfather" (Silko, 1991, 31). Symbolic of the godly grace that accompanied the Pueblo on their migration north to New Mexico, the stone figurines represent the protection of tradition by ancestral parents. An officious white curator's dismissal of the delegation and its authority allegorizes the white world's sacrilege in displaying artifacts as historic exhibits of conquest. One elderly Laguna collapses out of despair that his people have lost their spiritual grandsires.

To energize first peoples and outcasts with the strength and vision of rebels, Silko insists that individual pantheons of gods must merge, just as races and tribes must share the task of tossing out imperialists. Analyst Kathryn Hume, an expert in comparative lit-erature at Stanford University, explains the rejection of European faiths: "When slaves came to this country, some of their loas (voodoo spirits) survived transplantation and have flourished, whereas true Christianity ... has not" (Hume, 2002, 205). The Afro-Cherokee Viet vet Clinton, an amputee and fomenter of revolt, envisions a synthesis of non–Chris-tian tribal deities— Cimi, the Mayan personification of Death; Cinq-Jour Malheureux, Haitian inflictor of catastrophe; the Haitian demon Congo Zandor; and Damballah, the Yoruban snake god. To this pantheon, he allies Eurzulie, the Yoruban goddess of love and beauty; Gede-Brav, the Haitian phallic power; Gede Ge Rouge, the Yoruban cannibal god and master of the afterlife; Ogoun Ferraille, the Yoruban warrior god; and far-seeing Quet-zalcoatl, the Mesoamerican feathered snake and sky power worshiped by both the Olmec and Aztec. The force of so grand a rainbow coalition impels the anonymous underdogs from the south along desert trails through Mexico toward the apostates of Tucson. To ready himself for the coming cataclysm, Clinton reunites with his black Indian cousins in New York and moves south toward Haiti to buttress collaborators in a universal resistance of oppressive Christian capitalists.

## GLOBAL FAITHS

Through comparative anthropology and mythography, *Gardens of the Dunes* (1999) refutes male-dominated Catholicism by featuring Celtic, Minervan, and Gnostic gyno-centric alternatives to androcentric orthodoxy. For source material, Silko draws on the biblical visionary Ezekiel, Tarot readings, Arthurian Grail lore, and Celtic circles, groves, and runes. Analyst David Murray, an expert in American studies at the University of Not-tingham, declares that the bible "is actually premised on the exclusion of many disparate texts and divergent ideas ... that would share much more with 'primitive' and other reli-

gions than the present orthodoxy" (Murray, 2007, 146). The author returns to those primitive rites and icons in *The Turquoise Ledge* (2010), in which she interprets the legend of
St. Patrick ridding Ireland of snakes as a myth of the purging of the British Isles of aboriginal cults that revered the serpent. In the edenic opening of *Gardens*, Silko pictures the
fecundity of earth as a gift from Grandfather Snake, who settled his niece Sand Lizard in
terraced gardens of the Arizona sandhills. In return for amaranth greens, beans, corn,
pumpkins, roots, squash, and sunflowers, tillers of the dunes thank the Mother Creator
by offering the first picking to ancestral spirits, the second to birds and animals, and the
third to bees. By leaving choice fruits to the land, the gardeners anticipate a subsequent
year of lush harvests. For the sake of survival, Sand Lizard rules demand successive plantings because "human beings are undependable; they might forget to plant at the right
time or they might not be alive next year" (Silko, 1999, 15).

   In contrast to the inbred Amerindian devotion to animism, Silko juxtaposes the
atmosphere of Christian education at the Sherman Institute in Riverside, California, where
white teachers have sour faces and dormitory matrons pinch the children. Sensibly, Indigo,
a protagonist, prefers the safety of desert sandhills "far away from churches and schools"
(*ibid.*, 70). At the Parker Reservation on the Arizona-California boundary, Sister Salt views
proof of Christian greed in the unfruitful floodplain gravel given to the Apache, Chemehuevi, Cocopa, Mojave, and Yuma as opposed to rich Colorado River bottom land "allot-
ted to regular churchgoers" (*ibid.*, 204). Snide asides about the missionaries' obsession
with miscegenation and of warnings that coupling with black men will produce babies with
monkey tails indicate why Sister Salt has no wish to trust Christians. Upon her departure
from the reservation, she slashes the long sleeves and high neck from her blouse and cuts
her skirt into strips to combat the heat. On hotter days, she prefers nudity, an outrage to
prissy Protestant Europeans.

   A scene on the S.S. *Pavonia* illustrates the primal link between Indians and nature.
In the roll of the ship on its way to Bristol, England, Indigo pictures the water alive with
wave and wind. Realizing that "Ocean was Earth's sister," she grieves for Sister Salt (*ibid.*,
224). Indigo's weeping precedes a prayer to Ocean to deliver a message to her sister that
the two would reunite eventually. Indigo's natural affinity for prayerful communion with
spirits mirrors the enthusiasm of Hattie Abbott Palmer for protofeminist readings in Coptic scrolls. From her study of early church history at Dr. Rhinehart's library, she ventures
into the lives of the "Illumined Ones," the apostles of Jesus who obtain "secrets not revealed
to the bishops or cardinals or the pope himself" (Silko, 1999, 229). The epiphanies echo
Silko's belittlement of corrupt ecclesiastical hierarchy, who color her fiction with their
avarice and manipulation of believers. She speaks through Indigo a sorrow that "so many
greedy and cruel people did damage only the Messiah could repair" (*ibid.*, 455). The author
identifies with Aunt Bronwyn, a druidic rescuer of sacred stones in Somerset, England.
Storytelling sessions during a rainstorm heighten the affinity of Indigo for the old woman,
an enthusiast for Celtic myth and apostate from the church. To assist the child in her search
for Mama among the followers of the Indian Messiah and his dancers, Bronwyn admits
"Christ ... might be anywhere" (*ibid.*, 264).

   Silko concurs with the ubiquity of godhood. In *Turquoise Ledge* (2010), she returns
to the concept of deceased spirits returning to earth in the form of rainclouds. An unidentified critic for *Kirkus Reviews* notes that the author "argues that nature actually functions
as a spiritual go-between linking departed ancestors with living relatives" ("Review," 2010,
612). She relates the experience of a teacher at a Hopi school who recognizes the benefi-

cence of her dead seven-year-old son in a small rain cloud that pauses overhead, to "bring precious precipitation" (Silko, 2010, 13). The author extends the concept of ancestral visitation in the actions of birds and wild animals. Human survivors honor the deceased with a serving of fry bread dropped into the hot coals to feed the dead. Her family's difficulties with understanding a Presbyterian grandmother and pitying Grandma Lillie Ann Stagner's excommunication from the Catholic church for marrying a non–Christian, Grandpa Henry C. "Hank" Marmon, explain some of the author's antipathies toward legalistic and non-inclusive faiths.

*See also* hypocrisy; Palmer, Hattie Abbott; ritual; Wovoka.

- *References and further reading*

Avila, Monica. "Leslie Marmon Silko's *Ceremony*: Witchery and Sacrifice of Self," *Explicator* 67:1 (Fall 2008): 53–55.

"Grace Abounding in Botswana" (review), *New York Times Book Review* (23 March 1986): 7.

Grobman, Laurie. "(Re)Interpreting 'Storyteller' in the Classroom: Teaching at the Crossroads," *College Literature* 27:3 (Fall 2000): 88–110.

Hume, Kathryn. *American Dream, American Nightmare: Fiction since 1960*. Urbana: University of Illinois Press, 2002.

Jones, Tayari. "Folk Tale of Survival," *The Progressive* (2000): 43–44.

Keegan, Bridget, and James C. McKusick. *Literature and Nature: Four Centuries of Nature Writing*. New York: Prentice Hall, 2000.

Kutzbach, Konstanze, and Monika Mueller. *The Abject of Desire: The Aestheticization of the Unaesthetic in Contemporary Literature and Culture*. Amsterdam: Rodopi, 2007.

Lippy, Charles H. *Pluralism Comes of Age: American Religious Culture in the Twentieth Century*. Armonk, NY: M. E. Sharpe, 2002.

McClure, John A. *Partial Faiths: Postsecular Fiction in the Age of Pynchon and Morrison*. Athens: University of Georgia Press, 2007.

Murphy, Patrick D., Terry Gifford, and Katsunori Yamazato. *Literature of Nature: An International Sourcebook*. New York: Taylor & Francis, 1998.

Murray, David. *Matter, Magic, and Spirit: Representing Indian and African American Belief*. Philadelphia: University of Pennsylvania Press, 2007.

Niemann, Linda, and Leslie Marmon Silko. "Narratives of Survival," *Women's Review of Books* 9:10–11 (July 1992): 10.

Petrolle, Jean. *Religion without Belief: Contemporary Allegory and the Search for Postmodern Faith*. Albany: State University of New York Press, 2007.

Porter, Joy. *Place and Native American Indian History and Culture*. New York: Peter Lang, 2007.

Porterfield, Amanda. *American Religious History*. Malden, MA: Blackwell, 2002.

Powell, Brenda J. "Mythic Realism: Magic and Mystery in Marele Day's *Lambs of God*," *Christianity & Literature* 59:3 (April 2010): 479–502.

"Review: *The Turquoise Ledge*," *Kirkus Reviews* 78:13 (1 July 2010): 612.

Sadowski-Smith, Claudia. *Border Fictions: Globalization, Empire, and Writing at the Boundaries of the United States*. Charlottesville: University of Virginia Press, 2008.

Silko, Leslie Marmon. *Almanac of the Dead*. New York: Simon & Schuster, 1991.

_____. "Foreword" to *God Is Red*, by Vine Deloria, Jr. Golden, CO: Fulcrum, 2003.

_____. *Gardens in the Dunes*. New York: Scribner, 1999.

_____. "Grace Abounding in Botswana" (review), *New York Times Book Review* (23 March 1986): 7.

_____. "Humaweepi, Warrior Priest" in *The Man to Send Rain Clouds: Contemporary Stories by American Indians*, ed. Kenneth Rosen. New York: Viking, 1974.

_____. "The Indian with a Camera," foreword to *A Circle of Nations: Voices and Visions of American Indians*. Hillsboro, OR: Beyond Words Publishing, 1993.

_____. *The Turquoise Ledge: A Memoir*. New York: Viking, 2010.

_____. *Yellow Woman and a Beauty of the Spirit: Essays on Native American Life Today*. New York: Simon & Schuster, 1996.

_____, and Ellen L. Arnold. *Conversations with Leslie Marmon Silko*. Jackson: University Press of Mississippi, 2000.

# ritual

Silko extricates religious and healing ceremonies from the dismissive white perception of paganism to an integral part of the Amerindian understanding of suffering and agency. As a pre-schooler, she viewed the Navajo and Pueblo purification rites conducted for World War II veterans returning home from combat in Africa, Asia, Europe, and the Pacific. Practitioners of ritual intended for ritual to shield survivors from illness and harm generated by participation in combat. The failure of traditional chants, prayers, and sand paintings caused her to blame the indelible evil of 20th-century warfare on individuals, families, and tribes. She learned that residents of the Laguna community relate an individual's experiences to reassure traumatized tribe members that they did not suffer alone, the purpose of the legends of Yellow Woman, John Dillinger, and Geronimo. Eventually, corroborating stories about similar incidents from the past merged with all tales of violence and triumph to enroll the era's GIs in the tribe's battlefield histories.

In the author's view of culture, ritual combines symbolic acts and gestures to create a powerful attitude and pervasive motivation in practitioners, the focus of her coming-of-age story "Humaweepi, the Warrior Priest" (1974). Re-enactments counter anxiety and despair at ignorance, injustice, and human pain by transcending human experience with evidence of a metaphysical plain of being. For Humaweepi, his chant at the lakeside unites him with the spirit of the bear, an iconic animal in Amerindian beast lore reflected by a boulder that takes the bear's shape. In *The Turquoise Ledge* (2010), the novelist describes a Hopi pilgrimage in March 2006 from Hotevila, Arizona, to Mexico City to propitiate Tlaloc, the Aztec god of rain, to end 11 years of drought. To gain the aid of the deity, runners carry corn meal, pollen, and water from sacred springs, the liquid emergence of life-giving water from the underworld. In answer to their gifts, the ritual performers interpret the appearance of an eagle as a heavenly reply. Tlaloc's mercy appears on June 16 in the form of rain engulfing the Sierra Madre, followed in winter by ample snowstorms.

Some ritual objects, Silko observes, date back 18,000 years to the aborigines of the Southwest. According to Chip Colwell-Chanthaphonh, the curator of anthropology at the Denver Museum of Nature & Science, first peoples, since ancient times, "have been struggling to get things for humans to be able to carry on and thrive, not just scrape by" (Colwell-Chanthaphonh, 2005, 166). Silko's writings revive respect for their ritual objects, but the expert reminds the unwary, "You can't meddle with it too much, or there will be trouble" (*ibid.*). Consecrated ceremonies reaffirm belief in order and in the realistic wonder in faith, which supercedes belief in emotions, intellect, and morality. The individual benefits by envisioning the greater sphere and by acclimating the self to a universe that human efforts cannot change. Like the wizard Merlin in Camelot or Friar Tuck in Sherwood Forest, the enlightened celebrant must revere two paths—being and doing. Wisdom of the elders directs the worshiper to accept being as a nonconfrontational lifestyle as well as to learn how and when to take action to secure life and security.

## RITUAL PURPOSE

In her earliest parable, "The Man to Send Rain Clouds" (1969), published in the *New Mexico Quarterly*, the author depicts the simple, but touching respect of two cultures for Grandpa Teofilo, a deceased sheepherder and ceremonial dancer, found two days after his death. Ken and his brother-in-law Leon descend an arroyo to retrieve the body, wrap it in a red blanket, and honor it with a gray feather and blue, yellow, green, and white face paint, colors drawn from nature for the purpose of harmonizing the corpse with the earth. The bringing of food to the family serves a practical purpose — feeding gravediggers who cut through frozen turf to shape a burial site. In a touch of grace, Ken tosses corn meal and pollen over the corpse and prays for the soul to send rain, the element that ensures the pueblo's longevity. To Father Paul, a sign of devotion to deity requires weekly attendance at Mass; to Ken and Leon, the shepherd is "O.K. now" because a less rigid performance of ritual than the priest's has restored Teofilo's unity with nature and with tribal continuity (Silko, 1969, 135).

Elders continue the respectful ceremony with candles and medicine bags in a half-hidden sun, an emblem of a bicultural rite for Teofilo, whose name means "beloved of God." A final dusting of corn meal repeats the blessing as Grandpa Teofilo carries to the nether world his assignment to guard survivors. Despite suspicions of Indian trickery, the Franciscan priest, bound to serve the poor and outcast, violates his ritual of last rites and holy water to sprinkle the red blanket. His attempt to retrieve a forgotten thought suggests a Jungian perspective on universal human memory, a sharing of global history that unites all people. Possibly, Silko views Father Paul as a potential convert from orthodoxy to a less legalistic Pueblo view of life and death. The syncretism of Laguna graveside ritual with Catholic dogma discloses an early perspective that Silko later espouses in her study of clashing white and native cultures. Unlike the uncertainties of *Ceremony* and *Almanac of the Dead*, the story concludes on the phrase "for sure," an indication of the author's youthful idealism. A resilient character in her early stories, Teofilo returns in "Tony's Story" (1969) as a storykeeper, a bearer of culture.

RITUAL CLEANSING

In *Ceremony* (1977), Silko's first novel, ritual derives from both repeated actions and words and from intuitive propitiation of earth powers. In summer 1941, Tayo and his Uncle Josiah learn that holy men climb the mountains, study the night sky, and listen to dawn winds for signs of drought relief. On his own, Tayo picks yellow flowers and shakes pollen from them onto the pool in the cliff crevice, thus merging icons of fertility with a symbol of revival. The devotional gift seems, if not orthodox, at least appropriate. His observations of a spider, frogs, and dragonflies remind him of hopeful myths of Spider Woman (Ts'its'tsi'nako or Thought Woman) and of the sand frogs that crop up after years of drought. The two-tone blue of the dragonfly wings form a duality of blue daytime and dark blue night skies, an assurance that the 24-hour cycle will continue and life will go on changing as it always had. Silko graces Tayo's idyll at the pool with the flit of a hummingbird, a streak of green that promises the renewal of flowers and the seasons. In spring 1948, he experiences another intuitive study of ritual by striping his hands with the white markings of ceremonial dancers. The gypsum lines generate a gestalt (pattern) that he respects, the use of natural colorings to connect the dancers with earth.

Subsequent depictions of ritual pinpoint its weakness — the orthodox gestures, chants, and songs that fail to combat new forms of threat in the world. In the description of author Simon Joseph Ortiz, Tayo is "still not home ... far away from himself" (Ortiz, 2006, 258). The human actor of old world ritual, Ku'oosh, the tedious Laguna medicine man, leads Tayo to memories of the scalp ceremony, a cave ritual involving the warriors' bestowal of scalps on a subterranean altar. Tayo receives a limited boost from Ku'oosh's words and from a dose of Indian tea (Mormon tea or *Ephedra virida*), a stimulant that offers whiffs and a taste of rain-tinged air and damp green turf. The colors defeat momentarily the images of red, bloody wounds and the white fog that encases Tayo's mind and shields him from reliving the Bataan Death March, where his cousin/foster brother dies in April 1942. Silko exemplifies rigidity in Ku'oosh's meticulous adherence to past ceremony, which has little power to stem the sufferings of GIs returning from World War II. Nonetheless, it is the elderly shaman who insists, "You better get help soon" (Silko, 1977, 98). Although the author did not consciously structure the novel, tendencies from her youthful observation of derelict and alcoholic veterans express an immediacy and a demand for action to save them from ruin.

RITUAL MAGIC

Rehabilitation requires more effective ritual that employs potent, up-to-the-minute magic. At Betonie's stone hogan above Gallup, the old Chicano-Navajo healer puffs on hand-rolled cigarettes, a ritual that activates the power of tobacco, a medicinal plant featured in the myth of the purification of earth by Fly and Hummingbird. The smoky atmosphere and Betonie's smoke rings released in the night sky precede a sacred quest, the old man's four-stage assignment to Tayo: find stars, Mexican longhorns, the holy mountain, and a woman. At the third stage, Tayo searches for the constellation and his Uncle Josiah's wild speckled herd on the land of rustler Floyd Lee and locates the woman, Ts'eh Montaño, a wonder worker who cultivates medicinal plants. Among them, she grows the morning glory vine (*Ipomoea nil*), which links him directly to Spider Woman. The liminal plant, which twines around "four wide windows," the portal separating real and supernatural realms, prefigures the emergence of blue and yellow shades throughout the sexual idyll (*ibid.*, 170). The colors reflect blue sky, the source of a mountainous vista, life-giving rain, and sexual union conferring a welcome rejuvenation for Tayo, who greets the sunrise with prayer, "We come at sunrise to greet you.... Father of the clouds you are beautiful" (*ibid.*, 169).

Silko anticipates the destruction of earth through profligate use of the atomic bomb and asserts that new ceremonies and restored lore from ancient times must replace the standard ritual from the past. The text refers to the testing of atomic power in a blast at the Trinity Site in Los Alamos, New Mexico, on July 16, 1945, a white anti-ritual that produces a major breach in the flow of human history. The messianic "new man," Tayo, a hybrid Laguna with Mexican eyes, transcends outworn notions of race and ethnicity through flashback and introspection. During his testing in the wilderness, he re-enacts a deer ritual by concealing himself in a niche, shaking his head like a buck, and yelling "ahooouuuh!," his cry to the wild side of his nature (*ibid.*, 205). As in her story "The Two Sisters" (1981), Silko honors the deer as "the original food" that pueblo people depend on (Silko, 1981, 101). Tayo's bestial performance prefigures a meeting with a cougar and with Mountain Lion Man, the husband of Ts'eh and mythic hunter, both elements of Tayo's readying for normalcy.

The ritual quest unfolds with the propitiation of the she-elk pictograph that priests paint on the cliff and Tayo's retreat to the Laguna kiva, where his narrative adds to clan lore his unique story. Ortiz explains: "Tayo does return, not by magic or mysticism or some abstract revelation; instead the return is achieved through a ceremony of story, the tracing of story, rebuilding of story, and the creation of story" (Ortiz, 2006, 258). As proof of the renewal of old ceremony, Tayo confers with the elders who "thought maybe there might be something you should tell them" (*ibid.*, 212). Silko pictures Ku'oosh feeding the fire with kindling, a re-ignition of old lore with new energy. Optimistically, the ritual purges the war veteran of battle fatigue and readies him to embrace a messianic destiny for his people.

## RITUAL AND NATURES

In *Gardens in the Dunes* (1999), a neo–Victorian novel, Silko regards ritual as an everyday duty, a natural part of coexistence with earth. In the southwestern sandhills of Arizona, Grandma Fleet, the mentor and teacher of granddaughters Indigo and Sister Salt, insists on reverence for all living things. The female clan honors their matriarch, the Sand Lizard, by following the teachings of Grandfather Snake, the guardian of the spring. Sand Lizard combats greed with a three-fold harvest ceremony. The first fruits belong "to the spirits of our beloved ancestors," the sources of rain; the second fruit feeds the birds and wild animals for tolerate tender sprouts and seedlings (Silko, 1999, 15). The third fruit harvesters leave for "the bees, ants, mantises, and others who cared for the plants" (*ibid.*). A few thriving plants producing beans, pumpkins, and squash remain unharvested to return to earth the beginnings of next year's garden. The horticultural system reflects the workings of nature herself, a female deity who epitomizes generosity.

In *The Turquoise Ledge* (2010), the author's memoir, she returns to issues of ritual and to the disturbance of landmarks from anchorage in the earth. She describes visits by ethnographer Franz Boas and anthropologist Elsie Clews Parsons in 1917 and 1918 for the purpose of observing Laguna pueblo life. Of the deaths of residents from influenza and lightning strike, Silko refutes Parsons's "Notes on Ceremonialism at Laguna" (1919), which claim that the work of outside professionals had no part in the natives' demise. Based on Pueblo beliefs, Silko rebuts the claim of white outsiders: "Anyone who dared to reveal ceremonial secrets risked severe reprisals from the supernatural world," an animistic belief in retribution for sacrilege (Silko, 2010, 51).

*See also* Betonie; myth; religion; Tayo.

• *References and further reading*

Colwell-Chanthaphonh, Chip. "Portraits of a Stories Land: An Experiment in Writing the Landscapes of History," *Anthropological Quarterly* 78:1 (January 2005): 151–177.
Gohrisch, Jana. "Cultural Exchange and the Representation of History in Postcolonial Literature," *European Journal of English Studies* 10:3 (December 2006): 231–247.
Mitchell, Carol. "'Ceremony' as Ritual," *American Indian Quarterly* 5:1 (February 1979): 27–35.
Ortiz, Simon J. "Towards a National Indian Literature: Cultural Authenticity in Nationalism" in *American Indian Literary Nationalism*, eds. Jace Weaver, Craig S. Womack, and Robert Allen Warrior. Albuquerque: University of New Mexico Press, 2006.
Silko, Leslie Marmon. *Ceremony*. New York: Viking Press, 1977.
_____. "The Man to Send Rain Clouds," *New Mexico Quarterly* 38:4/39:1 (Winter-Spring 1969): 133–136.
_____. *Storyteller*. New York: Seaver, 1981.
_____. *The Turquoise Ledge: A Memoir*. New York: Viking, 2010.
Weso, Thomas F. "From Delirium to Coherence: Shamanism and Medicine Plans in Silko's 'Ceremony,'" *American Indian Culture and Research Journal* 28:1 (Winter 2004): 53–65.

# Rocky

A recruit to a nationalistic war, Rocky, the golden boy of *Ceremony* (1977), is the ghost soldier who fails to return home. Named Augustine at birth, he survives in the memories of his Laguna family as a Pueblo Indian acculturated to secular, self-aggrandizing white ways. Despite Auntie Thelma's distancing of her two boys from each other to prevent a sibling relationship, Rocky thinks of his maternal cousin and foster brother Tayo as a blood brother. When four-year-old Tayo separates permanently from his mother, "little sister" Laura, Rocky whispers the welcome "my brother" and shares his room (Silko, 1977, 236). Silko creates vulnerability in the off-kilter trio by picturing Auntie Thelma as a shadow that spooks a rabbit. The image captures both the amorphous menace of the resentful aunt/foster mother and the toned body and keen reflexes of Rocky, an all-state football and track hero at Albuquerque Indian School. The white coach drives a wedge between Rocky and the Laguna with the standard rah-rah ego boost: "Nothing can stop you now except one thing: Don't let the people at home hold you back" (*Ibis.*, 52).

A rover in heart and mind similar in daring to the title figure in Thomas Berger's historical novel *Little Big Man* (1964), Rocky symbolizes the striving for *arete* (Greek for "excellence"), which the narrative describes in the honing and testing of his knife, hunting with Uncle Robert and Tayo, and climbing "Bone Mesa, high above the valley" (*ibid.*, 17). Rocky serves Silko as a literary foil of an early protagonist, "Humaweepi, the Warrior Priest" (1974), who learns sacred ritual and philosophy by revering and obeying his elderly uncle, even when Humaweepi harbors a contrary opinion. In contrast to the neophyte priest, Rocky ignores his carping mother and tunes out her destructive comments by reading a sports magazine, visiting an out-of-town girlfriend, and fantasizing about becoming a pilot, a visual escape from his life at the pueblo. Critic Janet Zandy, a literature expert at the Rochester Institute of Technology, describes him as a victim of "'someday' individualistic ambitions," a contrast to Uncle Josiah's wild Mexican longhorns, a scraggly, sinewy herd that adapts to the reality of drought and sparse pasturage to survive collectively in the desert (Zandy, 2004, 139).

LEARNING TO BE WHITE

Silko speaks through Rocky the destabilizing influence of Anglo culture on Indian education. In the explanation of analysts Angie Chabram, a professor at the University of California at Davis, and Rosa Linda Fregoso, a specialist in Latino studies at the University of California at Santa Cruz, staff at Bureau of Indian Affairs schools "represent both the hope of escape from the poverty of the reservations ... and at the same time the destructive imperialism that has imprisoned and impoverished them in the first place" (Chabram & Fregoso, 2005, 78). During Rocky's first year boarding at the Albuquerque Indian school, he absorbs white orthodoxy and idolizes scientists who "know everything there is to know" (Silko, 1977, 76). From the science teacher, a disciple of logical secular truths, Rocky internalizes rationality in the classroom as refutation of "old-time superstition," his contemptuous term for animistic faith (*ibid.*, 181). Amid poverty and drought, he anticipates a future that projects the plans accessible only to whites (*ibid.*, 73). In an act of disrespect for an elder, Rocky refutes as ignorance his Uncle Josiah's plan to raise Ulibarri's resilient Mexican cattle from Magdalena. To Rocky, the modern method of herding devised by scientists demands belief by desert Indians who know nothing of cattle breeding. In the summation of critic John A. McClure, an English professor at Rutgers, Rocky suffers "an all-but-complete extinction of religious allegiances, intuitions, and impulses" (McClure, 2007, 139).

According to Silko, the white world's concept of secular heroism seduces Rocky and other impressionable high school graduates. As explained by critic Kimberly Roppolo, a Cherokee-Choctaw-Creek professor of native studies at the University of Oklahoma, Indians esteem military service as a way "to succeed off the reservation, but it is also the only legal way to earn war honors, a necessary function in the ceremonial continuance of the universe and life as we know it" (Roppolo, 2007, 541). To perpetuate brotherhood, Rocky proposes joining the military with Tayo as a pair in the same unit, but he looks to Tayo first "as if he wanted to ask him something," a suggestion of his dependence on Tayo's stability (Silko, 1977, 60). The deed done, it is Rocky who exclaims, "We can do real good," evidence of youthful idealism, the life's blood of armies (*ibid.*, 66). Before encountering the enemy, "those yellow Jap bastards," the two stroll the streets of Oakland and, at a bridge in San Diego, wish for safe deployment (*ibid.*, 39). From his teens, Rocky is the loner who "had his own way" and who becomes "the one to leave home" (*ibid.*, 67, 72). In the jungle, he asserts, "But, Tayo, we're *supposed* to be here. This is what we're supposed to do," an indication of his acceptance of white propaganda (*ibid.*, 8).

The loss of Rocky at age 19 or 20 burdens the family with unexpected tragedy. In the Philippines during an execution of captives before a firing squad, Rocky attempts to jolt Tayo out of a hallucination of Uncle Josiah by insisting, "Tayo, this is a Jap" (*ibid.*, 7). The battlefield pep talk places Rocky in the position of adviser and voice for realism. For all his macho spunk and self-assurance, he incurs a shrapnel wound to the leg and dies of a rifle blow to the head during the Bataan Death March of April 1942. Critics accord his death to his gullibility to recruiting claims that he fails to read critically. To Tayo, the dishonored corpse wrapped in a blanket in the monsoon rain is not Rocky's but Tayo's, a confusion in history that allows the second-best son to return alone from the Pacific war. In despair, Tayo yields to "the shivering" and sorrows at losing both his mother and blood brother to white destroyers (*ibid.*, 8). Roppolo explains that Tayo is under obligation as the only witness to confirm Rocky's honors for coups and battle, a requirement corroborated by Cheyenne chief Senator Ben Nighthorse Campbell.

For the survivor, Rocky exists only in memories and nightmares, which Tayo confides to Betonie, the Chicano-Navajo medicine man. Critic Kenneth Lincoln, an English professor at the University of California at Los Angeles, pictures the slain GI as "Superpatriot Rocky ... his skull squashed like a watermelon or water jug (perhaps the 'kill-hole' of an Ancestral pot spirit *released* from use)" (Lincoln, 2008, 116). The image of fragility under a deathblow foreshadows Emo's stomping of melons and Tayo's contemplation of piercing Emo's cranium with a rusty screwdriver. After Tayo's return from a veterans' hospital in 1948, he envisions his foster brother's face in the features of a Japanese boy. At the hovels outside Gallup, the protagonist realizes that his brother, had he survived war, would have succumbed to the enticements of alcoholism, fighting, and sex that lure Emo, Harley, Leroy Valdez, and Cousin Pinkie to their doom. On the first night at Betonie's hogan, Tayo interprets the detritus stacked in boxes and bags as the empty promises that whites made to Rocky. Grandma, who doted on the career-minded A student, insists that the family carry out Rocky's promise to buy a kerosene stove. Like the heat radiating against winter's coldest day, memories of Rocky penetrate Tayo's consciousness. Unfortunately for Tayo, who lies in their old iron bed, flashbacks of Rocky's last moments confer heat but no light.

*See also Ceremony*; Tayo.

• *References and further reading*

Chabram, Angie, and Rosa Linda Fregoso. "Decolonizing Imperialism: Captivity Myths and the Postmodern World in Leslie Marmon Silko's *Ceremony*" in *Exploding the Western: Myths of Empire on the Postmodern Frontier*, ed. Sara L. Spurgeon. College Station: Texas A&M University Press, 2005.

Chavkin, Allan Richard, and Nancy Feyl Chavkin. "The Origins of Leslie Marmon Silko's Ceremony," *Yale University Library Gazette* 82:1/2 (October 2007): 23–30.

Lincoln, Kenneth. *Speak Like Singing: Classics of Native American Literature*. Albuquerque: University of New Mexico Press, 2008.

McClure, John. *Partial Faiths: Postsecular Fiction in the Age of Pynchon and Morrison*. Athens: University of Georgia Press, 2007.

Roppolo, Kimberly. "Vision, Voice, and Intertribal Metanarrative: The American Indian Visual-Rhetorical Tradition and Leslie Marmon Silko's *Almanac of the Dead*," *American Indian Quarterly* 31:4 (Fall 2007): 534–558.

Silko, Leslie Marmon. *Ceremony*. New York: Viking, 1977.

Teuton, Sean Kicummah. *Red Land, Red Power: Grounding Knowledge in the American Indian Novel*. Durham, NC: Duke University Press, 2008.

Zandy, Janet. *Hands: Physical Labor, Class, and Cultural Work*. New Brunswick, NJ: Rutgers University Press, 2004.

## Seese's genealogy

The most pathetic of Silko's losers in *Almanac of the Dead* (1991), Seese entangles herself in a homosexual love triangle involving Beaufrey, David, and Eric. As the wife of David, she agrees to one abortion, then carries her second pregnancy to term. Beaufrey's jealousy motivates him to kidnap the infant Monte to Colombia and murder him. Silko depicts Seese as a seeker, a searcher for peace and recompense for theft of her son. Homophonically, her name invokes both "sees" and "cease," a cry for the end to the novel's cavalcade of murder and cannibalism.

Seese's grief sends her into the service of Lecha, the media psychic who locates remains of the dead for police investigators. To Seese's regret, Lecha never finds Monte, but the job of decoder of Mayan codices enlightens Seese to a groundswell resistance movement against voluptuaries like David and Beaufrey and their tangle of sex partners. Critic Deborah M. Horvitz notes, "Although she starts out a Destroyer, even naming her murdered baby after Montezuma, she evolves through her relationships with Lecha and the almanacs" and "casts in her lot with Lecha and the revolution" (Horvitz, 2000, 35).

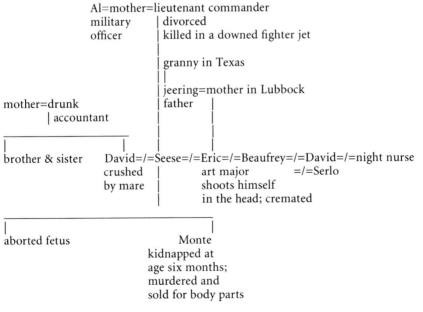

*See also* abortion; women.

• *References and further reading*

Horvitz, Deborah M. *Literary Trauma: Sadism, Memory, and Sexual Violence in American Women's Fiction.*
    Albany: State University of New York Press, 2000.
Silko, Leslie Marmon. *Almanac of the Dead.* New York: Simon & Schuster, 1991.

## sex

Silko values nonviolent sexual coupling, whether monogamous or extramarital, as a path to the inner self, an essential to Amerindian emotional stability. As she stated in the essay "As a Child I Loved to Draw and Cut Paper" (1996), from girlhood, she observed that sexual humor, unlike female-obsessed *Playboy* cartoons, involved male anatomy equally with women's bodies. She learned about copulation from studying her uncle Tony's billy goat, a model of macho pride that "mounted the nannies, powerful and erect with the great black testicles swinging in rhythm between his hind legs" (Silko, 1981, 173). So, too, her vignettes of human copulation display an overt strength and pride. Critic Suzanne Evertsen Lundquist, an English professor at Brigham Young University, notes a positive outcome of the celebration of sexuality and reproduction in Silko's respect for "healing intimacy," a bulwark against ill fate (Lundquist, 2005, 242).

The author flaunts her challenge to white Puritanism, which she charges with exclusion, patriarchy, intolerance, and repression of natural urges and fertility. In *Yellow Woman and a Beauty of the Spirit: Essays on Native American Life Today* (1996), she charges Christian missionaries with introducing sexual inhibitions to the Americas, where Indians view marital relations as a form of teamwork and source of subsequent generations. She asserts the role of sexuality in personhood and community interaction: "In the old Pueblo worldview, we are all a mixture of male and female, and this sexual identity is changing constantly" (Silko, 1996, 67). The difference in European and Amerindian attitudes toward recreational sex creates both humor and tension in "A Geronimo Story" (1974), in which Siteye, a Laguna regular, indirectly accuses Major Littlecock of lusting after horses. The challenge to manhood allows Siteye to ridicule a pompous superior while destabilizing the power of whites over the volunteers who perform the major's work for him.

### Woman as Amazon

Silko deals directly with female sexuality in her first compendium, *Laguna Woman: Poems* (1974). Her opening entry, "Poem for Myself and Mei-Mei: Concerning Abortion, Chinle to Fort Defiance April 1973," examines the issue of reproductive freedom in terms of the wealth of spring sun and butterflies. The obvious question of the right to personal liberty versus the value of a living fetus depicts a non-judgmental perception of all life, the gift of the Mother Creator. In conflict with the white world's polemics from the religious right over pro-life and pro-choice, the native view situates the struggle within the woman who chooses to end a pregnancy.

In the tale of Yellow Woman (Kochininako) and Buffalo Man, Silko uses their coital adventure to epitomize the union of the animal world with the spiritual plane. The universal power of libido enables Yellow Woman to pass through the divide between palpable and spiritual and to save her people from extinction by securing a new source of food. In "Buffalo Story" (1981), she exults, "They would bring home all that good meat. Nobody would be hungry then" (Silko, 1981, 76). Similar in tone to the sarcastic poem "Mesita Men" (1972), the image of female assertiveness and nonconformity accords to women a contemplative respect for coition, an opposite to males who prefer rapid, unthinking mating in the style of Uncle Tony's rutting goats. From the opposite perspective, the companion work, "Si'ahh Aash'" (1972), regards the lustiness of wives who seek adulterous relationships to supplement unsatisfying marital intercourse with their husbands. The brief verse sanctions women's needs and methods of achieving fulfillment and pleasure.

## HOLY AND UNHOLY INTERCOURSE

The author maintained a focus on sexuality in *Ceremony* (1977), her first novel, which features the fornication of Indian GIs with willing blondes. She depicts sensuality in Night Swan, the Mexican mistress of Uncle Josiah, through flamenco dance. Associated with the intense blue of her shawl and room decor, she takes on feline traits—"an old cantina dancer with eyes like a cat" (Silko, 1977, 87). Night Swan entrances in the style of Hispanic barroom entertainers—with hands lifting her skirts, back arched, and heels tapping a rapid tattoo: "She was the bull and at the same time the killer, holding out her full skirts like a cape" (*ibid.*, 86). She makes seductive eye contact with men on the periphery of her motions and hints at her bewitching of a man from Las Cruces, whose horses crush him to death.

The linking of seductiveness and bestial violence connects Night Swan with an earthbound magic. Josiah responds to her allure like a dog quivering from a dream, another animal reference exhibiting Silko's investment of male lust with feral elements. When Tayo has his first sexual encounter, probably arranged by Josiah, the blue of Night Swan's sheets wraps his ankles and thighs as though twisting time around his passion-aroused genitals. The imagery pictures their coupling as swimming in a sensual water flowing "away from all his life before that hour" (*ibid.*, 99). The implications of holiness in their ritual coitus during a refreshing rainstorm links Night Swan with sacred current and prefigures Tayo's rejuvenation with her counterpart, Ts'eh Montaño, an embodiment of Mother Earth. With the zeal of the Yupik heroine fighting a Gussuck pillager in "Interior and Exterior Landscapes" (1981), Ts'eh applies sexual glamour to perplexing situations that require intense interpersonal treatment of spiritual disorder. Critic Brewster E. Fitz connects the therapy of intercourse to storytelling, which he describes as "metaphorically united" for their limitless possibilities of communication (Fitz, 2004, 64).

In contrast to the aggressive dance, Helen Jean epitomizes the failure of a native woman to turn carnal appeal into a dynamic advantage. Locked into poverty at the Ute reservation at Towac, she seeks opportunity in Gallup to relieve the needs of Emma and the other children. Helen Jean's janitorial work at the Kimo Theater, an iconic venue in Albuquerque, devolves into sexual peonage to the manager. At the El Fidel bar, she solicits war veterans "laughing and whooping it up" and offers casual sex in exchange for handouts from their government disability checks (*ibid.*, 151). Unlike Night Swan and the semi-divine Ts'eh, Helen Jean achieves no self-assertion through casual sex, only degrading drudgery that pays in cash. After an Isleta man slaps her, she begins to see that parasitism on returning soldiers is a hazardous means of eking out a living. Silko uses Helen Jean's disillusion as a parallel to the rejection GIs feel upon return to civilian life.

## THE SEX OF LEGEND

In the sentient tale of "Yellow Woman" (1981), a modern setting of the Pueblo legend, Silko showcases the egalitarianism between male and female Indians. The speaker of the short story, who conceals her real name, admires the physique of her seducer, the tall

Navajo named Silva. Contrary to white romantic heroines of novels by Danielle Steel and Judith Krantz who coo over rippling backs and muscular arms, the protagonist thrills to his breathing and heartbeat and the touch of his hand on her neck. The torso-to-torso vignette replicates a scene from Silko's pueblo anecdote "Laughing and Laughing about Something That Happened at Mesita" (1974), which rhapsodizes briefly on being "deep into those places that people go when they are together like that" (Silko, 1974, 99). The sharing of physical attraction expresses a gender parity that places equal responsibility on each party for indulging in extramarital affairs.

In the criss-crossing sins and psychopathologies of *Almanac of the Dead* (1991), a sex-obsessed historical panorama, Silko carries legendary carnality to Gothic extremes. The narrative blends various forms of voyeurism, greed, cannibalism, and sybarism, which includes a federal court judge's bestiality with basset hounds, Serlo's collection of semen to create a pure race, and Angelita's hanging of Bartolomeo because of his racist and sexual sneers at her. The immoderation of crimes and fetishes caused Sven Birkerts, a literary critic at Bennington College, to compare the work to the *Satyricon* (ca. A.D. 60) of Petronius Arbiter, a carnal landmark dating to early imperial Rome. Sharon Patricia Holland, an English professor at the University of Illinois, accounts for carnality in *Almanac* as an historical cycle similar in source and purpose to the *Satyricon*: "Sexual acts serve as metaphors for the horrors of a continent ravaged by Europeans, foretold by the Maya and come round again in the present day" (Holland, 2000, 76). A tussle in the bushes unites the Marxist organizer Angelita with the Mayan El Feo, a vehicle of revolt. For him, imagination enhances intercourse with a fantasy of "the warmth of the darkest, deepest forest in an early-summer rain" as he buries himself "deeper and deeper into the core of the earth until he lost himself in eternity" (Silko, 1991, 522). In contrast to private encounter between consenting adults, Beaufrey's flourishing porn video business targets an unhealthy population, those who enjoy films of abnormal intercourse, abortions, ritual circumcision, and sex change operations. The literary foils represent the two sides of Silko's characterization—those who energize the world for change and those who drag down fetishists with perverse self-gratification.

Depravity and commerce in *Almanac* produce odd pairings in what critic Dorothea Fischer-Hornung calls "a set of constantly shifting and seemingly unending proliferations of erotic triangles" (Fischer-Hornung, 2007, 116). At Eddie Trigg's medical complex, an industry devoted to plasma and organ harvesting and spa treatments of cosmetic ills, perversion enhances the powers of the paraplegic CEO over people he considers social rejects. To the downsized and unemployed factory workers and homeless cripples who flock to his storefronts to sell their blood for cash, Trigg offers oral sex as a relaxant. In a Dracula pose, he fellates clients, who drift away permanently as machines strip their veins of blood. Trigg parlays his earnings through a relationship with Leah Blue, a venal real estate developer who plots with him a futuristic spa and health resort, theme park, and pleasure mall, consisting of sex toy vendors, a gallery of erotic arts, and a museum of animal and human penises and scrota. To maintain Leah's interest, Trigg, a paraplegic, offers his rigid erection—"dead as a dildo"—which satisfies his mistress without giving Trigg an orgasm (Silko, 1991, 659). Silko wrings a droll connection between illicit sex and land speculation: "Trigg had fucked her one way, and in typical Tucson fashion he was ready to try to fuck her with a slick real estate deal too" (*ibid.*, 382).

## SEX IN THE DUNES

In contrast to the darkly comic perversions of *Almanac*, in *Gardens in the Dunes* (1999), Silko accentuates a healthy Amerindian curiosity about human reproduction, including Indigo's spying of Susan Abbott James's adultery with Mr. Stewart, her Scots gardener, and the readings of Vedna, a Chemehuevi-Laguna laundress, of titillating episodes from the Old Testament. In revelations about Sand Lizard matings with outsider males, the author exonerates the mothers of random coitus producing light- and dark-skinned babies. The text gives a political reason for interbreeding: "Sex with strangers was valued for alliances and friendships that might be made" (Silko, 1999, 202). In later commentary, Silko describes sex as a business conduit because it creates "a happy atmosphere to benefit commerce and exchange with strangers" (*ibid.*, 219). Grandma Fleet adds another dimension by calling casual coupling "simply good manners," an interpersonal courtesy and welcome (*ibid.*).

The story develops the philosophy of the desert comfort girl. Sister Salt, a light-skinned Anglo-Sand Lizard, learns from the Chemehuevi twins, Maytha and Vedna, that the Havasu tribe smothers mixed-blood infants out of fear of murder and thievery by white armies. Because the Chemehuevi fear that Mr. Syrup, the reservation manager, will disrupt the girls' plan for a private laundry, Sister Salt promises that she can manage Syrup because she knows where to touch him. Silko adds, "Sand Lizards practiced sex the way they all used to, before the missionaries came," a joyous congress that the author spies in the firmament in *The Turquoise Ledge* (2010)(Silko, 1999, 206). The tumescent rain clouds over her home "resemble nude humans at an orgy" (Silko, 2010, 241). In her first romance, Sister Salt couples with Big Candy, an Afro–Red Stick Indian cook and brewer from Louisiana who pays her fine to liberate her from Mr. Syrup, the superintendent at the Yuma jail. In thanks, she moves in with him near the dam site, an engineering project on the Colorado River that enriches them both. In her subsequent relations with her laundry clients, particularly with Mexican laborer Charlie Luna, she hesitates to identify the sire of her unborn child, whom she imagines bearing traits from both Big Candy and Charlie.

In contrast to the light-hearted congress of Amerindian characters, the author posits the sexual battery of Hattie Abbott Palmer, a repressed wife. She sinks into psychosomatic despair after suffering robbery, assault, and rape. Dizzy with pain, she realizes the extent of the attack: "It wasn't until one of the Indian women wrapped a piece of cloth around her shoulders that she realized she was naked" (*ibid.*, 457). Hostility in the town of Needles, California, hints at the townspeople's exoneration of sexual assault as the just come-uppance to a white woman who meddles with Indian affairs. At a low point in her recovery, Hattie ponders "how much easier death would be than this" (*ibid.*, 458). In a fillip toward the white world's barbarity, Silko pictures young Indian girls solacing Hattie and restoring her to health. In a wordless defense of the victim, Sister Salt spits in the face of Mr. Abbott, a degradation of the worst in white males and yells at police officers and soldiers sexual aspersions, "Masturbators! Donkey fuckers!" (*ibid.*, 469). Through sisterhood, Hattie sips blue corn flour in water and observes the dance and Sister Salt's ministrations to the baby Bright Eyes, a rejuvenating empowerment of women against invasion and cruelty.

*See also* abortion; homosexuality; Montaño, Ts'eh; women.

• *References and further reading*

Avila, Monica. "Leslie Marmon Silko's Ceremony: Witchery and Sacrifice of Self," *Explicator* 67:1 (Fall 2008): 53–55.

Davidson, Michael. *Concerto for the Left Hand: Disability and the Defamiliar Body.* Ann Arbor: University of Michigan Press, 2008.

Fischer-Hornung, Dorothea. "'Now we know that gay men are just men after all': Abject Sexualities in Leslie Marmon Silko's *Almanac of the Dead*" in *The Abject of Desire: The Aestheticization of the Unaesthetic in Contemporary Literature and Culture*, eds. Konstanze Kutzbach and Monika Mueller. Amsterdam: Rodopi, 2007, 107–128.

Fitz, Brewster E. *Silko: Writing Storyteller and Medicine Woman.* Norman: University of Oklahoma Press, 2004.

Holland, Sharon Patricia. *Raising the Dead: Readings of Death and (Black) Subjectivity.* Durham, NC: Duke University Press, 2000.

Lorenz, Paul H. "The Other Story of Leslie Marmon Silko's 'Storyteller,'" *South Central Review*, 8:4 (Winter 1994): 59–75.

Lundquist, Suzanne Evertsen. *Native American Literatures: An Introduction.* New York: Continuum, 2005.

Silko, Leslie Marmon. *Almanac of the Dead.* New York: Simon & Schuster, 1991.

_____. *Ceremony.* New York: Viking, 1977.

_____. *Gardens in the Dunes.* New York: Scribner, 1999.

_____. "Laughing and Laughing" in *Come to Power*, ed. Dick Lourie. Trumansburg, NY: Crossing Press, 1974.

_____. *Storyteller.* New York: Seaver, 1981.

_____. *The Turquoise Ledge.* New York: Viking, 2010.

_____. *Yellow Woman and a Beauty of the Spirit: Essays on Native American Life Today.* New York: Simon & Schuster, 1996.

# siblings

Silko analyzes the unique relationship of siblings as evidence of deep, powerful emotion and sources of clan survival stories. She came of age at Laguna, where, after the Civil War, the brotherhood of Robert and Walter Marmon impacted local clans and pueblo governance. Sisterhood with sisters Wendy and Gigi embroiled them all in outdoor adventures and homey story sessions with Aunt Susie Reyes Marmon and Grandma A'mooh. Of the Pueblo, the author invokes unity through narrative: "We are all sisters and brothers because the Mother Creator made all of us—all colors and all sizes. We are sisters and brothers, clanspeople of all the living beings around us" (Silko, 1996, 64). The sibling relation fosters powerful conjunctions. Unlike whites, who accept the Cartesian separation of animal and human, the Laguna celebrate a unity in nature and a siblinghood in relationships with lower beings. In "Interior and Exterior Landscapes" (1996), Silko explains: "Life on the high, arid plateau became viable when the human beings were able to imagine themselves as sisters and brothers to the badger, antelope, clay, yucca, and sun" (*ibid.*, 38). Only through a cohesion of plant, animal, and mineral can the landscape balance life in "a viable relationship ... despite the vicissitudes of the climate and terrain" (*ibid.*).

The author expresses outcomes of the yoking of powers in the rescue of Yellow Woman (Kochininako) by the war twins Morning Star and Evening Star (Ma'see'wi and Ou'yu'ye'wi), the synergy of the sisters Earth and Sky, the birth of twin sons to an adulterous wife, the squabble between Corn Woman and Reed Woman (Nau'ts'ity'i and Iktoa'ak'o'ya) and the subsequent drought, and the cruel assault of Ahsti-ey upon her sister Hait-ti-eh's long hair. In "Tony's Story" (1969), the author peruses the antithesis of brotherhood in pseudo-siblings Leon and Antonio "Tony" Sousea. To Tony's offer of a matching arrowhead to protect Leon from a virulent state cop, Leon violates the pairing of fellow pueblo dwellers. Since his role in war, he puts faith in his .30-.30, a material protector he claims can "kill a white man" (Silko, 1981, 127). The separation of the two friends over the murder of an Indian-hating cop implies the two sides of the Indian psyche, the warrior who refuses to be cowed by a white authority and the traditional Indian who perceives evil as a supernatural force demanding the exorcism of fire.

## BROTHERS AND LOSS

In *Ceremony* (1977), Silko's first novel, she overlays vignettes of sibling relationships as testimonials to the complexity of family life within a closed clan society. For Auntie Thelma, her "little sister" Laura's offenses at cavorting naked with white and Mexican men and staying out all night drunk comprise a personal affront to an older sibling plus the burden of clan censure of the whole household. Auntie Thelma's relationship with Josiah, her and Laura's brother, devolves into false attempts at domestic harmony and sniping at Josiah for his affair with Night Swan, the Mexican cantina dancer. Thelma grouses, "I was the last one to know what my own brother has been doing" (Silko, 1977, 81). Out of social insecurity and Catholic hypocrisy, she makes covert swipes at the self-esteem of Tayo, a four-year-old nephew/foster son whose hazel eyes and light complexion set the child apart from full-blood Laguna. While Josiah and Grandma assuage Tayo's confusion and loss of mothering, the uncle/foster father comforts him with the assurance, "he had a brother now" (Silko, 1977, 61). Auntie Thelma inhibits the outsider's bonding with her son Rocky, a union that would supply both cousins with quasi-siblings.

Silko's "rocky" brother story puts its faith in love. She indicates that, for all Auntie Thelma's subversion of brotherhood, Rocky introduces Tayo as his birth sibling and plots a way for the two to serve in the military together. Tayo's sense of honor, the spoiler in Rocky's plan, compels him to remain behind to cultivate chili peppers and corn, herd sheep, and help Uncle Josiah brand his wild Mexican longhorns. The decision to go to war reignites family dissension. To Auntie Thelma, Rocky is the chosen one, the one to embrace freedom of choice. She demeans Tayo as the family disgrace, the Christian burden who must remain home to help with the farm work and to suffer her ongoing silent torment. Her brother Josiah urges her to let Tayo go; Grandma concurs for a practical reason — to make the boys mutual guardians on the battlefront. Silko reprises the character and unity of Rocky and Tayo in *Storyteller* (1981), in which the war twins, Ma'see'wi and Ou'yu'ye'wi tend the Corn Mother's altar.

## GOTHIC PAIRINGS

For her phantasmagoric *Almanac of the Dead* (1991), a nightmarish dystopian classic, Silko generates meaning from opposition: the beauty industry vs. blood and organ salvaging, capitalism vs. Marxism, and self-indulgence vs. self-sacrificing eco-terrorism by AIDS victims wrapped in explosives. To account for the upheaval caused by a cannibalistic society in conflict with indigenous peoples, the author creates contrasting duos, including innocent siblings who flee across the Sonoran Desert on a children's crusade to save the Mayan codices from destruction. On their way, like Hansel and Gretel, they confront a witchy crone, a terrorist who compels them to collaborate to save themselves and the Mayan almanacs. More prominent than the wandering children, the psychic Lecha and Zeta, 60-year-old Anglo-Yaqui twins, devote themselves to extremes, Zeta to gun running and drug smuggling and Lecha to decoding and reordering ancient Mayan codices that prophesy an end to European conquest and postcolonial victimization. Silko describes the coming chaos as a bloodbath: "They turned upon one another in the most bloodthirsty

manner; brother killed brother, sister devoured sister" (Silko, 1991, 478). The relationship attests to the violation of humankind's most sacred trusts.

Contemporary with the sisters' concerns, the labors of Mayan twins El Feo (Spanish
for "the Ugly") and Tacho press the underclass toward revolution. To gain inside information, the latter serves as chauffeur of the insurance mogul Menardo Panson. Tight-
lipped, but observant, Tacho communicates his spying to the loosely allied revolutionary
force that El Feo leads. Just as Lecha and Zeta gain wisdom and direction from their grandmother Yoeme, El Feo and Tacho rely on sacred macaws, who relay spirit messages from
the nether world. Tacho observes that "The macaws said the battle would be won or lost
in the realm of dreams, not with airplanes or weapons," a reference to a spiritual struggle between good and evil that is already killing off whites through suicide, overdosing,
war, and murder (*ibid.*, 475). Silko imposes the style of the Hero Twins from the *Popol
Vuh* (ca. 1554), a Quiché scripture that critic Philip Jenkins, the Edwin Erle Sparks Professor of Humanities at Pennsylvania State University, identifies as "America's true and
only Bible" (Jenkins, 2005, 228). The dynamic pair applies their powers to interpret visions
and to mobilize the dispossessed through charisma. In the mounting tension, the followers of El Feo "wait for the earth's natural forces already set loose, the exploding, fierce
energy of all the dead slaves and dead ancestors haunting the Americas" (Silko, 1991, 518).

## Sibling Imparity

Pairings of unequals energize the text with unclear alliances of power sources, a natural political outgrowth of democracy. To the Mayan snake god Quetzalcoatl, other gods—
Damballah, Ogoun, Eursulie, and the 30-foot stone snake icon at Laguna—impact fealty
and hope. Amid a roster of antagonists, Max "Mr. Murder" Blue, a contract killer from
Cherry Hill, New Jersey, who attracts a streak of lightning, and his grasping wife Leah, a
real estate developer, produce the Cain and Abel of the saga, brothers Bingo and Sonny
Blue, dissolute movers and shakers who exhibit the era's obsessive self-gratification. To
Bingo's annoyance, Sonny dominates him and disapproves of his cocaine addiction. Both
brothers indulge in sexual adventurism, Bingo with a pair of Mexican maids, and Sonny
with Algería Martinez-Soto, a Venezuelan architect and the second wife of insurance
wheeler-dealer Menardo Panson. Max's deviant family contrasts his brother Bill's more
normal rearing of Angelo, the orphaned horse specialist. The misalliance of siblings illustrates Silko's rejection of clear statements of heroism or villainy in favor of a character list
of checkered figures, each beset by individual demons and past sins.

Silko moves in a different direction in *Garden of the Dunes* (1999), an historical novel
describing Indian sisters separated in girlhood. During their growing up years in Needles,
California, the girls learn basketry from Grandma Fleet and sell their wares at the rail
depot. During a glowing four-night experience with the Ghost Dance, they fantasize about
a time of harmony and peace overseen by Jesus, who returns during the dance with his
mother and 11 children. The epiphany ends in violence and the flight of the girls south
along a river route to their childhood dugout in the sandhills. Sister Salt, who is perhaps
seven years older than Indigo, treats her sibling with motherly concern and urges her not
to cry after their grandmother leaves them alone overnight. Both girls display an understanding of self-preservation and a reverence for the spring, where they bless the grandfather rattlesnake that tends their water source. With appropriate respect for the food
supply, the girls entertain each other with a contest to see who can make dried apple slices
and venison jerky last longer. Critic Harold Bloom observes that the two dominant plots

"involving the two sisters diverges as a logical result of the conflict between intertribal gatherings and Anglo forces dislocating Indian lives" (Bloom, 2010, 125).

Through intercalary chapters, Silko juxtaposes the separated Sand Lizard sisters and their reunion alongside Dr. Edward G. Palmer and his sister, Susan Abbott James. Reared in affluence, the two lack human warmth and familial loyalty. The brother, a naturalist turned bio-pillager, maintains a loveless marriage akin to a brother-sister arrangement. During his visit to Oyster Cove, Long Island, he observes Susan's horticultural extremes in grubbing up an English garden to produce a blue-toned planting suited to one night's soiree with rich New Yorkers. The author creates satire out of Edward's sneers at Susan's profligacy, a sin less damaging than Edward's assaults on biota in Mexico, Guatemala, Surinam, Brazil, and Corsica. Still mulling over his failure to profit from plant thievery, Edward expires in an Albuquerque tuberculosis hospital. His disillusioned wife pays the bills and leaves his remains in an icehouse for Susan to sort out when she arrives. The wry closure of family business suits the cold-hearted pair, who profess no loyalty to kin.

*See also* Indigo; Sister Salt; Tayo.

• *References and further reading*

Bloom, Harold. *Native American Writers*. New York: Bloom's Literary Criticism, 2010.
Jenkins, Philip. *Dream Catchers: How Mainstream America Discovered Native Spirituality*. New York: Oxford University Press, 2005.
Lee, A. Robert. *Gothic to Multicultural: Idioms of Imagining in American Literary Fiction*. Amsterdam: Rodopi, 2009.
Schorcht, Blanca. *Stories Voices in Native American Texts: Harry Robinson, Thomas King, James Welch, and Leslie Marmon Silko*. New York: Routledge, 2003.
Silko, Leslie Marmon. *Almanac of the Dead*. New York: Simon & Schuster, 1991.
_____. *Ceremony*. New York: Viking Press, 1977.
_____. *Gardens in the Dunes*. New York: Scribner, 1999.
_____. *Storyteller*. New York: Seaver, 1981.
_____. *Yellow Woman and a Beauty of the Spirit: Essays on Native American Life Today*. New York: Simon & Schuster, 1996.

## Silko, Leslie Marmon

By eliding world literary genres, Laguna writer Leslie Marmon Silko perpetuates Old World cultures and lore while generating new meanings. Abby H. P. Werlock, a former English professor at St. Olaf College, refers to Silko's style as self-consciousness or self-reflexivity from "[becoming] more and more attracted to the world of illusion as opposed to the 'real' world of fact" (Werlock, 2010, xii). In an evaluation of the author as a person and writer, Laura Paskus, a journalist for *High Country News*, describes Silko as "notoriously private," but up-front about "her fierce sense of right and wrong, particularly when it comes to wildlife and developers, earth and bulldozers" (Paskus, 2010). As explained by critic Gabriella Morisco, on staff at the University of Urbino, from experience the author acknowledges that "to be a half-breed in the third millennium is not an obstacle but the only way" to revive humankind (Morisco, 2010, 146).

The author lives and writes her credo of hybridity. Whether in English, Keres, Spanish, or a blend of languages, she treasures stories that answer the age-old humanistic questions about love, birth, separation, suffering, and death. As she explains in the preface to *The Turquoise Ledge* (2010), she relies on chunks of memory, which she maneuvers into meaning by involving imagination and relying on subconscious backup. She explains, "We learn to ignore the discrepancies between our memory of an event and a sister's memory.

We can't be certain of anything" (Silko, 2010, 1). To bridge the gaps in autobiography, she envisions herself as a fictional character and sees herself scaling the narrow footpaths made by ancient Tucson tribes over past eons. As though absorbing Amerindian history, she channels the story of her people through respect for the land and for native artifacts, particularly a grinding stone left under a tree by a long-ago breadmaker.

## WOMANHOOD AND LIBERTY

Early on, Silko valued the gender freedom of female Laguna. As ego ideals, she emulates self-sufficient women who repaired cars and washing machines, chopped and stacked firewood, and plastered adobe walls alongside males and other females. She explained to interviewer Laura Coltelli, "There is not any of this peculiar Christian, Puritan segregation of the sexes. So there is very much wholeness there" (Coltelli, 1990, 137). Silko regards the division of labor among the Pueblo tribes as less gender specific than that of whites. She regards children's introduction to everyday work as more general, more preparatory for life than the training offered in schools. Like other Pueblo youth born in the matriarchy, she looked to female relatives as power wielders. Next in line of rank came her maternal uncles, who were more likely to upbraid or punish than her father, photographer Leland "Lee" Howard Marmon.

Silko and her sisters Gigi and Wendy matured Laguna style at the Pueblo Indian Reservation, where "Everyone was a teacher, and every activity had the potential to teach the child" (Silko, 2007, 210). Because of the author's love of New Mexico's vistas, she recalls in *Storyteller* (1981) how her father urged her to become a writer "because writers worked their own hours and they can live anywhere and do their work" (Silko, 1981, 161). As he predicted, she took to imaginative writing, but continued to draw on the Southwestern vistas and history for characters, motifs, and milieu. The Marmons lived in the shadow of the Los Alamos Jackpile uranium mine and the Trinity atomic bomb test site, settings that echo through her ecofeminist themes of injustice and exploitation of natural resources and of aborigines. A mile from Paguate Village and 159 miles from Laguna, the explosion blasted away apricot trees and melon vines. More insidious, the exposure of unsuspecting miners and residents deluged their bodies, homes, and food with toxic particulate, a residue her writings equate with white colonialism.

## LIBERATING WORDS

Silko rejects the absolutes of classic literature in favor of communal truths about people and land. Her book review "Here's an Odd Artifact for the Fairy-Tale Shelf" (1986) states a manifesto of how to liberate words of past cultural, historical, and political connections: "Any characters or plot are imagined within a world that answers only to 'itself,' the inner created world of the novel or poem itself" (Silko, 1986, 179). She describes how the brain favors narrative as a source of valuable data and "as a primary means of organizing and relating human experience" (Silko, 2010, 45). Cherokee critic Sean Kicummah Teuton, an expert on Amerindian studies at the University of Wisconsin at Madison, describes the author's violation of Baconian empiricism as a challenge to "the distinctions crucial to the sciences: pure/impure, past/present, orality/writing" (Teuton, 2008, 24). Rather than view stories as dry, static artifacts, she values them as a living entity, ever changing while ever referencing the wisdom and experience of the ancestry and legacy of first peoples. For the lapsed native and self-exile, the only reconnection is through reclaiming native healing, ritual, and origin stories. Survival lore, the collective memory of the elders, transmits proven strategies of surviving loss and despair and shortens the distance between the listener and the community. Teuton lists integral details as events that occur "on the peaks, in the hollows, at the banks of streams, within the whirlpools," the natural settings that link Indians to their homeland (Teuton, 2008, 50).

Like Spider Woman (Ts'its'tsi'nako or Thought Woman), the wise crone of Pueblo myth, Silko forms lyric, surreal, and narrative webs—flexible matrices that remain resilient, ever-shifting, dynamic, and collateral with world events. By recovering cultural myth and merging it with her own times, according to analysts Mary Loving Blanchard, an English professor at New Jersey City University, and associate Cara Falcetti, the author's "writing reflects, overall, her efforts to merge all the parts of herself" (Blanchard & Cara Falcetti, 2007, 237). In native thinking, the author's narrative provides a verbal map of her intellect, "a mosaic of memory and imagination" (Silko, 1991, 575). As she explains in *Almanac of the Dead* (1991), under the right conditions, a past experience, such as the abduction of the legendary heroine Yellow Woman (Kochininako), can recur in the present under current conditions. Even if the details vary, the essence remains the same, but the story acquires an updated applicability to prevailing situations.

Independent analyst Deborah M. Horvitz accounts for Silko's role as a teller of revamped lore: "Committed to change, Silko understands that cultural and political trends in history as well as individual psychological patterns of behavior will repeat unless victims and perpetrators alike consciously acknowledge and internalize their meanings" (Horvitz, 2000, 25). Silko's most disturbing jeremiad, the dystopian novel *Almanac of the Dead*, dramatizes in unsettling scenarios her anticipation of radical change in the Western Hemisphere. Rachel Adams, a professor of comparative literature at Columbia University, explains the impetus behind *Almanac*, which the novelist wrote in a fury: "Outraged at U.S. voters' rejection of the Mexican elements in their midst, she determined to write about the inextricable mixture of U.S. and Mexican cultures in North America" (Adams, 2009, 52). By revealing encrypted messages, religious myth, and prophetic tales and dreams, the author rescued readers from "the fatal consequences of ignorance" and from reliance on the faulty thinking of Europeans (Horvitz, 2000, 25).

One of Silko's methods of storytelling, the indeterminance of antecedents for personal pronouns—he, her, his, it, its, our, ours, she, their, they, us, we—incorporates all humanity, past and present, in actions. According to analyst A. Robert Lee, a Silko expert, the author's focus remains fixed—"to the politics of indigeneity, to embrace a sacral earth, a coming redress" (Lee, 2003, 91). Arising from what Lee terms a "native literary vacuum," she and fellow writers of the Native American Renaissance introduced to a Eurocentric nation the tribal ethnomythology that whites demeaned and banned (*ibid.*, 103). Through Tayo, the battle-weary veteran and protagonist of *Ceremony* (1977), the author explores what critic Linda J. Krumholz, an English professor at Denison University, terms "contact zones," the settings of racism, thievery, torment, and war that recurs in the author's memoir, *The Turquoise Ledge* (2010) (Krumholz, 1994, 89). Her text celebrates Pueblo unity, which Lee calls "a sustaining myth-world, a cosmos which coheres" (Lee, 2003, 106).

*See also* reclamation; storytelling; writing.

• *References and further reading*

Adams, Rachel. *Continental Divides: Remapping the Cultures of North America*. Chicago: University of Chicago Press, 2009.

Blanchard, Mary Loving, and Cara Falcetti. *Poets for Young Adults: Their Lives and Works.* Westport, CT: Greenwood, 2007.

Coltelli, Laura. *Winged Words: American Indian Writers Speak.* Lincoln: University of Nebraska Press, 1990, 135–153.

Horvitz, Deborah M. *Literary Trauma: Sadism, Memory, and Sexual Violence in American Women's Fiction.* Albany: State University of New York Press, 2000.

Krumholz, Linda J. "Reading and Subversion in Leslie Marmon Silko's 'Storyteller,'" *Ariel* 25 (January 1994): 89–113.

Lee, A. Robert. *Multicultural American Literature: Comparative Black, Native, Latino/a and Asian American Fictions.* Jackson: University Press of Mississippi, 2003.

Morisco, Gabriella. "Contrasting Gardens and Worlds: America and Europe in the Long Journey of Indigo, a Young Native American Girl" in *Nations, Traditions and Cross-Cultural Identities: Women's Writing in English in a European Context*, eds. Annamaria Lamarra and Eleonora Federici. Bern: Peter Lang, 2010, 137–148.

Paskus, Laura. "Of History and Home," *High Country News* (3 September 2010).

Silko, Leslie Marmon. *Almanac of the Dead.* New York: Simon & Schuster, 1991.

_____. "Here's an Odd Artifact for the Fairy-Tale Shelf," *Studies in American Indian Literatures* 10:4 (Fall 1986): 177–184.

_____. "'Not You,' He Said" in *What Wildness Is This: Women Write about the Southwest*, eds. Susan Wittig Albert and Susan Hanson. Austin: University of Texas Press, 2007.

_____. *Storyteller.* New York: Seaver, 1981.

_____. *The Turquoise Ledge: A Memoir.* New York: Viking Adult, 2010.

Teuton, Sean Kicummah. *Red Land, Red Power: Grounding Knowledge in the American Indian Novel.* Durham, NC: Duke University Press, 2008.

Werlock, Abby H. P. *Facts on File Companion to the American Short Story.* New York: Facts on File, 2010.

## Sister Salt

The child of rape committed on Mama by a Presbyterian preacher in Silko's eco-novel *Gardens in the Dunes* (1999), Sister Salt thrives on buoyant matriarchy. Bearing the name of the protagonist Salt in D'Arcy McNickle's *Runner in the Sun* (1987), she weathers the stress of capture and genocide by adapting from gardener, game tracker, and cook to camp follower and domestic. Wynne L. Summers, an English professor at Southern Utah University, explains her assimilation as a matter of survival "in the world of dominance that in turn dominates nature" (Summers, 2009, 98). The name "Salt" also alludes to Jesus' rhetorical question in the gospel of Matthew: "Ye are the salt of the earth: but if the salt hath lost his savour, wherewith shall it be salted?" (5:13). The passage links the character to a household staple and element of wellness that has served earth dwellers as a symbol of wealth and well being and as a medium of exchange.

Sister Salt and her sister Indigo, who is approximately seven years younger, form a family headed by their mother, a laundress at a train hotel in Needles, California, and by Grandma Fleet, a hardy survivor who once chewed through ropes to escape capture by white soldiers. The lessons in audacity and responsibility impact Sister Salt early with duties to Indigo and orders to sell dog- and frog-shaped baskets to white passengers at the rail depot. During a four-night Ghost Dance by the river, Sister Salt falls into a trance. Surrounded by love and light, she envisions ancestral spirits bearing affection to the living. In a later scene, as the grandmother sinks into the sleep of old age, Sister Salt feels affection welling up in her heart for the shrunken old lady who cares for them with the last of her energy. After Grandma's death, Sister Salt interprets the wind as saying "All gone, all gone," an introit to her advance to clan matriarch (Silko, 1999, 57). She lovingly tends to the burial and the grave offering of stew and fresh water while leaving Indigo to mourn in her own way. Duty to the past and attention to a sibling foretell Sister Salt's emergence as one of Silko's more resilient mother figures.

## SISTER BECOMES MOTHER

The text stresses the difference in age and maturity that makes Sister Salt the temporary mother and Indigo her child. Just as the siblings retain and recite the aphorisms taught by their grandmother, Indigo internalizes her sister's dicta "so she did not disappoint Sister Salt and Mama, or Grandma Fleet" (*ibid.*, 176). With the self-assurance of the next family matriarch, the older sibling follows domestic instructions on drying beans and corn and on storing the food in pottery jars cached under the sand floor. As enduring as mythic Yellow Woman (Kochininako), she reveres natural foods—amaranth dates, beans, squash, greens, datura, wild honeycomb, crushed seeds, spring water—as the source of life and survival. In a later episode, as Grandma Fleet taught, Sister Salt gathers amaranth greens to feed starving people, another gesture that links her to Christlike charity. Her cooking over a stone firepit inherited from her mother and grandmother allies her with generations of Indian women who valued food preparation as a duty and expression of familial love.

After capture and jailing at Yuma by Superintendent Syrup, in Part Two, Sister Salt impresses her assailants as a troublemaker and potential escapee requiring custody at the Indian agency at Parker, Arizona, north of Yuma. Jailed by a racist superintendent for petty theft, she uses her time in a women's cell to form a sisterhood of female criminals, including an antic duo, Chemihueva-Laguna twins Maytha and Vedna. Despite their high spirits, Sister Salt reveals "the numb half world only a step outside the everyday world" that she inhabits in grief for Indigo (*ibid.*, 202). During her work as a comfort girl to laborers on a dam project and washer of laundry and beer bottles at a tent city on the Colorado River outside Parker, she thrives on joy and female energy.

## SATISFACTIONS OF WOMANHOOD

Sister Salt values her body and works naked in the heat of the day. She delights in sex work by "[taking] her choice of the men willing to pay a dime for fun in the tall grass" (*ibid.*, 218). Sexual union with Afro–Big Stick Indian cook and brewer Big Candy produces a beloved son, called Bright Eyes, whom the young mother talks to each dawn in Sand Lizard language while the fetus is still *in utero*. Amelia V. Katanski, the Marlene Crandell Francis Assistant Professor of English at Kalamazoo College, interprets the conception as "a larger Pan-Indian alliance that stretches across national boundaries," allying Sister Salt with Indigo, her globe-trotting sibling (Katanski, 211). At the birth of the first male to the clan, miscegenation arouses no anxiety or hostility. As Silko affirmed to interviewer Per Seyersted, "The community is tremendously important. That's where a person's identity has to come from, not from racial blood quantum levels" (Seyersted, 1980, 15).

Three chapters on in Indigo's adventures, Silko returns to Sister Salt, who receives a metaphysical dream message that Indigo is happy and singing. The loss of Big Candy from Sister Salt's life replicates the marital history of Mama and Grandma Fleet, both of whom flourish as single parents and clan matriarchs. In the opinion of reviewer Frederick Luis Aldama of Stanford University, Silko dramatizes alternate methods of refuting "the racist, materialist elite that tries to displace and pathologize difference ... by seeking out like-minded peoples who are open to new visions and to change" (Aldama, 2000, 458). Living near the bones of Grandma Fleet with Apache, Chemehuevi, Cocopa, Mojave, and Yuma girls, Sister Salt rekindles her love of the land and arranges leaf-green stones into a "garden that needed no water" (Silko, 1999, 213). A reunion with her laundry partners, Chemehuevi twins Maytha and Vedna, relieves the tedium of working alone through their shared jokes and stories. Convivially, each twin teases "they wished Sister Salt were their twin, not the other" (*ibid.*, 334). Their survival methods exhibit what critic Laura Coltelli terms modern resistance to negative social and economic trends among the exploiters of the American Southwest.

   *See also Gardens in the Dunes*; Grandma Fleet; Indigo; Indigo and Sister Salt's genealogy.

• *References and further reading*

Aldama, Frederick Luis. "Review: *Gardens in the Dunes*," *World Literature Today* 74:2 (2000): 457–458.
Coltelli, Laura. *Reading Leslie Marmon Silko: Critical Perspectives through Gardens in the Dunes.* Pisa: Pisa University Press, 2007.
Katanski, Amelia V. *Learning to Write "Indian": The Boarding-School Experience and American Indian Literature.* Norman: University of Oklahoma Press, 2005.
Saguaro, Shelley. *Garden Plots: The Politics and Poetics of Gardens.* Burlington, VT: Ashgate, 2006.
Seyersted, Per. *Leslie Marmon Silko.* Boise: Boise State University, 1980.
Silko, Leslie Marmon. *Gardens in the Dunes.* New York: Scribner, 1999.
Summers, Wynne L. *Women Elders' Life Stories of the Omaha Tribe: Macy, Nebraska, 2004–2005.* Lincoln: University of Nebraska Press, 2009.

## social class

   Silko's canon examines the pecking order of humankind through surveys of family, clan, pueblo, race, and nation. Her depiction of Laguna life highlights the social acceptability of all comers and the sharing of food, even during drought and famine. In *Yellow Woman and a Beauty of the Spirit: Essays on Native American Life Today* (1996), the diatribe "America's Iron Curtain: The Border Patrol State" attests to racial profiling as a means of abasing and intimidating people living along the southwestern border with Mexico with guns and drug-sniffing dogs. Critic Barbara A. Arrighi, editor of Arrighi, Barbara A. *Understanding Inequality: The Intersection of Race/Ethnicity, Class, and Gender* (2007), states the obvious — that individuals and vehicles travel the Canada-U.S. border daily "with only random stops and searches" (Arrighi, 2007, 11). The targeting of brown-skinned people accounts for heavy surveillance by white police and Immigration and Naturalization Service officials who view Hispanics and Indians as *persona non grata*. Implications of border racism, which worsened in Arizona in summer 2010, imply that non-white members of the lower class are not only unwelcome, but also criminal. In the essay "Fences against Freedom," Silko refutes bigotry with logic she learn in girlhood: "We are all one family — all the offspring of Mother Earth — and no one is better or worse according to skin color or origin" (Silko, 1996, 101).

   In a Dickensian vignette in *Ceremony* (1977), the novelist investigates the nature of race as a creator of joblessness, exclusion, and poverty. She depicts the class of Gallup ghetto outcasts through the perspective of mixed-race children. Marked by black, Hispanic, Hopi, Laguna, Navajo, and Zuni traits, the young share shelters made of tin, cardboard, bricolage, and scrap wood from a dump ringed with wrecked cars, emblems of a hopeless existence. Far from the disapproval of bigots who might notice their "light-colored hair or light eyes, bushy hair and thick lips," the children survive in the arroyo along the river, a symbol of the flow of fate that leaves them washed up along the shore like flotsam (Silko, 1977, 108). Single-parent homes teach children the danger of flash flood. Everyday squalor acquaints them with the smell and muck of feces in the willow grove and the grief of a miscarriage or self-induced abortion. One boy, a latter-day Oliver Twist or Philip Pirrip, identifies with the buried remains choked with yellow sand while he sleeps in a hole in a clay bank, a grim parallel to an impromptu interment. In early boyhood, as adaptable as the title figure in Peter Carey's historical novel *Jack Maggs* (1998), the boy respects the economic necessity of his mother's night work. When the police raid the arroyo, he knows to scatter with the other youngsters and observes the burning and disinfecting of his former home that precedes the long wait for his mother's return.

The departure and return of prostitutes with wine bought by black, Mexican, and white clients demands that children stay out of sight. Haunted by hunger, the unnamed boy, a parallel to Tayo, the orphaned protagonist of *Ceremony*, suffers the absence of food the next morning and scrounges in garbage cans in an alley. A memory of play in a bar recalls a small boy digging at a heap of cigarette butts with a plastic straw. Without supervision, he devours discarded gum, coins, and cigarettes until he vomits. He is still a crib baby when the police rescue him from abandonment and place him in a receiving home, where he amuses himself by chewing paint from the crib rail, an oral satisfaction linked to lead poisoning. The child, like a puppy, identifies changes in his mother by smell and look. After her incarceration, she returns with short hair and the disinfectant smell of the receiving home, a social intervention that does nothing to relieve her family's destitution.

The arrival of Uncle Robert and Tayo shifts the point of view from the deserted child to two grown men who pity the hardscrabble existence of whores and winos in the Gallup arroyo. Robert refuses to feed the endless cycle of drunkenness by extending a handout to a glut of derelicts. Tayo tosses the winos two quarters, a reenactment of his last night in San Diego before deployment to the Pacific war, when he and Rocky make wishes on coins tossed into a pond. The allusion to blind luck dims hope for the homeless by reminding the reader that Rocky's wish for a safe return from combat went unfulfilled. The luckless vagrants suffer the first lay-offs, but take the risk because of their yearning to exit reservation life, an ambition they share with Helen Jean, a Ute wanderer from the Towac reservation. Like the riverside women, her ticket to escape lies in sexual bondage to her employer, the manager of the Kimo Theater in Albuquerque. The cynicism of Gallup whites damns the poorly educated Indians like Helen Jean to substandard wages and capricious firings. In the distance to the north near the railroad tracks and town dump, the Chicano-Navajo shaman Betonie chooses to live in sight of Gallup's unfortunates, a suggestion of his dedication to healing native people.

In *Almanac of the Dead* (1991), Silko returns to the downtrodden for whom the law is more punitive than just. The text envisions class warfare as a tool of indigenous people for restoring land seized by imperialists over the past five centuries. Critic Cathy Moses describes chapter five as a survey of "class-based resistance strategies [featuring] the critical role of discourse" rather than armies and artillery (Moses, 2000, 14). Her moral center, Sterling, the outcast Laguna yardman at Zeta's desert home outside Tucson, ponders "people who get away with murder because of who they are, and whom they know" (Silko, 1991, 26). Wisely, he avoids cops who "didn't need any excuse to go after Indians" (*ibid.*, 28). In the accumulation of wealth that obsesses the region's dope dealers, corrupt officials, and land developers, the novel sets medical technologists in the role of a murderous elite. Launched by Eddie Trigg, a paraplegic with his own agenda of self-rescue, a biomedical complex feeds off drifters, Viet vets, the disabled, and AIDS victims for plasma, corneas, hearts, kidneys, and skin. The sale of body parts posits a postmodern vampirism —

a social parasitism of the worthy on the down-and-out. Critic Ann Folwell Stanford, a literature expert at DePaul University, notes the duplicity of medical advancement, which impugns "our assumptions about worthiness and unworthiness and how those assumptions are linked to pernicious and tenacious foundations of racism, classism, and sexism" (Stanford, 1997, 38). She characterizes Trigg as infectious for profiteering on undesirables and for transforming medicine into a ghoulish factory system.

Silko surveys the self-important more minutely in *Gardens in the Dunes* (1999), a neo–Victorian novel replete with a hierarchy of social castes. At the Colorado River dam project outside Parker, Arizona, an overt ranking of peoples bases its assumptions on windfall earnings. Amid a tight economic order, visits by pompous inspectors require kowtowing to powerful Washington insiders. Within the tent city, Superintendent Wylie rewards himself with eggs, butter, and tasty entrees prepared by his personal chef, Big Candy, an Afro—Big Stick Indian cook and brewer from Louisiana. From Wylie's largesse, Candy distributes turkey skin and greasy leftovers to Sister Salt and other refugee Indians who wash beer bottles, launder clothes, and service male clients along the riverbank. The work camp comes to a quick and scorching halt after Delena, a Mexican gypsy, sets fire to the structures after robbing them of cash. Ironically, the money passes to arms dealers, who supply rifles to Mexican revolutionaries who struggle for land and justice.

The author contrasts Sister Salt's unstable milieu with that of her captive sister Indigo, a runaway from the Sherman Institute at Riverside, California. As the foster daughter of an intellectual couple, Dr. Edward G. Palmer and Hattie Abbott Palmer, Indigo takes the grand tour of Europe, a jaunt awarded daughters of the privileged and titled before their "coming out" in society. Heavy incongruity pictures the 11-year-old corroborating her Amerindian assumptions about life and spirit from the perusal of reclaimed seedbeds, terraced gardens, and orchards in Somerset, England, and Lucca, Italy. From comfortably rich gardeners—Aunt Bronwyn and *la professoressa* Laura—Indigo comforts herself from grief at the death of Grandma Fleet, the disappearance of Mama, and separation from Sister Salt. Upon the child's restoration to the sandhills of southwestern Arizona, she observes the collapse of the Palmer marriage and Hattie's bankruptcy, robbery, and rape by white males. Rich in wisdom and experience, Indigo gives generously to her foster mother and profits from their continued alliance. In terms of Sand Lizard social hierarchy, Indigo and Sister Salt rise in significance as the next generation of clan matriarchs.

*See also* abortion; hypocrisy; injustice; racism.

· *References and further reading*

Arrighi, Barbara A. *Understanding Inequality: The Intersection of Race/Ethnicity, Class, and Gender.* Lanham, MD: Rowman & Littlefield, 2007.
Moses, Cathy. *Dissenting Fictions: Identity and Resistance in the Contemporary American Novel.* New York: Routledge, 2000.
Silko, Leslie Marmon. *Almanac of the Dead.* New York: Simon & Schuster, 1991.
_____. *Ceremony.* New York: Viking Press, 1977.
Stanford, Ann Folwell. "'Human Debris': Border Politics, Body Parts, and the Reclamation of the Americas in Leslie Marmon Silko's *Almanac of the Dead,*" *Literature and Medicine* 16:1 (Spring 1997): 23–42.

## Spider Woman

According to native animists, Spider Woman (Ts'its'tsi'nako or Thought Woman) is the sacred thinker and generator of all and the prime mover of artistry and social integration. The "little grandmother" of the Holy Ones, she derives from the Olmec goddess

Teotihuacan, a deity of darkness and caves. She takes the unassuming pose of the elderly dispenser of tough love, chanter of Pueblo origin lore, extruder and namer of all things, preserver of memory, and the adapter of myths to new situations and challenges. In Laguna and Navajo tradition, Spider Woman, a parallel to the Greek spinner Arachne, is the guide for the lost and forgotten, the patterner of constellations in the sky. She recharges women's spirits and offers outlets to female thoughts and ambitions. Dominant in the iconography of Spider Woman, weaving dramatizes her skillful manipulations of tiny components of human activity. Her loom forms a cosmic union of female with male, which binds nature into an interconnected sanctuary of disparate bloodlines. The frame unites sky with earth as the weaver interlaces the sun's rays into lightning zigzags and streams of rain, symbols of fecundity, fruitfulness, and dynamism. For paths to enlightenment, she leaves gossamer strands for humankind to follow. The regard for the tribal crone influences the characterization of Grandma Baby in Toni Morrison's *Beloved* (1970), the dramas of Nigerian folkteller Osonye Onwueme, versions of the Inanna goddess cycle translated by Diane Wolkstein, and the Pueblo mythography of Paula Gunn Allen. Epicist Velma Wallis's Gwich'in tale *Two Old Women* (1993) updates the grandmother image by dramatizing the shimmering path to survival that saves two tribal outcasts from extinction.

## STORIES AS WEBS

Silko, a scion of Grandmother Spider, cherishes Pueblo storytelling as a literary wellspring of motifs and themes learned in childhood from Aunt Susie Reyes Marmon and Grandma A'mooh. Their oral narratives dramatized Spider Woman as the first mother of the Keres Indians. According to critic Kenneth Lincoln, an English professor at the University of California at Los Angeles, the author, inspired by the archetypal grandmother, "receives and writes the words that readers hold in their hands: her stories as medicine, her belly moving in procreative tale, and her lyric ceremonies a cure for today's crises by way of yesterday's song-stories" (Lincoln, 2008, 114–115). In *Storyteller* (1981), Silko's tales and verse contribute to a global acknowledgement of Mother Earth, the life-giver and sustainer. In her crisscrossing of historical strands, she complicates frontier history, forcing colonizers to reexamine their justification of imperialism and genocide.

A complex figure of divinity and destructive power, Spider Woman exists outside the either-or thinking of Christianity and Islam in a shadowy complex of human motivation and action. Analysts Clara Sue Kidwell, director of the Consortium for Graduate Opportunities for American Indians at the University of California at Berkeley, and Alan R. Velie, an English professor at the University of Oklahoma, explain: "Indians did not traditionally view spiritual forces as either inherently benevolent or malign" (Kidwell & Velie, 2005, 32). Ambiguity, the antithetical tension inherent in classic Greek, Roman, and Norse deities, heightens the drama of Spider Woman lore and relates it directly to stories of clownish tricksters and deceivers like Kaup'a'ta, the Evil Gambler, the extremes of human perversity. From these tales come models of foolish and wicked behaviors and the outcomes and punishments that await Grandmother Spider's wayward children.

Spider Woman perpetuates native truths through belief and retellings. Critic Sara L. Spurgeon, a professor in women's studies at the University of Arizona, explains the longevity of Spider Woman in Amerindian myth: "This witch is spinning a new myth that is being reified in the course of its telling—literally creating the world, as all myths do" (Spurgeon, 2005, 96). Silko's first novel, *Ceremony* (1977), opens with praise to the maternal wonder worker: "Thought-Woman, the spider,/named things and/as she named them/they appeared" (Silko, 1977, 1). Like the Grimm Brothers' 1812 version of Rapunzel isolated in her tower spinning straw into gold, the spider goddess, from her divine plane, channels words into objects through fiberwork, one of the domestic constants of womanhood. Simultaneously, she grooms a continuous line of storykeepers to preserve world mythos. According to Lois Parkinson Zamora, professor of art, English, and history at the University of Houston, the ins and outs of fragmented tales produces main lines, side trails, and cul de sacs—"not always parallel but sometimes ironic reflections, sometimes comic exaggerations, sometimes without clear connections" (Zamora, 2005, 281). Through ecofeminism, Spider Woman's scraps of wisdom activate female powers to shield fragile living filaments and to network all earth into a nurturing habitat. Following the cohesive introduction of *Ceremony*, the action honors the Amerindian worldview as a homey web which wanderers like the war-damaged veteran Tayo can always reclaim.

In "Lullaby" (1974), an existential short story based on Spider Woman's enigmatic fabrics, Silko sprinkles images of weaving over the text, beginning with the merger of snowflakes into ground cover. To depict the reverence of Ayah, a Navajo matriarch, for native womanhood, the narrative pictures her wrapping herself in a green army blanket that belonged to her deceased son Jimmie. Much as the web of circumstance draws him into a world war and leaves his remains grotesquely unidentifiable from a helicopter crash and fire, the raveling blanket wraps Ayah's head in an insubstantial protection from her family's gradual dissolution. To retrieve her husband Chato from wasting his monthly government allotment in Azzie's Bar, she stalks into the all-male assembly and dries the blanket by the stove. The men view her as a disgusting vermin, "a spider crawling slowly across the room (Silko, 1974, 16).

Ayah turns her startling appearance to her advantage. Immediately, she perceives "They were afraid; she could feel the fear. She looked at their faces steadily" (*ibid.*). According to critic Jordana Finnegan, an English instructor at Foothill College, the duality of Ayah's appearance in no-woman's land exemplifies a clash of perspectives, "the stark disparity between traditional Native reverence for the spider and Euroamerican anxiety about the spider's powers" (Finnegan, 2008, 115). The analyst interprets Ayah as an avatar of Spider Woman, calm and wise as she accepts Chato's concession to cold and death. With the grace of a divinity, Ayah tucks the blanket around Chato, retaining for herself the dignity of motherhood and matriarchy. In the crime and decadence saga *Almanac of the Dead* (1991), Silko relies more heavily on Grandmother Spider's webbing technique by bringing together more stories of substance abuse and despair in what critic Michael Davidson calls "paths crossing in ways that mimic new cosmopolitan movements in the global market" (Davidson, 2008, 215). The novelist speaks through the Yaqui mystic Lecha, the worth of Grandmother Spider's gifts of a "truly great legacy" (Silko, 1991, 569).

*See also* myth; storytelling.

• *References and further reading*

Carter, Nancy Corson. "Spider Woman as Healer: Donna Henes's *Dressing Our Wounds in Warm Clothes* and Leslie Marmon Silko's *Ceremony*," *Mythosphere* 1:3 (August 1990): 282–303.
Davidson, Michael. *Concerto for the Left Hand: Disability and the Defamiliar Body*. Ann Arbor: University of Michigan Press, 2008.
Finnegan, Jordana. *Narrating the American West*. Amherst, NY: Cambria Press, 2008.
Kidwell, Clara Sue, and Alan R. Velie. *Native American Studies*. Lincoln: University of Nebraska Press, 2005.
Lincoln, Kenneth. *Speak Like Singing: Classics of Native American Literature*. Albuquerque: University of New Mexico Press, 2008.
Silko, Leslie Marmon. *Almanac of the Dead*. New York: Simon & Schuster, 1991.

_____. *Ceremony*. New York: Viking, 1977.

_____. "Lullaby," *Chicago Review* 26:1 (Summer 1974): 10–17.

Spurgeon, Sara L. *Exploding the Western: Myths of Empire on the Postmodern Frontier*. College Station: Texas A&M University Press, 2005.

Zamora, Lois Parkinson. "Finding a Voice, Telling a Story: Constructing Communal Identity in Contemporary American Women's Writing" in *American Mythologies: Essays in Contemporary Literature*, eds. William Blazek and Michael K. Glenday. Liverpool, UK: Liverpool University Press, 2005, 267–294.

## *Storyteller* (1981)

A polyphonic masterwork, *Storyteller* integrates history, reminiscence, verse, myth, dialogue, varied typefaces, and photography into an organic paean to Laguna culture and ethos. According to critic Abby H. P. Werlock, formerly an English professor at St. Olaf College, the chronology is "like an ocean. Events occurring 500 years ago impact life as much as those occurring five minutes ago. And events occurring in time are often variations or reenactments of mythic events" (Werlock, 2010, 474). As fragile as heirloom handkerchiefs or fading photos, the nonlinear stories possess an ambiguity because of lost details, a natural attrition over time. In a letter to poet James Wright in October 1978, Silko stated that Laguna tellers repeat phrases and refuse to take credit as the final word on truth. The telling is so important to the narrative that the author introduces the teller, the setting, and relationships with hearers. Analyst Linda Krumholz, a specialist in ethnic literatures at Denison University, esteems the method and style for its introduction of readers to an Amerindian way of thinking: "The dissolution of generic categories, the shift of discursive ground, and the reformulation of the subject create a ritual of initiation," a welcoming of the newcomer to sacred tradition (Krumholz, 1999, 81). Like Moses removing his shoes to revere Yahweh on divine ground in Exodus 3:2–5, the reader awaits an experience with the ineffable.

By setting the stage, Silko exhibits the elements of cultural transmission. The dramatic encounter impacts her collection with meaning and purpose. Author Simon Joseph Ortiz summarizes: "Story is to engender life" (Ortiz, 2006, 258). Like Velma Wallis's Athabascan-centered epic *Two Old Woman: An Alaska Legend of Betrayal, Courage and Survival* (1993) and Ilie Ruby's Seneca-based novel *The Language of Trees* (2010), Silko composes stories to enlighten readers on the nature of human dilemmas and choices. She enlarges on human need for direction: "Sometimes we are weak, sometimes we recalculate, sometimes we do things just right [to get a] sense of all the possibilities we have in our lives" (Lopez, 1996, 6). To illustrate variance in human responses to such common quandaries as drought, thirst, hunger, infidelity, gossip, and witchery, the author accounts for "little changes here and there.... There were even stories about the different versions of the stories and how they imagined these differing versions came to be" (Silko, 1981, 227). As interconnected as the webs spun by Grandmother Spider, the network of narrative has neither beginning nor end.

GENRE AND THEME

The text of *Storyteller* celebrates truth, female divinity, and mystic nature as the cultural property of native literature, a legacy Silko shares with tellers Paul Gunn Allen, Linda Hogan, Johnny Moses, and Mourning Dove. Elizabeth Tallent, a critic for the *New York Times Book Review*, lauded Silko for "[honoring] the moral force of Native American tradition in conflict with intrusive, impoverishing Western European culture" (Tallent, 1991,

6). To interviewer Kim Barnes, the author defined her audience as "people who are interested in the relationship between the spoken and the written," a transformation of ages-old myth and legend to printed text (Barnes, 1986, 84). A favorite sexual adventure, "Yellow Woman," features a bold legendary female unmoved by the predations of a seducer, Buffalo Man, a ka'tsina (or kachina) spirit and guardian of rain and water. For its reclamation of a classic feminist episode, the tale became a favorite in women's studies courses for a description of a woman's survival of kidnap and her rejuvenation of a pueblo.

The finished product, in the description of critic A. Robert Lee, gives the visual effect of "celebration and mural, story-cycle and text-and-image collage" (Lee, 2003, 42). A rich oral olio, the genres blend and contrast—

- absurdism       "Uncle Tony's Goat"
- beast fable     Old Badger Man's resurrection story
- fool tale       the abduction of three men by four women
- history         Grandpa Stagner's water drilling business
- legend          "Yellow Woman"
- nature lyric    "Deer Dance/For Your Return"
- melodrama       "Estoy-eh-muut and the Kunideeyahs"
- memoir          reflections on the author's father
- myth            Pueblo creation lore
- parable         "The Go-Wa-Peu-Zi Song"
- revenge         tale"Storyteller"
- ritual          "Coyote Holds a Full House"
- satire          "A Geronimo Story"
- trickster tale  Pa'caya'nyi
- true crime      "Tony's Story"

The tone ranges from poignance at the slaying of an adulterous wife and reverence for the corn ritual to the humor of three males kidnapped by four females and the mystic migration of a people to Laguna because of the jealousy of two sisters. For the author's inclusion of personal memories, critic Lionel Larré, an expert on Amerindians at the Université Michel de Montaigne in Bordeaux, named Silko's imaginative postmodern genre *l'autobiographie hybride*, a blend of source materials that impact and shape her life story.

## HISTORIC SOURCES

The author dedicated the unplotted anthology to storytellers past and present, the truthkeepers who educate and guide the Laguna. In *The Turquoise Ledge* (2010), Silko identifies the poem "Deer Dance/For Your Return" as a gesture to Grandpa Hank Marmon, who died of heart attack on February 13, 1965. The poet was a teenager, the only family member who could perform mouth-to-mouth resuscitation, which failed to revive the 69-year-old patriarch. To honor his passing, Silko's lyrics describe a reverse birth into the mountains where "the people welcome you," her image of a reunion with ancestors (Silko, 1981, 188). She grieves for the old man who touched her life so intimately and names her grave gifts—blue corn meal, turquoise and silver, feathered antlers, and a red blanket, traditional offerings that sanctify and bless.

Critic Jan Castro noted the fluidity of Silko work at reflecting tribal consciousness and admired her experimentation with verbal structure. "The Storyteller's Escape" reflects the understated reverence for "the dear ones who do not come back," who achieve immortality through related lore (Silko, 1981, 247). The text — which Cynthia Carsten, a religion specialist at Arizona State University, labels *sui generis*— moves the reader from prose to verse to pictures "so that relativity of time, place, and writing style becomes secondary to the overall multigenerational picture and fabric of the tales" (Castro, 1981, 101). The stories tumble out like the weavings of Grandmother Spider, the matriarch of narration. Specialist Cathy Lynn Preston, a lecturer in the honors program at the University of Colorado at Boulder, numbered eight versions of the Yellow Woman myth, representing the eight legs of Grandmother Spider. By inventing a postmodern autobiographic genre, the author introduced to Western convention the Indian version of an individual life viewed within a cohesive community dating back to the beginnings of first peoples.

Silko outlined the overall view of a story as the placement of people in the larger context of history, a motif that empowers Peruvian novelist Mario Vargas Llosa's *The Storyteller* (1989). Her perusal of Pueblo values informs outsiders of a culture that emerged in North America before the intrusion of Western traditions. During a lengthy coexistence with the Spanish, French, Mexicans, Apache, and Anglos, abduction of Pueblo women presented an ongoing danger. To A'mooh, the Laguna narrator of abduction tales, the past and present co-exist in "enduring metaphysical truths" revealed in subsequent lives and actions (Lorenz, 1994, 61). According to analyst Paul H. Lorenz, the effect of stories nested within events parallels the "omniscient vision of the eagle," the embodiment of wisdom that looks from above from the past far into the future (*ibid.*). No consistent point of view dominates; unlike European literary conventions, the text lacks a hierarchy of primary and secondary characters and reveals no hero or villain. The resolution to conflict restores a natural balance, a "cosmic justice" that destroys the evildoers who challenge universal harmony (*ibid.*).

## STORY AS CONFLICT

As a contrast to Southwestern experience with white invaders, Silko tells an Alaskan story, "Storyteller," a revenge tale that employs the encroaching cold and dimming light as reflections of Yupik experience with oil drillers along the Kuskokwim River north of Anchorage. The young protagonist who tells her story in Yupik to a jailer voices her need to avenge her parents' death by enticing a storekeeper across a frozen river to a weak spot that collapses under his weight. A typical native resister, the girl demonizes Gussucks (whites) for corrupting the community with alcohol and debauchery of native women and for sullying the land with drills and machinery that rape Mother Earth. The ambiguous conclusion leaves the mythic hunter weaponless in confrontation with a bear, a symbolic depiction of Yupik people faced with white imperialism that imperils their lifestyle. In the assessment of Cynthia Carsten, style and genre are crucial to the girl's testimony: Silko "rejects the literary structures of the oppressor in the same way that the girl rejects the legal system," which favors whites over Indians (Carsten, 2006, 113). Both white literary convention and the dominator's laws prevent the Yupik from honoring traditional values.

The entry entitled "Tony's Story," first published in *Thunderbird* in 1969, takes place on August 10 on San Lorenzo's Day, marking the martyrdom on a gridiron in A.D. 258 of Saint Lawrence of Rome by the Roman emperor Valerian. The narrative reprises the tensions and culture clash of "The Man to Send Rain Clouds," which Silko published the previous spring. Leon, the returning veteran, prefigures the doubts of Emo and Harley in *Ceremony* (1977) by forgetting steps to the Corn Dance and by scorning the power of a token arrowhead, an amulet meant to protect both Leon and his blood brother Antonio "Tony" Sousea. The violent resolution results from Tony's trance state, in which he kills "it," the incarnation of witchery. Silko's version re-examines a real incident in 1947, when a victim of police brutality shot a cop who appeared to take the form of a witch. The fiery conclusion and the gathering of rain clouds in Silko's fiction dramatizes opposites — good versus evil and the pueblo's need for water and for healing from the post-war angst brought home by veterans. The most dramatic contribution to the collection, "Tony's Story" magnifies the tensions in Pueblo natives who attempt to merge their own life episodes with those of the white world.

*See also* "A Geronimo Story"; "Lullaby"; storytelling; "Yellow Woman."

• *References and further reading*

Barnes, Kim. "A Leslie Marmon Silko Interview," *Journal of Ethnic Studies* 13.4 (1986): 83–105.
Carsten, Cynthia. "Storyteller: Leslie Marmon Silko's Reappropriation of Native American History and Identity," *Wicazo SA Review* 21:2 (Autumn 2006): 105–126.
Castro, Jan. "The Threads of Life," *Greenfield Review* 9.3–4 (1981): 101.
Hernandez, Dharma Thornton. "*Storyteller*: Revising the Narrative Schematic," *Pacific Coast Philology* 31:1 (1996): 54–67.
Iftekharrudin, Farhat. *The Postmodern Short Story: Forms and Issues.* Westport, CT: Praeger, 2003.
Karem, Jeff. *The Romance of Authenticity: The Cultural Politics of Regional and Ethnic Literatures.* Charlottesville: University of Virginia Press, 2004.
Krumholz, Linda J. "Native Designs: Silko's *Storyteller* and the Reader's Initiation," *Leslie Marmon Silko: A Collection of Critical Essays*, eds. Louise Barnett and James Thorson. Albuquerque: University of New Mexico Press, 1999.
Larré, Lionel. *Autobiographie amérindienne: pouvoir et résistance de l'écriture de soi.* Pessac, Fr.: Presses universitaires de Bordeaux, 2009.
Lee, A. Robert. *Multicultural American Literature: Comparative Black, Native, Latino/a and Asian American Fictions.* Jackson: University Press of Mississippi, 2003.
Lopez, Ruth. "Finding Justice Through Words," *Santa Fe New Mexican* (3 March 1996): D6.
Lorenz, Paul H. "The Other Story of Leslie Marmon Silko's 'Storyteller,'" *South Central Review*, 8:4 (Winter 1994): 59–75.
Ortiz, Simon J. "Towards a National Indian Literature: Cultural Authenticity in Nationalism" in *American Indian Literary Nationalism*, eds. Jace Weaver, Craig S. Womack, and Robert Allen Warrior. Albuquerque: University of New Mexico Press, 2006.
Preston, Cathy Lynn. *Folklore, Literature, and Cultural Theory: Collected Essays.* New York: Taylor & Francis, 1995.
Silko, Leslie Marmon. *Storyteller.* New York: Seaver, 1981.
Tallent, Elizabeth. "Storytelling with a Vengeance," *New York Times Book Review* (22 December 1991): 6.
Werlock, Abby H. P. *Facts on File Companion to the American Short Story.* New York: Facts on File, 2010.

# storytelling

Silko treasures oral lore as a human energizer, the antidote to lethargy, sickness, and victimhood. The author stresses the reassurance of stories that set precedents for such common human situations as humiliation and sorrow. Because of the clan sharing of story cycles, "You are never the first, and you understand that you probably will not be the last to commit or be victimized by a repugnant act," such as the victimization of the war veteran Leon by a racist state trooper in "Tony's Story" (1969) (Silko, 1986, 93). Analyst Abby H. P. Werlock, a former English professor at St. Olaf College, affirms Silko's faith in stories: "They can literally restore us to life, helping us to sharpen our awareness and our understanding of the seemingly mundane as well as the inexplicable and the spiritual" (Werlock, 2010, xiv). According to *Storyteller* (1981), in Laguna tradition, clan narrators "passed down an entire culture by word of mouth an entire history an entire vision of the world which depended on memory and retelling by subsequent generations" (Silko, 1981, 5–6). British critic Laurelyn Whitt, a philosopher at Utah Valley University, comments that oral tellings transmit "information about the nature of the world, its beings and processes" and imparts "a means of relating knowledge and of correlating behavior" (Whitt, 2009, 53).

In the essay "Interior and Exterior Landscapes" (1996), the author accounts for the ongoing amassing of lore of Pueblo cliff dwellers as the collective wisdom of all witness into "innumerable bundles of other stories" (Silko, 1996, 31). Thus, no one expert holds claim to absolute truth, which honors all levels of human experience and shifts and alters with each succeeding generation. In *The Turquoise Ledge* (2010), the author names her Aunt Alice Marmon Little, Aunt Susie Reyes Marmon, and Grandpa Henry C. "Hank" Marmon as the sources of her evocative language and her "sense of narrative structure, of how a story needs to be told" (Silko, 2010), 46). She defines the inclusivity of lore as a form of divine omniscience: "Whether we know the stories or not, the stories know about us" (Silko, 1996, 150). The worth of oral narrative permeates her fiction, particularly the lives of Lecha, the mystic manuscript keeper in *Almanac of the Dead* (1991) and of Indigo, the orphaned Sand Lizard tribe member in the neo–Victorian novel *Gardens in the Dunes* (1999). From her upbringing by a storytelling native grandma to her introduction to Chinese monkey tales during a long train ride from Riverside, California, to Grand Central Station in New York City, she retreats into historical events and bestial shapeshifting to escape numerous personal travails.

## HEALING THE SPIRIT

The communal process of piecing together and relating events involves even the smallest child in "storylistening," a form of spiritual centering. A session involves a question-and-answer element to correct misperceptions and to encourage the youngest clan member to train for the next generation of oral transmissions. Because the topics cover triumphs as well as failures and shame, the inclusion of all clan members reduces the isolation suffered by the disgraced and guilt-ridden. Silko insists, "One doesn't recover by oneself" (Silko, 1996, 52). A session begins with the opening of the door to admit ancestral spirits. She remarks, "Even if a key figure, an elder who knew much more than others, were to die unexpectedly, the system would remain intact" (*ibid.*). The network of an inclusive organic history contrasts white history, by which a single chronicler can dominate and pollute a nation's background with bias and distortions. In contrast, the Pueblo system is self-correcting and tolerant of conflicting versions. The elders insist, "What is forgotten is what is no longer meaningful. What is true will persist" (*ibid.*, 134).

In recalling the Hopi basket filled with her Grandpa Hank Marmon's candid photos, Silko enjoyed the commentary that linked her family with events and people in the 1920s. She and her sisters and cousins delighted in an ongoing identification of people and places provided by Grandma Lillie, Hank's wife. The use of photos to trigger narrative produced a layering of time indigenous to the Laguna. In the essay "The Indian with a Camera" (1993), she recalls, "The identification of the faces and the places in the photographs never failed to precipitate wonderful stories about the 'old days,' which in turn brought out even older stories that stretched far beyond the confines of the snapshots in the grasshopper basket" (Silko, 1993, 5). The image of the grasshopper on the container suggests the continuum of past and present that moves, like the insect, in hops and leaps across the Laguna landscape. More than mere entertainment, "the stories and reminiscences that enliven all Pueblo social gatherings are densely encoded with expression and information" (*ibid.*, 7).

## REDRESSING INJUSTICE

In *Almanac of the Dead* (1991), Silko's saga of decadence and crime, she depicts storykeeping as a form of political activism. The perpetuation of past narrative in stories-within-stories undergirds Indian revival because "Ignorance of the people's history had been the white man's best weapon" (Silko, 1991, 742). Because of the cyclic style of transmission among Indian tellers, she creates Root, a white biker listening to the rambling wisdom of his employee Calabazas, a Yaqui smuggler. Befuddled at the maddeningly meandering installments, Root "wanted to yell at the old man to just tell him what it was, what was bothering him or what had gone wrong" (*ibid.*, 215). In the layered telling, Silko praises a European polemicist, Karl Marx, for recognizing the inviolability of history as "the sacred text": "Within 'history' reside relentless forces, powerful spirits, vengeful, relentlessly seeking justice" (*ibid.*, 316). Because of his European background, Marx did not fully grasp the significance of communal Amerindian consciousness; nonetheless, Silko advances his theory with a native writer's certainty. The reason for the power of narrative lies in its preservation of tribal identity: "The maker of a thing pressed part of herself or himself into each object made," formulating immortality for the teller who "lived on in the imaginations and hearts of their descendents" (*ibid.*, 520). Because of the individual contributions to tribal lore in the act of story sharing, ancestry remains vigorous and rejuvenative.

Of her role as teller/writer and justice seeker, Silko admits, "What we call 'memory' and what we call 'imagination' are not so easily distinguished" (Silko, 1981, 227). In the style of her ancestors, she relates crazy, funny, and silly stories as well as historic events to restore land, justice, and sovereignty to Indians disheartened and weakened by genocide. In the words of analyst Kenneth Lincoln, an English professor at the University of California at Los Angeles, the lore of first peoples should be prized: "The descriptive language precise, the action encoded naturally, the words tensile, these ancient oral narratives are well-told works of art from first words to last" (Lincoln, 2008, 40). Analyst Mary Aswell Doll, on staff at the Savannah College of Art and Design, depicts the oral culture as "speakings that communicate through voice's timbre, language's rhythm, embodied gesture and the melodies of conversation," all part of the Laguna tradition (Doll, 2000, xix). The performance creates two narrative stars—the teller and the stories themselves, survivors of long years of recitation.

For maximum impact, Silko resacralizes storytelling in its pre–Columbian purity, a performance of words, gestures, and expression that establish the precedent of the *hummah-hah* (old lore). In her role as storykeeper in the Laguna Film Project script "Running on the Edge of the Rainbow" (1978), she characterizes her storytelling ability as a birthright, a natural resource she shares with fellow native writers Navarre Scot Momaday and Simon Joseph Ortiz. Through a "truly great legacy," she literally invokes deity into everyday presence of Amerindian society (Silko, 1991, 569). In the estimation of analyst Brewster E. Fitz, a Silko expert, the author's urge to write rather than tell "conflicted between a writerly acceptance of Laguna culture as literate and a desire to live and paradoxically to write in a culture that is primarily oral" (Fitz, 2004, x). The telling, begun by Thought Woman (Ts'its'tsi'nako or Spider Woman) and embedded in *Ceremony* (1977), replicates human decision-making and prolongs the vital relationship between humankind and all forms of life, a source of primal strength and longevity. She believes that oral narrative requires a reciprocity between teller and hearer, a patterning that draws all participants into the circle of wisdom. If the story generates a creditable impact, the hearer may reiterate it for another occasion or purpose. If not, the narrative dies.

## STORIES AS COMMUNITY

In Laguna tradition, the ritual passage of tribal lore sets the tone for a new year by reminding listeners that survival depends on daring actions and escapes, such as those of Geronimo and the mythic Yellow Woman. The retelling occurs at the winter solstice, December 21 or 22, when members assemble for a four-day, four-night recap of Pueblo creation and migration, which connects the individual with infinity. The winter ritual endows hearers with new configurations of ancient wisdom. It requires annual transmission at the collective telling to meet the challenges of the future and to admonish natives who "misbehave" (Silko, 1977, 47). Through group participation, tribe members acknowledge the communal outlook — the human responsibility to shed selfishness and to look after and care for others.

Story modifications account for changes in culture, history, language, and memories of the past, for example, an explanation of the early morning flash that Grandma sees in *Ceremony*, which reprises the atomic bomb test at Trinity site outside Los Alamos, New Mexico, on July 16, 1945. As the novel reveals, stories become a grounding to sanity in unprecedented times, notably, the air attack on civilians at Hiroshima and Nagasaki that ended World War II. As the writer creates coherence from chaotic fragments, like the bomb blast itself, a logical and moral philosophy guides the reader in interpreting the alteration of uranium rocks into earth-threatening atomic power. The verbal image of a sorcerer releasing a whirling power makes palpable to the uninitiated the nature of atomic weaponry, which the military can detonate, but not control. The ancient story of a wizards' contest depicts the dreadful weapon as the result of posturing and grandstanding, a primal human fault that the Greeks called *hubris* (pride), a power lust and greed expressed through irreverence toward the importance of the individual to life on earth.

## STORIES AND THE INDIVIDUAL

For the sake of morality and right thinking, Silko's stories are proactive. Through cautionary tellings, *Ceremony* invokes the community to counter threats to the Laguna from atomic war and post-war despair. The telling confers cure through the I-thou relationship of speaker to listener. Tayo, her war-damaged protagonist, invokes oral telling as a way to give strength to a corporal, who slips through the mud while carrying Tayo's cousin/foster brother Rocky in a blanket stretcher during the Bataan Death March of April 1942. At a low point in the convoy, Tayo vents his frustration in a double "Goddamn" and finds the "words gathered inside him," conferring strength (*ibid.*, 12). He continues assuaging himself with stories at the Dixie Tavern in Budville, where he numbs himself on beer and relates to former GIs Emo, Harley, and Leroy Valdez adventures with a blonde, who lets Tayo drive her '38 Buick. In memories of boyhood, Tayo recalls esteeming narrative as guidance — "exactly which way to go and what to do to get there," directions passed on from others who had trod the same path, whether physical or metaphorical (*ibid.*, 19). His reliving of past story times prefaces his placement in his own saga, which requires following a shaman's prophetic patterns.

Of the dangers of weaponry and post-combat drugs and ennui, Silko declared, "I realize now how the telling at Laguna was meant to prevent the withdrawal and isolation at times like these" (Silko, 1986, 121). Her admission of the storykeeper's skills and obligations attests to the Indian notion of communal power, a sharing of individual talents and observations to defeat alienation and gloom. Unlike the white world's tradition of shaping the action hero as a model of probity, Silko's style turns from outward performance inward to tribal and clan associations with timeless strands of myth, which confer the protection of Thought Woman, the universal prime mover. The struggle itself becomes the object of Silko's narrative, a model of shifting and growing that affirms the life of Tayo and the Laguna people. Thus, listeners intuit from the storykeeper the process by which they can return to wholeness and fidelity.

The text of *Gardens in the Dunes* (1999) places narration in natural settings. The siblings Indigo and Sister Salt grow up loved and nurtured by the oral wisdom of Mama and Grandma Fleet, the family matriarch whose lessons become a cultural conduit, the trunk line of wisdom. Among the tales and fun stories, Grandma issues cautionary tales of the theft of Indian children for sale in the slave markets of Tucson and Yuma. After the separation of the foursome, Indigo retreats into storybooks, which lessen the monotony of a cross-country train trip from Arizona to Oyster Bay, New York. During ongoing seasickness aboard the S.S. *Pavonia*, she listens to Hattie Palmer's reading of Buddhist fables about a mischievous Chinese monkey. The accounts of beast fable — "taking bites from the apples of longevity, stealing the golden pills of immortality and gobbling them down with the special wine for the banquet of the immortals"—steady Indigo with the magic of imagination (Silko, 1999, 227). Upon meeting Aunt Bronwyn in Somerset, Indigo accepts the old woman's belief in magic stones and in brownies and fairies in "the land of the stones that dance and walk after midnight" (*ibid.*, 237). Edward dismisses the old lady's belief in the "good folk," her rescue of stones, and the hand-feeding of pet cows as proof Bronwyn has "gone native" (*ibid.*, 252). Edward's money-hungry thoughts make him restless in England and in the gardens at Lucca, Italy, where the *la professoressa* Laura tells Hattie and Indigo the myth of the white snake with the golden crown. In annoyance, Edward looks at his pocket watch, an indication of his inability to connect with the mythos of past eras. In contrast, Hattie, his misaligned mate, recalls luminous glows, her graphic ties to mystic experiences. Subdued by decorum and Edward's empiricism, Hattie chooses to leave her questions about the glow unasked, but Indigo mulls them over as esoteric way markers that may lead her back to Mama.

In company with elders as well versed in lore as Grandma Fleet and Aunt Bronwyn — "the old folks, the people back home"— Silko stores scraps of narrative from the normal Laguna conversation to direct her life path (Lorenz, 1994, 60). As meticulous as Old Man Badger, the "Skeleton Fixer," she labors to reposition "words like bones scattered all over the place," a parallel of the Grandma Fleet's bean rows and the stones and icons that Bronwyn places throughout her terraced garden and orchard (Silko, 1981, 244, 242). Upon encountering a Laguna resident, Silko extends details of local events by mimicking dialogue with a "sense of story ... what elements need to be there and which don't" (Seyersted, 1985, 21). Increasing her command of technique is the appetite of natives for her stories, the oral sustenance that feeds the pueblo on accounts of "the North Star, who acted as a spy for Estoyehmuut, Arrowboy, the time his wife, Kochinanako, Yellow Woman, ran off with Buffalo Man" (Silko, 1999, 417). To Silko, the stories possess a mystic vision. In turn, they empower listeners to act in their own time. With the courage of Geronimo, Indigo, Tayo, and Yellow Woman, hearers dare to make choices that prevent tribal extinction, an end-time that Silko foresees as the chilling of the universe when winter constellations subsume the sun. In the opinion of literary analyst Dharma Thornton Hernandez, Silko's gift for written transmission of anecdote, beast fable, chant, humor, song, talk-story, and trickster lore alters the traditional telling, "thus changing the Euroamerican narrative schematic for both Native Americans and non–Native Americans" (Hernandez, 1996, 54–55).

*See also* feminism; Grandma Fleet; Indigo; *Storyteller*; Tayo.

• *References and further reading*

De Ramírez, Susan Berry Brill, and Edith M. Baker. "'There Are Balances and Harmonies Always Shifting; Always Necessary to Maintain': Leslie Marmon Silko's Vision of Global Environmental Justice for the People and the Land," *Organization Environment* 18 ( June 2005): 213–228.

Doll, Mary Aswell. *Like Letters in Running Water: A Mythopoetics of Curriculum.* New York: Routledge, 2000.

Fitz, Brewster E. *Silko: Writing Storyteller and Medicine Woman.* Norman: University of Oklahoma Press, 2004.

Hernandez, Dharma Thornton. "Storyteller: Revising the Narrative Schematic," *Pacific Coast Philology* 31:1 (1996): 54–67.

Lincoln, Kenneth. *Speak Like Singing: Classics of Native American Literature.* Albuquerque: University of New Mexico Press, 2008.

Lorenz, Paul H. "The Other Story of Leslie Marmon Silko's 'Storyteller,'" *South Central Review,* 8:4 (Winter 1994): 59–75.

Petrolle, Jean. *Religion without Belief: Contemporary Allegory and the Search for Postmodern Faith.* Albany: State University of New York Press, 2007.

Seyersted, Per. "Interview with Leslie Marmon Silko," *American Studies in Scandinavia* 13 (1985): 17–25.

Silko, Leslie Marmon. *Almanac of the Dead.* New York: Simon & Schuster, 1991.

_____. *Gardens in the Dunes.* New York: Scribner, 1999.

_____. "The Indian with a Camera," foreword to *A Circle of Nations: Voices and Visions of American Indians.* Hillsboro, OR: Beyond Words Publishing, 1993.

_____. "Landscape, History, and the Pueblo Imagination," *Antaeus* 51 (1986): 83–94.

_____. *Storyteller.* New York: Seaver Books, 1981.

_____. *The Turquoise Ledge: A Memoir.* New York: Viking 2010.

Walther, Berenice. *Storytelling in Leslie Marmon Silko's Ceremony.* Munich: Ravensburg Grin Verl, 2006.

Werlock, Abby H. P. *Facts on File Companion to the American Short Story.* New York: Facts on File, 2010.

Whitt, Laurelyn. *Science, Colonialism, and Indigenous Peoples: The Cultural Politics of Law and Knowledge.* Cambridge: Cambridge University Press, 2009.

Yuknavitch, Lidia. *Allegories of Violence: Tracing the Writing of War in Late Twentieth Century Fiction.* New York: Routledge, 2001.

## substance abuse

Silko's survey of addictive behavior depicts the imbalance that intoxication thrusts on normal life. More destructive to Amerindians, the use of the "drunk Indian" stereotype promulgated by whites downgrades first peoples as weak and worthless. In *The Turquoise Ledge* (2010), she describes her mother Virginia's steady drinking from seventh grade, her coffee cup filled with whiskey, and her impairment on weekends and at "picnics and parties, and Christmas Eve and New Year's Eve" (Silko, 2010), 39). Critic Suzanne Evertsen Lundquist, an English professor at Brigham Young University, describes Silko's dramatization of "the self-gratifying nature of addictive behavior [that] separates family members, social units, and humans from the natural world" (Lundquist, 2005, 242).

The alcoholism of the Marmon cousins stemmed from World War II and the Korean War, severe breaches with normality. The addition of a criminal element expands individual experience with drugs and alcohol to a post-war syndrome imposing "global suffering" (*ibid.*). In *Ceremony* (1977), Silko draws on memories of Laguna GIs who returned from World War II in pitiable mental disorder. Among them was her cousin, Robert Leslie Evans, the prototype for Tayo, her shell-shocked protagonist. In "Fifth World: The Return of Ma ah shra true ee" (1996), the author regrets that alcohol drove army veterans to suicide. She recalls, "I knew they were not bad people, yet something had happened to them. What was it?" (Silko, 1977, xvi).

The text of *Ceremony* makes an obvious contrast between the drunkenness of slouching, argumentative winos and the serenity of nature. As analyzed by John Emory Dean, an English professor at Texas A&M International University, the protagonist Tayo's retreat into beer and whiskey replicates Ron Kovic's despair in *Born on the Fourth of July* (1976) and Winnie Smith's *American Daughter Gone to War* (1992). The soulless aridity and aimlessness following the dissolution of tribalism and spirituality attack Pueblo soldiers returning from World War II in a form of buddy ritual. Harley, suffering a "desperate thirst for alcohol," initiates his downward spiral to destruction (*ibid.*, xvi). He and fellow veterans, recipients of Purple Hearts from action in Iwo Jima and Wake Island, escape from memories of "bodies ... dismembered beyond recognition" into bar-hopping, a source of momentary relief and a profanation of life forces through carousing, promiscuity, fighting, and violation of friendship (*ibid.*, 240). Their self-medication on alcohol exemplifies the insidious nature of Ck'o'yo witchery.

For Tayo, the son of a wino mother, bingeing is a diversionary technique to fool his army pals: "They wouldn't be suspicious then: They wouldn't think he was crazy. He'd just be another drunk Indian, that's all" (*ibid.*, 241). Worsening the physical situation, Tayo suffers cyclical vomiting and an inability to take nourishment. To create camaraderie, Emo speaks of "we," a post-war community of men who understand the demands and regrets of a brutal war. Through a drunken fog, Tayo perceives the racist nature of a non-white soldier fighting the white man's war against the Japanese. As out of place as the black Buffalo Soldiers killing Indians in the Old West, Tayo and his buddies drink away the self-hatred for being used. He cringes from memories of refusing to execute Japanese prisoners of war, for whom he holds mutual respect as victims of imperialist whites. Silko enhances the racial oneness by picturing Tayo's hallucination that a Japanese captives morphs into Uncle Josiah, Tayo's foster father.

Squirming in the grip of regret and chronic nausea, Tayo knows that "Liquor was medicine for the anger that made them hurt," a relief from choking and tight guts at wartime loss and butchery (Silko, 1977, 40). Silko sets Indian veterans Emo, Harley, Leroy, and cousin Pinkie among merrymakers in Gallup bars escaping through whiskey and beer at Eddie's club, juke box music, and stumbling around the dance floor. They advance to fighting, rowdy behavior, reckless driving, trespass and poaching, sexual promiscuity, and lawlessness. In a dissolute scenario, the text invokes drunks "against the dirty walls of the bars along Highway 66, their eyes staring at the ground as if they had forgotten the sun in the sky" (*ibid.*, 107). Seduced by dreams of alcoholic bliss, they appear to "[look] for it somewhere in the mud on the sidewalk" (*ibid.*). By comparing wholeness to daylight and alcohol to filth, the text stresses the degradation that boozing brings on an animistic people who normally draw strength from oneness with nature.

The rampant insanity of drug abuse chokes human reason in an apocalyptic saga, *Almanac of the Dead* (1991), Silko's voyage of the damned through the Tucson underworld. Sterling, the Laguna gardener and moral center of the novel, gazes at a death-world littered with "pistols, shotguns, and cartridges scattered on the kitchen counters, and needles and pills all over the table. The Devil's kitchen doesn't look this good" (Silko, 1991,

20). Critic David Murray summarizes the controlling theme as "the logic of capitalist supply and demand that can and does extend to trade in bodies, body parts, and pornographic images of the abuse of bodies, as well as drugs.... Absolutely anything becomes a commodity.... Consumers become figures of nightmare, literally vampires and cannibals" (Murray, 2007, 136). Populated by the self-indulgent wealthy and privileged as well as sex addicts and homeless derelicts, the city teems with the dissolute lives paralleling America in its seamy decline. Of the effects of addiction on blacks, Clinton, a disaffected Afro-Cherokee Vietnam vet, pinpoints sickness, hunger, and endangerment by cops, "the white man's allies," because "only dope stopped young black men from burning white America to the ground" (Silko, 1991, 426).

Critic Katherine Sugg, an English professor at Central Connecticut State University, summarizes Silko method of diagnosing social ills as "hyperrealistic mode ... a fantastic, repulsive quality further emphasized by the blunt, cold, and flat affect of the characters' personas" (Sugg, 2008, 70). The malaise in street addicts allows Eddie Trigg to sucker bums into detox centers and blood donation centers, where he drains them dry in a Dracula-esque act of commercialization of their life force. Silko wrings irony from Trigg's co-conspirators, West German buyers and U.S. medical colleges, who contribute to the dehumanization of the poor and downtrodden through the marketing of biomaterials and profiteering on detox and rehab centers. Of critical response, which ranges across the continuum, analyst Linda Grant Niemann, an English professor at the University of California at Santa Cruz, felt the "reader might need to detox after reading the book, it is so dusted with cocaine, torture, and depraved sexuality" (Niemann, 1992, 3). For the moral degeneracy of *Almanac*, Niemann called the work "an ark filled with the stories and the voices and the people who will create a new world out of the destruction of the old" (*ibid.*, 1).

*See also Almanac of the Dead; Ceremony; Emo; Harley; Tayo.*

• *References and further reading*

Andrade, Susan Z. *Atlantic Cross-Currents: Transatlantiques.* Trenton, NJ: Africa World Press, 2001.
Dean, John Emory. *Travel Narratives from New Mexico: Reconstructing Identity and Truth.* Amherst, NY: Cambria, 2009.
Lundquist, Suzanne Evertsen. *Native American Literatures: An Introduction.* New York: Continuum, 2005.
Murray, David. *Matter, Magic, and Spirit: Representing Indian and African American Belief.* Philadelphia: University of Pennsylvania Press, 2007.
Niemann, Linda. "New World Disorder," *Women's Review of Books* 9:6 (March 1992): 1–4.
Silko, Leslie Marmon. *Almanac of the Dead.* New York: Simon & Schuster, 1991.
_____. *Ceremony.* New York: Viking Press, 1977.
_____. *The Turquoise Ledge: A Memoir.* New York: Viking Adult, 2010.
_____. *Yellow Woman and a Beauty of the Spirit: Essays on Native American Life Today.* New York: Simon & Schuster, 1996.
Stanford, Ann Folwell. "'Human Debris': Border Politics, Body Parts, and the Reclamation of the Americas in Leslie Marmon Silko's *Almanac of the Dead*," *Literature and Medicine* 16:1 (Spring 1997): 23–42.
Sugg, Katherine. *Gender and Allegory in Transamerican Fiction and Performance.* New York: Palgrave Macmillan, 2008.

## superstition

Silko expresses first peoples' metaphysical beliefs, which range from human conversations with serpents and prayers to the sunrise to an Amerindian fear that posing for a photograph saps the spirit. Her definition of nonrational spirituality manifests itself in intersections between individuals, between nature and people, and between the dead and the living. As a result, the connection between people and their ancestors strengthens ties with the past, the focus of "How to Hunt Buffalo" (1994), a reprise of Indian ritual from ancient times to the annihilation of free-roving herds in the mid–1900s. In an interview with Ellen L. Arnold, the author mused on "similarities in the effect of the so-called post–Einsteinian view of time and space and the way the old [Indian] people looked at energy and being and space-time" (Silko & Arnold, 2000., xi). The flexibility of native cosmology and the blend of history with ritual and healing provokes Silko's antipathies for missionaries and for Indian schools managed by white Christian proselytizers. The author denounces legalistic, bible-based curriculum for dissuading youth from "pagan" and "savage" nativism and from respect for clan and tribal beliefs. In place of white-directed education, she favors storytelling, the traditional Amerindian method of directing emotional energy to a cosmic worldview.

Silko's quest novel *Ceremony* (1977) clarifies the difference between devotion to tradition and dismissal of the old ways as superstition. Through irony, she pairs Rocky, the full-blood Laguna, with his half-breed cousin/foster brother Tayo, both U.S. Marines during the Pacific war. Tayo, the unwanted nephew/foster son of his Auntie Thelma, honors tradition in the style of Grandma and his uncles, Josiah and Robert. Rocky, the A student and football and track hero at the Albuquerque boarding school, denies the sanctity of ritual, dissociates himself from Pueblo tradition, and aims to succeed in the white world far from the primitivism of the reservation. The false advisers warn, "Don't let the people at home hold you back," but it is the white man's war that steals his youth (Silko, 1977, 51). Tayo grieves at the cruel fate that extinguishes Rocky in April 1942 during the Bataan Death March of World War II, when a grenade wound to the leg and the blow of a Japanese rifle butt kill Rocky, the family pet. His naive boast that "he was always going to win" haunts Tayo in war's aftermath, a debilitating regret that Tayo outlives his "golden boy" cousin (*ibid.*).

In reflection over their shared boyhood, the author pictures the boys' response to hunting. Tayo relives the gutting of a deer in early fall. Silko describes "the ritual of the deer," a reverence for animal life that places the kill on the same plane as that of its human hunters (*ibid.*, 52). A ceremonial preparation of the deer for eating requires covering the cooling carcass so the eyes can't watch the disemboweling, a grotesque image of dismemberment that foretells Rocky's sufferings in the Philippines. While Uncle Josiah and Uncle Robert kneel in respect and sprinkle cornmeal to feed the deer's spirit and ensure successful hunts in the coming year, Rocky turns aside from tradition in embarrassment at a mystic gesture toward nature that includes spreading the carcass on a Navajo blanket and decorating its neck and antlers with silver and turquoise. While Rocky regards the meat only as well cured venison, Tayo experiences love from the deer's heart and liver, which he wraps and carries carefully to the truck. Ironically, the transfer foreshadows his devoted treatment of Rocky, whom litter bearers carry on a blanket stretcher through monsoon rain to a prisoner of war camp. Along the way, Tayo soothes the company with narrative: "He made a story for all of them, a story to give them strength" (*ibid.*, 12).

As the result of heroic healing through converging powers, Tayo recovers. From failed treatments in a Los Angeles military hospital by white psychiatrists, Tayo enters ritual curing via chant, smoking sacred tobacco, storytelling, and following the bear's tracks and the sacred geometrics of Betonie's hoop ceremony and sandpainting. At the right moment, according to Cherokee critic Sean Kicummah Teuton, an expert on Amerindian studies at the University of Wisconsin at Madison, "Time is stilled, this world yields to that of myth and legend, the natural and the supernatural meld; and the present moment, which joins past and future, becomes a centering process, a locus of consciousness and being forever becoming" (Teuton, 2008, 136). Another strand of tradition, Tayo's reverence for Grandma, leaves him open to her insistence that the old times were an era of magic when animals spoke to humans. In war's aftermath, Silko returns Tayo full circle to sacred turf and reunites him during a snowstorm with Uncle Josiah's speckled Mexican longhorns. A mythic hunter, a mirror image of Josiah, fosters Tayo's growth in reverence. Overhead, a starry cluster, perhaps Orion, reassures Tayo of the authenticity of nature's path.

SYNCRETIC DEITIES

Silko ventures into a more convoluted study of myth, fetishism, and third world beliefs in the Gothic saga *Almanac of the Dead* (1991), her most ambitious work. She builds a New World perspective on animism through the blending of gods from black Africans, Mexicans, and Amerindians. Among the Pueblo, the loss of stone idols known as "little grandmother" and "little grandfather" grieves elders for the tender spirits that watch over the tribe (Silko, 1991, 31). Yaqui stories promulgate believes about "energies" that crave blood, "stories that good Christians were not supported to believe" (*ibid.*, 512). Among them are tales of "wise homemakers" who feed "goat or pig blood to knives, scissors, and other sharp or dangerous" domestic objects to keep themselves safe from harm (*ibid.*). In a garbage dump, the Yaqui Tacho discovers a bleeding, crying, sweating, urinating opal the size of a macaw egg. The human effluvia that ooze from the stone cause him to think about white "energies that craved blood" (*ibid.*, 512). The serendipity of locating a sacred talisman in debris fills Tacho with respect for blood. Thinking over the ritual Aztec blood-letting, he concludes: "Long before Europeans ever appeared, the people had already disagreed over the blood and the killing.... Spirits were not satisfied with just any blood.... The spirits must be fed with the blood of the rich and the royal" (*ibid.*, 336–337). The mystique of the bleeding opal forces Tacho into an urgent mission to join his twin, El Feo. With guidance from the sacred spirit macaws, the twins, like Moses and Aaron in Exodus, lead the dispossessed from Mesoamerica toward a reclamation of Amerindian land to the north.

Clinton, Silko's Afro-Cherokee veteran of the Vietnam War, voices the affinity of the Cherokee for West African slaves who hid in the Appalachian Mountains, bringing with them the giant serpent Damballah, the twin warriors, and the Maize Mother, an avatar of the Native American Earth Mother. Because the Cherokee welcomed runaways, their two belief systems melded into a strong consciousness of earth powers. Clinton reveres his knife as the sanctuary of the voodoo spirit Ogou Feraille (or Ogou-Feray), the armored Yoruban combat deity. When Ogou reached the Western Hemisphere, he transformed himself from the African blacksmith to "the guerrilla warrior of hit-and-run scorched earth and no prisoners" (*ibid.*, 417). By clinging to his amulet-weapon, Clinton feels himself safe from shrapnel. On return to the moral muck of Tucson, he reveres Ogou as the leader of the people's revolution and the avenger for "the bitterness and blood spilled since the Europeans had arrived" (*ibid.*, 418).

*Almanac* emphasizes the similarities between the West African Damballah and Quetzalcoatl or Maah'shra-True'-Ee, the feathered snake of Aztec and Olmec lore from Mesoamerica. In both cases, the serpent icons mediate between the spiritual realm and earth by crawling into holes to retrieve messages and warnings from the underworld to disseminate to humankind. Because of Quetzalcoatl's power to endow people with knowledge and literacy, from the 16th century onward, the priests of the *conquistadores* defamed snake legends as satanic idol worship. For substantiation, Catholic fathers cited the duplicitous Old Testament snake from the Garden of Eden, who denied knowledge to Adam and Eve, tempted them to doubt God, and precipitated their disobedience and expulsion from the earthly paradise. Silko's text develops the African Damballah into the great stone water snake of the Laguna, the icon that restores the exile Sterling in the falling action and welcomes him home.

## MYSTIC POWERS

For *Gardens in the Dunes* (1999), the author inserts abrupt adventures in metaphysics to contrast the ordered empiricism of Dr. Edward G. Palmer, a field botanist. In the Tampico market, his offer of cash for iron meteorites outrages a black Mayan seer with a face painted blue. Her prediction of recompense alerts sailors who fight a storm in the Gulf of Mexico. Presumably sent by the "Black Indian of Tampico, who kept two sets of altar saints," the gale incites rumors of the spite of "a daughter of the African spirits and the Maya spirits as well" (Silko, 1999, 88, 89). The text endows the seer with syncretic power, which she manipulates by burning rum and black dog hair in a white bowl, color coding that suggests the eternal war between good and evil. The terror generated by her double realms causes sailors to jettison valuables overboard to still the tropical storm. The impact of superstition on the crew continues far to the south in the protection of Campeche Bay, where the men pour holy water and toss bananas and gold beads into the waves to silence the wind.

Silko dramatizes metaphysical payback to punish doubters. Edward's bold irreverence toward amulets recurs in Bath, England, where he handles artifacts—chalcedony carved with three cattle, a bloodstone idol of the Roman god Jupiter holding a staff and an eagle, Fortuna in brown and white agate holding a poppy and ear of corn, a carnelian image of Minerva and a serpent, and lead curse tablets—retrieved from the Celtic layer of the sacred spring of Sulis, a Romano-Celtic mother goddess. Upon lifting a tin mask to his face, Edward notices the distancing that the object causes between the wearer and his observers. As Mary Stewart demonstrates in the Druidic and Mithraic rituals pictured in *The Hollow Hills* (1973), Silko implies that a separation from the ordinary is a purpose of masking. The collapse of the Palmer marriage begins in frequent separations and reaches a climax in Bastia, Corsica, where Hattie palmer experiences a vision of the Holy Mother, a conversion to a sacred female aura that Edward ridicules. On his deathbed, he continues to covet worldly goods, which lead him to bankruptcy, despair, and doom. Silko contrasts his restless material quest to Hattie's search for the eternal female, which she locates in gardens.

As in the author's fiction, animistic concepts dominate *The Turquoise Ledge* (2010), Silko's memoir and paean to life in the desert. The text repeats a consultation theory from *Almanac of the Dead*, that macaws deliver oracles from the dead to human interpreters. She believes that Star Beings from the sky protect the east side of her house and that bees, lizards, birds, snakes, stones, and rain bring messages from the afterlife and from newly departed friends and family. During the deathwatch over her dog Dolly, she feels ghost dogs visiting during her last three nights. After Dolly's passing on the fourth night, the author digs a grave and unearths a stone shaped like a dove's heart, a farewell from Dolly. Silko concludes, "She's not far away" (Silko, 2010, 188). The statement captures the Amerindian affinity for past generations, who hover near earth to sustain and direct the living.

*See also* Betonie; Lecha and Zeta's genealogy; religion; symbolism; Tayo; Wovoka.

• *References and further reading*

Olmstead, Jane. "The Uses of Blood in Leslie Marmon Silko's *Almanac of the Dead*," *Contemporary Literature* 40:3 (Fall 1999): 464–490.

Rainwater, Catherine. *Dreams of Fiery Stars: The Transformations of Native American Fiction*. Philadelphia: University of Pennsylvania Press, 1999.

Shapiro, Colleen. "Silko's Ceremony," *Explicator* 61:2 (Winter 2003): 117–119.

Silko, Leslie Marmon. *Almanac of the Dead*. New York: Simon & Schuster, 1991.

_____. *Ceremony*. New York: Viking Press, 1977.

_____. *Gardens in the Dunes*. New York: Scribner, 1999.

_____. *The Turquoise Ledge*. New York: Viking, 2010.

_____, and Ellen L. Arnold. *Conversations with Leslie Marmon Silko*. Jackson: University Press of Mississippi, 2000.

Teuton, Sean Kicummah. *Red Land, Red Power: Grounding Knowledge in the American Indian Novel*. Durham, NC: Duke University Press, 2008.

## symbolism

In an ecofeminist worldview, Silko regards symbols in nature much as her ancestors revered petroglyphs. For the title of her memoir, *The Turquoise Ledge* (2010), the author chooses one of the desert's more startling formations, a colorful mineral formed by water on volcanic rock. Because of the use of turquoise by the paleo–Pueblo as trade items, the blue-green semi-precious stone represents commerce to relieve the poverty that threatens life for dwellers of the Sonoran Desert of Arizona. To interviewer Steve Bennett, a journalist with the San Antonio *Express News*, Silko confided the various meanings of "treasure in the desert"—"wishful thinking, a daydream ... things we seek in the distance but then discover close by, things that we think to be true but later find out are wrong ... the sudden surprise of beauty, which the earth and the desert offer us so generously whether we deserve them or not" (Bennett, 2010, 4K). A symbolic serendipity, shards of the bright stone infuse the author with hope in her mental conflict with the desert destroyer with his bulldozer.

Silko fills her imagery in *Laguna Woman: Poems* (1974) with the shapes of rainclouds, encounters with deer and birds, and the efforts of characters to wrest meaning from objects. In *Sacred Water: Narratives and Pictures* (1993), dominant in a dry land is the snake messenger, a harbinger of rain or occupant of a pool of fresh water, which Silko described as "life itself" (Silko & Arnold, 2000, 122). For *Ceremony* (1977), the author applies cumulative symbolism to express human qualities. For inborn strength, she implies that Ulibarri's spotted Mexican cattle, the wild longhorns descended from desert strains, parallel the Laguna, a pueblo people drawn south to their ancestral homeland. As wiry as desert antelope, the herd is capable of surviving on mesquite and scarce water. The recovery of the cattle from the fenced pasture of rustler Floyd Lee centers the quest novel, providing direction and purpose to Tayo, the protagonist.

Tayo, too, parallels natural elements, which he views in a grotto, a sacred niche for its shielding of life in an arid land. As frogs bury themselves in dry sand until rejuvenating rain sets them free, Tayo lives in the shadow world of lies and war, combat flashback and nightmare until his grandmother's stories and Betonie's ceremonial myths set him on a path to understanding. Organizing Tayo's actions are sets of four—four fellow veterans (Emo, Harley, Leroy Valdez, and cousin Pinkie), the four cardinal directions, the fourth world below, "Auntie's brand, a rafter 4," and the four sacred mountains of the sandpainting, a spiritual map that transcends political boundaries (Silko, 1977, 81). Sheathed in Laguna lore and legend, Tayo follows the fours and cleanses his spirit of the white world's deceit and a malaise that Mary Aswell Doll, a history and art teacher at Savannah College of Art and Design, calls a "psychic sleep of forgetting" (Doll, 2000, 212). As imprinted with being and instinct as the frogs, Tayo takes on the identity and purpose that nature intended for him.

## SYMBOLS AS DIRECTION

Tayo's symbolic quest advances along a symbolic map toward action. He survives separation from Ts'eh Montaño, his surreal beloved, and retreats to his homeland at Laguna. After a rejuvenating summer with her at Pa'to'ch, he realizes that he is strong enough to withstand the pain of loss from September until their reunion in May. By questing for the cattle to fulfill his promise to Uncle Josiah, Tayo rids himself of trauma, bonds with his horse, and begins to feel normal again. Even after his fall from the horse on Mount Taylor, he stops resisting and lies fearlessly on the ground, "close to the earth, where the core was cool and silent as mountain stone ... a returning rather than a separation" (Silko, 1977, 201). Because he had "proved something to himself," his spirit responds to the positive energy of achievement, as opposed to the negative exertions of fighting a war on foreign soil (*ibid.*, 198).

For contrast to Tayo's emerging heroism, Silko betokens fragility in blue pollen, a bloody fetus bundled in rags for burial in the sand, a blind grandmother and blind mule, a beat-up GMC pickup, elderly counselors, shanties destroyed in the ravine, rainbows, sand painting, wildflower roots and stems, a decrepit kiva, and a spring pooling at the base of a crevice in rock. A direct image of Tayo, the tough U.S. marine, the bull with a broken foreleg bears intact muscles, but a structure too damaged to support them. In native style, Silko wraps these insubstantial icons in light, the alpha and omega of her narrative, which opens and closes on the curative power of dawn. For the fever-ridden ex-infantryman, the coalescing of daylight on a patch of wall foreshadows his healing through nature and a firm grip on life forces. No longer confused like the thread tumbling from Grandma's wicker sewing basket, his thoughts return to sunlight, the source of human life that dispels the emotional fog that prevents his showdown with hurtful memories. In contrast to his healing, his contemporaries, Harley and Leroy, die mangled in the balky pickup. Buried under American flags in shiny army-issue coffins, the two receive honors as "if they had died at Wake Island or Iwo Jima" (ibid., 295). Critic Sharon Holm, on staff at the University of London, associates the allusion to the flag-raising on Iwo Jima and the two Indian corpses with that of Pima soldier Ira Hamilton Hayes of Sacaton, Arizona. After honoring the American flag on Mount Suribachi, Hayes also returned home to rootlessness, 52 arrests for public drunkenness, and an early death following a fight over a card game.

## SYMBOLS AS WARNINGS

For *Almanac of the Dead* (1991), Silko ramps up Gothic symbolism in an era of criminality and fervid bloodletting. In a review of the troubling characterization, Paul West, book critic for the *Los Angeles Times*, complained of a procession of beings and "their virtual interchangeability contrasted with the personae, gargoyles, incubuses, demons and revenants of another dimension" (West, 1992, 8). Menardo Panson, a traitorous Mexican Indian and self-made tycoon of Universal Insurance, becomes obsessed with his bullet-proof vest, a frail techno-shield that entombs him while assuaging his fear of death. Anticipating the revival of Wovoka's Ghost Shirts, which followers misunderstood as actual guarantees of immortality, Menardo engineers his own execution by posing in his vest for his driver to test with real gunfire. Silko turns others of her narcissists into victims as she prepares indigenous people for the recolonization of stolen land. The overarching emblem, a giant stone snake, a twentieth-century version of African and Mayan vision serpents, flourishes between worlds, crawling into its hole to retrieve spirit messages from the nether world. At Laguna Pueblo, it emerges outside the Jackpile uranium mine, evidence of earth's recompense for the injuries white conquerors and polluters have done to the Americas. A prophetic symbol, the reptile foreshadows doom for Caucasian rule of North America. Silko's memoir *The Turquoise Ledge* (2010) returns to the appearance of M'ashra'true'ee in spring 1980 at the heaps of radioactive tailings at the mine, where reverent visitors leave offerings of pollen, cornmeal, coral, turquoise, and mother of pearl in thanks for a symbol of hope.

The guardian serpent returns to prominence in the opening and closing of *Gardens in the Dunes* (1999), an historical novel mixed with Silko's usual mythic, poetic, and allegorical elements. Of the allegorical implications, German critic Hartwig Isernhagen, a specialist in American studies at the University of Basel, translates gardens as "pastoral fusions of nature and art and moments of heightened insight and affectivity in exactly those places in which in [Nathaniel] Hawthorne's or [Henry] James's texts, for instance, 'high art' would occur" (Isernhagen, 2002, 177). Isernhagen characterizes the settings as "existential or quasi-religious" (*ibid.*). While the last four-member matriarchy of the Sand Lizard people survives in Arizona's sandhills, an old rattler, the iconic high priest, presides over the spring. Reviewer William Willard, an anthropology professor at the University of Arizona, notes that "The concept of the snake guardian is one that is present in mythology all over the U.S. Southwest and the Mexican Northwest" (Willard, 2000, 140). Grandma Fleet honors the serpent as both protector and mediator between the living and ancestral spirits. The murder of the old snake in the falling action precludes despair by the crowning of a new warden, the beautiful daughter serpent who takes her father's place. Symbolically, the female reptile prefigures a revival of the matriarchy and betokens the blossoming of Sister Salt and Indigo, the new mother figures in the sand dunes. While Sister Salt nurtures her son Bright Eyes, Indigo, the new storykeeper, introduces new seeds for the garden and the rare black gladiolus for both food and beauty. Thus, the death of the old rattler augurs further episodes in the drama of Sand Lizard revitalization.

*See also* wisdom.

- *References and further reading*

Bennett, Steve. "Author Silko Isn't Concerned about Time," *Express News* (25 July 2010): 1K, 4K.

Dean, John Emory. *Travel Narratives from New Mexico: Reconstructing Identity and Truth.* Amherst, NY: Cambria, 2009.

Doll, Mary Aswell. *Like Letters in Running Water: A Mythopoetics of Curriculum.* New York: Routledge, 2000.

Holm, Sharon. "The 'Lie' of the Land: Native Sovereignty, Indian Literary Nationalism, and Early Indigenism in Leslie Marmon Silko's Ceremony," *American Indian Quarterly* 32:3 (Summer 2008): 243–274.

Isernhagen, Hartwig. "Of Deserts and Gardens: The Southwest in Literature and Art, 'Native' and 'White'" in *Literature and Visual Arts in Twentieth-Century America*, ed. Michele Bottalico. Bari: Palomar Eupalinos, 2002, 173–187.

Silko, Leslie Marmon. *The Turquoise Ledge.* New York: Viking, 2010.

_____, and Ellen L. Arnold. *Conversations with Leslie Marmon Silko.* Jackson, MS: University Press of Mississippi, 2000.

Stanford, Ann Folwell. "'Human Debris': Border Politics, Body Parts, and the Reclamation of the Americas in Leslie Marmon Silko's *Almanac of the Dead*," *Literature and Medicine* 16:1 (Spring 1997): 23–42.

West, Paul. "When a Myth Is as Good as a Mile," *Los Angeles Times* (2 February 1992): 8.

Willard, William. "Review: *Gardens in the Dunes*," *Wicazo Sa Review* 15:2 (Fall 2000): 139–141.

# Tayo

One of Silko's vivid portrayals of postcolonial damage, Tayo, the mixed-breed war veteran in *Ceremony* (1977), becomes a voluntary Indian by siding with his matrilineage and sorrowing for his cousin/near-brother Rocky. Critic John A. McClure, an English professor at Rutgers, calls Tayo a "semioutcast ... drawn out of traditional ways and off the reservation by the spell of the secular West's products and power ... dismantled and nearly destroyed by alcohol and modern war" (McClure, 2007, 139). During an epic journey modeled on the post-war gropings of the author's cousin Robert Leslie Evans, Tayo dramatizes the Homeric motif of *nostos* (homecoming), a journey haunted by heart-sickness. Replicating the epic voyages of Odysseus, Aeneas, and Bran, Tayo's quest epitomizes the displaced survivor's obsession with past horrors and with the humiliation of being a half-breed. Rather than view time through the Judeo-Christian concept of linear chronology, he returns to the cyclical cosmology found in ancient Greek narrative and Amerindian stories. Thus, his recovery of Uncle Josiah's speckled Mexican longhorns keeps his promise to an old man who died six years earlier. The continuity of life from age to age comforts Tayo and reunites him spiritually with Josiah and with Rocky, whom Tayo fails to save from combat in the Philippines. On an epic scale, according to analyst John Emory Dean, an English professor at Texas A&M International University, Tayo must accept the quest "or he and his people will dry up and vanish, thereby fulfilling the Western narrative of manifest destiny" (Dean, 2009, 165).

While remapping his homeland on horseback and on foot, Tayo attempts to mask from his family shattering internal strife from captivity in the Philippines in 1945 and shell-shock on Iwo Jima in early 1945. He becomes the existential hero who must work out for himself historic and personal disintegration. At the depth of crisis, he views the geo-economic rape of New Mexico by logging and uranium mining and realizes the cultural duality in his homeland, a dominant theme that Silko returns to in *Almanac of the Dead* (1991) and *The Turquoise Ledge* (2010). To reconcile blended parentage, he undergoes a psychic power struggle that maneuvers the shards of his identity into a whole being. As explained by critic Alexandra Ganser, a lecturer at the University of Oklahoma, Tayo must transform himself by finding "a heritage of his own" (Ganser, 2004, 150). In Darwinian terms, he is the resilient hybrid who survives the adversity that kills his full-blood cousin Rocky, a brittle individual incapable of accommodating threats to his rigid worldview. Rather than an embarrassment to the family and clan, Tayo becomes a bridge mediating between two historically grafted cultures. In recovery, he lives in the moment, glorying in the dawn, when "a single moment gathered all things together — the last stars, the mountaintops, the clouds, and the winds—celebrating this coming" (Silko, 1977, 182).

## THE CULTURAL HERO

In the analysis of Kenneth Lincoln, an English professor at the University of California at Los Angeles, Tayo draws on a prototype from world literature — "the divine child of ancient myth — a martyred Christ, stuttering Moses, or swollen-footed Oedipus who redefines communal life and evolving culture" (Lincoln, 2008, 111). Lincoln expands on the uniqueness of the mixed-blood Indian: "Like the half-breed Hermes, son of Zeus and earth mother Maia, Tayo will serve both as culture bearer and messenger to and from the gods" (Lincoln, 2008, 111). Standing at the threshold of the divine like the unproven Celtic princeling Arthur Pendragon, the Hebrew warrior Gideon, the Scandic Beowulf, and the

Indian archer Arjuna in the *Bhagavad-Gita* (ca. 200 B.C.), Tayo must embrace the god-hood within to revitalize himself to become "story-carrier and gene-crosser ... intercultural traveler, a water-woman-hunter, a sun-and-rain balancer" (*ibid.*, 117). Only by reclaiming the true self can he redirect focus and complete his mission to a damaged people as "culture bearer and messenger to and from the gods" (*ibid.*). Critic Ronald Strickland, the chairman of humanities at Syracuse University, points out Silko's ability to make her hero simultaneously courageous and tender, a postmodern advance over assumptions about Gilgamesh, Saul, and other warlord victors of early world literature.

A literary twin of the disoriented Blackfoot in James Welch's psychological novel *Winter in the Blood* and the transported convict in Peter Carey's *Jack Maggs* (1997), Tayo appears as an anti-hero, a wraith shamed, enraged, and unbalanced by schizoid dreams and a dehydrated spirit. As defeated as Chato, the crippled Navajo ranch hand in "Lullaby" (1974), Tayo survives world war disempowered, scarred by white exploitation, and incapable of accepting the arbitrary labeling of the Japanese as enemies. The protagonist suffers a colonization of the mind by white materialism, stereotypes, and exploitation, a wrong-headedness he shares with Abenaki writer Joseph Bruchac, autobiographer of *Bowman's Store* (1997). From age four, Tayo survives fatherlessness and the disgrace triggered by his mother Laura's alcoholism and sexual libertinism with white and Mexican males. In 1926, she abandons him to relatives. Following her death, he knows intuitively that his foster mother, Auntie Thelma, considers him a family embarrassment, the residue of taboo behavior and a burden requiring care and upbringing. In May 1940, he remains true to his Uncle Josiah's dream of a cattle business, a source of manly pride. Unlike Rocky, who tunes out his mother's disparaging comments about the family herd, Tayo listens to her prediction of doom and recognizes her usual premise, perpetual family failure because of "little sister" Laura's sexual transgression and her conception of an illegitimate mixed-breed son. Tayo maintains spiritual stasis by actively promoting family prosperity. In June, he maintains his belief in Josiah's plan and helps him brand the wild herd, which migrates steadily south.

## Spiritual Demons

In a postmodern version of Western captivity lore, Silko plots a new frontier myth depicting the hybrid protagonist overwhelmed by a demon — a technological evil far from his Laguna core. After he promises to bring his cousin Rocky safely back to the pueblo from war, which erupts in the Pacific on December 7, 1941, Tayo discerns in Auntie Thelma's look a chilling curse, her hope that "something" happens to Tayo, not her beloved son (Silko, 1977, 73). During the Bataan Death March through the Philippines in April 1942, Tayo perceives defeat in the form of mud. The slough, quickened by a monsoon, fills tire ruts, turns wounds green, encourages malarial fever, and impairs Tayo and a corporal, who slip while carrying his cousin Rocky in a blanket stretcher. Tayo commits a cosmic error — the Greek *hamartia*, the missing of the mark — by praying for an end to rain rather than an end to soldiering. According to critic Laurie Champion, a specialist in comparative literature at San Diego State University, by cursing the rain, he insults Corn Woman (Nau'ts'ity'i) and her sister (Iktoa'ak'o'ya or Reed Woman). To be absolved of combat regrets and purged of self-medication with alcohol, the 26-year-old survivor must accept purification and the inevitable changes of people and places, including the death of Rocky from a grenade round to leg and a blow to the head from a Japanese rifle butt. Under these burdens, Tayo becomes the prototypical victim of sorcery.

The ensuing struggle for wholeness and fidelity mirrors a peacetime form of imprisonment in a secularized world that is empty and moribund. Faced by the awful power of the white military, Tayo "had no reasons to believe" in the pueblo's sacred lore (*ibid.*, 94). Ambivalence and internal hurts set him adrift in time, a disunion with the motions of the heavens. As deracinated as True Son, the bicultural protagonist of Conrad Richter's *The Light in the Forest* (1953), the veteran has reason to challenge all that is holy to bring him safely home again. At the shabby hogan of Betonie, a Chicano-Navajo shaman north of Gallup, "all of it seemed suddenly so pitiful and small compared to the world [Tayo] knew the white people had," a material wealth that caused World War II (*ibid.*, 127). While living it up with his fellow veterans Emo, Harley, Leroy Valdez, and cousin Pinkie, Tayo incurs the bewitching, which Silko describes as Ck'o'yo medicine. A destructive force counter to birth and vitality, the negative power confines his companions in a cycle of wickedness that devours them in the style of the snake that swallows its own tail. Tayo admits that fractious carouses precipitate arguments and brawls that destroy short-term peace. Rather than grieve for himself, he regrets that life's promise falls short for Rocky.

Silko symbolizes Tayo's emptiness as a lack of human substance in the presence of a palpable, unyielding pain. He shapeshifts into white smoke, a hollow, fading outline lacking consciousness and volition and "[waiting] to die the way smoke dies" (Silko, 1977, 15). He inhabits a "gray winter fog ... a twilight cloud," the drug-induced nothingness that shields him from suffering and combat memories (*ibid.*). The detritus of evil—the reek of urine and vomit in Harley's pickup truck—forces Tayo outdoors toward the freshness of desert air, the balm that restores him to sanity and wellness. During a six-year drought, the atmosphere of dry air and desert sand vivifies the sterility of his spirit. Without moisture to soothe human skin and dwindling pasturage, the lengthy dry period re-bruises his hurts, creating fresh wounds. The contrast between the New Mexico climate and his memories of a Philippine monsoon forces him to relive interminable rain hammering his skull and the effort to evacuate Rocky from combat on a blanket stretcher. The drenching downpour in Tayo's nightmares and panic attacks increase his guilt for returning home without his cousin. To Emo, a war-crazed Army veteran, Tayo and his ravings over post-war racism exacerbate malice and depression. Emo sees his old friend as "a skinny light-skinned bastard" intent on ruining the fun of a drunken brag session (*ibid.*, 42–43). Tayo conceals the source of his weeping, which is pity for his comrades, whose seduction by white technology takes the form of aimless truck rides. Because the antipathies morph into fury, Tayo departs the Dixie Tavern in Budville in a police car and bears on his hand reminders of his loss of control in the fight with Emo—"thick welted scars from the shattered bottle glass" that Tayo rammed into his comrade's gut (*ibid.*, 139).

## Finding Home Again

After a period of estrangement, Tayo embraces the Laguna affinity for the open spaces of New Mexico by walking and observing nature's minutia. A man of good heart, he pities the suffering in Gallup's Hopi, Laguna, Navajo, and Zuni derelicts and wishes them safe harborage in their reservations. From Betonie's hoop ceremony and sand painting, he perceives a boundaryless homeland bathed in cool mountain air. He looks toward the sacred slopes of Tse-pi'na (Mount Taylor) as a source of hope. His memories return to the spring that Josiah showed him inside a cave, a symbol of the internal wellsprings that nourish the soul. Outside of bars and the fetid smell of the pickup truck, he retreats into nature by scanning sky and earth for antidotes to battle fatigue. As part of his post-war purification, searches for Josiah's spotted Mexican cattle restore the family's positive outlook and conclude with success for the hunter, who locates the herd in the corral of Ts'eh Montaño, an avatar of nature and spirit of place. The exertions of herding, like priestly duties to the Earth Mother, fulfill part of Betonie's vision of healing. In Montaño's company, he experiences sacred coitus, relaxation of neck and belly, and a normal lapse into sleep, suggestions of the pre–Columbian utopia. He enjoys an Edenic summer idyll free of Emo's hurtful rumors and the possibility of recommitment to a veterans' mental ward. In May 1949, Tayo can safely declare that "love had outdistanced death" (*ibid.*, 219).

## CHARACTERIZATION OF THE SURVIVOR

The text creates urgency in the gaps that remain in the protagonist's homing. In the resolution, Tayo returns to the incomplete gestalt to examine the source of his anxiety and precarious mental state. Because he is "unchurched, untutored, and only semiliterate in the ways of [Pueblo] tradition," he blames himself for the deaths of Rocky and the Japanese prisoners (McClure, 2007, 141). As he once punished himself for killing flies, he views his infractions as the cause of Uncle Josiah's death by breaking a promise to help him raise the wild-eyed Mexican herd. The fly image alludes to a line from Shakespeare's *King Lear*: "As flies to wanton boys are we to th' gods,/They kill us for their sport" (IV, i, 36–27), a token of ill fortune. A spiritual neophyte, Tayo lacks the theological expertise and language to refute doubt in divine beneficence. Because of his naïveté, Silko sends the ghost of Uncle Josiah to remind Tayo that Rocky's mathematical logic and empirical truths can no longer explain a world threatened by the massacre of innocents by the American atomic bomb.

Significantly, Silko subverts the Caucasian trope of the doomed Indian, the stock character in the works of James Fenimore Cooper and Oliver La Farge reactualized in Ken Kesey's novel *One Flew Over the Cuckoo's Nest* (1962) and Hal Borland's *When the Legends Die* (1963). As the sacred strings unwind from his skull like the unraveling of yarn from a corpse wrapping, Tayo gains release from soldiery and from the curse of mixed blood. Silko ends Tayo's years of confusion on the autumn solstice, September 22, 1949, at what critic Kurt Caswell, a literature professor at Texas Tech University, calls "the totem meal ceremony (an ancient sacrificial ritual in which the members of a clan affirm their identification with their god)" (Caswell, 2008, 175). At a pivotal moment in reshaping his beliefs, he realizes that "he had learned the lie by heart—the lie which they had wanted him to learn: only brown-skinned people were thieves" (Silko, 1977, 191). Rather than cringe from memories of World War II, he grasps a piece of uranium ore and recognizes the monstrous capitalist plan to turn earth's power into a hellmouth—the atomic bomb, "a great spiral, swallowing the universe endlessly into the black mouth" (*ibid.*, 247). The coalescing of the pattern of lies and trickery relieves his terror of insanity and connects the stories, much as he recovers the scattered Mexican cattle and rejects the witchery of panic and an urge to murder Emo by driving a rusty screwdriver into his cranium.

## TAYO'S PROMISE

Similar in tone to John Irving's *A Prayer for Owen Meany* (1989), Karen Tei Yamashita's play *Through the Arc of the Rain Forest* (1990), and Tim O'Brien's auto-reflexive novel *The Things They Carried* (1990), Silko's novel projects hope for the future. Rather than actualize the white stereotype of "another drunk Indian war veteran settling an old feud," Tayo retreats from warrior mode to the contemplative man, the humanist in action, a character who prefigures the exiled Sterling in *Almanac of the Dead* (*ibid.*, 253). No longer distracted by the white world's evil, he hunts, tracks, and herds, grounding practices on childhood training by Uncle Josiah that restores Tayo's reverence for earth's creatures. His choices, according to critic A. Robert Lee, a Silko expert, return him "to a sustaining myth-world, a cosmos which coheres" (Lee, 2009, 506). In ecofeminist terms, Spanish literary analysts Jesús Benito Sánchez, Ana Ma Manzanas Calvo, and Begoña Simal González conclude that only by realizing "that the personal and the political and that the local and the global interpenetrate each other does he start on his path toward recovery" (Sánchez, Calvo, & González, 2009, 219).

The closeness to nature generates spirituality that the author revisits in the essay "How to Hunt Buffalo" (1994), the coming-home scenes in *Gardens in the Dunes*, and her own life in *The Turquoise Ledge* (2010). By reconfiguring his place in time and space, Tayo, like the title figure in "Humaweepi, the Warrior Priest," shapes himself into a sage in "a coherent cosmos informed by principles of harmony, balance, and reciprocal relatedness" (McClure, 2007, 151). Author Simon Joseph Ortiz pictures Tayo as "wealthy with story and tradition," a hero, like Marco Polo, returning to the pueblo with treasure for all (Ortiz, 2006, 258). He nurtures himself once more with the beliefs and rituals of the sacred kiva, where he becomes, like the orphaned Humaweepi, both healed and healer. Among revered elders, he combines the feminine force of nature and language to tell Mother Earth's story as it coalesced, as sturdy as the Mexican herd, "in bone and muscle" (*ibid.*, 236). Humanist critic Marion W. Copeland asserts, "The planting of a new life, the telling of a new tale — these are the natural outcome of Tayo's vision and ceremony" (Copeland, 1983, 171). For his complexity, the character of Tayo has taken his place alongside Cooper's Deerslayer, Conrad's Marlowe, Camus's Meursault, and Heller's Yossarian.

*See also* Emo; Harley; madness; Montaño, Ts'eh; reclamation; siblings; substance abuse; Tayo's genealogy.

• *References and further reading*

Caswell, Kurt. "The Totem Meal in Leslie Marmon Silko's *Ceremony*," *ISLE* 15:2 (2008): 175–183.

Champion, Laurie. *Contemporary American Women Fiction Writers: An A-to-Z Guide*. Westport, CT: Greenwood Press, 2002.

Copeland, Marion W. "*Black Elk Speaks* and Leslie Marmon Silko's *Ceremony*: Two Visions of Horses," *Critique* (Spring 1983): 158–172.

Dean, John Emory. *Travel Narratives from New Mexico: Reconstructing Identity and Truth*. Amherst, NY: Cambria, 2009.

Ganser, Alexandra. "Violence, Trauma, and Cultural Memory in Leslie Silko's *Ceremony*," *Atenea* 24:1 (June 2004): 145–149.

Hernández-Avila, Inés. *Reading Native American Women: Critical/Creative Representations*. Lanham, MD: Altamira, 2005.

Lee, A. Robert. *Multicultural American Literature: Comparative Black, Native, Latino/a and Asian American Fictions*. Jackson: University Press of Mississippi, 2003.

Lincoln, Kenneth. *Speak Like Singing: Classics of Native American Literature*. Albuquerque: University of New Mexico Press, 2008.

Martin, Holly E. "Hybrid Landscapes as Catalysts for Cultural Reconciliation in Leslie Marmon Silko's *Ceremony* and Rudolfo Anaya's *Bless Me, Ultima*," *Atenea* 26:1 (June 2006): 131–149.

McClure, John. *Partial Faiths: Postsecular Fiction in the Age of Pynchon and Morrison*. Athens: University of Georgia Press, 2007.

Ortiz, Simon J. "Towards a National Indian Literature: Cultural Authenticity in Nationalism" in *American Indian Literary Nationalism*, eds. Jace Weaver, Craig S. Womack, and Robert Allen Warrior. Albuquerque: University of New Mexico Press, 2006.

Roppolo, Kimberly. "Vision, Voice, and Intertribal Metanarrative: The American Indian Visual-Rhetorical Tradition and Leslie Marmon Silko's *Almanac of the Dead*," *American Indian Quarterly* 31:4 (Fall 2007): 534–558.

Sánchez, Jesús Benito, Ana Ma Manzanas Calvo, and Begoña Simal González. *Uncertain Mirrors: Magical Realisms in US Ethnic Literatures*. New York: Rodopi, 2009.
Silko, Leslie Marmon. *Ceremony*. New York: Viking, 1977.
Strickland, Ronald. *Growing Up Postmodern: Neoliberalism and the War on the Young*. Lanham, MD: Rowman & Littlefield, 2002.
Teuton, Sean Kicummah. *Red Land, Red Power: Grounding Knowledge in the American Indian Novel*. Durham, NC: Duke University Press, 2008.
Zandy, Janet. *Hands: Physical Labor, Class, and Cultural Work*. New Brunswick, NJ: Rutgers University Press, 2004.

## Tayo's genealogy

The extended family in *Ceremony* (1977) conveys a sense of loose clan ties, even between Auntie Thelma's household and her brother Josiah's wife and Cousin Pinkie, whom Josiah hires to herd sheep. Sexual connections link an unusual group to Tayo's kin, including a cantina dancer and a mountain demigoddess, the consort of Mountain Lion Man.

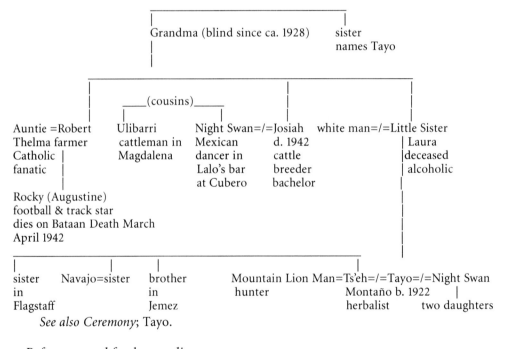

See also *Ceremony*; Tayo.

• *References and further reading*

Beidler, Peter G., and Robert M. Nelson. "Grandma's Wicker Sewing Basket: Untangling the Narrative Threads in Silko's *Ceremony*," *American Indian Culture and Research Journal* 28:1 (2004): 5–13.
Silko, Leslie Marmon. *Ceremony*. New York: Viking, 1977.

## *The Turquoise Ledge* (2010)

In her self-portrait *The Turquoise Ledge*, the author repeats autobiographical material found in *Storyteller* (1981) and *Yellow Woman and a Beauty of the Spirit: Essays on Native American Life Today* (1996). Inspired by her 60th birthday in 2008, Silko replaces the vigor of her earlier works with introspection. She retreats into solitude in a step back from pollution, crowding, native involvement in casinos, the war in Afghanistan, and "the local earth-gouger," who reshapes the landscape with a bulldozer (Johnson, 2010). In an interview with Tom Ashbrook, a journalist for National Public Radio, she established then memoir's perspective as Amerindian — "What I loved the most.... Where my heart is. My identity is fixed" (Ashbrook & Silko, 2010). At a time when Arizona politics resounded with "rancorous shrieking" over land use and the presence of undocumented aliens, she validated communion with nature as "beyond price" (*ibid.*) She concluded, "We need that reconnection" with the wild (*ibid.*). Her own daily walks freed her from linear time and suggested to her mind variances in gravity and light, the basics of physics. On days that light shifted, she determined that the "shimmerings and glints ... are alive" (*ibid.*).

The author's reflections on family include heightened tensions of her Laguna and non–Laguna relatives. Concerning a gathering in April in Denver, she joked about old age, retirement, and the composition of memoirs and family tell-alls. Instead of sinking into nostalgia, she smirked, "Oh, I'm an enemy of genres," an admission of her aversion to tight Western parameters and writing styles (Richey, 2010). To explode expectations of memoir, she cultivates an organic rendering of her reflections on the outdoors through episodes, vignettes, myth, diary, translation and etymology, quotations of Emily Dickinson's poems, and incidental imagistic verse about her 25-acre Arizona oasis. Among anecdotes of longevity and recovery are accounts of women who survive appendicitis without surgical intervention and of dogs with loose neck and throat skin that survive rattlesnake bites that don't penetrate muscle. Valuers of turquoise save Bull Durham tobacco bags and remove the blue tax stamps to paste on the forehead to quell headache. The unsigned critique from *Kirkus Reviews* admires the themes and desert setting, but regrets that the lack of a cohesive style and method restricts the reader from "a much-needed treatise on renewing our relationship with the natural world" ("Review," 2010, 612).

In an interview with critic Steve Bennett, a journalist with the San Antonio *Express News*, Silko remarked on the need for recording deeply personal meditations: "Writing provides the solitude necessary to reflect on being in this world" (Bennett, 2010, 1K). She embeds the text with insights into Indian trade routes from Arizona and New Mexico as far south as Guatemala, where worshipers of Tlaloc, the Aztec Lord of the Rain, bartered for powdered turquoise to blend into teal body paint for ritual dances. With respect for the outdoors, she communicates with nature's sounds from rivers, winds, rocks, and shi-wah nah (cloud beings) and awaits respite from heat waves when her "overheated brain wasn't much good for writing or anything else" (Silko, 2010, 13, 125). Much of the action involves interpreting clouds and anticipating even a light shower of rain, which appears over the precipices as a translucent wave, a paradox replete with power and fragility. Against the conflict of dry, hot weather and baking sun, she counterbalances dragging the water hose and misting bird cages, but her persistent spritzing with water drowns her favorite flowers— the brugmansia, alyssum, datura, and rain lily, even a hapless cactus. The loss epitomizes both the delicacy of desert plants and the mistaken benevolences of human dwellers who meddle with nature. Of those who precede her, she muses, "What happened? Where did they go?" (*ibid.*, 274). Of the cycle of appearances and disappearances of humankind, she warns, "So we eat and then one day some hungry creature eats us" (*ibid.*, 290). Because of her animistic beliefs, the statement contains more humor than fear.

## SILKO AND THE OUTDOORS

Far from the high desert plateau she grew up on in New Mexico, Silko makes friends with rattlesnakes, whom she protects from her mastiffs Lyon and Snapper, bulldogs Thelma and Tigger, the gray parrot Gray Bird, the cockatoo Mrs. Rambo, and the macaws Binny, Bolee, Brittney, Paco, Prophecy Bird, Rudy Scruffy, Sandino, Sugar, and Tony. For the sake of wild quadrupeds and birds, she retains the horse trough long after the deaths of her Arabians, Hudson Bay and Prince Charming. Sprinkled among first-person observations and events, a poem to a pansy moth reprises Silko's poetic style from *Laguna Woman: Poems* (1974). Lyric passages recall the song of the coyotes, night calls of birds and owls, a stir of breezes, and a glimpse of constellations, reminders of Star Beings in parallel universes. At times, she relishes total silence: "No human sounds (unless you count my breathing), no engines, no trains, no barking dogs, no airplanes" (*ibid.*, 226). The absence of technological noise makes her think of life ten millennia past. In a later encounter with an aged tortoise, she remarks, "Truly we were blessed," her interpretation of "the generosity of the world" (*ibid.*, 277, 294). An unsigned review in *Publishers Weekly* lauds her free movement between earthlings and spirits as "a fluid and delicate life's balance between human and nature" ("Review," 2010, 41).

The author introduces her text by picturing herself in motion on the desert surface. She opens on her cardiovascular workouts by walking through the dense sand of arroyos behind her house northwest of Tucson, Arizona. Of her oneness with the big arroyo near her residence, she asserts, "I can think of no better place to die than out on the trail in these hills with the saguaros and all the other beings I love" (Silko, 2010, 231). Among the keepsakes she finds on the path, she treasures colored gems and ancient grinding stones, evidence of woman's work dating to prehistory. She reports metaphysical visits from the dead from rainclouds, a burrowing owl, and an exuberant grackle, the raucous squawker at the top of an electric pole that announces a visit from her deceased friend Sheila. Another episode with an attention-getting wren foretells the death of Silko's cousin Lana. A surprise discovery of a quartz knife left from paleo–Indian residency explains her visions of past lives: "No wonder some nights I saw figures in the darkness or heard women's voices singing grinding songs" (*ibid.*, 259). The outrage she feels for the gouging of the earth by an unidentified bulldozer driver — "the man and his machine" — expresses her love of earth and long-ago ancestors and a wish to protect the desert in its pristine state (*ibid.*, 295).

## TIME FOR REFLECTION

Silko reprises an unhurried, unruffled life without thought to calendar or clock, a theme she developed earlier in the short story "Bravura" (1974). To interviewer Steve Bennett, she explains, "Losing all sense of time is actually the way to reality" (Bennett, 2010, 1K). She recalls toddlerhood when "there was always time for everything as long as the sun was up" (Silko, 2010, 47). Her eccentric Aunt Charity Alice Marmon Little finds opportunities to recycle glass and tin containers along with string and aluminum foil. Aunt Lillie Stagner Marmon salvages coffee cans, stones, lumber, posts, wire, and galvanized roofing. Memories of a relaxed childhood account for her adult rhythms. Of meanderings at the town dump, the author recalls "solitude and self-reliance," which accompany her to the river with her dogs to play with minnows and toads (*ibid.*, 52). With her father, Leland "Lee" Howard Marmon, she learns gun safety with a .22 rifle and enjoys Fourth of July fireworks, homemade rockets, slingshots, and flying saucers catapulted upward by string. Her father takes her to Quick, Arizona, to buy a colt named Joey. A riding accident in 1959 leaves Silko groggy for three days.

In musings on an upbringing involving the entire Laguna community, she relives the issue of whether to speak Keres or English. She values her grandfather Henry C. "Hank" Marmon's skill at language and the early years she spent with Grandma A'mooh, the family matriarch, who spoke only Keres to Silko until she entered kindergarten. A rhetorical question interrupts the discussion of communication: "Why do people choose not to teach their children their mother tongues — something unthinkable under normal circumstances" (*ibid.*, 43). A conversion to Presbyterianism, part of the conflict in Grandma A'mooh, sets up barriers to the Amerindian past, particularly the *hummah-hah* lore, an alternate worldview to Protestantism based on ancient communication between humans and animals that Grandma mentions in *Ceremony* (1977). Additional language obstacles arise from the Spanish conversations of Great Grandma Helen Whittington Stagner and her daughter, Grandma Lillie Stagner Marmon, and the English communication between Grandpa Hank and his sons, Richard and Leland. The concept of learning a new language raises a psychological obstacle in Silko, who experiences "all the ghosts of the past ... the anxiety and sense of guilt and inadequacy and the loss," her memories of being a mixed-breed child in a Laguna milieu (*ibid.*, 44).

## Language and Art

The author particularizes diverse languages and reverence for the heavens as compartments in the world's survival kit. Should earth suffer disaster, she asserts that indigenous grammar and syntax will ensure that a part of humankind will endure. The centrality of vocabulary derives from "the nouns, the names of the plants, insects, birds and mammals important locally to human survival" (*ibid.*, 46). During 2006, the year she leaves writing to paint extraterrestrial Star Beings, she values antique culture, its icons, deities, and words. She experienced an "aha" moment: "When you're a servant to the Star Beings you have to completely humble yourself" (Jeffries, 2010). She reflects on the trade route north from Teotihuacan in southern Mexico to Arizona, from 200 B.C. to A.D. 750, when merchants bargained with macaws and feathers for the rare turquoise "most desired by the deities for their ornaments and ceremonies" (Silko, 2010, 151). To enhance her knowledge of Mesoamerica, she buys two Nahuatl-English dictionaries. From a page-by-page study of vocabulary, she learns that ancient Mesoamericans had a term for "space ship," a corroboration of theories that aliens inspired petroglyphs and stone paths (*ibid.*, 139).

Silko's memoir enhances her reputation as writer, storyteller, and artist. She perceives life in her paintings and receives supernatural aid in composing *The Turquoise Ledge* and in emulating the fresco style of kiva painters of the 14th century , whose icons took shape in the same century as Geoffrey Chaucer's *The Canterbury Tales* (1385). Her interest in the spirits from constellations derives from a cycle of communications — "dreams and visions to artists of all kinds all over the planet so they will begin to make images of the Star Beings" to prepare humankind for the next visitation from the Milky Way (*ibid.*, 141). For Silko's talent at expressing the Pueblo worldview, critic Steve Bennett named the author "one of the strongest native voices in American literature" (Bennett, 2010, 10B).

• *References and further reading*

Ashbrook, Tom, and Leslie Marmon Silko. "The Storyteller: Leslie Marmon Silko," www.onpointradio.org/2010/10/storyteller-leslie-marmon-silko, accessed on October 22, 2010.

Bennett, Steve. "Author Silko Isn't Concerned About Time," *Express News* (25 July 2010): 1K, 4K.
_____. "'Nuevo Mundo' Celebrates Women," *Express News* (31 July 2010): 10B.
Jeffries, Kim. "A Conversation with Leslie Marmon Silko on *The Turquoise Ledge*," *Seattle Times* (19 October 2010).
Johnson, Cat. "Silko Heads for Santa Cruz," *Santa Cruz News* (21 October 2010).
Mellas, Laurie. "Memory and Promise: Leslie Marmon Silko's Story," *Mirage* 24 (Spring 2006): 11–14.
"Review: *The Turquoise Ledge*," *Kirkus Reviews* 78:13 (1 July 2010): 612.
"Review: *The Turquoise Ledge*," *Publishers Weekly* (23 August 2010): 41.
Richey, Joe. "Women Writers Shine Brightly at Denver Events," *Boulder Reporter* (12 April 2010).
Silko, Leslie Marmon. *The Turquoise Ledge*. New York: Viking, 2010.

# vengeance

Silko tinges the antipathy and violence of her works with retribution, including the sneers at posturing womanizers in "Mesita Men" (1972) and the murder of a corrupt policeman in "Tony's Story" (1969). For Tony, a cop killer, the shapeshifting of a law officer into a witch requires immediate extermination of "it," one of the recognizable two-legged threats that "take on strange forms" (Silko, 1969, 4). In the luring of a murdering Gussuck (white man) onto ice in "Storyteller" (1981), the unnamed avenger targets another alien, a white trader, "a parasite, exploiting not only the fur-bearing animals and the fish but also the Yupik people themselves" (Silko, 1981, 45). The author enlarges in *Yellow Woman and a Beauty of the Spirit: Essays on Native American Life Today* (1996) that his death in a well-laid trap atones for the protagonist's loss of her parents. The girl refuses to conceal her murderous intent: "I intended that he die. The story must be told as it is" (*ibid.*, 31). For her aim to redress racist crimes, critic Lionel Larré, a specialist in Americana at the University Michel de Montaigne at Bordeaux, declares her vengeance "un acte politique" (Larré, 2005, 173).

The author is adept at minimizing reprisal with comedy. A less retribution, "A Geronimo Story" (1974) adds a layer of drollery to legends of the hardy Apache leader who keeps ranks of military pursuers and their Laguna scouts confused while he roams the Southwestern badlands. As wily as Br'er Rabbit in the briarpatch, Geronimo does little more than hide in home country while cavalrymen waste money and horseflesh on forays over ancient lava flows. Not only do they kill off their mounts, the trackers inadvertently feed the renegades, who turn horse carcasses into jerky. The comeuppance to white imperialists typifies Silko's slick Laguna humor, which she embeds with irritants.

## RETALIATION AS MOTIF

In *Ceremony* (1977), Silko's first novel, close relationships spawn incidence of cruel, even deadly requital. Auntie Thelma, Tayo's caregiver, appears to tend her nephew/foster son and to guide him from emotional isolation toward wellness. From age four, Tayo knows otherwise. Her eyes disclose resentment toward the biracial child of "little sister" Laura, a wino and carouser who shamed the family by coupling with a white man. Thelma's posture and expression bear a long-term animus. She exudes Christian piety and uses gossip and fanatic attendance at Catholic Mass as a goad to prod and torment Tayo for surviving the war. Because her son Rocky dies in the Philippines from a grenade blast, her hatred for Tayo turns virulent. Like Emo, another war veteran, she harbors a palpable loathing that prevents her nephew from returning to normal. The poisonous atmosphere evokes in Tayo a sense of obligation to the people who reared him after Laura's death. He confides to Betonie, the Chicano-Navajo shaman north of Gallup, "I was supposed to help [Rocky] ... I owed them that much" (Silko, 1977, 132).

A parallel to Thelma, Emo, a fellow veteran of Wake Island and Iwo Jima, endorses a patriotism that takes the form of bloodlust bolstered by false honor and duty. He requires tactile and carnal violence to relieve his internalization of colonialism and his self-blame for America's betrayal of first peoples. Out of envy of whites, Emo glories in sexual conquest of Caucasian females. In standard postcolonial lacklogic, he exults, "They took our land, they took everything! So let's get our hands on white women!" (*ibid.*, 55). According to his hyped-up view of the military hero, war sanctions his knocking teeth from the corpse of a Japanese officer and his treasuring the trophies in a Bull Durham bag, which he rattles like a totem rattle, a sacred token of combat. The *ad hoc* ritual suits his drunken prating, but Tayo silently rejects the ongoing bender as a soulless, self-deceptive numbing of damaged spirits.

Silko carries Emo's taunts and baiting to the limit for Tayo, who retaliates with a broken beer bottle thrust into Emo's gut. In contrast to Emo's misdirected rant, Tayo turns constructive rage into self-liberation from evil and witchery. At the fictional climax, restraint prevails over an eye for an eye. Tayo observes the demonic sacrifice of Harley under Emo's knife in an iron maiden formed of barbed wire. Buttressed with wisdom from spiritual healers Ku'oosh, Betonie, and Ts'eh Montaño, Tayo chooses to let evil devour itself. As typified by Sara L. Spurgeon, a specialist in women's studies at the University of Arizona, the protagonist refuses to be hustled into an either-or logic, an "insistence on violent retribution or passive acceptance of death" (Spurgeon, 2005, 98). For his prudent choice, Laguna elders invite him to join their coterie and to share his experiences and foresight.

## REQUITING HISTORY

The author heightens the stakes of conquest and compensatory evil in the allegorical novel *Almanac of the Dead* (1991), a Gothic prophecy of doom to morally bankrupt white usurpers. The author claims to have composed the novel on two slants—a voodoo hex and an act of salvation and antidote to imperialism, particularly the destruction of indigenous libraries in 1540 by Spanish conquerors. Katherine Sugg, an English professor at Central Connecticut State University, admires the novel's tone and style: "Because Silko writes so clearly against the expectations and comfort zones of all its readers—both minority identified and cosmopolitan, white, U.S.-oriented—*Almanac* illustrates the ability of particular narratives to use allegory 'with a vengeance'" (Sugg, 2008, 32). A cast of 77 characters engages in adultery, beheadings, infanticide, and murder for hire as well as drug and gun running, dumping of aliens in the desert, jail torture, and the filming of snuff murders and suicides for sale to purveyors of exotic death. A more productive cabal, the Green Vengeance eco-warriors, modeled on agents of Earth First!, yields hard-core avengers, one of whom martyrs himself "blowing up Glen Canyon Dam" (Silko, 1991, 729). Influential on the recovery of stolen land are the stories of Karl Marx, who "had understood that the stories or 'histories' are sacred; that within 'history' reside relentless forces, powerful spirits, vengeful, relentlessly seeking justice" (*ibid.*, 316). Critic Shari Michelle Huhndorf, an expert in ethnic studies at the University of Oregon, describes Silko's nemesis as an unstinting stalker, the image of "the original possessors of the land [that] seem to haunt the collective unconscious of the white man" (Huhndorf, 2001, vii). As implied in the title of Vine Deloria's *Custer Died for Your Sins: An Indian Manifesto* (1988), the crimes of previous centuries remain unexpiated, a staggering wrong as implacable as Frankenstein's monster or Marley's Ghost in refusing exorcism without recompense.

Fictional vengeance in *Gardens in the Dunes* (1999), a neo–Victorian novel, fits historical events of the late nineteenth century at the end of the Indian Wars. In images of "Paiute children begging for money from passengers at the depot," Silko specifies the damage to indigenous people after white engineers and dam builders begin shifting the course of the Colorado River outside Parker, Arizona, to water Los Angeles (Silko, 1999, 21). Profiteering takes the form of after-hours card games, whoring, and tippling on local brew in "gambling and brewery tents ... packed with miners and cowboys" (*ibid.*, 219). Delena, a Mexican Gypsy, observes the concentration of cash in the hands of exploiters and plots a way to steal their ill-gotten gains. By ending a dog show with fighting and arson in the tent city, she manages to locate the strongbox with the aid of a money-sniffing dog and to channel it south to gun runners who supply repeating rifles and ammunition to the Mexican revolt. The author epitomizes fire and theft as a worthy reprisal against white avarice.

In *The Turquoise Ledge* (2010), Silko muses on violent frontier myths and legends, including the pursuit of Geronimo. She makes an example of the kidnap by Apache raiders who seize Placida Romero and her infant from a slave market in Cubero, New Mexico, to repay Americans and Mexicans for ravishing young Apache girls. Catholic officialdom abets the trafficking in underage victims by rewarding Pueblo scouts with Apache slave children. The author develops her racial antipathies and recompense against Mexican households for stripping their Navajo servants and whipping them, "a common perversion with the founding families of New Mexico" (Silko, 2010, 34). Upon learning the truth about Juana, a family nanny, Silko rages that the old woman lived most of her 100 years in service to the brother of Josephine Romero Whittington, a brutish elder known as "Grandma Whip." Juana's three older sisters go to the gallows after they retaliate against the enslaver by poisoning him. Terrorism repays Grandma Whip by making her leery of poison in the sugar bowl. Silko's black-edged humor reminds readers of the price paid for preying on the vulnerable.

*See also* Emo; injustice; vulnerability.

• *References and further reading*

Holm, Sharon. "The 'Lie' of the Land: Native Sovereignty, Indian Literary Nationalism, and Early Indigenism in Leslie Marmon Silko's Ceremony," *American Indian Quarterly* 32:3 (Summer 2008): 243–274.
Huhndorf, Shari Michelle. *Going Native: Indians in the American Cultural Imagination*. Ithaca: Cornell University Press, 2001.
Larré, Lionel. "Autorité et Discours: L'Auteurité en Question," *Annales du CRAA* 29 (2005): 165–179.
Silko, Leslie Marmon. *Almanac of the Dead*. New York: Simon & Schuster, 1991.
_____. *Ceremony*. New York: Viking, 1977.
_____. *Storyteller*. New York: Seaver, 1981.
_____. "Tony's Story," *Thunderbird* (1969): 2–4.
_____. *The Turquoise Ledge: A Memoir*. New York: Viking Adult, 2010.
_____. *Yellow Woman and a Beauty of the Spirit: Essays on Native American Life Today*. New York: Simon & Schuster, 1996.
Spurgeon, Sara L. *Exploding the Western: Myths of Empire on the Postmodern Frontier*. College Station: Texas A&M University Press, 2005.
Sugg, Katherine. *Gender and Allegory in Transamerican Fiction and Performance*. New York: Palgrave Macmillan, 2008.

## violence

Lawlessness and aggression undergird Silko's writings about person-to-person wrongdoing. Her compendium *Yellow Woman and a Beauty of the Spirit: Essays on Native American Life Today* (1996) stresses past destruction — the burning of Maya and Mixtec libraries beginning in 1540 "to foster the notion that the New World was populated by savages," a necessary stereotype to exonerate Europeans for land theft, enslavement, and genocide (Silko, 1996, 157). Because international law protected conquered peoples, but not savages or beasts, Spanish *conquistadores* found it necessary to expunge evidence of Mesoamerican humanity. Other of her writings bring malevolence up to date. In "On Photography" (1996), she notes the electrical charge that infuses a mob: "The greed and violence of the last century in the United States are palpable; what we have done to one another and to the earth is registered in the very atmosphere and effect, even in the light" (Silko, 1996, 182). By copying, cutting, pasting, and sewing copies of *Sacred Water: Narratives and Pictures* (1993), she made the work into "the route towards a genuinely regenerative ceremony" and "a soothing, healing antidote to the relentless horror loose in this world" (Coltelli, 1996, 26). For her application of storytelling to rancor, critics have dubbed her a postmodern medicine woman.

In her mid-twenties, when she published "Tony's Story" (1969) in *Thunderbird*, Silko spoke through the title character, Antonio Sousea, a post–World War II puzzle, "why men who came back from the army were troublemakers on the reservation" (Silko, 1981, 125). The story suggests the power of the law enforcement uniform when a state policeman assaults Leon, a returning veteran no longer dressed like a soldier. Contributing to the story's atmosphere, Silko depicts a drought and the menace of a police face behind silvery dark glasses. The shift in status demeans Leon to the stereotypical drunk Indian tossed into the paddy wagon for simply existing. In revolt against white injustice against first peoples, Leon words the mantra of the rebel: "We are just as good as them" (*ibid.*). The assertion cites good reason for non-whites to demand their rights.

## THE VIOLENT IMAGE

In *Ceremony* (1977), Silko focuses on trickery and barbarism — a deceptive deal to buy a used GMC pickup, a patrolman's illegal arrest of a bar brawler, the gutting of a deer, the herding of prisoners on a Philippine island, the plunge of broken glass into Emo's gut, a rifle butt hitting Rocky's skull, slaughter of sheep and herd dogs, white theft of Indian lands, capricious shooting of the puma, and the writhing of an infantry veteran wrapped in barbed wire. In an episode involving Helen Jean, a Ute who works off the Towac Reservation in Colorado as a cook and a janitor at the Kimo movie theater in Albuquerque, she recalls a beating by Pawnees from Oklahoma. At the El Fidel bar in July 1948, the veterans express aggression dating to the landing on Omaha Beach, France, on June 6, 1942. Silko specifies bar brawls by turning from Helen Jean to Harley, whom Leroy and Tayo must carry to the truck. Dawn confers sobriety and wisdom on Tayo, who realizes that, eventually, he and his war buddies will die of a stabbing or a head-on collision if they continue bar hopping. Rather than a threat of destruction, the violence proceeding from their beery fights and drunken rides down Highway 66 anticipates "waiting for it to end," his summation of a life of aimlessness and victimization (Silko, 1977, 168).

Through Tayo, Silko categorizes types and aims of violence. During merrymaking with his buddies, his only self-defense, regurgitating alcohol by the roadside, relieves him of the urine and vomit smell in the truck and of sorrow at "defending the land they had already lost" (*ibid.*, 169). Only on the flight from betrayal by Leroy Valdez and Harley does Tayo put together the immense picture of violence, the reason that Japanese faces looked like the Laguna. Tayo realizes the circle of life on the planet that bonds all clans in the fight for survival against atomic power, "a circle of death that devoured people in cities twelve thousand miles away" (*ibid.*, 246). He recalls "dismembered corpses and the atomic heat-flash outlines, where human bodies had evaporated" (*ibid.*, 37). Conrad Shumaker, an American literature specialist at the University of Central Arkansas, accounts for the protagonist's choice of inaction rather than vengeance: "By refusing to kill Emo, Tayo keeps the story and the ceremony intact, and the witchery, having been seen for what it is, will turn on itself" (Shumaker, 2008, 33). Like the Greek voyager Jason tossing a stone in the midst of a ghoulish army in Apollonius's *Argonautica* (ca. 220 B.C.), Tayo allows the evil to implode.

INTERNATIONAL SAVAGERY

Silko's *Almanac of the Dead* (1991), a grim allegory, centers its survey of colonial and postcolonial persecutions on Tucson. Sara L. Spurgeon, author of *Exploding the Western* (2005), interprets the tangle of crimes and vindication as a variation of the classic Western, "filled with cowboys and Indians, ambushes and gunfights, outlaws, bandits, smugglers, and captives" (Spurgeon, 2005, 108). In the evaluation of critic Sharon Patricia Holland, an English professor at the University of Illinois, the author's "focus on sexual and physical violence exposes the underbelly of American society as its topcoat" (Holland, 2000, 70). The text claims that the city based its economic rise on bootlegging and other illicit profiteering on the late 19th-century Indian Wars. Chief among the symbolic exploiters are Christians, who "all feared illness and physical change; since life led to death, consciousness terrified them, and they had sought to control death by becoming killers themselves" (Silko, 1991, 718). In an interview with Ellen L. Arnold issued during the presidency of George W. Bush, the author justified the extremes of havoc in the text by comparing them to the realities of war in Operation Desert Storm and in the genocide that threatened Bosnia and Serbia. Silko charged, "Nothing in *Almanac* approximates the depravity of the white men leading the U.S. today; nothing in *Almanac* reveals the 'lynch mob' mentality of the ruling class in the U.S. today" (Silko & Arnold, 2000, 134).

Initially, the allegory predicates its survey of 20th-century venality and crime on the example of North America's historical forebears, including U.S. Cavalry, slave dealers, and de Guzman, a torturer of first peoples. While cataloguing faults of the Death-Eye Dog, her metaphor for Europeans, Silko concedes a human failing, an innate bloodlust in all races and ethnicities. Lecha, the Yaqui clairvoyant who reveres the ancient Mayan manuscript, perceives that the *conquistador* Hernán de Cortés and the Aztec cacique Montezuma II were two warriors different in ethnicity, but alike in their love of barbarism. The acknowledgement rids the novel of an us-against-them premise and opens the motifs and themes to an inclusive study of global inhumanity, focusing primarily on the Americas and the Caribbean.

THE ERA OF BLOODLETTING

From the first Hispano-Mayan clash in Mexico City in 1519 derives a hellish list of neocannibalism — the elderly hunchbacked woman who eats children to stave off starvation, de Guzman's phallo-torture of Indian women by seating them on sharpened stakes and piling bags of silver on their laps, the execution of the undercover cop known as Jamey, the commercialization of Eric's suicide and snuff films, the removal of testicles from a victim in an interrogation chair, and the assassination for hire that Mafioso Max "Mr. Murder" Blue engineers by telephone from a private golf course. Worse than one-on-one torture and murder, Silko inserts privatized health care and the biotech industry, a grisly form of commercialization that relies on boundary-invasive migrants for labor. In the description of critic Michael Davidson, a specialist in gender and disability studies at the University of California at San Diego, "global instabilities in one part of the world are acted out in first-world tourism and commodity society" (Davidson, 2008, 216).

Silko embroiders the Gothic nature of vampirism by picturing a cripple as the chief ghoul. Dubbed "Wheelie" and "Steak-in-a-Basket," Eddie Trigg, the paraplegic blood and organ harvester, dehumanizes his victims as "Human debris. Human refuse" (Silko, 1991, 444). A blatant form of ethnic cleansing, the corporate model profiles humans into saleable commodities and sources of plasma. For his megabusiness— Alpha-Bio Products, Alpha-Hemo-Science Limited, Bio Mart, Bio Materials, Inc., and Tucson's biotourist industry— he engineers the commercial transport of civil war victims, hoboes, and wetbacks in Mexico to biomaterials chop shops. He manages the kidnap and murder of the infant Monte and the harvesting of his organs for sale. At his most cannibalistic extreme, he fellates unemployed factory workers and disabled, homeless donors while draining them of blood. The oral element connects him with Dracula, the Transylvanian monster who sates himself on the blood of innocents.

Critics categorize as neocannibalism Silko's horror scenes, which date back to the use of adipose fat of slaughtered Aztec to salve the wounds of Cortés's soldiers. Calabazas, the Yaqui drug smuggler, reports that the bones still wash up in arroyos, turning skulls into trail markers. Analyst Jeff Berglund, an English professor at Northern Arizona University, classifies the roster of sadism as "a soul-disease that has laid the groundwork for its own eventual destruction" (Berglund, 2006, 151). To redirect victims of colonialism from infighting and greed, Silko schedules a Marxist seminar of propaganda abetted by a revival of Wovoka's prophecy that indigenous people will one day oust Europeans from the Western Hemisphere and revive pre–Columbian societies. The discrediting of ideology takes shape in the execution of Comrade Bartolomeo, the Cuban revolutionary who tries to make the uprising of the disaffected in the Western Hemisphere fit the Marxist doctrine. His declaration that tribalism is "the whore of nationalism and the dupe of capitalism" incriminates him with Indian leaders, who summarily hang him (Silko, 1991, 526). The expendability of Bartolomeo is implicit in Korean-American computer hacker Awa Gee's prophecy that "no leaders of chains of command would be necessary" for a revolt destined to arise spontaneously (*ibid.*, 686). American literary theorist Walter Benn Michaels outlines the dilemma: "It is history, not socialism, that will redeem the Indians— hence Comrade Bartolomeo must die" (Michaels, 2006, 23).

APOCALYPSE NOW

Silko is as adamant about human rights in nonfiction as she is in novels and stories. In "America's Iron Curtain: The Border Patrol State" (1994), a personal essay on freedom of travel, she allows a late-night experience with highway patrol officers to merge in her imagination with "more than 12,000 'disappearances' during Argentina's 'dirty war' in the late 1970s" (Silko, 1994, 413). She merges bodily with people seized, interrogated, and shot on the roadside at random. As she frequently does in prose and verse, she identifies with the drug-sniffing German shepherd, a mishandled female terrorized by the ruthless direction of the border watchers. Endowed with "innate dignity that did not permit her to serve the murderous impulses of those men," the dog makes no complaint against Silko or her companion, Gus (*ibid.*). Implicit in the juxtaposition of border guard with dog lies the subtextual congratulation to the German shepherd for displaying more decency than her master.

Silko expounds on the incident to denounce racial profiling and the interference of a new incarnation of the U.S. cavalry — the Immigration and Naturalization Service — on the free travel of U.S. citizens across the Southwest. She impugns two types of violence, verbal and nonverbal, in a new police state in which security patrols wield an ominous power over anyone not white or not dressed traditionally. In addition to armed patrols, the essay vilifies journalists and politicians who "dehumanize and demonize undocumented immigrants" as though they deserve no rights (*ibid.*, 415). Of particular concern to natives is the violation of the Treaty of Guadalupe Hidalgo of 1848, which guaranteed the right of the Papago to cross the Mexico boundary unmolested to visit other Uto-Aztecan speakers to north and south of the international line. In tune with Robert Frost's "Mending Wall" (1914), Silko agrees with the poet that "Something there is that doesn't love a wall." As though facing down intimidating patrols, she declares, "It is no use; borders haven't worked, and they won't work" (*ibid.*).

WOMEN VS. VIOLENCE

Memories of terror open *Gardens in the Dunes* (1999), a novel featuring a lone matriarchy of the Sand Lizard tribe of southwestern Arizona. Grandma Fleet, who heads the family, instructs her granddaughters, Indigo and Sister Salt, on eluding the invaders who kidnap the "messiah," the author's designation for the leader of the Ghost Dance (Silko, 1999, 13). On the fourth night of the Ghost Dance at the riverbank outside Needles, California, a raid by white men scatters participants. While the raiders seize Mormons, the sisters run south along the river and hide in the willows and cattails. The girls, well trained in self-sufficiency, know not to speak a word during their concealment. With the instincts of animals bred for desert survival, the sisters seek the terraced gardens in the dunes, a time-honored retreat to the Mother Creator. In subsequent scenes of danger, the siblings examine the remains of Mrs. Van Wagnen's burned dwelling. The wasteful destruction of canned food accompanies a willful destruction of the orchard. In shock at such deliberate waste, Sister Salt surveys the remains of apricot and peach trees and weeps at a stunning realization, "This was what the white people did to one another" (*ibid.*, 61). Silko differentiates between the girls, stressing Indigo's innocence of human motivations and Sister Salt's silent tears for the homeowner's distress at wanton ruin.

A separate set of white characters contrasts the Sand Lizard people's experience with persecution. Hattie Abbott, a graduate student researching heresy during a seminar at Harvard Divinity School, immerses herself in Dr. Rhinehart's Coptic scrolls and studies the Crusades in her first semester. From her readings in apocryphal texts, she deduces that "the Crusades accustomed Christians to killing for the sake of religion" (*ibid.*, 98). Subsequent commentary on European wars and "crimes against the old stones and the sacred groves of hazel and oak" allude to the battle against Celtic paganism and druids during the Christianizing of Great Britain (*ibid.*, 252–253). Much as Tacho and El Feo predict recompense against white usurpers in *Almanac*, Aunt Bronwyn foresees "violent retribution" against English Protestants, which she predicts within two decades or less (*ibid.*, 253). The corresponding images of colonial violence in Southwestern Arizona and Somerset, England, impose the author's surmise about the gendering of world history — it is males who destroy and females who reassemble the pieces.

*See also* abortion; Emo; genocide; Gothic; injustice; Tayo; war.

• *References and further reading*

Berglund, Jeff. *Cannibal Fictions: American Explorations of Colonialism, Race, Gender and Sexuality*. Madison: University of Wisconsin Press, 2006.

Coltelli, Laura. "Leslie Marmon Silko's *Sacred Water*," *Studies in American Indian Literatures* 8:4 (1996): 21–29.

Davidson, Michael. *Concerto for the Left Hand: Disability and the Defamiliar Body*. Ann Arbor: University of Michigan Press, 2008.

Holland, Sharon Patricia. *Raising the Dead: Readings of Death and (Black) Subjectivity*. Durham, NC: Duke University Press, 2000.

Hume, Kathryn. *American Dream, American Nightmare: Fiction since 1960*. Urbana: University of Illinois Press, 2002.

Michaels, Walter Benn. *The Shape of the Signifier: 1967 to the End of History*. Princeton, NJ: Princeton University Press, 2006.

Shumaker, Conrad. *Southwestern American Indian Literature: In the Classroom and Beyond*. New York: Peter Lang, 2008.

Silko, Leslie Marmon. *Almanac of the Dead*. New York: Simon & Schuster, 1991.

_____. "The Border Patrol State," *Nation* 259:12 (17 October 1994): 412–416.

_____. *Ceremony*. New York: Viking, 1977.

_____. *Gardens in the Dunes*. New York: Scribner, 1999.

_____. *Storyteller*. New York: Seaver, 1981.

_____. *Yellow Woman and a Beauty of the Spirit: Essays on Native American Life Today*. New York: Simon & Schuster, 1996.

_____, and Ellen L. Arnold. *Conversations with Leslie Marmon Silko*. Jackson: University Press of Mississippi, 2000.

Spurgeon, Sara L. *Exploding the Western: Myths of Empire on the Postmodern Frontier*. College Station: Texas A&M University Press, 2005.

Wynn, Judith. "Nightmare Vision of 'Almanac' Succeeds," *Boston Herald* (22 December 1991): 62.

## vulnerability

The author specializes in setting characters in a milieu of overwhelming odds, such as Navajo parents Ayah and Chato in "Lullaby" (1974), the Indian wannabe in the vignette "Bravura" (1974), the neophyte holy man in "Humaweepi, the Warrior Priest" (1974), a mixed-race school child in "'Not You,' He Said" (2007), and a harmless ne'er-do-well misidentified as Geronimo in "Old Pancakes" (2008). In an animistic one-on-one with herd animals in "How to Hunt Buffalo" (1994), Silko opens on "all of us who are born into this world," a subtextual image of infancy and helplessness (Silko, 1994, 2). By urging the would-be hunter to visit "the old folks who fed you and held you in their arms," she leads into the subject of "[asking] for the buffalo's life" and singing to nature while awaiting the appearance of a herd (*ibid.*). Shifting the qualms from the animals to the solitary hunter, the essayist stresses unease in the human perception of bestial strength. The composition closes on the gift that the sacrificial beast offers. In acknowledgement of the impermanence of life, the hunter must preface the fatal rifle shot with thanksgiving and an admission to the buffalo, "we cherish you" (*ibid.*, 3).

In a more complex study of stalking and killing one's own kind, Silko's first novel, *Ceremony* (1977), renders a standard situation for young war veterans. When peace ends battlefield slaughter after the bombing of Hiroshima and Nagasaki on August 6 and 8, 1945, GIs return to a home, community, and self markedly changed. Tayo, the protagonist, repatriates himself to the New Mexico pueblo and finds it beset by ills, a situation that Silko symbolizes in an "early storm [that] had caught the tree vulnerable with leaves that caught the snow and held it in drifts until the branches dragged the ground" (Silko, 1977, 194). The tempest, which crops up again in *The Delicacy and Strength of Lace: Let-*

*ters between Leslie Marmon Silko and James Wright* (1986), betokens the sudden unleashing of atomic power during World War II with bombs made from ore unearthed from Laguna terrain. In a comment on Herman Melville's *Moby-Dick* (1851) and Henry David Thoreau's *Walden* (1854), critic Lawrence Buell, the Powell M. Cabot Professor of American Literature at Harvard University, accounts for the value of Silko's queries into threats to earth's integrity as "contemporary ecoglobalist imagination ... about the ongoing conquest of natural environment on a planetary scale" (Buell, 2007, 242).

The novelist hyperbolizes the contrast in genders by picturing Tayo as bowed with grief and regret over the Pacific war as opposed to flirty Night Swan, resilient Ts'eh Montaño, and the GI's blind Grandma and blustery Auntie Thelma, who steamroll the men of the clan. A once-over of Emo, Harley, Leroy Valdez, and cousin Pinkie, Laguna survivors of the Pacific war, reveals men addicted to alcohol and aimlessness funded by government checks. Silko faults materialism with besetting the men with temptation to carouse and waste their youth. More troubling is the attack on the sacred at Laguna Pueblo, where the Jackpile mine exploits uranium at a cost to miners of lethal disease as well as pollution in the air and groundwater by potent technology. In an introduction to the 30th edition of *Ceremony*, novelist Larry McMurtry regrets that "Evils have been unleashed, witches have increased in power, and the indigenous people are more vulnerable than ever to spiritual and physical defilement" (McMurtry, 2007, xxii). The issue of exploitation of the unwary returns in Silko's memoir, *The Turquoise Ledge* (2010), in which the author states her concern for the people of Paguate, who live amid radioactive groundwater and the tailings of the Jackpile mine, a pernicious waste of nature and a source of human maladies. One antidote to technological tyranny lies in the use of American stories to confront the government with its exploitation of first peoples. Choctaw archeologist Dorothy Lippert, on staff at the Smithsonian National Museum of Natural History, comments on narrative like Silko's that "[collaborates] on a common goal": "Traditional histories may be taken into account when a tribe petitions for federal recognition, so in a concrete sense, stories do represent survival for the people" (Lippert, 2008, 128).

THE THREAT OF CONQUEST

The motif of threat to the susceptible broadens in Silko's pitiless hell on earth in *Almanac of the Dead* (1991), a diatribe damning tyranny against peasant society on a par with Peruvian Nobelist Mario Vargas Llosa's *Death in the Andes* (1993) and *The Feast of the Goat* (2000). In a sinkhole of crime around Tucson, Arizona, the defenseless become fodder for cannibalistic fantasy and sexual manipulation. From the time of the Maya and Aztec, overlords acquire wealth and delusions of power and prestige through ritual bloodletting of pregnable humans. Silko lobs a dark jest at the affinity of Montezuma II for Spanish imperialist Hernán de Cortés, both of whom belong to the "same secret clan" of demons (Silko, 1991, 760). Over five centuries later, preying on the weak takes the form of draining the homeless of blood, skinning victims of Mexican revolutions of saleable tissue, gelding male victims as proof of dominion, and beheading U.S. legates to suppress the peace process. An Argentine distributor of pornographic videos feeds on prisoners, degrading them with torture and emasculation. In the Freudian framing of life and death urges, filmmakers choose death by obliterating sentiment and pity in the objectification of female sexuality and human extermination, for example, in Beaufrey's delight in Seese's abortion of her first pregnancy. The narrative focuses on the southern border, which is "particularly vulnerable to secret agents and rabble-rousers, sewage that had seeped out of Guatemala to pollute 'the pure springs of Mexican democracy,'" a token of the author's idealistic view of vulnerable peasants (*ibid.*, 272).

In a parody of the Nazi strategy of the big lie, perpetrators of hurt on the hungry and helpless reach nimbly for rationales of their cruelty. Cloaking their depravity in righteous fascism, the pornographers claim to warn "leftwingers and subversives ... criminals of all types.... This is what's waiting for anyone out there who dares violate the law" (*ibid.*, 344). The feminist critique of Jane Olmstead, a language expert at the University of Connecticut, connects the underworld hunger for pornographic images with the Christian metaphysics of crucifixion: "The Church created the ultimate model of pornography: the ordeal of Christ's humiliation, suffering, and slow death on display; the mind/body split; the hatred of women apparent in the virgin/whore dichotomy," a reference to the extreme characterizations of the Virgin Mary and Mary Magdalene (Olmstead, 1999, 477). Silko indicts Christian scripture — a deity's sacrifice of his human son — and church history — holy wars, witch hunts, pogroms, and the torment and burning of heretics—for a portion of responsibility for the commercialization of savagery and sacrifice of social expendables.

## SUBJECTION AND GENDER

The author shifts from ideological to personal empowerment by espousing the feminist manifesto that women should repudiate a weak self-image. In a 1995 issue of *Hungry Mind Review*, she published "In the Combat Zone," a tough, no-nonsense essay describing concern for women's safety from stalkers and rapists. The text states Silko's own experience with a stalker in city traffic and her intent to carry a concealed weapon for self-protection. She blames female socialization for making their gender vulnerable: "It isn't height or weight or strength that make women easy targets; from infancy women are taught to be self-sacrificing, passive victims.... Women are TAUGHT to be easy targets by their mothers, aunts, and grandmothers" (Silko, 1995, 44). To circumvent helplessness, the essay charges women with "the primary responsibility for the health and safety of their bodies" (*ibid.*, 46). Her edict poses a countermeasure to an economic climate that produces "more desperate, angry men with nothing to lose" (*ibid.*).

For *Gardens in the Dunes* (1999), a summation of the novelist's social themes, female characters stand out from males by recolonizing the earth and safeguarding holy flowerbeds, niches, and orchards. Custodial matrons and their children turn expanses of turf into sources of sustenance from "succulent little roots and stems growing deep beneath the sand" (Silko, 1999, 17). Their unassuming gardens and dugouts furnish food and shelter as well as sanctuary from marauders. In a paradox on subjection, Indigo, the daughter of a Sand Lizard matriarchy, rescues herself from the Sherman Institute, an Indian indoctrination center in Riverside, California. Fostered by wealthy intellectuals, Dr. Edward G. Palmer and Hattie Abbott Palmer, Indigo, in turn, enriches their lives with the sanity and earth-based wisdom of first peoples. Because the Palmer marriage founders, leaving Hattie both bankrupt and widowed, the foster child sets an example of resilience and flexible philosophy that strengthens both Indigo and Hattie for a return to a guileless existence in the Arizona sandhills. Weathering a flood and adversity among Indian and white residents and police, Indigo relies on the pedagogy of her elders, who taught her "to remember other locations of water and places of shelter, just in case something happens," a sensible caveat as whites usurp more of the Southwest (*ibid.*, 447). Bolstered by the spirits of her female ancestors, Indigo prevails by rejecting victimhood and defeat through gardening and storytelling, the weapons of empowered women.

*See also* powerlessness.

• *References and further reading*

Buell, Lawrence. "Ecoglobalist Affects: The Emergence of U.S. Environmental Imagination on a Planetary Scale" in *Shades of the Planet: American Literature as World Literature*, eds. Wai-chee Dimock and Lawrence Buell. Princeton, NJ: Princeton University Press, 2007, 227–247.

Lippert, Dorothy. "Not the End, Not the Middle, But the Beginning: Repatriation as a Transformative Mechanism for Archaeologists and Indigenous Peoples," *Collaboration in Archaeological Practice: Engaging Descendant Communities*, eds. Chip Colwell-Chanthaphonh and T. J. Ferguson. Lanham, MD: AltaMira, 2008, 119–130.

McMurtry, Larry. "Introduction" to *Ceremony*. New York: Penguin, 2007.

Olmstead, Jane. "The Uses of Blood in Leslie Marmon Silko's *Almanac of the Dead*," *Contemporary Literature* 40:3 (Fall 1999): 464–490.

Silko, Leslie Marmon. *Almanac of the Dead*. New York: Simon & Schuster, 1991.

_____. *Ceremony*. New York: Viking, 1977.

_____. *Gardens in the Dunes*. New York: Scribner, 1999.

_____. "How to Hunt Buffalo" (1994), an unpublished fourfold housed in the Bienecke archives at Yale University Library, New Haven, Connecticut.

_____. "In the Combat Zone," *Hungry Mind Review* (Fall 1995): 44, 46.

## war

With the same disdain as novelists Amy Tan and Cormac McCarthy, Silko investigates war from a tribal perspective, which views individuals as part of a collective. Throughout *Ceremony* (1977), a quest novel, she demonizes American militarism as an outgrowth of global materialism. Critic Charles E. Wilson, an English professor at Old Dominion University, notes the glamour of a uniform and rifle to teenaged boys and comments that "Their subsequent participation in the war [is] rendered offensive in hindsight," a regret that heightens group animosities (Wilson, 2005, 84). At fault for disillusion is phony patriotism, "at once seductive and lethal ... existing only as another empty label which serves to divide human beings and compromise humanity" (*ibid.*). The indoctrination of high school graduates with falsehoods takes shape as flesh hunger, which "devoured white hearts, ... for more than two hundred years white people had worked to fill their emptiness; they tried to glut the hollowness with patriotic wars and with great technology and the wealth it brought" (Silko, 1977, 191). Wilson compares the protagonist's rejection of propaganda generated to support U.S. imperialism in the form of weaning goats at the ranch, a maturation that restores his right thinking about the perversion of science to produce better killing machines.

During her sojourn in Ketchikan, Alaska, the novelist created Tayo, the haunted GI, from fellow Laguna who return from World War II in fragile mental condition. Silko expert Brewster E. Fitz summarizes the "death-dealing insanity of the Western worldview" that foregrounds the novel: "In writing of Tayo's return to health and harmony, she was literally writing her own way back from a dicey encounter between two perspectives (Laguna and Inuit) that risked leaving her insane" (Fitz, 2004, 52). The text dramatizes her censure of a horrendous world conflict that ends in unprecedented atomic cataclysm against civilians. The bombing leaves "atomic heat-flash outlines, where human bodies had evaporated" (Silko, 1977, 34). At its end, the Pacific war earns for the United States the questionable honor of being the first and only superpower to unleash the atom in weapon form. Historically the Pacific war caused Pyrrhic losses on Iwo Jima and Wake Island and concluded with blasts in Japan that had been engineered and refined on New Mexican soil. The dropping of two atomic bombs on major cities altered the outlook of civilians and soldiers worldwide. Unlike the realistic protest novels of optimists Mark Twain and Upton Sinclair, Silko doubts America's future and proposes a grassroots revolt against corruption, greed, and the technology of mass murder. Analyst Elizabeth Cook-Lynn, a scholar of native–American studies, sums up Silko's outlook on atrocities against humanity: "She is intent upon retribution, which means that America must pay for its crimes; something must be given up in payment — if not death, at least punishment" (Cook-Lynn, 2007, 51).

*Ceremony* stresses the drastic escalation of warfare from infantry clashes and the execution of Japanese prisoners of war to the dropping of radioactive material on cities filled with noncombatants. To Tayo's hallucinations and weeping over Pacific killing fields, his less cerebral cousin/foster brother Rocky asserts, "We're *supposed* to be here. This is what we're supposed to do," a naive truism establishing the success of military indoctrination of 18-year-olds straight out of high school (Silko, 1977, 8). She describes Ku'oosh as the traditional medicine man whose scalp ceremony, a time-honored warrior cleansing, lacks the power to counter the nightmares of combat that horrify Tayo. Sara L. Spurgeon, an English professor at Texas Tech University, characterizes the GI's dilemma as alienation — "a despised half-breed in his own community, [who] has no place of original purity to which he might be restored" (Spurgeon, 2005, 88). Echoing Toni Cade Barbara's sensitivity to human rights in *The Salt Eaters* (1981), Tayo's recall of a gentle Japanese American internee and her children at a Los Angeles depot reminds the reader that World War II overturned the lives of U.S. citizens because of their genetic and cultural ties to Japan. Ironically, no such diminution of German–Americans occurred. From a civilian perspective, Ku'oosh admits the intensification of racism since the global conflict: "I'm afraid of what will happen to all of us if you and the other [veterans] don't get well" (Silko, 1977, 38).

For the backdrop of *Almanac of the Dead* (1991) and *Gardens in the Dunes* (1999), Silko makes repeated references to conflict and post-war politics. In the former novel, gloom engulfs Tucson's Viet vets, who return home from Southeast Asia to disrespect and blame for a war that they neither started nor condoned. Clinton, an Afro-Cherokee veteran wearing a prosthetic foot, protects himself from a pacifist backlash by "[wearing] his full Green Beret uniform every day. Otherwise there would be trouble" from lower-class residents he vilifies as "Arizona honkie-trash crackers" (Silko, 1991, 404). Silko builds satire from the manipulations of Rambo-Roy, musterer of an army of derelicts: "He had to laugh. Americans got paralyzed with fear every time they saw a Vietnam veteran still wearing combat clothes" (*ibid.*, 390). The terror of seeing former GIs in uniform implies guilt at the nation's prolonged attempt to save Vietnam from the advance of communism.

In *Gardens in the Dunes*, world upheaval echoes the fallout from the Indian Wars. On the approach of Edward and Hattie Palmer and Indigo to Italy, rumors of banditry in Corsica and of revolutionary violence to the south infringe on their travel plans. Meanwhile, Indigo's sibling, Sister Salt, has her own fears of soldiers and conflict stemming from the Indian holocaust. Upon meeting the Gypsy Delena, Sister Salt learns that Mexican soldiers kill every captive — even women and children. Sister Salt deduces, "War explained the scar down [Delena's] face; war answered the question of whether she had any family" (Silko, 1999, 354). The text wrests black humor from the fact that the Messiah's promises of peace contrast the words of Nuestra Señora de Guadalupe, the female divinity who warns Mexicans to arm themselves with quality U.S. repeating rifles. Delena's plot to rob the labor camp and empty Mr. Wylie's floor safe focuses on escape to Tucson to buy "as many boxes of rifles and cartridges as she wanted to buy for cash" (*ibid.*, 386). On her trudge over the Sand Tank Mountains northwest of Tucson, she exults that Mexican rebels fighting federal troops with rocks and sticks will appreciate repeating rifles. The image of a peasant war against an institutionalized militia repeats from *Almanac of the Dead* Silko's defense of the underclass who fight for their rights.

*See also* Geronimo; injustice; madness; Tayo; violence.

• *References and further reading*

Cook-Lynn, Elizabeth. *New Indians, Old Wars*. Urbana: University of Illinois Press, 2007.
Fitz, Brewster E. *Silko: Writing Storyteller and Medicine Woman*. Norman: University of Oklahoma Press, 2004.
Parrish, Timothy. *From the Civil War to the Apocalypse: Postmodern History and American Fiction*. Amherst: University of Massachusetts Press, 2008.
Silko, Leslie Marmon. *Almanac of the Dead*. New York: Simon & Schuster, 1991.
_____. *Ceremony*. New York: Viking Press, 1977.
_____. *Gardens in the Dunes*. New York: Scribner, 1999.
Spurgeon, Sara L. *Exploding the Western: Myths of Empire on the Postmodern Frontier*. College Station: Texas A&M University Press, 2005.
Wilson, Charles E. *Race and Racism in Literature*. Westport, CT: Greenwood, 2005.

## wisdom

In humanistic situations, Silko transforms into contemporary writing the wisdom of Amerindians. More than light amusement or children's narratives, oral tradition is a mainstay to the Laguna and other Pueblo. She muses that the Mayans, inventors of the zero, kept "all knowledge in history, technology, and religion embedded in narrative," a nonscholarly source of anecdote and wonder available to each tribe member, even the youngest (Silko & Arnold, 2000, 157). To journalist Ruth Lopez, Silko asserted that such amassed pragmatism and prudence continue to bolster tribal strength and resilience: "It is the only way human culture survives, by learning from our mistakes" (Lopez, 1996, D6). The author actualizes the pronouncement in the lives of her erring characters—Ayah and Chato on "Lullaby" (1974), two female figures in "Poem for Myself and Mei-Mei: Concerning Abortion" (1974), "little sister" Laura and Emo in *Ceremony* (1977), the title figure in "Coyote Holds a Full House in His Hand" (1981), and the white conqueror in "500 Years from Now, Everyone in Tucson Speaks Nahuatl Not Chinese" (2007). Rather than judge people as sinners or villains, Silko's Indian philosophy pictures them as learning through trial and error. Of her own discovery of duty to self, she confided to Cat Johnson, an interviewer for *Santa Cruz News*, "In order to have a peaceful death, it's very important to do everything that you passionately want to do…. You won't regret what you've done, you'll only regret what you didn't do" (Johnson, 2010).

In childhood, like the title figure in Forrest Carter's coming-of-age story *The Education of Little Tree* (1976) and Laura and Mary Ingalls, characters in the *Little House on the Prairie* series, Silko relied on Laguna elders for guidance and philosophy. Of the oldest folk, she recalls the keen insights of women "who remember way back in time and had a much clearer memory of terrible things that had happened" (Mellas, 2006, 12). To interviewer Laurie Mellas, Silko expressed gratitude for stories that retain her people's suffering. In the late 19th and early 20th centuries, the U.S. government used a divide-and-conquer approach by jailing boys and men of the Rio Grande valley in Santa Fe. The separation left Acoma, Hopi, Laguna, and Zuñi girls and women to starve because they could not manage home duties and childcare as well as agriculture. The author admires the fact that the women never gave in to defeat and that they fought bureaucrats who attempted to destroy the pueblo animistic religion, a mainstay against despair. According to what novelist Larry McMurtry terms "the native people's long-accumulated and reverently guarded wisdom about the natural world," Silko asserts that white legalities fail to bolster conquerors whose imperialism is totally corrupt (McMurtry, 2007, xxi). Instead, she declares, "The way you change human beings and human behavior is through a change in consciousness and that can be effected only through literature, music, poetry — the arts" (*ibid.*, 14).

## A PLACE IN TIME

By honoring mythic truth over tyranny and capitalism, Silko restores power and identity to first peoples, who revere Mother Earth as their progenitor. Novelist Maxine Hong Kingston admired the ancestral voices in Silko's works and of the spiritual guidance from the time of creation to the present and future. Silko's texts model the value of elders teaching youngsters, including her own education in use of firearms from her father, Leland "Lee" Marmon, and in earth stories from her Great Grandma A'mooh. The concept of learning by doing infuses the lives of Silko's characters, including Andy in *Storyteller* (1981), who acquires camping and horse handling training from his uncle Siteye. In an early vignette, "Bravura" (1974), the title figure learns by doing after he leaves the university to write poetry in a Southwestern hamlet at Moquino, New Mexico. Tricked by Dan Gonzales into wasting his pittance of cash on exorbitant rent, Bravura refuses to let Dan's opportunism dampen his enthusiasm for living in the desert. The prioritizing of residency over the cost of rent establishes Bravura's resolve to seize an opportunity to know the desert, whatever the cost.

In a contrasting *bildungsroman*, "Humaweepi, the Warrior Priest" (1974), Silko dramatizes an apprenticeship that readies a novice for holy service. On a par with protagonists in Mary Stewart's *The Crystal Cave* (1970) and *The Hollow Hills* (1973) and Lois Lowry's novel *The Giver* (1993) and *Messenger* (2004), the title figure, the orphaned Humaweepi, endures belittling from his peers for clinging to the mentoring of his uncle, whose pedagogy clings to the old ways. A similar mentoring of a war veteran by an elder in *Ceremony* (1977), a quest novel, retrieves Tayo, a survivor of the Bataan Death March of April 1942, from a mental maelstrom. In adulthood, the GI learns by participation the insight housed in the shaman Betonie's sand painting and hoop ceremony. Tayo realizes the worth of stories he took for granted in boyhood and reacquaints himself with tribal erudition. Novelist Larry McMurtry recognizes the "haunting, heartbreaking" story of a damaged soldier that commends the returnee for right thinking: "Tayo, like the wisest of his people, turns for protection to the tribe's saving stories," the oral storehouse that acknowledges and forgives a range of human foibles (*ibid.*, xxi, xxii). McMurtry states the worth of age-old oral wisdom: "If [the stories] are faithfully kept and honored, the people will survive and perhaps in time recover their primal strength" (*ibid.*).

## WRITTEN TRUTHS

Silko differentiates between the wisdom of storytelling and the truth-telling of writing, the theme of Senegalese author Mariama Bâ's feminist novel *So Long a Letter* (1981). To interviewer Steve Bennett of the San Antonio *Express News*, Silko explained, "Writing and the attention one must give to words seem to open a window in the subconscious, words on the page seem to generate more words, certain images and scenes from the dream consciousness begin to appear on the page" (Bennett, 2010, 4K). From the effort come wrestlings with meaning consistent with her philosophy of thriving in an earthly environment and respecting human and animal rights. For *Almanac of the Dead* (1991), she innovates a tactile image of inscribed wisdom in the Yaqui psychic Lecha's translation of an ancient Mayan codex, a compendium of magic inscribed on material from horse stomachs and pocked with parenthesis-shaped arcs where gastric parasites chewed. The source of feminist enlightenment, the focus of *Gardens in the Dunes* (1999), takes a similar archaic palpability in the Coptic scrolls of Dr. Rhinehart. From them, Hattie Abbott Palmer, a participant in a seminar on heresy at Harvard Divinity School, extracts something to believe in, the matriarchy of creation: "Wisdom, Sophia, sent Zoe, Life, her daughter who is called Eve, as an instructor to raise up Adam," a female view of the transfer of womanly thought to alleviate male inadequacy (Silko, 1999, 100). After a series of marital and personal setbacks, Hattie remains anchored in "incorruptible Wisdom, Sophia" and clings to the belief that "there are no sins of the flesh, spirit is everything" (*ibid.*, 450).

In her memoir, *The Turquoise Ledge* (2010), the novelist continues to propitiate the spirit through daily rambles in the Sonora Desert. She turns from a written guidebook to the nature-written evidence of wind, rain, and heat on the Sonora Desert. She characterizes a retreat into timelessness as a form of intuitive reality she learned from Laguna elders: "There are the seasons; there are the risings and settings of the moon, the planets and the constellations. There are intervals between heartbeats" (Bennett, 2010, 4K). Among the inklings she elicits from her study of the paleo–Pueblo, she locates a means of combating a despoiler of the terrain, a man with a bulldozer, whom she confronts with symbols of Star Beings painted on rocks in a child's tempera. The significance of her confrontation appears to catch the man's attention, at least for the time being. With the self-confidence of a sage, she takes comfort from even a small victory "consistent with my sense of the world and my place in it" (Bennett, 2010, 4K).

*See also* Betonie; Grandma Fleet; Spider Women; writing.

• *References and further reading*

Bennett, Steve. "Author Silko Isn't Concerned about Time," *Express News* (25 July 2010): 1K, 4K.
Johnson, Cat. "Silko Heads for Santa Cruz," *Santa Cruz News* (21 October 2010).
Lopez, Ruth. "Finding Justice Through Words," *Santa Fe New Mexican* (3 March 1996): D6.
McMurtry, Larry. "Introduction" to *Ceremony*. New York: Penguin, 2007.
Mellas, Laurie. "Memory and Promise: Leslie Marmon Silko's Story," *Mirage* 24 (Spring 2006): 11–14.
Silko, Leslie Marmon. *Gardens in the Dunes*. New York: Scribner, 1999.
_____. *The Man to Send Rain Clouds: Contemporary Stories by American Indians*, ed. Kenneth Rosen. New York: Viking, 1974.
_____. *Storyteller*. New York: Seaver, 1981.
_____. *The Turquoise Ledge*. New York: Viking, 2010.
_____, and Ellen L. Arnold. *Conversations with Leslie Marmon Silko*. Jackson: University Press of Mississippi, 2000.
West, Paul. "When a Myth Is as Good as a Mile," *Los Angeles Times* (2 February 1992): 8.

## women

Silko highlights the uniqueness of womanhood through actions rather than poses. She derives from the Laguna Pueblo, a matriarchal, matrilineal tribe educated and enlightened by oral tradition. Central to native ethnomythology stand concepts of womanhood derived from Spider Woman (Thought Woman or Ts'its'tsi'nako) and a culture hero, Yellow Woman, the temporary sex partner of Silva, the tall Navajo. Silko expands on the assertive woman with memorable scenarios—the beneficence of Ayah to guide her husband Chato into an easeful death, the curse of the Black Indian of Tampico, the wiliness of Grandma Fleet in rescuing her granddaughters from tribal police, and the seductive kinetics of Night Swan, who uses her powerful swirls to dance a man to death. An outstanding model is the determination of the twins Maytha and Vedna, admirable Chemehuevi-Laguna figures in *Almanac of the Dead* (1991), comfort girls from Winslow, Arizona, who survive jailing and the collapse of their laundry business outside a dam-building project outside Needles, California. Critic Gabriella Morisco points out the significance of female empowerment and sisterhood to the author's writing. The female characters "become the unquestionable protagonists who finally come together to form an alliance among themselves," a solidarity underlying *Storyteller* (1981), *Yellow Woman* (1993), and *Gardens in the Dunes* (1999) (Morisco, 2010, 139).

According to the essay "As a Child I Loved to Draw and Cut Paper" (1996), Silko absorbed a liberal view of gender in girlhood, when her parents displayed no prudery toward nudity and sex. In a discussion of Amerindian womanhood in literature, Cherokee scholar Rayna Green lauds the native writer's subversion of seventeenth-century European stereotypes of squaws enslaved to warriors. Thanks in part to Silko's role in the Native American Literary Renaissance, dominant female characters emerge from a tribal perspective of balanced gender roles rather than male subjugation of women, a standard of white literature. In *Yellow Woman and a Beauty of the Spirit: Essays on Native American Life Today* (1996), Silko admires her Grandma Lillie Ann Stagner Marmon, a fearless horseback rider who avoided female garb except on Christmas Eve, Palm Sunday, and Easter. From Silko's mother, Mary Virginia Lee Leslie Marmon, the author observed the deft handling of rattlesnakes. Silko learned from Virginia that "Humans are the most dangerous of all animals" (Silko, 1996, 17).

## WOMEN SUPPORT WOMEN

In *The Turquoise Ledge* (2010), the author's memoir, she describes how women support their tribal sisters. With the grace of Mariama Bâ's Senegalese epistolary novel *So Long a Letter* (1989) and of Velma Wallis's Athabascan-centered epic *Two Old Woman: An Alaska Legend of Betrayal, Courage and Survival* (1993), Silko honors women for their insistence on apportioning goods, even in hard times. Her Pueblo females dress each other in a communal oneness involving the sharing of jewelry and garments and mutual hair grooming. Old women cling to their aging houses, ignoring leaks and drafts. To the younger generation, the matriarchs request to remain at home until death "and then they may tear it down" (Silko, 2010, 190). The choice of disposal for inherited property becomes a rite of passage and test of the wisdom and fortitude of the subsequent generation of women.

In her writings, Silko empowers women against adversity, such as the resilience of country club gossips in Tuxtla, the grandmother who trades a sewing machine for a Navajo horse, the neo–Druid who protects ancient plantings at Somerset, and the old Yupik woman who causes planes to crash near Bethel, Alaska, by dragging a fox pelt over the television screen. Of Laguna women, the author extols the individual native female as historian or culture keeper, "the [human] tie that binds her people together, transmitting her culture through song and story from generation to generation" (Mainiero, 1982, 82–83). The lore that the Indian wisewoman relays establishes continuity with change, the source of enlightenment in Amy Tan's mother-to-daughter talk-story in *The Kitchen God's Wife* (1991). During historic transitions, such as the upheaval of World War II, the female mediator relates strategies for countering the corruption and genocide wrought by European culture.

ROUNDED CHARACTERS

In pre–Christian style, the gendered roles of Silko's female characters blend positive and negative character traits and choices, a testimony to their humanity and versatility:

| woman | title | role |
|---|---|---|
| Alegría | *Almanac of the Dead* | ambitious professional |
| Amalia | *Almanac of the Dead* | weak mother |
| Angelita, La Escapía | *Almanac of the Dead* | Mayan organizer, Marxist revolutionary |
| Auntie Kie | "Auntie Kie" | elder, savant, defender of Indian rights |
| Auntie Thelma | *Ceremony* | martyr, caregiver, religious fanatic |
| Aunt Susie | *Storyteller* | scholar, teacher, storyteller, survivor |
| | *The Turquoise Ledge* | |
| Aunt Marie | *Almanac of the Dead* | doting aunt |
| Ayah | "Lullaby" | weaver, elderly survivor |
| Black Indian | *Gardens in the Dunes* | guardian, shaman |
| blonde | *Ceremony* | siren, risk taker |
| Dahlia | *Gardens in the Dunes* | freedwoman |
| Delena | *Gardens in the Dunes* | Gypsy trickster, revolutionary, thief, liberator |
| Grandma | *Ceremony* | kind rescuer, storyteller |
| Grandma A'mooh | "People and the Land" | mother, traditional educator, self-sufficient female |
| | *The Turquoise Ledge* | |
| Grandma Fleet | *Gardens in the Dunes* | matriarch, scavenger, traveler |
| Grandmother | "Lullaby" | yarn maker, crone |
| Hattie | *Gardens in the Dunes* | heretical scholar |
| Helen Jean | *Ceremony* | Ute prostitute, victim of Anglo materialism, protector |
| Holy Mother | *Gardens in the Dunes* | maternal goddess |
| Iliana | *Almanac of the Dead* | aristocrat, deceived wife |
| Indigo | *Gardens in the Dunes* | autodidact, experimenter |
| Juana | *Storyteller* | Navajo foster mother, kidnap victim |
| Kochininako | "Yellow Woman" | sensual, vital female survivor |
| Laura | *Ceremony* | risk taker, deceased mother, family embarrassment |
| Leah Blue | *Almanac of the Dead* | Mafiosa, entrepreneur |
| Lecha | *Almanac of the Dead* | psychic, addict, failed mother |
| Lillie | *Storyteller* | storykeeper, store clerk |
| Mahawala | *Almanac of the Dead* | storyteller, tribal historian |
| Maytha & Vedna | *Gardens in the Dunes* | twin survivors, entrepreneurs |
| Mrs. Abbott | *Gardens in the Dunes* | protective mother, conformist |
| Mrs. Palmer | *Gardens in the Dunes* | garden designer |
| Mrs. Van Wagnen | *Gardens in the Dunes* | homemaker, widow, food preserver |
| Nayah | *Storyteller* | grieving mother |
| Night Swan | *Ceremony* | siren, dancer |
| Riverwoman | *Laguna Woman* | abandoned lover, survivor |
| Rose | *Almanac of the Dead* | companion, interpreter |
| Seese | *Almanac of the Dead* | grieving mother, addict |
| Silko | *Storyteller* | hunter, observer of nature |
| | *Turquoise Ledge* | activist, memoirist, guardian of animals |

| Sister Salt | *Gardens in the Dunes* | rescuer, homemaker, entrepreneur |
| social worker | "Lullaby" | outsider, disrupter |
| Susan James | *Gardens in the Dunes* | entertainer, social climber |
| Ts'eh Montaño | *Ceremony* | semi-divine seer, herbalist |
| Waithea | *Storyteller* | willful child, suicide |
| woman | "Storyteller" | Yupik victim, avenger |
| Yoeme | *Almanac of the Dead* | obnoxious crone, Yaqui savant |
| Yupik woman | *Almanac of the Dead* | sorcerer |
| Zeta | *Almanac of the Dead* | entrepreneur, foster mother |

Under clan logic, in *Ceremony* (1977), "Little Sister" Laura's promiscuity and drunken sprees with white and Mexican men disorder the extended family and invite approbation. She willingly embraces the colonizer in a temporary form of miscegenation that repulses whites. While the Catholic priest, Father Kenneth, clucks over her venal sins, the clan experiences the loss of Laura as well as a personal loss of clan dignity and honor. Auntie Thelma, out of devotion to the church and to family, has no choice but to act in the role of Laura's parent to retrieve the infantilized "little sister" from profligacy. Auntie's depiction depicts the reversion of female strength into abuse. Worsening the subtextual hints of female diminution, Silko mirrors the sexual depravity of Laura with that of Helen Jean, a resident of the Ute reservation at Towac. Helen Jean cozies up to a Mexican railroad worker on payday in hopes of sending cash from prostitution to her sister Emma on the reservation. Analyst Sara L. Spurgeon, a specialist in women's studies at the University of Arizona, regrets that Helen Jean's "downward spiral is apparent and virtually identical to Laura's. Both of them ... are lost beyond escape or redemption ... cannibalized and consumed by their captor's culture" (Spurgeon, 2005, 82). Spurgeon particularizes the destruction of Indian women "by Anglo racism and by Anglo misogyny — a two-pronged attack Indian men are not subject to" (*ibid.*, 81).

Tayo and his uncle experience a mundane sharing of womanhood at the Dixie Tavern in Budville. During Night Swan's affair with Uncle Josiah in summer 1940, the brazen, cat-eyed cantina dancer at Cubero speaks confidently to him of her peripatetic career in El Paso, Las Cruces, and Socorro. To her, people and places matter less than performances, which she remembers in detail. Silko depicts her as Amazonian, a superwoman on a par with the witch-goddess Circe in Homer's *Odyssey*, who saps the power from lovers while stoking the potency of her dances. Mimicking both the bull and the matador, Night Swan awes Lalo the bartender, his patrons, and the guitarist, who stops strumming before the dance ends. Recalling a wife's claim that horses had trampled her husband, Night Swan accounts for her presence at Cubero. The image of the deceased lying in the corral at his home suggests the wild animal passions that seize the man, the same passions that terrify Uncle Josiah. Fearful of atrophy of her female juices, Night Swan flees to Cubero in sight of a symbolic mountain, Tse'pi-na (Mount Taylor), the mythic "woman veiled in clouds" (Silko, 1977, 87). The image captures the dancer's mysticism, a veil that separates her from men longing for a human female. Her departure in 1942 after Uncle Josiah's funeral ends her sexual adventures with him and Tayo, who spends only one evening with her, perhaps at the instigation of Uncle Josiah. The one night of love suggests a standard ploy among adult males globally who tutor youths in sexuality by pairing them with experienced women.

## WOMEN AND RESILIENCE

In *Almanac of the Dead* (1991), Silko pictures resistance as gendered and empowered by such female leaders as Yoeme, Lecha, Rose, and Angelita or La Escapía, the student of

Marxism. Critic Cathy Moses, an expert on feminist fiction, describes the Mayan codices in the title as "a text passed down through generations of women that both foretells and enacts the unraveling of Western patriarchal hegemony" (Moses, 2000, 12). The author follows native tradition of the Indian wisewoman by according unusual powers of prophecy and agency to Lecha. Taking her cue from her grandmother Yoeme, the Yaqui culture keeper, Lecha devotes herself to a sacred text by hiring Seese, the blonde transcriber of ragged, splotchy Mayan manuscripts. Upon growing into her destiny, Lecha realizes a truth that Yoeme had failed to reveal — that clairvoyance comes at a price, an internal pain that Lecha describes as cancer. While exercising her ability to locate missing corpses for the police, Lecha lounges in hotel rooms and numbs her post-performance headaches with fat marijuana cigarettes, red wine, and Percodan, a potent painkiller. The fusion of heroics with addiction relieves Lecha of the role of protagonist in the European literary sense and accords her a humanity essential to the story she preserves for future generations.

Seese, too, pays a price for her sensitivity and heightened humanity. A first-time mother searching for her abducted six-month-old son Monte, she lives in a penthouse with her lover David. The homosexual triangle that ties David to his model Eric and to Beaufrey, a merchant of abortion and death videos, confuses Seese. In a blur of alcohol and drugs, she struggles to survive the sorrow of losing Monte while warding off despair at David's ambivalence toward a monogamous relationship and fatherhood. Upon Eric's suicide, Seese releases a womanly compassionate that supercedes David's cold-blooded photographic shoot of the death scene. Unlike her lover, a self-destroyer and embracer of emotional and spiritual aridity, Seese is able to take in the wet red chenille bedspread and human remains and to shiver with the brutality of Eric's self-murder. Critic Jane Olmstead differentiates between Seese's humanity and David's professional "crimes against nature": "In contrast to David's attempts to use technology to control death (and to reap fame and fortune as a result), Seese's face becomes the technology that relentlessly exposes the reality behind the aesthetic constructions of depth and color and planes" (Olmstead, 1999, 475).

## WOMAN AS CARETAKER

Silko celebrates female hardihood, beneficence, and survivalism in *Gardens in the Dunes* (1999), a gynocentric novel featuring needlework and holistic horticulture as tokens of womanly energy. Critic David Murray, a professor of American studies at the University of Nottingham, pinpoints the author's source as "the conventions of the nineteenth-century sentimental novel [which] revolves largely around women and their sensibilities and vulnerabilities in their society" (Murray, 2007, 145). Mama, a laundress at the depot hotel in Needles, California, displays an age-old female talent for recycling by sewing ragged towels and burned blankets into a family quilt, a monument to womanly thrift. Grandma Fleet scours the city dump for seeds and apricot and peach pits to refurbish their desert garden when the family returns to Sand Lizard territory. German analyst Hartwig Isernhagen, an American literature specialist at the University of Basel, accentuates the "pervasive gendering that associates the 'good' garden with a female principle" that unifies a span of gardeners, "the indigenous American, the immigrant American, and the European [into] a global ecofeminist alliance" (Isernhagen, 2002, 178–179). The paradox of womanhood declares "I am the first and the last," an echo of the alpha and omega identifying Christ in Revelation 1:8, 21:6, and 22:13 (Silko, 1999, 229).

Silko's text opens on the Sand Lizard people, an indigenous tribe living in the time of the Ghost Dance, which critic Amelia V. Katanski, the Marlene Crandell Francis Assistant Professor of English at Kalamazoo College, reveres as "the ultimate reversal of Eurocentrism" (Katanski, 2005, 213). In addition to the scarcity of water, the dwindling tribe faces the police roundup of dancers and followers of the Paiute Messiah Wovoka. Grandma Fleet, a widowed survivor, escapes captivity at Fort Yuma in 1849 by chewing through ropes and crawling away through desert sage. Skilled at making do, she returns to the sandhills and survives on amaranth and sunflower seeds, pumpkins, and squash, which she tends "as if the plants were babies" (Silko, 1999, 179). Amid grief for her husband and daughter, she resides alone anticipating a reunion with people who never return. Late in her pregnancy with Sister Salt, Mama rejoins the family. After the imprisonment of the men, more stragglers return from Parker, Arizona, and form a women's commune. Grandma Fleet takes responsibility for Mama, Sister Salt, and the birthing of Indigo. Similarly stoic, Mama conceals her knowledge of English and stands guard while Sister Salt displays dog- and frog-shaped baskets at the train depot in Needles, California, a tourist trade that the author recalls from Laguna depot history of children selling pottery and beaded pine. While other children beg for candy and pennies, Mama retains family dignity by "[standing] nearby and [watching] for trouble" and forbidding panhandling (*ibid.*, 19).

From hands-on lessons in domesticity, the protagonists learn homemaking and survival in the woman-to-girl style of paleo–Indians. Silko introduces menarche as a landmark of womanhood, an anatomical development to be celebrated. The change in Sister Salt's body causes a rift with Indigo, whose curiosity about menstrual flow annoys her older sibling. The confusion in Indigo captures the pre-teen angst of a budding female who mistakes her sister's modesty for rejection. Private thoughts in both girls conceal worry about Mama's absence and their concern for a life deprived of male company, the source of adult relationships and babies. In native style, Sister Salt looks to the evening star and solaces her loneliness with the thought of Mama viewing the same sky. In times of danger, early alerts return to protect Sister Salt and Indigo: "When they were on the run, no one must speak even one word" (*ibid.*, 33). In silence after Mama's captivity, the sisters accept a hard truth: "Mama might be gone a long while" (*ibid.*, 45). The girls are so immersed in nature lore that they can picture Mama dead and devoured, "crawling around as a worm or running as a coyote" (*ibid.*, 51).

## WOMAN AS SCHOLAR

The literary foil of the earth-educated Sand Lizard sisters, Hattie Abbott Palmer represents the rise of female scholasticism and professionalism in the 1890s. Educated at Vassar and Harvard Divinity School, Hattie rejects Christian patriarchal cant by delving into Dr. Rhinehart's library of Coptic scrolls, a treasure of feminist history. One text expresses the eternal all-woman in a translation of a manuscript written by Mary Magdalene. By studying heretical doctrines, Hattie opens her mind to the anti-church, which rejects hierarchies and tithes, and to the myths of Sophia (wisdom) and Eve, the eternal female who rescues Adam from God's jealousy and vengeance. By composing a thesis for a seminar on heresy concerning Mary Magdalene's discipleship to Jesus, Hattie herself incurs ostracism similar to that initially ousting the Gnostics from the first Christian church for their open-minded study of belief systems. Rejuvenated by the concept of female empowerment, Hattie proposes as a thesis topic "The Female Principle in the Early Church," an overt defiance of patristic domination of orthodoxy (Silko, 1999, 101). Public humiliation for broaching so heterodox a topic weakens her from nervous prostration, but strengthens her resolve. Because of her receptivity toward women's plight in an androcentric world, she rebukes Edward, her husband, for trying to tie Indigo with a rope and fulminates against the Indian school for abandoning the search for the missing child. Building the vehemence of Hattie's words is the realization that callous authorities "didn't care if she was lost or died — that meant one less Indian they had to feed" (*ibid.*, 107).

Silko enlarges on the difference between the maternal wife and scholarly husband by picturing Edward, a merchant collector, searching tomes for data on the history, culture, and language of the first people of the Mojave Desert and Colorado River basin for "a tribe never before studied by anthropologists" (*ibid.*, 111). Unlike his altruistic wife, Edward hopes to find a unique research niche that will secure his place in history. The couple continues on separate paths of learning in Bath, England, where Edward confers with greedy botanists at Kew Gardens while Hattie enjoys Aunt Bronwyn, a cultural plant collector at Somerset. Eager for insight, Bronwyn ventures into Druidic lore and ancient toad sculptures "worshiped as incarnations of the primordial Mother" (*ibid.*, 241). In a woodsy setting, Bronwyn identifies circles and spirals cut into limestone as "the eyes of the original Mother, the Mother of God, the Mother of Jesus," an example of the old woman's syncretism of the sacred (*ibid.*, 265). In Lucca, Italy, another female horticulturist, *la professoressa* Laura, hybridizes gladioli and acknowledges her success with Indo-Mediterranean fertility runes, emblems of the longevity and power of female divinity. After the collapse of the Abbott-Palmer marriage and Edward's death in a tuberculosis hospital, Hattie returns to her European friends and the comfort of female gardeners. The resolution pictures Silko's overturn of the male-dominated Garden of Eden with terraced flower and vegetable beds and orchards resplendent in woman-centered art.

*See also* abortion; Auntie Thelma; ecofeminism; Grandma Fleet; Indigo; Indigo and Sister Salt's genealogy; Lecha and Zeta's genealogy; marriage; Montaño, Ts'eh; mothering; sex; Sister Salt; Spider Woman; "Yellow Woman."

• *References and further reading*

Christie, Stuart. *Plural Sovereignties and Contemporary Indigenous Literature*. New York: Palgrave Macmillan, 2009.

Erdrich, Heid Ellen, and Laura Tohe. *Sister Nations: Native American Women Writers on Community*. St. Paul: Minnesota Historical Society Press, 2002.

Ganser, Alexandra. "Violence, Trauma, and Cultural Memory in Leslie Silko's *Ceremony*," *Atenea* 24:1 (June 2004): 145–149.

Hollrah, Patrice E. M. *"The Old Lady Trill, the Victory Yell": The Power of Women in Native American Literature*. New York: Routledge, 2003.

Isernhagen, Hartwig. "Of Deserts and Gardens: The Southwest in Literature and Art, 'Native' and 'White'" in *Literature and Visual Arts in Twentieth-Century America*, ed. Michele Bottalico. Bari: Palomar Eupalinos, 2002, 173–187.

Katanski, Amelia V. *Learning to Write 'Indian': The Boarding-School Experience and American Indian Literature*. Norman: University of Oklahoma Press, 2005.

Lauter, Paul. *A Companion to American Literature and Culture*. Malden, MA: Blackwell-Wiley, 2010.

Mainiero, Linda, ed. *American Women Writers*. New York: Frederick Ungar, 1982.

May, Janice Susan. *Healing the Necrophilia of Euro-American Society in Leslie Marmon Silko's Gardens in the Dunes*. Radford, VA: Radford University, A.D. 2000.

Morisco, Gabriella. "Contrasting Gardens and Worlds: America and Europe in the Long Journey of Indigo, a Young Native American Girl" in *Nations, Traditions and Cross-Cultural Identities: Women's Writing in English in a European Context*, eds. Annamaria Lamarra and Eleonora Federici. Bern: Peter Lang, 2010, 137–148.

Moses, Cathy. *Dissenting Fictions: Identity and Resistance in the Contemporary American Novel*. New York: Routledge, 2000.

Murray, David. *Matter, Magic, and Spirit: Representing Indian and African American Belief.* Philadelphia: University of Pennsylvania Press, 2007.

Olmstead, Jane. "The Uses of Blood in Leslie Marmon Silko's *Almanac of the Dead*," *Contemporary Literature* 40:3 (Fall 1999): 464–490.

Olsen, Erica. "Silko's Ceremony," *Explicator* 64:3 (Spring 2006): 190–192.

Silko, Leslie Marmon. *Gardens in the Dunes.* New York: Scribner, 1999.

_____ "Introduction," *On the Rails: A Woman's Journey,* by Linda Niemann. Berkeley, CA: Cleis, 1996.

_____. *Yellow Woman and a Beauty of the Spirit: Essays on Native American Life Today.* New York: Simon & Schuster, 1996.

Spurgeon, Sara L. *Exploding the Western: Myths of Empire on the Postmodern Frontier.* College Station: Texas A&M University Press, 2005.

## Wovoka

Silko uses the reclamation of the teachings of Wovoka (renamed Jack Wilson), a Northern Paiute seer, as an emblem of reclaimed Indian faith through the power of the Ghost Dance. Born around 1856 in Mason Valley, Nevada, he developed from shaman to magician. After he received a revelation from the spirit world, he prophesied an Amerindian revival led by dead ancestors returned to earth. Historically, Wovoka's Ghost Dance movement swept the frontier in the late 1800s, involving the Havasupai, Mormons, Paiute, and Walapai and plains tribes to the north in episodes of glossolalia, trances, and spiritual ecstasy sparked by rejoicing at a renewal of the environment and a return of the buffalo. Because of the upsurge of hope in a demoralized people, in 1890, the U.S. government banned native ceremony and religion.

Dutch critic Hans Bak, an expert in native Americana, characterizes Silko's fictional dance ritual as the "antidote to the poisonous meeting of Cortés and Montezuma, a meeting which was orchestrated by sorcerers called 'destroyers'" (Bak, 2005, 133). In *Almanac of the Dead* (1991), Silko's chronicle of North American sins against minorities, she applies the Mayan concept of time and imports from the past a spiritual uprising capable of crushing boundaries and cleansing the hemisphere of its wickedness. She justifies the overlay of the past on the present as an element of the sacred, which is always now. To interviewer Ellen L. Arnold in "Of Apricots, Orchard, and Wovoka" (2000), the novelist explained the involvement of European immigrants in the syncretism of Christianity with native animism: "They weren't here long, and they had to see their Jesus, their Mary, their Joseph, their saints, go native" (Silko & Arnold 2000, 187).

Instead of an adult perception of the Wovoka dance cult, Silko envisions hypnotic events through the ambiguous perspective of Indigo. On the fourth night of the dance, she witnesses the collapse of a young Mormon man who "suddenly fell to his knees with his face in his hands, babbling and weeping" (Silko, 1999, 32). Critic David Murray, a professor of American studies at the University of Nottingham, comments, "By presenting the Ghost Dance mainly as experienced by a child, the visionary and prophetic aspects are foreground, and it is these elements that Indigo recognizes in the other religions she encounters" (Murray, 2007, 145). Like the original Ghost Dancers, Silko's characters express personal viewpoints and sufferings by "[claiming] their own performative space," a contrast to the enforced conformity of legalistic Christian missionaries (*ibid.*). In *The Turquoise Ledge* (2010), Silko invests the performers with militaristic personas by calling them "descending ghost warriors, a shower of revenants" (Silko, 2010, 138). In the view of analyst Carlton Smith, a literature teacher at Palomar College, *Almanac* resonates with "both the historic occasion of the ghost dance and the body politic of contemporary ghost dancers" (Smith, 2000, 47).

## SUPERNATURAL ARMOR

Modern versions of the protective Ghost Shirt take the form of technological fetishes and obsessions—*mestizo* insurance magnate Menardo Panson's bulletproof vest, Eddie Trigg's medical research facilities that plot solutions to spinal cord injury, and Serlo's storage of the ejaculate of a pure-blood white at a *finca* (plantation) in Chile and his dream of an Alternative Earth module to house only the "select few" (Silko, 1991, 543). On a grander scale, Leah Blue builds a gated city at Venice, Arizona, an elitist shield against intermingling with the poor, homeless, and outcast of Tucson. In a subsequent essay, "Fences against Freedom," published in the fall 1994 issue of *Hungry Mind Review*, Silko claims that Americans are erecting their own magic shield: The "U.S. government is building a steel wall twelve feet high which eventually will span the entire length of the Mexican border," a bulwark against an onslaught of undocumented aliens (Silko, 1994, 20). Rather than generate a unified choreography of hope, the dissension aroused by racial bitterness and rage produces anarchy as the nation allows xenophobia to subsume democracy and welcome to outsiders.

In *Almanac*, Silko, like Wovoka himself, reminds Indians of their failure to protect themselves from white terrorism. At the darkly comic International Holistic Healers Convention in Tucson, Wilson Weasel Tail, the Lakota law student and healer, whips an audience to a frenzy in the plot resolution by calling on tribal memory. He skewers listeners with a rhetorical question: "Where were you when the people first discussed the Europeans? Tell the truth. You forgot everything you were ever told" (Silko, 1991, 721). Instead of sounding the alarm at the death of Miniconjou Sioux chief Big Foot at the massacre at Wounded Knee on December 29, 1890, Amerindians allowed whites to manipulate Indian greed and to corrupt them into thievery from neighbors. Wilson explains that, through dance-chant from Canada to Chile, the Ghost Dance still revives oneness with ancestors killed during the post–Columbian era. To pump up enthusiasm for revolt, he warns that the 60 million spirits of the deceased will harangue Indians until they hide in whiskey. As proof of indigenous power, Wilson informs his listeners that universal destruction from meteors can trample rich nations. In their retreat, the buffalo once more will roam the Great Plains, just as Wovoka predicted.

## AWAITING THE APOTHEOSIS

In the opening scenes of *Gardens in the Dunes* (1999), a neo–Victorian novel, Silko pictures a family of Sand Lizard women fleeing the roundup of Ghost Dancers and followers of the Indian Messiah, an evangelist who replaces Wovoka. She bases the event on a Ghost Dance held in Kingman, Arizona, in 1893, but, for the sake of her story, she resets the gathering in Needles, California. She describes how fearful whites respond to an era of native rejuvenation: "Indian police grabbed all the Indians they could, while the soldiers arrested the white people, mostly Mormons, who came to dance for the Messiah" (Silko, 1999, 14). Silko imparts the syncretic teachings of Wovoka, who foretold an Indian revival through ecstatic dance, peace making, and moral living based on the life of Jesus: "If the Paiutes and all other Indians danced this dance, then the used-up land would be made whole again..., then they would be able to visit their dear ones and beloved ancestors.... Great storms would purify the Earth of her destroyers" (*ibid.*, 25).

Silko's fictional account of the Ghost Dance details face paint, robing, and shared anticipation of a godly presence. Under the Indian Messiah, the evangelist who continued the cult after Wovoka's withdrawal from the movement, the Paiute revere piñon nuts and water as sacred food. In a broad interpretation of "family," they include all comers to their gatherings (*ibid.*, 24). In the estimation of reviewer Tayari Jones, a specialist in minority literature at Rutgers-Newark University, Silko's liberated version of Jesus depicts "a family man, a part of a community. He is not a mystery to be understood only by clergy" (Jones, 2000, 43). The text weaves wisps of spiritual yearning with cultural grief for Sioux victims of the Wounded Knee Massacre and for other losses. Meanwhile Delena, a Mexican Yaqui revolutionary, suffers her own terrors of the final solution to indigenous populations. In a book review, William Willard notes the similarity between persecution of Indians and of Latter Day Saints: "Joseph Smith, their prophet, had been murdered by a mob in Illinois; they too needed deliverance from the sorrows of this world" (Willard, 2000, 140).

The evening dance, told through the perspective of Indigo and Sister Salt, begins peacefully, but grows intense with expectation. Participants paint their faces with white clay, mark doorways with red ocher streaks, and dress in white canvas robes and shawls for the dance. In a circle moving right to left in mimicry of the sun, they drag their feet along the river sand outside Needles, keeping in close contact with Mother Earth and sleeping by their campfire ashes over a four-night assembly. Words to their songs point upward from snow on the ground to the Milky Way, the pathway the dead take to the spirit world. A second song mentions metaphoric clear water pouring from a cleft in a black rock. Later singing describes a wind stirring the grass and willows, an allusion to revolt from nature and, by extension, from nature worshippers. Wovoka's disciples await a time when "the used-up land would be made whole again and the elk and the herds of buffalo killed off would return" (Silko, 1999, 23). The U.S. Cavalry use native unity and resistance as justification for genocide and for attacks on Mormons, who threaten to ally with Indians against the government. In the aftermath of betrayal and mass arrest, Indigo retains the salvific message: "All who are lost will be found, a voice inside her said; the voice came from the Messiah, Indigo was certain" (*ibid.*, 320).

*See also Gardens in the Dunes*; powerlessness; symbolism.

• *References and further reading*

Bak, Hans. *First Nations of North America: Politics and Representation*. Amsterdam: VU University Press, 2005.
Huhndorf, Shari Michelle. *Going Native: Indians in the American Cultural Imagination*. Ithaca: Cornell University Press, 2001.
Jones, Tayari. "Folk Tale of Survival," *The Progressive* (2000): 43–44.
Lee, A. Robert. *United States: Re-viewing American Multicultural Literature*. València: Universitat de València, 2009.
Murray, David. *Matter, Magic, and Spirit: Representing Indian and African American Belief*. Philadelphia: University of Pennsylvania Press, 2007.
Ruoff, A. Lavonne Brown. "Images of Europe in Leslie Marmon Silko's *Gardens of the Dunes* and James Welch's *The Heartsong of Charging Elk*" in *Comparative Site of Ethnicity: Europe and the Americas*, eds. Boelhower, William, Carmen Birkle, and Rocio Davis. Heidelberg: Winter Verlag, 2004.
Ruta, Suzanne, "Dances with Ghosts," *New York Times* (18 April 1999).
Silko, Leslie Marmon. *Almanac of the Dead*. New York: Simon & Schuster, 1991.
_____. "Fences against Freedom," *Hungry Mind Review* 31 (Fall 1994): 6–20.
_____. *Gardens in the Dunes*. New York: Scribner, 1999.
_____. *The Turquoise Ledge: A Memoir*. New York: Viking, 2010.
_____, and Ellen L. Arnold. *Conversations with Leslie Marmon Silko*. Jackson: University Press of Mississippi, 2000.
Smith, Carlton. *Coyote Kills John Wayne: Postmodernism and Contemporary Fictions of the Transcultural Frontier*. Hanover, NH: University Press of New England, 2000.
Willard, William. "Review: *Gardens in the Dunes*," *Wicazo Sa Review* 15:2 (Fall 2000): 139–141.

# writing

Through a variety of media, settings, and tonalities, Silko extols the role of the culture custodian. She commented to interviewer Chip Colwell-Chanthaphonh, curator of the Denver Museum of Nature & Science, on the danger of empowering only a few people with automated systems from outer space, an alert borne by the Greek myth of Daedalus and Icarus: "It's terribly important to have somebody, a humanist, who can reclaim that perspective because soaring has always been in humans" (Colwell-Chanthaphonh, 2005, 164). She characterized the fantasy of flying over earth and looking down from a heightened perspective as natural to earth-bound humankind: "We are always looking for revelations" as antidotes to "a very tenuous hold here" (*ibid.*). Among the handholds Silko validates are ancient, weathered artifacts—some as old as the arrival of paleo–Indians to the Southwest in 18,000 B.C. She exonerates the repatriation of past keepsakes for ritual rather than locking them into glass museum cases, where they remain unhandled and sterile. She recalls her elders admonishing her in childhood to let things remain undisturbed. The abandonment and reclamation are normal aspects of culture: "They have to go out and they have to deteriorate and disintegrate. They have to continue their cycle," an oblique reference to her own role as reviver of past symbols (*ibid.*).

The author's early writings preceded an outpouring of brilliance and enthusiasm for filmmaking and the visual arts, which she compared to oral tradition. She explained that film "operates on a highly refined, simultaneous, personal level.... Film gives the feeling that we get going for a walk, experiencing many things at once in a simple elemental way" (Silko & Arnold, 2000, 47). She confided to poet James Wright her intent to launch the Laguna Film Project—a trio of works entitled *Stolen Rain* that she initiated on July 21, 1979. By photographing Laguna locations against a storyteller's voice, she intended to relate the pueblo's beginnings and to honor storykeeping as a sacred trust. To Wright she confided problems with cinematography: "Film is so tedious and expensive — I'm so thankful to work with words on paper, depending on no one" (Silko & Wright, 1986, 62). By September, she vowed, "Never again film projects," which taxed her skill to control the dissemination of theme and motif (*ibid.*, 88).

## WRITING AS RITUAL

In her description of composition methods, Silko expresses views on customs in terms of ritual details. Her instinct for worth guides her composition. She describes artists as sponges soaking up "hints and clues" and relies on the feeling that "you can tell by the fabric of the narrative what's right and what's wrong" (Jeffries, 2010). In her classroom, she urges would-be writers to preserve their best self and best energy for composition. The most promising time to work is dawn, "closer to the dream state. Your resistance is still low; the regular world — the electric bill, the flat tire — has yet to invade" (Mellas, 2006, 14). The elements of humanistic short fiction, she explains, are "fractals," increments of a shape to be (Fedderson, 1998). According to her essay "Breaking Down the Boundaries: 'Earth, Air, Water, Mind'" (1998), she begins in the morning and, hours later, feels ready to "just push the big nuclear button and get rid of it all" (Silko, 1998, 91). To do her best work, she claims, "You cannot jar the body or move it around. The closer you can be to the dream state, to waking up, the better, and so nightgowns are good. Actually no clothes at all are" (*ibid.*).

Silko informed Kim Jeffries, an interviewer for the *Seattle Times*, that character and action derives in part from people she has known and memories of her experiences. One of Silko's incorporations of a free-floating mental state occurred in 1981, when she heard helicopters overhead and turned them into a fictional medevac of wounded U.S. infantrymen from Mexico. The reverie of war in Mexico impacted the surreal mustering of a peasant army in *Almanac of the Dead* (1991), in which she predicted the revolt of Mesoamericans against native displacement and dispossession from ancestral land. Additional global uprisings against Marcos in Manila, outside the Berlin Wall, and in Los Angeles and Tiananmen Square against the repressive Chinese government impacted her imagination. According to the tribal view of time as an ocean, people continue to fight injustice from past centuries in battles that are "absolutely necessary, absolutely unavoidable" (*ibid.*, 93). She validates women as warriors against obstacles and intellectual and political boundaries, in part by telling clan stories to prepare the younger generation for their role as reclaimers of Amerindian rights.

## ON HUMAN RIGHTS

The author anchors her storytelling amid native needs. She typified to interviewer Kim Barnes the writer's obligation to universal humanity, "The most deeply felt emotions, like the deepest kind of fear or loss or bereavement of ecstasy or joy, those kinds of deep, deep, deep level feelings and emotions, are common in all human beings" (Barnes, 1986, 90). To transform oral narrative from the past into the written word of the present, she transcends literary rules and boundaries that diminish the sacred power of Laguna oral storytelling. In the description of critic Kenneth R. Lincoln, an expert on Amerindian studies at the University of California at Los Angeles, "Silko's sentences flow like high-desert waters, mountain snowmelt feeding down the New Mexico ravines in spring runoff, as it has for millennia, swelling creeks and pooling streams over summer fields of corn, beans, and squash, the legendary three sisters" (Lincoln, 2008, 110). His praise encompasses her skill at turning landscape into character.

More illustrative of Silko's naturalized text is *Sacred Water: Narratives and Pictures* (1993), which critic Hertha Wong, an English teacher at the University of California at Berkeley, terms an "imagetext ... all linked by the central motif of water — a scarce, life-generating resource and the focus of most of the rituals among the peoples of the arid Southwest" (Wong, 2000–2001, 154). In the blend, Silko cultivates a segue from image to action to create the flavor of storytelling as an adjunct to photography. The result seeks "to translate auto/geography into verbal/visual narrative" (*ibid.*, 155). Her enjoyment of the book's compilation and integration aroused "the sheer sensual pleasure of the paper, glue, and the [laser] copy machine images of my photographs" (Silko, 1993, 15). The purity of the work contrasts her previous immersion in the contamination and evil of Tucson for *Almanac of the Dead* (1991), her most pointed diatribe against Euro-American usurpation.

## NATURAL METHOD

Silko's style is organic, like cascades replenishing cisterns and springs with life-sustaining water. She explains in "Notes on *Almanac of the Dead*" (1996), "I work by intuition and instinct; I don't make outlines or plans because whenever I do, they turn out to be useless" (Silko, 1996, 136). She relates both history and social order through cautionary tales and escape strategies that educate youth on behavior and morality and prepare them for life conflicts. Her inventions turn stories from mundane narration into life celebrations of a culture that resists intrusion, dismissal, and erasure. By re-embroidering themes and motifs in new tellings, she refutes white stereotypes that belittle and discount native Americans. While interlayering images, myths, and vignettes in nonlinear order, she impacts the hearer with the value of past and present struggles on future courses of action.

In her first novel, *Ceremony* (1977), the author imposes the order of the universal matrix, the structure on which Thought Woman (also Spider Woman or Ts'its'tsi'nako) created the world. The image of neat threads replaces the initial confusion of knotty tangles, the metaphor for mental chaos that grips Tayo, a survivor of World War II. To shed the guilt and sorrow that benights his mind, he must reconnect with his Laguna homeland. Within nature, Silko predicts the way to sanity. She valorizes the early morning spider webs outlined in the dawn's rays. German critic Jana Gohrisch, a literature professor at Leibnitz University, interprets the strands as "both fragile and strong because of its segmented construction, which ensures that its function is maintained even if some of the filaments are broken" (Gohrisch, 2006, 237). She finds in the spider's lair a "symbol of universal cohesion, of death ... and of the continuity of life conveyed through the circle," a pervasive symbol in Amerindian cosmology of unending being on earth and in the afterlife (*ibid.*).

Spiritual Guidance

During the composition of *Gardens in the Dunes* (1999), Silko recovered from the dark, doom-laden office atmosphere that gripped her while she completed *Almanac of the Dead*. She told a reporter from the *Santa Fe New Mexican*: "Somehow the creation of [*Gardens*], with so much positive energy, made me so much more vulnerable.... I really felt that the ancient spirits ... wanted me to write this book and give their voices a form and so they protected me" ("Exploring," 1998, 30). Sustaining her during normal life vicissitudes, imaginary flowers and plants conferred peace and light as well as emotional uplift. In summary, she described a fundamental change that overtakes her with each new work, notably, the realization that communal need permeates all phases of human activity.

In composing *The Turquoise Ledge* (2010), Silko aimed her contemplation of turning 60 into a self-portrait. Essential to composition, solitude reveals subconscious thoughts and attitudes as well as "images and scenes from the dream consciousness" (Bennett, 2010, 4K). The title, according to her remarks to interviewer Steve Bennett, refers to "the sudden surprise of beauty, which the earth and the desert offer us so generously whether we deserve them or not" (*ibid.*). Publication of her memoir introduces a more settled phase of her writing career in which she treasures the bits of turquoise emerging from ancient lava flows and the snakes that guard her residence west of Tucson. A touch of grace accompanies her discovery of grinding stones left under a tree by ancient desert dwellers. To protect the sacred presence of past generations, the author puts a hex on a bulldozer driver, raining down on him the curses of star spirits that she paints in tempera on rocks. The memoir rounds out the periods of artistic unrest and humanistic drive that place Silko in the vanguard of the Native American Renaissance.

*See also* Silko, Leslie Marmon.

• *References and further reading*

Barnes, Kim. "A Leslie Marmon Silko Interview," *Journal of Ethnic Studies* 13.4 (1986): 83–105.
Bennett, Steve. "Author Silko Isn't Concerned about Time," *Express News* (25 July 2010): 1K, 4K.
Brice, Jennifer. "Earth as Mother, Earth as Other in Novels by Silko and Hogan," *Critique* 39, no. 2 (Winter 1998): 127–138.

Colwell-Chanthaphonh, Chip. "Portraits of a Stories Land: An Experiment in Writing the Landscapes of History," *Anthropological Quarterly* 78:1 (January 2005): 151–177.

"Exploring Passions," *Santa Fe New Mexican* (13 November 1998): 30.

Fedderson, Rick, Susan Lohafer, Barbara Lounsberry, and Mary Rohrberger. *The Tales We Tell: Perspectives on the Short Story*. London: Greenwood, 1998.

Gohrisch, Jana. "Cultural Exchange and the Representation of History in Postcolonial Literature," *European Journal of English Studies* 10:3 (December 2006): 231–247.

Jeffries, Kim. "A Conversation with Leslie Marmon Silko on *The Turquoise Ledge*," *Seattle Times* (19 October 2010).

Lincoln, Kenneth. *Speak Like Singing: Classics of Native American Literature*. Albuquerque: University of New Mexico Press, 2008.

Saunders, Michael. "Alexie Sends 'Smoke Signals,'" *Boston Globe* (5 July 1998): N1.

Silko, Leslie Marmon. "Breaking Down the Boundaries: 'Earth, Air, Water, Mind'" in *The Tales We Tell: Perspectives on the Short Story*, ed. Barbara Lounsberry. London: Greenwood, 1998.

_____. *Sacred Water: Narratives and Pictures*. Tucson: Flood Plain Press, 1993.

_____. *The Turquoise Ledge: A Memoir*. New York: Viking Adult, 2010.

_____. *Yellow Woman and a Beauty of the Spirit: Essays on Native American Life Today*. New York: Simon & Schuster, 1996.

_____, and Ellen L. Arnold. *Conversations with Leslie Marmon Silko*. Jackson: University Press of Mississippi, 2000.

_____, and James Wright. *The Delicacy and Strength of Lace Letters*. St. Paul, MN: Graywolf, 1986.

Wong, Hertha D. Sweet. "Native American Visual Autobiography: Figuring Place, Subjectivity, and History," *Iowa Review* 30:3 (Winter 2000-2001): 145–156.

## "Yellow Woman" (1974)

Silko genders primordial creative power in females, including goddesses and demi-goddesses, the life-affirming mediators between evil and good. According to Amerindian playwright and poet Carolyn Dunn, Silko's writing depicts the Laguna proto-feminist Kochininako (Yellow Woman) as an Amazon, "self-definitive, assertive, decisive, and continuous," a source of "sacred knowledge from the wilderness" (Dunn, 2005, 198–199). An earthly manifestation of Ts'its'tsi'nako, the arachnid Thought-Woman (Grandmother Spider), the prototypical female hero dwells apart from ordinary humans. The concept of fecundity extends from Yellow Woman across other characters, including Ayah, the Navajo matriarch in "Lullaby" (1974); Tayo, the bringer of rain, and the semi-divine herbalist Ts'eh Montaño in *Ceremony* (1977); clan matrons Indigo and Sister Salt from *Gardens in the Dunes* (1999); and rattlesnakes and Silko herself, the mother figure in the garden in *The Turquoise Ledge* (2010).

Much as Chicano/Chicana writers reset the La Llorona story cycle both in indeterminate and modern times, Silko presents her subversive females in what feminist critic Roumania Velikova calls "a continuous chain of communal experience" (Velikova, 2002, 61). In *Yellow Woman and a Beauty of the Spirit: Essays on Native American Life Today* (1996), the author differentiates between the Puritan view of sexual inhibitions and rigid monogamy and the Pueblo concept of a married couple as a team. Before Christian missionaries shamed and degraded Indians for their flexible mores, married people, female and male, were unashamed to take lovers or produce love children. Conrad Shumaker, an English professor at the University of Central Arkansas, accounts for the strengths of the matriarchy: "Because a child belonged to its mother's clan, there was no problem of illegitimacy—every child was cared for" (Shumaker, 2008, 78). The pattern recurs in *Gardens in the Dunes* (1999), in which Sister Salt claims the happiness of unfettered sexual relationships that leaves her "as free and joyous as that River Girl character," a direct reference to Yellow Woman (Silko, 1999, 400).

## AN ICON OF EMPOWERMENT

The use of immediate, historical, and mythic voices reveals the complex humanity of native women through past ages. Like the realm of the classic Artemis/Diana, virgin hunter and moon goddess, Yellow Woman's superintendence of creation elevates her to the equal of males. In her teens, Silko walked the banks of the river and fantasized how she would react of she happened upon a handsome male and faced Yellow Woman's dilemmas and choices. The placement of the legend along the river indicates the life of a risk taker who welcomes challenge at the boundary between worlds. With the duality of the Hindu creator/destroyer Kali Ma, Yellow Woman is an ambivalent figure who chooses membership in the Destroyer Clan, the fomenters of capricious destruction and death. The author identifies with Yellow Woman because the mythic self-sacrificer violates traditional taboos to rescue the Pueblo from crises. Abby H. P. Werlock, a former English professor at St. Olaf College, justifies the use of the mythic Yellow Woman as a prototype "whose adventures cause her suffering yet fulfill the pressing needs of her community" (Werlock, 2010, 474). Yellow Woman bolsters tribal fertility and confronts Buffalo Man, a virile bestial challenger at an eastern spring, a symbol of sexual union with human female and of rejuvenation for her thirsting family. Because of her willing carnal union with the aggressor, she convinces the Buffalo People to sacrifice themselves so the Pueblo can survive famine.

By resetting the metastory in her own time, Silko carries out the basic function of the storyteller—"There is always, always the dynamic of bringing things together, of interrelating things.... Through narrative you can begin to see a family identity and an individual identity" (Gelfant, 2000, 513). Analyst Joan Thompson corroborated Silko's view of ongoing story building as the growth of a live being in unending flux who adapts to changes in human circumstances. In the introduction of Yellow Woman, Whirlwind Man sets her on a global journey, the introit to her saga of off-site rendezvous with men and male deities. Silko's updated version, "Yellow Woman," enables the protagonist to identity her 20th-century self in terms of a long-respected archetype. As analyst Paul John Eakin, a literature specialist at Indiana University, explains the union of past with present, Al's wife voluntarily sees herself as her clan's mythic hero, Yellow Woman: "Hers is a storied consciousness, first and last, in which then and now coalesce in a narrative continuum" (Eakin, 1999, 71). By imagining a permanent alliance with Silva, her seducer, she allows herself to disappear as a real woman and fade into a story figure.

## SYMBOL OF SENSUALITY

The text of Silko's version stresses an overt sexual chemistry in a culture that perpetuates flexible gender roles and sexual mores. Bold and blatantly sensual, the protagonist, Al's wife, enters the story with a damp thigh adhered to the naked leg of Silva, her tall, swarthy Navajo abductor, a model of the dark, evil wanderer, a sinister destroyer whose names echoes the Latin for "woods." Silko examines the dramatic situation from the female perspective. Yellow Woman consciously observes the gradual shift in terrain from cottonwood and willow by the riverbank to junipers and piñons further north, yet, she can't differentiate between stories of the mythic Yellow Woman and her own identity. Because of her grandfather's storytelling, she accepts her abduction as an episode in tribal heritage that makes palpable a standard Pueblo motif of female ventures beyond the community. Silva, clad in Levis, looks toward Concho Valley, Arizona, where he steals cattle from the

Texans' ranches. His admission of rustling causes Yellow Woman to see shadows filling in the vista, hints of her intimidation by a menacing womanizer.

As though viewing her fate, Yellow Woman recedes from "the edge that dropped forever into the valleys below," a reflection of her choices that change clan history (Silko, 1981, 58). The image introduces his undressing of his prey and his demand, "You will do what I want," the words of a dominator (*ibid.*). Her sexuality, a celebration of procreation and continuity, emboldens her advance into a "shaky crossroads," a treacherous milieu, for the sake of tribal survival (Dunn, 2005, 200). Theorist Dunn explains "It is Coyotesse who must venture into the darkness to bring back the knowledge to the tribe" (*ibid.*) Like the current in the river, his forcefulness parallels her will to resist his vigor and to return home to Al and the children and a non-mythic time when people drive pickup trucks and make Jell-O. According to Dunn, the kidnap initiates the "Coyotesse quest," the trickery of the nontribal kidnapper, and a regenerative return to Pueblo tradition for the birth of a magical child. Because female saviors like Yellow Woman bear "a gift to the people," once they are abducted "by Evil Katsina, the people love their ... connection to the divine" (*ibid.*, 198). Dunn elucidates the danger of breaching the divide between human and deity: "The people and the land are no longer one because once the corn is gone, there can be no longer a sacred connection between people, land, and goddess" (*ibid.*).

## SUBSEQUENT VERSIONS

In "Cottonwood" and "Buffalo Story" (1981), traditional dramas of love and destiny, Silko presents alternate episodes in the adventures of Yellow Woman. In the first stave, she represents ecofeminism, the performer of "drastic things ... for the world to continue out of love for this earth" (*ibid.*, 65). Blinded by the radiance and majesty of Sun Man, Yellow Woman abandons a husband and three children. At the autumnal equinox, she hurries to a rendezvous under the fall leaves of the cottonwood to martyr herself "so the earth continued" (*ibid.*, 66). Her feat involves stopping the sun from plunging earth into perpetual night, a mythic self-sacrifice reminiscent of Persephone in the Greek underworld. The parallel strand, "Buffalo Story," depicts Yellow Woman's self-sacrifice as the result of attraction to Buffalo Man. On her journey to find water for her distraught family, she senses a great animal presence in the roiling of a muddy pool in an arroyo, a foreshadowing of a vigorous sexual union. Her migration to the land of the Buffalo People prefaces her people's cyclical search for the buffalo on the plains and their drying of jerky from buffalo meat to feed the Pueblo during droughts.

Silko incorporates a double martyrdom in the slaughter of Buffalo Man and his abductee by Estoy-eh-muut (Arrowboy). Through supernatural spying by the North Star and disguise from the red clay dust offered by Spider Woman, Estoy-eh-muut tracks his errant wife through chest-high buffalo grass (*Bouteloua dactyloides*), a perennial drought-resistant ground cover and model of plains fecundity before the coming of white pioneers with their plows and cattle herds. Estoy-eh-muut senses a shift of loyalty in his beloved wife. Ostensibly, he sacrifices her to allow him to return to the people with news of meat, but the story maintains a subtextual hint of vengeance by a cuckolded husband. Critic Janis P. Stout, an English professor at Texas A&M University, summarizes the dramatic double death as a "story of magical transformations and redemptive scapegoating" (Stout, 2007, 212).

An exploit narrated by Aunt Alice Mormon Eckerman in Silko's childhood tells of a Laguna girl named Kochininako, a possessor of unisex courage and cunning. The choice of protagonist acknowledges Silko's hunting ability. Upon meeting the giant Estrucuyu, a brute on the mesa, Kochininako keeps him at bay by giving him her morning kill of four rabbits, her bow and arrows, a flint *hadti* (knife), and buckskin leggings, moccasins, belt, and the manta over her smock. Aunt Alice accords the girl propriety in refusing to disrobe before the giant and concludes the story with the hunter's rescue. Upon the arrival of the war twins, Ma'see'wi and Ou'yu'ye'wi (Morning and Evening Star), they slay the giant with throws of their flint knives and gut him like a deer. By tossing the *yash'ka* (heart) toward the road by the railroad tracks, the twins confer on the place a connection to Pueblo myth and a narrative episode explaining how a crag between Laguna and Paguate got its name. Subtextually, the story demeans the white world's transcontinental railroad by identifying it only peripherally as a landmark near an amazing rock.

A later episode, set in summer 1967 and narrated in flint-edge dialogue, pictures the elopement of a weak woman with four Navajo males. Silko relieves the story of terror and pathos by mocking three Navajo males as they explain to state police and the FBI why they couldn't escape from four Laguna women, avatars of the mythic Yellow Woman. The septet flees in a 1956 Ford, leaving a trail of wine bottles and size 42 panties in the underbrush. Unlike Kochininako and Buffalo Man, the pairing of an elusive wife with the tall Navajo from Alamo leads to illicit sex, metaphorized by an overturned water jar and by muddy roads during the rainy season. The author speaks through the angry husband, who demands "a damn good story" to explain a ten-month absence and the birth of twin sons, the bumper crop of lusty coitus (Silko, 1981, 95). The witty fillip at the end charges the straying wife less with adultery than with failure to tell a convincing story. Her musing on a rationale offers multiple meanings to the title, "Storytelling," which tends toward "lies" rather than "narration."

*See also* Yellow Woman's genealogy.

## • *References and further reading*

Anderson, Mark Cronlund, and Irene Maria Blayer. *Interdisciplinary and Cross-Cultural Narratives in North America*. New York: Peter Lang, 2005.

Dunn, Carolyn. "The Trick Is Going Home: Secular Spiritualism in Native American Women's Literature" in *Reading Native American Women: Critical/Creative Representations*, ed. Inés Hernández-Avila. Lanham, MD: Altamira, 2005.

Eakin, Paul John. *How Our Lives Become Stories: Making Selves*. Ithaca: Cornell University Press, 1999.

Gelfant, Blanche H. *The Columbia Companion to the Twentieth-Century American Short Story*. New York: Columbia University Press, 2000.

Harrington, Ellen Burton. *Scribbling Women & the Short Story Form: Approaches by American & British Women Writers*. New York: Peter Lang, 2008.

Katanski, Amelia V. *Learning to Write "Indian": The Boarding-School Experience and American Indian Literature*. Norman: University of Oklahoma Press, 2005.

Larré, Lionel. "Autorité et Discours: L'Auteurité en Question," *Annales du CRAA* 29 (2005): 165–179.

Mann, Karen B. "Context and Content in Women's Stories," *Eureka Studies in Teaching Short Fiction* 2:1 (Fall 2001): 13–20.

McClure, John. *Partial Faiths: Postsecular Fiction in the Age of Pynchon and Morrison*. Athens: University of Georgia Press, 2007.

Preston, Cathy Lynn. *Folklore, Literature, and Cultural Theory: Collected Essays*. New York: Taylor & Francis, 1995.

Shumaker, Conrad. *Southwestern American Indian Literature: In the Classroom and Beyond*. New York: Peter Lang, 2008.

Silko, Leslie Marmon. *Storyteller*. New York: Seaver, 1981.

_____. *Yellow Woman and a Beauty of the Spirit: Essays on Native American Life Today*. New York: Simon & Schuster, 1996.

Stout, Janis P. *Picturing a Different West: Vision, Illustration, and the Tradition of Cather and Austin*. Lubbock: Texas Tech University Press, 2007.

Thompson, Joan. "Yellow Woman, Old and New: Oral Tradition and Leslie Marmon Silko's Storyteller," *Wicazo SA Review* 5:2 (Autumn 1989): 22–25.

Velikova, Roumiana. "Leslie Marmon Silko: Reading, Writing, and Storytelling," *MELUS* 27:3 (22 September 2002): 57–74.

Werlock, Abby H. P. *Facts on File Companion to the American Short Story*. New York: Facts on File, 2010.

## Yellow Woman's genealogy

Yellow Woman, the salvific figure in three of Silko's Laguna myths, copulates willingly with a seducer who abducts her from the pueblo. In "Cottonwood" and "Buffalo Story," her mating with Sun Man and Buffalo Man rescue her people and ensure their continuance. In "Yellow Woman" (1981), Silko's postmodern adaptation of the story, Al's wife rationalizes her one-time fling with Silva, the cattle thief from the mountains, as another episode in the ongoing adventures of a lusty Amerindian woman.

```
grandmother=grandpa (dead)
            |
      mother            relatives north of Laguna
        |                      |
   Al=Yellow Woman=/=Silva the cattle rustler
    |                      | abductor from the north
   baby                    |
                     twin sons
```

- *References and further reading*

Silko, Leslie Marmon. *Storyteller*. New York: Seaver, 1981.

Stout, Janis P. *Picturing a Different West: Vision, Illustration, and the Tradition of Cather and Austin*. Lubbock: Texas Tech University Press, 2007.

"Yellow Woman and a Beauty of the Spirit," *Los Angeles Times* (19 December 1993): 52.

# Glossary

Throughout the canon of Leslie Marmon Silko, spellings of terms vary, for example, *ahhh moot/a'moo'ooh/A'mooh, amate/amati, Bun'yah'nah/byn'yah'nah; Gunideeyah/ Gunnadeyah/Kunideeyah, hummah-hah/humma-ha; Huracan/Hurucan; kachina/ Ka't'sina; Kawaik/Ka'waik/Kha-waik; Ka-waik'meh/Kwakemeh/Kawaikameh; Ma ah shra true ee/Maah' shra-True'-Ee/Maahastryu/Marsha-true'ee; Ogou/Ogoun; Shiwana- /shi-wah nah; yashtoah/yastoah.*

**Ahau** (*Almanac of the Dead*, pp. 575, 578) the Mayan flower symbol.

**Ahau Kan** (*The Turquoise Ledge*, pp. 106–107) the Mayan rattlesnake and lord of wisdom.

*Ahe'yuhe'yu* (*Almanac of the Dead*, p. 724) a Paiute cry of alarm.

**Ahmoo'uut** (*Storyteller*, p. 70; *Gardens in the Dunes*, p. 217) the tribal name of Arrowboy, husband of Kochininako in "Buffalo Story." In *The Delicacy and Strength of Lace*, p. 86, Silko credits Arrowboy with shooting an arrow through the earth's crust to allow the first people to emerge. In *Gardens in the Dunes*, the North Star informs Arrowboy of the location of Kochininako, who runs off with Buffalo Man. *See also Kochininako.*

**Ahsti-ey** and **Hait-ti-eh** (*Storyteller*, pp. 100–103) rivals for Estoy-eh-muut in "The Two Sisters," a story of jealousy, betrayal, and migration.

*amatl* (*Yellow Woman and a Beauty of the Spirit: Essays on Native American Life Today*, p. 156; *The Turquoise Ledge*, pp. 241, 246–247) bark paper, also called *amate*, made from the boiled inner bark of the ficus and pounded to produce a delicate writing surface.

*amedicana* (*Yellow Woman and a Beauty of the Spirit: Essays on Native American Life Today*, p. 41) an Amerindian term for mixed-blood white and Laguna.

**a'moo'ooh** (*Ceremony*, pp. 33, 230, 257; *Storyteller*, pp. 33–34, 75, 93, 245, 250; *Almanac of the Dead*, p. 94; *Yellow Woman and a Beauty of the Spirit: Essays on Native American Life Today*, pp. 61–62; *The Turquoise Ledge*, pp. 16, 18, 28, 43, 175, 180) a Laguna expression of endearment and solace to a child or animal or of mourning for a beloved relative.

**Anasazi** (*Yellow Woman and a Beauty of the Spirit: Essays on Native American Life Today*, p. 204) Navajo for "ancient ones," a reference to paleo–Indians who inhabited Arizona, Colorado, New Mexico, and Utah.

**bahana** (*Almanac of the Dead*, p. 85) Hopi term for white people or white culture.

**BIA** (*Ceremony*, pp. 70, 84, 215; *Storyteller*, pp. 18, 20, 46, 127; *Yellow Woman and a Beauty of the Spirit: Essays on Native American Life Today*, pp. 57, 63, 73, 85, 94; *Almanac of the Dead*, p. 27; *Gardens in the Dunes*, p. 216; *The Turquoise Ledge*, pp. 40, 68, 69) Bureau of Indian Affairs, an official U.S. government agency. In the 1950s, the BIA censured native languages so children in government schools would learn English and develop independence from reservation life.

**Boukman** (*Almanac of the Dead*, p. 418) Jamaican priest who spurred the Haitian Revolution.

**bun'yah'nah** (*Storyteller*, p. 10; *Yellow Woman and a Beauty of the Spirit: Essays on Native American Life Today*, p. 55) Keresan for "west lake."

caca (*Almanac of the Dead*, p. 163) Spanish euphemism for excrement or feces.

ca'cazni (*The Turquoise Ledge*, p. 82) the word for "rattlesnakes" in Seri, the language of Sonora, Mexico..

cacique (*Almanac of the Dead*, pp. 32–35, 420–421) a titled leader or political boss of indigenous tribes.

Calabazas (*Almanac of the Dead*, pp. 216–218) Spanish for the globular red-orange squash or calabash that grow the size of pumpkins.

cenote (*Yellow Woman and a Beauty of the Spirit: Essays on Native American Life Today*, p. 181) sinkhole or poole connected to underground water bodies.

centavos (*Gardens in the Dunes*, p. 87) Mexican pennies, each worth one-hundredth of a peso.

cerro (*The Turquoise Ledge*, pp. 55, 143, 206) Spanish for "hill or upland."

chac (*The Turquoise Ledge*, p. 278) the Mayan god of lightning and rain, the equivalent of the Aztec god Tlaloc.

chaparral (*Yellow Woman and a Beauty of the Spirit: Essays on Native American Life Today*, p. 182; *The Turquoise Ledge*, pp. 269, 311) an impenetrable thicket of shrubs and dwarf trees common to the American Southwest.

Chichan (*Almanac of the Dead*, p. 573) Mayan serpent deity who generates creativity, energy, and charisma.

chongo knot (*Ceremony*, p. 107) a plaited clump of hair looped into a figure eight on the back or top of the head "like the oldtimers wore."

Chumayel manuscript (*Almanac of the Dead*, p. 572) a handwritten copy of a sacred Mayan chronicle dating as early as 1775. The Spanish inscribed and illustrated the text in Chumayel, Yucatan. It contains nine manuscripts divided into 24 chapters consisting of calendars, details of the Spanish conquest and a yellow fever epidemic in 1648, an incantation and ritual of angels, the story of Antonio Martinez, creation mythology, a history of Yucatan and mound building, medical and astrological texts, an apocalypse, and the allusive prophecy of Chilam Balam or Balam the Priest, a late 15th-century prophet who predicted a new religion brought by strangers from the east.

Cimi (*Almanac of the Dead*, p. 573) the Mayan personified Death.

Cinco de Mayo (*Almanac of the Dead*, pp. 204, 488) a patriotic holiday for Chicanos and Latinos in Texas and the Southwest, Cinco de Mayo (Fifth of May) notes Mexico's victory over the French invasion force at Puebla, Mexico, north of Veracruz on May 5, 1862.

Cinq-Jour Malheureux (*Almanac of the Dead*, p. 430) Haitian bringer of five days of ill luck.

Ck'o'yo (*Ceremony*, pp. 47–49, 54, 170, 172, 173, 192, 204, 247, 256; *Storyteller*, pp. 111, 113, 115, 121, 161, 166; *Yellow Woman and a Beauty of the Spirit: Essays on Native American Life Today*, pp. 130, 134) destructive power, the equivalent of modern materialism and spiritual vapidity. Corn Woman indicates that Ck'o'yo evil makes regular appearances among good people. In *Almanac of the Dead*, p. 416, Corn Woman reappears as the Maize Mother.

Cliff House (*Almanac of the Dead*, pp. 87, 97; *Yellow Woman and a Beauty of the Spirit: Essays on Native American Life Today*, pp. 59, 137, 186; *Gardens in the Dunes*, p. 69; *The Turquoise Ledge*, p. 47) a Laguna term for the afterlife.

*compadres* (*Almanac of the Dead*, p. 340) Spanish for "male friends, pals."

"Company" (*Almanac of the Dead*, p. 331) slang for the Mafia.

Congo Zandor (*Almanac of the Dead*, p. 429) Haitian demon.

*corrido* (*The Turquoise Ledge*, p. 33) Spanish for "ballad," a form of oral journalism in northern Mexico in the form of folksongs carrying crime alerts, propaganda, and border protests from the 1820s and afterward and performed by an itinerant *corridista* (balladeer). Episodic narratives signed off in the last stanza in the style of the cautionary tale.

*Cuetzalan* (*Yellow Woman and a Beauty of the Spirit: Essays on Native American Life Today*, p. 156) Nahuatl for a town in the Mexican state of Puebla.

*cuetzalli* (*Yellow Woman and a Beauty of the Spirit: Essays on Native American Life Today*, p. 156) Nahuatl for "beautiful or precious red feathers."

*Cuk Do ag* (*The Turquoise Ledge*, p. 81) Tohono O'Odom for "Black Mountains or the Tucson Mountains."

*Cuk Son* (*The Turquoise Ledge*, p. 81) Tohono O'Odom for "place by Black Mountains or the Tucson Mountains."

*curandero* (*Almanac of the Dead*, p. 602) folk healer and shaman.

Damballah (*Almanac of the Dead*, pp. 416–417, 422–423, 429, 735; *Yellow Woman and a Beauty of the Spirit: Essays on Native American Life Today*, p. 147) Yoruban serpent deity and husband of the goddess of creation.

deeni (*Storyteller*, pp. 9, 12, 39; *Yellow Woman and a Beauty of the Spirit: Essays on Native American Life Today*, p. 54) Keresan for "upstairs."

*dicho* (*Gardens in the Dunes*, pp. 362, 363, 367–369, 442) Spanish for "proverb" or "wise saying."

*dioses* (*The Turqoise Ledge*, p. 246)    Spanish for "gods or supreme beings."

*le droit du seigneur* (*Almanac of the Dead*, pp. 535, 541)    French for "the lord's right," a medieval custom that allowed a feudal lord to deflower peasant girls.

dun cow (*Gardens in the Dunes*, p. 225)    a character common to English beast fables.

Eb (*Almanac of the Dead*, p. 573)    the Mayan spirit of rebirth and regeneration.

Estoy-eh-muut (*Storyteller*, pp. 70, 72–75, 101–102, 140, 144–154; *Gardens in the Dunes*, p. 417)    Arrowboy, the phallic name of the husband of Yellow Woman in "Buffalo Story." "The Two Sisters" translates his name as "great young hunter."

Estrucuyu (*Storyteller*, pp. 83–88; *Yellow Woman and a Beauty of the Spirit: Essays on Native American Life Today*, p. 33; *The Turquoise Ledge*, p. 53)    a giant destroyer, symbolic of supernatural threat to Kochininako or Yellow Woman.

Eurzulie (*Almanac of the Dead*, pp. 417, 429)    Yoruban goddess of love and beauty.

*Eye'ae'yuhe'yu* (*Almanac of the Dead*, p. 724)    A mournful Paiute exclamation.

*finca* (*Almanac of the Dead*, pp. 535, 537–542, 544–545, 547, 556–557, 559, 560)    Spanish for "rural real estate or ranch."

folding books (*Yellow Woman and a Beauty of the Spirit: Essays on Native American Life Today*, p. 21; *The Turquoise Ledge*, p. 246)    Mayan hieroglyphic scripts that professional bookmakers encoded on sturdy bark cloth from the amate or wild fig.

gambling sticks (*Ceremony*, pp. 158, 179; *Storyteller*, p. 162; *Gardens in the Dunes*, p. 205)    the Indian equivalent of playing cards, which bear animal engravings as suit marks.

Gede-Brav (*Almanac of the Dead*, p. 430)    Haitian phallic deity.

Gede Ge Rouge (*Almanac of the Dead*, p. 429)    Yoruban cannibal deity and master of the dead.

Ge Rouge (*Almanac of the Dead*, pp. 424, 429)    Yoruban for "red-eyed."

glyph (*Almanac of the Dead*, pp. 128, 569; *The Turquoise Ledge*, pp. 107, 241, 308)    a symbol for a sound or word.

Gnostic (*Gardens in the Dunes*, pp. 77, 79, 93, 95, 97, 99, 261, 450)    concerning religious views and belief systems that differ from orthodox Christianity.

graahdunt (*The Turquoise Ledge*, p. 47)    Keresan for "cilantro or coriander."

Gunadeeyah (*Conversations with Leslie Marmon Silko*, p. 170; *Almanac of the Dead*, pp. 759–760; *Yellow Woman and a Beauty of the Spirit: Essays on Native American Life Today*, pp. 28, 167)    the Destroyers, a mythic explanation of evildoers, exploiters, sorcerers, and witches. **See also** *Kunideeyah.*

Gussuck (*Storyteller*, pp. 18–25, 28–31)    native Alaskan term for a white man.

Guumeyosh (*The Turquoise Ledge*, p. 136)    a Hopi spirit that cannibalizes children.

hadti (*Storyteller*, pp. 84, 86–87)    flint knife.

Hani'a (*Storyteller*, p. 100)    Keresan for "east country" and another name for La Cienega, New Mexico, southwest of Santa Fe.

*haute* (*Almanac of the Dead*, p. 504)    French for "high" or "extreme."

Hero Brothers (*Yellow Woman and a Beauty of the Spirit: Essays on Native American Life Today*, p. 33)    twin hunters who rescue Kochininako from Estrucuyo. See Ma'see'wi and Ou'yu'ye'wi.

Hohokam (*Yellow Woman and a Beauty of the Spirit: Essays on Native American Life Today*, p. 181)    a paleo–Indian culture of Arizona and ancestral tribe of the Pima.

Huitzilopochtli (*The Turquoise Ledge*, pp. 131, 229)    the Aztec hummingbird god, a sun and war deity.

hummah-hah ("'Not You,' He Said," p. 210; *Storyteller*, p. 38; *Yellow Woman and a Beauty of the Spirit: Essays on Native American Life Today*, pp. 31, 63, 204; *The Turquoise Ledge*, pp. 27, 43–45, 48–49, 69)    Keresan for "long ago," a reference to stories of creation, when people talked with animals. To preserve native history, the Pueblo gather during the winter solstice (December 21 or 22)    for a four-day, four-night retelling of the people's history.

Huracan (*Almanac of the Dead*, p. 479; *The Turquoise Ledge*, p. 171)    Mayan god of fire, storm, and wind.

ideograph (*Yellow Woman and a Beauty of the Spirit: Essays on Native American Life Today*, pp. 156, 168)    a symbol representing an abstract idea or concept rather than a word.

Iktoa'ak'o'ya (*Ceremony*, pp. 1, 48; *Storyteller*, pp. 158–159)    Reed Woman, the sister of Corn Woman (Nau'ts'ity'I and Ts'its'tsi'nako, the arachnid Spider Woman or Thought Woman, and the creators of the world and the four underworlds that make up the universe. Iktoa'ak'o'ya's enjoyment of river splashes generates the sibling squabble that precedes her departure to the underworld, leaving the earth in drought. **See also** *Nau'ts'ity'i.*

I'tcts'ity'i (*Yellow Woman and a Beauty of the Spirit: Essays on Native American Life Today*, p. 125)    Corn Woman, the mother of white people and daughter of Thought Woman. With her sister Nau'ts'ity'i, I'tcts'ity'i created the universe.

*I'yche! ana'nisa'na'* (*Almanac of the Dead*, p. 724) Paiute for "Oh! my children."

*I'yehe'! ha'dawu'hana'* (*Almanac of the Dead*, p. 724) Paiute for "Oh, we have oppressed [the children].

kachina (*Almanac of the Dead*, pp. 31, 33, 87). See Ka't'sina.

Ka't'sina (*Ceremony*, pp. 94, 103, 182; *Storyteller*, pp. 55–57, 59, 229; *Yellow Woman and a Beauty of the Spirit: Essays on Native American Life Today*, pp. 29, 41, 162, 203; *The Turquoise Ledge*, pp. 44, 124, 136, 151, 248–249, 274–275) a benevolent Hopi spirit, also called a Kachina. *See also* Whirlwind Man under "Kochininako," Guumeyosh, and Kaup'a'ta.

Katun (*Almanac of the Dead*, pp. 575, 577, 578) a Mayan unit of time equal to 7,200 days.

Kaup'a'ta (*Ceremony*, pp. 170–176, 192; *Storyteller*, pp. 161, 166; *Yellow Woman and a Beauty of the Spirit: Essays on Native American Life Today*, pp. 29–30) the Gambler, a snazzily dressed trickster from Reedleaf Town who causes a three-year drought by imprisoning storm clouds. A tinge of cannibalism colors his story, in which he feeds his guests blue cornmeal mixed with human blood drained from the victims he cheats and hangs upside down in his storeroom.

Kawaik (*Storyteller*, pp. 10, 11–13; *The Delicacy and Strength of Lace*, pp. 70–71; *Almanac of the Dead*, pp. 135, 577; *Sacred Water: Narratives and Pictures*, p. 23; *Yellow Woman and a Beauty of the Spirit: Essays on Native American Life Today*, pp. 127, 152; *The Turquoise Ledge*, p. 45) Keresan for "lake."

Ka-waik'meh (*Almanac of the Dead*, pp. 135, 577; *Yellow Woman and a Beauty of the Spirit: Essays on Native American Life Today*, pp. 18, 127; *The Turquoise Ledge*, p. 21) Keres for "the Laguna, the residents of Kawaik."

kiva ("Humaweepi, the Warrior Priest," p. 161; *Ceremony*, pp. 230, 238–239, 256–258; *Yellow Woman and a Beauty of the Spirit*, 68, 176; *Storyteller*, p. 263; *Almanac of the Dead*, pp. 31–32, 90) among the Pueblo, a subterranean ceremonial chamber reserved for spiritual ritual, priestly training, and religious conferences.

Kochininako (*Storyteller*, pp. 54, 66, 68, 70–75, 82–88, 141, 143, 144; *Yellow Woman and a Beauty of the Spirit: Essays on Native American Life Today*, pp. 33, 70–72; *Gardens in the Dunes*, pp. 400, 417; *The Turquoise Ledge*, pp. 49, 53) Yellow Woman, a straying wife who travels the world with Whirlwind Man, a ka't'sina or spirit. She returns in "Cottonwood" as the mate of Sun Man and in "Buffalo Story" as the woman abducted by Buffalo Man. An updated tale depicts

Kochininako as a young Laguna who outsmarts the giant Estrucuyu. In "Estoy-eh-muut and the Kunideeyahs," the unfaithful wife places purple corn near her husband Estoy-eh-muut to keep him asleep while she consorts with witches of the Kunideeyah clan of destroyers.

K'oo'ko (*Ceremony*, p. 37) a fanged female deity of recompense who haunts dreams and disturbs the order of nature.

Kunideeyah clan (*Storyteller*, pp. 140, 145) a coven of witches known as "the destroyers."

ladino (*Almanac of the Dead*, p. 261) hispano–Indians of Central America.

Legba-Gede (*Almanac of the Dead*, pp. 429–430) Yoruban intermediary between humans and deities; keeper of the crossroads.

*llano* (*Almanac of the Dead*, pp. 550, 554–555, 558, 563–565) Spanish for "treeless plain; flatland."

*locos* (*Almanac of the Dead*, pp. 316, 601, 610, 617, 634, 719) madmen, lunatics.

maaht'zini (*Storyteller*, p. 35) the Keresan word for piki bread, a thin tortilla baked on a stone and rolled up. *See also* piki.

maas-guuts (*Storyteller*, p. 153) a coiled trivet woven of yucca fiber that cushions a water jar on the bearer's head.

Mah'de'haths (*Storyteller*, p. 147) a cliff named in Keresan "place of no escape."

Maah' shra-True'-Ee (*Almanac of the Dead*, pp. 135, 57; *Sacred Water: Narratives and Pictures*, pp. 23–24; *Yellow Woman and a Beauty of the Spirit: Essays on Native American Life Today*, pp. 95, 124, 127, 147) the "divine snake of the beautiful lake" and serpent messenger from the Fourth World to people on earth who warns of the end-time. *See also* Quetzalcoatl.

malpais (*Storyteller*, p. 216) badlands, the setting of pursuit in "A Geronimo Story."

manta (*Storyteller*, pp. 12, 15, 85; *The Delicacy and Strength of Lace*, p. 71; *Yellow Woman and a Beauty of the Spirit: Essays on Native American Life Today*, pp. 55–56; *The Turquoise Ledge*, pp. 58, 61) the traditional dress of a Hopi woman, comprised of a square yoke and straight tunic-length bodice worn with sashes and over under-dresses and buckskin leggings.

maroons (*Almanac of the Dead*, p. 428) blacks on the run from slavery who sheltered in maroon communities, free societies that protected their liberty by guerrilla warfare.

Ma'see'wi and Ou'yu'ye'wi (*Ceremony*, pp. 46, 48; *Storyteller*, pp. 86, 111, 113; *Almanac of the Dead*, p. 475; *Yellow Woman and a Beauty of the Spirit: Essays on Native American Life Today*, pp. 129–130) the war twins, Morning and Evening Star, who neglect Corn Woman's altar to watch Pa'-caya'nyi's magic tricks. In the episode of Kochininako and the Estrucuyu, the twins rescue her by beheading the giant with their flint knives. In the display of Pa'caya'nyi's power, the war twins exhibit gullibility before a false sorcerer.

**menudo** (*Ceremony*, p. 100)    a traditional Mexican soup comprised of clear of red broth containing hominy and tripe.

**Mestizo** (*Almanac of the Dead*, pp. 11, 257, 510; *Yellow Woman and a Beauty of the Spirit: Essays on Native American Life Today*, pp. 112, 119, 123, 202; *Gardens in the Dunes*, pp. 87, 137, 143–147, 175, 312; *The Turquoise Ledge*, p. 144)    mixed-blood Mexican Indians.

**metate** (*The Turquoise Ledge*, p. 176)    Nahuatl for "grinding stone or mortar."

**migra** (*Almanac of the Dead*, p. 620)    U.S. immigration agent and border patrol.

**milagros** (*Yellow Woman and a Beauty of the Spirit: Essays on Native American Life Today*, p. 133)    Spanish for "miracles."

**Mixtec** (*Yellow Woman and a Beauty of the Spirit: Essays on Native American Life Today*, p. 15)    Mesoamerican people dating to pre–Columbian times and occupying Guerrero, Oaxaca, and Puebla, Mexico.

**Monahwee** (*Yellow Woman and a Beauty of the Spirit: Essays on Native American Life Today*, p. 184)    a hostile leader who fought removal of the Muscogee from the Southeast to Oklahoma in 1834.

**mosca** (*Almanac of the Dead*, pp. 194–195)    Spanish for "housefly."

**mota** (*Almanac of the Dead*, p. 217)    Latin American term for marijuana.

**mukluk** (*Storyteller*, p. 20)    soft-soled Eskimo books made of reindeer of seal hide.

**museo** (*Yellow Woman and a Beauty of the Spirit: Essays on Native American Life Today*, p. 157)    Spanish for "museum."

**Nahuatl** (*Yellow Woman and a Beauty of the Spirit: Essays on Native American Life Today*, p. 156; *The Turquoise Ledge*, pp. 40, 138, 139, 144, 191, 197, 238, 241, 246, 258, 278)    an Aztecan language of central Mexico spoken by the Nahua and closely related to the Hopi language.

**Nau'ts'ity'i** (*Ceremony*, pp. 48–49, 255–256; *Storyteller*, p. 114; *Yellow Woman and a Beauty of the Spirit: Essays on Native American Life Today*, pp. 25, 130)    Corn Woman, the source of nurturance and goodness who punishes the war twins Ma'see'wi and Ou'yu'ye'wi (Morning Star and Evening Star)    for preferring magic to agriculture. At the end of their punishment for

disloyalty, she commands in motherly fashion, "Stay out of trouble from now on" (Silko, 1981, 121). *See also* Iktoa'ak'o'ya.

**Nayah** (*Storyteller*, p. 9; *Yellow Woman and a Beauty of the Spirit: Essays on Native American Life Today*, p. 54)    Keresan for "mother."

***Nuestra Señora de Guadalupe*** (*Yellow Woman and a Beauty of the Spirit: Essays on Native American Life Today*, p. 133; *Gardens in the Dunes*, pp. 354, 362)    a manifestation of the Virgin Mary who appeared in Mexico City on December 9, 1531.

***Ni'athu'-a-u'a'haka'nith'ii*** (*Almanac of the Dead*, p. 724)    Paiute for "Because white people are insane."

***norteño*** (*Almanac of the Dead*, p. 214)    the syncretic music of northern Mexico written for accordion and the 12-string guitar in the style of Czech and German polkas and waltzes.

**ocotillo** (*Yellow Woman and a Beauty of the Spirit: Essays on Native American Life Today*, p. 181–182)    a branchy desert shrub that blossoms after rain.

**Ogou** (*Almanac of the Dead*, pp. 413–414, 417, 419, 429–431)    Yoruban warrior deity who controls fire, iron, politics, and combat.

**Ogou Ge Rouge** (*Almanac of the Dead*, pp. 424, 430)    *See* Ge Rouge.

**Ogoun Ferraille** (*Almanac of the Dead*, p. 431)    Yoruban warrior deity in armor.

**Pa'caya'nyi** (*Ceremony*, pp. 47–49; *Storyteller*, pp. 111, 113; *Yellow Woman and a Beauty of the Spirit: Essays on Native American Life Today*, p. 128–130)    a Ck'o'yo medicine man and trickster-witch, K'yo's illegitimate son from reedleaf town. Pa'caya'nyi lures the Laguna away from devotion to Corn Woman's altar.

**pansón/pansóna** (*Almanac of the Dead*, pp. 180, 258)    Spanish slang for "fatty."

***paragua*** (*Almanac of the Dead*, p. 240)    Spanish for "lady's parasol."

***patrón*** (*Almanac of the Dead*, p. 270)    wealthy, powerful shielder of lower class people.

**Petro-Mait-Carre-Four** (*Almanac of the Dead*, p. 430)    Haitian satanic power of the *carré-four*, French for "crossroads."

**Peruvian pink flake** (*Almanac of the Dead*, p. 181)    cocaine.

**petroglyph** (*Ceremony*, p. 231; *Sacred Water: Narratives and Pictures*, p. 29; *Yellow Woman and a Beauty of the Spirit: Essays on Native American Life Today*, pp. 4, 156, 181; *The Turquoise Ledge*, pp. 129–130, 140, 141, 153, 178, 253–255, 257–258, 274, 308, 318)    a rock engraving tapped, carved, cut, or scraped into a mineral surface.

**peyote** (*Almanac of the Dead*, pp. 615, 618)    a

small cactus containing mescaline, a psychedelic used for native worship, trances, and healing.

**pictograph** (*Ceremony*, p. 101; *Yellow Woman and a Beauty of the Spirit: Essays on Native American Life Today*, p. 156; *The Turquoise Ledge*, p. 140, 317)   a picture representing a tangible object. *See also* petroglyph.

**piki** (*Ceremony*, p. 107; *Storyteller*, p. 264; *The Turquoise Ledge*, p. 19)   a blue-gray corn ground into meal on a grindstone and mixed with stove ash to make piki bread, a Hopi tortilla or crepe cooked rapidly on a sandstone griddle.

**pit house** (*Gardens in the Dunes*, p. 13)   a partially subterranean dugout lined with stone and used for food storage, ritual, and celebration of dance, song, and storytelling.

***Pues! Qué guapo!*** (*Almanac of the Dead*, p. 318)   Spanish for "Well! How gorgeous!"

**Quechua** (*The Turquoise Ledge*, p. 158)   the largest Amerindian language family, spoken largely in western South America.

**Quetzalcoatl** (*Almanac of the Dead*, pp. 136, 429, 572, 576, 735; *Yellow Woman and a Beauty of the Spirit: Essays on Native American Life Today*, p. 147; *The Turquoise Ledge*, p. 152)   an iconic Central American divinity that takes the blended form of feathered snake. Worshipped by the Aztec from 400 B.C. to A.D. 600 and a thousand years earlier by the Olmec, it represents a dualism in the acquisition of knowledge and literacy which enabled humankind to creep on the ground with the other creatures and to fly like the gods.

**quinella** (*Almanac of the Dead*, pp. 364, 366)   a type of betting in which the winner names the first and second horses across the finish line.

***ramada*** (*Almanac of the Dead*, pp. 259, 332, 633–634; *Gardens in the Dunes*, p. 205)   an arbor or trellis roofed with vines and branches to form a breezy shelter.

**Raramuri** (*The Turquoise Ledge*, p. 132)   a tribe of first peoples in Northern Mexico.

***reina de la noche*** (*The Turquoise Ledge*, p. 89)   Spanish for "queen of the night," a night-blooming cereus cactus.

***Res accident lumina rebus*** (*Almanac of the Dead*, p. 715)   Latin for "One thing will illuminate other things," an observation of the Roman scientist Lucretius.

***Res ipsa loquitur!*** (*Almanac of the Dead*, p. 714)   Latin for "The thing speaks for itself," a wise saying of the philosopher Cicero.

***Res judicata*** (*Almanac of the Dead*, p. 715)   the legal term for a matter already decided in court.

***roja*** (*Almanac of the Dead*, p. 557)   Spanish for "red."

***Rosa, Rosita, Rosaura*** (*Gardens in the Dunes*, p. 362)   Spanish for "rose, rosebud, rosie," a symbol on fortune-telling cards.

***sala*** (*Almanac of the Dead*, p. 550)   Spanish for "parlor or sitting room."

***sangre limpia*** (*Almanac of the Dead*, pp. 259, 534)   Spanish for "pure blood," an obsession of Spanish nobility.

***sangre pura*** (*Almanac of the Dead*, pp. 534, 535, 541–542, 549, 554, 556)   *See sangre limpia.*

**screenfold** *Yellow Woman and a Beauty of the Spirit: Essays on Native American Life Today*, pp. 156–158)   a picture book from ancient southern Mexico meant to be read as a mural.

**Sendero** (*Almanac of the Dead*, p. 316)   *See* Shining Path.

**Shalako** (*The Turquoise Ledge*, p. 152)   a Zuni harvest ceremony marked by dancing celebrating the harvest.

**Shining Path** (*Almanac of the Dead*, p. 316)   the Maoist party of Peru.

**Shiwana** (*Yellow Woman and a Beauty of the Spirit: Essays on Native American Life Today*, p. 29; *The Turquoise Ledge*, p. 13)   the rain clouds, children of the sun and restorers of life on earth.

**si'ahh aash'** (*Laguna Woman*, p. 19)   a male who seeks casual sex with married women.

**si'ash** (*Yellow Woman and a Beauty of the Spirit: Essays on Native American Life Today*, p. 67)   the Keres term for a lover.

**Simbi** (*Almanac of the Dead*, p. 422)   Congolese serpent spirit.

***sin semilla*** (*Almanac of the Dead*, p. 233)   Spanish for "without seeds," a powerful marijuana harvested in the bud stage.

**Spañada** (*Laguna Woman*, p. 3)   a brand of sangria, a Spanish red wine.

**Spiderwoman** (*Ceremony*, pp. 173, 175; *Storyteller*, pp. 70, 141, 165; *Yellow Woman and a Beauty of the Spirit: Essays on Native American Life Today*, p. 30; *The Turquoise Ledge*, p. 19)   a benevolent grandmother and defeater of the tricksters Coyote and the gambler Kaup'a'ta. *See* Ts'its't-si'nako.

**Squaw Man** (*Storyteller*, p. 16)   slang pejorative for a white man married to an Indian woman.

**Star Beings** (*The Turquoise Ledge*, pp. 129–133, 135–137, 140, 149, 183, 207, 209, 229, 308–309, 315, 317)   Amerindian sky deities who impregnated human women with Star Children and who visit earth at 600 year intervals. Native artists symbolize the Star Begins as white crosses.

**Stro'ro'ka** (*Storyteller*, pp. 229–234)   masked dancers who mime Coyote stories.

**stsamaku** (*Storyteller*, p. 13)   Keresan for "my daughter."

*Tengo los dientes* (*Almanac of the Dead*, p. 605) Spanish for "I have teeth."

*tlacuilos* (*Yellow Woman and a Beauty of the Spirit: Essays on Native American Life Today*, p. 156) Nahuatl term for "painter-scribe," the creator of ancient Mesoamerican screenfolk books.

Tlahuizcalpantecuhtli (*The Turquoise Ledge*, p. 229) Aztec god of Venus, the morning star.

Tlaloc (*The Turquoise Ledge*, pp. 133, 135, 144–145, 160, 175, 183, 197, 260) an Aztec god of fertility, water, and rain propitiated by dancers coated in blue-green body paint.

Tlalocan (*The Turquoise Ledge*, p. 197) the Nahua concept of the upper level of heaven.

*tlantli* (*Yellow Woman and a Beauty of the Spirit: Essays on Native American Life Today*, p. 156) Nahuatl for "tooth rooted in place."

Toe'osh (*Laguna Woman*, pp. 3, 5) the Laguna name for Coyote, a pervasive trickster in native fable.

toloache (*Almanac of the Dead*, p. 488) toxic moonflower or datura.

toot (*Almanac of the Dead*, p. 205) a single dose or "snort" of powdery cocaine.

tribal police (*Storyteller*, p. 56) non-hereditary reservation peace officers.

Ts'eh (*Ceremony*, p. 223) the Navajo word for rock.

Ts'its'tsi'nako (*Ceremony*, p. 1; *Yellow Woman and a Beauty of the Spirit: Essays on Native American Life Today*, pp. 50, 64, 125, 204) the Laguna spider deity Thought Woman, who inspires Silko's short story "Lullaby" and her telling of *Ceremony*. See also Spiderwoman.

Tucson (*Almanac of the Dead*, p. 190) the Papago word for "fresh water."

*turpis causa* (*Almanac of the Dead*, p. 715) the legal term for "shameful case."

*Uhi'yeye'heye'* (*Almanac of the Dead*, pp. 724–725) an untranslatable Paiute exclamation.

wacah (*Almanac of the Dead*, pp. 339, 468, 472, 476) Spanish for "macaw."

Xiutecuhtli (*The Turquoise Ledge*, p. 152) an Aztec god of fire and volcanoes.

Xolotl (*Almanac of the Dead*, p. 572) Mayan god of lightning, fire, ill fortune, and death.

yash'ka (*Storyteller*, p. 88) Keresan for "heart" and the name of a landmark between Laguna and Paguate.

yashtoah (*Storyteller*, pp. 8, 11–13, 15; *The Delicacy and Strength of Lace*, pp. 70–71; *Yellow Woman and a Beauty of the Spirit: Essays on Native American Life Today* pp. 54–57) the curled upper crust on corn meal mush

Yeibechei (*Storyteller*, p.43) Navajo holy people or spirits of natural forces and sacred sites.

*Yo volveré* (*Ceremony*, pp. 6, 97) a scrap of a love ballad meaning "I will return" that haunts Tayo's nightmares.

yucca (*Storyteller*, pp. 13, 34) fibrous desert plant used for cordage and yarn for weaving bags and sandals and its juice for shampoo.

Yupik(*Storyteller*, pp. 18, 30, 31; *Almanac of the Dead*, pp. 151, 154–155) language of Central Alaskan aborigines, also called Yupik.

zah-zee hadti (*The Turquoise Ledge*, p. 41) Laguna for "there's no more."

## • *Sources*

Cutter, Martha J. *Lost in Translation: Contemporary Ethnic American Writing and the Politics of Language Diversity.* Chapel Hill: University of North Carolina Press, 2005.

Mitchell, Carol. "'Ceremony' as Ritual," *American Indian Quarterly* 5:1 (February 1979): 27–35.

Hoil, Juan José, and Ralph Loveland Roys. *The Book of Chilam Balam of Chumayel.* Washington, D.C.: Carnegie Institution, 1933.

Olmstead, Jane. "The Uses of Blood in Leslie Marmon Silko's *Almanac of the Dead*," *Contemporary Literature* 40:3 (Fall 1999): 464–490.

Silko, Leslie Marmon. *Storyteller.* New York: Seaver Books, 1981.

# Appendix A:
# Events in Silko's History

**32,000 B.C.** Lake Bonneville, a pluvial lake, takes shape in the North American Great Basin at Utah. (*The Turquoise Ledge*, p. 17)

**28,000 B.C.** The Laguna date their arrival in North America in a story about sea turtles swimming from China to the Pacific Coast. ("Prayer to the Pacific," 1972)

**18,000 B.C.** Humans called "San José man" settle on the San José River, raise beans and corn, and domesticate turkeys. (*Laguna Woman*, pp. 44–45; *Yellow Woman and a Beauty of the Spirit: Essays on Native American Life Today*, p. 185; *The Turquoise Ledge*, p. 17)

Paleo-Indians of the pueblos carve petroglyphs on rock outcroppings along the river and in kivas. ("The Indian with a Camera," p. 4)

**16,800 B.C.** The drying of Lake Bonneville left behind Utah's Great Salt Lake. (*The Turquoise Ledge*, p. 17)

**11,000 B.C.** Folsom man leaves spear points as evidence of his residency near Folsom, New Mexico. (*The Turquoise Ledge*, p. 17)

**10,500 B.C.** Volcanic action in Arizona leaves evidence of an explosion in black basalt, ash, and tufa. (*Yellow Woman and a Beauty of the Spirit: Essays on Native American Life Today*, pp. 187–188)

**900 B.C.** Maya build a temple at Tampico, Mexico. (*Gardens in the Dunes*, p. 87)

**400 B.C.** The Aztec begin a thousand years of worship of Quetzalcoatl, the feathered serpent and bringer of knowledge. (*Almanac of the Dead*, p. 136)

**200 B.C.–A.D. 750** During the classical period of the Mexican city of Teotihuacan, merchants bring macaws and feathers to Arizona and New Mexico to trade for turquoise. (*The Turquoise Ledge*, p. 151).

**ca. A.D. 30** Mary Magdalene serves Jesus as a disciple. (*Gardens of the Dunes*, pp. 77, 94–95, 99, 101, 220, 261)

Simon of Cyrene helps Jesus carry his cross and takes his place at the execution site. (*Gardens of the Dunes*, pp. 97, 100)

Simon Magus of Samaria claims to possess Jesus' magical powers of healing. (*Gardens of the Dunes*, p. 97)

**ca. 100** An Asian heretic, Cerinthus, denies Jesus' divinity. (*Gardens in the Dunes*, p. 97)

The Ophites of Egypt and Syria revere knowledge over faith. (*Gardens in the Dunes*, p. 99)

**ca. A.D. 117** Basilides refutes the Gospel details of Jesus' crucifixion. (*Gardens in the Dunes*, p. 97)

**ca. A.D. 150** Valentinus, a gnostic philosophy from Egypt, outlines the layers of heaven. (*Gardens in the Dunes*, pp. 93, 98–99)

Carpocrates of Alexandria denies Jesus' divinity. (*Gardens in the Dunes*, p. 97)

Marcion of Sinope organizes a separate Christian church. (*Gardens in the Dunes*, pp. 99, 175)

**ca. 325** Eusebius issues *Church History*. (*Gardens in the Dunes*, p. 118)

**385** The Roman emperor Maximus condemns the heretic Priscillian to beheading. (*Gardens in the Dunes*, pp. 97–98)

**ca. 500** The historical King Arthur assembles knights around a round table. (*Gardens in the Dunes*, pp. 246, 249)

**ca. 520** St. Columba orders the protection of a sacred grove at Derry, Ireland. (*Gardens in the Dunes*, p. 261)

**658** Church leaders at the Council of Nantes order bishops to hide stones venerated by pagans. (*Gardens in the Dunes*, p. 261)

**850** Chaco Canyon becomes a trade nexus at Four Corners. (*The Turquoise Ledge*, p. 17)

**1000** Native miners excavate turquoise from Mount Chalchihuitl, New Mexico. (*The Turquoise Ledge*, p. 191)

**March 1095** The First Crusade introduces a period of revenge killings of Muslims that continues until 1291. (*Gardens in the Dunes*, p. 98)

**1100** Residents of Chaco Canyon thrive in clusters of apartment buildings. (*Yellow Woman and a Beauty of the Spirit: Essays on Native American Life Today*, p. 30)

**1200s** The Navajo flourish in the Southwest along with the Apache. ("Slim Man Canyon," *Laguna Woman*, p. 19)

The Anasazi build stone villages at Mesa Verde, Colorado. (*The Turquoise Ledge*, pp. 17, 20)

**1441** The Portuguese initiate the European trade in African slaves. (*Almanac of the Dead*, pp. 419–420)

**November 1, 1478** The Spanish Inquisition legitimates subsequent cruelties perpetrated by *conquistadores* against Amerindians. (*Yellow Woman and a Beauty of the Spirit: Essays on Native American Life Today*, p. 147)

**October 12, 1492** The arrival of Spanish ships to the New World initiates war against first peoples. (*Almanac of the Dead*, pp. 133, 220; *Yellow Woman and a Beauty of the Spirit: Essays on Native American Life Today*, p. 185)

**ca. 1500** The Peruvian Inca mummify their dead. (*Almanac of the Dead*, p. 64)

**1502** Bartolomé de las Casas journeys to Hispaniola and observes Spanish genocide of the Taíno. (*Almanac of the Dead*, p. 314)

**April 7, 1504** A Mayan almanac predicts the arrival of Hernán de Cortés in Santo Domingo, Hispaniola. (*Almanac of the Dead*, p. 570; *Yellow Woman and a Beauty of the Spirit: Essays on Native American Life Today*, pp. 137, 146)

**February 2, 1512** On Hispaniola, Spanish invaders burn alive Hatuey, a Taíno cacique. (*Almanac of the Dead*, pp. 314, 315)

**November 8, 1519** Hernán de Cortés first encounters Aztec cacique Montezuma II. (*Almanac of the Dead*, p. 570)

**1520** Beginning in 1520, Europeans kill 70 million Amerindians over the next decade. (*Yellow Woman and a Beauty of the Spirit: Essays on Native American Life Today*, pp. 147, 185)

Because the Maya and Mixtec offer blood gifts to screenfold books, Spanish missionaries and colonial authorities begin burning Mesoamerican libraries. (*Yellow Woman and a Beauty of the Spirit: Essays on Native American Life Today*, p. 157)

**September 1524** Spain finances the voyage of Portuguese explorer Estevan Gomez to North America. (*Almanac of the Dead*, p. 237)

**Early 1527** Cabeza de Vaca sets out from Spain to explore the Caribbean and Mexico. (*Almanac of the Dead*, p. 237)

**December 21, 1529** Nuño Beltrán de Guzmán, a Spanish *conquistador* and colonial governor of New Spain, begins a systematic extermination of the Yaqui. (*Almanac of the Dead*, pp. 216, 234; *Yellow Woman and a Beauty of the Spirit: Essays on Native American Life Today*, pp. 139, 147)

**December 9, 1531** A version of the Virgin Mary appears in Mexico City. (*Yellow Woman and a Beauty of the Spirit: Essays on Native American Life Today*, p. 133)

**1540** The Spanish march into Laguna. (*Yellow Woman and a Beauty of the Spirit: Essays on Native American Life Today*, p. 103; *Gardens in the Dunes*, p. 15)

**1540s** Coronado mounts an expedition across the Southwest and encounters hail in Texas. (*Almanac of the Dead*, pp. 31, 46, 237; *Yellow Woman and a Beauty of the Spirit: Essays on Native American Life Today*, p. 31)

To obliterate the past, Spanish bishop of Yucatán Diego de Landa Calderón burns Indian libraries. (*Almanac of the Dead*, p. 315; *Yellow Woman and a Beauty of the Spirit: Essays on Native American Life Today*, pp. 21, 136, 165; "Bingo Big," p. 856)

The absence of a national literature enables Europeans to convince the Roman Catholic Pope Paul III that Indians are subhuman. (*Yellow Woman and a Beauty of the Spirit: Essays on Native American Life Today*, p. 21) ca. 1550   England enters the triangular slave trade. (*Gardens of the Dunes*, p. 231)

1560   Mexico and Peru suffer an influenza epidemic. (*Almanac of the Dead*, p. 577)

May 1566   An earthquake strikes the Maya of Yucatan. (*Almanac of the Dead*, p. 577)

January 3, 1590   An epidemic of whooping cough strikes the Maya of Yucatan. (*Almanac of the Dead*, p. 577)

Late October 1598   Conquistador Don Juan de Oñate attacks San Juan Pueblo and reduces the population from 2,000 to 250 by firing cannon at the Indians. (*Ceremony*, p. 136)

As a punishment for Acoma males, the Spanish lop off one hand and one foot of every captured male over the age of seven. (*The Turquoise Ledge*, p. 20)

1620   Indians own nearly two billion acres of land when the pilgrims arrive. ("Auntie Kie," p. 28; *Yellow Woman and a Beauty of the Spirit: Essays on Native American Life Today*, p. 81)

August 10–21, 1692   Popé's Rebellion drives Spanish colonizers from New Mexico. (*The Turquoise Ledge*, p. 21)

March 2, 1699   Black Indians initiate Mardi Gras celebrations in New Orleans. (*Almanac of the Dead*, p. 420)

1700–1780   The Catholic Church participates in the slave trade in New Mexico by baptizing 800 abducted Apache children and placing them in Spanish homes as servants. (*The Turquoise Ledge*, p. 34)

1750   Escaped African maroons intermarry with the Carib Indians of St. Vincent, producing Black Indians. (*Almanac of the Dead*, p. 410)

1760   Koromantin blacks from the Gold Coast launch a revolt in St. Mary's, Jamaica. (*Almanac of the Dead*, p. 425)

1776   Cubero, New Mexico, becomes a Mexican military post and thriving slave market. (*The Turquoise Ledge*, pp. 33–35)

August 22, 1791   Boukman, a Jamaican priest, inspires the resistance movement of Biassou and Jean François that precedes the Haitian Revolution. (*Almanac of the Dead*, pp. 418, 428)

January 3, 1801   Toussaint L'Ouverture invades Santo Domingo and frees slaves. (*Almanac of the Dead*, pp. 428–429)

1806   Noah Webster attempts to standard pronunciation, spelling, and usage with *A Compendious Dictionary of the English Language*. (*Yellow Woman and a Beauty of the Spirit: Essays on Native American Life Today*, p. 173)

May 3, 1814   Napoleon begins his exile at Elba. (*Gardens of the Dunes*, pp. 308–309)

1823   Restorers of Tampico, Mexico, use the stones of a Mayan temple to lay the foundation of the Cathedral of the Immaculate Conception. (*Gardens in the Dunes*, p. 87)

1832   Andrew Jackson defies the decision of U.S. Supreme Court Chief Justice John Marshall that the Georgia government exile Cherokees from the state on the Trail of Tears. ("Auntie Kie," p. 30; *Almanac of the Dead*, p. 415; *Yellow Woman and a Beauty of the Spirit: Essays on Native American Life Today*, pp. 83, 199; *The Turquoise Ledge*, p. 59)

1840s   White assimilators of first peoples institute the Canadian Industrial School for Indians. (*Yellow Woman and a Beauty of the Spirit: Essays on Native American Life Today*, p. 182)

1845   Philosopher Margaret Fuller publishes *Woman in the Nineteenth Century*. (*Gardens in the Dunes*, pp. 101–102)

1846   The Irish Potato Famine initiates emigration that continues until 1852. (*Gardens in the Dunes*, p. 252)

The U.S. seizure of New Mexico Territory does not halt the Indian slave trade. (*The Turquoise Ledge*, p. 34)

February 2, 1848   According to the Treaty of Guadalupe Hidalgo, the peace accord that ends the Mexican-American War, the United States guarantees citizenship and property rights of the 80,000 Mexicans in Arizona, California, New Mexico, and Texas. (*Almanac of the Dead*, pp. 213, 236–237, 643; *Yellow Woman and a Beauty of the Spirit: Essays on Native American Life Today*, p. 160)

1849   Indians flee gold prospectors and enter imprisonment at Fort Yuma, Arizona. (*Gardens of the Dunes*, p. 16)

ca. September 1856   Apache raiders stalk and kill two herders in Swahnee southeast of Laguna Pueblo and rustle the sheep. (*Yellow Woman and a Beauty of the Spirit: Essays on Native American Life Today*, p. 34)

March 6, 1858   Mexican troops murder Geronimo's wife Alope, his mother Juana, and his three children. (*Almanac of the Dead*, p. 39)

1860   Psychophysicist Gustav Fechner publishes his belief that plants share human emotions. (*Gardens in the Dunes*, p. 240)

**1861**   Mexicans slay Geronimo's second wife, Nana-tha-thtith, and their child. (*Almanac of the Dead*, p. 39)

July At the formal proclamation of Arizona Territory, citizensally politically with pro–South factions in New Mexico. (*Gardens in the Dunes*, p. 405)

**May 5, 1862**   Mexicans defeat the French forces of Napoleon III at Puebla, Mexico. (*Almanac of the Dead*, p. 488)

**July 8, 1862**   The Morrill Anti-bigamy Act criminalizes polygamy. (*Gardens in the Dunes*, p. 38)

**July 15, 1862**   Geronimo joins Cochise, Mangas Coloradas, and Jute to ambush the only source of water at Apache Pass, Arizona. (*Almanac of the Dead*, p. 227; *Yellow Woman and a Beauty of the Spirit: Essays on Native American Life Today*, p. 139)

**January 1, 1863**   President Abraham Lincoln's Emancipation Proclamation begins the freeing of slaves. (*The Turquoise Ledge*, p. 32)

**April 10, 1864**   Maximilian I of Austria and Charlotte of Belgium begin their three-year rule of Mexico. (*Almanac of the Dead*, pp. 215, 281)

**1865**   Confederate general John Bankhead Mc-Gruder superintends the settlement of secessionists in northeastern Mexico. (*Almanac of the Dead*, p. 488)

**June 14, 1866**   Prussia invades Bohemia, thus launching the Austro-Prussian War. (*Almanac of the Dead*, p. 488)

**August 8, 1866**   Charlotte, the Empress of Mexico, travels to Paris to beg the Empress Eugénie to help save the empire. (*Almanac of the Dead*, p. 488)

**August 26, 1866**   Colonel Charles "Chuck" Goodnight and Oliver Loving establish the Goodnight-Loving Trail from Fort Belknap, Texas, to Denver, Colorado. (*Yellow Woman and a Beauty of the Spirit: Essays on Native American Life Today*, p. 159)

**September 27, 1862**   Charlotte visits the Vatican to beg Pope Pius IX to help Mexico. (*Almanac of the Dead*, p. 489)

**1867**   Karl Marx publishes *Das Kapital*. (*Almanac of the Dead*, p. 311)

**May 15, 1867**   The fall of Mexico City to Republicans precipitates a court martial and the execution of Maximilian on June 9. (*Almanac of the Dead*, p. 215)

**1868**   Mexicans massacre 150 Yaqui. ("The People and the Land ARE Inseparable," p. 110; *Almanac of the Dead*, p. 190; *Yellow Woman and a Beauty of the Spirit: Essays on Native American Life Today*, p. 87)

**1869**   In collaboration with his egalitarian wife, Harriet Taylor Miller, John Stuart Mill, a progressive English philosopher, champions female liberation in *The Subjection of Women*. (*Gardens in the Dunes*, pp. 74, 93)

**1871**   Only 140 million acres of land remain in Indian hands. ("Auntie Kie," p. 28; *Yellow Woman and a Beauty of the Spirit: Essays on Native American Life Today*, p. 81)

Citrus growers plant the first orange trees in Riverside, California. (*Gardens in the Dunes*, pp. 69–70, 90)

**January 6, 1871**   A post office establishes the town of Parker, Arizona, an Indian reservation on the Colorado River. (*Gardens in the Dunes*, p. 18)

**April 10, 1871**   P. T. Barnum initiates a traveling circus aboard the Pennsylvania Railroad. (*Gardens in the Dunes*, p. 154)

**1870s**   Paiute Indian schools open at Pyramid Lake and Walker River reservations. (*Gardens in the Dunes*, p. 21)

**1874**   Resettlement of the Walapai to La Paz, Arizona, results in heavy mortality and a threat to the tribe's survival. (*Gardens in the Dunes*, pp. 18, 21, 29, 57, 63)

**June 8, 1874**   Before his death, Cochise reminds the Apache that the white world will collapse. (*Almanac of the Dead*, p. 235)

**1875**   Prospectors locate copper at the Gila Monster Mine in Maricopa County, Arizona. (*The Turquoise Ledge*, pp. 11, 149–150, 160, 231, 233–234, 269, 294–295, 314, 316)

**1876**   In 1876, John Warne Gates introduces barbed wire in Antonio, Texas, the beginning of the end for independent foraging rights. (*Yellow Woman and a Beauty of the Spirit: Essays on Native American Life Today*, p. 159)

Henry Wickham steals 70,000 rubber tree seeds from Brazil. (*Gardens in the Dunes*, p. 129)

**November 1, 1878**   Captain Richard H. Pratt begins the white eradication of Indian nativism by opening an Indian acculturation school in Carlisle, Pennsylvania. (*Storyteller*, p. 6; *Almanac of the Dead*, p. 234; *Yellow Woman and a Beauty of the Spirit: Essays on Native American Life Today*, pp.

60–61, 159–160; *Gardens in the Dunes*, p. 168; *The Turquoise Ledge*, p. 28)

**1881**    Marion Bergess publishes *Stiya, the Story of an Indian Girl*, a propaganda fiction for the U.S. War Department. (*Yellow Woman and a Beauty of the Spirit: Essays on Native American Life Today*, p. 162)

Mary Baker Eddy founds Massachusetts Metaphysical College at Boston. (*Gardens in the Dunes*, p. 101)

**1882**    General George Crook takes command of the cavalry hunt for Geronimo. (*Almanac of the Dead*, pp. 225–226)

The Cunard line adds to its fleet the S. S. *Pavonia*. (*Gardens in the Dunes*, p. 197)

**Spring 1882**    Nana, leader of Apache raiders, shoots José Domingo Gallegos, a Navajo ranch hand, and kidnaps his wife, Plácida Romero Gallegos, their daughter, and a nephew. (*The Turquoise Ledge*, p. 33)

**1884**    Except on federal parkland at Yellowstone, the buffalo, numbering 1,200 to 2,000, near annihilation. (*Yellow Woman and a Beauty of the Spirit: Essays on Native American Life Today*, p. 147)

**1885**    New Orleans hosts the World's Industrial and Cotton Centennial Exposition. (*Gardens in the Dunes*, p. 92)

**September 3, 1886**    General Nelson Appleton Miles takes custody of Geronimo, who surrenders at Skeleton Canyon in southeastern Arizona, and ships him by boxcar to Fort Marion, Florida. (*Almanac of the Dead*, pp. 74–75, 129, 220–221, 230–232, 234)

**January 1, 1889**    Wovoka, a Paiute holy man, experiences a vision of the return of Amerindian dead to life. (*Almanac of the Dead*, p. 721; *Gardens in the Dunes*, pp. 13–14, 22–24, 124–125, 196–197, 220, 262)

**April 22, 1889**    The Oklahoma Land Rush threatens Indian families, forcing the Wagon People to drive to Casa Grandes, Mexico, in search of a place open to Cherokee settlers. (*Storyteller*, p. 52)

**1890s**    The U.S. government begins forcible transfer of Pueblo students to East Coast boarding schools as a form of cultural erasure. ("The Indian with a Camera," p. 7; *Yellow Woman and a Beauty of the Spirit: Essays on Native American Life Today*, pp. 161–162; *Gardens in the Dunes*, p. 49)

**1891**    The United States Industrial Indian School opens at Phoenix. (*Gardens in the Dunes*, p. 63)

**December 29, 1891**    The Ghost Dance comes to an end after U.S. cavalry massacres Sioux at Wounded Knee, South Dakota. (*Gardens in the Dunes*, p. 262)

**May 5, 1893**    A panic on Wall Street initiates an economic depression. (*Gardens in the Dunes*, pp. 129, 387)

**October 21, 1893**    Clark Stanley kills rattlesnakes and produces snake oil medicine at the Chicago World Exposition. (*The Turquoise Ledge*, p. 82)

**October 4, 1894**    The U.S. army moves Geronimo from Florida to Fort Sill, Oklahoma. (*Almanac of the Dead*, p. 88)

**1896**    The Ethiopian army fears Italians will invade Eritrea at Aduwa. (*Gardens in the Dunes*, p. 326)

**January 4, 1896**    Utah achieves statehood. (*Gardens in the Dunes*, p. 205)

**1897**    A fire destroys the depot at Needles, California. (*Gardens in the Dunes*, pp. 384–386)

**August 12, 1898**    The end of the Spanish-American War concludes the 1893 depression with an economic recovery. (*Gardens in the Dunes*, p. 162)

**1900**    Slavehunting of Navajo people ends in territorial New Mexico. (*Storyteller*, p. 89)

The Hopi, Zuñi, and the Pueblo at Acoma and Laguna experience a drought. (*Yellow Woman and a Beauty of the Spirit: Essays on Native American Life Today*, p. 30)

**July 29, 1900**    Anarchists murder Italy's King Umberto I. (*Gardens of the Dunes*, p. 326)

**Early 1900s**    White ranchers from Texas take possession of a canyon above Encinal, New Mexico. (*Ceremony*, p. 185)

**September 5, 1902**    Some 600 Mexican *federales* capture 400 Yaqui returning from exile and murder them at Hermosillo. (*Almanac of the Dead*, pp. 216, 233–234)

**1904**    At the World's Fair in St. Louis, Missouri, attendees gawk at Geronimo, then 75 years old. (*Ceremony*, p. 122)

U.S. courts partition 200,000 acres of the Cebolleta Land Grant, leaving only 20,000 acres to the people. (*Ceremony*, p. 127; *The Turquoise Ledge*, p. 26)

**January 1905**    President-elect Theodore Roosevelt invites Geronimo, Red Cloud, Quanah Parker, and chiefs of the Blackfoot, Sioux, and Ute to ride in the inaugural parade. ("Auntie Kie," 30; *Almanac of the Dead*, p. 40; *Yellow Woman and a*

*Beauty of the Spirit: Essays on Native American Life Today*, p. 83)

**February 1, 1905**   The Department of Agriculture superintends the use of 21 million acres of the Cibola National Forest above Encinal, New Mexico, for lumbering, mining, forage, and ranching. Hunters shoot the deer and wild turkeys to feed loggers and sport shooters kill bears and mountain lions. (*Ceremony*, p. 203)

**1906**   Taos Pueblo begins a 67-year fight to recover the sacred Blue Lake, which the U.S. Government claims as part of Taos National Forest. (*Yellow Woman and a Beauty of the Spirit: Essays on Native American Life Today*, p. 43)

**1908**   During the archeological excavation of Enchanted Mesa (Katsi'ma), Henry C. "Hank" Marmon drives workers from the Smithsonian Institution to the dig. (*Storyteller*, p. 198)

**February 14, 1914**   Arizona gains statehood. (*The Turquoise Ledge*, p. 251)

**July 14, 1914**   World War I begins in Europe. (*Almanac of the Dead*, p. 32)

**August 1914**   The French introduce gas grenades to warfare during the first world war. (*Almanac of the Dead*, p. 351)

The legislature in Santa Fe struggles to cope with famine among Indians. (*Almanac of the Dead*, p. 32)

**1917–1918**   Ethnographer and linguist Franz Boas and his pupil, Elsie Clews Parsons, collect Laguna texts as sources of a Keresan grammar. (*Storyteller*, p. 254, *The Turquoise Ledge*, pp. 50–51)

According to Silko, a train robbery occurs in Grants, New Mexico. (*The Delicacy and Strength of Lace*, p. 27)

**1919**   Fearing that the Pueblo are a dying culture, ethnographer Franz Boas begins a two-year project collecting Keresan texts, which the American Ethnological Society publishes in 1928. ("'Not You,' He Said," p. 210; *Storyteller*, p. 38)

**November 1919**   Marcus Garvey begins the Back to Africa movement. (*Almanac of the Dead*, p. 414)

**1920s**   Laguna suffers a drought, when cows eat cactus pulp. Loggers strip canyons of timber and shoot bears and puma for sport. (*Ceremony*, pp. 10, 186)

**October 29, 1929**   The "Crash" begins the Great Depression. (*Almanac of the Dead*, p. 40)

**1930s**   The Dust Bowl engulfs the Southwest in drought that forces herders to sell their livestock to opportunists in Albuquerque and Gallup. (*Ceremony*, p. 74)

**January 22, 1934**   After a fire in the Hotel Congress, firemen identify John Dillinger and his gang for the police. (*Almanac of the Dead*, pp. 29, 39, 76–78)

**March 3, 1934**   John Dillinger escapes from the "escape-proof" Lake County Jail in Terre Haute, Indiana. (*Almanac of the Dead*, p. 78; *Yellow Woman and a Beauty of the Spirit: Essays on Native American Life Today*, p. 139)

**July 22, 1934**   The FBI shoots John Dillinger at the Biograph Theater in Chicago. (*Almanac of the Dead*, p. 78)

**1939**   Anthropologist Carleton Stevens Coon publishes a theory of the superiority of European races in *The Races of Europe, the White Race and the New World*. (*Yellow Woman and a Beauty of the Spirit: Essays on Native American Life Today*, p. 102)

**September 1940**   Rocky and Tayo enlist during the U.S. military buildup that precedes the American entrance into world war. (*Ceremony*, pp. 64–65)

**1941**   Hitler begins the mass extermination of European Jews. (*Almanac of the Dead*, pp. 406, 495)

The Indian Reorganization Act forces Indian communities to adopt a tribal council form of government. (*Yellow Woman and a Beauty of the Spirit: Essays on Native American Life Today*, p. 93)

**December 7, 1941**   Japanese pilots bomb Pearl Harbor and Wake Island. During the war, Leland "Lee" Marmon learns photography.(*Ceremony*, p. 18, *Storyteller*, p. 1)

**Weeks later**   Emo, Harley, and Leroy ship out from Oakland, California, to Wake Island. (*Ceremony*, pp. 41, 43, 120, 163, 165)

**December 23, 1941**   The Battle of Wake Island ends with an American surrender. (*Ceremony*, pp. 20, 40, 259)

**February 19, 1942**   The U.S. government ships 110,000 Japanese-Americans and Japanese from the Pacific coast to internment camps in Arizona, Arkansas, California, Colorado, Idaho, Utah, and Wyoming. (*Ceremony*, pp. 17, 190)

**April 9–21, 1942**   Rocky dies on the 60-mile Bataan Death March, perhaps from the thrust of a Japanese gun butt into his moribund body. During the march, Tayo senses Uncle Josiah's presence. (*Ceremony*, pp. 28, 30, 44, 102)

**Late April 1942**   At the end of the march, Tayo suffers fever in a prisoner of war camp at San Fernando. (*Ceremony*, p. 44)

**November 1942**   The U.S. government chooses Los Alamos as the test site for the atomic bomb and pays Indians $5,000 for the land. (*Ceremony*, pp. 37, 246)

**Spring 1943**   The mine on the Cebolleta Land Grant floods with underground spring water. (*Ceremony*, pp. 243–244)

**Late Summer 1943**   A second flood overwhelms the mine. (*Ceremony*, p. 244)

**June 6, 1944**   Allies invade German-occupied France near the Douve River at Normandy, France, where total casualties reach 4,200. (*Ceremony*, p. 161)

**December 18, 1944**   The U.S. Supreme Court declares Japanese internment legal, but, under *Ex parte Endo*, frees internees. (*Ceremony*, pp. 17, 190)

**February 19–March 26, 1945**   Combat on Iwo Jima shellshocks Tayo. (*Ceremony*, pp. 8, 259)

**July 16, 1945**   Grandma observes the A-bomb at the Trinity Site at Los Alamos. (*Ceremony*, pp. 245–246)

**August 1945**   The mining company stops guarding the diggings at the Cebolleto Land Grant. (*Ceremony*, p. 244)

**August 6, 1945**   An American plane drops an A-bomb on Hiroshima, Japan, killing over 140,000 civilians. (*Ceremony*, pp. 169, 246; *Almanac of the Dead*, pp. 424, 515, 628, 718; *The Turquoise Ledge*, pp. 70–71)

**August 8, 1945**   A second A-bomb destroys Nagasaki, killing 40,000 and maiming another 40,000. (*Ceremony*, pp. 169, 246; *Almanac of the Dead*, p. 515; *The Turquoise Ledge*, pp. 70–71)

**September 4, 1945**   Japanese holding Wake Island surrender to American Marines. (*Ceremony*, p. 20)

**September 14, 1945**   Japanese soldiers surrender on Wake Island. (*Ceremony*, p. 259)

**February–April 1948**   Wind blows sand during the drought at Laguna. (*Ceremony*, p. 11)

**1949**   A uranium discovery in Cibola County draws entrepreneurial attention to Paguate, New Mexico, as a source of atomic weaponry for the Cold War. (*Almanac of the Dead*, p. 34)

A black retarded killer strangles a white librarian in Washington, D.C. (*Yellow Woman and a Beauty of the Spirit: Essays on Native American Life Today*, pp. 20, 127)

**July 18, 1949**   Anthropologist Ashley Montagu reports to the UNESCO inquiry into race that the term itself has no validity. (*Yellow Woman and a Beauty of the Spirit: Essays on Native American Life Today*, pp. 101–102)

**1952**   The Anaconda Copper Mine begins removing uranium ore from 7,000 acres of Laguna property. (*Ceremony*, p. 245; *Almanac of the Dead*, pp. 758–759, 762; *Yellow Woman and a Beauty of the Spirit: Essays on Native American Life Today*, pp. 43–44, 95, 128; *The Turquoise Ledge*, p. 69)

**July 26, 1953**   Fidel Castro leads the Cuban underground against Cuban dictator Fulgencio Batista. (*Almanac of the Dead*, p. 315)

**1954**   The Laguna hire a lawyer to press suit against the state of New Mexico for stealing six million acres of Indian land. (*Yellow Woman and a Beauty of the Spirit: Essays on Native American Life Today*, p. 18; *The Turquoise Ledge*, p. 26)

**Early 1960s**   The Anaconda company proposes removing Indians from Paguate village to unearth rich uranium ores. (*The Turquoise Ledge*, p. 72)

**November 22, 1961**   A conspiracy theory connects J. Edgar Hoover with the assassination of John F. Kennedy. (*Almanac of the Dead*, p. 405)

**Fall 1962**   At Fairbanks, Alaska, Eskimo editor Howard Rock founds the *Tundra Times*, reaching a circulation of 5,000 in the first decade. (*The Delicacy and Strength of Lace*, pp. 29–30)

**April 4, 1963**   A subsequent conspiracy theory connects J. Edgar Hoover with the assassination of Martin Luther King, Jr. (*Almanac of the Dead*, pp. 405, 408)

**November 24, 1963**   President Lyndon B. Johnson expands the Vietnam War. (*Almanac of the Dead*, p. 407)

**1964**   Polingasi Qoyawayma publishes *No Turning Back*, a memoir of life at a government boarding school. (*Yellow Woman and a Beauty of the Spirit: Essays on Native American Life Today*, p. 163)

**1967**   A federal court judgment awards the Laguna $.25 per acre for stolen land worth $100 per acre. (*The Turquoise Ledge*, p. 26)

**January 21, 1968**   The ten-week Battle of Khesanh begins in Vietnam. (*Almanac of the Dead*, p. 449)

**March 16, 1968**   An army unit tortures and murders some 500 unarmed Vietnamese civilians. (*Almanac of the Dead*, p. 449)

**1969** Helen Sekaquaptewa publishes *Me and Mine*, a memoir of the Carlisle Indian School. (*Yellow Woman and a Beauty of the Spirit: Essays on Native American Life Today*, p. 163)

**January 20, 1969** After the election of Richard Nixon, racism dominates national politics. (*Yellow Woman and a Beauty of the Spirit: Essays on Native American Life Today*, pp. 106–107)

**November 20, 1969** American Indians seize Alcatraz Island and occupy it until June 11, 1971. (*Yellow Woman and a Beauty of the Spirit: Essays on Native American Life Today*, p. 73)

**1973** The Army Corps of Engineers begins flooding sacred shrines and terrain near Cochiti Pueblo, where they begin work in 1965. In 2001, the military apologizes to the Indians for destroying agricultural tracts. (*The Delicacy and Strength of Lace*, p. 28)

A Congressional act recognizes the Arizona Yaqui as native Americans. ("The People and the Land ARE Inseparable," p. 110; *Yellow Woman and a Beauty of the Spirit: Essays on Native American Life Today*, p. 87)

A suicide pact claims the lives of seven teenagers from Paguate. (*Yellow Woman and a Beauty of the Spirit: Essays on Native American Life Today*, pp. 130–131; *The Turquoise Ledge*, pp. 72–73)

**February 27, 1973** The American Indian Movement seizes Wounded Knee, South Dakota. (*Yellow Woman and a Beauty of the Spirit: Essays on Native American Life Today*, pp. 73–74)

**late 1970s** The Green Party forms in Belgium and Germany. (*Almanac of the Dead*, p. 415)

**July 21, 1979** The Atlanta child murders begin and continue until March 12, 1981, with a total of 28 black victims. (*Almanac of the Dead*, p. 139)

**Spring 1980** A 30-foot stone snake appears at the Jackpile uranium mine near Paguate, New Mexico. (*Almanac of the Dead*, pp. 31, 35, 91–93, 95, 576, 577, 761–762; *Yellow Woman and a Beauty of the Spirit: Essays on Native American Life Today*, pp. 126, 138, 143, 148; *The Turquoise Ledge*, p. 73)

**1981** The U.S. Commission on Civil Rights issues "Indian Tribes: A Continuing Quest for Survival." (*Yellow Woman and a Beauty of the Spirit: Essays on Native American Life Today*, pp. 74–75)

The Rev. John Fife begins the Sanctuary Movement to undocumented immigrants from El Salvador. (*Yellow Woman and a Beauty of the Spirit: Essays on Native American Life Today*, p. 111)

Digging at the Jackpile mine continues in a strip mine two miles wide and hundreds of feet deep, worked by around 640 miners from the pueblo. (*Ceremony*, p. 245; *Almanac of the Dead*, pp. 758–759, 762; *Yellow Woman and a Beauty of the Spirit: Essays on Native American Life Today*, pp. 43–44, 95, 128, 139)

**August 1, 1983** Ferdinand Marcos orders Benigno Aquino shot in the head at Manila International Airport in the Philippines. (*Almanac of the Dead*, p. 354)

**September 1, 1983** A Korean Air Lines Flight 007 crashes on a flight path from Bethel, Alaska, to the Sea of Japan. (*Almanac of the Dead*, pp. 157)

**1984** During the Reagan era, Indians retain 52 million acres in the continental U.S. in 38 states and 40 million acres in Alaska, only five percent of the original native homeland. ("Auntie Kie," 28; *Yellow Woman and a Beauty of the Spirit: Essays on Native American Life Today*, p. 81)

**January 1, 1984** The Zapatistas outside Tuxtla Gutierrez revolt. ("Listening to the Spirits: An Interview with Leslie Marmon Silko," pp. 7–8; *Yellow Woman and a Beauty of the Spirit: Essays on Native American Life Today*, pp. 152–154, 158)

**April 26, 1984** A meltdown at the Chernobyl Nuclear Power Plant in Ukraine spreads concern for nature and humankind. (*Sacred Water: Narratives and Pictures*, p. 116)

**March 23, 1984** An assassin shoots Luis Donaldo Colosio Murrieta, a candidate for Mexican president. (*Yellow Woman and a Beauty of the Spirit: Essays on Native American Life Today*, p. 158)

**1993** Hazel O'Leary, U.S. Secretary of Energy, declassifies documents revealing past abuses of citizens by feeding plutonium to handicapped children and injecting plutonium into poor black Alabamans. (*The Turquoise Ledge*, pp. 70–71)

**September 11, 2001** Terrorist planes impact and destroy the twin towers and much World Trade Center in downtown Manhattan. (*The Turquoise Ledge*, p. 99)

**2006** The U.S. government begins building a 12-foot wall between Southwestern states and Mexico. (*Yellow Woman and a Beauty of the Spirit: Essays on Native American Life Today*, p. 107)

**March 2006** Hopi runners journey from Hotevila, Arizona, to Mexico City to petition Tlaloc, the Aztec god of rain, to end the drought. (*The Turquoise Ledge*, p. 175)

**2010**   Marcelo Luis Ebrard, a finalist for the 2010 World Mayor prize, urges employees of Mexico City to learn Nahuatl, the Aztec language. (*The Turquoise Ledge*, pp. 46–47)

## Sources

Arnold, Ellen. "Listening to the Spirits: An Interview with Leslie Marmon Silko." *Studies in American Indian Literature* 10:3 (Fall 1998): 1–33.

Jacobs, Connie. "A Toxic Legacy: Stories of Jackpile Mine," *American Indian Culture and Research Journal* 28:1 (Winter 2004): 41–52.

# Appendix B:
# Writing and Research Topics

1. Arrange a literature seminar to compare the amorous attraction between Uncle Josiah and Night Swan in *Ceremony* or of Seese and David in *Almanac of the Dead* with similarly problematic pairings in Ariana Franklin's *The Serpent's Tail*, Peter Carey's *Oscar and Lucinda*, Isabel Allende's *The House of the Spirits*, Sandra Cisnero's *Woman Hollering Creek*, Michel Faber's *The Crimson Petal and the White*, Nora Roberts's *Montana Sky*, Mario Vargas Llosa's *The War of the End of the World*, and Amy Tan's *The Hundred Secret Senses*. Focus on shared elements, including gender restrictions on libido and the power of disapproval and gossip to shame lovers.

2. Compose an annotated map of the American Southwest featuring these landmarks: Tucson, Albuquerque, Mount Taylor, Rio San José, Laguna, Paguate, Acoma Pueblo, Sherman Institute, Isleta, Sonora Desert, Colorado River, Parker reservation, Gallup, Flagstaff, Jackpile mine, Needles, Cebolleta Mountains, Canyon de Chelly, Mission San José, University of New Mexico, Sedillo Grant, Chinle, Mesita, Patoch Butte, Dripping Springs, Cubero, Denver, Canyon del Muerto, and Atchison, Topeka, and Santa Fe Railroad.

3. Characterize the motivation and purpose of ecofeminism in the works of Silko, Mary Austin, Rachel Carson, Marjorie Stoneman Douglas, Kathy Reichs, Marjorie Kinnan Rawl-

ings, and Barbara Kingsolver. Which author predicts vengeance on the desecrators of Mother Earth? What works depict women as healers and saviors of earth's wonder and fecundity? Which author valorizes women's work at the peasant level?

4. Summarize the effects of multiple threats to survival in Silko's *Almanac of the Dead* and one of these works: Sebastian Faulks's *Birdsong*, Kathy Reichs's *Grave Secrets*, Victor E. Villasenor's *Rain of Gold*, Karen Tei Yamashita's *Through the Arc of the Rain Forest*, Chinua Achebe's *Things Fall Apart*, Gloria Anzaldúa's *Borderlands/La Frontera*, Thomas King's *Green Grass, Running Water*, Orson Scott Card's *Ender's Game*, Jean Giono's *Horseman on the Roof*, Marge Piercy's *Woman on the Edge of Time*, Greg Sarris's *Mabel McKay*, Marilynne Robinson's *Housekeeping*, Nevil Shute's *On the Beach*, Susan Straight's *I Been in Sorrow's Kitchen and Licked Out All the Pots*, or Margaret Atwood's *The Handmaid's Tale*.

5. Summarize the vagaries of the dying in the death scene of Silko's "Lullaby" and in similar views of the moribund in Rudolfo Anaya's *Bless Me, Ultima*, Michael Ondaatje's *The English Patient*, Margaret Edson's *Wit*, Katherine Anne Porter's "The Jilting Granny Weatherall," Velma Wallis's *Two Old Woman: An Alaska Legend of Betrayal, Courage and Survival*, Kaye Gibbons's *On the Occasion of My Last Afternoon*,

Cormac McCarthy's *The Road*, or Winnie Smith's *American Daughter Gone to War*.

6. Propose the choice of Silko's *The Turquoise Ledge* or *Storyteller* as a community read or a celebration of Women's History Month. Suggest taped readings, improvised scenes, an extended character web, historical timelines, or the use of fiction to clarify family concerns and actions during periods of change, particularly the postcolonial era. Provide a list of corroborative texts by Navarre Scott Momaday, Mary Hunter Austin, Barbara Kingsolver, John Muir, Jamaica Kincaid, Cathy Song, Yoko Kawashima Watkins, Simon Joseph Ortiz, Gayle Ross, Joseph Bruchac, Carmen Deedy, or Joy Harjo.

7. Compare the peace and solitude of the arroyo in *The Turquoise Ledge* with one of these literary settings: ranch land in Conrad Richter's *The Sea of Grass*, sharecropping in James Agee's *Let Us Now Praise Famous Men: Three Tenant Families*, the outback in Peter Carey's *Oscar and Lucinda*, the *llano* in Rudolfo Anaya's *Bless Me, Ultima*, the muck in Zora Neale Hurston's *Their Eyes Were Watching God*, islanders along the Carolina coast in Pat Conroy's *The Water Is Wide*, the Florida swamps in Marjorie Kinnan Rawlings's *Cross Creek*, and a former plantation in Walter Dean Myers's *The Glory Field*. Include music and dance, food, superstition, religion, learning, daily labor, ritual, fear, betrayal, love, and child rearing.

8. Analyze the survivalism of the historian Old Mahawal and the "wild ones" in *Almanac of the Dead* and of the Sand Lizard people in *Gardens in the Dunes*. Contrast the fears and strategies of a February departure to the mountain retreat and escape from the European fever with Donald Davidson's advice in the poem "Sanctuary," the post-war trauma in Virginia Ellis's *The Wedding Dress*, talk-story in Amy Tan's *The Kitchen God's Wife*, and the climb featured in John Krakauer's *Into Thin Air*.

9. Account for variant images of journeys in Silko's fiction, particularly the journey to Oakland for Tayo and other recruits in *Ceremony*, Alegría Panson's flight from coyotes in *Almanac of the Dead*, the route home for the abducted wife in "Yellow Woman," and Indigo's long route from Riverside to Oyster Bay and Eu-

rope. Draw parallels from the outer space battles in Scott Card's *Ender's Game*, the abduction in *The Captivity of Mary Rowlandson*, the missionary trek to the Congo in Barbara Kingsolver's *The Poisonwood Bible*, the wartime travels of soldiers and medical workers in Michael Ondaatje's *The English Patient*, kidnap from Africa and impressment into slavery in Toni Morrison's *Beloved*, whaling voyages in Sena Naslund's *Ahab's Wife*, transportation of captives in Thomas Keneally's *Schindler's Ark*, and Santiago's travels to Egypt in Paulo Coelho's *The Alchemist*.

10. Contrast parenting styles in several of Silko's works. Include the following models:

- among Indian women in Needles, California, in *Gardens in the Dunes*
- by Grandma A'mooh in *Storyteller*
- in Yoeme's family in *Almanac of the Dead*
- among Navajo matriarchs in "Lullaby"
- by Grandma and Uncle Josiah in *Ceremony*
- by Leslie Marmon Silko and James Wright in *The Delicacy and Strength of Lace*
- by Edward and Hattie in *Gardens in the Dunes*.

11. Cite advice to the young in *Gardens in the Dunes* that compares with cautionary storytelling in Sylvia Lopez-Medina's *Cantora*, Jane Smiley's *The All-True Travels and Adventures of Lidie Newton*, Isabel Allende's *Daughter of Fortune*, John Irving's *The World According to Garp*, August Wilson's *Piano Lesson*, Toni Morrison's *Song of Solomon*, Forrest Carter's *The Education of Little Tree*, Maxine Hong Kingston's *Woman Warrior*, Lois Lowry's *The Giver*, Jamaica Kincaid's *The Autobiography of My Mother*, or Julia Alvarez's *In the Time of the Butterflies*.

12. Contrast the emotional and moral faults of the bourgeoisie in Silko's depiction of the socially prominent Abbotts and Palmers in *Gardens in the Dunes* with Edith Wharton's *The Age of Innocence*, Henry James's *Washington Square*, Emilia Pardo Bazan's *The House of Ulloa*, Kate Chopin's *The Awakening*, Gabriel García Marquéz's *Love in the Time of Cholera*, Jim Harrison's *Legends of the Fall*, or Margaret Atwood's *Alias Grace*.

13. Typify Silko's views on displacement of first peoples with the same theme in Nikolai

Gogol's *Dead Souls*, Jamaica Kincaid's "Ovando," Rigoberta Menchú's *I, Rigoberta*, Alex Haley's *Roots*, Daisy Bates's *The Passing of the Aborigines*, John Batchelor's *The Ainu of Japan*, and Sherman Alexie's *The Lone Ranger and Tonto Fistfight in Heaven*.

14. Determine the source of female strength in Silko's "Lullaby." Compare the Navajo matriarchs to strong women in Ilie Ruby's *The Language of Trees*, Peter Carey's *The Unusual Life of Tristan Smith*, Robert Harling's *Steel Magnolias*, Terry McMillan's *Getting to Happy*, Kaye Gibbons's *Charms for the Easy Life*, Alice Walker's *The Color Purple*, and the satiric stage comedy *Tent Meeting* by Larry Larson, Levi Lee, and Rebecca Wackler.

15. Account for tyrannic methods of citizen control in "America's Iron Curtain: The Border Patrol State" or *Almanac of the Dead* and for despotism in Alexander Solzhenitsyn's *One Day in the Life of Ivan Denisovich*, Marjane Satrapi's *Persepolis*, Pierre Boulle's *The Bridge on the River Kwai*, Linda Sue Park's *When My Name Was Keoko*, Boris Pasternak's *Doctor Zhivago*, Melba Beals's *Warriors Don't Cry*, Richard Adams's *Watership Down*, or Julie Otsuka's *When the Emperor Was Divine*.

16. Compare barriers to female aspirations in *Garden in the Dunes* with similar obstacles in Joyce Carol Oates's *We Were the Mulvaneys*, Laura Esquivel's *Like Water for Chocolate*, Zora Neale Hurston's *Their Eyes Were Watching God*, Jane Smiley's *One Thousand Acres*, Marylynne Robinson's *Housekeeping*, Beth Henley's *Crimes of the Heart*, or Barbara Kingsolver's *The Lacuna*.

17. Discuss variances in the presentation of community in a timeline of native American writings. How does Silko's emphasis on Laguna unity compare with the homelands described by these native American writers: Sherman Alexie (Spokane), Paula Gunn Allen (Laguna), Betty Louise Bell (Cherokee), Black Elk (Oglala Sioux), Joseph Bruchac (Abenaki), George Copway (Ojibwa), Ella Cara Deloria (Yankton Sioux), Vine Deloria (Yankton Sioux), Charles Eastman (Santee Sioux), Louise Erdrich (Chippewa), Joy Harjo (Muscogee), Linda Hogan (Chickasaw), Winona LaDuke (Ashinaabe), Susette LaFlesche (Ponca/Iowa), William Least Heat-Moon (Osage), Wilma Mankiller (Cherokee), Navarre Scott Momaday (Kiowa), Mourning Dove (Colville/Okanaga), Simon Joseph Ortiz (Acoma), Louis Owens (Choctaw/Cherokee), Pretty Shield (Crow), Wilson Rawls (Cherokee), Wendy Rose (Hopi/Miwok), Rigoberta Menchú Tum (Quiché Maya), Gerald Vizenor (Anishinaabe), Velma Wallis (Athabascan), Anna Lee Walters (Oto/Pawnee), James Welch (Blackfeet/Gros Ventres), and Sarah Winnemucca (Paiute).

18. Summarize the types of advice and counsel shared by these characters: *la professoressa* Laura/visitors, Grandma Fleet/Indigo, Ku'oosh/Tayo, Old Pancakes/soldiers, Beaufrey/Seese, Alegría/Menardo Panson, Grandma/Tayo, Siteye/Andy, Yoeme/granddaughters, Grandma A'mooh/Leslie Marmon Silko, Big Candy/Mr. Wylie, Maytha and Vedna/Sister Salt, Ts'eh Montaño/Tayo, Harley/Tayo, Betonie/Tayo, Chato/Ayah, Mr. Abbott/Hattie Abbott, Aunt Bronwyn/visitors, Major Littlecock/soldiers, Auntie Thelma/Uncle Josiah, recruiter/Rocky and Tayo, and Sister Salt/Indigo.

19. Account for Gothic images in Leslie Marmon Silko's writings, including Harley wrapped in barbed wire, macaw prophets, Zeta's bloodthirsty guard dogs, a stone snake that appears at the Jackpile mine, drunks in an alley at Gallup, a snake mural painted on the wall at Tucson, Shush's trauma, abduction of Yellow Woman, Silva's shots at pursuers, the rape of Hattie Abbott Palmer, a failed bullet-proof vest, a fall down a marble staircase, suicide on a chenille bedspread, dismemberment of Monte, Tayo's dreams of becoming smoke, a sudden flash over the desert, Dr. William Gates's medical treatments, and a hallucination of Uncle Josiah as a Japanese warrior.

20. Select contrasting scenes and describe their pictorial qualities, for example:

- homesickness in Ketchikan/Sterling's return to Laguna
- an army of homeless/children eating pages
- women laughing at an adulterer/Tayo planting wildflowers
- dogs in costumes/meeting Matinnecock gardeners

- arson in a barn/a cantina dancer at Lalo's bar
- Aunt Susie translating testimony/filmmakers at the Jackpile mine
- the bombing of Hiroshima and Nagasaki/ playing golf with Max Blue
- a child custody suit/Auntie Kie's tirade
- Edward's broken leg/coyotes dumping passengers in the desert.

21.  Discuss the cultural and familial value of food and healing in Silko's works and in other feminist writing, e.g., Gish Jen's "Fish Cheeks," Barbara Kingsolver's *The Bean Trees*, Jessamyn West's *The Friendly Persuasion*, Kaye Gibbons's *On the Occasion of My Last Afternoon*, Erica Jong's *Witches*, Kathryn Stockett's *The Help*, Maxine Kumin's "Making the Jam without You," Jean Auel's *The Clan of the Cave Bear*, Cathy Song's *The Picture Bride*, Laurel Thatcher Ulrich's *Good Wives*, Anna Quindlen's *One True Thing*, Toni Cade Bambara's *The Salt Eaters*, or Isak Dinesen's *Babette's Feast*.

22.  Contrast flaws and strengths in two of these characters: Sterling, Zeta, Uncle Josiah, Susan Abbott James, Mr. Hyslop, Reed Woman, Dr. William Gates, Leah Blue, Ramboy Roy, Delena, Chato, Aunt Kie, Geronimo, Grandpa Hank, Al, James Wright, John Dillinger, Thought Woman, Mr. Stewart, Father Paul, Juana, Shush, and Japanese-Americans at the depot. Which characters recognize weaknesses? faults? inescapable dilemmas? temporary obstacles?

23.  Write an extended definition of *conflict* using as examples Edward's arrest at Bastia, Juana's enslavement, Father Paul's blessing of Teofilo's remains, Silko's freeing of a diamondback rattlesnake from bird netting, Tony's shooting of a cop, the fire at Needles, Old Pancakes's arrest, Geronimo's escapes, Lecha's abandonment of Ferro, Tayo's departure from the Los Angeles veteran's hospital, Uncle Josiah's purchase of Ulibarri's longhorns, removal of Silko from the schoolyard photo, rejection of Hattie Abbott's treatise on female Christians, Yellow Woman's return to Al, the use of a police dog to inspect Silko's car, and the attack on Mrs. Van Wagnen's home and garden.

24.  Compare female nurturing in these scenes: Silko's protection of her birds, Grandma A'mooh's reading bible stories to the Marmon sisters, Seese's admiration of Monte, Delena's concern for thirsty dogs, Indigo's nurse care to a rape victim, Hattie's reading to Indigo on the train to Oyster Bay, Ts'eh Montaño's welcome to Tayo, Silko's farewell to Dolly, Mama's sewing of a quilt from burned blankets, Aunt Bronwyn's storytelling to Indigo, and Night Swan's romance with Uncle Josiah.

25.  Compare shifts in the family power structure in *Ceremony* with scenes from Alice Sebold's *The Lovely Bones*, James Agee's *A Death in the Family*, Sandra Cisneros's *Caramelo*, Peter Carey's *True History of the Kelly Gang*, Kaye Gibbons's *Ellen Foster*, August Wilson's *Fences*, Marion Zimmer Bradley's *The Mists of Avalon*, Ann Petry's *Tituba of Salem Village*, Jean Rhys's *Wide Sargasso Sea*, Khaled Hosseini's *The Kite Runner*, or Pat Conroy's *The Great Santini*. Emphasize the compromises that allow individuals to cope with unlovable people.

26.  Improvise a dialogue among Sterling, Emo, Geronimo, Yoeme, Yellow Woman, Grandma Fleet, Delena, Uncle Josiah, Siteye, Max Blue, Rocky, Big Candy, and Tayo on the subject of poverty and dispossession as determiners of disempowerment. As a model, explain through character dialogue the Amerindian attitude toward home, food, clothing, children, healing, stories, land, spirits, nativism, and personal belongings.

27.  Contrast the use of the supernatural in Silko's *Almanac of the Dead* to Carlos Ruiz Zafón's *The Shadow of the Wind*, Dan Brown's *The Lost Symbol*, Paula Gunn Allen's *Spider Woman's Granddaughters*, Albert Sánchez Piñol's *Cold Skin*, or Louise Erdrich's *Four Souls*.

28.  Cite occasions for storytelling in Silko's works, such as encouragement of children to behave, warnings about white enslavers, review of tribal creation stories, or introduction of places where crucial events occurred, such as Mount Taylor and Rio San José. Contrast the tales with models of talk-story in Isabel Allende's *The House of the Spirits*, Marsha Norman's '*night, Mother*, Lee Smith's *Oral History*, Beth Henley's *Crimes of the Heart*, and Amy Tan's *Saving Fish from Drowning*.

29. Discuss the repeated motif of colonialism in Silko's works. Explain how she applies the setting and themes of white infringement on the sovereignties of North America through fable, *bildungsroman*, satire, jeremiad, polemic, psychological novel, Gothic cautionary tale, dreamscape, vignette, anecdote, article, personal essay, speech, travelogue, biography, and autobiography.

30. Account for the significance of secondary characters, such as the ranch owner in "Lullaby," Ileana and Jamey in *Almanac of the Dead*, Helen Jean and cousin Pinkie in *Ceremony*, the rooster and Annie in *The Delicacy and Strength of Lace*, Laura and the Messiah in *Gardens in the Dunes*, the photographer in "'Not You,' He Said," the hunter in *How to Hunt Buffalo*, the elk and coyote in *Laguna Woman*, the uncle in "Humaweepi, the Warrior Priest," Lee Marmon in *Storyteller*, Leon in "The Man to Send Rain Clouds," Cazimir in *The Turquoise Ledge*, and Bishop Lando in *Yellow Woman and a Beauty of the Spirit*.

31. Contrast the drama in these situations: collecting blood from the homeless, breaking in a new saddle, spoon-feeding mush and Indian tea to Tayo, halting the telling of Keres stories, cutting Lloyd Lee's steel wolf-proof fence, entering the priesthood, conducting a ceremony over a deer carcass, making soup from a codex, watering Grandma's hollyhocks, welcoming the enemy to a harvest feast, working in a uranium mine, threatening to burn a book defaming Indians, suffering the blow of a rifle butt to the head, shooting a witch, and locating the body of Teofilo.

32. Characterize the importance of setting to these scenes: hanging Bartolomeo, stopping at a road block outside Albuquerque, consulting with an architect on building a mansion at the edge of the jungle, smuggling marijuana from Mexico in a wagonload of gourds, luring a white man onto ice, locating caves used by desert travelers, sitting on a boulder shaped like a bear, betraying a Pueblo monument to filmmakers, carrying a blanket stretcher through the rain, panhandling at the riverbank near Gallup, and writing a novel in Ketchikan.

33. Summarize the significance of these terms to Silko's canon: Marx, Yaqui, Chilam Balam, *Popol Vuh*, Bureau of Indian Affairs, Elsie Parsons, Apache Wars, hoop ceremony, Damballah, Fourth World, battle fatigue, apocalypse, Toe'osh, Sulis Minerva, Les Evans, Quetzalcoatl, pollen, Montezuma, Ck'o'yo medicine, Kaup'a'ta, *conquistadores*, Olmec, Ghost Dance, Nahua, sex mall, ecofeminism, Ogou Feraille, Yupik, *hummah-hah*, and diaspora.

34. Explain the implications of the following titles:

"Sangre Pura"
"Indian with a Camera"
"Kill the Rich"
"Bio-Materials, Inc."
"'Not You,' He Said"
"The Border Patrol State"
"TV Talk Show Psychic"
"Bataan Death March"
"Green Vengeance — Eco-Warriors"
"Prayer to the Pacific"
"Masque of the Blue Garden"
"How to Hunt Buffalo"

35. Locate examples of journeys and visits as symbols of ambition, vengeance, and healing, particularly Aunt Bronwyn's pilgrimage to Celtic groves, Indigo's night at the American embassy, the Messiah's pilgrimage, Hattie Abbott's carriage ride with Mr. Hyslop, the long walk to the burned house, Tayo's return to the dripping spring, the retrieval of Indigo from the Matinnecock village, Edward's search for meteorites, Emo's exile, the planting of Laura's gladiolus corms in Arizona, Delena's journey south to sellers of repeating rifles, the children's retreat from a desert cannibal, and the return of the female snake to the spring.

36. Debate the wisdom of the following choices: Silko's decision to leave Ketchikan, drawing Star Beings with tempura paint, burning a rainforest, learning to fire a rifle, giving manuscripts to a granddaughter for safekeeping, opening a riverbank laundry, burning a barn, escaping from the Sherman Institute, clipping Rainbow's wings, painting a grasshopper's portrait, hiding in a glass greenhouse, and killing a goat.

37. Outline elements of history from Silko's works. Include the Indian Wars, Treaty of

Guadalupe Hidalgo, bombing of Hiroshima and Nagasaki, arrest of John Dillinger, Battle of Wake Island, interning Japanese-Americans, burning Mayan libraries, carving petroglyphs, the building of Mesa Verde, suing the U.S. government for land theft, the Zapatista uprising, and the opening of the Jackpile mine.

38.  Discuss the effectiveness of the following rhetorical devices:

- *euphony* "die softly" ("Poem for Myself and Mei-Mei: Concerning Abortion")
- *pun* Major Littlecock ("A Geronimo Story")
- *double entendre* "all the way" (*Ceremony*)
- *sobriquet* "Skeleton Fixer" (*Storyteller*)
- *myth* "Fly and Hummingbird" (*Ceremony*)
- *romanticism* "deep down, somewhere behind his belly, near his heart" (*Ceremony*)
- *dialogue* "I have been learning all this time and I didn't even know it" ("Humaweepi, the Warrior Priest")
- *personification* "How many chances did Death get in five years?" (*Almanac of the Dead*)
- *repetition* "if the stories had somehow been lost, then the people were lost" (*Almanac of the Dead*)
- *vernacular* "That damn goat got pissed off too easy anyway" ("Uncle Tony's Goat")
- *emphasis* "But you see, he *was* the sun" ("Cottonwood")
- *visual image* "Auntie's brand, a rafter 4" (*Ceremony*)
- *allusion* "Chariots of fire! Beasts with seven heads!" (*Gardens in the Dunes*)
- *detail* "the grasshopper basket" (*Yellow Woman and a Beauty of the Spirit*)
- *internal rhyme* "Clackety-clack! Never get back, never get back, get back, get back" (*Gardens in the Dunes*)
- *versification* "Whirling darkness/has come back on itself./It keeps all its witchery/to itself" (*Ceremony*)
- *simile* snow "like birds' feathers" ("Lullaby")
- *boast* "he was always going to win" (*Ceremony*)
- *inversion* "Whether we know the stories or not, the stories know about us" (*Yellow Woman and a Beauty of the Spirit*)
- *parallelism* "the blood of the rich and the royal" (*Almanac of the Dead*)
- *invocation* "Sunrise, accept this offering, Sunrise" (*Ceremony*)

- *epithet* "Squaw Man" ("Fences against Freedom")
- *sense impression* "I smell you in the silver leaves, mountainlion man" ("Indian Song: Survival")
- *alliteration* "Prayer to the Pacific" (*Laguna Woman*)
- *foreign terms* "the *americanos* came in and set up their own courts" (*Almanac of the Dead*)
- *hyperbole* "sweat hogs of capitalism" (*Almanac of the Dead*)
- *humor* "Holy Ghost, hallelujah, savior, sinners, sins, crucify, whore, damned to hell, bastard, bitch" (*Gardens in the Dunes*)
- *confessional* "It was not so easy for me to learn where we Marmons belonged" (*Yellow Woman and a Beauty of the Spirit*)
- *metaphor* "the Destroyers" (*Almanac of the Dead*)

39.  Survey the rewards and recriminations of old age in two of Silko's characters. Consider Tayo's grandma, old Guzman, Old Mahawal, Grandma Fleet, Zeta, Lecha, Grandma A'mooh, Yoeme, Betonie, Ayah and Chato, Ayah's grandmother, Mr. Abbott, Virginia Lee Leslie Marmon, Old Pancakes, and Grandpa Hank.

40.  Summarize the following feminist situations in Silko's works: diminution of sex workers, child custody, women's role in tribal politics, abduction, squabbles between sisters, womanizing males, biracial children, on-the-job sexual harassment, devaluation of female professionals, illegitimate children, and bisexual mates.

41.  What are Silko's strongest comments about underclass health care? child abandonment? foster care? poverty? racism? housing? white schools? urban crime? substance abuse? pollution? war? land despoliation?

42.  Describe how Silko presents social issues, such as an adulterous husband and pedophilia in *Almanac of the Dead*, alcoholism and miscegenation in *Ceremony*, poverty in old age in "Lullaby," racism in "'Not You,' He Said," displacement and dispossession in "A Geronimo Story," outrage in "Tony's Story," legalistic religion in "The Man to Send Rain Clouds," violation of civil rights in "America's Iron

Curtain: The Border Patrol State," and androcentric institutions of higher learning in *Gardens in the Dunes*.

43. Contrast the fear of incorporeality in Tayo in *Ceremony* with that of the title figure in H. G. Wells's *The Invisible Man*, Frodo Baggins in J. R. R. Tolkien's *The Lord of the Rings*, or Paul Moreaux in Robert Cormier's *Fade*. Characterize events that cause the sundering of mind from body. Which characters find invisibility useful? salvific? debilitating? life-threatening?

# Bibliography

## Primary

### Long Works

*After a Summer Rain in the Upper Sonoran.* Roswell, NM: Black Mesa, 1984.

*Almanac of the Dead.* New York: Simon & Schuster, 1991.

*Boomer: Railroad Memoirs* (co-authored with Linda Grant Niemann). Bloomington: Indiana University Press, 2011.

*Ceremony.* New York: Viking, 1977.

*The Delicacy and Strength of Lace: Letters between Leslie Marmon Silko and James Wright.* St. Paul, MN: Graywolf, 1986.

*Gardens in the Dunes.* New York: Scribner, 1999.

*How to Hunt Buffalo: for Linda Grant Niemann.* Tucson: self-published, 1994.

*Laguna Woman: Poems.* New York: Greenfield Review Press, 1974.

*Love Poem and Slim Man Canyon.* Tucson: University of Arizona Poetry Center, 1996.

*Ordinary Places.* Minneapolis: Coffee House, 1985.

*Rain* (with co-author Lee Marmon). New York: Grenfell, 1996.

*Sacred Water: Narratives and Pictures.* Tucson: Flood Plain, 1993.

*Storyteller.* New York: Seaver, 1981.

*The Turquoise Ledge: A Memoir.* New York: Viking Adult, 2010.

*Yellow Woman.* New Brunswick, NJ: Rutgers University Press, 1993.

*Yellow Woman and a Beauty of the Spirit: Essays on Native American Life Today.* New York: Simon & Schuster, 1996.

### Short Works

"America's Debt to the Indian Nations: Atoning for a Sordid Past." *Los Angeles Times* (12 July 1981): 2; *Yellow Woman and a Beauty of the Spirit: Essays on Native American Life Today.* New York: Simon & Schuster, 1996, 73–79.

"America's Iron Curtain: The Border Patrol State." *Nation* 259:12 (17 October 1994): 412–416; under the title "The Border Patrol State" in *Yellow Woman and a Beauty of the Spirit: Essays on Native American Life Today.* New York: Simon & Schuster, 1996, 115–123.

"Auntie Kie Talks about U.S. Presidents and U.S. Indian Policy." *Mother Jones* 9:8 (October 1984): 28–30; *Yellow Woman and a Beauty of the Spirit: Essays on Native American Life Today.* New York: Simon & Schuster, 1996, 80–84.

"Bingo Big." *Nation* 260:23 (12 June 1995): 856–860.

"Bravura" in *The Man to Send Rain Clouds: Contemporary Stories by American Indians*, ed. Kenneth Rosen. New York: Viking, 1974.

"Breaking Down the Boundaries: 'Earth, Air, Water, Mind'" in *The Tales We Tell: Perspectives on the Short Story*, ed. Barbara Lounsberry. London: Greenwood, 1998.

"Chapulin's Portrait." *Kenyon Review* 32:1 (1 January 2010): 109–134.

"Commentary" to *Mabel McKay*, by Greg Sarris. Berkeley: University of California Press, 1994.

"Coyote Holds a Full House in His Hand." *TriQuarterly* 48 (Spring 1980): 166–174.

"Criminal Justice in American Indian Literature." *Oshkaabewis Native Journal* 1:1 (1990): 31.

"Deer Dance/For Your Return." *Columbia* 1:2 (Fall 1977): 9–11.

"Deer Song." *Journal of Ethnic Studies* 2:2 (Summer 1974): 69.

"An Essay on Rocks." *Aperture* 139 (Summer 1995): 60–63; *Yellow Woman and a Beauty of the Spirit: Essays on Native American Life Today.* New York: Simon & Schuster, 1996, 187–191.

"An Expression of Profound Gratitude to the Maya Zapatistas." *People's Tribune* (29 February 1994);

*Yellow Woman and a Beauty of the Spirit: Essays on Native American Life Today.* New York: Simon & Schuster, 1996, 152–154.

"Fences against Freedom." *Hungry Mind Review* 31 (Fall 1994): 6, 20, 58–59; *Yellow Woman and a Beauty of the Spirit: Essays on Native American Life Today.* New York: Simon & Schuster, 1996, 100–114.

"500 Years from Now, Everyone in Tucson Speaks Nahuatl Not Chinese," speech to the Indigenous Languages Conference in Tucson on June 14, 2007.

"Foreword." *God Is Red: A Native View of Religion,* by Vine Deloria, Jr. Golden, CO: Fulcrum, 2003, vii–ix.

"Foreword." *Yardbird Reader* 3 (1974): 98–103; *Border Towns of the Navajo Nation.* Alamo, CA: Holmganger, 1975.

"The Fourth World." *Artforum* 27:10 (Summer 1989): 125–126; under the title "Fifth World: The Return of Ma Ah Shra True Ee, the Giant Serpent." *Yellow Woman and a Beauty of the Spirit: Essays on Native American Life Today.* New York: Simon & Schuster, 1996, 124–134.

"From a Novel Not Yet titled." *Journal of Ethnic Studies* 3:1 (Spring 1975): 72–87.

"Gallup, New Mexico—Indian Capital of the World." *New America* 2:3 (Summer-Fall 1976): 30–32.

"A Geronimo Story" in *Come to Power: Eleven Contemporary American Indian Poets,* ed. Dick Lourie. New York: Crossing, 1974, 81–94; *The Man to Send Rain Clouds: Contemporary Stories by American Indians,* ed. Kenneth Rosen. New York: Viking, 1974.

"Grace Abounding in Botswana" (review). *New York Times Book Review* (23 March 1986): 7.

"Hawk and Snake." *Chicago Review* 24:4 (Spring 1973): 98.

"Here's an Odd Artifact for the Fairy-Tale Shelf." *Impact/Albuquerque Journal* (8 October 1986): 10–11; *Studies in American Indian Literatures* 10:4 (Fall 1986): 177–184.

"Horses at Valley Store." *Chicago Review* 24:4 (Spring 1973): 99–100; *Carriers of the Dream Wheel: Contemporary Native American Poetry,* ed. Duane Niatum. New York: Harper & Row, 1975.

"How to Hunt Buffalo" (1994), unpublished fourfold housed in the Bienecke archives at Yale University Library, New Haven, Connecticut.

"Humaweepi, the Warrior Priest" in *The Man to Send Rain Clouds: Contemporary Stories by American Indians,* ed. Kenneth Rosen. New York: Viking, 1974.

"Hunger Stalked the Tribal People." *People's Tribune* (Thanksgiving 1994); *Yellow Woman and a Beauty of the Spirit: Essays on Native American Life Today.* New York: Simon & Schuster, 1996, 96–99.

"A Hunting Story." *Journal of Contemporary Literature* 1:1 (Fall 1976): 11–13.

"In Cold Storm Light." *Quetzal* 2:3 (Summer 1972): 46.

"Indian Song: Survival." *Chicago Review* 24:4 (Spring 1973): 94–96.

"The Indian with a Camera," foreword to *A Circle of Nations: Voices and Visions of American Indians,* Hillsboro, OR: Beyond Words, 1993, 4–5; *Yellow Woman and a Beauty of the Spirit: Essays on Native American Life Today.* New York: Simon & Schuster, 1996, 175–179.

"Interior and Exterior Landscapes: The Pueblo Migration Stories" in *Landscape in America,* ed. George F. Thompson. Austin: University of Texas Press, 1995, 155–169; *Yellow Woman and a Beauty of the Spirit: Essays on Native American Life Today.* New York: Simon & Schuster, 1996, 25–47.

"In the Combat Zone." *Hungry Mind Review* (Fall 1995): 44, 46.

"Introduction." *On the Rails: A Woman's Journey,* by Linda Niemann. Berkeley, CA: Cleis, 1996.

"Introduction." *The Pueblo Imagination: Landscape and Memory in the Photography of Lee Marmon,* by Lee Marmon. Boston: Beacon, 2003, 12–13.

"The Invention of White People" in *Shaking the Pumpkin: Traditional Poetry of the Indian North Americas,* ed. Jerome Rothenberg. New York: Alfred Van Der Marck, 1986.

"A Laguna Portfolio." *Studies in American Indian Literatures* 5:1 (Spring 1993): 63–74.

"Landscape, History, and the Pueblo Imagination." *Antaeus* 51 (Autumn 1986): 83–94.

"Language and Literature from the Pueblo Indian Perspective" in *English Literature: Opening Up the Canon,* eds. Leslie Fiedler and Houston Baker, Jr. Baltimore: Johns Hopkins University Press, 1981; *Yellow Woman and a Beauty of the Spirit: Essays on Native American Life Today.* New York: Simon & Schuster, 1996, 48–59.

"Laughing and Laughing" in *Come to Power: Eleven Contemporary American Indian Poets,* ed. Dick Lourie. New York: Crossing, 1974, 99.

"Lullaby," *Chicago Review* 26:1 (Summer 1974): 10–17.

"The Man to Send Rain Clouds." *New Mexico Quarterly* 38:4/39:1 (Winter–Spring 1969): 133–136; *The Man to Send Rain Clouds: Contemporary Stories by American Indians,* ed. Kenneth Rosen. New York: Viking, 1974.

"Mistaken Identity" in *Reckonings: Contemporary Short Fiction by Native American Women,* eds. Hertha Dawn Wong, Lauren Muller, and Jana Sequoya Magdaleno. New York: Oxford University Press, 2008, 143–147.

"'Not You,' He Said" in *What Wildness Is This: Women Write about the Southwest*, eds. Susan Wittig Albert and Susan Hanson. Austin: University of Texas Press, 2007.

"Old Pancakes," in *Reckonings: Contemporary Short Fiction by Native American Women*, eds. Hertha Dawn Wong, Lauren Muller, and Jana Sequoya Magdaleno. New York: Oxford University Press, 2008, 147–149.

"An Old-Time Indian Attack Conducted in Two Parts." *Yardbird Reader* 5 (1976): 77–84; *The Remembered Earth: An Anthology of Contemporary Native American Literature*, ed. Geary Hobson. Albuquerque: University of New Mexico Press, 1979.

"On Photography" in *Partial Vision*, ed. Lucy Lippard. New York: Free Press, 1992; *Yellow Woman and a Beauty of the Spirit: Essays on Native American Life Today*. New York: Simon & Schuster, 1996, 180–186.

"The People and the Land ARE Inseparable" in *Yellow Woman and a Beauty of the Spirit: Essays on Native American Life Today*. New York: Simon & Schuster, 1996, 85–91; *What Wildness Is This: Women Write About the Southwest*, eds. Susan Wittig Albert and Susan Hanson. Austin: University of Texas Press, 2007.

"Poem for Myself and Mei-Mei: Concerning Abortion." *Journal of Ethnic Studies* 2:2 (Summer 1974): 66.

"Prayer to the Pacific." *Chicago Review* 24:4 (Spring 1973): 93–94; *Carriers of the Dream Wheel: Contemporary Native American Poetry*, ed. Duane Niatum. New York: Harper & Row, 1975.

"Preface" to *Partial Recall: With Essays on Photographs of Native North Americans*, eds. Lucy R. Lippard and Don Desmett. Philadelphia: Temple University Press, 1993, 8–10.

"Preparations." *Chicago Review* 24:4 (Spring 1973): 100.

"Private Property" in *Earth Power Coming*, ed. Simon Joseph Ortiz. Tsaile, AZ: Navajo Community College Press, 1983.

"Prophecy of Old Woman Mountain." *Journal of Ethnic Studies* 2:2 (Summer 1974): 70.

"Reasserting Our Claims." *New Letters* 59:1 (1992): 43, 51.

"Replacing Confusion with Equity: Alternatives for Water Policy in the Colorado River Basin" (co-authored by Helen M. Ingram and Lawrence A. Scarr) in *New Courses for the Colorado River*, ed. Gary Weatherford and F. Lee Brown. Albuquerque: University of New Mexico Press, 1986, 177–199; reprinted in *A River Too Far: The Past and Future of the Arid West*, eds. Joseph Finkhouse and Mark Crawford. Reno: Nevada Humanities Commission, 1991, 83–103.

"Rooster and the Power of Love" in *Stories That Shape Us*. New York: Norton, 1995.

"Skeleton Fixer's Story." *Sun Tracks* 4 (1978): 2–3.

"Stone Avenue Mural." *City Lights Press* (1994); *Yellow Woman and a Beauty of the Spirit: Essays on Native American Life Today*. New York: Simon & Schuster, 1996, 149–151.

"Story from Bear Country," *Journal of Contemporary Literature* 1:1 (Fall 1977): 4–6; *Antaeus* 27 (Autumn 1977): 62–64.

"Storyteller." *Puerto del Sol* 14:1 (Fall 1975): 11–25.

"Story-telling." *Journal of Ethnic Studies* 2:2 (Summer 1974): 72–74.

"Sun Children." *Quetzal* 2:3 (Summer 1972): 47.

"They Were the Land's" (review). *New York Times Book Review* (25 May 1980): 10, 22.

"Through the Stories We Hear Who We Are," *Amicus Journal* 14:4 (1993): 19.

"The Time We Climbed Snake Mountain." *Chicago Review* 24:4 (Spring 1973): 99.

"Tony's Story." *Thunderbird* (1969): 2–4; *The Man to Send Rain Clouds: Contemporary Stories by American Indians*, ed. Kenneth Rosen. New York: Viking, 1974, 69–71.

"Tribal Prophecies" in *Encuentro: Invasion of the Americas and the Making of the Mestizo*, Venice, CA: SPARC, 1991; *Blue Mesa Review* 4 (Spring 1992): 12–13; *Yellow Woman and a Beauty of the Spirit: Essays on Native American Life Today*. New York: Simon & Schuster, 1996, 92–95.

"Uncle Tony's Goat" in *The Man to Send Rain Clouds: Contemporary Stories by American Indians*, ed. Kenneth Rosen. New York: Viking, 1974.

"Videomakers and Basketmakers." *Aperture* 119 (Summer 1990): 72–73.

"When I Was Thirteen" in *Storyteller* (1981); *Voices under One Sky*, ed. Trish Fox Roman. Freedom, CA: Crossing, 1994, 26–27.

"When Sun Came to Riverwoman." *Greenfield Review* 3:2 (1973): 67–68.

"Where Mountainlion Laid Down with Deer." *Northwest Review* 13:2 (1973): 34–35.

"Yellow Woman" in *The Man to Send Rain Clouds: Contemporary Stories by American Indians*, ed. Kenneth Rosen. New York: Viking, 1974.

"Yellow Woman and A Beauty of the Spirit." *Los Angeles Times* (19 December 1993): 52; *Yellow Woman and a Beauty of the Spirit: Essays on Native American Life Today*. New York: Simon & Schuster, 1996, 60–72.

## Drama

*Lullaby* (unpublished), with Frank Chin, 1976.

## Film

*Arrowboy and the Witches*, produced with Dennis Carr, North Hollywood, CA: Video Tape, 1980.

*Black Elk*, written for Marlon Brando.

## Audiotape

"The Laguna Regulars and Geronimo." *Ahwasasne Notes*. Rooseveltown, NY: Mohawk Nation, 1977.

# Secondary

## General

Adams, Rachel. *Continental Divides: Remapping the Cultures of North America*. Chicago: University of Chicago Press, 2009.

Alcoff, Linda. *Visible Identities: Race, Gender, and the Self*. New York: Oxford University Press, 2005.

Anderson, Lorraine, and Thomas S. Edwards. *At Home on This Earth: Two Centuries of U.S. Women's Nature Writing*. Hanover, NH: University Press of New England, 2002.

Archuleta, Elizabeth. "Securing Our Nation's Roads and Borders or Re-circling the Wagons? Leslie Marmon Silko's Destabilization of 'Borders,'" *Wicazo Sa Review* 20:1 (Spring 2005): 113–137.

Armstrong, Gene. "Invigorated by Poetry: Top Native American Writers Get Together for a Three-Day UA Symposium," *Tucson Weekly* (7 June 2007).

Arnold, Ellen. "Listening to the Spirits: An Interview with Leslie Marmon Silko," *Studies in American Indian Literature* 10:3 (Fall 1998): 1–33.

Assmann, Aleida. "Space, Place, Land — Changing Concepts of Territory in English and American Fiction" in *Borderlands: Negotiating Boundaries in Post-Colonial Writing*. Amsterdam: Rodopi, 1999.

Ballenger, Bruce P., ed. *The Curious Writer*. White Plains, NY: Pearson Longman, 2005.

Barnes, Kim. "A Leslie Marmon Silko Interview," *Journal of Ethnic Studies* 13.4 (1986): 83–105.

Barnett, Louise, and James Thorson, eds. *Leslie Marmon Silko: A Collection of Critical Essays*. Albuquerque: University of New Mexico Press, 1999.

Beck, John. *Dirty Wars: Landscape, Power, and Waste in Western American Literature*. Lincoln: University of Nebraska Press, 2009.

Beidler, Peter G. "'The Earth Itself War Sobbing': Madness and the Environment in Novels by Leslie Marmon Silko and Louise Erdrich," *American Indian Culture & Research Journal* 26:3 (2002): 113–124.

Beier, J. Marshall. *International Relations in Uncommon Places: Indigeneity, Cosmology, and the Limits of International Theory*. Hampshire, NY: Palgrave Macmillan, 2005.

Bellinelli, Matteo. *Leslie Marmon Silko*. Princeton, NJ: Films for the Humanities, 1995. Video.

Beste, Helga. "*What's that, crazy?*": zur Funktion verruckter Charaktere bei John Kennedy Toole, Joseph Heller, Marilynne Robinson und Leslie Marmon Silko. Trier, Ger.: Wissenschaftlicher Verlag, 2003.

Blackmarr, Amy. *Above the Fall Line: The Trail from White Pine Cabin*. Macon, GA: Mercer University Press, 2003.

Blanchard, Mary Loving, and Cara Falcetti. *Poets for Young Adults: Their Lives and Works*. Westport, CT: Greenwood, 2007.

Bloom, Harold. *Native American Writers*. New York: Bloom's Literary Criticism, 2010.

Bowers, Maggie Ann. "Eco-Criticism in a (Post-) Colonial Contest and Leslie Marmon Silko's *Almanac of the Dead*" in *Towards a Transcultural Future: Literature and Human Rights in a 'Post'-Colonial World*, ed. Peter H. Marsden. Amsterdam: Rodopi, 2004.

Brice, Jennifer. "Earth as Mother, Earth as Other in Novels by Silko and Hogan," *Critique* 39, no. 2 (Winter 1998): 127–138.

Brown, Alanna Kathleen. "Pulling Silko's Threads Through Time: An Exploration of Storytelling," *American Indian Quarterly* 19:2 (Spring 1995): 171–179.

Brown, Julie. *American Women Short Story Writers: A Collection of Critical Essays*. New York: Routledge, 2000.

Brown-Guillory, Elizabeth. *Women of Color: Mother-Daughter Relationships in 20th-century Literature*. Austin: University of Texas Press, 1996.

Buell, Lawrence. "Ecoglobalist Affects: The Emergence of U.S. Environmental Imagination on a Planetary Scale" in *Shades of the Planet: American Literature as World Literature*, eds. Wai-chee Dimock and Lawrence Buell. Princeton, NJ: Princeton University Press, 2007, 227–247.

_____. *The Future of Environmental Criticism: Environmental Crisis and Literary Imagination*. London: Wiley-Blackwell, 2005.

_____. "Leslie Silko: Environmental Apocalypticism," in *The Environmental Imagination: Thoreau, Nature Writing, and the Formation of American Culture*. Cambridge, MA: Harvard University Press, 1995.

Cheyfitz, Eric. "The (Post)Colonial Predicament of Native American Studies," *Interventions* 4:3 (November 2002): 405–427.

Clarke, Deborah. *Driving Women: Fiction and Automobile Culture in Twentieth-Century America*. Baltimore: Johns Hopkins University Press, 2007.

Claviez, Thomas, and Maria Moss. *Mirror Writing: (Re-)Constructions of Native American Identity*. Berlin: Galda & Wilch, 2000.

Coltelli, Laura. *Winged Words: American Indian*

*Writers Speak*. Lincoln: University of Nebraska Press, 1990, 135–153.

Colwell-Chanthaphonh, Chip. "Portraits of a Stories Land: An Experiment in Writing the Landscapes of History," *Anthropological Quarterly* 78:1 (January 2005): 151–177.

Connors, Philip, "Talking with Leslie Marmon Silko," *Newsday* (4 April 1999): B11.

Corbett, Thomas. "Acclaimed Native American Artist and Author Lee H. Marmon Takes Top Honors in Regional Book Awards Competition," www.leemarmongallery.com/pressrelease_-MPBA-award.html, 2005.

Cortese, Romana, and James Cortese. "A Labyrinth of Mirrors: Carlos Ruiz Zafón's *The Shadow of the Wind*" in *21st-Century Gothic: Great Gothic Novels since 2000*, ed. Danel Olson. Lanham, MD: Scarecrow, 2011, 527–538.

Cucinella, Catherine. *Contemporary American Women Poets: An A-to-Z Guide*. Westport, CT: Greenwood, 2002.

Cutchins, Dennis. "'So That the Nations May Become Genuine Indian': Nativism and Leslie Marmon Silko's Ceremony," *Journal of American Culture* 22:4 (Winter 1999): 79–91.

Cutter, Martha J. *Lost in Translation: Contemporary Ethnic American Writing and the Politics of Language Diversity*. Chapel Hill: University of North Carolina Press, 2005.

David, Gary A. *The Orion Zone: Ancient Star Cities of the American Southwest*. Kempton, IL: Adventures Unlimited, 2006.

Dennis, Helen May. *Native American Literature: Towards a Spacialized Reading*. New York: Taylor & Francis, 2007.

Denzin, Norman K., Yvonna S. Lincoln, and Linda Tuhiwai Smith, eds. *Handbook of Critical and Indigenous Methodologies*. Los Angeles: Sage, 2008.

De Ramírez, Susan Berry Brill, and Edith M. Baker. "'There Are Balances and Harmonies Always Shifting; Always Necessary to Maintain': Leslie Marmon Silko's Vision of Global Environmental Justice for the People and the Land," *Organization Environment* 18 (June 2005): 213–228.

Desai, Gaurav Gajanan, and Supriya Nair. *Postcolonialisms: An Anthology of Cultural Theory and Criticism*. New Brunswick, NJ: Rutgers University Press, 2005.

Dirda, Michael. "Stylists and Visionaries: 25 years of American Fiction," *Washington Post* (1 June 1997).

Donovan, Kathleen M. *Feminist Readings of Native American Literature: Coming to Voice*. Tucson: University of Arizona Press, 1998.

Elliott, Gayle. "Silko, Le Sueur, and Le Guin: Storytelling as a 'Movement Toward Wholeness'" in *Scribbling Women & the Short Story Form: Approaches by American & British Women Writers*, ed. Ellen Burton Harrington. New York: Peter Lang, 2008, 178–192.

Erdrich, Heid Ellen, and Laura Tohe. *Sister Nations: Native American Women Writers on Community*. St. Paul: Minnesota Historical Society Press, 2002.

Evers, Larry, and Denny Carr. "A Conversation with Leslie Marmon Silko," *Sun Tracks* 3:1 (Fall 1976): 28–33.

Fear-Segal, Jacqueline. *White Man's Club: Schools, Race, and the Struggle of Indian Acculturation*. Lincoln: University of Nebraska Press, 2007.

Fedderson, Rick, Susan Lohafer, Barbara Lounsberry, and Mary Rohrberger. *The Tales We Tell: Perspectives on the Short Story*. London: Greenwood, 1998.

"Finding Justice through Words," *Santa Fe New Mexican* (3 February 1996): 6.

Finnegan, Jordana. *Narrating the American West*. Amherst, NY: Cambria, 2008.

Fisher, Dexter. "Stories and Their Tellers—A Conversation with Leslie Marmon Silko" in *The Third Woman: Minority Women Writers of the United States*. Boston: Houghton Mifflin, 1980.

Fitz, Brewster E. *Silko: Writing Storyteller and Medicine Woman*. Norman: University of Oklahoma Press, 2004.

Gannon, Thomas C. *Skylark Meets Meadowlark: Reimagining the Bird in British Romantic and Contemporary Native American Literature*. Lincoln: University of Nebraska Press, 2009.

Gelfant, Blanche H. *The Columbia Companion to the Twentieth-Century American Short Story*. New York: Columbia University Press, 2000.

Hanne, Michael. *Creativity in Exile*. Amsterdam: Rodolpi, 2004.

Harmsen-Peraino, Suzanne. "The Ghost Dance Vision in Leslie M. Silko's *Almanac of the Dead* and *Gardens in the Dunes*," *Canada cahiers* 12 (8 September 2008): 128–140.

Hart, George, and Scott Slovic. *Literature and the Environment*. Westport, CT: Greenwood, 2004.

"History's Great, Grave Whole," *New York Times* (29 December 1991).

Ho, Wendy. *In Her Mother's House: The Politics of Asian American Mother-Daughter Writing*. Blue Ridge Summit, PA: AltaMira, 1999.

Hoil, Juan José, and Ralph Loveland Roys. *The Book of Chilam Balam of Chumayel*. Washington, DC: Carnegie Institution, 1933.

Hölbling, Walter. *US Icons and Iconicity*. Münster, Austria: Wien Lit, 2006.

Holt-Fortin, C. "The Intersection of Fantasy and Native America: From H. P. Lovecraft to Leslie Marmon Silko," *Choice* 47:10 (1 June 2010): 1920.

Huhndorf, Shari Michelle. *Going Native: Indians in the American Cultural Imagination.* Ithaca: Cornell University Press, 2001.

_____. *Mapping the Americas: The Transnational Politics of Contemporary Native Culture.* Ithaca: Cornell University Press, 2009.

_____. "Picture Revolution: Transnationalism, American Studies, and the Politics of Contemporary Native Culture," *American Quarterly* 61:2 (June 2009): 359–381.

Hunt, Alex. "The Radical Geography of Silko's *Almanac of the Dead,*" *Western American Literature* 39:3 (Fall 2004): 256–278.

Irr, Caren. *Pink Pirates: Contemporary American Women Writers and Copyright.* Iowa City: University of Iowa Press, 2010.

Jacobs, Karen. "Optic/Haptic/Abject: Revisioning Indigenous Media in Victor Masayesva, Jr. and Leslie Marmon Silko," *Journal of Visual Culture* 3 (December 2004): 291–316.

Jacobs, Margaret D. *Engendered Encounters: Feminism and Pueblo Cultures, 1879–1934.* Lincoln: University of Nebraska Press, 1999.

Jaskoski, Helen. *Leslie Marmon Silko: A Study of the Short Fiction.* New York: Twayne, 1998.

Jolivétte, Andrew. *Cultural Representation in Native America.* Lanham, MD: Altamira, 2006.

Joshi, S. T. "Foreword," *21st-Century Gothic: Great Gothic Novels since 2000,* ed. Danel Olson. Lanham, MD: Scarecrow, 2011, xi–xviii.

Joyce, Graham. "Narrative and Regeneration: *The Monsters of Templeton* by Lauren Groff in *21st-Century Gothic: Great Gothic Novels since 2000,* ed. Danel Olson. Lanham, MD: Scarecrow, 2011, 445–452.

Justice, Daniel Heath. *Our Fire Survives the Storm: A Cherokee Literary History.* Minneapolis: University of Minnesota Press, 2006.

Karem, Jeff. *The Romance of Authenticity: The Cultural Politics of Regional and Ethnic Literatures.* Charlottesville: University of Virginia Press, 2004.

Karno, Valerie. "Legal Hunger: Law, Narrative and Orality in Leslie Marmon Silko's Storyteller and Almanac of the Dead," *College Literature* 28:1 (Winter 2001): 29–45.

Katz, Jane B., ed. *This Song Remembers: Self Portraits of Native Americans in the Arts.* Boston: Houghton Mifflin, 1980.

Keen, Suzanne. *Empathy and the Novel.* New York: Oxford University Press, 2007.

Kennedy, J. Gerald. *Modern American Short Story Sequences: Composite Fictions and Fictive Communities.* Cambridge: Cambridge University Press, 1995.

Kidwell, Clara Sue, and Alan R. Velie. *Native American Studies.* Lincoln: University of Nebraska Press, 2005.

Kirchmayer, Katharina. *Sites of Resistance in Alice Walker and Leslie Silko.* Norderstedt, Ger.: Bruck und Bindung, 2010.

Krupat, Arnold. *Red Matters: Native American Studies.* Philadelphia: University of Pennsylvania Press, 2002.

_____. *The Turn to the Native: Studies in Criticism and Culture.* Lincoln: University of Nebraska Press, 1998.

_____, and Michael A. Elliott. "American Indian Fiction and Anticolonial Resistance" in *The Columbia Guide to American Indian Literatures of the United States since 1945.* New York: Columbia University Press, 2006.

Kuokkanen, Rauna Johanna. *Reshaping the University: Responsibility, Indigenous Epistemes, and the Logic of the Gift.* Vancouver: University of British Columbia Press, 2007.

Lavender, Catherine Jane. *Scientists and Storytellers: Feminist Anthropologists and the Construction of the American Southwest.* Albuquerque: University of New Mexico Press, 2006.

Lincoln, Kenneth. *Sing with the Heart of a Bear: Fusions of Native and American Poetry, 1890–1999.* Berkeley: University of California Press, 1999.

_____. *Speak Like Singing: Classics of Native American Literature.* Albuquerque: University of New Mexico Press, 2008.

Lippert, Dorothy. "Not the End, Not the Middle, but the Beginning: Repatriation as a Transformative Mechanism for Archaeologists and Indigenous Peoples," *Collaboration in Archaeological Practice: Engaging Descendant Communities,* eds. Chip Colwell-Chanthaphonh and T. J. Ferguson. Lanham, MD: AltaMira, 2008, 119–130.

Lippy, Charles H. *Pluralism Comes of Age: American Religious Culture in the Twentieth Century.* Armonk, NY: M. E. Sharpe, 2002.

Lopez, Ruth. "Exploring Passions," *Santa Fe New Mexican* (13 November 1998): 30.

_____. "Finding Justice Through Words," *Santa Fe New Mexican* (3 March 1996): D6.

Low, Denise. "Two Aspects of Western Landscape: Migration Trail and Landmarks," *Midwest Quarterly* 49:2 (January 2008): 200–216.

Lundquist, Suzanne Evertsen. *Native American Literatures: An Introduction.* New York: Continuum, 2005.

Lynch, Tom. *Xerophilia: Ecocritical Explorations in Southwestern Literature.* Texas Tech University Press, 2008.

Lyons, Scott Richard. *X-Marks: Native Signatures of Assent.* Minneapolis: University of Minnesota Press, 2010.

Mainiero, Linda, ed. *American Women Writers.* New York: Frederick Ungar, 1982.

Mariani, Philomena, ed. *Critical Fictions: The*

*Politics of Imaginative Writing.* Seattle, WA: Bay Press, 1991.

Markowitz, Harvey, and Carole A. Barrett. *American Indian Biographies.* Ann Arbor: University of Michigan Press, 2005.

Marmon, Lee. *The Pueblo Imagination: Landscape and Memory in the Photography of Lee Marmon.* Boston: Beacon, 2003.

Marsden, Peter H. *Towards a Transcultural Future: Literature and Human Rights in a "Post"-colonial World.* Amsterdam: Rodopi, 2004.

McAdams, Janet. "A Conversation with Simon Ortiz," *Kenyon Review* 32:1 (January 2010): 1–8.

McClure, John. *Partial Faiths: Postsecular Fiction in the Age of Pynchon and Morrison.* Athens: University of Georgia Press, 2007.

McMurtry, Larry. *Sacagawea's Nickname: Essays on the American West.* New York: New York Review of Books, 2004.

Mellas, Laurie. "Memory and Promise: Leslie Marmon Silko's Story," *Mirage* 24 (Spring 2006): 11–14.

Michaels, Walter Benn. *The Trouble with Diversity: How We Learned to Love Identity and Ignore Inequality.* New York: Metropolitan Books, 2006.

Moore, Lucy. *Into the Canyon: Seven Years in Navajo Country.* Albuquerque: University of New Mexico Press, 2006.

Moore, MariJo. *Genocide of the Mind: New Native American Writing.* New York: Nation Books, 2003.

Morgan, Thomas D. "Native Americans in World War II," *Army History* 35 (Fall 1995): 22–27.

Murray, David. *Matter, Magic, and Spirit: Representing Indian and African American Belief.* Philadelphia: University of Pennsylvania Press, 2007.

Nelson, Robert M. "Settling for Vision in Silko's *Ceremony*: Sun Man, Arrowboy, and Tayo," *American Indian Culture and Research Journal* 28:1 (2004): 67–73.

Nevill, Adam L. G. "Wonder and Awe: Mysticism, Poetry, and Perception in Ramsey Campbell's *The Darkest Part of the Woods*" in *21st-Century Gothic: Great Gothic Novels since 2000*, ed. Danel Olson. Lanham, MD: Scarecrow, 2011, 149–157.

Nguyen, B. Minh, and Porter Shreve. *Contemporary Creative Fiction.* White Plains, NY: Pearson/Longman, 2005.

Niemann, Linda, and Joel Jensen. *Railroad Noir: The American West at the End of the Twentieth Century.* Bloomington: Indiana University Press, 2010.

Norman, Brian. *The American Protest Essay and National Belonging: Addressing Division.* Albany: State University of New York Press, 2007.

Olson, Danel, ed. "Introduction" to *21st-Century Gothic: Great Gothic Novels since 2000*, ed. Danel Olson. Lanham, MD: Scarecrow, 2011, xxi–xxxiii.

Palumbo-Liu, David. *The Ethnic Canon: Histories, Institutions, and Interventions.* Minneapolis: University of Minnesota Press, 1995.

Parker, Robert Dale. *The Invention of Native American Literature.* Ithaca: Cornell University Press, 2003.

Parrish, Timothy. *From the Civil War to the Apocalypse: Postmodern History and American Fiction.* Amherst: University of Massachusetts Press, 2008.

Perry, Donna. *Backtalk: Women Writers Speak Out.* New Brunswick, NJ: Rutgers University Press, 1993.

Petrilli, Susan. *White Matters.* Roma: Meltemi, 2007.

Pierotti, Raymond. *Indigenous Knowledge, Ecology, and Evolutionary Biology.* New York: Routledge, 2011.

Porter, Joy, and Kenneth M. Roemer. *The Cambridge Companion to Native American Literature.* Cambridge: Cambridge University Press, 2005.

Powers, Peter Kerry. *Recalling Religions: Resistance, Memory, and Cultural Revision in Ethnic Women's Literature.* Knoxville: University of Tennessee Press, 2001.

Pratt, Mary Louise. "Arts of the Contact Zone" in *Ways of Reading: An Anthology for Writers*, eds. David Bartholomae and Anthony Petrosky. Boston: St. Martin's, 1993.

Pulitano, Elvira. *Transatlantic Voices: Interpretations of Native American Literatures.* Lincoln: University of Nebraska Press, 2007.

Rader, Pamela J. *Multi-Ethnicity as a Resource for the Literary Imagination: The Creative Achievements of Women Artists, Poets, and Novelists.* Lewiston, NY: Edwin Mellen, 2009.

Rainwater, Catherine. *Dreams of Fiery Stars: The Transformations of Native American Fiction.* Philadelphia: University of Pennsylvania Press, 1999.

Ramsey, Jarold, and Lori Burlingame, eds. *In Beauty I Walk: The Literary Roots of Native American Writing.* Albuquerque: University of New Mexico Press, 2008.

Rand, Naomi R. *Silko, Morrison, and Roth: Studies in Survival.* New York: Peter Lang, 1999.

Ridington, Robin, and Jillian Ridington. *When You Sing It Now, Just Like New: First Nations Poetics, Voices, and Representations.* Lincoln: University of Nebraska Press, 2006.

Roberts, Kathleen Glenister, and Ronald C. Arnett. *Communication Ethics: Between Cosmopolitanism and Provinciality.* New York: Peter Lang, 2008.

Robinett, Jane. "Looking for Roots: Curandera and

Shamanic Practices in Southwestern Fiction," *Mosaic* 36:1 (March 2003): 121–134.

Roeder, Fred. "The Marmon Brothers of Laguna," *Storyteller*. New York: Arcade, 1981.

Round, Phillip H. *Removable Type: Histories of the Book in Indian Country, 1663–1880*. Chapel Hill: University of North Carolina Press, 2010.

Ruoff, A. LaVonne. "Ritual and Renewal: Keres Traditions in the Short Fiction of Leslie Silko," *MELUS* 5:4 (Winter 1978): 2–17.

Sadowski-Smith, Claudia. *Border Fictions: Globalization, Empire, and Writing at the Boundaries of the United States*. Charlottesville: University of Virginia Press, 2008.

San Juan, Epifanio. *Beyond Postcolonial Theory*. New York: St. Martin's, 1999.

Saunders, Michael. "Alexie Sends 'Smoke Signals,'" *Boston Globe* (5 July 1998): N1.

"Save the Snake," *Arizona Daily Star* (23 February 1997).

Schweninger, Lee. "Claiming Europe: Native American Literary Responses to the Old World," *American Indian Culture and Research Journal* 27:2 (2003): 61–76.

Seed, David. *A Companion to Twentieth-Century United States Fiction*. Malden, MA: Wiley-Blackwell, 2010.

Seyersted, Per. "Interview with Leslie Marmon Silko," *American Studies in Scandinavia* 13 (1985): 17–25.

Shumaker, Conrad. *Southwestern American Indian Literature: In the Classroom and Beyond*. New York: Peter Lang, 2008.

_____. *Leslie Marmon Silko*. Boise: Boise State University, 1980.

Silko, Leslie Marmon, and Ellen L. Arnold. *Conversations with Leslie Marmon Silko*. Jackson: University Press of Mississippi, 2000.

Stein, Rachel. *Shifting the Ground: American Women Writers' Revisions of Nature, Gender, and Race*. Charlottesville: University Press of Virginia, 1997.

Stigter, Shelley. *Double-Voice and Double-Consciousness in Native American Literature* (thesis). Lethbridge, Alta.: University of Lethbridge, 2005.

Stout, Janis P. *Picturing a Different West: Vision, Illustration, and the Tradition of Cather and Austin*. Lubbock: Texas Tech University Press, 2007.

Stromberg, Ernest. *American Indian Rhetorics of Survivance: Word Medicine, Word Magic*. Pittsburgh: University of Pittsburgh Press, 2006.

Sturgis, Amy H., and David D. Oberhelman. *The Intersection of Fantasy and Native America: From H. P. Lovecraft to Leslie Marmon Silko*. Campbell, CA: Mythopoeic Press, 2009.

Teuton, Sean Kicummah. *Red Land, Red Power: Grounding Knowledge in the American Indian Novel*. Durham, NC: Duke University Press, 2008.

Thornton, Matthew. "Deals," *Publishers Weekly* 254:19 (7 May 2007): 14–15.

Van Gelder, Lawrence. "Footlights," *New York Times* (27 September 2000).

Velie, Alan R. *Four American Literary Masters*. Norman: University of Oklahoma Press, 1982.

Vizenor, Gerald Robert. *Narrative Chance: Postmodern Discourse on Native American Indian Literatures*. Norman: University of Oklahoma Press, 1993.

_____. *Shadow Distance: A Gerald Vizenor Reader*. Hanover NH: Wesleyan University Press, 1994.

Waldron, Karen E. "The Land as Consciousness: Ecological Being and the Movement of Words in the Works of Leslie Marmon Silko" in *Such News of the Land: U.S. Women Nature Writers*, eds. Thomas S. Edwards and Elizabeth A. De Wolfe. Hanover, NH: University Press of New England, 2001, 178–203.

Wenzel, Jennifer. *Bulletproof: Afterlives of Anticolonial Prophecy in South Africa and Beyond*. Chicago: University of Chicago Press, 2009.

Werlock, Abby H. P. *Facts on File Companion to the American Short Story*. New York: Facts on File, 2010.

White, Daniel. "Antidote to Desecration: Leslie Marmon Silko's Nonfiction" in *Leslie Marmon Silko: A Collection of Critical Essays*, eds. Louise Barnett and James Thorson. Albuquerque: University of New Mexico Press, 1999, 135–148.

Whitt, Laurelyn. *Science, Colonialism, and Indigenous Peoples: The Cultural Politics of Law and Knowledge*. Cambridge: Cambridge University Press, 2009.

Wilentz, Gay Alden. *Healing Narratives: Women Writers Curing Cultural Dis-ease*. New Brunswick, NJ: Rutgers University Press, 2000.

Wilson, Sharon Rose. *Myths and Fairy Tales in Contemporary Women's Fiction: from Atwood to Morrison*. New York: Palgrave Macmillan, 2008.

Wisenberg, S. L. "Rethinking the Melting Pot Arguments about Assimilation, Race and American Society," *Chicago Tribune* (17 August 1997): 8.

Wolfreys, Julian. *Modern North American Criticism and Theory: A Critical Guide*. Edinburgh: Edinburgh University Press, 2006.

Womack, Craig S. "A Single Decade: Book-Length Native Literary Criticism between 1986 and 1997" in *Reasoning Together: The Native Critics Collective*. Norman: University of Oklahoma Press, 2008.

Wright, Anne, ed. *The Delicacy and Strength of Lace: Letters between Leslie Marmon Silko and James Wright*. St. Paul, MN: Graywolf, 1986.

Wright, Gregory. "Narrating the American West: New Forms of Historical Memory," *Studies in American Indian Literatures* 22:1 (Spring 2010): 132–134.

Zamora, Lois Parkinson. "Finding a Voice, Telling a Story: Constructing Communal Identity in Contemporary American Women's Writing" in *American Mythologies: Essays in Contemporary Literature*, eds. William Blazek and Michael K. Glenday. Liverpool, UK: Liverpool University Press, 2005, 267–294.

Zax, David. "Q&A," *Smithsonian* 38:5 (August 2007): 36.

## Almanac of the Dead

Abbott, Carl. *How Cities Won the West: Four Centuries of Urban Change in Western North America*. Albuquerque: University of New Mexico Press, 2008.

Acoose, Janice, Craig S. Womack, Daniel Heath Justice, and Christopher B. Teuton. *Reasoning Together: The Native Critics Collection*. Norman: University of Oklahoma Press, 2008.

Adamson, Joni. *American Indian Literature, Environmental Justice, and Ecocriticism: The Middle Place*. Albuquerque: University of Arizona Press, 2001.

_____, and Scott Slovic. "The Shoulders We Stand On: An Introduction to Ethnicity and Ecocriticism," *MELUS* 34:2 (1 June 2009): 5–24.

Ammons, Elizabeth. *Brave New Words: How Literature Will Save the Planet*. Iowa City: University of Iowa Press, 2010.

Andrade, Susan Z. *Atlantic Cross-Currents: Transatlantiques*. Trenton, NJ: Africa World Press, 2001.

"Author's Novel Calls for Reconciliation with Earth," *St. Paul Pioneer Press* (7 February 1993).

Bak, Hans. *First Nations of North America: Politics and Representation*. Amsterdam: VU University Press, 2005.

Barbieri, Richard. "A Richly Barren Land," *Independent School* 60:2 (Winter 2001): 100–102.

Baringer, Sandra. *The Metanarrative of Suspicion in Late Twentieth Century America*. New York: Routledge, 2004.

Beck, John. *Dirty Wars: Landscape, Power, and Waste in Western American Literature*. Lincoln: University of Nebraska Press, 2009.

Bell, Virginia E. "Counter-chronicling and Alternative Mapping in *Memoria del Fuego* and *Almanac of the Dead*," *MELUS* 25:3/4 (2000): 5–30.

Bergland, Renée. *The National Uncanny: Indian Ghosts and American Subjects*. Hanover, NH: Dartmouth College, 2000.

Berglund, Jeff. *Cannibal Fictions: American Explorations of Colonialism, Race, Gender and Sexual-

ity*. Madison: University of Wisconsin Press, 2006.

Birkerts, Sven. "Apocalypse Now," *New Republic* 205:19 (4 November 1991): 39–41.

Bomberry, Victoria. "Refounding the Nation: A Generation of Activism in Bolivia," *American Behavioral Scientist* 51:12 (August 2008): 1790–1800.

Brigham, Ann. "Productions of Geographic Scale and Capitalist-Colonialist Enterprise in Leslie Marmon Silko's *Almanac of the Dead*," *Modern Fiction Studies* 50:2 (2004): 303–331.

Brooks, Lisa Tanya. *The Common Poet: The Recovery of Native Space in the Northeast*. Minneapolis: University of Minnesota Press, 2008.

Butler, Martin. *Hybrid Americas: Contacts, Contrasts, and Confluences in New World Literatures and Cultures*. Tempe, AZ: Bilingual Press, 2008.

Carlin, Margaret. "Apocalypse Any Day Now: Angry Indian Writer Calmly Predicts End of Rule by White Man," *Rocky Mountain News* (19 January 1992).

Carter, Nancy Corson. "Apocalypse Imminent Series," *St. Petersburg Times* (24 November 1993): 6D.

Cherniavsky, Eva. *Incorporations: Race, Nation, and the Body Politics of Capital*. Minneapolis: University of Minnesota Press, 2006.

_____. "Tribalism, Globalism, and Eskimo Television in Leslie Marmon Silko's *Almanac of the Dead*," *Angelaki: Journal of Theoretical Humanities* 6:1 (1 April 2001): 111–126.

Cheyfitz, Eric. "The (Post)Colonial Predicament of Native American Studies," *Interventions* 4:3 (November 2002): 405–427.

Collier, George. *BASTA! Land and the Zapatista Rebellion in Chiapas*. Chicago: Institute for Food and Development Policy, 1994.

Cook-Lynn, Elizabeth. *Anti-Indianism in Modern America: A Voice from Tatekeya's Earth*. Urbana: University of Illinois Press, 2001.

_____. *New Indians, Old Wars*. Urbana: University of Illinois Press, 2007.

_____. *Why I Can't Read Wallace Stegner and Other Essays: A Tribal Voice*. Madison: University of Wisconsin Press, 1996.

Cotten, Angela L., and Christa Davis Acampora. *Cultural Sites of Critical Insight: Philosophy, Aesthetics, and African American and Native American Women's Writings*. Albany: State University of New York Press, 2007.

Cryer, Dan. "Native Uprising," (Long Island) *Newsday* (17 November 1991): 35.

Cutter, Martha J. *Lost and Found in Translation: Contemporary Ethnic American Writing and the Politics of Language Diversity*. Chapel Hill: University of North Carolina Press, 2005.

Dauterich, Edward, IV. "Time, Communication,

and Prophecy: Prodigious Unity in *Almanac of the Dead*," *CLA Journal* 50:3 (March 2007): 348–363.

Davidson, Michael. *Concerto for the Left Hand: Disability and the Defamiliar Body*. Ann Arbor: University of Michigan Press, 2008.

D'haen, Theo. *How Far Is America from Here?: Selected Proceedings of the First World Congress of the International American Studies Association, 22–24 May 2003*. Amsterdam: Rodopi, 2005.

Dimock, Wai-chee, and Lawrence Buell. *Shades of the Planet: American Literature as World Literature*. Princeton, NJ: Princeton University Press, 2007.

Douglas, Christopher. *A Genealogy of Literary Multiculturalism*. Ithaca: Cornell University Press, 2009.

"Fatal Flaw Kills 'Dead' as It Offers Apologia for Yaqui People," *Washington* (D.C.) *Times* (19 January 1992).

Fischer-Hornung, Dorothea. "'Now we know that gay men are just men after all': Abject Sexualities in Leslie Marmon Silko's *Almanac of the Dead*" in *The Abject of Desire: The Aestheticization of the Unaesthetic in Contemporary Literature and Culture*, eds. Konstanze Kutzbach and Monika Mueller. Amsterdam: Rodopi, 2007, 107–128.

Foster, Tol. "Of One Blood: An Argument for Relations and Regionality in Native American Literary Studies" in *Reasoning Together: The Native Critics Collective*. Norman: University of Oklahoma Press, 2008.

Graham, Shane. "Re-reading Leslie Marmon Silko's *Almanac of the Dead* after 9/11," *English Studies in Africa* 48:2 (2005): 75–88.

Harder, Bernie. "The Power of Borders in Native American Literature: Leslie Marmon Silko's *Almanac of the Dead*," *American Indian Culture and Research Journal* 24:4 (2000): 95–106.

Harjo, Joy. "Review: *Almanac of the Dead*," *Blue Mesa Review* (Spring 1992): 207–210.

Hobby, Blake, ed. *Exploration and Colonization*. New York: Bloom's Literary Criticism, 2010.

Holland, Sharon Patricia. *Raising the Dead: Readings of Death and (Black) Subjectivity*. Durham, NC: Duke University Press, 2000.

Horvitz, Deborah M. *Literary Trauma: Sadism, Memory, and Sexual Violence in American Women's Fiction*. Albany: State University of New York Press, 2000.

Hume, Kathryn. *American Dream, American Nightmare: Fiction Since 1960*. Urbana: University of Illinois Press, 2002.

Hunt, Alex. "The Radical Geography of Silko's *Almanac of the Dead*," *Western American Literature* 39:3 (Fall 2004): 256–278.

Irr, Caren. "The Timelessness of *Almanac of the Dead*, or a Postmodern Rewriting of Radical Fiction" in *Leslie Marmon Silko: A Collection of Critical Essays*, eds. Louise Barnett and James Thorson. Albuquerque: University of New Mexico Press, 1999, 223–234.

Jacobs, Karen. "Optic/Haptic/Abject: Revisioning Indigenous Media in Victor Masayesva, Jr., and Leslie Marmon Silko," *Journal of Visual Culture* 3:3 (December 2004): 291–316.

Jarman, Michelle. "Exploring the World of the Different in Leslie Marmon Silko's *Almanac of the Dead*," *MELUS* 31:3 (Fall 2006): 147–168.

Jenkins, Philip. *Dream Catchers: How Mainstream America Discovered Native Spirituality*. New York: Oxford University Press, 2005.

Katerberg, William H. *Future West: Utopia and Apocalypse in Frontier Science Fiction*. Lawrence: University Press of Kansas, 2008.

Kelleher, Kathleen. "Predicting a Revolt to Reclaim the Americas," *Los Angeles Times* (13 January 1992): E1.

Kelsey, Penelope Myrtle. *Tribal Theory in Native American Literature: Dakota and Haudenosaunee Writing and Indigenous Worldviews*. Lincoln: University of Nebraska Press, 2008.

Kincaid, James R. "Who Gets to Tell Their Stories?" *New York Times* (3 May 1992): 24–29.

Ku, Chung-Hao. "The Kid Is All the Rage: (Bi)-Sexuality, Temporality and Triangular Desire in Leslie Marmon Silko's *Almanac of the Dead*," *Journal of Bisexuality* 10:3 (July–September 2010): 309–349.

Larson, Charles. "'Almanac': Tribal Assault," *Washington Post* (26 November 1991).

Lauter, Paul. *A Companion to American Literature and Culture*. Malden, MA: Blackwell-Wiley, 2010.

Lee, A. Robert. *Gothic to Multicultural: Idioms of Imagining in American Literary Fiction*. Amsterdam: Rodopi, 2009.

_____, ed. *Loosening the Seams: Interpretations of Gerald Vizenor*. Bowling Green, KY: Bowling Green University Press, 2000.

_____. *United States: Re-viewing American Multicultural Literature*. València: Universitat de València, 2009.

Libretti, Tim. "The Other Proletarians: Native American Literature and Class Struggle," *Modern Fiction Studies* 47:1 (Spring 2001): 164–189.

Michaels, Walter Benn. *The Shape of the Signifier: 1967 to the End of History*. Princeton, NJ: Princeton University Press, 2006.

Miles, Tiya, and Sharon Patricia Holland. *Crossing Waters, Crossing Worlds: The African Diaspora in Indian Country*. Durham, NC: Duke University Press, 2006.

Mogen, David. "Native American Vision of Apocalypse: Prophecy and Protest in the Fiction of

Leslie Marmon Silko and Gerald Vizenor" in *American Mythologies: Essays in Contemporary Literature*, ed. William Blazek. Liverpool, UK: Liverpool University Press, 2005.

Moses, Cathy. *Dissenting Fictions: Identity and Resistance in the Contemporary American Novel*. New York: Routledge, 2000.

Murphy, Jacqueline Shea. *The People Have Never Stopped Dancing: Native American Modern Dance Histories*. Minneapolis: University of Minnesota Press, 2007.

Muthlaya, John. "*Almanac of the Dead*: The Dream of the Fifth World in the Borderlands," *Literature Interpretation Theory* 14:4 (2003): 357–385.

Niemann, Linda. "New World Disorder," *Women's Review of Books* 9:6 (March 1992): 1–4.

_____, and Leslie Marmon Silko. "Narratives of Survival," *Women's Review of Books* 9:10–11 (July 1992): 10.

O'Donnell, Patrick. *The American Novel Now: Reading Contemporary American Fiction since 1980*. Chichester, UK: Wiley-Blackwell, 2010.

Olmstead, Jane. "The Uses of Blood in Leslie Marmon Silko's *Almanac of the Dead*," *Contemporary Literature* 40:3 (Fall 1999): 464–490.

O'Meara, Bridget. "The Ecological Politics of Leslie Silko's *Almanac of the Dead*," *Wicazo Sa Review* 15:2 (Fall 2000): 63–73.

Piatote, Beth Hege. "Bodies of Memory and Forgetting: 'Putting on Weight' in Leslie Marmon Silko's *Almanac of the Dead*," *Paradoxa* 6:15 (2001): 198–210.

Porter, Joy. *Place and Native American Indian History and Culture*. New York: Peter Lang, 2007.

Prince-Hughes, Tara. "Worlds In and Out of Balance: Alternative Genders and Gayness in the *Almanac of the Dead* and *The Beet Queen*" in *Literature and Homosexuality*, ed. Michael J. Meyer. Amsterdam: Rodopi, 2000.

Reed, T. V. "Toxic Colonialism, Environmental Justice, and Native Resistance in Silko's 'Almanac of the Dead,'" *MELUS* 34:2 (Summer 2009): 25–42.

Romero, Channette. "Envisioning a 'Network of Tribal Coalitions': Leslie Marmon Silko's *Almanac of the Dead*," *American Indian Quarterly* 26:4 (1 September 2002): 623–640.

_____. "The Politics of the Camera: Visual Storytelling and Sovereignty in Victor Masayesva's Itam Hakim, Hopiit," *Studies in American Indian Literatures* 22:1 (Spring 2010): 49–75.

Roppolo, Kimberly. "Vision, Voice, and Intertribal Metanarrative: The American Indian Visual-Rhetorical Tradition and Leslie Marmon Silko's *Almanac of the Dead*," *American Indian Quarterly* 31:4 (Fall 2007): 534–558.

Rorty, Richard. *Achieving Our Country: Leftist Thought in Twentieth-Century America*. Cambridge, MA: Harvard University Press, 1998.

Salaita, Steven. *The Holy Land in Transit: Colonialism and the Quest for Canaan*. Syracuse, NY: Syracuse University Press, 2006.

Sarkowsky, Katja. *AlterNative Spaces: Constructions of Space in Native American and First Nations' Literatures*. Heidelberg, Ger.: American Studies, 2007.

Schacht, Miriam. "'Movement Must Be Emulated by the People': Rootedness, Migration, and Indigenous Internationalism in Leslie Marmon Silko's *Almanac of the Dead*," *Studies in American Indian Literatures* 21:4 (Winter 2009): 53–70.

Schorcht, Blanca. *Stories Voices in Native American Texts: Harry Robinson, Thomas King, James Welch, and Leslie Marmon Silko*. New York: Routledge, 2003.

Schueller, Malini Johar. *Locating Race: Global Sites of Post-Colonial Citizenship*. Albany: State University of New York Press, 2009.

Shackelford, Laura. "The Resistance of Counter-Networks in Leslie Marmon Silko's *Almanac of the Dead*," *Postmodern Culture* 16:3 (May 2006): 1.

Shukla, Sanhya Rajendra, and Heidi Tinsman. *Imagining Our Americas: Toward a Transnational Frame*. Durham, NC: Duke University Press, 2007.

Skow, John. "The People of the Monkey Wrench," *Time* 138:23 (9 December 1991): 86.

Smith, Carlton. *Coyote Kills John Wayne: Postmodernism and Contemporary Fictions of the Transcultural Frontier*. Hanover, NH: University Press of New England, 2000.

Smith, Lindsey Claire. *Indians, Environment, and Identity on the Borders of American Literature: From Faulkner and Morrison to Walker and Silko*. New York: Palgrave Macmillan, 2008.

Sol, Adam. "The Story as It's Told: Prodigious Revisions in Leslie Marmon Silko's 'Almanac of the Dead,'" *American Indian Quarterly* 23:3–4 (Summer-Autumn 1999): 24–48.

Spurgeon, Sara L. *Exploding the Western: Myths of Empire on the Postmodern Frontier*. College Station: Texas A&M University Press, 2005.

Stanford, Ann Folwell. "'Human Debris': Border Politics, Body Parts, and the Reclamation of the Americas in Leslie Marmon Silko's *Almanac of the Dead*," *Literature and Medicine* 16:1 (Spring 1997): 23–42.

St. Clair, Janet. "Cannibal Queers: The Problematics of Metaphor in *Almanac of the Dead*" in *Leslie Marmon Silko: A Collection of Critical Essays*, eds. Louise Barnett and James Thorson, eds. Albuquerque: University of New Mexico Press, 1999, 207–222.

_____. "Death of Love/Love of Death: Leslie Marmon Silko's *Almanac of the Dead*," *MELUS* 21:2 (1996): 141–156.

St. John, Edward B. "Review: *Almanac of the Dead*," *Library Journal* 116:17 (15 October 1991): 124.

Su, John J. *Ethics and Nostalgia in the Contemporary Novel*. Cambridge: Cambridge University Press, 2005.

Sugg, Katherine. *Gender and Allegory in Transamerican Fiction and Performance*. New York: Palgrave Macmillan, 2008.

Tallent, Elizabeth. "Storytelling with a Vengeance," *New York Times Book Review* (22 December 1991): 6.

Teale, Tamara. "The Silko Road from Chiapas, or Why Native Americans Cannot Be Marxists," *MELUS* 23:4 (1998): 157–166.

Tewinkel, Wim. "Elders' Stories Saved for Future," *Windspeaker* 21:8 (November 2003): 23.

Tillett, Rebecca. "The Indian Wars Have Never Ended in the Americas: The Politics of Memory and History in Leslie Marmon Silko's *Almanac of the Dead*," *Feminist Review* 85:1 (2007): 21–39.

_____. "The Price of Free Trade: NAFTA and the Economies of Border Crossing in George Rabasa's *The Floating Kingdom* and Leslie Marmon Silko's *Almanac of the dead*," *Comparative American Studies* 6:4 (December 2008): 329–343.

_____. "Reality Consumed by Realty: The Ecological Costs of 'Development' in Leslie Marmon Silko's *Almanac of the Dead*," *European Journal of American Culture* 24:2 (August 2005): 153–169.

_____. "'Resting in Peace, Not in Pieces': The Concerns of the Living Dead in Anna Lee Walters's *Ghost Singer*," *Studies in American Indian Literature* 17:3 (Fall 2005): 85–114.

Voparil, Christopher J., and Richard J. Bernstein. *The Rorty Reader*. Malden, MA: Wiley-Blackwell, 2010.

Weaver, Jace, Robert Allen Warrior, and Craig S. Womack. *American Indian Literary Nationalism*. Albuquerque: University of New Mexico Press, 2006.

Weinstein, Sharon. "A Radical Premise About America as a Stolen Land," *Virginian-Pilot* (12 January 1992): C3.

West, Paul. "When a Myth Is as Good as a Mile," *Los Angeles Times* (2 February 1992): 8.

Wynn, Judith. "Nightmare Vision of 'Almanac' Succeeds," *Boston Herald* (22 December 1991): 62.

Yuknavitch, Lidia. *Allegories of Violence: Tracing the Writing of War in Late Twentieth Century Fiction*. New York: Routledge, 2001.

## Ceremony

Alexie, Sherman. "Root Juice," *American Poet* 31 (Fall 2006): 32–33.

Allen, Paula Gunn. "Special Problems in Teaching Leslie Marmon Silko's Ceremony," *The American Indian Quarterly* (Fall 1990): 379–386.

Avila, Monica. "Leslie Marmon Silko's *Ceremony*: Witchery and Sacrifice of Self," *Explicator* 67:1 (Fall 2008): 53–55.

Bassett, Troy J. ""My Brother': The Recovery of Rocky in Leslie Marmon Silko's *Ceremony*," *American Indian Culture and Research Journal* 28:1 (2004): 35–40.

Beidler, Peter G. "Bloody Mud, Rifle Butts, and Barbed Wire: Transforming the Bataan Death March in Silko's *Ceremony*," *American Indian Culture and Research Journal* 28:1 (2004): 23–33.

_____, and Robert M. Nelson. "Grandma's Wicker Sewing Basket: Untangling the Narrative Threads in Silko's *Ceremony*," *American Indian Culture and Research Journal* 28:1 (2004): 5–13.

Bell, Betty Louise. "Indians with Voices: Revisiting *Savagism and Civilization*" in *American Mythologies: Essays in Contemporary Literature*, eds. William Blazek and Michael K. Glenday. Liverpool, UK: Liverpool University Press, 2005, 15–28.

Bell, Robert. "Circular Design in *Ceremony*," *American Indian Quarterly* 5.1 (February 1979): 47–62.

Bird, Gloria. "Toward a Decolonization of the Mind and Text: Leslie Marmon Silko's *Ceremony*" in *Reading Native American Women: Critical/Creative Representations*, ed. Inés Hernández-Avila. Lanham, MD: Altamira, 2005, 93–106.

Blazek, William, ed. *American Mythologies: Essays in Contemporary Literature*. Liverpool: Liverpool University Press, 2005.

Brennan, Jonathan. *Mixed Race Literature*. Stanford, CA: Stanford University Press, 2002.

Brown, Harry John. *Injun Joe's Ghost: The Indian Mixed-Blood in American Writing*. Columbia: University of Missouri Press, 2004.

Brown, Ray Broadus. *Murder on the Reservation: American Indian Crime Fiction: Aims and Achievements*. Madison: University of Wisconsin Press, 2004.

Burlingame, Lori. "Empowerment Through 'Retroactive Prophecy'" in D'Arcy McNickle's *Runner in the Sun: A Story of Indian Maize*, James Welch's *Fools Crow*, and Leslie Marmon Silko's *Ceremony*," *American Indian Quarterly* 24:1 (Winter 2000): 1–18.

Carlisle, Janice, and Daniel R. Schwarz. *Narrative and Culture*. Athens: University of Georgia Press, 2010.

Carroll, Al. *Medicine Bags and Dog Tags: American Indian Veterans from Colonial Times to the Second Iraq War*. Lincoln: University of Nebraska Press, 2008.

Carter, Nancy Corson. "Spider Woman as Healer: Donna Henes's *Dressing Our Wounds in Warm Clothes* and Leslie Marmon Silko's *Ceremony*," *Mythosphere* 1:3 (August 1990): 282–303.

Caswell, Kurt. "The Totem Meal in Leslie Marmon Silko's *Ceremony*," *ISLE* 15:2 (2008): 175–183.

Caton, Louis Freitas. *Reading American Novels and Multicultural Aesthetics: Romancing the Postmodern Novel*. New York: Palgrave Macmillan, 2008.

Chabram, Angie, and Rosa Linda Fregoso. "Decolonizing Imperialism: Captivity Myths and the Postmodern World in Leslie Marmon Silko's *Ceremony*" in *Exploding the Western: Myths of Empire on the Postmodern Frontier*, ed. Sara L. Spurgeon. College Station: Texas A&M University Press, 2005.

Chavkin, Allan Richard. *Leslie Marmon Silko's Ceremony: A Casebook*. New York: Oxford University Press, 2002.

_____, and Nancy Feyl Chavkin. "The Origins of Leslie Marmon Silko's *Ceremony*," *Yale University Library Gazette* 82:1/2 (October 2007): 23–30.

Churchill, Ward. *A Little Matter of Genocide: Holocaust and Denial in the Americas, 1492 to the Present*. San Francisco: City Lights Books, 1997.

Clarke, Deborah. *Driving Women: Fiction and Automobile Culture in Twentieth-Century America*. Baltimore: Johns Hopkins University Press, 2007.

Clayton, Jay. *The Pleasures of Babel: Contemporary American Literature and Theory*. New York: Oxford University Press, 1994.

Concannon, Kevin. "Deer-Hoof Clackers and Coke Bottles: The Construction of the Postcolonial Nation in Leslie Marmon Silko's *Ceremony*," *Ariel* 35:3/4 (July-October 2004): 183–200.

Copeland, Marion W. "*Black Elk Speaks* and Leslie Marmon Silko's *Ceremony*: Two Visions of Horses," *Critique* (Spring 1983): 158–172.

Cox, James H. *Muting White Noise: Native American and European American Novel Traditions*. Norman: University of Oklahoma Press, 2006.

Cutchins, Dennis. "'So That the Nations May Become Genuine Indian': Nativism and Leslie Marmon Silko's *Ceremony*," *Journal of American Culture* 22:4 (1999): 77–89.

Dean, John Emory. *Travel Narratives from New Mexico: Reconstructing Identity and Truth*. Amherst, NY: Cambria, 2009.

Doll, Mary Aswell. *Like Letters in Running Water: A Mythopoetics of Curriculum*. New York: Routledge, 2000.

Evans, Robert Leslie. "A Real Life Model for Tayo in Silko's *Ceremony*," *American Indian Culture and Research Journal* 28:1 (2004): 15–22.

Ferguson, Laurie L. "Trickster Shows the Way: Humor, Resiliency, and Growth in Modern Native American Literature," *Sciences and Engineering* 63 (April 2003): 4880.

Ganser, Alexandra. "Violence, Trauma, and Cultural Memory in Leslie Silko's *Ceremony*," *Atenea* 24:1 (June 2004): 145–149.

Giles, James R. *Violence in the Contemporary American Novel: An End to Innocence*. Columbia: University of South Carolina Press, 2000.

Gohrisch, Jana. "Cultural Exchange and the Representation of History in Postcolonial Literature," *European Journal of English Studies* 10:3 (December 2006): 231–247.

Goldstein, Coleman. "Silko's *Ceremony*," *Explicator* 61:4 (Summer 2003): 245–248.

Hailey, David E., Jr. "The Visual Elegance of Ts'its'tsi'nako and the Other Invisible Characters in *Ceremony*," *Wicazo Sa Review* 6:2 (Autumn 1990): 1–6.

Holm, Sharon. "The 'Lie' of the Land: Native Sovereignty, Indian Literary Nationalism, and Early Indigenism in Leslie Marmon Silko's *Ceremony*," *American Indian Quarterly* 32:3 (Summer 2008): 243–274.

Huffstetler, Edward W. "Leslie Marmon Silko's *Ceremony*: The Recovery of Tradition," *American Indian Culture & Research Journal* 33:1 (2009): 160–161.

Jacobs, Connie. "A Toxic Legacy: Stories of Jackpile Mine," *American Indian Culture and Research Journal* 28:1 (Winter 2004): 41–52.

Johnson, Loretta. "Greening the Library: The Fundamentals and Future of Ecocriticism," *Choice* 47:4 (December 2009): 623–630.

Kalogeras, Yiorgos, Eleftheria Arapoglou, and Linda Joyce Manney. *Transcultural Localisms: Responding to Ethnicity in a Globalized World*. Ann Arbor: University of Michigan Press, 2006.

Karem, Jeff. "Keeping the Native on the Reservation: The Struggle for Leslie Marmon Silko's *Ceremony*," *American Indian Culture and Research Journal* 25:4 (2001): 21–34.

Karoui-Elounelli, Salwa. "Unsounded Vocality: The Trope of Voice and the Paradigm of Orality in American Postmodern Fiction," *Mosaic* 43:1 (March 2010): 111–126.

Keating, AnaLouise. *Teaching Transformation Transcultural Classroom Dialogues*. New York: Palgrave Macmillan, 2007.

Kennedy, Virginia. "Unlearning the Legacy of Conquest: Possibilities for 'Ceremony' in the Non-Native Classroom," *American Indian*

*Culture and Research Journal* 28:1 (Winter 2004): 75–82.

Killingsworth, M. Jimmie. *Appeals in Modern Rhetoric: An Ordinary-Language Approach*. Carbondale: Southern Illinois University Press, 2005.

Larson, Charles R. "The Jungles of the Mind," *Washington Post* (24 April 1977): E4.

Lewis, Randolph. *Alanis Obomsawin: The Vision of a Native Filmmaker*. Lincoln: University of Nebraska Press, 2006.

Low, Denise, and Peter G. Beidler. "Preface," *American Indian Culture and Research Journal* 28:1 (Winter 2004): 104.

Mackenthun, Gesa. "Storytelling as Cultural Survival in Leslie Silko's *Ceremony*" in *Erzahlkulturen im Medienwandel*, ed. Christoph Schmitt. Munster, Ger.: Waxmann, 2006.

MacShane, Frank. "Review: *Ceremony*," *New York Times Book Review* (12 June 1977): 15.

Magdaleno, Jana Sequoya. "How(!) Is an Indian? A Contest of Stories," *Lake Berryessa* (California) *News* (3 August 2010).

Magoc, Chris J. *So Glorious a Landscape: Nature and the Environment in American History and Culture*. Wilmington, DE: SR Books, 2002.

Martin, Holly E. "Hybrid Landscapes as Catalysts for Cultural Reconciliation in Leslie Marmon Silko's *Ceremony* and Rudolfo Anaya's *Bless Me, Ultima*," *Atenea* 26:1 (June 2006): 131–149.

Mayo, James. "Silko's *Ceremony*," *Explicator* 60:1 (Fall 2001): 54–56.

McClure, John A. *Partial Faiths: Postsecular Fiction in the Age of Pynchon and Morrison*. Athens: University of Georgia Press, 2007.

McKibben, Bill, and Albert Gore. *American Earth: Environmental Writing since Thoreau*. Ann Arbor: University of Michigan Press, 2008.

McMurtry, Larry. "Introduction" to *Ceremony*. New York: Penguin, 2007.

Meyers, Karen. *Contemporary American Literature (1945–Present)*. New York: Chelsea House, 2010.

Miller, Carol. "Telling the Indian Urban: Representations in American Indian Fiction," *American Indian Culture & Research* 22:4 (1998): 43–65.

Mitchell, Carol. "'Ceremony' as Ritual," *American Indian Quarterly* 5:1 (February 1979): 27–35.

Miura, Noriko. *Marginal Voice, Marginal Body: The Treatment of the Human Body in the Works of Nakagami Kenji, Leslie Marmon Silko, and Salman Rushdie*. Boca Raton, FL: Universal Publishers, 2000.

Nelson, Elizabeth Hoffman, and Malcolm Nelson, eds. *Telling the Stories: Essays on American Indian Literatures and Cultures*. New York: Peter Lang, 2001.

Nelson, Robert M. "The Kaupata Motif in Silko's *Ceremony*: A Study of a Literary Homology,"

*Studies in American Indian Literatures* 11.3 (Fall 1999): 221.

_____. *Leslie Marmon Silko's Ceremony: The Recovery of Tradition*. New York: Peter Lang, 2008.

Niezen, Ronald. *The Origins of Indigenism: Human Rights and the Politics of Identity*. Berkeley: University of California Press, 2003.

Olsen, Erica. "Silko's Ceremony," *Explicator* 64:3 (Spring 2006): 190–192.

Ortiz, Simon J. "Towards a National Indian Literature: Cultural Authenticity in Nationalism" in *American Indian Literary Nationalism*, eds. Jace Weaver, Craig S. Womack, and Robert Allen Warrior. Albuquerque: University of New Mexico Press, 2006.

Peters, Ariane. *Living In-between: The Search for Identity in Leslie Marmon Silko's Ceremony*. Munich: Ravensburg GRIN Verlag, 2003.

Petrolle, Jean. *Religion Without Belief: Contemporary Allegory and the Search for Postmodern Faith*. Albany: State University of New York Press, 2007.

Piper, Karen. "Police Zones: Territory and Identity in Leslie Marmon Silko's *Ceremony*," *American Indian Quarterly* (22 June 1997): 483–501.

Porterfield, Amanda. *American Religious History*. Malden, MA: Blackwell, 2002.

Powell, Brenda J. "Mythic Realism: Magic and Mystery in Marele Day's *Lambs of God*," *Christianity & Literature* 59:3 (April 2010): 479–502.

Purdy, John Lloyd. *Writing Indian, Native Conversations*. Lincoln: University of Nebraska Press, 2009.

Rains, Frances. "From the Eyes of the Colonized: Rethinking the Legacy of Colonization and Its Impact on American Indians," *Journal of Philosophy and History of Education* 52 (2002): 125–131.

Rainwater, Catherine. "The Semiotics of Dwelling in Leslie Marmon Silko's *Ceremony*," *American Journal of Semiotics* 9:2/3 (1992): 219–240.

Ridington, Robin, and Jillian Ridington. *When You Sing It Now, Just Like New: First Nations Poetics, Voices, and Representations*. Lincoln: University of Nebraska Press, 2006.

Roberson, Susan L. *Defining Travel: Diverse Visions*. Jackson: University Press of Mississippi, 2007.

Roberts, Kathleen Glenister. *Alterity and Narrative: Stories and the Negotiation of Western Identities*. Albany: State University of New York Press, 2008.

Roppolo, Kimberly. "Sacred Sexuality in Leslie Marmon Silko's *Ceremony*," *Red Ink* 11:1 (2002): 70–77.

Rosier, Paul C. "Fond Memories and Bitter Struggles: Concerted Resistance to Environmental Injustices in Postwar Native America" in *Echoes from the Poisoned Well: Global Memories of Environmental Injustice,* eds. Heather Goodall, Paul C. Rosier, and Sylvia Hood Washington. Lanham, MD: Lexington Books, 2006.

Ruppert, James. "Dialogism and Mediation in Leslie Silko's *Ceremony,*" *Explicator* 51:2 (Winter 1993): 129–134.

Sánchez, Jesús Benito, Ana Ma Manzanas Calvo, and Begoña Simal González. *Uncertain Mirrors: Magical Realisms in US Ethnic Literatures.* New York: Rodopi, 2009.

Sánchez, María Rutgh Noriega. *Challenging Realities: Magic Realism in Contemporary American Women's Fiction.* València: Universitat de València, 2002.

Sarairah, Dafer Yousif. "Leslie Marmon Silko's *Ceremony* as a Viable Path of Resistance and Agency," *Scientific Journal of King Faisal University* 4:2 (2003): 155–168.

Schwarz, Daniel R. *Narrative and Culture.* Athens: University of Georgia Press, 2010.

Schweninger, Lee. "Reading, Learning, Teaching N. Scott Momaday, Leslie Marmon Silko's *Ceremony*: The Recovery of Tradition," *Western American Literature* 45:2 (Summer 2010): 201–203.

Shapiro, Colleen. "Silko's Ceremony," *Explicator* 61:2 (Winter 2003): 117–119.

Siemerling, Winfried. *The New North American Studies: Culture, Writing and the Politics of Re/cognition.* New York: Routledge, 2005.

Singh, Amritjit, ed. *Memory and Cultural Politics.* Boston: Northeastern University Press, 1996.

_____, and Peter Schmidt. *Postcolonial Theory and the United States: Race, Ethnicity, and Literature.* Jackson: University Press of Mississippi, 2000.

Sokolowski, Jeanne. "Between Dangerous Extremes: Victimization, Ultranationalism, and Identity Performance in Gerald Vizenor's *Hiroshima Bugi: Atomu 57,*" *American Quarterly* 62:3 (September 2010): 717–738.

Strickland, Ronald. *Growing Up Postmodern: Neoliberalism and the War on the Young.* Lanham, MD: Rowman & Littlefield, 2002.

Suarez, Ray, "Leslie Marmon Silko's Book *Ceremony,*" *Talk of the Nation* (NPR) (17 June 1999).

Tarter, James. "Locating the Uranium Mine: Place, Multiethnicity, and Environmental Justice in Leslie Marmon Silko's Ceremony" in *The Greening of Literary Scholarship: Literature, Theory, and the Environment,* ed. Steven Rosendale. Iowa City: University of Iowa Press, 2002.

Teorey, Matthew. "Spinning a Bigendered Identity in Silko's *Ceremony* and Puig's *Kiss of the Spider Woman,*" *Comparative Literature Studies* 47:1 (2010): 1–20.

Todd, Jude. "Knotted Bellies and Fragile Webs: Untangling and Re-Spinning in Tayo's Healing Journey," *American Indian Quarterly* 19:2 (Spring 1995): 155–170.

TuSmith, Bonnie. *All My Relatives: Community in Contemporary Ethnic American Literatures.* Ann Arbor: University of Michigan Press, 1994.

Wagner, Ole. *The Stolen Land Will Eat Their Hearts — Leslie Marmon Silko's Ceremony from an Environmentalist Perspective.* Norderstedt, Ger.: GRIN Verlag, 2004.

Walther, Berenice. *Storytelling in Leslie Marmon Silko's Ceremony.* Munich: Ravensburg Grin Verl, 2006.

Welch, Sharon D. *Real Peace, Real Security: The Challenges of Global Citizenship.* Minneapolis: Fortress, 2008.

Weso, Thomas F. "From Delirium to Coherence: Shamanism and Medicine Plans in Silko's 'Ceremony,'" *American Indian Culture and Research Journal* 28:1 (Winter 2004): 53–65.

West, Rinda. *Out of the Shadow: Ecopsychology, Story, and Encounters with the Land.* Charlottesville: University of Virginia Press, 2007.

Whitley, David S. *Cave Paintings and the Human Spirit.* Amherst, NY: Prometheus Books, 2009.

Wilentz, Gay Alden. *Healing Narratives: Women Writers Curing Cultural Dis-ease.* New Brunswick, NJ: Rutgers University Press, 2000.

Wilson, Charles E. *Race and Racism in Literature.* Westport, CT: Greenwood, 2005.

Wilson, Michael D. *Writing Home: Indigenous Narratives of Resistance.* East Lansing: Michigan State University Press, 2008.

Wilson, Norma C. "Ceremony: From Alienation to Reciprocity" in *Teaching American Ethnic Literatures,* ed. John R. Maitano and David R. Peck, 69–82. Albuquerque: University of New Mexico Press, 1996.

Winsbro, Bonnie C. *Supernatural Forces: Belief, Difference, and Power in Contemporary Works by Ethnic Women.* Amherst: University of Massachusetts Press, 1993.

Wolf, Werner. *Description in Literature and Other Media.* Amsterdam: Rodopi, 2007.

## The Delicacy and Strength of Lace

Barillas, William David. *The Midwestern Pastoral: Place and Landscape in Literature of the American Heartland.* Athens: Ohio University Press, 2006.

Lincoln, Kenneth. *Indi'n Humor: Bicultural Play in Native America.* New York: Oxford University Press, 1993.

Margolies, Diane Rothbard. *The Fabric of Self: A Theory of Ethics and Emotions.* New Haven, CT: Yale University Press, 1998.

Mason, David. "The Inner Drama of James Wright," *Hudson Review* 58:4 (2006): 667–674.

Show, Gene. "Review: *The Delicacy and Strength of Lace*," *Library Journal* 135:1 (1 January 2010): 107–108.

Simon, Caroline Joyce. *The Disciplined Heart: Love, Destiny, and Imagination.* Grand Rapids, MI: W. B. Eerdmans, 1997.

Wright, James, Anne Wright, and Saundra Rose Maley. *A Wild Perfection: The Selected Letters of James Wright.* Middletown, CT: Wesleyan University Press, 2008.

Wrye, Harriet Kimble. "Sitting with Eros and Psyche on a Buddhist Psychoanalyst's Cushions," *Psychoanalytic Dialogues* 16:6 (April 2007): 725–746.

## Gardens in the Dunes

Aldama, Frederick Luis. "Review: *Gardens in the Dunes*," *World Literature Today* 74:2 (2000): 457–458.

Averbach, Margara. "*Gardens in the Dunes* by Leslie Marmon Silko: Stories as Resistance" in *Raízas e rumos: perspectivas interdisciplinares em estudos americanos*, ed. Sonia Torres. Rio de Janeiro: 7Letras, 2001.

Azima, Rachel Mieko Pouri. *Alien Soil: Ecologies of Transplantation in Contemporary Literature.* Madison: University of Wisconsin Press, 2008.

Bak, Hans. *First Nations of North America: Politics and Representation.* Amsterdam: VU University Press, 2005.

Bataille, Gretchen M. *Native American Representations: First Encounters, Distorted Images, and Literary Appropriations.* Lincoln: University of Nebraska Press, 2001.

Boelhower, William Q, Rocio G. Davis, and Carmen Birkle. *Sites of Ethnicity: Europe and the Americas.* Heidelberg: Universitatsverlag, 2004.

Bomberry, Victoria Jean. *Indigenous Memory and Imagination: Thinking beyond the Nation.* Stanford, CA: Stanford University, 2001.

Castro, Michael, "Silko Explores Themes of Religion, Nature, Family," *St. Louis Post-Dispatch* (4 April 1999).

Cheyfitz, Eric. *The Columbia Guide to American Indian Literatures of the United States since 1945.* New York: Columbia University Press, 2006.

Christie, Stuart. *Plural Sovereignties and Contemporary Indigenous Literature.* New York: Palgrave Macmillan, 2009.

Cohen, Robert. "An Interview with Leslie Marmon Silko," *Southwest American Literature* 24:2 (Spring 1999).

Coltelli, Laura. *Reading Leslie Marmon Silko: Critical Perspectives through Gardens in the Dunes.* Pisa: Pisa University Press, 2007.

Dennis, Helen May. "Felicitous Spaces: Places of Refuge in the Writings of Paula Gunn Allen, Linda Hogan, and Leslie Marmon Silko in *Comparative Site of Ethnicity: Europe and the Americas*, eds. Boelhower, William, Carmen Birkle, and Rocio Davis. Heidelberg: Winter Verlag, 2004.

Fauntleroy, Gussie. "In Silko's Garden," *Santa Fe New Mexican* (23 May 1999): 2.

Ferguson, Suzanne. "Europe and the Quest for Home in James Welch's *The Heartsong of Charging Elk* and Leslie Marmon Silko's *Gardens in the Dunes*," *Studies in American Indian Literatures* 18:2 (Summer 2006): 34–53.

Flint, Kate. *The Transatlantic Indian, 1776–1930.* Princeton, NJ: Princeton University Press, 2008.

"Gathering the Gardens in the Dunes: Leslie Marmon Silko Makes the Flora Central to Her Latest Fiction," *Kansas City Star* (20 June 1999): K5.

Hamilton, Patrick Lawrence. *Reading Space: Narratives of Persistence and Transformation in Contemporary Chicana/o Fiction.* Denver: University of Colorado Press, 2006.

Harmsen-Peraino, Suzanne. "The Ghost Dance Vision in Leslie M. Silko's *Almanac of the Dead* and *Gardens in the Dunes*," *Canada cahiers* 12 (8 September 2008): 128–140.

Hebebrand, Christina M. *Native American and Chicano/a Literature of the American Southwest.* New York: Routledge, 2004.

Ingram, Annie Merrill. *Coming into Contact: Explorations in Ecocritical Theory and Practice.* Athens: University of Georgia Press, 2007.

Isernhagen, Hartwig. "Of Deserts and Gardens: The Southwest in Literature and Art, 'Native' and 'White'" in *Literature and Visual Arts in Twentieth-Century America*, ed. Michele Bottalico. Bari: Palomar Eupalinos, 2002, 173–187.

Jones, Tayari. "Folk Tale of Survival," *The Progressive* 64:2 (February 2000): 43–44.

Katanski, Amelia V. *Learning to Write 'Indian': The Boarding-School Experience and American Indian Literature.* Norman: University of Oklahoma Press, 2005.

Köhler, Angelika. "'Our human nature, our human spirit, wants no boundaries': Leslie Marmon Silko's *Garden in the Dunes* and the Concept of Global Fiction," *Amerikastudien* 47:1 (2002): 237–244.

Kowinski, William Severini. "Review: *Gardens in the Dunes*," *Orion* 19:1 (Winter 2000): 70–71.

Li, Stephanie. "Domestic Resistance Gardening, Mothering, and Storytelling in Leslie Mamon Silko's *Gardens in the Dunes*," *Studies in American Indian Literature* 21:1 (Spring 2009): 18–37.

Madsen, Deborah L. *American Aesthetics.* Tübingen, Ger.: Gunter Narr, 2007.

Mariani, Andrea. *Riscritture dell'eden: il giardino nell'immaginazione letteraria angloamericana.* Naples: Liguori, 2003.

Martinez, C. "Un giardino color indaco: *Gardens in the Dunes* di L. M. Silko" in *Riscritture dell'Eden*, ed. A. Mariani. Naples: Liguori, 2003.

May, Janice Susan. *Healing the Necrophilia of Euro-American Society in Leslie Marmon Silko's Gardens in the Dunes*. Radford, VA: Radford University, 2000.

Messer, Jane. "Mothering and Resistance," *Australian Feminist Studies* 23:56 (June 2008): 271–273.

Morisco, Gabriella. "Contrasting Gardens and Worlds: America and Europe in the Long Journey of Indigo, a Young Native American Girl" in *Nations, Traditions and Cross-Cultural Identities: Women's Writing in English in a European Context*, eds. Annamaria Lamarra and Eleonora Federici. Bern: Peter Lang, 2010, 137–148.

Naparsteck, Martin, "The West under Cover," *Salt Lake Tribune* (12 December 1999): D4.

Pulitano, Elvira. *Transatlantic Voices: Interpretations of Native North American Literatures*. Lincoln: University of Nebraska Press, 2007.

Regier, A. M. "Revolutionary Enunciatory Spaces: Ghost Dancing, Transatlantic Travel, and Modernist Arson in Gardens in the Dunes," *Modern Fiction Studies* 51:1 (Spring 2005): 134–157.

Ruoff, A. Lavonne Brown. "Images of Europe in Leslie Marmon Silko's *Gardens of the Dunes* and James Welch's *The Heartsong of Charging Elk*" in *Comparative Site of Ethnicity: Europe and the Americas*, eds. William Boelhower, Carmen Birkle, and Rocio Davis. Heidelberg: Winter Verlag, 2004.

Ruta, Suzanne, "Dances with Ghosts," *New York Times* (18 April 1999): 31.

Ryan, Terre. "The Nineteenth-Century Garden: Imperialism, Subsistence, and Subversion in Leslie Marmon Silko's Gardens in the Dunes," *Studies in American Indian Literatures* 19:3 (Fall 2007): 115–132.

Sackman, Douglas C. "A Garden of Worldly Delights" in *Land of Sunshine: An Environmental History of Metropolitan Los Angeles*, ed. William Deverell. Pittsburgh: University of Pittsburgh Press, 2005.

_____. *Orange Empire: California and the Fruits of Eden*. Berkeley: University of California Press, 2005.

Saguaro, Shelley. *Garden Plots: The Politics and Poetics of Gardens*. Burlington, VT: Ashgate, 2006.

Seaman, Donna, "Earthwork a Rich, Panoramic Tale About the Relationship Between People and the Natural World Around Them," *Chicago Tribune* (8 August 1999): 5.

Stanton, Therese. "Review: *Gardens in the Dunes*," *Ms.* 9:3 (April/May 1999): 110.

Steinberg, Sybil, and Jeff Zaleski. "Forecasts: Fiction," *Publishers Weekly* 246:9 (1 March 1999): 59–60.

Summers, Wynne L. *Women Elders' Life Stories of the Omaha Tribe: Macy, Nebraska, 2004–2005*. Lincoln: University of Nebraska Press, 2009.

Udel, Lisa J. "Revision and Resistance: The Politics of Native Women's Motherwork," *Frontiers* 22.2 (2001): 43–62.

Willard, William. "Review: *Gardens in the Dunes*," *Wicazo Sa Review* 15:2 (Fall 2000): 139–141.

Wood, Karenne. "Review: *Gardens in the Dunes*," *American Indian Quarterly* 23:2 (1999): 71–72.

## "A Geronimo Story"

Anderson, Eric Gary. *American Indian Literature and the Southwest: Contexts and Dispositions*. Austin: University of Texas Press, 1999.

Bentley, Nancy. *Frantic Panoramas: American Literature and Mass Culture, 1870–1920*. Philadelphia: University of Pennsylvania Press, 2009.

Muthyala, John. *Reworlding America: Myth, History, and Narrative*. Athens: Ohio University Press, 2006.

Warrior, Robert Allen. *The People and the Word: Reading Native Nonfiction*. Minneapolis: University of Minnesota Press, 2005.

## "Here's an Odd Artifact for the Fairy-Tale Shelf"

Wilson, Sharon Rose. *Myths and Fairy Tales in Contemporary Women's Fiction: from Atwood to Morrison*. New York: Palgrave Macmillan, 2008.

## Laguna Woman: Poems

Domina, Lynn. "'The Way I Heard It': Autobiography, Tricksters, and Leslie Marmon Silko's Storyteller," *Studies in American Indian Literatures* 19:3 (Fall 2007): 45–67.

Lyon, Thomas J. *Updating the Literary West*. Fort Worth: Texas Christian University Press, 1997.

Roemer, Kenneth. "Bear and Elk: The Nature(s) of Contemporary Indian Poetry," *Journal of Ethnic Studies* 10 (1975): 233–236.

## Landscape, History, and the Pueblo Imagination

Killingsworth, M. Jimmie. *Appeals in Modern Rhetoric: An Ordinary-Language Approach*. Carbondale: Southern Illinois University Press, 2005.

Kane, Adrian Taylor. *The Natural World of Latin American Literatures: Ecocritical Essays on Twentieth Century Writings*. Jefferson, NC: McFarland, 2010.

## Lullaby

Bird, Julie. "What Is the Role of Nature in 'Lullaby'?" in *The Curious Writer*, ed. Bruce P. Ballenger. White Plains, NY: Pearson Longman, 2005.

Champion, Laurie. *Contemporary American Women Fiction Writers: An A-to-Z Guide.* Westport, CT: Greenwood, 2002.

Clouse, Barbara Fine. *Patterns for a Purpose with Instructor Access to Catalyst.* New York: McGraw-Hill Education, 2005.

Cullum, Linda E. *Contemporary American Ethnic Poets: Lives, Works, Sources.* Westport, CT: Greenwood, 2004.

Fallon, Erin. *A Reader's Companion to the Short Story in English.* Westport, CT: Greenwood, 2001.

Friedman, Susan Stanford. "Bodies on the Move: A Poetics of Home and Diaspora," *Tulsa Studies in Women's Literature* 23:2 (Fall 2004): 189–212.

Hollrah, Patrice E. M. *"The Old Lady Trill, the Victory Yell": The Power of Women in Native American Literature.* New York: Routledge, 2004.

Keegan, Bridget, and James C. McKusick. *Literature and Nature: Four Centuries of Nature Writing.* New York: Prentice Hall, 2000.

Madsen, Deborah L. *Feminist Theory and Literary Practice.* London: Pluto Press, 2000.

McBride, Mary. "Shelter of Refuge: The Art of Memesis Leslie Marmon Silko's Lullaby," *Wicazo SA Review* 3:2, 15–17.

Minh-ha, Trinh T. "Difference: A Special Third World Women Issue" in *The Feminism and Visual Culture Reader,* ed. Amelia Jones. New York: Routledge, 2003, 151–173.

Stoller, Eleanor Palo, and Rose Campbell Gibson. *Worlds of Difference: Inequality in the Aging Experience.* Thousand Oaks, CA: Pine Forge, 2000.

Zandy, Janet. *Hands: Physical Labor, Class, and Cultural Work.* New Brunswick, NJ: Rutgers University Press, 2004.

## Running on the Edge of the Rainbow: Laguna Stories and Poems

Velikova, Roumiana. "Leslie Marmon Silko: Reading, Writing, and Storytelling," *MELUS* 27:3 (22 September 2002): 57–74.

## Sacred Water

Aveni, Anthony F. *Behind the Crystal Ball: Magic, Science, and the Occult from Antiquity through the New Age.* Denver: University Press of Colorado, 2002.

Cevasco, George A., and Richard P. Harmond. *Modern American Environmentalists: A Biographical Encyclopedia.* Baltimore: Johns Hopkins University Press, 2009.

Chamberlain, Gary. *Troubled Waters: Religion, Ethics, and the Global Water Crisis.* Lanham, MD: Rowman & Littlefield, 2008.

Coltelli, Laura. "Leslie Marmon Silko's *Sacred Water,*" *Studies in American Indian Literatures* 8:4 (1996): 21–29.

Cook, Barbara. *Women Writing Nature: A Feminist View.* Lanham, MD: Rowman & Littlefield, 2008.

Irland, Basia. *Water Library.* Albuquerque: University of New Mexico, 2007.

Murphy, Patrick D., Terry Gifford, and Katsunori Yamazato. *Literature of Nature: An International Sourcebook.* New York: Taylor & Francis, 1998.

Ruland, Vernon. *Conscience across Borders: An Ethics of Global Rights and Religious Pluralism.* San Francisco: University of San Francisco, 2002.

Weaver, Janice. *That the People Might Live: Native American Literatures and Native American Community.* New York: Oxford University Press, 1997.

Wong, Hertha D. Sweet. "Native American Visual Autobiography: Figuring Place, Subjectivity, and History," *Iowa Review* 30:3 (Winter 2000–2001): 145–156.

_____. *Sending My Heart Back Across the Years: Tradition and Innovation in Native American Autobiography.* New York: Oxford University Press, 1992.

## Storyteller

Arnold, Ellen L. "Silko: Writing Storyteller and Medicine Woman," *Modern Fiction Studies* 51:1 (Spring 2005): 194–197.

Ballinger, Franchot. *Living Sideways: Tricksters in American Indian Oral Traditions.* Norman: University of Oklahoma Press, 2006.

Brooks, Joanna. "'This Indian World': A Petition/Origin Story from Samson Occom (Mohegan) and the Montaukett Tribe" in *Early Native Literacies in New England: A Documentary and Critical Anthology,* eds. Kristina Bross and Hilary E. Wyss. Amherst: University of Massachusetts Press, 2008.

Brown, Alanna Kathleen. "Pulling Silko's Threads Through Time: An Exploration of Storytelling," *American Indian Quarterly* 19:2 (Spring 1995): 171–179.

Cajete, Gregory, Donnna Eder, and Regina Holyan, eds. *Life Lessons through Storytelling: Children's Exploration of Ethics.* Bloomington: Indiana University Press, 2010.

Carsten, Cynthia. "Storyteller: Leslie Marmon Silko's Reappropriation of Native American History and Identity," *Wicazo SA Review* 21:2 (Autumn 2006): 105–126.

Castro, Jan. "The Threads of Life," *Greenfield Review* 9:3–4 (1981): 101.

Cohen, Robin. "Silko: Writing Storyteller and Medicine Woman," *Southwestern American Literature* 30:2 (Spring 2005): 85–87.

Danielson, Linda L. "Storyteller: Grandmother Spider's Web," *Journal of the Southwest* 30:3 (Autumn 1988): 325–355.

_____. "The Storytellers in *Storyteller*," *Studies in American Indian Literatures* 1:2 (Fall 1989): 21–31.

Donahue, James J. "Silko: Writing Storyteller and Medicine Woman," *MELUS* 31:1 (Spring 2006): 156–158.

Elgue-Martini, Cristina. *Espacio, memorie e identidad: configuraciones en la literatura comparada.* Houston: Comunicarte, 2005.

Finnegan, Jordana. *Narrating the American West: New Forms of Historical Memory.* Amherst, NY: Cambria, 2008.

Fitz, Brewster E. "Coyote Loops: Leslie Marmon Silko Holds a Full House in Her Hand," *MELUS* 27:3 (October 2002): 75–91.

Grobman, Laurie. "(Re)Interpreting 'Storyteller' in the Classroom: Teaching at the Crossroads," *College Literature* 27:3 (Fall 2000): 88–110.

Hernandez, Dharma Thornton. "*Storyteller*: Revising the Narrative Schematic," *Pacific Coast Philology* 31:1 (1996): 54–67.

Hirsch, Bernard A. "'The Telling Which Continues': Oral Tradition and the Written Word in Leslie Marmon Silko's 'Storyteller,'" *American Indian Quarterly* 12:1 (Winter 1988): 1–26.

Iftekharrudin, Farhat. *The Postmodern Short Story: Forms and Issues.* Westport, CT: Praeger, 2003.

Krumholz, Linda J. "Native Designs: Silko's *Storyteller* and the Reader's Initiation" in *Leslie Marmon Silko: A Collection of Critical Essays*, eds. Louise Barnett and James Thorson. Albuquerque: University of New Mexico Press, 1999.

_____. "Reading and Subversion in Leslie Marmon Silko's 'Storyteller,'" *Ariel* 25 (January 1994): 89–113.

Langen, T. C. S. "Estoy-eh-muut and the Morphologists," *Studies in American Indian Literatures* 1:1 (Summer 1989): 1–12.

Lee, A. Robert. *Multicultural American Literature: Comparative Black, Native, Latino/a and Asian American Fictions.* Jackson: University Press of Mississippi, 2003.

Lorenz, Paul H. "The Other Story of Leslie Marmon Silko's 'Storyteller,'" *South Central Review* 8:4 (Winter 1994): 59–75.

Marshall, Leni. "Kiss of the Spider Woman: Native American Storytellers and Cultural Transmission," *Journal of Aging, Humanities and the Arts* 1:1/2 (January 2007): 35–52.

Nelson, Robert M. "He Said/She Said: Writing Oral Tradition in John Gunn's 'Kopot Kanat' and Leslie Silko's *Storyteller*," *Studies in American Indian Literatures* 5:1 (1993): 31–50.

Preston, Cathy Lynn. *Folklore, Literature, and Cultural Theory: Collected Essays.* New York: Taylor & Francis, 1995.

Ramirez, Susan Berry Brill. "Storytellers and Their Listener — Readers in Silko's 'Storytelling' and 'Storyteller,'" *American Indian Quarterly* 21:3 (22 June 1997): 333–357.

Shanley, Kathryn W. "The Indians America Loves to Love and Read: American Indian Identity and Cultural Appropriation," *American Indian Quarterly* 21:4 (22 September 1997): 675–702.

Tanner, Travis J. "Reading from Sand Creek," *Kenyon Review* 32:1 (Winter 2010): 142–165.

Van Dyke, Annette. "Silko, Writing Storyteller and Medicine Woman," *Studies in American Indian Literatures* 21:3 (Fall 2009): 102–105.

## The Turquoise Ledge

Ashbrook, Tom, and Leslie Marmon Silko. "The Storyteller: Leslie Marmon Silko," www.onpo intradio.org/2010/10/storyteller-leslie-marmon-silko, accessed on October 22, 2010.

Bennett, Steve. "Author Silko Isn't Concerned About Time," (San Antonio) *Express News* (25 July 2010): 1K, 4K.

_____. "'Nuevo Mundo' Celebrates Women," (San Antonio) *Express News* (31 July 2010): 10B.

Carmin, Jim. "Review: *The Turquoise Ledge*," www.oregonlive.com/books/index.ssf/2010/10/nonfiction_review_the_turquois.html, accessed on October 24, 2010.

Johnson, Cat. "Silko Heads for Santa Cruz," *Santa Cruz News* (21 October 2010).

"Mondo Nuevo Mundo: The Macondo Foundation Brings Literary Superstars to SATX," *San Antonio Current* (28 July 2010).

Paskus, Laura. "Of History and Home," *High Country News* (3 September 2010).

"Review: *The Turquoise Ledge*," *Kirkus Reviews* 78:13 (1 July 2010): 612.

"Review: *The Turquoise Ledge*," *Publishers Weekly* 15:42 (23 August 2010): 41.

Richey, Joe. "Women Writers Shine Brightly at Denver Events," *Boulder Reporter* (12 April 2010).

Scher, Steve, and Leslie Marmon Silko. "Rattlesnakes, Star Beings, and Native American Stories with Writer Leslie Marmon Silko," http://kuow.org/program.php?id=21666, accessed on October 22, 2010.

## Yellow Woman

Arrighi, Barbara A. *Understanding Inequality: The Intersection of Race/Ethnicity, Class, and Gender.* Lanham, MD: Rowman & Littlefield, 2007.

Allen, Paula Gunn. "Kochinnenako in Academe: Three Approaches to Interpreting a Keres Indian Tale," *Yellow Woman*, eds. Leslie Marmon Silko and Melody Graulich. New Brunswick, NJ: Rutgers University Press, 1993.

Barnett, Louise K. "Yellow Women and Leslie Marmon Silko's Feminism," *Studies in American Indian Literatures* 17:2 (Summer 2005): 18–31.

Campedelli, Lauren. "The 'Don't Miss' List," *Los Angeles Downtown News* (18 October 2010).

Cohen, Robin. "Landscape, Story, and Time, as Elements of Reality in Silko's Yellow Woman," *Weber's Studies: An Interdisciplinary Humanities Journal* 12:3 (Fall 1995): 141–147.

Dunn, Carolyn. "The Trick Is Going Home: Secular Spiritualism in Native American Women's Literature" in *Reading Native American Women: Critical/Creative Representations*, ed. Inés Hernández-Avila. Lanham, MD: Altamira, 2005, 189–203.

_____, and Carol Comfort. *Through the Eye of the Deer: An Anthology of Native American Women Writers*. San Francisco: Aunt Lute Books, 1999.

Eakin, Paul John. *How Our Lives Become Stories: Making Selves*. Ithaca: Cornell University Press, 1999.

Graulich, Melody, ed. *Yellow Woman*. New Brunswick, NJ: Rutgers University Press, 2003.

Harrington, Ellen Burton. *Scribbling Women & the Short Story Form: Approaches by American & British Women Writers*. New York: Peter Lang, 2008.

Huber-Warring, Tonya. *Storied Inquiries in International Landscapes: An Anthology of Educational Research*. Charlotte, NC: Information Age, 2010.

Jeffries, Kim. "A Conversation with Leslie Marmon Silko on *The Turquoise Ledge*," *Seattle Times* (19 October 2010).

Katanski, Amelia V. *Learning to Write "Indian":*

*The Boarding-School Experience and American Indian Literature*. Norman: University of Oklahoma Press, 2005.

Klaus, Carl H. *The Made-Up Self: Impersonation in the Personal Essay*. Iowa City: University of Iowa Press, 2010.

Larré, Lionel. *Autobiographie amérindienne: pouvoir et résistance de l'écriture de soi*. Pessac, Fr.: Presses universitaires de Bordeaux, 2009.

_____. "Autorité et Discours: L'Auteurité en Question," *Annales du CRAA* 29 (2005): 165–179.

Mann, Karen B. "Context and Content in Women's Stories," *Eureka Studies in Teaching Short Fiction* 2:1 (Fall 2001): 13–20.

Metz, Nina. "Author Silko Makes a Point to Tell Story," *Chicago Tribune* (16 October 2010).

Morel, Pauline. "Counter-Stories and Border Identities: Storytelling and Myth as a Means of Identification, Subversion, and Survival in Leslie Marmon Silko's 'Yellow Woman' and 'Tony's Story'" in *Interdisciplinary and Cross-cultural Narratives in North America*, eds. Mark Cronlund Anderson and Irene Maria Blayer. New York: Peter Lang, 2005.

Smith, Sidonie. *Moving Lives: Twentieth-Century Women's Travel Writing*. Minneapolis: University of Minnesota Press, 2001.

Thompson, Joan. "Yellow Woman, Old and New: Oral Tradition and Leslie Marmon Silko's *Storyteller*," *Wicazo SA Review* 5:2 (Autumn 1989): 22–25.

# Index

The coded titles after entries identify the following works from Silko's canon: AD *Almanac of the Dead* (1991); C *Ceremony* (1977); DS *The Delicacy and Strength of Lace* (1986); GD *Gardens in the Dunes* (1999); GS "A Geronimo Story" (1974); L "Lullaby" (1974); LW *Laguna Woman* (1974); MS "The Man to Send Rain Clouds" (1969); S *Storyteller* (1981); TL *The Turquoise Ledge* (2010); YW *Yellow Woman* (1993); YWBS *Yellow Woman and a Beauty of the Spirit* (1996). Numbers in **bold italics** indicate main entries.

LaVergne, TN USA
02 February 2011
214997LV00001B/1/P